Java in a Time of Revolution

Occupation and Resistance, 1944 - 1946

JAVA IN A TIME OF REVOLUTION

Occupation and Resistance, 1944-1946

Benedict R. O'G. Anderson

Cornell University Press

ITHACA AND LONDON

First published 1972 by Cornell University Press.
Published in the United Kingdom by Cornell University Press Ltd.,
2–4 Brook Street, London W1Y 1AA.

Prepared under the auspices of the Cornell Modern Indonesia Project.

This book has been published with the aid of a grant from
the Hull Memorial Publication Fund of Cornell University.

International Standard Book Number 0-8014-0687-0
Library of Congress Catalog Card Number 74-174891

PRINTED IN THE UNITED STATES OF AMERICA BY VAIL-BALLOU PRESS, INC.

Library of Congress Cataloging in Publication Data
(For library cataloging purposes only)

Anderson, Benedict Richard O'Gorman, date.
    Java in a time of revolution.

    "Prepared under the auspices of the Cornell Modern
Indonesia Project."
    Bibliography: p.
    1. Indonesia—Politics and government—1942–1949.
2. Nationalism—Indonesia. I. Cornell University.
Modern Indonesia Project. II. Title.
DS644.A6936   959.8'022   74-174891
ISBN 0-8014-0687-0

for W.

My sympathy is for those
who have sacrificed everything
for the freedom of the nation, the state,
    and the people of Indonesia,
those on the left side and those on the right . . .
                                                —the late Soe Hok-gie

Foreword

A relatively small number of this century's revolutions have been studied in sufficient depth, and the analytical concepts and causal patterns developed in these studies have often been borrowed rather indiscriminately in the analysis of other revolutions that have been the object of less thorough scholarly scrutiny. Surely the base provided by the seminal studies has been much too narrow to support the edifice of generalizations subsequently erected.

This book by Benedict Anderson significantly broadens the foundation provided by the rare in-depth treatments. His intensive and detailed analysis of the genesis of the Indonesian revolution discloses important characteristics which are not evident in accounts of other modern revolutions. In carrying our understanding of the formative period of the Indonesian revolution much further than any previous author he shows how its sociopolitical pattern departs considerably from those of other modern revolutions, and that its outbreak cannot be satisfactorily explained through conventional Marxian analysis, or in terms of either an alienation of the intelligentsia or a frustration of rising expectations. The central thrust of revolutionary power in the critical generative stage of the struggle for independence, he makes clear, lay primarily, and indeed to a decisive degree, with Indonesian youth.

In describing the extraordinary revolutionary role of a suddenly militant Indonesian youth, Anderson explains how special

traditional cultural factors and the nature of the Japanese occupation conditioned this group's political consciousness, in particular its perception of its place in the struggle for national independence and social change. Thanks to his intensive study of
both the Japanese occupation and the revolution, his account
provides a continuum bridging the two phenomena and showing
the impact of Japanese political culture on traditional and de-
traditionalized elements of Indonesian society and the effect of
this on the revolution—especially with respect to the youth
groups and the army.

This book provides a much more extensive account than any
previous work of the origins of the political parties and the military, as well as of the youth organizations—relating their development to the problem of building national political power
while pursuing a revolutionary policy. The description of the
growth of the Indonesian army and the important part which it
came to play in the revolution contributes a great deal to an
understanding of the army's present position in Indonesian society and its perception of its own political role.

Of major importance are this study's unusually deep insights
into the often contradictory impulses of national independence
and social revolution and why the strategies for securing one can
easily conflict with those for attaining the other. Indeed, I believe
that this is one of its significant contributions to the literature of
revolution. The dilemma emerges clearly in Anderson's account
of the intense debate and conflict in 1945–46 over revolutionary
strategy, with its exacerbation of the cleavages within both the
political elite and the army. He brings this into sharp focus in
his discussion of the opposing ideas of Sutan Sjahrir and Tan
Malaka—particularly the outstanding difference between them
and their adherents as to whether in the context of the international power balance a successful national revolution could
permit a concurrent social revolution, and whether a national
revolution could develop sufficient political thrust without a social
revolution. This he describes as an ongoing process coloring

the whole intra-revolutionary struggle for power. With Sukarno, Hatta, and Amir Sjarifuddin backing Sjahrir in his insistence that realism dictated assigning a heavy priority to national revolution, Tan Malaka, disadvantaged by the lack of any political organization of his own, was defeated despite his powerful attraction for and initial support by much of the youth. Anderson believes that this defeat over the issue of immediate social revolution not only reinforced the position of the political moderates in Indonesian society but considerably reduced the likelihood that, once national independence was attained, far-reaching social reforms would actually be carried out.

In his account Anderson helps set the record straight concerning the character of Tan Malaka and his capacity and potential for leadership. This nationalist-communist leader, whose early career so closely paralleled Ho Chi Minh's (whom he preceded as Comintern agent for Southeast Asia, and whom he appears to have surpassed in asserting an independent attitude within the Comintern) is assigned a place in Indonesia's revolutionary history which previous authors through ignorance or prejudice have denied him.

This book constitutes an important contribution both to our understanding of the revolutionary process, particularly in colonial countries, and to our knowledge of a critical period in Indonesian history that until now has been only superficially described.

GEORGE McT. KAHIN

Singapore

Preface

There is a tide in the affairs of men
Which, taken at the flood, leads on to fortune;
Omitted, all the voyage of their life
Is bound in shallows and in miseries.

—Shakespeare, *Julius Caesar*

Most studies of a society's politics are heavily influenced in their scope, focus, and orientation by their writers' personal encounters with that society at particular historical conjunctures. This book is no exception. When I first went to Indonesia in 1962, I intended to continue research I had begun in the United States dealing with the impact of the Japanese occupation on Indonesian society during the Second World War. But the experience of living in Indonesia under Guided Democracy gradually but decisively shifted my interests and altered my perspectives.

As I worked through the documentary materials of the late Japanese occupation and interviewed Indonesians about their experiences during that period, I was increasingly struck by similarities between the social conditions and the political atmosphere of the society I was studying and those of the society I observed around me. I was reading about catastrophic inflation, declining production, widespread corruption, oppressive military rule, bureaucratic demoralization, forced labor, incipient famine, compulsory rice deliveries, and the flight of peasants to the cities. Outside the libraries these were matters of daily conversation and experience. From the sources it was evident that in 1944 and

1945 there was a growing sense that the Japanese rule was near-
ing its end; the nearer this end drew, the more feverish political
life became. I felt the same curious mixture of hope, fear, excite-
ment, and misery in the Indonesia of 1963 and 1964, since the
tense political stalemate of Guided Democracy seemed unlikely
to persist beyond the life of its aging architect, President Sukarno.
It was difficult to avoid the feeling that, as in 1945, Indonesia
was rapidly moving toward a major historical crisis, the resolution of which would decide the destiny of a generation.

Accordingly, I became increasingly interested in how the
earlier crisis had been resolved and what the effects of that
resolution had been. As I turned to work on the materials of the
early revolution, I came to the conclusion that from this perspective it was possible, indeed reasonable, to conceive the months
from November 1944 to July 1946 as a largely self-contained
historical period. It was all the easier to adopt this time frame and
perspective in view of the fact that George Kahin had already
described and analyzed the revolution as a whole in his classic
Nationalism and Revolution in Indonesia.

Two other considerations eventually came to shape the scope
and content of my research. In the first place, the time span
chosen seemed to encompass naturally a significant segment not
only of Indonesia's domestic political history, but of international
events: in it the power of Japan declined and finally collapsed,
while the surviving imperial powers had not yet reimposed their
oppressive weight on the destiny of Southeast Asia. In most of
the countries of the area, the experience of Japanese domination
had aroused revolutionary forces that, for a short period, created
possibilities for radical change and regeneration. For a time the
Hukbalahap guerrillas stood at the gates of Manila; the Malayan
Peoples' Anti-Japanese Army was unchallenged on the Malay
Peninsula; and the Viet Minh extended its power virtually unchecked down the long Vietnamese coastline. In Indonesia, too,
for some critical months, revolutionary forces were in the ascendant. It was as if for one brief moment the societies of Southeast

Asia could begin to shape their own futures without dictation from the outside.

In the second place, the time span chosen allowed me to focus attention on an aspect of the revolution I felt had been largely neglected, but which my materials and interviews convinced me was of considerable historical and cultural significance. I found that the contemporary accounts of Indonesians, Dutch, and British alike stressed that the central role in the outbreak of the revolution was taken, not by an alienated intelligentsia, nor in the main by oppressed classes, but by the young, or, as Indonesians refer to them, the *pemuda*. My research strongly confirmed this judgment. Since it was difficult to explain the pemuda's revolutionary activities on the conventional basis of economic deprivation, alienation, or the frustration of "rising expectations," I was led to think increasingly in cultural terms. The experience of living among the pemuda of Guided Democracy gave me the idea that an identifiable pemuda consciousness existed, the product of both ancient traditions and a specific type of modern experience. Finally, I became convinced that the special character and course of the early Indonesian revolution could to a considerable degree be explained by this pemuda consciousness. A major part of this book has therefore been devoted to its description and analysis.

Although I was able to gather a considerable amount of data on developments in the Outer Islands of Indonesia, it did not compare in richness or quantity with what I accumulated on Java. Given the limited scope and the cultural emphasis of my research, I decided, for the sake of economy and clarity, to concentrate my attention on Java. After living there for more than two years, I felt I was still only beginning to understand Javanese society and its traditions. It therefore seemed presumptuous even to try to deal with the other cultures of Indonesia in the way I thought might be possible for Java.

This book, then, is bound by very narrow limits. It covers little more than a year and a half in the history of one island; and it is the product of a highly personal interplay of study, intuition, and experience. Perhaps I should add that most of the actual writing was done after the crisis of Guided Democracy was resolved in the massacres of 1965–66, and with this resolution the Indonesia I had known first and best was gone for good. It was impossible not to be deeply affected by these events, and I have no doubt that they have left their mark on the pages that follow.

In dealing with the perplexing problem of variations in the spelling of Indonesian names, I have found no satisfactory solution. Many Indonesians continue to prefer the Dutch-derived *oe* to the English-derived *u,* and I have spelled many personal names with this *oe,* though for purposes of alphabetization (in the bibliography and the index) I have treated *oe* as *u* except where it occurs at the beginning of a name. Another problem arises from the fact that many Javanese names may be written with either an *a* (reflecting the conventions of Javanese script) or *o* (reflecting speech patterns); thus, for example, Sastrawidagda may also be spelled Sastrowidagdo. The only rule followed here is that each name of an individual person is spelled consistently one way throughout the text.

For simplicity in dealing with Japanese names, I have followed the Western practice of placing the personal name before the family name, rather than the traditional Japanese convention which requires the order to be reversed.

I would like to take the opportunity to acknowledge here my intellectual and imaginative debt to Harry Benda, the late Claire Holt, George Kahin, James Siegel, and John Smail, all of whom have in different ways fundamentally shaped my thinking about Indonesia. A very special debt of gratitude is due to George Kahin, whose book *Nationalism and Revolution in Indonesia* first inspired me to study Indonesia, and who by his personal example, unending patience, and unfailing support made this book possible. Special thanks are also due to John Echols and

Mario Einaudi for their generous advice and guidance over the years.

I am also deeply grateful to Don Emmerson, Herbert Feith, Daniel Lev, Ruth McVey, Nugroho Notosusanto, Ong Hok-ham, T. B. Simatupang, and the late Soe Hok-gie, who read the manuscript in whole or in part, offered many invaluable suggestions and criticisms, and generally made available materials of their own for my benefit.

The list of friends whose thoughts, writings, and experiences have helped me in so many ways is too long to be included here, but my gratitude is no less deep for this. My debt is particularly great to Frederick and Alice Bunnell, Lance Castles, Arlene Lev, Soemarsaid Moertono, Malik Munir, Oey Kok-khioe, Nusjirwan Tirtaamidjaja, Mildred Wagemann, and Linda Weinstein.

Special thanks are due to Mrs. H. A. Joustra and Mr. Rodney de Bruin of the Rijksinstituut voor Oorlogsdocumentatie in Amsterdam and to Miss Mastini Hardjoprakoso of the National Museum Library in Djakarta for their generous help and cooperation.

I would also like to express my appreciation to the Social Science Research Council and the Southeast Asia Program of Cornell University for the financial support that sustained my research in Indonesia, Holland, and the United States.

Finally, many thanks are due to Mrs. Eleanor Parker and Mrs. Roberta Ludgate, who typed successive versions of the manuscript with exceptional skill, patience, and understanding.

BENEDICT R. O'G. ANDERSON

Ithaca, N.Y.

Contents

Chapter 1

Youth and Crisis in Java

The central role of the Angkatan Muda (Younger Generation) in the outbreak of the Indonesian national revolution of
1945 was the most striking political fact of that period. For
the returning Dutch and their British allies, as well as for the
Eurasian and Chinese communities, the once innocent word
pemuda (youth) rapidly acquired an aura of remorseless terrorism.[1] On the Indonesian side, a whole literature of glorifica-
tion attests to an exultant consciousness of the sudden emergence
of youth as a revolutionary force in those critical times. Students
of the development of nationalism in Indonesia have also stressed
the relative newness of this phenomenon in a society where the
values of respect for and submission to the aged were traditionally paramount.[2]

It has been customary to attribute the rise of the Angkatan
Muda primarily to the remarkable efforts made by the Japanese
occupation authorities to rally the youth of Java behind the
struggle against the advancing Allies. There can be little doubt

[1] See, for example, David Wehl, *The Birth of Indonesia* (London,
1948), chap. 2; I. J. Brugmans, et al., eds., *Nederlandsch-Indië onder
Japanse bezetting: Gegevens en documenten over de jaren 1942–1945*
(Franeker, 1960), pp. 599ff.; H. J. van Mook, *The Stakes of Democracy
in Southeast Asia* (New York, 1950), pp. 146–54, 210–11.

[2] George McT. Kahin, *Nationalism and Revolution in Indonesia*
(Ithaca, N.Y., 1952), pp. 129–32; Harry J. Benda, *The Crescent and the
Rising Sun: Indonesian Islam under the Japanese Occupation, 1942–1945*
(The Hague, 1958), p. 172.

1

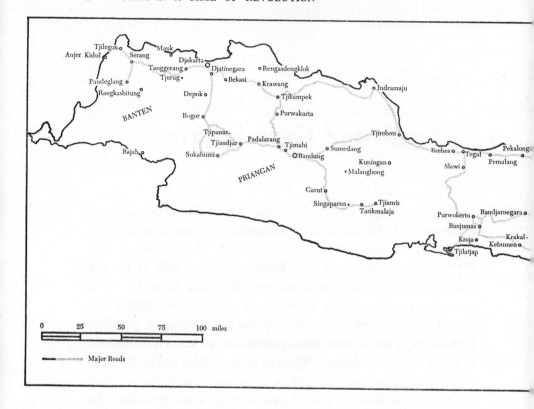

that by intensive propaganda and the creation of a multitude of youth organizations, whether military, paramilitary, political, or even sporting, the Japanese did help to crystallize a powerful self-consciousness among those they mobilized. Yet it should not be supposed that Japanese policy would have had such significant results had it not been for certain deep-rooted aspects of Javanese life, for youth was itself an essential category of traditional Javanese society, to which Javanese culture assigned a style and meaning of its own.

Youth in Javanese Society

In one sense youth was defined by traditional society as a distinct stage in the linear trajectory of the life-arc between childhood and maturity. But in another sense the meaning of youth

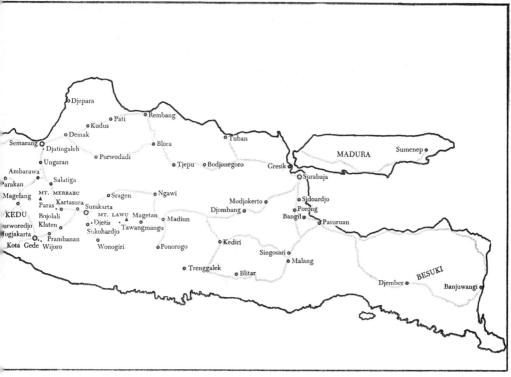

JAVA

transcended the life-arc, and by its autonomous cultural style defined traditional society by systematic oppositions. Only by envisaging the category of youth both as part of the life-arc and as a cultural means of transcending that arc can one understand the role of the youth of Java in a time of revolution.

The life-arc of the Javanese male was traditionally conceived as divided into four distinct stages—childhood, youth, maturity, and old age.[3] The period of childhood lasted until circumcision.[4] Until about the age of six, the boy was habitually indulged by

[3] Cf. Robert R. Jay, *Javanese Villagers: Social Relations in Rural Modjokuto* (Cambridge, Mass., 1969), chap. 3.

[4] Hildred Geertz says that while some pious Islamic families like to have their boys circumcised as early as eight, most wait until they are between ten and fourteen years old. *The Javanese Family: A Study of Kinship and Socialization* (Glencoe, Ill., 1961), p. 120.

parents and kin. Thereafter he was slowly initiated into the elaborate hierarchical norms of his society, a process primarily effected by the gradual withdrawal of the Javanese father from his earlier warm and intimate relationship with his son. From this experience the boy learned that his father was no longer the caressing and protecting presence which enfolded him when his mother was not at hand, but a figure toward whom he was expected to display the central Javanese attitude of *hormat*— respect and deference to the stated or unstated wishes of any person older or higher in social status than himself.[5] Indeed it was only when he had started to master the social problems of handling the ramifications of the hormat system, including the complex honorifics of the Javanese language, that he was said to be *wis Djawa,* or to have become a Javanese.[6]

With the ceremony of circumcision, the boy passed out of childhood. He was henceforth regarded, and encouraged to regard himself, as a man and a Moslem.[7] The time now came for him to move out of the home. No longer a child, not yet the father of children, he entered the liminal period of youth, suspended between two modes of being.

If, heretofore, the boy had been defined by society, the opportunity now was opened for him to define society in turn. The liminal period was conceived as a time for withdrawal, concentration, and preparation. Tradition prescribed that the youth attach himself to a *guru* (teacher) from whom he would acquire knowledge and wisdom. And traditional society itself provided a variety of such teachers. The guru might be an elderly relative with a

[5] "For the Javanese, it does not matter whether a person actually 'feels' respectful 'inside' or merely acts as if he did. In fact a significant aspect of all Javanese social relationships is that the important thing is not the sincerity of the action but the successful concealment of all dissonant aspects of the relationship." *Ibid.,* p. 11.

[6] Before this he is referred to as *durung Djawa,* or not yet Javanese. *Ibid.,* p. 105.

[7] This is beautifully described in Pramoedya Ananta Toer, *Tjerita dari Blora* (Djakarta, 1952), particularly in the story called "Sunat," pp. 77–86.

reputation as a wise man. He might be a local *djago*—a practitioner of magical arts, an expert in *pentjak* (the Javanese art of self-defense), and an adept of the esoteric *ngèlmu kedotan* (science of invulnerability). Or he might be a well-known *kjai* (religious teacher), to whose "school," the *pondok* or *pesantrèn,* the youth would find himself drawn. Traditionally, the pupil lodged with his teacher, who fed and clothed him while initiating him into the secrets of his lore. In return, the youth obeyed his teacher unconditionally and served him by helping to work his land or performing any other task he might impose.

Of these alternatives, it was perhaps the pesantrèn that best reflected traditional society's conception of the appropriate institution to prepare its youth for re-emergence into society. Not only were the pesantrèn the direct descendants of the pre-Islamic *asrama,* the educational institutions of the legendary past, but in their location, routine, spirit, and institutional structure they provided the ideal framework for this process of preparation.[8]

It was not by chance that the pesantrèn were situated outside the larger community, either at the periphery of a village or in the remoter countryside. This physical isolation symbolically represented, but also concretely reinforced, the real withdrawal of the *santri* (students) from society. Since many of the pesantrèn were also economically self-contained units in which the santri lived from the produce of pesantrèn land, the sense of isolation was compounded with a strong consciousness of communal autonomy. In addition, the austere routine of work in the fields, prayer, meditation, and study contributed to building the special atmosphere and spirit that sharply distinguished the pesantrèn from its surroundings.

As described by Samudja Asjari, the spirit of the pesantrèn was molded by four values: simplicity, cooperativeness, solidarity, and selfless sincerity (*keichlasan*).[9] Simplicity was not only

[8] Samudja Asjari, "Kedudukan kjai dalam pondok pesantrèn" (M.A. thesis, University of Gadjah Mada, 1967), p. 84.

[9] *Ibid.,* pp. 102–5.

the natural product of a closed community of unmarried males, without servants or womenfolk. It also expressed the inner sense of the pesantrèn—withdrawal from the ties and hierarchies of Javanese society, and the search for a meaning to life deeper than that contained in social relationships. Cooperativeness and solidarity too signified the drive toward the submergence of self in a community whose purpose was the single-minded pursuit of transcendence. And in the concept of keichlasan, sincere devotion without calculation of profit and loss, was expressed the heart of the relationship not only between the santri themselves, but chiefly between the santri and their kjai. It was a central part of the conception of the pesantrèn that the santri would learn nothing save insofar as he was *ichlas:* only if his attitude toward his kjai was pure, sincere, devoted, and unquestioning would he be able to penetrate the mysteries of which the kjai was master. The teacher was regarded as the student's spiritual father, and their relationship was often closer and deeper than that previously existing between the youth and his biological father.[10]

Removal from society in the closed community of the pesantrèn tended to create in itself a sense of weightlessness, a free-floating intuition of liberation from the tightly ordered rural society, a feeling of exaltation, and a deepening, however transitory, of religious consciousness. But in addition, since the teachings of the pesantrèn, even when strongly Islamic in form, were usually initiations into the secret sources of illumination and

[10] This is particularly well exemplified in the relationship between Ardjuna and Durna in the traditional *wajang* (shadow-play) stories. Durna was the chief strategist of the Kurawa faction, Ardjuna the champion of the Pandawa, yet Ardjuna never forgot, even in the final battle, that Durna was the teacher to whom he owed his prowess. He himself refused to attack his teacher, and bitterly rebuked his ally, Drestadjumena, for the treacherous manner in which he slew Durna. The play *Palgunadi* depicts the choice Durna makes between two of his favorite pupils, Ardjuna and Palgunadi. The fact that he betrays Palgunadi to help Ardjuna is regarded as one of the reasons for his subsequent death by treachery on the battlefield Kurusétra.

cosmic energy, they created a vital élan of their own.[11] Both for
the santri themselves, as well as for the community from which
they stood apart, the pesantrèn were concentrations of contained
power.[12]

For many Javanese, this period in the development of a boy's
life was purely transitory, a genuine rite of passage from childhood into maturity. Conceived within the framework of the life-
arc it was a necessary stage before his rebirth into the sexuality,
hierarchy, and routine of adult existence. Nonetheless there always remained a minority in the pesantrèn who found its way of
life permanently fulfilling. These became the wandering santri
of Javanese classics such as the *Serat Tjentini*,[13] moving from
pesantrèn to pesantrèn in quest of wiser teachers, deeper experiences, and higher truths. Within the settled order of rural Javanese society, circulating santri formed a recognized but deviant
group.[14] They formed part of that essential class of what Pigeaud

[11] This was usually done through various types of ascetic practice
and meditation, known as *tapa* or *semadi*. An important part of pesantrèn
education consisted of learning religious incantations, and their esoteric
meaning, as well as gaining an intuitive comprehension of the absolute
by means of special riddles and conundrums. See, Benedict O'Gorman
Anderson, "The Languages of Indonesian Politics," *Indonesia*, no. 1
(April 1966), pp. 89–116; and for a specifically Javanese explanation
of this phenomenon, K. G. P. A. A. Mangkunagara VII, *On the Wajang
Kulit (Purwa) and Its Symbolic and Mystical Elements*, trans. Claire
Holt (Ithaca, N. Y., 1957).

[12] For an analysis of Javanese thinking about power, see Benedict
O'Gorman Anderson, "The Idea of Power in Javanese Culture," in Claire
Holt, ed., *Culture and Politics in Indonesia* (Ithaca, N.Y., 1972).

[13] This extraordinary encyclopaedic work has been published in
romanized script, but as yet no one has attempted its translation. See
Serat Tjentini, transcribed and edited by R. Ng. Soeradipoera, R. Poerwasoewignja, and R. Wirawangsa (Batavia, 1912–15). A Dutch-language
summary of the contents may, however, be found in Theodoor Pigeaud,
De Serat Tjabolang en de Serat Tjentini: Inhoudsopgaven (Batavia, 1933).

[14] The word *santri* is used here in its ancient and general sense of
"pupil." Only in comparatively modern times has it come to mean the
devout Moslem minority in Java (as opposed to the *abangan* majority of

has called *trekkers en zwervers* (travellers and wanderers), which provided the unpredictable element in the traditional community —*satria lelana* [15] looking for adventure, strolling players, magicians, gamblers, and brigands. Such groups were never sharply differentiated, and individuals might assume various of these roles at different times.[16] For example, the santri who had studied

---

nominal Moslems, who primarily adhere to a syncretic traditional religion based largely on animist and Hindu-Buddhist beliefs).

[15] *Satria lelana* were wandering aristocratic warriors, unattached to any particular kingdom or royal master. They were traditionally the source of political and other disturbances, and were a favorite subject of popular legend. See Theodoor Pigeaud, *Javaanse volksvertoningen* (Batavia, 1938), p. 35.

[16] Compare, for example, the legendary folk hero, Radèn Pandji, and the more historical figure of Kèn Angrok, founder of the East Javanese dynasty of Singosari. Of the latter, Vlekke writes that "the young man started on a career of crime, committing theft, murder, rape, and all manner of violence, not out of baseness of mind, but because the magic power received from the gods ran too strongly in him to be controlled. He had to find an outlet for his superhuman strength; the laws of man were not made for him." See Bernard H. M. Vlekke, *Nusantara: A History of Indonesia* (rev. ed.; The Hague, 1959), p. 54. The theme of the magical gambler-brigand-prince regularly recurs in classical Javanese literature. See, for example, W. L. Olthof, trans., *Babad Tanah Djawi in proza* (The Hague, 1941). This type of figure was by no means confined to the ethnically Javanese areas of Indonesia, but existed in various forms throughout the archipelago. The best-known example outside Java was perhaps the *paréwa* of Minangkabau—"wild" members of the traditional community who broke many of its rules and defied many Islamic precepts, yet were the guardsmen of the mosques. The writer Hamka gives a fine picture of the paréwa ideal: "They live by gambling, cockfighting, etc. They are also experts in pentjak and *silat* [traditional art of self-defense]. Their society is widespread, and paréwa from different *kampung* [neighborhoods] hold each other in mutual esteem and admiration. . . . If a paréwa once makes a friend, he will defend that friend to the death, and will take his family as his own: it is as though they have the same mother, the same brothers and sisters, the same relatives. They are forbidden to flirt with girls. If one of them loses everything at gambling, the winner will give him clothes and money, and the cost of his travel home." See H. A. M. K. Amrullah [Hamka], *Tenggelamnja kapal Van der Wijck* (5th ed.; Djakarta, 1957), p. 111. Here and subse-

the science of invulnerability in the pesantrèn might well turn his skill to practical use in his subsequent travels. The pupil of the djago specializing in pentjak might be no less inclined to test what he had learned.

Throughout Javanese history there were always such self-contained pools of single males, within or between pesantrèn, or attached to the djago: some of them were boys going through their rites of passage into adulthood, while others were older men for whom the esoteric wandering life, mediating between the natural and invisible world, was permanently appealing. It was in these pools that the utopian, voluntarist, and transcendent elements of traditional Javanese thought found their most ardent adherents. In times of tranquillity and order, utopia was the world within—whether the search for the absolute through study, asceticism, and prayer, or the quest for power through physical and magical exercises. In times of crisis, however, utopia often assumed an external aspect in response to the social disintegration and natural catastrophes which were traditionally regarded as the visible signs of dynastic decline and danger in the cosmological order. Under these conditions, the santri and their like flowed out into society in many guises: as the zealous supporters of new dynastic pretenders, as propagandists for religious brotherhoods, and even simply as magico-religious bandits. It is scarcely surprising, therefore, to find that such groups were a traditional source of leadership for the countless localized peasant uprisings in the last century of Dutch colonial rule.[17]

But the significance of the pesantrèn in times of crisis was not simply that they often provided leadership for rural rebellions,

quently, translations from the Indonesian and Dutch are mine, except as otherwise specified.

[17] See G. W. J. Drewes, *Drie Javaansche goeroe's: Hun leven, onderricht en messiasprediking* (Leiden, 1925), pp. 10–49; Sartono Kartodirdjo, *The Peasants' Revolt of Banten in 1888* (The Hague, 1966); and Sartono Kartodirdjo, "Agrarian Radicalism in Java—Its Setting and Development," in Holt, ed., *Culture and Politics.*

for the pools of santri themselves naturally swelled in periods of stress, when the normal rhythms of the community were *gontjang,* or out of kilter. When society itself succumbed to chaos and disintegration, the counter-institutions of the pesantrèn and the djago band offered a model of a transcendent order. As the meaning of the regular life-arc was undermined by war, oppression, or economic disaster, the asceticism and élan within pesantrèn-like communities took on a general significance unimaginable in times of peace. Traditional deviant aspects of santri existence—sexual abstinence, fraternal solidarity, selfless devotion, nomadic wandering, and dealings with the supernatural— were now seen as in harmony with the times. The sense that everything was in suspension while disorder raged in the cosmos seemed to be reflected in the suspended quality of the pesantrèn's inner order. The society itself became a larger pesantrèn, in which the pesantrèn life-style assumed the mode of normality and necessity. For in periods of great crisis the whole society moved to free itself from the cycle of routine and regularity, and accepted the suspended soaring of the spirit which underlay the pesantrèn's conception of itself. Outside the pesantrèn marriages were postponed, agricultural work was cut short, and families were abandoned. When times of peace returned and society resumed its "normal" aspect, the temporary santri went back to their families and labors, while the committed santri withdrew to their retreats. Over the years, the pools of santri might increase or decline, but they were always there, built into traditional society, and ready to provide that society with a transcendent conception of itself when the times demanded it.

A Time Out of Joint

Only by bearing this tradition in mind is it possible to understand the situation of the pemuda in the period of the later Japanese occupation, for by 1945 the disruptions caused by the collapse of the Dutch colonial regime in 1942 and three years of war and military rule had begun to precipitate Javanese society into that sense of *kegelisahan* (tremblingness),[18] of being loose from its moorings, which traditionally signaled the emergence of the santri into the outer world.

At the close of the Japanese occupation there was a widespread feeling of impending catastrophe. Social and economic conditions had deteriorated rapidly under a combination of natural calamities, chaotic administration, and dislocations caused by the war. The harvest of 1944 was almost completely ruined by drought. The army-imposed economic policy of strict autarchy within each residency created great hardships. The policy was partly necessitated by the critical shortage of transportation both in and around Java, but it was also designed to permit self-supporting local resistance to an anticipated Allied invasion. In practice, however, the autarchy system made little allowance for the existence in Java of surplus and deficit areas, with the result that the deficit areas were especially hard hit. The pressures thereby created to evade the autarchy regulations led to extensive rice smuggling,[19] black-marketeering, and, since the blind eye of officialdom was needed, bribery. Furthermore, the military government's extravagant deficit spending drove the rupiah down to one-sixtieth of its value in three and a half years.[20] Indonesia's first taste of the inflation which was to haunt her subsequent history rapidly undermined the probity of the civil service, and petty corruption became endemic. The inflation also accentuated class differences and exacerbated other social tensions.[21]

[18] The evocative word used by Sutan Sjahrir in *Our Struggle,* trans. Benedict O'Gorman Anderson (Ithaca, N.Y., 1968).

[19] This is well described in Idrus' superb short-story "Och . . . Och . . . Och," translated in *Indonesia,* no. 2 (Oct. 1966), 129–34.

[20] For figures on the inflation, see *Star Weekly* (Djakarta), no. 6 (Feb. 10, 1946).

[21] For excellent material on the socioeconomic situation in Java in the late occupation period, see "Tjatatan stenografis sidang Sanyō Kaigi ke-empat pada tanggal 8 bulan 1, 2605," doc. no. 036626–55 in the Indies Collection at the Rijksinstituut voor Oorlogsdocumentatie in Amsterdam (hereinafter cited as IC-RVO). Part of this document has

The dangerous effect of scarcity and inflation on the morale of the official class was clear enough to the Japanese. It was one of the reasons, in addition to the need to ensure regular, smooth supplies of food and war materiel to the Japanese army and its auxiliaries throughout the archipelago, that the notorious system of enforced rice deliveries was set up in 1943. Under this system, the peasants were compelled to sell large portions of their rice crop to government agencies at very low controlled prices.[22] The rice so obtained was in part passed on to the military and civilian bureaucracies, which were thus subsidized by the plundering of the rural poor. The supply system in general rapidly sclerosed under the twin pressures of the rapacity of the military administration and growing corruption within the military-controlled distribution system. A widespread breakdown of health services and pest control caused several outbreaks of epidemics. The ratio of deaths to births rose to unexampled heights.[23] The precipitous decline of Java's prewar export economy in plantation products also created large pools of unemployment.[24] The plight of the peasantry, particularly in the deficit areas of the northern

---

been translated in Benedict O'Gorman Anderson, "The Problem of Rice," *Indonesia,* no. 2 (Oct. 1966), pp. 77–123. For a good short analysis of the reasons why this kind of inflation accentuates class conflict, see J. A. C. Mackie, *Problems of the Indonesian Inflation* (Ithaca, N.Y., 1967), pp. 62f.

[22] See Anderson, "Problem of Rice." For example (pp. 88–89), in the Residency of Bogor the levies varied from 40 per cent of the crop for those owning and working less than one hectare up to 75 per cent for those owning and working over five hectares. In the Residency of Banten 75 per cent of the crop had to be sold to the government regardless of the pattern of landholding.

[23] See *ibid.,* p. 93, for the grim statistics for the residencies of Pati and Kedu in late 1944.

[24] This can readily be deduced from the statistics on sugar production cited in Theodoor de Bruin, "Gevolgen der internering van Nederlanders voor de economie van Nederlands-Indië tijdens de Japanse bezetting (Maart 1942–Augustus 1945)" (M.A. thesis, Rotterdam, 1962), p. 8. For example, whereas in 1942 there were 85 sugar mills in operation producing a total of 1,326,000 tons of sugar, by 1945 there were only 13 mills, and production dropped to 84,000 tons.

littoral and the mountainous southern coast, caused alarm even in the comfortably situated circles of the Djakarta political elite.[25] The critical conditions in the hinterland accelerated a decades-old flight to the cities, which absorbed a great deal of the unemployed and underemployed misery of the Japanese period, but on a highly unstable and short-term basis.

The institution of the *rōmusha* program of forced labor further eroded any sense of stability and order within Javanese society. The rōmusha were mostly peasants from the poorer areas of East and Central Java,[26] who were induced by various means to contract themselves out for work on military construction projects. Many were sent to Sumatra and even farther afield to Burma, Siam, and the eastern islands. They were usually treated with great brutality and callousness. Of the estimated 500,000 who were mobilized for work outside their own areas, not more than a small fraction returned home after the war.[27] The evil effects of the rōmusha system were compounded by the actual

[25] This comes out very clearly in the "Tjatatan stenografis," though the elite had very little idea of the roots of the disastrous economic situation, or how to set about improving it.

[26] See Tan Malaka, *Dari pendjara ke pendjara,* II (Jogjakarta, n.d.), 170. See also John R. W. Smail, *Bandung in the Early Revolution, 1945–1946* (Ithaca, N.Y., 1964), p. 12. My own interviews generally confirm the picture given by these two authors.

[27] According to W. F. Wertheim, almost 300,000 were sent overseas, of whom barely 70,000 returned alive after the war. See *Indonesian Society in Transition: A Study of Social Change* (Bandung, 1956), p. 228. These figures are probably inflated. John O. Sutter indicates that the rōmusha program started toward the end of 1943. See *Indonesianisasi: Politics in a Changing Economy, 1940–1955* (Ithaca, N.Y., 1959), pp. 187–88. If this is the case, the program would have had only a year and a half to operate before the Japanese surrender. Moreover, in these years Allied attacks on Japanese shipping were causing increasing paralysis in the internal sea communications of the Greater East Asia Co-prosperity Sphere. The figures should be compared with those for transmigration from Java to the Outer Islands in the post-independence era. According to Indonesia, Biro Pusat Statistik, *Statistical Pocketbook of Indonesia, 1961* (Djakarta, 1962), pp. 16–17, the number averaged approximately 21,000 a year.

application of the program, which made it possible to buy exemption either by bribing the recruiting officials or by paying a poverty-stricken compatriot to take one's place. In this way the more powerful and prosperous groups of the community (rich traders, officials, the Chinese) were able to profit further from their good fortune, while the sufferings of the poorer strata of the population were multiplied.[28]

No less serious than the social consequences of the rōmusha program (which indeed may have helped "solve" the unemployment problem when the export plantations closed down), were its political consequences. In the first place, almost every echelon of the Indonesian official class was compelled by the Japanese to assume some responsibility for the program, whether by organizing recruitment at the village level, by propagandizing at higher levels, or simply by doing nothing to obstruct it. Village headmen and district officers in charge of running the program in a good number of cases made its effects all the worse by designating for rōmusha service those elements in rural society they disliked or feared.

The complicity the Japanese imposed on the established politicians, officials, and businessmen was a major factor in the secular decline in the prestige and authority of these groups throughout the Japanese period. Each in its own way, by helping operate the program or buying exemption from it, or by profiting from the corruption, black-marketeering, and forced rice deliveries, earned the hostility and distrust of the victims of these policies, and indeed all those strata of Indonesian society most ruthlessly ravaged by the occupation government.

From the point of view of the dispossessed, the peasants, the

[28] See, for example, Tjamboek Berdoeri [pseud.], *Indonesia dalem api dan bara* (Malang, 1947), pp. 150–52, 155. He notes that when the Japanese began recruiting Chinese youths for various types of guard duties, it was typically the sons of poor Chinese who were caught. Rich parents paid doctors to certify that their sons had weak hearts. Within the Chinese community, recruiters used their power extensively for corruption and blackmail.

workers, the unemployed and the forcibly recruited, the close of the Japanese occupation was a time of growing darkness and desolation. For the first time in living memory, people were falling dead in the streets from starvation or disease, mendicancy spread silently but horrifyingly through the cities, and the sense of being precipitated out of a stable order increased with every month that passed. From the point of view of all strata in society not directly associated with the Japanese government, a sense of moral crisis, of the traditional order's being upturned, of a transvaluation of normal values also swiftly developed. The classical images of the *Djaman Édan* gained renewed currency as traditional culture strove to define and shape unprecedented experiences.[29] The times were once again out of joint; it was an age in which fools profited from their folly and the wise suffered for their wisdom.

It was thus in a society already *gelisah* with these sufferings and premonitions that the pemuda of the war years grew up. One cannot doubt that the suspension of traditional society in times of crisis was now reexperienced with unusual intensity under conditions of total war and the harsh administration of the Japanese occupation army.

[29] See Drewes, *Drie Javaansche goeroe's,* pp. 154–63; R. W. Dwidjosugondo [Tjantrik Mataram], *Peranan ramalan Djojobojo dalam revolusi kita* (Bandung, n.d. [1954?]), pp. 29ff. Both give lists of the signs of an oncoming crisis of the world order. See Brugmans et al., eds., *Nederlandsch-Indië* (pp. 599f.), for the appearance of such signs in Japanese-occupied Java in 1945, as observed by members of the population.

Chapter 2

Experience and Vision

While the youth of Java were deeply affected by the changes taking place in the society around them, their own immediate experiences were at least as significant in the shaping of pemuda consciousness. As will become evident, various sectors of the youthful population underwent very different experiences, largely in accordance with their position in the class and educational structure of late colonial society. Yet at the same time the institutions created for youth by the Japanese authorities bore certain common features that, by an irony of history, replicated some of the essential characteristics of the traditional pesantrèn. Accordingly, the experience of being part of these institutions reinforced the cultural power of that tradition no less than it instilled new conceptions and cemented new relationships.

In 1940, it has been reliably estimated, there were probably just under five million young people on Java between fifteen and nineteen.[1] In that same year, in all of Indonesia (to which Java contributed two-thirds of the total population), there were 1,789 students enrolled in senior high schools offering a Western type of education, and 637 attending college-level institutions.[2] In very rough terms, then, it could be said that less than one in every two thousand of the youth of Java in that year was under-

[1] Widjojo Nitisastro, *Population Trends in Indonesia* (Ithaca, N.Y., 1970), p. 161. Here and subsequently "Java" is used to refer both to Java itself and to the smaller adjacent island of Madura.

[2] Kahin, *Nationalism and Revolution,* pp. 31–32.

16

going the experience of upper-level nontraditional education. The tiny size of this minority reflected not merely the conservative character of colonial educational policy but also the fact that right up to the outbreak of the war Javanese (and Indonesian) society remained overwhelmingly rural.[3]

The minority was not only exceedingly small, but highly privileged. Most of the students were the children of prominent members of the *prijaji*,[4] of the small group of successful professional men in the largest urban centers, or of well-established migrant families from the Outer Islands. Many were also related to the more notable politicians of the prewar nationalist movement. They were a group that sprang from those select milieux in which Dutch was the language of the home and everyday conversation, and all were highly conscious of their elite status within native society.

During the latter years of the Dutch era, youth politics had been principally confined to this group.[5] Its leadership was heavily concentrated in the two cities of Djakarta (or Batavia, as it was known at the time) and Bandung, where the Medical and

[3] According to W. Brand the population of Java was 95.3 per cent rural in 1930, and even as late as 1961 the figure had only dropped to 84.4 per cent. "Some Statistical Data on Indonesia," *Bijdragen tot de taal-, land- en volkenkunde,* CXXV, 3 (1969), 308.

[4] *Prijaji* refers to the traditional ruling class of Java, which the Dutch turned into an obedient, privileged instrument by incorporating it into the colonial administrative apparatus. For a good description of this group and its culture, see Clifford Geertz, *The Religion of Java* (New York, 1960), Part III.

[5] See J. M. Pluvier, *Overzicht van de ontwikkeling der nationalistische beweging in Indonesië in de jaren 1930 tot 1942* (The Hague, 1953), pp. 151–54 and *passim;* J. B. Amstutz, "The Indonesian Youth Movement, 1908–1955" (Ph.D. thesis, Fletcher School of Law and Diplomacy, 1958), pp. 1–74; and Indonesia, Departemen Pendidikan Dasar dan Kebudajaan, Biro Pemuda, *Sedjarah perdjuangan pemuda Indonesia* (Djakarta, 1965), pp. 23–96 (hereinafter cited as Biro Pemuda, *Sedjarah perdjuangan pemuda Indonesia*). Amstutz estimates (p. 1) that at no time in the colonial era were more than 10,000 young people active in political organizations. Compare the figures for the Japanese period given below.

Law faculties and the Technical Institute were located. It was indeed the experience of life in these institutions, to which students were attracted from all parts of Indonesia, that explains why it was among the ranks of these youths that the explicit ideology of Indonesian nationalism was first formulated and disseminated. The young Sukarno graduated from the Technical Institute in Bandung in 1926 and founded the Indonesian National Party (Partai Nasional Indonesia, or PNI) the next year.[6] His fellow founders all had university degrees.[7] And it was at the second Congress of Indonesian Youth, held October 26–28, 1928, that the song that would become the Indonesian national anthem, "Indonesia Raja," was sung for the first time, and the red and white flag flown. At that same congress the participating youth took the historic oath of commitment to one people, the Indonesian people, one nation, the Indonesian nation, and one language, the Indonesian language. In a real sense the development of nationalism among these educated youths was less the result of their readings in European history or their encounters with racist colonial authorities than of their experiences in schools whose raison d'être derived directly from the centralized structure of the Netherlands Indies in the twentieth century. Nationalism was the only explanation that could be given for each student's having made the journey from whatever home he had left to enter one classroom with the others. Only nationalism made sense of the new life on which they were collectively embarked. But insofar as this nationalism was a response to experience, it was necessarily limited to those who could participate more or less directly in that experience. The politically-minded youth of the 1930's were profoundly isolated from the rest of their contemporaries. It was not until the Japanese period that nationalism spread deeply into small-town and

[6] For a full discussion of Sukarno's early career and involvement in the nationalist movement, see Bernhard Dahm, *Sukarno and the Struggle for Indonesian Independence* (Ithaca, N.Y., 1969), pp. 21–126.

[7] Kahin, *Nationalism and Revolution,* p. 90.

rural Java; and it did so then because of the new experiences encountered there, to which it gave coherent meaning.

For the Western-educated minority the initial effect of the occupation was decidedly a shock. The military government closed all the faculties. Dutch was no longer permitted as the language of instruction in any type of school. Since virtually all upper-level textbooks were in Dutch, this meant that much of higher education was suspended for the duration of the war years, though the Medical Faculty was reopened on an ad hoc basis in 1943.[8] The Japanese did eventually open certain "educational centers" of their own, but these could scarcely be described as academic institutions. Deprived of the chance to continue their formal education, and often without means to support themselves when deteriorating communications disrupted contact with their families, unemployed students went in various directions. Some, indeed, returned to their homes. Others went to work in various capacities for the military government, most notably in the Sendenbu (Department of Propaganda), where they were given significant roles to play. Still others, thanks to their financial means, were able to withdraw into private life, meeting with friends, holding informal discussions, reading intensively on all manner of subjects that seemed relevant to their condition, and reflecting on their future. Later on in the occupation, some of these youths were drawn slowly into the underground groups that grew up on the base of such intimate daily interactions.

The most significant aspect of the experience of the elite and educated youth, who were, it should be stressed, largely confined to the cities of Djakarta and Bandung, was that it involved a break in the expected trajectory of their careers. Suspension of

[8] According to Amstutz there were 850 Indonesians enrolled in university-level educational institutions in 1941. "The Indonesian Youth Movement," p. 3. In an interview granted to the author on June 4, 1967, Subadio Sastrosatomo, who was a student in Djakarta at the time, estimated that at the height of the occupation there were not more than 150 students engaged in formal study there.

classes meant, in a war of unpredictable duration, a suspension of their lives. Normal routines and expectations no longer held good. Willy-nilly, it was a time for withdrawal and self-preparation. The accidents of war had created for those few youths whose education had removed them from the traditional cultural sphere a complex of experiences that moved them back toward it.

But while the Japanese closed down some institutions for the education of the youth of Java, they created new ones that were to prove of decisive importance for the future. Of these, the most important was the Pembela Tanah Air (Fatherland Defense Force), or "Peta," established in October 1943.[9] The Peta was designed by the Japanese Sixteenth Army authorities as a decentralized auxiliary guerrilla force to be deployed in the event of an Allied invasion of Java. It was specifically stated that the new military force would be stationed in its area of recruitment, and would be used solely for local defense.[10] In view of the type of fighting that it was expected to carry on, the Peta was organized only up to the battalion (*daidan*) level, each battalion containing on the average about five to six hundred men.[11] Generally speaking, the Peta commands coincided with the administrative districts of the island, or *kabupatèn,* though in the case of very large kabupatèn like Djakarta and Bandung there might be two or even three.

Those chosen for training as battalion commanders (*daidanchō*) were in most cases not school-age youths but somewhat older men believed by the Japanese to have influence among and au-

[9] On the founding of the Peta, see Benda, *The Crescent and the Rising Sun,* chap. 4, notes 35, 36; O. D. P. Sihombing, *Pemuda Indonesia menantang fasisme Djepang* (Djakarta, 1962), pp. 153–74; Sedjarah Militer Kodam VI Siliwangi, *Siliwangi dari masa kemasa* (Djakarta, 1968), pp. 31f.; Radèn Gatot Mangkupradja, "The Peta and My Relations with the Japanese," *Indonesia,* no. 5 (April 1968), pp. 105–34; and George S. Kanahele, "The Japanese Occupation of Indonesia: Prelude to Independence" (Ph.D. thesis, Cornell University, 1967), pp. 120–27.

[10] Smail, *Bandung,* p. 25.

[11] By the end of the occupation, the Japanese had built up 66 such battalions in Java, and three in Bali.

thority over the youth. Significantly enough, they were often local schoolteachers, officials, or Islamic notables.[12] They were not given intensive military training, and were usually not confined to the asrama (barracks), as were the more junior officers. Their essential function was to give moral leadership and exercise political supervision over their subordinates.

If youths were normally excluded from the senior echelon of the Peta, the ranks of company commanders (*chūdanchō*) and especially platoon commanders (*shōdanchō*) were largely composed of them.[13] The chūdanchō and shōdanchō were given extensive and effective military training suited to their rank, and were subjected to strict military discipline.[14] Peta trainees were

[12] A picture of the types of men recruited as daidanchō emerges from comparing the following: Kasman Singodimedjo, an urban Islamic teacher and politician, in Djakarta; K. H. Sjam'oen, a conservative, rural kjai, in Banten; Sudarsono, a well-placed police official from the Dutch period, in Jogjakarta; Mustopo, from the family of the *bupati* (administrative head) of Kediri, and a dentist by profession, in Surabaja; and Sudirman, an Islamic schoolteacher, in Kroja. Kasman, Mustopo, and Sudirman, at least, were men in their early and middle thirties. Mohammed Saleh, a daidanchō in Jogjakarta, related that in his case the Japanese authorities asked the local branches of the Muhammadijah (modernist Islamic social and educational organization) to give them a list of candidates for the job. He himself was only fourth on the list, but was finally selected over the others because of his robust physique and organizing capacities. Interview with Mohammed Saleh Werdisastro, Jan. 3, 1963. Probably his record as a scout and youth leader also recommended him to the Japanese military.

[13] Sedjarah Militer Kodam VI, *Siliwangi dari masa kemasa*, p. 32, makes this point explicitly. Kanahele, "Japanese Occupation," p. 124, stresses that this was particularly true of the shōdanchō.

[14] See Nugroho Notosusanto, "Instansi jang melaksanakan pembentukan tentara Peta," *Madjalah Ilmu2 Sastra Indonesia*, II (June 1964), 285–88; Anonymous, untitled document found in Sixteenth Army Headquarters by the Allies, IC-RVO doc. no. 006501-6; Capt. Munenari Yanagawa, "Statement" of Oct. 14, 1945, IC-RVO doc. no. 006508-16; Capt. Kisō Tsuchiya, "Statement" of March 3–8, 1947, in Tjipinang Prison, IC-RVO doc. no. 00625-35; and esp. Oemar Bahsan, *Tjatatan ringkas tentang: Peta ("Pembela Tanah-Air") dan Peristiwa Rengasdengklok* (Bandung, n.d. [1955?]), sections 3 and 7, and esp. pp. 9–14.

schooled in asrama set up outside urban and village communities. This isolation served practical purposes, but was also intended to encourage the youths to absorb the pure spirit of Bushidō, undistracted by the routine world outside.

At first the tough military discipline shocked some of the recruits. Soehoed Prawiroatmodjo, who went through this training himself, wryly recalls that "the boys had been used to drinking coffee and smoking cigarettes early in the morning, and sitting in a dream, with their thoughts far away. When they were forced to get up and do an early run, they couldn't control their bodies and their pants often got wet—not from sweat. Some of them lost as much as 35 pounds in the first weeks." But it was not long before the impressive rigor and commitment of the Japanese military code had their effect. Soehoed notes that the training period was not primarily intended by the Japanese "for intensive study of the history of the military arts, military strategy, combat tactics and weapons technology . . . but rather for acquiring physical and spiritual strength." They insisted that "victory or defeat did not depend on the size of one's military forces. Smaller forces could always conquer their adversaries, provided they had a burning spirit of struggle and had undergone complete training. . . . Thus they implanted the idea that the single most important quality of a soldier was the soldierly spirit [*semangat roch kepradjuritan*]." [15]

A similar impression emerges from the recollections of another former Peta officer, Kemal Idris, who described his experience of Japanese training as follows:

I entered the Seinendōjō [training school at Tanggerang] *in order not to be out of work.* . . . With 49 others I was there for about four months in all. *None of our families knew where we were going.* We were given very heavy and harsh training. Discipline was very extreme, we were beaten over the head with shoes and things like that.

[15] *Perlawanan bersendjata terhadap fasisme Djepang* (Djakarta, 1953), pp. 50, 54, 57, 59.

Yanagawa was the commander, and we admired and respected him enormously. He was very brave, quite honest and ruthlessly impartial. . . . To give two examples. We were divided into two platoons of 25 men each, A and B. Someone in A lost a cartridge on exercises. We spent twelve hours, all of us, including him [Yanagawa], looking for it, without eating or drinking. Again, we were taught to regard our rifles as part of our bodies. Once one of our boys broke a rifle cleaner, but didn't own up. We were all summoned and made to kneel on two vertical wooden slats for about ten hours. Of course we were trained to sit on our heels, but not on slats, on the floor. Yanagawa and the other Japanese did the same thing, only getting up to slap someone around who couldn't take it. . . . I remember one other incident, when we couldn't take the raw fishy food that the Japanese gave us to eat, so a group of us broke bounds and went to get *saté* [barbecued shish-kebab] in the village. We were hauled over the coals afterwards because *we were absolutely forbidden to leave the asrama.* It was supposed to be secret. But when we explained honestly, we were hardly punished at all. The Japanese had the idea that it was always better to tell the truth. Their belief was that if you could lie, your *djiwa* [spirit] couldn't be straight, it must be *béngkok* [crooked, bent], not sincere. This meant you couldn't be a wholly committed fighter. Too much thinking. A large part of our training was simply in a kind of semi-meditation.[16]

The institution at which Kemal Idris was trained, the Seinendōjō (Youth Training School for Military Arts), was set up in secret prior to the formation of the Peta, and was designed to create a small corps of Japanese-speaking Indonesians to help train prospective Peta volunteers. The name derives from the Japanese word for youth (*seinen*) and the ancient Japanese institution of *dōjō*. Dōjō were schools where *kendō* and other forms of traditional combat were taught by highly revered masters. The schools were usually located in remote places, and their teachings stressed

[16] Interview with Kemal Idris, at that time a brigadier general, Jan. 18, 1964; italics mine. It is of interest to note that Kemal was himself a member of the privileged minority discussed earlier; for biographical details, see the Appendix.

self-denial, meditation, and unquestioning devotion to the master.[17]

The resemblance between the dōjō and the pesantrèn is self-evident. But the Seinendōjō and the Peta were more than reminiscences of traditional forms. Their purpose, the defense of the fatherland, was entirely modern. Whereas the nationalism of the educated youth of the prewar years had been the necessary but indirect outcome of the implicit logic of the colonial educational structure, in the Peta structure and explicit meaning coincided. It was not only the experience of being in the Peta but the specific ideological training the institution provided that created and heightened the nationalist political consciousness of its members. Soehoed, for example, describes an occasion on which he and his comrades were asked by their Japanese trainer where their weapons came from. Some said from Holland; others mentioned various other foreign countries. The trainer told them that they were all wrong. "Your weapons come from the Indonesian people. They are the products of the sweat of the Indonesian people, squeezed out of them by the Dutch, and used for their oppression. Now these weapons have been turned back to the sons of Indonesia themselves, to be used to defend the people and the fatherland. Use them well, so that the trust the people have bestowed on their sons is not betrayed." [18] On the one hand, the Peta provided military training in preparation for the day the fatherland would have to be defended. On the other hand, it was also a withdrawal from society, and an initiation into secret learning. In the Peta asrama power was being concentrated, ready to be released into society when the impending crisis broke.

It has been noted that the Peta ranks below that of daidanchō were largely filled by the youth. But it was also true that those recruited for leadership positions in the organization were not randomly distributed throughout the youthful population. There

[17] For this information on the dōjō, the author is indebted to Dr. Akira Nagazumi.

[18] Soehoed, *Perlawanan bersendjata*, p. 66.

is convincing evidence to suggest that they were drawn predominantly from lower-level prijaji families, from the ranks of
village and small-town schoolteachers, and from the kin of prominent rural kjai.[19] In daidan close to the larger cities, sons of
upper-level prijaji and professional families could be found. For
example, the sons of the well-known conservative official and
politician Soetardjo Kartohadikoesoemo and the lawyer Mr.
Singgih held middle-level Peta ranks in the areas of Purwakarta
and Djakarta. In the Priangan, the prominent Peta figure Sukanda
Bratamenggala came from the dominant *ménak* (Sundanese
upper prijaji) stratum.[20] Farther out in the hinterland, connections with the higher elites were less apparent, and the links with
local elites more significant. Levels of education were lower,
and ties with the countryside more deeply felt.[21]

While the 37,000-man Peta was the most prominent of the
new educational institutions created by the military authorities,
it was paralleled by a variety of other institutions of scarcely less
significance for the future. In mid-1943 the Heihō (Auxiliary
Forces) was formed as an integral part of the Imperial armies.
By contrast with the Peta, which was stationed in the areas of
its recruitment, the Heihō was liable to service wherever the
interests of the Japanese required it. Also, unlike the Peta, its
officers were Japanese: it contained no Indonesians above the

[19] Soehoed gives the backgrounds of the ten candidates for Peta officer
training recruited from the rural East Java Residency of Kediri. Six
were small-town officials, three were teachers, and one a Moslem notable.
In fact, all were from small urban centers. Soehoed adds drily, "It is clear
that in general these people belonged to the upper echelons of [provincial]
Indonesian society." *Ibid.,* p. 41. On the other hand, he insists (p. 51)
that the Peta as a whole was drawn from all levels of society (peasants,
workers, traders, and officials), all religious groups, and all educational
strata (graduates of colleges, high schools, primary schools, and pesantrèn). There may be an ideological element in this assertion, however,
since the Indonesian military has always officially stressed its broad popular base.

[20] For biographical details on Sukanda, see the Appendix.

[21] A certain minimum of education was required for effective performance in the technical aspects of Peta training programs.

rank of sergeant. By the end of the war it had grown to an estimated 25,000 men.[22] On December 4, 1944, the Barisan Hizbullah was established specifically to prepare activist Moslem
youth for the anticipated defense of Java. Training began in
February 1945 under the redoubtable Captain Yanagawa, who
had so impressed the recruits of the Seinendōjō. It started more
than a year after the Peta, however, and did not manage to train
more than 500 cadres.[23]

While these organizations were set up primarily for military
purposes, others were established to secure the more immediate
goals of internal security and political mobilization. The Seinendan (Youth Corps) was inaugurated on April 29, 1943.[24] Operating under the control of the Education Bureau of the Internal
Affairs Department of the military government, it was designed
as a sort of militant, politicized scout organization that could be
employed for mobilizing the population behind the authorities
for various tasks connected with local defense, for transmitting
government propaganda to the young, and as a recruiting base
for an expanding Peta. The age limits set for membership were
initially 14 to 25, but this was later narrowed to between 14 and
22. Its lowest unit of organization was the kabupatèn, and it

[22] On the Heihō, see the excellent description given in Sihombing,
Pemuda Indonesia, pp. 137–42. Sihombing himself was a member of the
Heihō.

[23] On the Hizbullah, see the discussion in Benda, *The Crescent and the
Rising Sun,* pp. 179–81, and Yanagawa, "Statement." Yanagawa judged
the Hizbullah a failure, primarily on account of quarrels within the
Moslem community and diminishing enthusiasm for the project on the
part of his superiors. According to a participant, each residency of
Java was required to produce 25 candidates for training. They were to be
between the ages of 17 and 25, and unmarried. As in the Peta, great emphasis was laid on spiritual discipline, and Yanagawa made his usual
deep impression. Interview with Munawar, Aug. 1967. According to
IC-RVO doc. no. 005116, the 500 cadres returned to their home areas and
began training local youths, so that by the time of the surrender the
Hizbullah numbered 50,000. The figure is probably much exaggerated.

[24] See Sihombing, *Pemuda Indonesia,* pp. 109–27, for an extended
description of the Seinendan.

tended accordingly to have a primarily urban character. If Japanese documents are to be believed, it eventually numbered more than half a million strong.[25] The Keibōdan (Vigilance Corps), formed at the same time as the Seinendan, was intended as an auxiliary police force to help maintain order and security and to watch out for spies and saboteurs. Membership was open to healthy men between 20 and 35. Its hierarchy extended down to the village level, where local Keibōdan units were put under the authority of the headman. Because it performed primarily police functions, the Keibōdan was open to Chinese youths, while the more political Seinendan was not. Its membership was believed to have grown ultimately to well over a million.[26]

Finally, the youth of Java were drawn into the lower structures of the central political organization of the later Japanese period, the Jawa Hōkōkai (Java Service Association), inaugurated in March 1944. At the start of the occupation the Japanese had dissolved all overtly political organizations, but as the war proceeded they created first the Triple-A Movement, and subsequently the Pusat Tenaga Rakjat (Center of People's Strength), or the "Putera," with the aim of mobilizing popular support and enthusiasm for the Imperial cause.[27] Neither of these movements was particularly successful, in part because they were silently obstructed by the traditional civil service, which observed that

[25] Figures for this and other organizations are drawn, with some reservations, from IC-RVO doc. no. 005116. Figures reported to the central authorities tended to be inflated, since local officials were anxious to be obliging and also could often obtain extra supplies and financial support by exaggerating the number of their charges.

[26] See Sihombing, *Pemuda Indonesia,* pp. 133–35; Soehoed, *Perlawanan bersendjata,* p. 28; and IC-RVO doc. no. 005116, where a detailed breakdown of the Keibōdan by residency is given.

[27] On these movements, and the Japanese policy behind them, see Kahin, *Nationalism and Revolution,* pp. 103, 106–10; Benda, *The Crescent and the Rising Sun,* pp. 112–13, 117–19; and Kanahele, "Japanese Occupation," chaps. 2, 4. The Triple-A Movement derived its name from the letter "A" which occurred three times in the movement's slogan, "Nippon, the Leader of Asia, Nippon, the Protector of Asia, Nippon, the Light of Asia."

leadership was in the hands of their old adversaries, the prewar
nationalist politicians, and in part because of internal divisions
among the politicians themselves. Essentially, however, the movements failed because in 1942 and 1943 the war was not yet
going badly enough for the Japanese to feel any urgent commitment to political development. By 1944, however, the war was
clearly going badly, economic conditions in Java were deteriorating, and popular morale was low. The Hōkōkai, therefore, was
instituted for the purposes not only of serious mobilization but
also of deeper control of the population, on whose productive
labor the military was increasingly dependent.[28] In several important respects it differed from its predecessors. By contrast to
the Putera, whose leadership was formally in Indonesian hands,
the Hōkōkai was directly under the authority of the *gunseikan*
(the head of the military administration). The Hōkōkai also
reached out beyond the indigenous Indonesian society to which
the Putera had been confined, and incorporated the Eurasian,
Chinese, and Arab minorities. Where the Putera had been led by
politicians, Hōkōkai branches were headed at each level by the
appropriate *pangrèh pradja* official.[29] Within the framework of
the new organization were not only older organizations such as
the Madjelis Sjuro Muslimin Indonesia (Consultative Council of
Indonesian Moslems), or "Masjumi," [30] but all sorts of conflict-

[28] Fuller discussions of the Hōkōkai are contained in Kanahele, "Japanese Occupation," pp. 142–44; and Kahin, *Nationalism and Revolution*,
pp. 110–11. Kanahele notes that the Hōkōkai was modeled on the Imperial Rule Assistance Association, the official political movement of
wartime Japan.

[29] *Pangrèh pradja* refers to the core of generalist regional administrators
in the colonial bureaucracy, as opposed to government employees in
specialized or technical agencies. They formed the elite of the native administrative corps. After 1946, the name was changed to *pamong pradja*.

[30] The Masjumi, a typical occupation portmanteau organization, was
formed by the Japanese in November 1943 to encompass and unify the
notoriously fissiparous elements of prewar Islam. For a superb analysis
and discussion of this organization and Japanese Islamic policy in general,
see Benda, *The Crescent and the Rising Sun*, esp. chaps. 7, 8.

ing leadership groups—conservative prijaji administrators, nationalist politicians of every stripe, traditionalist and modernist
Islamic notables, professional men, and regional elites. At its
lower levels, the Hōkōkai was linked to the villages and urban
kampung (neighborhoods) by the *tonarigumi* (neighborhood
associations), which usually encompassed about twenty house-
holds under a *kumichō* (neighborhood chief).[31] This large organizational complex had no inner coherence of its own; it expressed the desires of none of its major constituents. But it was
admirably suited to the purposes of its creators, who used it
effectively to maintain surveillance over the population, facilitate
the collection and distribution of supplies, disseminate government propaganda, and mobilize all strata of society for rallies,
parades, and public rituals, which, as will be seen, were essential
elements in the political style of the military rulers.

Attached to the body of the Hōkōkai was the Suishintai or
Barisan Pelopor (Vanguard Corps).[32] The Barisan Pelopor was
intended to be the driving activist vanguard of the Hōkōkai.
Under the nominal leadership of Sukarno himself, but operation-
ally directed by the radical nationalist Dr. Muwardi, it attracted
into its ranks young people of all strata. But since its formal
organization, like that of the Seinendan, did not descend below
the kabupatèn level, the Barisan Pelopor drew its strength from
the increasingly politicized youth of the larger urban centers,
particularly Djakarta. It organized paramilitary drilling with
sharpened bamboo spears; it brought people to hear the speeches
given by Sukarno and other nationalist notables; and it even

[31] On the tonarigumi, see the interesting material contained in Brugmans et al., eds. *Nederlandsch-Indië*, pp. 162ff.; and IC-RVO doc. no.
011199-212. Harry Benda has pointed out to the author that the tonarigumi had become an important element in domestic Japanese administration during the 1930's, when many features of Tokugawa despotism (including this one) were resuscitated and strengthened.

[32] See Kanahele, "Japanese Occupation," pp. 165–67. IC-RVO doc. no.
005116 gives a figure of 80,000 for the Barisan Pelopor by the end of
the occupation. This again is certainly an exaggeration.

disseminated the content of those speeches to those who had not come. In essence, it taught its members the techniques of mass mobilization. Through its structure, independent links were created between the elite youths working in the Hōkōkai central office and the youths of the nonelite urban wards—the slums and the belt of shantytowns around the fringes of the city. Some of these nonelite youths were unemployed; others were attached to the local djago for which Djakarta has always been famous, or to pesantrèn outside the city limits. In this process the rigid educational stratification which was the legacy of the colonial years began to break down. While the nationalist ideology propagated by the Barisan Pelopor was clearly significant in itself, it was the *experience* of being in an organization that pushed the elite youth out into the masses and sucked uneducated youth up towards the elite that gave the ideology its concrete meaning. To youths of all strata who encountered one another through the Barisan Pelopor, the experience generated that sense of mass power, of fraternal solidarity, of immense possibilities, that lies at the heart of popular nationalism. It was a new nationalism, very different from that of their elders, precisely because it grew out of an unprecedented experience.

All the youth organizations of the occupation were products of crisis. None could be seen, in those days, as steps in a career or as part of the orderly progression of the life-arc. They were all created for an impending historical moment, the meaning of which, it became increasingly clear, was to be the destiny of the nation. Not only did the Japanese say so, but the character of youth experience itself. Nor was the meaning of the experience closely confined to the thousands of youths who participated directly in these organizations, for each of these youths was also inextricably tied to the network of informal relationships between youths in the larger society. Friends met with friends; the sons of village headmen talked with the members of the village pentjak groups or theatrical troupes that they led; information was passed on through neighborhood gangs, at football matches, and in classrooms; and small boys watched their elder brothers with fascination. The sense of waiting and preparation spread slowly but inexorably. By the end of the occupation it was as if a gigantic engine was being accelerated ever more furiously, but not yet put into gear.

But it was not simply the experience of the times and the cultural traditions through which the experience was mediated that created the pemuda vision. The political style of the occupation authorities was equally important.[33] The Dutch had ruled in a calm, businesslike, bourgeois style, buttressing their authority with the myths of white superiority, rationalism, technological prowess, and the historic world mission of Western civilization. The business of the colonial state was essentially conceived of as administrative business. Politics, and especially Indonesian politics, tended to be regarded as a troublesome irritation, to be kept, as far as possible, at the periphery of colonial life. The shattering blow of General Imamura's military victory in 1942, and the subsequent humiliations visited on the Dutch both inside and outside the internment camps, dethroned the old myths. In their place new myths appeared—myths of spiritual power, of the ascendant East, and of self-sacrificing valor. The style of Japanese rule derived not from the utilitarian calculus of tropical capitalism, but from the military and imperial traditions of Japan, and from the violent and radical thought of the Young Officers of the 1930's, not a few of whom served in the Sixteenth Army in Java. It was a profoundly theatrical style, compounded of pageantry, military discipline, public violence, and inexplicable silences. For maximum effect, it required a massive and participating audience.

The official politics of the occupation period were grand charades, dramatizing movement and action, but like the theater

[33] For a fuller discussion of the ideas outlined here, see Benedict O'Gorman Anderson, "Japan: 'The Light of Asia,' " in Josef Silverstein, ed., *Southeast Asia in World War II: Four Essays* (New Haven, Conn., 1966), pp. 13–50.

merely the shadow of events. The formation of the Peta, for example, was not, on the public stage at least, the product of the administrative calculations of the military authorities. It was depicted as a generous response to an open letter from Gatot Mangkupradja, written in his own blood, in which he urged the commander of the Sixteenth Army to establish a volunteer force for the defense of the fatherland.[34] In addition parades, elaborate celebrations of public holidays, hortatory broadcasts, public swearings of solemn oaths, mass gymnastics, and the dissemination of heady slogans formed part of a panoply of rituals created to give the impression that important and decisive events were taking place.[35] And, in a sense, despite administrative cynicism, they were. For throughout Java, the new style of politics was experienced as a revelation of hitherto unimagined potentialities.

At the same time, the impact of the Japanese style was powerfully enhanced by the familiar traditional resonances it evoked. The great importance attached by the Japanese military to spiritual strength has already been noted. Official spokesmen never tired of stressing its superiority over technological skills and material prosperity. In countless lectures and speeches they

[34] The text of the letter, dated September 7, appears in *Pandji Poestaka* (Djakarta), Sept. 15, 1943. In his own later account of this affair Gatot insisted on the spontaneity of his gesture (see "The Peta.") Djèn Amar states that the letter was timed by the Japanese with some care. *Bandung lautan api* (Bandung, 1963), p. 63. The signal was given only when the first group of trainees at the Seinendōjō had completed the course and thus were ready to act as a skeleton staff for the Peta. The first class of the Seinendōjō graduated in June 1943. Kanahele ("Japanese Occupation," pp. 120–22) confirms this view on the basis of Japanese documents.

[35] It should be noted that here and throughout this chapter developments are seen from the perspective of their impact on youth. The Japanese were in fact careful to maintain a high degree of separation between the expressive and the administrative aspect of their rule. Participation in expressive politics was largely confined to prewar politicians at the upper level and youths at the lower. For administrative tasks, they relied heavily on the traditional administrative corps of the pangrèh pradja, as the Dutch had done before them, and as a succession of nationalist governments would do when they had gone.

insisted that victory in the war and independence for Indonesia depended on the *semangat* (spiritual power) and discipline of the Indonesian people themselves. The similarity between these ideas and traditional Javanese conceptions of power as cosmic energy, to be concentrated and accumulated by ascetic purity and spiritual discipline, was quite apparent. The value attached to semangat also implied a contempt for the rationalist calculus of marginal advantage, and conversely, a confirmation of the traditional importance ascribed to sudden inspiration (*ilham*). The new prestige of the military in the occupation order could also be seen as a kind of restoration. Under the Dutch the native military had been merely the abject and mercenary appendages of colonial power. But in the collective memory of precolonial greatness, constantly renewed by the wajang shadow-plays, the warrior-knight, selfless and valiant, was remembered as the guarantor of society's happiness and prosperity. The fact that these ancient ideas seemed to be reflected in the state doctrines of the Japanese Empire can only have reinforced the sense of their inherent truth.

The Japanese political style, then, presented the youth of Java with a new mode of political life and action that by sheer contrast implied a radical critique of the values and political ideas Dutch rule had instilled in their fathers. Yet the new mode was also deeply compatible with the traditional world from which most of the youths had come. Moreover, in spite of the conservative intentions of the military authorities, their political style was vulnerable to unexpected transformations. If semangat could prevail against superior technology, was the overthrow of even Japanese rule not suddenly conceivable? Mass movements had only to move off stage into living reality. Symbolic rallies against imperialism and colonial oppression had only to abandon the stadium and pour into the streets. Rituals of solidarity with the Japanese Empire had only to change the object of their devotion. Self-sacrifice, austerity, fraternity, and heroism had only to be given concrete opportunities for their realization. Violence and death had only to flow out of the lecture room, the radio program, and the movie house toward the military prisons, the arsenals, and the army headquarters itself. A political vision was already there; it had only to be put into effect. Well before the revolution broke out, its style had already been discovered.

Chapter 3

Opposition

While the Japanese had been greeted as liberators from colonial oppression on their arrival in Java in March 1942, their initial popularity was not long-lived. Rape, looting, black-marketeering, and racial arrogance aroused widespread resentment, all the greater in that the terror inspired by the Kenpeitai (Military Police) necessitated its concealment. The ravages and exactions of the occupation authorities were most acutely felt among the peasantry, the victims of both the forced rice-delivery and the rōmusha program. In 1944, a year marked by widespread crop failures, resentment turned into the despair and hatred of the destitute. In a poignant renewal of a century-old tradition of hopeless agrarian protest,[1] sporadic instances of open resistance to the Japanese began to occur. Not surprisingly, in the first such instance, the uprising in Singaparna (Tasikmalaja) on February 25, 1944, leadership was assumed by an elderly traditionalist kjai supported by the members of his pesantrèn.[2] In this and sub-

[1] See Sartono Kartodirdjo, "Agrarian Radicalism," *passim.*

[2] On this uprising, led by K. H. Zainal Mustofa, see Sjarief Hidajat, *Riwajat singkat perdjuangan K. H. Z. Mustofa* (Tasikmalaja, 1961); Djèn Amar, *Bandung lautan api,* p. 17; Benda, *The Crescent and the Rising Sun,* pp. 160–61, 268–69; *Kan Pō* (Djakarta) (39), pp. 29f. (the official Japanese account); and *Harian Rakjat* (Djakarta), Sept. 29, 1957. Following this affair there were two revolts in the area of Indramaju. The first took place in Karangampel in May 1944, and the second in Lohbener in August of that same year. In both instances leadership was provided by local *hadji* (returned pilgrims from Mecca). On these revolts, see Djèn Amar, *Bandung lautan api,* pp. 17f.; and G. Pakpahan, *1261 hari dibawah sinar "Matahari Terbit"* (n.p., n.d.), p. 55.

sequent cases the resistance was swiftly and harshly quelled. In 1945 there were two serious mutinies within rural Peta units involving the loss of Japanese lives. Both disturbances appear to have been the result of local grievances—disputes over women, corruption, and unwarranted punishments within the barracks—without real political perspectives.[3]

Undergrounds

With one notable exception, to be discussed below, consciously political resistance to the Japanese does not seem to have become significant until late in 1944, after the Japanese prime minister, Kuniaki Koiso, made his historic promise on September 7 before the Eighty-fifth Imperial Diet that the "East Indies" would definitely be given its independence "in the future." [4] When this resistance did begin to crystallize, it found adherents not among the peasants and youthful santri of the hinterland, but among the Western-educated pemuda of the larger urban centers, especially Djakarta. And whereas the agrarian insurgents proclaimed their hostility in acts of public defiance that cost some of them their lives, the opposition of the urban pemuda

[3] The first and most serious of these was the mutiny in Blitar on February 14 and 15, 1945. The best account is given in Soehoed, *Perlawanan bersendjata*, pp. 141–91, but see also *Soeara Asia* (Surabaja), June 14, 1945; Kanahele, "Japanese Occupation," pp. 185–87; Sidik Kertapati, *Sekitar proklamasi 17 Agustus 1945* (2d ed.; Djakarta, 1961), pp. 30–40; and Benedict O'Gorman Anderson, *Some Aspects of Indonesian Politics under the Japanese Occupation, 1944–1945* (Ithaca, N.Y., 1961), pp. 46f. References to the second mutiny, which occurred shortly afterward in Kroja, may be found in Kanahele, "Japanese Occupation," p. 315; and S. M. Gandasubrata, *An Account of the Japanese Occupation of Banjumas Residency, Java, March 1942 to August 1945,* trans. Leslie H. Palmier (Ithaca, N.Y., 1953), p. 19.

[4] For the text of this promise, see Harry J. Benda, James K. Irikura, and Kōichi Kishi, eds., *Japanese Military Administration in Indonesia: Selected Documents* (New Haven, Conn., 1965), p. 259. General discussions of Japanese policy toward Indonesia in this period can be found in Anderson, *Some Aspects,* chap. 1; and Kanahele, "Japanese Occupation," chap. 8.

was expressed more circumspectly in shadowy, informal underground groups that were careful not to provoke reprisals from
the Kenpeitai.

It was not merely the lesson to be drawn from the fate of the
rural rebels that encouraged circumspection. The history of the
one serious urban resistance movement of the war years sufficiently demonstrated the military authorities' ruthless way with
any organized group they considered subversive. Shortly before
the collapse of the Dutch colonial government, P. J. A. Idenburg,
then director-general of the Department of Education, and one
of the more enlightened, progressive officials in the Netherlands
Indies bureaucracy, had contacted Amir Sjarifuddin, a former
chairman of the Gerakan Rakjat Indonesia (Indonesian People's
Movement), or "Gerindo," the most left-wing of the legal parties
of the late thirties, and asked him whether he would be willing to
organize an underground intelligence network in the event of a
Japanese occupation.[5] To Amir, as to other committed left-wing
Asian nationalists at the time, cooperating with bourgeois-demo-
cratic colonial states against the rising powers of fascism and
militarism was a choice whose rationality seemed confirmed by
the alliance of those states with the Soviet Union after June 1941.
It was therefore not difficult to reach an understanding. Amir
agreed to accept the rather large sum of 25,000 guilders to
finance the projected underground network.[6] Into the organization he recruited those he could: members of the very small segment of Indonesian society that shared his perspective on the

[5] For biographical details on Amir, see the Appendix.
[6] For fuller details see P. J. A. Idenburg, "Het Nederlandse antwoord
op het Indonesisch nationalisme," in Henri Baudet and I. J. Brugmans,
eds., *Balans van beleid: Terugblik op de laatste halve eeuw van Nederlandsch-Indië* (Assen, 1961), pp. 121–51. In an interview given to the
author in August 1964, Dr. Idenburg related that Charles van der Plas,
then governor of East Java, had obtained money from the Indies government for the purpose of organizing a resistance movement, but being
little acquainted with nationalist circles in Djakarta, he entrusted some
of the money to Idenburg. It was on Idenburg's initiative that Amir was
chosen as organizer of the underground.

coming Japanese onslaught. From what little subsequently transpired about his organization, it seems clear that its members
were drawn from the left wing of the Gerindo and from the so-
called Illegal PKI (Partai Komunis Indonesia, or Indonesian
Communist Party), which had been clandestinely reconstituted
by Muso in 1935 after the disastrous uprisings of 1926 and
1927. Perhaps in part because the core of the Illegal PKI lay in
Surabaja, the main strength of Amir's group seems to have been
concentrated in that city and generally in East Java. In spite of
Idenburg's high opinion of Amir's abilities, Amir was no match
for the Kenpeitai's army of informers and spies. In January 1943
he was arrested along with 53 other people. In February 1944
some of his top aides were executed, and others sentenced to
long terms in prison.[7] Amir himself was saved from death only
by the personal intervention of the two best-known nationalist
leaders of the time, Sukarno and Hatta, who warned the Japanese
that his execution would seriously damage the cause of mobilizing the population behind the Japanese war effort. In the event
Amir's sentence was commuted to life imprisonment.[8]

Amir's underground had been essentially a continuation of
the politics of the colonial period into that of the Japanese occupation. It was oriented toward the international struggle between
the Allied and Axis powers. And it was a complete failure. The
undergrounds that succeeded it had precisely the opposite character. They grew up at a time when the defeat of Japan was
becoming virtually inevitable, and thus had the character of
preparations for the future rather than the defense of the past.

[7] Kahin, *Nationalism and Revolution,* pp. 111–12; *Antara* (Djakarta),
Feb. 12, 1946; Kanahele, "Japanese Occupation," p. 286; and Pusat SBPI
[Sarikat Buruh Pertjetakan Indonesia?], *Dokumentasi pemuda: sekitar
proklamasi Indonesia Merdeka* (Jogjakarta, 1948), p. 45, (hereinafter
cited as *Dokumentasi pemuda*). This rare booklet is based on notes left
by D. N. Aidit, Lagiono, Wikana, and Mustapha. It gives a full list of
those executed.

[8] Kahin, *Nationalism and Revolution,* pp. 111f.; and Pakpahan, *1261
hari,* pp. 97–99. For biographical details on Sukarno and Hatta, see the
Appendix.

They were oriented toward the immediate destiny of Indonesia. And they were by no means the disasters that Amir's had been. They were not maquis, or undergrounds in the sense of groups engaged in sabotage, spying, or subversion. In most cases their activities amounted to little more than exchanging political gossip, discussing Indonesia's future, speculating on Allied intentions, and criticizing Japanese policy within the privacy of closed groups of friends. A few individuals listened clandestinely to Allied broadcasts and passed along what information they gleaned to those they trusted. The significance of these groups lay not in their effect on the occupation government, but in the political identities they generated, which were to be of signal importance after the end of the war.

While such informal groups existed in most of the larger towns of Java, their size was usually too small and their information too limited for them to have any but local consequences. In the capital city, however, and to a somewhat lesser extent in Bandung, only four hours away by car, the opposition groups not only were larger and better informed but also had institutional bases that gave them more coherence and self-confidence. Perhaps not surprisingly, the key institutional bases for the metropolitan undergrounds were asrama, or dormitories, for various types of pemuda. Indeed, to an overwhelming degree, the undergrounds were pemuda phenomena. (The number of older political leaders or government officials who played a role in them was probably less than a dozen.) The asrama provided a refuge from families, beds for students stranded in the capital or visiting it from the provinces, a forum for intense and reasonably private discussion, and a focus for solidarity. The three main undergrounds that developed in Djakarta drew their style and membership largely from the asrama that served as their institutional bases.

The first of these groups was centered in the asrama of the Medical Faculty, situated at Prapatan 10, in the heart of the best residential section of the city. We have already noted that the

Medical Faculty was the one Dutch institution of higher learning permitted to function in the occupation years. It catered to an extremely small group of students of high academic attainments, most of whom spoke Dutch among themselves and were intimately connected to the elite of native society. While these students were certainly powerfully affected by the general crisis atmosphere of the occupation, their outlook on events was also conditioned by the fact that their Faculty, their asrama, and the scientific studies they were engaged in were extensions of the Dutch period that had not been markedly changed by the advent of the Japanese. Accordingly, it is not surprising that as a group they were considerably more Western in their orientation than other undergrounds, and that many of them came strongly under the influence of Sutan Sjahrir.[9]

Sjahrir had been among the exceedingly few prewar nationalist politicians who refused to participate in public life during the occupation.[10] While his social-democratic views would in any case have made it ideologically difficult for him to work for or with the Japanese, he was also convinced that the Allies were bound to win the war eventually and that the country's future would in part be determined by the degree to which Indonesians resisted the occupation authorities. Very much concerned, as we shall see, with the effects of Japanese indoctrination on the youth

[9] For biographical details on Sjahrir, see the Appendix. Among the more prominent Medical Faculty pemuda were Sjarif Thajeb, Djohar Nur, Darwis, and Tadjuludin.

[10] According to Kahin (*Nationalism and Revolution*, p. 104), Sukarno, Hatta, and Sjahrir decided early in the occupation that the nationalist struggle could best be prosecuted at two levels—above ground and underground. Sukarno and Hatta were to work above ground through the Japanese, and Sjahrir, while maintaining contact with Sukarno and Hatta, was to organize an underground resistance. Hatta certainly gave Sjahrir financial support during this period, and the two remained in very close touch. But Sjahrir's *Out of Exile* does not give the impression of any close contact between Sjahrir and Sukarno. See Soetan Sjahrir, *Out of Exile*, trans. Charles Wolf, Jr. (New York, 1949), esp. pp. 246–47; see also Kanahele, "Japanese Occupation," pp. 53–54.

of Indonesia, he naturally found contacts most congenial with the students of the Medical Faculty, who were least affected by that indoctrination. In them he found a ready audience for his conception of a resistance whose focus was opposition to Japanese political culture and adherence to international social-democratic values. His refusal to collaborate with the authorities at a time when collaboration was becoming increasingly odious as a result of the forced rice deliveries, the rōmusha program, and so forth, marked him as a man of principle, and gave him great prestige with the opposition elements at Prapatan 10. Later, when the war had ended and when Sjahrir made his bid for power largely on the basis of his opposition role, exaggerated claims were made for his resistance activities, less by himself than by his political supporters. However courageous his refusal to participate in the activities of the military regime may have been, it should be understood that the underground he led consisted of little more than an informal network of contacts with university students and with friends and family outside Djakarta.[11]

The second underground centered around the Asrama Angkatan Baru Indonesia (Asrama of the New Generation of Indonesia) at Menteng 31, also in the heart of residential Djakarta, which was set up early in the occupation under the auspices of the military administration, more particularly its Department of Propaganda, the Sendenbu. Among the better-known figures in this asrama were two young men particularly in the confidence of the eccentric activist Hitoshi Shimizu, who for the earlier period of the occupation was entrusted with work among the pemuda.[12] These two were Chaerul Saleh and Sukarni, both of whom held positions in the Sendenbu until June 1945. The asrama was set

---

[11] A good indication of the relatively subdued nature of Sjahrir's underground activities is the brief, blurred account of the Japanese period in *Out of Exile.* Outside Djakarta, his closest connections were with Dr. Sudarsono's group in Tjirebon and that of Djohan Sjahroezah in Surabaja, discussed below in Chapter 10.

[12] See Hitoshi Shimizu, "Statement" of Dec. 5, 1945, IC-RVO doc. no. 006580–4.

up by Shimizu with the intention of creating a core of pemuda activists who after an initial period of training would pass on the education they had received to potential cadres in the provinces. Under Shimizu's direction most of the training given at the asrama was strongly nationalist in content; the teachers summoned to give lectures at the asrama were such well-known nationalist politicians of the thirties as Sukarno, Hatta, Yamin, Mr. Sunarjo, and Amir Sjarifuddin (at least until his arrest).[13] The official training period of the Menteng 31 asrama appears to have ended in April 1943, just about the time the Putera got under way, but the asrama itself remained a place where many of the pemuda who had been trained there, together with their friends and hangers-on, continued to gather and discuss politics.

The membership of the asrama, which does not seem to have numbered more than fifty or sixty at any one time, differed from that of the Medical Faculty asrama chiefly in two respects. First, whereas most of the leaders of the Medical Faculty group had not been politically active in the Dutch colonial period, the leading members of the Menteng 31 asrama had, however ineffectively, been involved in anti-Dutch nationalist activities.[14] Second, while some members of the Menteng 31 asrama were former students at the Law Faculty, there was also a fair admixture of pemuda who had lower educational qualifications but had been on the fringes of the youth movements of the thirties. The varied composition of the asrama is shown by the contrast between its senior members, who were from the prewar educated elite, like

---

[13] *Dokumentasi pemuda,* p. 14.

[14] According to Biro Pemuda, *Sedjarah perdjuangan pemuda Indonesia,* p. 114, members were drawn from such prewar political organizations as the Gerindo; the Barisan Pemuda Gerindo (Gerindo Youth Corps); Indonesia Muda (Young Indonesia); the Suryawirawan (Sun Corps), which was the youth organization of the conservative cooperating nationalist Partij Indonesia Raja (Greater Indonesia Party), or the "Parindra"; the Perhimpunan Peladjar-Peladjar Indonesia (Association of Indonesian Students), or PPPI; and the Suluh Pemuda Indonesia (Torch of Indonesian Youth), or SPI. For details on these organizations and their orientations, see *ibid.,* pp. 61–96.

Chaerul Saleh, Sukarni, A. M. Hanafi, and Ismail Widjaja, and
the nonelite, such as the youthful Aidit, Lukman, and Sjamsuddin Tjan.[15] Chaerul Saleh, for example, was a close relative of
Hatta. In the later colonial period he had become an *anak buah*
of Yamin, who had acted as his guru and financial guarantor
when quarrels with his family left him without means of supporting himself.[16] M. H. Lukman, a future leader of the PKI, while
not of elite origins himself, had been in contact with Hatta during
Hatta's exile in the Boven Digul concentration camp in the middle
thirties.[17]

It should not be forgotten that though Menteng 31 was primarily an asrama whose members were being given political
training under Japanese auspices, it was also a regular meeting
place for their friends. Older pemuda—such as B. M. Diah,
Adam Malik, and the Tjokroaminoto brothers—who worked for
the Japanese news agency Dōmei or at the metropolitan newspaper *Asia Raya,* were in regular communication with the Menteng 31 habitués, and an informal network of communication
existed from early in the occupation.[18] Thus there was always a
secondary Menteng 31 group considerably larger than the official
membership of the asrama.[19]

[15] For biographical details on Chaerul Saleh, Sukarni, Hanafi, Ismail
Widjaja and Aidit, see the Appendix.

[16] *Anak buah* is a key phrase, describing a man or boy who is in moral,
financial and social subordination to another. The relationship of the
bapak (father; patron; leader) to the anak buah is a complex one, involving strong mutual claims. The anak buah are expected to give full
public support to their bapak, carry out his instructions faithfully, and
follow his ideological lead. In return he is expected to support them
financially (at least in part), shelter them, protect them from punishment, and give them moral and intellectual guidance. The relationship
normally, though not invariably, implies a difference in generations between the bapak and the anak buah.

[17] For biographical details on Lukman, see the Appendix.

[18] For biographical details on B. M. Diah, Adam Malik, and Anwar
and Harsono Tjokroaminoto, see the Appendix.

[19] According to Biro Pemuda (*Sedjarah perdjuangan pemuda Indonesia,* p. 115) and Sidik Kertapati (*Sekitar proklamasi,* p. 48), in mid-

The third asrama, the Asrama Indonesia Merdeka (Free Indonesia Asrama), has since been the subject of some controversy, mainly because of the problematic political activities of its sponsor, Rear Adm. Tadashi Maeda, who during the war years headed the Bukanfu, the naval office for liaison with the army in Djakarta.[20] This asrama was set up at Kebon Sirih 80 in October 1944, shortly after the Koiso Declaration promising Indonesia her independence.[21] Maeda himself subsequently said of this asrama:

The asrama was set up after the Koiso Declaration, which was very disappointing, since there was no follow-up. I felt very strongly that Indonesia would need capable leaders of the younger generation. I invited almost all the top Indonesian leaders to lecture there on whatever they liked. Even Sjahrir appeared—of course not collaborating with us! The first group of candidates (about thirty people) graduated in April 1945; a second, larger group, about eighty strong, began training in May, but their training had to be stopped halfway through due to the surrender.[22]

While the Admiral was the asrama's patron, its actual operations were supervised by his two capable assistants, Tomegorō Yoshizumi and Shigetada Nishijima. Both Yoshizumi and Nishijima were civilian Japanese with extensive experience in prewar Indonesia as businessmen and intelligence agents. Both came in time

---

1943 the leaders of the Menteng 31 asrama organized a so-called Barisan Banteng (Wild Buffalo Corps) for Djakarta youths of all classes between the ages of 12 and 15 (Sidik says 12 to 25, which is perhaps more likely). The youths practiced drill with bamboo rifles, learned patriotic songs and slogans, and were given a rudimentary political education. The number of 10,000 given for the organization is obviously a vast exaggeration.

[20] Maeda's function was to ensure the supply of food and other materiel to the naval area administration in Makasar. The naval area, comprising all of Indonesia except for Sumatra, Java, and Madura, was a food deficit area, and required economic support from the army-controlled regions. For biographical details on Maeda, see the Appendix.

[21] Sidik Kertapati, *Sekitar proklamasi*, p. 109.

[22] Interview with Admiral Maeda, April 8, 1962.

to identify strongly with Indonesian nationalist aspirations.[23]

After the occupation period, some effort was made by groups associated with Sjahrir to discredit the activities of Maeda and his aides, mainly for internal political reasons that will be dealt with below. It was sometimes charged that the Kaigun (Japanese navy) group had set up the asrama to train infiltrators who would penetrate the communist or near-communist "undergrounds" and either capture them (and direct them against the Allies) or split them along prewar lines, between an orthodox Stalinist group and a more nationalistic communist group associated with the followers of Tan Malaka. On other occasions, it was argued that Maeda and his aides, anticipating a Japanese defeat, had reasoned that Japan would fall under the control of communist or at least far-left groups, that the Allies themselves would soon fall out, with the Anglo-Saxon powers pitted against the Soviet Union, and that Japan might thus find herself in alliance with Russia. Japan would then benefit greatly from having cultivated in the asrama a younger generation of leaders in the strategic center of Southeast Asia with strongly anti-Western, possibly communist, sympathies.[24]

In fact there is little evidence to support either of these claims. The testimony of Wikana, who was certainly no friend of the Japanese, explicitly confirms the sincerity of Maeda and his assistants with regard to Indonesian independence.[25] Others have testified that Maeda repeatedly attempted to intervene with the Kenpeitai on behalf of Indonesians suspected of subversive activities. The so-called Kaigun group of older politicians close to Maeda, including Mr. Subardjo, Mr. Iwa Kusumasumantri, Mr. Singgih, Mr. Latuharhary, Dr. Ratulangie, Mr. Maramis, and Dr. Buntaran, was ideologically speaking not really a group at

[23] For biographical details on Yoshizumi and Nishijima, see the Appendix.

[24] See Kahin, *Nationalism and Revolution,* pp. 117–20.

[25] Interview with Wikana, Jogjakarta, Nov. 1, 1962.

all, though all were friends of Subardjo. Among them were anti-Western Javanese nationalists as well as moderately conservative politicians from East Indonesia whom Maeda, as the Djakarta representative of the naval area administration in Makasar, was responsible for assisting and supporting.[26] Moreover, the lecturers at the asrama were virtually identical with the teachers at the army-sponsored Asrama Angkatan Baru Indonesia, including Sukarno, Hatta, Yamin, Subardjo, Sunarjo. The most striking addition was Sjahrir.[27] It is not necessary to presuppose any complicated speculations on Japan's future in a postwar world to understand that the Maeda group, particularly since they were not responsible for the actual administration of Java, felt free to devote themselves to what they viewed as the long-range interests of both Indonesia and Japan. Since they felt certain that Indonesia would eventually become independent, it was only prudent for them to try to win some friends for Japan in the strategically located and potentially rich archipelago. It seems clear, too, that they saw themselves as playing the historic role of midwife to the birth of a new nation.[28]

The Indonesian directorate of the asrama consisted of Subardjo, an older-generation politician of traditionalist Javanist

[26] According to Kanahele ("Japanese Occupation," pp. 18, 251), Subardjo, Maramis, Dr. Samsi, and Tadjoeddin Noor were among the prominent Indonesians recruited by Maeda and Nishijima in early 1941 for fifth-column work against the Dutch. Kanahele cites as his source Jusuf Hasan, *Riwajat hidup ringkas* (Bogor, 1957). Jusuf Hasan was apparently a member of the fifth column, and the above work contains his sworn testimony about his activities and associates.

[27] For Sjahrir's version of this, see *Out of Exile,* pp. 251f. This version, however, never explains why, if Subardjo was the fascist Machiavelli he was later made out to be, Sjahrir was invited to lecture there at all.

[28] See Anderson, "Japan," p. 16. This interpretation was generally confirmed by the author's interviews with Nishijima, Maeda, and Malik. It is also borne out by the fact that when Maeda and Nishijima reappeared in Indonesia after the war as agents of Japanese oil interests, they were able to establish excellent relations not only with the old Kaigun group but also with almost all the former teachers at the asrama.

leanings, and Wikana, a former Gerindo activist.[29] This some-what surprising alliance has been part of the reason for the much-discussed communist element in the Asrama Indonesia Merdeka. It is not altogether clear whether or not Wikana was a com-munist at the time of the Japanese occupation, and if he was, what the significance of being a communist at this time might be. He had been arrested by the Dutch in 1940 for helping distribute the illegal communist news sheet *Menara Merah,* along with other pemuda such as Adam Malik and Pandu Kartawiguna. Subardjo himself stated subsequently that he had decided to offer the job of running the asrama to Wikana because he was known to have wide influence among former Gerindo pemuda, because he was destitute, and because he was in danger of arrest as a communist by the Kenpeitai.[30] While this may be true, it is also possible that Nishijima, playing a lone hand, helped to make the choice, in view of his prewar contacts with Gerindo people.

In any case the asrama cannot be defined in ideological terms. Wikana was then fairly close to Sjahrir, and later said that he had discussed with him the question whether he should accept Su-bardjo's offer. He also talked the matter over with Sukarno.[31] He also had close personal relations with members of the Men-teng 31 group, especially Chaerul Saleh and Hanafi. Moreover, the young men assigned to study at the asrama seem to have been a heterogeneous mixture, including former Gerindo friends of Wikana, younger relatives of Subardjo and Iwa, and stranded pemuda elements from the eastern islands. Perhaps the most prominent member of the asrama was Mr. Jusuf, the mystically

[29] For biographical details on Subardjo and Wikana, see the Appendix.

[30] Interview with Mr. Subardjo in early 1962. Subardjo added that he took Wikana on as a result of a request by his aide, Sudiro (mBah). No judgment can be made of Wikana's views at this time from Kenpeitai accusations, since the Japanese military police were very liberal in their classification of communists.

[31] Interview with Wikana, Jogjakarta, Nov. 1, 1962. There is no con-firmation of this in Sjahrir's writings.

inclined Indramaju lawyer who was to lead the first post-independence PKI.[32] It was a period in which the clear ideological lines of the postwar years were not yet drawn, and in which hopes for independence were uppermost in the minds of all concerned.

The fluidity of relationships among the members of the asrama (which were in any case scarcely fifteen minutes' walking distance from each other) was exemplified by the appearance within the Barisan Pelopor of a smaller body known as the Barisan Pelopor Istimewa (Special Vanguard Corps). It consisted of about a hundred picked pemuda under the direct leadership of Sudiro who acted as Sukarno's bodyguards and personal emissaries. Into the membership of the Barisan Pelopor Istimewa were drawn young people from all the asrama, though Menteng 31 was especially well represented. Among them were Supeno, Aidit, Lukman, Djohar Nur, Asmara Hadi, Sidik Kertapati, Inu Kertapati, and Kakung Gunadi, as well as somewhat older men like Ir. Sakirman and Sukardjo Wirjopranoto.[33]

It must be stressed once again that the asrama groups were not underground in the same sense as the maquis in occupied France or Holland during the Second World War. With the exception of Amir's short-lived group, the Indonesian undergrounds did not attempt to combat Imperial Japan. Many of the pemuda were closely related by family and other ties to the most prominent collaborators of the late occupation period. Moreover, the Japanese administration was generally aware of what was going

[32] For Mr. Jusuf, see below, Chapter 10. Since Indramaju was also the home area of Mr. Subardjo, it is quite possible that good neighborhood relations rather than ideology may account for this particular recruit.

[33] Sidik Kertapati, *Sekitar proklamasi,* pp. 48–49. Generally speaking, Sidik's account of the underground is the most complete and satisfactory in the Indonesian language. See also the article by Angkasa Darma, "Sebelas tahun nan lalu," in *Merdeka* (Djakarta), Aug. 16, 1956. Some of the information on the Barisan Pelopor Istimewa was derived from interviews with Ir. Sakirman on Nov. 3, 1963, and Sudiro on Jan. 15, 1963.

on in pemuda circles.[34] The underground can best be seen as a frame of mind rather than as a complex of organizations or even groups. It represented a growing willingness on the part of metropolitan pemuda to think of themselves as "thinking dangerous thoughts." If one was outraged by the increasing misery of the population, disgusted by the complicity of the older politicians and officialdom in the face of the rōmusha and compulsory rice-delivery programs, and cynical about the Japanese promise of independence, one was already in the underground. The awareness that these attitudes were shared by others, particularly among the young, generated the intuition of a potential for resistance that made the underground so convincing an apparition. Moreover, it was an apparition that made sense vis-à-vis the ideological coerciveness and the conspiratorial style of the Japanese rulers. After the Koiso Declaration the underground gradually changed its character, and moved out of the shadowy limbo between legality and illegality. For the declaration's promise of independence appeared to confirm the most ardent aspirations of the pemuda themselves. The Japanese authorities were no longer in a position openly to oppose the pemuda objectives, but only the pace and means demanded for their achievement. It was a weakness the pemuda were able to exploit, and in so doing they abandoned the psychological withdrawal of resistance for an increasingly open opposition.

Confrontations

By the early months of 1945 the course of events exerted increasing pressure on the military authorities both in Tokyo and in Djakarta to fulfill the promise of the Koiso Declaration. The American landings on Leyte in October 1944 had led to the rapid destruction of Japanese power in the Philippines. By the end of February 1945 the battle of Manila was over, and civil

[34] See, e.g., Lt. Col. Tetsu Nomura, "Statement," IC-RVO doc. no. 059328. Nomura was head of the Kikakuka, or Planning Bureau, the top political organ within the military administration.

administration had been turned over to President Osmeña by General MacArthur. Beginning in March 1945 the British offensive in Burma rapidly picked up speed, culminating in the fall of Rangoon in May. It was also becoming clear that the collapse of Germany was imminent. In that event it would be unreasonable to expect Russia to remain neutral in the Pacific war, and accordingly, Japan would probably soon be left to face the combined power of the Allies all alone. Under the circumstances it became much more urgent than before to enlist local support in Java, by giving greater scope to nationalist sentiment. The bargaining position of Indonesian nationalists, both young and old, improved markedly as the military situation of the Japanese deteriorated. One of the most obvious signs of this shift was the Youth Congress held at the Villa Isola in Bandung from May 16 to 18, 1945, just a week after the German surrender.

The convening of the congress was presaged by orchestrated demands in the controlled Djakarta press that the Younger Generation be "brought out of the wings" and allowed to push itself forward into all fields, political and social, "since it is the youth who will be the builders and defenders of free Indonesia." [35] As a result of these "demands," the Japanese were able to present the holding of the congress as a sign of their responsiveness and sincerity, in spite of the fact that the purpose and the agenda of the congress remained strictly in their own hands. While the overall planning of the congress was primarily the responsibility of the Sendenbu (especially of Shimizu and Kaneko), the actual preparations were entrusted to Djamal Ali, an older pemuda who had been prominent in Indonesia Muda (Young Indonesia) before the war, and who during the occupation worked in the offices of *Tjahaja*, Bandung's sole wartime newspaper. Through his close contacts with Beppan, the military counterintelligence organization headed by Obana and Masugi, he enjoyed the confidence of powerful figures within the military administration. Technically,

[35] See Pakpahan, *1261 hari*, pp. 118f., and *Soeara Moeslimin Indonesia* (Djakarta), III, 12 (June 15, 1945), 17f.

the congress was sponsored by the so-called Angkatan Muda, the name given to the more prominent pemuda activists in the Bandung area as they were given more and more freedom to operate and organize out in the open. But since Djamal Ali and the Sendenbu were able to arrange for activist pemuda from all parts of Java to attend the sessions, the congress was not monopolized by a local Bandung group, but rather became the first Java-wide assemblage of youth leaders since the onset of the occupation.[36]

In spite of the fact that the Sendenbu did not intend the congress to accomplish much (no detailed agenda was issued beforehand to the participants), the opportunity provided for pemuda from the whole island to meet and exchange ideas was eagerly seized, and evidently most of those invited attended.[37] Accordingly, after the initial session the proceedings took place on two levels: a series of fairly official speeches along lines laid down by the Japanese, and a continuing flow of intense, informal discussions between the different delegations, cementing their growing solidarity. After three days of lobbying and debate, the pemuda passed two significant resolutions. First, all Indonesian groups should be united and centralized under a single leadership. Second, Indonesian independence should be realized as soon as possible: the Angkatan Muda was constantly prepared to devote its physical and spiritual energies toward the coordination of all efforts in that direction. As the Dōmei news agency

[36] Among the Djakarta delegates were Sukarni, Chaerul Saleh, Sjamsuddin Tjan, and Aidit from Menteng 31, and Zus E. A. Ratulangie from the Medical Faculty; from Surakarta came Suharti, Suwarti, and Harsono; from Jogjakarta, Sudarisman and Adisumarto; from Semarang, S. Karno; and from Surabaja, Surjono. Biro Pemuda, *Sedjarah perdjuangan pemuda Indonesia*, pp. 122–23. The best accounts of the congress are contained in Sidik Kertapati, *Sekitar proklamasi*, pp. 58–61; and Djèn Amar, *Bandung lautan api*, pp. 31–40.

[37] According to Djèn Amar (*Bandung lautan api*, p. 35) there were about 150 delegates. According to monitored Japanese broadcasts, however, there were 300. See United States, Federal Broadcasting Intelligence Service, "Daily Reports," May 26, 1945, section Q2.

reported ambiguously from Djakarta, only two alternatives could now be accepted by the youth of Indonesia—freedom or death.[38]

The second resolution clearly revealed the delegates' impatience with the slow pace of official preparations for independence, which so far had not proceeded much beyond the announcement on March 1 that an Investigating Committee for the Preparation of Indonesian Independence would be set up to study the question.[39] The first resolution, however, was somewhat more ambiguous. It has been interpreted as being aimed at the clear division during the later Japanese period between the leadership of the Hōkōkai (dominated, as we have seen, by the pangrèh pradja and nationalist politicians of the older generation) and that of the Masjumi (incorporating the Islamic elite), and as urging that the two be united—that the Masjumi lose its autonomy and be fully subordinated to the nationalist leadership of the Hōkōkai in some larger organization.[40] This interpretation seems unlikely, however, since it was Isa Anshary, later to achieve some fame as the leader of militant younger Moslem elements, who gave the keynote address at the Villa Isola Congress, and since a major theme of his address was harsh criticism of the Hōkōkai.

[38] Pakpahan, *1261 hari*, pp. 118f.

[39] Neither the committee's composition nor its first meeting date had yet been announced. For the announcement that the committee would be set up, see *Soeara Asia*, March 1, 1945; and for a fuller account of the committee, see Anderson, *Some Aspects*, pp. 17–32. A fascinating glimpse of the high-level Indonesian politics behind the setting up of this committee and the establishing of its objectives is contained in "Tjatatan pendek sidang Sanyō Kaigi, April 18, 2605 [1945]," IC-RVO doc. no. 038861–77, Appendix 3.

[40] Anderson, *Some Aspects*, pp. 52–53; Benda, *The Crescent and the Rising Sun*, pp. 191f. Benda concluded from the major speech given by the chief of the General Affairs Department (*sōmubuchō*), Maj. Gen. Otoshi Nishimura, on May 15, 1945, that at this point the Japanese abandoned their general support for Islamic claims to political ascendancy (see pp. 188–89). I disagree with Benda's interpretation, but with some hesitation, having earlier followed it completely (see *Some Aspects*, pp. 22–23).

Isa's sharp-tongued attack on the Hōkōkai focused not only on its unnational and repressive aspects, but particularly on the one-sided character of its leadership, which was in the hands of the older collaborationist elements. The implications of his speech were not that Islamic autonomy needed to be defended against the aggressive claims of secular nationalists and prijaji officials, but that the demands of the younger generation, whatever their *aliran*,[41] were being ignored by their conservative, timid elders. Unity meant unity between generations as much as unity between rival elites. Significantly, at the end of the congress a delegation was sent under Djamal Ali to see Sukarno, then holidaying in Sukabumi, to present him with the resolutions of the congress and to urge him to make further efforts to bring about independence sooner. With his habitual tact Sukarno added to the resolutions: "In the hands of our Youth lies the future of the Indonesian People."[42]

The Villa Isola Congress was followed by a series of youth conferences and discussions all over Java, led by the returning delegates in their own home areas. The sense of pemuda solidarity and self-confidence, which had been strongly stimulated by the congress, became increasingly marked in all the political activities that developed from then on until the proclamation of independence.

The growing pressure of the youth groups was next made

[41] *Aliran* (literally, "stream") refers primarily to the two major cultural traditions in Javanese life and the communities that embody them. These traditions are the abangan, a mélange of animism, magic, and Hindu-Buddhist residues under a thin Islamic veneer, and the santri, oriented much more exclusively toward Islam. Within each aliran there are, as it were, sub-aliran; for example, the abangan tradition is divided into an urban prijaji, and a rural folk variant. The santri tradition also contains significant urban-rural divergences. By 1955 these sub-aliran came to form the basis of Indonesia's four largest political parties. For an excellent discussion of the aliran and their emergence as political forces in twentieth-century Indonesia, see Ruth T. McVey's introduction to Sukarno, *Nationalism, Islam and Marxism* (Ithaca, N.Y., 1970).

[42] Djèn Amar, *Bandung lautan api*, p. 38.

evident at the eighth session of the Central Advisory Council
(Chūō Sangi-in), or CAC, which met from June 18 to 21.[43] For
the first time in the history of this generally timid organization,
voices were heard urging a greater role for the youth. Speaking
particularly through Mr. R. M. Sartono, the well-known prewar
leader of the Partij Indonesia (Indonesia Party; the "Partindo"),
the council urged the Japanese to bring more young people into
the administrative structure, to expand their military training,
and most important, to incorporate them into the leadership of
the projected Gerakan Rakjat Baru (New People's Movement),
or GRB, a mass organization the Japanese had announced would
be set up in July, superseding (and possibly unifying) the Hōkōkai, the Masjumi, and the plethora of other mass organizations
that already existed without clear relationships to one another.[44]

While the main pressure on the older nationalist politicians
like Sukarno and Hatta still came in this period from the educated pemuda of the metropolis, particularly those who had
direct personal relationships with the older leaders, these pemuda
were on occasion able to enlist nonelite pemuda in their cause.
One striking incident recorded by an Indonesian writer deserves
mention in this regard. According to this account, a mass meeting of Djakarta high-school students was held at the Djakarta
Zoo, close by Menteng 31 and Prapatan 10, and the following
resolutions were adopted: first, the youth should prepare themselves to carry on the struggle, however bloody [no indication
against whom]; second, they should stand firmly on the principle
of the total unity of all sectors of society; and third, they must

[43] The CAC, set up in the autumn of 1943, was the successor of the
prewar Volksraad (People's Council), with the difference that the CAC
was not even allowed, as the Volksraad had been, to interpellate the
government. It was supposed to act as a purely advisory body, answer-
ing specific questions put to it by the military administration. Residency
advisory councils (sangikai) along the same lines were set up at the
same time. For the composition of the CAC in early 1945, see Anderson,
Some Aspects, pp. 10–11. A good account of its origins is contained in
Benda, *The Crescent and the Rising Sun,* p. 137.

[44] Cf. Pakpahan, *1261 hari,* p. 126.

be prepared to undergo intensive military training in order to be able to defend their country. A student from the Medical Faculty then declared: "Everywhere throughout the world, it is the youth who are always revolting to combat inappropriate modes of acting and thinking. The youth must now agree to undergo training in military barracks." The mood of the meeting being now sufficiently aroused, the pemuda marched off to Sukarno's house, where they were received with the following words: "I will work as hard as I know how to have your resolution put into effect. . . . I see that my younger friends out there are carrying a banner reading 'Freedom for the People!' That is completely in accord with our Pantja Dharma." [45] When the crowd then proceeded to Hatta's house, they were told: "I am delighted to see all of you young people here. Unity among the youth like this is something I have long dreamed of. Be sure that you will, all of you, soon replace the present leaders, who are getting old. I myself will work hard to see that all your aspirations are fulfilled." The Indonesian commentator adds: "It was as though they were still uneasy about the urgings of the youth, so that they only answered that they would work hard to get things done." [46]

It seems to have been about the same time that a very small group of the leading pemuda in Djakarta met to set up an informal political liaison group called the Angkatan Baru (New Generation), coordinated by B. M. Diah, the pemuda journalist of the metropolitan newspaper *Asia Raya*. Since Diah was married to a niece of Subardjo, he had good contacts with both Menteng 31 and the Kaigun. His position in the newspaper world gave him, together with the pemuda in the Sendenbu, strategic access to news about the rapidly developing war situa-

[45] The Pantja Dharma (Five Duties) was a sort of code of loyalty to the Japanese Empire accepted at the sixth session of the CAC. See Benda, *The Crescent and the Rising Sun,* p. 278.

[46] Pakpahan, *1261 hari,* p. 125. See also Pusat Sedjarah Militer Angkatan Darat, *Peranan TNI Angkatan Darat dalam perang kemerdekaan* (Bandung, 1965), p. 20. The initiative for the rally seems to have come from Prapatan 10.

tion. These advantages seem to have led to his designation as central coordinator. The leadership of the new group varies according to different accounts, but it certainly included Chaerul Saleh, Sukarni, Supeno, and Anwar Tjokroaminoto, Diah's colleague at *Asia Raya,* who was both the son of the deceased Sarekat Islam (Islamic Union) leader H. O. S. Tjokroaminoto and the former brother-in-law of Sukarno. Some accounts add Wikana, Sudiro (of the Barisan Pelopor Istimewa), Harsono Tjokroaminoto, Pandu Kartawiguna, and others.[47]

The formation of the Angkatan Baru had little or no organizational significance, but it did represent the converging of most of the more prominent and well-connected pemuda leaders in the capital city onto the public stage as an open political bloc. This became quite apparent shortly afterward when the Japanese authorities organized a high-level meeting to discuss the establishment of the Gerakan Rakjat Baru, which had been foreshadowed in the demands aired at the Villa Isola Congress.

The official announcement on the formation of this movement was issued on July 2. In line with what seem to have been the expectations of the pemuda, the direction of the movement was to be entrusted to a new version of the Putera leadership: Sukarno and Hatta (as before); R. A. A. Wiranatakusumah, per-

---

[47] Differing accounts are contained in Tan Malaka, *Dari pendjara ke pendjara,* III (Djakarta, n.d.), 53; and Darmosugondo, "Mengenang peristiwa sekitar 17 Agustus 1945," in Darius Marpaung, ed., *Bingkisan nasional: Kenangan sepuluh tahun revolusi Indonesia* (Djakarta, n.d.), pp. 42ff. Other leading pemuda mentioned in these sources include Sjarif Thajeb, a student at the Medical Faculty and a scion of one of Djakarta's elite families (migrant Atjehnese), and Asmara Hadi, a young migrant from Bengkulu who had made a name for himself as a poet and journalist before the war, and who was related by marriage to Sukarno. In an interview granted on February 7, 1963, Diah said that the core of the Angkatan Baru consisted of himself, Chaerul Saleh, Anwar Tjokroaminoto, Supeno, Sukarni, Sudiro, and Soetomo (Bung Tomo). He added that Adam Malik, though close to the Angkatan Baru, was not a member and that Asmara Hadi was a latecomer. He confirmed that there was some rivalry and mistrust between the Angkatan Baru and the Angkatan Muda leadership in Bandung.

haps the most politically prominent member of the Sundanese aristocracy; and Wachid Hasjim, a notable of the Islamic movement in the Japanese period, and son of K. H. Hasjim Asjari, the head of the Religious Affairs Department and founder of the prewar Nahdatul Ulama (Council of Moslem Scholars).[48] The four men proceeded to select an eighty-man Preparatory and Organizational Committee that gave the youth significant representation in a national organization for the first time.[49] The pemuda appointees included Diah, Supeno, Sukarni, Asmara Hadi, Adam Malik, Sudiro, Harsono Tjokroaminoto, Wikana, Chalid Rasjidi, Pandu Kartawiguna, Soetomo, and S. K. Trimurti.[50] With the exception of Soetomo, all were pemuda from the metropolis, and the great majority were members of the Angkatan Baru or were closely associated with its leaders. The new importance of the pemuda was made very clear by Diah's appointment as secretary of the GRB's Working Committee.

On July 6, just before the first session of the Working Committee opened, the Angkatan Baru leaders met to discuss their position. It was agreed that above all they should demand a more forceful and nationalist attitude from the older leaders. Shortly after the session began, the issue came to a head in the discussions of the proposed GRB charter, into which the pemuda demanded that the words "Republic of Indonesia" be inserted.

[48] Wiranatakusumah thus, as it were, replaced Ki Hadjar Dewantoro, while Wachid Hasjim took over the position K. H. Mansjur had held in the old Putera directorate. K. H. Hasjim Asjari was the most famous traditionalist kjai in Java, and the huge pesantrèn of Tebu Ireng in Djombang which he headed was the spiritual center of the conservative Moslem organization Nahdatul Ulama. On K. H. Hasjim Asjari and the formation and growth of the Nahdatul Ulama in the prewar period, see the excellent account given in Deliar Noer, "The Rise and Development of the Modernist Muslim Movement in Indonesia during the Dutch Colonial Period, 1900–1942" (Ph.D. thesis, Cornell University, 1963), pp. 373–84.

[49] For full details on the leadership of the GRB, see Anderson, *Some Aspects,* pp. 39–41.

[50] For biographical details on Supeno, Pandu Kartawiguna, Soetomo, and Trimurti, see the Appendix.

This was, of course, unacceptable to the Japanese. In the first place, Tokyo itself had not yet made any final decisions on when and in what form independence would be given to Indonesia.[51] In the second, the Investigating Committee, which had been first convened on May 31 to consider all questions relating to the state structure of an independent Indonesia, had not yet held its final session, and one of the major issues it was concerned with was whether Indonesia would be a monarchy or a republic.[52] In any case the GRB was clearly not the appropriate forum for the consideration of these constitutional questions, and one of the Japanese officials present handed Sukarno a note reminding him that whether or not Indonesia would be a republic was for the Emperor alone to decide. The older politicians, such as Subardjo, Sukarno, Hatta, Yamin, and Abikusno, proposed a compromise in which the word "republic" would remain in parentheses, indicating a future state of affairs.[53] It appears that this compromise was put to the vote and was overwhelmingly accepted, except by the pemuda.[54]

Their reaction to defeat set a pattern for the future. Adam Malik rose and made a speech strongly critical of the whole prospective program of the GRB. He was followed by Chaerul Saleh, who denounced the proceedings even more strongly and warned the older leaders that if they persisted in their cautious

---

[51] Tokyo was not to do so until the Supreme War Council met on July 17. Its decision, confirmed by the Cabinet on July 21, was to set a provisional target for the granting of independence in September, but with the last minute timing to be left to the discretion of the local military and naval authorities. See Kōichi Kishi, Shigetada Nishijima, et al., *Indoneshia ni okeru Nihon gunsei no kenkyu* (Tokyo, 1959), p. 419. I have relied on the regrettably unpublished translation prepared under the direction of Harry J. Benda at Yale University.

[52] This second session was held from July 10 to 17. For details see Anderson, *Some Aspects*, pp. 29–32; and Muhammad Yamin, ed., *Naskah persiapan Undang-Undang Dasar 1945* (Djakarta, 1959–1960), I, 145–396.

[53] Tan Malaka, *Dari pendjara*, III, 54.

[54] In talks with the author Diah said that the vote went roughly 70–7 in favor, with only the "bravest" of the pemuda voting no.

tactics, their efforts would be sabotaged by the youth.[55] He reportedly also stated that if the voted decision was pushed through, he personally could not guarantee the consequences. Finally, Diah himself spoke. The vote indicated, he said, that the pemuda had lost on the basic principles of the GRB, which had been intended to bring the pemuda and the older leaders closer together; hence the pemuda felt they could not continue to bear responsibility for carrying out the GRB program. The meeting became increasingly unruly. Finally Sukarno called for a temporary adjournment, which was later made permanent. The pemuda group, led by Chaerul Saleh, Malik, and Diah, left the building in protest, and most of the small Angkatan Baru group followed suit. As punishment for this hostile behavior, Chaerul Saleh and Sukarni were removed from their posts in the Sendenbu, and the Sixteenth Army seems to have taken the opportunity presented by the fiasco to get rid of their patron, Shimizu, who on July 20 was flown out of Djakarta to Singapore in the charge of Kyūjirō Hayashi, the top political adviser of the *saikōsikikan* (commander-in-chief).[56]

The general reaction to the meeting's outcome among the metropolitan pemuda was bitterness and frustration. As one of them later put it: "We got smiles, serious warnings against adventurism. They told us not to believe in rumors. The number

[55] For slightly differing versions of what happened, see Tan Malaka, *Dari pendjara,* III, 54; Brugmans et al., eds., *Nederlandsch-Indië,* pp. 566f.; Indonesia, Kementerian Luar Negeri, *Fakta dan dokumen2 untuk menjusun buku "Indonesia memasuki gelanggang internasional,"* Subperiode: Kabinet Presiden Soekarno dari tanggal 17.8.45 sampai 14.11.45 (Djakarta, 1958) (hereinafter cited as *Fakta dan dokumen2*), p. 153; Sidik Kertapati, *Sekitar proklamasi,* p. 64.

[56] Hitoshi Shimizu, "Statement" of Nov. 27–Dec. 2, 1945, IC-RVO doc. no. 059815; Nomura, "Statement"; Shizuo Saitō, "Statement" of June 4–5, 1946, IC-RVO doc. no. 00538–42; Maj. Gen. Otoshi Nishimura, "Statement" of May 31–June 6, 1946, IC-RVO doc. no. 005815–21. In his "Statement" of June 21, 1946, IC-RVO doc. no. 041204–5, the commander of the Kenpeitai on Java, Maj. Gen. Shōzō Nishida, declared that he personally had been responsible for Shimizu's removal, thinking that he was causing trouble for the Japanese army.

of leaders who encouraged the younger generation was very small, indeed could be counted on the fingers of one hand." [57] The smiles and serious warnings expressed the older politicians' failure to comprehend pemuda goals. The humiliating events of July 6 clearly revealed to the pemuda leaders the growing gap between their consciousness and that of the older generation. The pemuda opposition stance developed precisely as the pemuda moved into the political arena, for it was then that they first felt the depth of their estrangement from the established leadership.

[57] *Dokumentasi pemuda,* p. 8.

Chapter 4

Proclaiming Independence

The Gerakan Rakjat Baru fiasco marked the end of the era of purely occupation politics, in which the rules were determined by the Japanese army's ultimate disposition of power. At the same time it clearly foreshadowed the pattern of conflict that was to emerge as the Japanese Empire moved toward its ruin.

On July 14, 1945, a week after the collapse of the Gerakan Rakjat Baru, the War Cabinet met in Tokyo to hear the results of ambassador Satō's discussions in Moscow. The envoy indicated in no uncertain terms that the Russians could be expected to enter the war momentarily. On July 16 the Potsdam conference opened, and on July 17 the Saikō sensō shidō kaigi (Supreme War Guidance Council) held a decisive meeting at which Foreign Minister Tōgō persuaded his colleagues that immediate "puppet" independence should be given to the former Netherlands East Indies, but that the initiative should be taken, or appear to be taken, by the Indonesian people themselves.[1] On July 21 this decision, after ratification by the War Cabinet, was transmitted to the Sixteenth Army commander, Gen. Yūichirō Nagano, in Djakarta. On July 29 Field Marshal Hisaichi Terauchi, the commander of the Southern Area Armies, with headquarters in Saigon, received instructions from Tokyo to go ahead with independence preparations as rapidly as possible but to

[1] See Benda et al., eds., *Japanese Military Administration,* p. 274, for the final policy document; see also K. A. de Weerd, "Prepared Statement," Nov. 1946, pp. 121–22, IC-RVO, doc. no. 059679ff.

make no announcement until Russia's entry into the war became imminent.[2] Accordingly, a hurried conference was held in Singapore on July 30 to discuss the final details of making Indonesia an independent state.[3] On August 6 Hiroshima fell victim to American atomic attack. Terauchi was warned by Tokyo that the end of Russia's neutrality was only hours away,[4] for Molotov had advised Satō that Russia would declare war at midnight on August 8.

The PPKI

On August 7 Saigon announced the creation of the Panitia Persiapan Kemerdekaan Indonesia (Committee for the Preparation of Indonesian Independence), or PPKI, as the successor to the now defunct Investigating Committee,[5] "to hasten all efforts in relation to final preparations for forming a government of an independent Indonesia." Gen. Moichirō Yamamoto, the gunseikan in Java, added: "This preparatory committee will be set up in Java, with the aim of completing endeavors for preparing independence for the whole of Indonesia, so that when all the preparations in Java are completed, this will mean that the whole territory of Indonesia will become independent as a new state." The membership would include representatives of the Outer Islands who had already been selected by the Southern Area commander

[2] See *Aneta* (New York), Aug. 30, 1945, citing an interview of Nathan Brock (*Christian Science Monitor*) with Colonel Yano, the trusted political adviser of Marshal Terauchi.

[3] See Nishimura, "Statement," May 31–June 6, 1946. The conference was attended by the sōmubuchō, or chiefs of the General Affairs departments of the military administrations of Java, Sumatra, Malaya, and the naval area, together with their staff aides. For details, see Kanahele, "Japanese Occupation," p. 215. In Java, the office of sōmubuchō was the second most important in the military administration after that of the gunseikan. It was held at this time by General Nishimura.

[4] *Aneta*, Aug. 30, 1945.

[5] Before being disbanded, the Investigating Committee had succeeded in preparing a draft constitution. It was later to be accepted almost *in toto* by the PPKI as the constitutional basis of the new Indonesian state. See Chapter 5 below.

himself on the basis of their "ability, experience, knowledge and discretion." Sukarno greeted this announcement by observing that whereas "the Investigating Committee I could term an organ of the military government, the Preparatory Committee is an organ of the Indonesian people themselves." [6]

Early on the morning of August 9, Sukarno, Hatta, Dr. Radjiman Wediodiningrat (the chairman of the Investigating Committee), Dr. Suharto (Sukarno's private physician), Lieutenant Colonel Nomura, and Miyoshi left by military plane for Singapore.[7] There Nomura reported to the military authorities.[8] Later that day they left Singapore for Saigon. On August 11 Marshal Terauchi received the three Indonesian leaders in his villa at Dalat, and at 11:40 A.M. a ceremony was held to inaugurate Sukarno and Hatta as chairman and vice-chairman of the new PPKI. After further discussion it was agreed that the PPKI would hold its first meeting on August 18, and that independence would be declared formally as soon as the final preparations on the Japanese side had been concluded.[9] After an evening cere-

[6] *Asia Raya,* Aug. 7, 1945.

[7] As noted before Nomura was head of the Planning Section of the military administration on Java. Miyoshi was an old Indonesia hand from far back. He had been a consular officer in The Hague, 1921–25, and later in Surabaja, 1926–32. From 1936 to 1939 he had been vice-consul in Djakarta, and in 1940, a member of the Kobayashi trade mission. In 1941 he had gone back to Tokyo, only to return with the invading army. He was a confidant of Nishimura and, because of his fluency in Indonesian, generally acted as interpreter for high army personnel. Shunkichirō Miyoshi, "Statement," IC-RVO doc. no. 005846–7.

[8] These were Lt. Gen. Seishirō Itagaki, commander of the Seventh Area Armies with headquarters in Singapore, and Maj. Gen. Fumie Shimura, formerly gunseikan on Sumatra, and since July 1945, deputy chief of staff to Itagaki. See Maj. Gen. Fumie Shimura, "Statement" of June 13, 1946, IC-RVO doc. no. 009402–6.

[9] In accordance with instructions issued by Tokyo on August 2, the PPKI was to be unofficially subordinated to a parallel committee, called the Liaison Guidance Committee for the Preparation of Independence, for the duration of the war. Its members were Nagano, Shimura, Maeda, Nishimura, Hamada (Shimura's successor as gunseikan in Sumatra), and Captain Yanagihara, head of the Seimuka (Political Section) in the

mony in which the Marshal paid his guests the courtesy of serving saté, the consultations closed. The next day, Hatta's birthday,
the leaders were given a final official word from Terauchi and
then left for Saigon. On August 13 the party flew back to Singapore, where they picked up the three nominated Sumatran members of the PPKI; the following day they returned to Djakarta,
where they were given an impressive welcome by General
Nagano and Admiral Maeda.[10]

At the same time the membership of the PPKI was announced: Ir. Sukarno, Drs. Mohammed Hatta, B. P. H. Poeroe-
bojo, Dr. K. R. T. Radjiman Wediodiningrat, Soetardjo Kartohadikoesoemo, Andi Pangeran, Mr. I. G. K. Pudja, Dr. Mohammed Amir, Oto Iskandardinata, R. Pandji Soeroso, B. P. K. A.
Soerjohamidjojo, Ki Bagus Hadikusumo, Mr. Abdul Abbas, Mr.
Latuharhary, A. A. Hamidhan, Abdul Kadir, Dr. Soepomo,
K. H. Wachid Hasjim, Mr. Teuku Mohammed Hassan, Dr. G. S.
Ratulangie, and Drs. Yap Tjwan Bing.[11] In addition, Mr. Subardjo was appointed special adviser to the committee.[12]

In formal terms the PPKI contained respectively twelve, four,
and five representatives of the territories of the Sixteenth Army,
the Twenty-fifth Army, and the navy. In reality, however, it was
overwhelmingly dominated by non-Islamic politicians of the
older generation.[13] Not a single member of the younger genera-

---

General Affairs Department of the naval administration in Makasar. See
Nishimura, "Statement," May 31–June 6, 1946. Cf. Kishi, et al., eds.,
Indoneshia ni okeru, p. 430. It is notable that these authors do not
mention Maeda's presence on this committee.

[10] Nomura, "Statement"; see also *Asia Raya*, Aug. 14, 1945.

[11] See *Soeara Moeslimin Indonesia*, III (Aug. 15, 1945); and Abdul
Gaffar Pringgodigdo, *Sedjarah singkat berdirinja negara Republik Indonesia* (Surabaja, 1958), p. 30.

[12] *Asia Raya*, Aug. 14, 1945.

[13] Of the twenty-one members, twelve can be classified as older generation non-Islamic nationalist leaders. In addition there were two representatives of the pangrèh pradja, three of the principalities of Jogjakarta
and Surakarta, two of Islamic organizations, one of the Peta, and one of
the Chinese minority. Broken down ethnically, there were ten Javanese,

tion was included. The roster of names reflected not only the gunseikan's expressed concern for men of experience, ability and discretion, but also the fact that the PPKI was not established within the context of occupation politics, in which it would have been important to give the pemuda a voice. The PPKI was rather a part of the new politics of independence, aimed at the problem of creating an Indonesian state, like the older states of Burma and the Philippines, inside the Greater East Asia Co-Prosperity Sphere. For this purpose the older nationalist leaders were clearly the men required, since they alone enjoyed the public authority and international salience necessary to give the new government an air of authenticity.

On the eve of the Japanese surrender, the military authorities had thus laid the groundwork for an orderly transfer of sovereignty, however limited its real scope, to a largely Javanese group of middle-aged non-Islamic politicians, with whom they had worked in reasonable harmony throughout the occupation. The Japanese had also taken care to minimize the threat of friction between this group and the bureaucratic establishment of the pangrèh pradja by appointing to the PPKI Soetardjo Kartohadikoesoemo and Soeroso. Both of these men came from the most sophisticated and metropolitan sectors of the bureaucracy, and while commanding wide loyalty within it, had long experience of working with nationalist leaders of their own generation.[14] The Japanese were also aware that whatever hostilities did exist between the politicians and the administrators ran little deeper than rivalry between competing skill-groups. Both largely belonged to the traditional indigenous ruling class. Moreover, the experience of the Japanese occupation had done much to lessen the distance between them. They had been compelled to work

---

two Minangkabau, and one each for the eight most important *suku* (ethno-cultural groups) in Indonesia. It is striking that no less than eleven members had university degrees—five in medicine, four in law, one in engineering, and one in economics.

[14] For biographical details on Soetardjo and Soeroso, see the Appendix.

together in the Hōkōkai, an organization in which provincial leadership was in the hands of the pangrèh pradja, while the central office was headed by Sukarno and his associates. Many of the nationalist leaders who had been strongly antipathetic to the pangrèh pradja in the thirties found their antagonism abating when the Japanese appointed them to administrative positions where they found themselves willy-nilly absorbing something of the pangrèh pradja ethos.

Questions of Independence

But all these plans were rapidly overtaken by events. When Sukarno and Hatta returned with their party from Saigon on August 14, rumors that Japan was about to surrender were already in the air. Pemuda working in the Sendenbu reported that according to broadcasts from San Francisco, Japan had accepted the Allied ultimatum for an unconditional surrender and would make a formal declaration in a matter of hours.[15] The elite grapevine was quick to spread the news across the capital. At about four o'clock that afternoon, Sjahrir went to see Hatta, told him of the surrender stories, and urged him to make a proclamation of independence outside the framework of the PPKI on the ground that the victorious Allies would have nothing to do with a Japanese-sponsored state. Dutch radio broadcasts from Papua and Australia had indicated that significant sections of the returning Allied forces in Southeast Asia were preparing to take stern action against those they regarded as having collaborated with the Japanese.[16] It is instructive to note, in the light of later

[15] Interview with Brig. Gen. Latief Hendraningrat, Jan. 22, 1963. Latief was deputy chief of the Djakarta Peta at the time.

[16] See the remarkable document "Beschouwingen over de algemeene en financiele voorbereiding van de Indonesische onafhankelijkheidsbeweging door de Japanners," IC-RVO doc. no. 059397ff. This document is anonymous, but internal and other evidence clearly indicates that it was drawn up by Capt. Hiroshi Nakamura of the Planning Section. The reason for the anonymity appears to be that Nakamura wrote it while serving a very long sentence in prison for his role in the so-called Nakamura Affair—the wholesale looting of the state pawnshops at the end of the war.

developments, that Sjahrir was at this point concerned with institutions, not individuals. He was urging that the proclamation of
independence be made outside a particular committee the Japanese had officially sponsored, and not that it be made by persons
who were clear of the collaborationist taint. There is no evidence
that he thought it possible for either himself or his underground
followers to declare independence on their own, or as yet to by-
pass the main group of nationalist politicians and their pangrèh
pradja associates.

To Sjahrir's argument Hatta replied with his usual phlegmatic
realism that to the Allies it was a matter of indifference what
body declared independence; they would be looking first at individuals. Whether he and Sukarno declared independence inside
or outside the PPKI, they would still probably be regarded as
collaborators.[17] Since Sjahrir appeared to accept that independence would have to be declared by Sukarno and Hatta, and
since it was necessary to avoid trouble with the Japanese, who
still held physical control of Java, the most prudent course was
to follow the procedures the Japanese had already outlined. After
arguing for some time, the two men went to Sukarno's house at
Pegangsaan Timur 56 and continued the discussion. Not surprisingly, Sukarno supported Hatta's viewpoint. They were already in trouble with the Allies; there was little point in antagonizing the Japanese as well. The meeting ended inconclusively,
with Sukarno and Hatta insisting on waiting for further news
about international developments and the attitudes of the Japanese authorities before proceeding further.

It was at noon on August 15 that the Emperor's broadcast

The "Beschouwingen" relates (pp. 18f.) the impact of broadcasts by
Colonel Abdulkadir, adviser to Lieutenant-Governor General van Mook,
from Papua and Australia. The colonel's repeated threat was: "When we
go back to Java, we shall never forget those who cried 'Amerika kita
seterika, Inggeris kita linggis!' ['Let's flatten America with an iron, let's
use a crowbar on England!']."

[17] From the reminiscences of Mohammed Hatta, recorded on tape by
Mr. Subardjo, who kindly allowed me to hear them.

announcing Japan's surrender was received in Djakarta. In spite
of the rapid decline of Japan's military fortunes in the last few
months, the shock to the Japanese in Java was immense. Yanagawa, the martinet of the Seinendōjō, recalled that he "felt such
a big shock that it was like a rushing train in full speed suddenly
stopping." [18] Hatta later remarked that the most convincing confirmation of the surrender rumors was the silence and emptiness
of the gunseikan's office that afternoon. At about three o'clock
he went with Sukarno and Subardjo to try to get confirmation
from Admiral Maeda at Maeda's offices on Gambir Prapatan,
close by the Medical Faculty asrama. Maeda told them unofficially that he was sure the surrender had taken place, but there
had still been no confirmation from the government in Tokyo.[19]
Nishijima noted the first reactions of the three nationalist politicians:

Mr. Sukarno said, "It matters much to us, I feel as if I caught something like a big stone in my throat." . . . Mr. Subardjo suddenly
cried out firmly, "Why did you say so? We already had the course
Indonesia is going! It cannot be changed according to the circumstances. . . . Whether Japan surrenders or not does not influence
our possible independence. We have only one way to go—ahead!"
The Rear-Admiral nodded his head and replied, "Please wait, take it
easy, we shall have an official announcement before long. Until that
time please take care of yourselves."

Nishijima added: "We realized for the first time that there were
persons besides us who were shocked by the sudden change of
the situation. Immediately before the long-awaited Independence

[18] Capt. Munenari Yanagawa, "Further Statement," IC-RVO doc. no.
006517–22.

[19] Adm. Tadashi Maeda, "Statement," April 20, 1946, IC-RVO doc.
no. 006830–44. I have also relied heavily on a private translation of
an article entitled "On the Eve of Indonesian Independence," by Maeda,
which appeared in the *Sunday Mainichi* (Tokyo), March 12, 1950. Included with this translation are excerpts of dictated reminiscences by
Shigetada Nishijima and Dr. Nakatani. The English is poor, but without
access to the original Japanese I hesitated to tamper with it.

of Indonesia was about to be achieved, the Goddess of Fortune showed them her back. How miserable and pitiful their fates would be!" [20]

The exchange illustrates very well the shock and disappointment felt by the older politicians when the Japanese surrendered. It was not so disappointing that the Japanese had been defeated as that the defeat should have occurred just as the transfer of power was about to be tidily arranged. The collapse of the Japanese appeared to set an immovable block across the path to independence. The Indonesian leaders had expected that their independent regime would have at least a few months' grace, and possibly longer, before the Japanese accepted defeat. In this period the new state, like Burma, would hopefully become a *fait accompli* to the outside world. The sudden collapse of the Japanese not only destroyed any real possibility of a legal transfer of power but promised a much speedier Allied presence in Java. In spite of Subardjo's brave words, the immediate prospects for the older nationalists appeared bleak, since they were less interested in a symbolic declaration of independence than in the transfer of government power into their own hands. Any chance of achieving the actual transfer of power now seemed to have been lost.

In the circumstances it appeared that there was nothing to be done except push ahead with the course set in Saigon and hope for the best. Accordingly Hatta took the initiative, asking Subardjo to inform the PPKI members that an extraordinary meeting would be held at ten o'clock the next day.[21] Since the main body of the delegates from the Outer Islands was lodged at the

[20] Nishijima, in the document referred to in the previous note.

[21] See the interesting anonymous "Report on the Sulawesi Representatives' Journey to Java" (for the PPKI), IC-RVO doc. no. 006009–21. This was confirmed by Teuku Mr. Mohammed Hassan in an interview with the author, Dec. 1, 1963. See also the "Notes" of Dr. Mohammed Amir, finished on June 14, 1946, and sworn to before a Dutch court in Sabang (IC-RVO doc. no. 005936–8), though they are not in general very reliable.

Hotel Des Indes, this was readily accomplished. It was also agreed that Hatta and the others would assemble later that evening at Sukarno's house to discuss what steps should be taken when the PPKI convened. Hatta himself recalls that he returned to his home and began work on an independence proclamation, which he was to bring in draft form to the evening meeting.[22]

In the meantime the news of the surrender, or at least rumors that it had occurred, spread rapidly through the pemuda network in the capital. At the initiative of the Medical Faculty students, an emergency meeting was held in the Bacteriological Laboratory in Pegangsaan, quite close to Sukarno's house. The fluidity of the underground is well illustrated by the variety of those attending the meeting: they included Menteng 31 people (Chaerul Saleh, Abubakar Lubis, Aidit); Medical Faculty (Darwis, Djohar Nur); Kaigun (Wikana); and several others. After considerable discussion, it was decided to send a delegation led by Wikana to see Sukarno that night, urging him to make a proclamation outside the framework of the PPKI as soon as possible.[23]

Though the pemuda no doubt attached some significance to the international factors uppermost in the minds of their elders, their attitude toward the PPKI and a PPKI-sponsored declaration of independence was primarily shaped by their own developing political consciousness. Ever since the Youth Congress the pemuda had been pressing the Japanese authorities to move

[22] From the taped reminiscences of Hatta.

[23] Adam Malik, *Riwajat dan perdjuangan sekitar proklamasi kemerdekaan Indonesia 17 Agustus 1945* (Djakarta, 1950), p. 33; Sidik Kertapati, *Sekitar proklamasi,* p. 76; *Dokumentasi pemuda,* p. 22. Cf. D. N. Aidit, *Pilihan tulisan,* I (Djakarta, 1959), 508. Malik says it was Wikana and Darwis who called on Sukarno. Sidik, Aidit, and *Dokumentasi pemuda* give Wikana, Subadio Sastrosatomo, Suroto Kunto, and D. N. Aidit. Not only is Sidik's account generally more reliable than Malik's, but the inclusion of Subadio's name in his list at a time when Subadio was at the opposite end of the political spectrum from Sidik and Aidit indicates his objectivity. Sidik's version was confirmed by Subadio in an interview with the author on June 4, 1967.

more rapidly toward independence, and had criticized the older leaders for their timidity and passivity. The PPKI had been minimally acceptable, in spite of the absence of any pemuda representation, so long as it pointed directly toward the goal of independence (*merdeka*), and so long as there was no practical alternative. With the Japanese surrender, however, all kinds of possibilities opened up, and the PPKI's justification in the eyes of the pemuda vanished overnight. That a defeated Japan should still have the power to determine the shape and form of Indonesian independence was clearly intolerable. The pemuda, unlike their elders, had no direct stake in an orderly transfer of power, nor were they at this point particularly concerned about their acceptability to the Allies. An immediate and autonomous declaration of independence was imperative for its own sake, as a symbolic expression of liberation and self-determination. The period of the underground was almost at an end. The long-anticipated moment of crisis had arrived. The Japanese had now lost whatever authority they had ever had; if the older leaders failed to do what was expected of them, then the pemuda must take the destiny of the nation into their own hands.

The Wikana delegation left the Bacteriological Laboratory and proceeded to the Kaigun offices, where they found Subardjo and his intimates, Iwa, Buntaran, and Samsi, drinking and talking. It is probable that Wikana asked Subardjo for the latest information on the Japanese surrender and learned of the plans for the next day's meeting of the PPKI. The pemuda then set off for Pegangsaan Timur to confront Sukarno. Subardjo and his friends followed, stopping by at Hatta's, only to find him still busy with his draft. Promising to come back for him later on, they hurried after Wikana.[24] At Pegangsaan Timur 56, meanwhile, the atmosphere had become increasingly heated, as Wikana pressed Sukarno to declare immediate independence on his own. The older man urged the pemuda to be patient, adding that in any case he could do nothing without consulting the other

[24] Interview with Subardjo, May 11, 1962.

members of the PPKI, especially Hatta. He made it clear that he was unwilling to risk antagonizing the Japanese authorities when everything was still uncertain, most particularly whether the Japanese would still go through with the arrangements for independence. It was, after all, only three days since he and Hatta had been given the fullest assurances on this point by Terauchi himself. Wikana, who had been an *anak mas* (favorite pupil or protégé) of Sukarno, brought the meeting to an emotional climax by clearly implying that Sukarno was failing to live up to his role as *bapak* (patron or leader). The break came when Wikana declared, "If Bung Karno will not declare this proclamation tonight, tomorrow there will be murder and bloodshed!" Enraged, Sukarno shouted, "Here is my throat! Drag me into a corner and finish me off tonight! Don't wait till tomorrow!" [25]

In the meantime Subardjo had gone off to alert Hatta to what was afoot at Pegangsaan Timur 56. Dropping his work Hatta left at once to join the debate. But his appearance seems only to have heightened the conflict. Even less impressed with Wikana's emotional appeals than Sukarno had been, he told the pemuda that the news of Japan's surrender was not yet official and that it made no sense to take any action until it was clear how the military authorities would react to an earlier proclamation.[26] Above all, he said, he wanted to avoid any foolhardy action that could lead to chaos. When Wikana angrily warned that the pemuda had already collected their strength, Hatta replied that neither he nor Sukarno would be coerced into doing anything rash, and challenged the pemuda to declare independence on their own if they thought they could carry it off. Nonplussed, Wikana could only reply that the pemuda "would not answer for the consequences if the proclamation was not made the next

[25] *Fakta dan Dokumen2,* p. 139; see also Mohammed Ibnu Sajuti [Sajuti Melik], "Proklamasi Kemerdekaan seperti jang saja saksikan," *Berita Yudha,* Aug. 16, 1968.

[26] Malik, *Riwajat,* p. 34.

morning at noon"; then he led his followers out of the house.[27]

From the point of view of the older leaders, the meeting had ended satisfactorily, and there is little reason to believe that they regarded the pemuda's behavior as any different from what it had been in previous months—youthful bravado, quixotic romanticism, and irrational attitudinizing. It was only the story of the Gerakan Rakjat Baru over again. From the point of view of the pemuda, however, the meeting had great psychological importance. The threat of mobilizing the pemuda was the unplanned outcome of emotions aroused in the debate with Sukarno and Hatta. But the threat had been made, and Hatta's direct challenge to Wikana, intended as a rebuke to what he saw as the latter's childishness, was deeply felt. In Hatta's own words, the pemuda delegation "dibikin malu [had been shamed]." [28] Subsequent developments clearly had their origin in this humiliation. Wikana was quite well aware that a declaration by himself and his fellow pemuda would have no significance. None were well-known outside a tiny circle of educated students. The only leaders with the prestige and authority to make a politically meaningful declaration of independence were Sukarno and Hatta.

Returning from the fruitless confrontation, Wikana was met by Darwis and taken to Tjikini 71, where the rest of the pemuda were awaiting the result of his mission. By now the number of youths assembled had swelled considerably.[29] And while the first cables officially confirming Japan's surrender were coming into Djakarta, Wikana gave a full report on what had happened.[30]

---

[27] *Ibid.;* see also Ali Moechtar Hoeta Soehoet, "Sedikit sekitar saat lahirnja R. I. Proklamasi," in Marpaung, ed., *Bingkisan nasional,* pp. 27–34; Aidit, *Pilihan tulisan,* p. 508; Sidik Kertapati, *Sekitar proklamasi,* p. 77.

[28] Taped reminiscences of Hatta.

[29] Sidik Kertapati notes the addition of Dr. Muwardi, Jusuf Kunto, and Singgih (shōdanchō in the Djakarta area Peta), among others (*Sekitar proklamasi,* p. 77).

[30] Maeda, "Statement," April 20, 1946; Maeda, "On the Eve."

The personal humiliation Wikana had suffered appears to have been taken by the assmbled pemuda as a collective challenge. In the early hours of the morning it was decided that some action would have to be taken to prove the sincerity of the pemuda group as a whole.

It is not clear who originated the plan to kidnap Sukarno and Hatta, but the eventual executors were Chaerul Saleh, Sukarni, Wikana, Dr. Muwardi, Jusuf Kunto, Singgih, and Dr. Sutjipto (a Peta officer from the Rengasdengklok district to the northeast of Djakarta). While Sukarni, Singgih, Muwardi, and Jusuf Kunto carried out the kidnapping, Chaerul Saleh and Wikana were to alert the pemuda in the capital, preparing them if necessary for rioting or even some kind of *putsch*.[31] The plan was faultlessly begun. About four o'clock on the morning of August 16, Hatta and Sukarno (together with his wife and infant son) were aroused and told that an uprising led by youths of the Heihō and Peta was imminent, and that they must therefore be moved to safety outside the city. Should they remain, the Japanese would very likely arrest or kill them, or in some way use them against the pemuda groups.[32] No physical coercion was employed against the two leaders. They seem at least initially to have believed the story. Packed into two cars, Sukarno and Hatta were driven away to Rengasdengklok, a small town well off the main roads, where the local Peta commander had arrested the very few Japanese trainers present and had raised the Indonesian flag on his own.[33]

[31] Sidik Kertapati, *Sekitar proklamasi*, p. 83; Malik, *Riwajat*, pp. 36–38; Anderson, *Some Aspects*, pp. 70–71.

[32] This had happened in the Blitar uprising, when a number of high Indonesians, including Oto Iskandardinata, Kasman Singodimedjo, Sudiro (mBah), Abikusno Tjokrosujoso, Dr. Soepomo, Sukarno, and A. Kahar Muzakkir were forced to attend the trials of the mutineers and by their presence sanction their punishment. See Pakpahan, *1261 hari*, p. 110.

[33] See Bahsan, *Tjatatan ringkas*, pp. 38–48, for a detailed eyewitness account. According to both Bahsan and Sidik Kertapati (*Sekitar proklamasi*, p. 78), Rengasdengklok was chosen not only because of its isolation but because a small underground group calling itself the Sapu Mas (Golden Broom) had been active in the local Peta since about

To this day opinions are divided about which of two general alternatives the pemuda leaders had in mind when they kidnapped Sukarno and Hatta, and it may be that they themselves were uncertain of the outcome. On the one hand, it has been suggested that by removing Sukarno and Hatta from Djakarta, the pemuda hoped to prevent them from being compelled to speak against an uprising the pemuda planned to start in the city. This would mean that the pemuda genuinely hoped to seize power from the Japanese. On the other hand—and this seems the more probable in the light of subsequent developments—the pemuda may have intended to force Sukarno and Hatta to accede to their wishes, and so atone for the incident at Pegangsaan Timur the night before. In any event neither prospect was realized. At Rengasdengklok, Sukarno and Hatta began to realize what was really happening and refused to budge from their position of the previous night. Until they had some firm commitment from the Japanese authorities, they were not prepared to make any move on their own. In Djakarta, once the removal of Sukarno and Hatta had been accomplished, the waiting began. The pemuda gathered in each other's houses and in the asrama. But nothing happened. There was no uprising.

In the morning Subardjo appeared at Maeda's residence on Diponegoro to inquire whether there was confirmation of surrender from Tokyo. He had just called at Sukarno's and discovered from Sukarno's private secretary, Sajuti Melik, who had witnessed something of the events of the previous night, that Sukarno had left the house early that morning under mysterious circumstances.[34] The first thought in the minds of Maeda, Nishi-

---

January 1945. Dr. Sutjipto acted as liaison between the Sapu Mas and the Djakarta pemuda.

[34] Maeda, "On the Eve." Sitting in Sukarno's study, Sajuti was an unseen observer of the clash between Sukarno, Hatta, and the Wikana delegation. After Wikana left, Sukarno discussed the situation with him and asked him to sleep at the house. He recalled later that he had been awakened at about four o'clock in the morning by Muwardi, who told him that Sukarno and Hatta had been taken away to carry out the proc-

jima, and Subardjo seems to have been that the military administration had arrested Sukarno and Hatta, or possibly that the two
leaders, for reasons best known to themselves, had left town.
But it soon became clear from conversations with the gunseikan's
office that the army was as much in the dark as everyone else,
though the Kenpeitai had been ordered to start a search.

From Subardjo the Kaigun people learned something of what
had happened the night before. Nishijima was accordingly sent
to locate Wikana and succeeded in finding him at the Asrama
Indonesia Merdeka. An emotional argument ensued in which
Nishijima tried to persuade Wikana to reveal the location of the
two leaders, promising that if Wikana did so Nishijima and
Maeda would cooperate fully in having Indonesian independence
declared. Without revealing the whereabouts of Sukarno and
Hatta, Wikana finally agreed to try to arrange for their return.[35]
He immediately went to see Subardjo at the latter's offices in
Prapatan. There he found Jusuf Kunto, who had been sent back
to Djakarta by Sukarni to report Sukarno's unchanged attitude
and to inquire whether there was final confirmation of the surrender from Tokyo. After further debate it was agreed that
Subardjo should go to Rengasdengklok with Jusuf Kunto, Sudiro
(mBah), and Yoshizumi and bring the leaders back to town.
Yoshizumi's presence was required to make sure that the group
was not interfered with by the military authorities. Through
Nishijima, Maeda guaranteed all concerned personal immunity
from the Kenpeitai and offered his own house as a safe place for
further negotiations.

The emissaries set off for Rengasdengklok late in the afternoon
and reached their destination about nightfall. Subardjo was able

---

lamation of independence. See Mohammed Ibnu Sajuti [Sajuti Melik],
"Kenangan dimasa lampau bagaikan seorang purnawirawan," *Mahasiswa
Indonesia* (Djawa Barat), Sept. 1968, Minggu ke-3; and Sajuti, "Proklamasi Kemerdekaan." For biographical details on Sajuti, see the Appendix.

[35] Nishijima's commentary on Maeda, "On the Eve."

to inform Sukarno and Hatta of the new situation in the capital, and also to assure them that the declaration of independence would in fact go through, since Maeda had offered his fullest cooperation. Sukarni was eventually convinced, largely by Kunto's confirmation of Subardjo's story, and about eight o'clock the whole group drove back to Djakarta.

In the meantime Subardjo had left instructions for the PPKI to assemble at Maeda's and await the return of the kidnapped leaders. The majority of the PPKI had in fact met that morning at ten o'clock for the emergency opening meeting. When Sukarno, Hatta, and Subardjo failed to appear, the group had broken up, each member returning to his home or hotel to await further developments. Now, as word of Subardjo's mission spread, they started to reassemble at Maeda's house, in considerable doubt and confusion about what had actually happened.

The pemuda groups in Djakarta were also told by Wikana of the steps he had taken, and of the guarantees offered by Maeda.[36] Nonetheless the atmosphere was increasingly tense. No one could be sure that the Japanese would not go back on their word and arrest both Sukarno and Hatta, as well as the most prominent youth leaders. Contact was therefore made with members of the Peta stationed in Djakarta, and warnings spread throughout the informal network of pemuda groups to prepare for an emergency situation.

Subsequently much has been made by certain representatives of the pemuda groups of the seriousness of the preparations for an uprising in Djakarta.[37] But what evidence exists indicates extreme confusion and disorganization. Contact with the Peta seems to have been on a purely individual basis. The commander of the Djakarta Peta, Kasman Singodimedjo, was in Bandung,

[36] Details can be found in Sidik Kertapati, *Sekitar proklamasi,* pp. 96–97.

[37] Aidit, *Pilihan tulisan,* pp. 508f.; Malik, *Riwajat,* pp. 41–43; Sidik Kertapati, *Sekitar proklamasi,* p. 83; see also Nawawi Dusky, "Hari proklamasi," *Abadi* (Djakarta), Aug. 22, 1955.

and his second-in-command, Latief Hendraningrat, was evidently unwilling to act without authorization (including orders from Sukarno and Hatta).[38] Various small groups did gather at certain points in the city, and plans seem to have been made for an attack on the radio station, the primary target of the pemuda, since it would allow them to spread news of the proclamation instantly. It is probably fair to assume that the pemuda had no real idea of seizing power in the city, but rather of taking over the radio transmitter on Gambir Barat so that a proclamation of independence could be relayed to the provinces and to the outside world. The Japanese were well aware of this likelihood, and the only major military step taken that day by the Japanese high command was to strengthen the guard outside the radio station.[39] Nonetheless the atmosphere was very tense, and the pemuda groups were in a highly excitable state. While Maeda may subsequently have exaggerated his fear of a pemuda uprising in order to avoid Allied charges of excessive zeal in promoting Indonesian independence, the situation was in reality explosive enough that had an incident broken out, a good deal of blood might have been shed, mainly by the Japanese troops stationed in the capital.

It was chiefly this consideration—the threat of massive repression by depressed and panicky army authorities—that led Maeda to take a major hand in pushing ahead with a declaration of independence. He was above all determined to carry through the orderly transfer of sovereignty that the Rengasdengklok affair had endangered, and to put authority once again firmly in the hands of the older leaders. Accordingly, when Sukarno and Hatta arrived back in Djakarta, Maeda immediately offered to intervene with the military authorities and try to work out some arrangement whereby the interests of all parties could be secured.[40]

[38] Sidik Kertapati, *Sekitar proklamasi*, p. 83. For biographical details on Kasman, see the Appendix.

[39] Nishimura, "Statement" of April 25, 1947, IC-RVO doc. no. 059334. Shōzō Miyano, the head of the Chianbu (Security Department), was assigned this task.

[40] The account that follows relies heavily on Maeda's "On the Eve."

Maeda then asked the gunseikan, General Yamamoto, for an immediate interview. In the meantime, however, the General had received word from Tokyo via General Itagaki in Singapore that the terms of the surrender bound Japan to maintain the status quo in all occupied territories; General Yamamoto was thus ordered to freeze all political activities and programs as of the date the Allied ultimatum was accepted. While he was quite sympathetic to the aims of Indonesian independence, the General knew he would be held personally responsible for any infraction of these terms. Accordingly he refused to see either Maeda or Sukarno and Hatta, and referred them to his subordinate, General Nishimura, head of the General Affairs Department of the military administration. Only after a prolonged conversation on the telephone, in which Maeda stressed the dangers of widespread rioting in the city, did even Nishimura consent to be approached.

Sukarno and Hatta then followed Maeda to Nishimura's official residence, where they found the General with his chief political advisers, Colonel Nomura, Captain Nakamura, Saitō, Miyoshi, and Nakatani. With Maeda's backing, the two Indonesian leaders asked for a full statement of the Japanese position. Could Nishimura guarantee that independence would go forward as originally planned now that Tokyo surrendered? If not, would the Japanese permit an immediate declaration of independence, backdated as it were to before the surrender, and then let the practical questions be worked out informally by the PPKI? Further, was there any definite news of when the Allies were expected to arrive, and what their attitude would be toward an independent Indonesian regime? Nishimura replied that any move to declare independence would be unacceptable, since the military authorities had an explicit responsibility for maintaining the status quo and would be liable to severe penalties if the PPKI was permitted to continue its work. The PPKI had been publicly set up by the Japanese, and therefore came under the terms of the surrender agreement.

Sukarno and Hatta then proposed that the Japanese "should

not complain if the activities of pemuda rioters would break
Japanese controls," in other words that the Japanese should permit a "revolutionary" declaration ostensibly initiated by youth
elements outside Japanese control. Nishimura replied that he
could not accept any such proposal "as long as he knew about
it," but that it might be permissible if it were done "without his
knowledge." [41] This decision on Nishimura's part represented a
compromise acceptable to all, since it gave the army's tacit
promise not to intervene should the Indonesians make their own
declaration of independence outside the framework of the PPKI.
The prime interest of the military authorities was to be able to
deny responsibility for any further political developments in
Indonesia. It should be remembered, too, that Nishimura represented a considerable group within the Sixteenth Army that was
by now quite sympathetic to Indonesian aspirations, and moreover felt a strong moral obligation to the Indonesians in view of
the Koiso Declaration and the whole ideological rationale for
Japan's Greater East Asia Co-prosperity Sphere. The arrangement with Sukarno and Hatta permitted the higher military authorities to fulfill at the same time this moral obligation and their
legal responsibilities to Tokyo. It would probably not be unreasonable to credit them with a certain *schadenfreude* toward the
victorious Allies.[42]

With the assurance that the military authorities would permit
a proclamation of independence as long as it was not associated
with the Japanese and did not result in disorders, Sukarno, Hatta,
and Maeda returned to Maeda's house. To make sure nothing
was done that would be unacceptable to the military, Miyoshi, a
trusted confidant of Nishimura, was sent along to observe the
proceedings.

Meanwhile, Nishijima had been assigned to help Sukarni and
Sajuti Melik warn the pemuda stationed in various parts of Dja-

[41] Nakatani's and Nishijima's notes on Maeda, "On the Eve."
[42] In any case what they were doing was similar to, if less bold than,
Idenburg's plotting with Amir Sjarifuddin on the eve of the occupation.

karta not to make any moves that would endanger the negotiations. The key places in the darkened city were the temporary headquarters of the more militant pemuda at the Prapatan 10 asrama, Dr. Muwardi's home, which was the headquarters of the Barisan Pelopor, and finally the radio station itself. Sukarni and Sajuti Melik handled dealings with the pemuda, and Nishijima handled dealings with the Japanese guards, who sometimes challenged their car. This joint patrol managed to complete its task successfully, though there were apparently some close shaves. At one point the whole group was detained by the Kenpeitai outside the radio station, and only a confirming telephone call to Maeda secured their release.[43] In any event the threatened uprising was called off.

It was about three o'clock in the morning when the various groups returned to the house. Word had been sent to Sjahrir of what was afoot. Indeed, a special party had been sent out to look for him—but he was nowhere to be found.[44] The main body of the pemuda gathered at Prapatan 10 agreed to have Chaerul Saleh and Sukarni represent them, and various other figures associated with these pemuda, such as Dr. Muwardi and B. M. Diah, were also assembled.[45] The PPKI members had been waiting patiently since early evening. The first step taken by Sukarno and Hatta was to assure them that the Japanese military had permitted a sub rosa declaration of independence and that they had

[43] Nishijima's notes on Maeda, "On the Eve." See also Shigetada Nishijima, "Verklaring betreffende de Indonesische onafhankelijkheidsbeweging en de bijeenkomsten ten huize van Maeda op 16/17 Augustus 1945," March 10–13, 1947, IC-RVO doc. no. 006076–89; Hasjim Mahdan, "Prapatan sepuluh," *Indonesia Raya* (Djakarta), Aug. 16, 1955; and Sajuti "Proklamasi Kemerdekaan."

[44] Sidik Kertapati, *Sekitar proklamasi*, pp. 96–97; cf. Sjahrir, *Out of Exile*, pp. 257–58.

[45] For details see Sidik Kertapati, *Sekitar proklamasi*, pp. 96–97. Diah had been arrested by the Kenpeitai following the Gerakan Rakjat Baru fiasco, and was apparently released just before the proclamation. See Kishi et al., eds. *Indoneshia ni okeru*, p. 422; Tan Malaka, *Dari pendjara*, III, 58.

nothing to fear as a result. Maeda, Sukarno, Hatta, Nishijima, Subardjo, Miyoshi, and Yoshizumi then retired into the Admiral's study to work out the actual wording of the proclamation. A fiery text drafted by the pemuda group at Prapatan 10 was not seriously considered, since the essence of the deal worked out at Nishimura's was that no group's major interests would be jeopardized. Thus it was important to devise a wording that would satisfy not only the Indonesians but also the Japanese, who were anxious that the phrasing used neither explicitly contain a formal, legal-style transfer of sovereignty, nor encourage rioting against the authorities by the pemuda. The final form of the independence proclamation, drafted by Sukarno himself, achieved these aims admirably. The text ran simply: "We, the people of Indonesia, hereby declare Indonesia's independence. Matters concerning the transfer of power and other matters will be executed in an orderly manner and in the shortest possible time." It was signed "In the name of the Indonesian People, Sukarno-Hatta, 17 August 2605." [46]

The phrase "transfer of power" was designed, Nishijima recalled, as a rough translation of the words *gyōseiken no iten* (transfer of administrative control) rather than *shuken no jōto* (cession of legal sovereignty). Thus Miyoshi was able subsequently to report that nothing beyond administrative authority had been claimed by the Indonesians, whereas the vaguer Indonesian phrase *pemindahan kekuasaan* could be taken to mean a far broader assumption of political power, and certainly was.[47] The wishes of Nishimura and the older nationalists were evident in the phrase "in an orderly manner," or in other words, without any pemuda action; and those of all Indonesians were evident in the phrase "in the shortest possible time," or before the anticipated landing of the Allied forces. All in all, it was a highly satisfactory text for the older nationalists and the Japanese. The drafters now

[46] A reproduction of the text can be found in Sidik Kertapati, *Sekitar proklamasi*, p. 93.

[47] Nishijima's notes on Maeda, "On the Eve."

emerged to face the PPKI and the representatives of the pemuda. Sukarni and Chaerul Saleh protested against the proclamation's tame character, but the initiative had now passed out of their hands. The working arrangement between the Sukarno-Hatta leadership and the authorities was quite acceptable to most of the PPKI. It was at first suggested that all present sign the document, but the pemuda representatives refused to sign any proclamation together with the PPKI, whom Chaerul Saleh termed "Kenpei nominees." Instead the pemuda asked that six of their representatives be allowed to sign exclusively with Sukarno and Hatta—a clearly unacceptable proposal that was evidently intended as a strategy to release the pemuda from having to take responsibility for a document unpalatable to them. Since the pemuda could not sign, and since it was now important that the proclamation be disassociated from the PPKI as such, the document was ultimately signed only by Sukarno and Hatta.[48]

It was now five o'clock in the morning and the group began to disperse, with the understanding that a public announcement of the proclamation would take place later that day. The initial plan was to call a mass meeting on Djakarta's central square. But the military authorities, evidently afraid that the meeting might get out of hand, sent troops to patrol the whole area, with the result that the proclamation was made instead at Sukarno's own home. Yamamoto and Nishimura also refused to permit the radio station to be used to announce independence to the outside world, since such an action would look too much like overt collusion with the nationalists in defying Allied orders. Nor were the newspapers initially permitted to announce it. But through the assistance of Maeda and Nishijima, the Naval Office press was used to run off copies of the proclamation for distribution in the capital, and the internal telephone and telegraph systems were used to spread the news across the island.[49] Later in the morning a simple ceremony was held at which Muwardi read the preface

[48] Tan Malaka, *Dari pendjara*, III, 59; and Malik, *Riwajat*, p. 52.
[49] Nishijima's notes on Maeda "On the Eve."

to the draft constitution drawn up by the Investigating Committee a month before, Sukarno read the proclamation, Latief Hendraningrat, as the senior Peta officer present, raised the Dwiwarna, the red and white national flag, and all present joined in singing "Indonesia Raya."

Through the telecommunications system of the Dōmei news agency, the text of the proclamation reached Bandung and Jogjakarta by noon.[50] The pemuda in Bandung had better success than their Djakarta colleagues in arranging for radio transmission. Beginning at 7 P.M. on August 17, broadcasts of the independence proclamation in English and Indonesian were made at hourly intervals from Radio Bandung.[51] The local radio system was hooked up to the Central Telegraph Office's shortwave transmitter and thus broadcast to the outside world. Only at 11:30 that night did the local Japanese military appear to give a formal reprimand. And there was no further interference in the process of disseminating the news that Indonesia was, at least on paper, free. In Djakarta, Admiral Maeda held a celebration banquet for those members of the PPKI who came from the naval area.[52]

[50] Djèn Amar, *Bandung lautan api,* pp. 45–47; *Kota Jogjakarta dua ratus tahun, 7 Oktober 1756–7 Oktober 1956* (Jogjakarta, 1956), p. 29.
[51] Djèn Amar, *Bandung lautan api,* pp. 47–48.
[52] "Report on the Sulawesi Representatives' Journey to Java."

Chapter 5

Toward a
Republican Government

In keeping with the unstated bargain between the older nationalist leaders and the Japanese military, the first steps to insti-
tutionalize the now independent state were taken on the morning
of August 18. General Yamamoto, indeed, solemnly and officially told Sukarno and Hatta:

Japan has accepted the Potsdam Declaration, and accordingly assistance toward independence is impossible; the military administration on Java will be continued under the command of the supreme
commander-in-chief of the Japanese army, in conformity with the
principles of maintaining the status quo, while firmly securing peace
and good order, until the day when the transfer of everything to the
Allies is completed.[1]

But this affirmation of Japanese intentions was made after the
PPKI had already held its first full meeting that same morning—
a meeting General Yamamoto would have prevented had he been
serious about obeying literally his orders to maintain the status
quo. Moreover, a denunciation of the meeting prepared by
Yamamoto was not actually delivered until the morning of
August 19.[2]

Though in essence the body that met on the morning of August
18 was the PPKI, certain adjustments were made in its member-

[1] Nishimura, "Statement" of April 10, 1947, IC-RVO doc. no. 059331.
[2] *Ibid.;* Kishi et al., eds., *Indoneshia ni okeru,* p. 491.

85

ship to fit the new situation. On an informal basis Kasman Singodimedjo, Peta commander in Djakarta, R. A. A. Wiranatakusumah, adviser to the Internal Affairs Department, Iwa Kusumasumantri, Ki Hadjar Dewantoro, and Sajuti Melik were asked to
attend.[3] To these were added the three most prominent pemuda
representatives of the moment: Chaerul Saleh, Sukarni, and
Wikana. After discussing the matter with other pemuda leaders,
the three had agreed to go. On their arrival, however, and perhaps also by prearrangement, Chaerul Saleh launched into a
violent attack on the legitimacy of the body as it was then constituted, claiming it "stank" of the Japanese. He demanded that
since Indonesia was now independent, all links with the Japanese period be broken, and urged that the meeting be moved to
a public place where the masses could participate in what was
going on. He also insisted that the PPKI change its name to
Komité Nasional Indonesia (Indonesian National Committee).
Hatta tried to appease the pemuda group, saying that he and
Sukarno found it difficult to separate their responsibility to the
Japanese from their responsibility to the people. "For this reason,"
he added, "we tell the Japanese that this is a meeting of the
PPKI, while we guarantee to the people that this is the first
meeting of the Komité Nasional Indonesia." [4] Sukarno assented
to Hatta's statement of their position.[5] In an exact repetition of
the scene at the opening of the Gerakan Rakjat Baru seven
weeks earlier, the youth representatives then left the meeting in

[3] "Report on the Sulawesi Representatives' Journey to Java"; Yamin
ed., *Naskah persiapan*, pp. 399–473; Abdul Gaffar Pringgodigdo,
Perubahan kabinet presidensil mendjadi kabinet parlementer (Jogjakarta,
n.d.), p. 16; Malik, *Riwajat*, p. 61; and Kishi et al., eds., *Indoneshia ni
okeru*, p. 512.

[4] Malik, *Riwajat*, p. 61; Sidik Kertapati, *Sekitar proklamasi*, pp. 100–
101; and Kishi et al., eds., *Indoneshia ni okeru*, p. 413. Malik incorrectly
gives the date as August 23.

[5] It is interesting that Sidik does not mention this, while Malik does.
Perhaps the relationship of the Left to Sukarno in 1961 does something
to explain the omission.

protest against being overruled by the older leaders.[6] While the clash was genuine enough, the departure of the youth leaders had advantages for both groups. The older nationalists were able to handle the constitutional and institutional matters before them very much along the lines set by the Investigating Committee, while the pemuda could abjure the caution and compromise by which Sukarno and Hatta were slowly endeavoring to pry an independent Indonesian government loose from the structures of the Japanese military administration.

Left to themselves the older leaders made some major decisions. They approved the draft constitution drawn up earlier by the Political Subcommittee of the Investigating Committee, while eliminating the obsolete passages praising Japan's imperial ideals in Asia.[7] The provisions that had aroused the greatest controversy in previous sessions of the Investigating Committee—those requiring that the president of the republic be a Moslem and that all professing Moslems adhere to the *sjariah* (requirements of Moslem law)—were also successfully disposed of. Sukarno and Hatta approached Teuku Hassan, the Atjehnese representative on the PPKI, and urged him to intervene with the strongest supporter of the Islamic position on the committee, Ki Bagus Hadikusumo, the modernist Muhammadijah leader from Jogjakarta. Although Teuku Hassan came from a well-known *uleëbalang* (feudal) family in Sigli, the reputation of the Atjehnese for religious zeal was apparently enough to persuade the Javanese kjai to accept the virtual elimination of any mention of Islam in the Constitution. Hassan stressed the importance of national unity. It was imperative not to drive the important Christian minorities (Batak, Menadonese, and Ambonese) into the arms of the returning Dutch by provisions at least one of which appeared

[6] Such walkouts were as essential a part of the pemuda style as the subsequent mass onslaughts on Japanese-held offices and the *daulat* (kidnapping) operations discussed below in Chapters 7 and 15.

[7] See Yamin, ed., *Naskah persiapan*, pp. 276, 401.

to relegate Christians to second-class citizenship.[8] Unanimity having been achieved by this maneuver, the meeting proceeded to add to the Constitution a group of transitional regulations allowing for the election of a president and vice-president by the PPKI and confirming the temporary authority of the PPKI until an official Indonesian National Committee could be formed. This committee would arrange eventually for the convening of the Parliament and Supreme Consultative Assembly stipulated by the Investigating Committee's draft. A further regulation was added giving the president elected by the PPKI virtually un-limited powers for six months after the end of the war. Once these preliminary steps had been taken, the Constitution was unani-mously accepted, and in the afternoon the PPKI, on Oto Iskan-dardinata's nomination, elected Sukarno and Hatta president and vice-president.[9] It was informally agreed that as soon as possible the president and vice-president would nominate addi-tional members to the PPKI so that it would fully represent all major Indonesian groups.

On August 19, in spite of Yamamoto's *pro forma* remon-strances, the PPKI met again, now calling itself for the first time the Komité Nasional Indonesia (KNI), in accordance with the terms of the new Constitution. General agreement was reached on the division of the former Netherlands East Indies into eight provinces, each headed by a governor. Each governor was to be assisted by a local Komité Nasional. Below the provincial level, the two main levels of local government were to be the residency and the village. The main reason for instituting this system of

[8] Interview with Teuku Mr. Mohammed Hassan, Dec. 1, 1963; essen-tially the same story emerges from the taped reminiscences of Hatta mentioned above.

[9] Yamin, ed., *Naskah persiapan,* pp. 34, 425–31. Cf. Tan Malaka, *Dari pendjara,* III, 60, for some critical comments on the proceedings. Kishi et al., eds., (*Indoneshia ni okeru,* p. 493) say that it was Latuhar-hary, not Oto Iskandardinata, who made the two nominations. Since Nishijima was an uninvolved eyewitness, his testimony is perhaps the most reliable. But common lore affirms the role of Oto.

government was to give maximum prestige and flexibility to leading members of the PPKI representing the Outer Islands, who
would proceed as rapidly as possible to their home territories to
form republican governments there. It was felt that communications, already difficult in the Japanese period, would remain uncertain while the Allies entered the archipelago. On the other
hand, the retention of the residency as the key unit of local administration was one more indication of the PPKI's intention of
adhering to Japanese administrative practice. As we have already
noted, in Java, at least, the residency was the major unit of
regional government, within which the autarchic economic policies of the military government were carried out. The highest
Indonesian officials in the provinces were usually the so-called
vice-residents (*fuku-shūchōkan*), and it was felt that the transfer
from Japanese to Indonesian control could be made smoothly by
keeping the older administrative units and at the same time encouraging the vice-residents to try to assume the powers of the
Japanese residents. Teuku Hassan, Ratulangie, Latuharhary, and
Pudja (all PPKI members) were then appointed governors of the
provinces they had come to represent in the PPKI (Sumatra,
Sulawesi, Maluku, and Sunda Ketjil), while Pangéran Mohammed Noor, also a member of the older nationalist elite, was
made governor of Kalimantan. In addition, a whole series of
regulations were passed dealing with administrative problems
likely to face the new state. The most interesting of these, as we
shall see, implied a commitment to purge the bureaucracy and
the police of undesirable elements. It was also decided to issue a
general political amnesty for those imprisoned for political of-
fenses under the Japanese regime.[10]

A special subcommittee under Subardjo considered the question of how the functions of the government should be divided
up among the ministries—particularly the distribution of jurisdictions and responsibilities. Controversy arose mainly over the
proposed establishment of ministries for religion and youth

[10] Yamin, ed., *Naskah persiapan*, pp. 438–52.

affairs. The impotence of Islam in the PPKI was remarkably illustrated when Latuharhary, representing Christian Maluku, strongly opposed the creation of a Ministry of Religion on the ground that it would become a bone of contention between the Islamic and Christian communities, and won the support of the KNI as a whole by a vote of nineteen to six.[11] Dr. Amir, personal physician to the Sultan of Langkat, urged the formation of a Youth Ministry to "enable us as soon as possible to start militarizing and training the ideology of our youth." [12] Though he received a certain amount of support from Iwa Kusumasumantri, his proposal seems to have found little favor in the eyes of a PPKI-KNI on which no youth representatives sat, and it was quietly dropped. Finally, Sukarno himself broached the idea of a Staatspartij (State Party), which would serve to mobilize the population behind the new government.[13] The idea appears to have been generally well received, but further discussion of it was deferred to a later meeting.

On August 21 the PPKI reconvened in secret session to discuss the forthcoming San Francisco conference and the possibility of sending a delegation to plead Indonesia's cause. A subcommittee was also set up to formulate the organizational structure and goals of the projected Staatspartij, which was now to be given the name Partai Nasional Indonesia (PNI) in nostalgic reminiscence of Sukarno's prewar party of that name.[14]

[11] Ibid., pp. 457, 462. An abangan-Christian alliance against the spokesmen for the santri community was very much in evidence in this decision.

[12] Ibid., 457. Ironically, it was precisely the militarized pemuda who eventually terrorized Dr. Amir into fleeing to the Dutch and British in Medan on April 25, 1946.

[13] See ibid., pp. 458, 460, where the conception is credited to Iwa. But the "Report on the Sulawesi Representatives' Journey to Java," which is in the form of a diary with detailed notes on events, hour by hour, explicitly states that the suggestion came from Sukarno. This is more probable in view of Sukarno's political history and the fact that the new party was soon to be named after his prewar nationalist party, with which Iwa had had only fleeting connections.

[14] "Report on the Sulawesi Representatives' Journey to Java." The subject of the San Francisco conference is not mentioned at all in Yamin's ostensibly complete edition of the PPKI's discussions.

Meeting again on August 22, the PPKI decided to establish a formal Komité Nasional Indonesia Pusat (Central Indonesian National Committee), or KNIP, and negotiations were begun to determine its membership. By August 27 a final list was reached through informal consultation by Sukarno and Hatta with the leaders of most of the prewar political organizations, as well as the relatively few new men who had come to the fore during the Japanese period. The full list of 137 members was then announced by Sukarno, and on the same day the PPKI disappeared into the newly established KNIP.[15]

The balance of power in the emerging national leadership at this time is well illustrated by the membership of the KNIP. A great majority of the 137 members (at least 85) were abangan Javanese. At the highest estimate, Islamic leaders numbered less than twenty. The pemuda fared little better, with no more than twenty or twenty-five positions.[16] An even larger majority consisted of nationalist politicians, of pangrèh pradja, and of professional men who had been appointed to the various top-level pseudo-legislative and pseudo-party organizations of the Japanese period. At the same time two of the best-known prewar politicians who had not been involved in the Japanese administration, Sjahrir and Amir Sjarifuddin, were now appointed to the KNIP.

Progress was also made with the formation of the PNI-Staatspartij. On August 23 Sukarno had made a radio speech warmly promoting the concept of the PNI, which he felt would unite all groups and become the "motor of the people's struggle in every sphere and every field. . . . [While] the National Committee is

[15] Full lists of the members of the first KNIP are contained in the issues of *Soeara Asia* and *Tjahaja* (Bandung) for Aug. 27, 1945.

[16] *Sinar Baroe* (Semarang) (Aug. 27, 1945) divided the membership as follows: fourteen leaders, nine pangrèh pradja, three police, nineteen civil servants, four businessmen, twelve doctors, two teachers, four lawyers or judges, five minority members, ten pemuda, five women, eight religious leaders, nine journalists, two Barisan Pelopor, and thirty-one others. This classification, though quite informal, gives an idea of contemporary ways of looking at the early KNIP and its makeup. My analysis of the KNIP is based on it only in part.

a committee, the Indonesian National Party is a party. The Committee is set up for a temporary period, the party we need also
to continue into the future. . . . [It will] strengthen the Unity of
the Nation and State, increase feelings of love, loyalty and
service to our native land; make efforts to work out the economic and social program as specified in the Constitution of the
Indonesian Republic; and assist in the achievement of social
justice and the principle of humanity by means of international
peace." [17] On August 27 the day-to-day leadership was announced: Sajuti Melik, Iwa Kusumasumantri, Mr. Sudjono,
Wikana, and Maramis.[18] Of this group, Iwa and Maramis were
closely associated with the Kaigun; Wikana was a former Kaigun
official and now one of the top pemuda leaders. Sudjono was a
second-level nationalist politician who had lived in Japan before
the war and returned to Indonesia in 1942 with the Japanese
warships. Sajuti, on the other hand, had only recently emerged
from a stay in a Kenpeitai jail for subversive actions and was
now Sukarno's confidential secretary. It was not really a board
likely to unite all groups, as Sukarno had urged. Discontent with
this narrowly based leadership resulted in a further announcement two days later of an expanded permanent leadership of
the new PNI, which was organized as follows:

First Great Leader: Sukarno
Second Great Leader: Hatta
General leadership: Mr. Gatot Tarunamihardja (party head),
    Iwa, Sajuti Melik, Mr. Sudjono, Maramis
Political section: Abikusno (chief), Iwa, Wikana, Suroto, Oto
    Iskandardinata, Wondoamiseno, Maramis, Dr. Sukiman,
    Sunarjo, Trimurti, Sajuti Melik, A. Baswedan, Liem Koen
    Hian, P. F. Dahler

[17] Sukarno, "The Change of the Times and Our Duty," cited in *Fakta
dan dokumen2*, pp. 4–10. For the announcement of the PPKI decision
to establish the PNI, see Koesnodiprodjo, ed., *Himpunan undang2,
peraturan2, penetapan2 pemerintah Republik Indonesia, 1945* (rev. ed.;
Djakarta, 1951), p. 118.
[18] *Soeara Asia*, Aug. 27, 1945.

Organizational section: Muwardi (chief), Sartono, Sukardjo Wirjopranoto, Sudiro (mBah), Sudiro, Supeno, Latuharhary, Sakirman, Sukarni, Harsono Tjokroaminoto, Winoto Danuasmoro, Sjarif Thajeb, Gaos Hardjasumantri, Nj. S. Mangunpuspito, Mr. Soeprapto and M. Tabrani.[19]

Since there has been some misunderstanding of this Staatspartij in subsequent writing about Indonesian politics, it might be worthwhile to take a close look at the structure of independent Indonesia's first so-called political party. The single most important aspect of this PNI was its direct continuity with the Hōkōkai. Sukarno and Hatta, Great Leaders of the new organization, had been head and deputy head of the Hōkōkai central office. Other prominent Hōkōkai members who reappeared in the new organization were Oto Iskandardinata, Abikusno, Winoto Danuasmoro, Sakirman, Sartono, Tabrani, and Sukardjo. Nj. Mangunpuspito was head of the Fujinkai, the women's affiliate of the Hōkōkai, while Muwardi and Sudiro were the top leaders of the Barisan Pelopor, the Hōkōkai's militant arm. Moreover, Muwardi, the organizer of the activist Barisan Pelopor, was assigned to be in charge of the PNI's organization, while Abikusno, formerly the director of the General Affairs (political) bureau of the Hōkōkai central office, took responsibility for the PNI's political division.

Islam was thinly represented by a few members of the prewar Islamic political parties personally congenial to Sukarno (Abikusno, Sukiman, and Wondoamiseno); none of the top Masjumi leadership was included. Pemuda members (Wikana, Suroto, Trimurti, Supeno, Sukarni, Harsono, Sjarif Thajeb, and Gaos) were prominent, but they were mainly pemuda with close ties to Sukarno.[20] The remaining members of the PNI leadership fell into two clear-cut categories: representatives of the Eurasian, Chinese, and Arab minorities (Dahler, Liem Koen Hian, and

[19] *Ibid.*, Aug. 29, 1945, and, with slight variations, *Tjahaja*, Aug. 29, 1945. For biographical details on Gatot, see the Appendix.

[20] This is a further indication that the PNI was the brainchild of Sukarno rather than of Iwa.

Baswedan), and what was often loosely referred to as the Kaigun group (Iwa, Maramis, Latuharhary, Gatot, Sudiro mBah, Soeprapto, and Sunarjo). The Kaigun group was primarily composed of men who had studied law together in Holland in the 1920's and had maintained close ties of friendship on their return. Its name was a result of the role one of its leading figures, Subardjo, played in Maeda's office, and the inclusion of Kaigun group members in the PNI leadership should probably be largely attributed to the services Subardjo had rendered in the proclamation crisis. (Why Subardjo himself did not join the PNI directorate is not clear.) But it is also true that the members of the group had by and large not been prominently associated with the major organizations sponsored by the Japanese army, and had not participated in the Hōkōkai. Insofar as some of them, such as Latuharhary and Maramis, were associated with the naval authorities, their incorporation in the PNI high command can be interpreted as a consolidation of the nationalist leadership in Djakarta, now that the wartime divisions between army and navy were no longer relevant.[21]

The PNI-Staatspartij, then, essentially represented a continuation of the central office of the Hōkōkai with the addition of the Kaigun group and a solid admixture of pemuda personally attached to Sukarno and Hatta. For those who looked forward to an orderly continuity of leadership from the Japanese to the independence period, it seemed a realistic and pragmatic solution.[22] Nonetheless, within a matter of days after its central

[21] For a discussion of the deep traditional rivalries between the Japanese army and navy, see Anderson, *Some Aspects,* chap. 1. It was partly to alleviate the consequences of these rivalries in Indonesia that Maeda's office had been set up. We have already seen an example of competition between the services in the separate asrama they established.

[22] Confirmation of this can be found in the announcement in *Soeara Asia,* Aug. 29, 1945, of the leadership of the PNI for the city of Djakarta, "after changes and additions to the Perhimpoenan Kebaktian [Hōkōkai]." The head of this PNI was Mr. Wilopo, who had been vice-chairman of the Barisan Pelopor for Greater Djakarta under Muwardi (*Djawa Baroe* [Djakarta], 1944, no. 20). This interpretation is also sup-

leadership had been announced, the party was formally dissolved.[23]

The reasons for the PNI's dissolution are of great importance for understanding the political climate of the time. The party was immediately criticized as being unrepresentative because it contained very few Islamic leaders and excluded major figures from the underground. While the first charge was largely justified, the second was somewhat dubious, since Sajuti, Wikana, Suroto, Supeno, Sakirman, Sukarni, and Sjarif Thajeb could all be loosely identified as underground figures.

Objections were also raised on the ground that the party would tend to duplicate the KNIP. This was the case only to a limited extent. It was certainly true that of the 34 leaders of the PNI, only four were not in the KNIP, and these four—Wondoamiseno, Gaos, Sjarif Thajeb, and Suroto—were not especially prominent at that time.[24] But this was largely beside the point, since the KNIP's functions were to be quasi-legislative, while the PNI would take over from the Hōkōkai the function of mobilizing the population on a continuing basis behind the national leadership. As Sukarno's speech of August 23 indicated, in the President's mind at least, the PNI would not yield to the KNIP, but the

---

ported by the announced aims of the PNI, which were apparently first drawn up at an informal meeting on August 24. Included was a statement that the PNI "has the duty to organize the forces of the people and mobilize the whole people at all times, on the basis of the coordination of all aliran and political viewpoints. . . . The establishing of this party will not only be adjusted to the wishes of the parties in the past [of the prewar period], but will also receive assistance from leaders of the people throughout the Indonesian archipelago, who came to Djakarta not long ago. The party will be based on people's sovereignty, as contained in the Constitution of the State of the Republic of Indonesia." See *Soeara Asia*, Aug. 27, 1945.

[23] Word of the dissolution took a long time to reach the provinces, with the result that in certain areas local branches of the PNI continued to be set up for a considerable period after the central leadership had been abolished.

[24] As president and vice-president, Sukarno and Hatta, of course, did not sit in the KNIP.

KNIP to the PNI, since the former would soon be transformed by general elections into a representative assembly, the Dewan Perwakilan Rakjat (People's Representative Council), or DPR.[25]

In fact, the demise of the PNI cannot be explained by these overt objections, but rather by the hostility it evoked from Sjahrir and his following, and by its own internal contradictions. From the start Sjahrir was strongly opposed to the PNI. He saw it as dominated by political leaders who had enjoyed high positions and comfortable lives in the midst of the population's sufferings. To him these men were collaborators who on moral grounds alone had no claim to the leadership of a free Indonesia.[26] But it was not only for moral reasons that Sjahrir worked to undermine the PNI. He was also convinced that Sukarno's wartime activities, especially his radio speeches against the Allies, would severely weaken his position in the international arena as the spokesman for Indonesia's aspirations for independence. Since the Allies were expected to land in Indonesia any day, he felt strongly—and so persuaded a great many of the younger metropolitan pemuda who had no stake in the continuity policy of the Sukarno-Hatta leadership—that these aspirations must be given an unequivocally non-Japanese cast and be expressed in organizational forms that owed as little as possible to the occupation period. To these convictions were added the natural promptings of self-interest. Sjahrir was well aware that aside from Amir, he alone of the well-known prewar politicians had the kind of wartime record likely to impress the Allied authorities. It may be

[25] For the constitutional position of the DPR and the provisions for its formation, see chapter 7 of the 1945 Constitution as contained in Osman Raliby, *Documenta Historica* (Djakarta, 1953), app. 1.

[26] In the attacks launched by Sjahrir and his following, the PNI was alleged to have a monolithic and fascist character, neither acceptable to contemporary international opinion nor tolerable from the point of view of Indonesia's own internal well-being. Neither epithet was really very apt. The PNI was so far from being monolithic that it disintegrated from within shortly after its birth. It was so far from being fascist that its top leadership included not only the staunchly anti-fascist Hatta, but Sajuti and others who had been imprisoned by the Kenpeitai.

wondered why Sjahrir did not bring his friends into the PNI and try to mold it to his own purposes. He did, after all, accept a seat in the KNIP (indeed, as its first member), and there is no reason to suppose that Sukarno, Hatta, and the PNI leaders would have been anything but pleased if he had joined them in the Staatspartij.

The answer appears to lie in the unusual combination of strengths and weaknesses in the political cards Sjahrir had to play. His major strength was his anti-Japanese wartime record. Yet to play this card by taking a strong public position against his "collaborationist" compatriots, though it would increase his standing with many pemuda and with the returning Allies, would isolate him from the existing leaders and incur their lasting enmity. By contrast, his major weakness was his lack of any organized political base. This was in part the result of his long political exile in the thirties and his retreat during the war years, and in part the result of his temperamental lack of interest in organizational activity. But most of all it was the result of the particular character of the Indonesian underground itself. As we have seen, this underground, unlike the undergrounds that developed in war-torn areas like Burma, Vietnam, and the Philippines, was neither rural, nor armed, nor highly structured. At bottom it amounted to little more than an informal communications network between urban intellectuals in a few cities on Java. Thus at the close of the occupation, Sjahrir's instruments for attaining power were severely restricted. Without organized backing of his own, he had no guarantee of being able to control the PNI-Staatspartij if he entered it. Furthermore, in the PNI his major strength, his anti-Japanese record, would go by the board, since the organization's Japanese parentage was clear. In the KNIP, however, especially in the greatly expanded KNIP of August 27, his talents might be turned to better advantage. The KNIP-PPKI relationship was much less direct than the PNI-Hōkōkai connection. The constitutional semiautonomy of the KNIP from the presidency permitted considerably greater free-

dom of maneuver than the PNI appeared to offer. The very structure of the KNIP allowed for the possibility of formal opposition
to the government, while that of the PNI presumably did not.

While the main attack on the PNI came from the former underground and pemuda elements who regarded it as a relic of
the Japanese period, the party also faced internal problems. Personal and ideological differences between important members,
for example between Sartono and Abikusno, broke out almost
immediately.[27] But more important, precisely insofar as the PNI
represented a continuation of the Hōkōkai it was condemned to
internal instability. We have seen how the Hōkōkai was created
by the Japanese and led at the highest level by Japanese officers.
While effective enough for the narrow aims for which it was
designed, the organization had no autonomous raison d'être of
its own. The groups incorporated in it were not natural allies in
any sense, and the fissiparous character of the prewar nationalist
movement was not altered by the experiences of the war years.
These divisions could not be eradicated nor, in the absence of the
strong external discipline imposed by the Japanese, could they
be easily contained within a single organization. Attacked from
without and disunited within, the PNI never had a chance to
develop a life of its own.

On August 31, Sukarno issued the following executive order:
"In view of the overweening importance and significance of the
national committees in concentrating all actions and organization of the people, the activity and preparations of the PNI are
temporarily suspended. All activities must be channeled into the
national committees. These national committees should be acti-
vated down to the village level." [28] The order was followed by a
full statement from the PNI leadership itself, signed by Sajuti
Melik. It said that in view of the President's order and "to avoid
disappointment and doubts among comrades already building

[27] I owe information on the internal divisions of the PNI to talks
with Mohammed Hatta on February 13 and September 27, 1962.
[28] *Soeara Asia,* Aug. 31, 1945.

branches," an explanation was necessary for the decision. Actually, the party had deeper aims and larger responsibilities than the national committees. But in light of the critical situation, all energies should be devoted undividedly to the national committees, since "in fact the work of the party in this period is identical with the work of the national committees, . . . as what is most necessary now is the organization of Indonesian independence and its recognition by the international world. The PNI should therefore work hard to become the backbone of the national committees, with no lessening of its members' responsibilities and tasks." The executive hoped that the members would not misunderstand the decision; they should continue to be the motor of the national struggle.[29] The day before the President's postponing of the PNI's formation, the Hōkōkai had been officially disbanded.[30]

While the politique of the Sukarno-Hatta leadership was, as we have seen, directed toward maintaining maximum continuity between the later Japanese era and the initial period of independence, and this politique was tacitly accepted by the Japanese military, there were clear limits beyond which it was unlikely that it could be pursued. The most striking instance of lack of continuity, and one that was to have critical and permanent consequences for Indonesian politics, was the Japanese decision to dissolve the Peta and the Heihō, thus depriving the infant republic of a coherent armed defense force to sustain its internal and external authority.

From the Japanese point of view, the decision was eminently sensible. While the maintenance of the structures of civilian government and their gradual appropriation by the Indonesians might pass muster with the Allies, it was clear that there could be no easy justification for continuing an armed force created for the sole purpose of fighting against them. Moreover, with the memory of the Blitar uprising still fresh in their minds, the high

[29] *Ibid.*, Sept. 3, 1945. The announcement is dated Sept. 1, 1945.
[30] *Ibid.*, Aug. 31, 1945.

command of the Sixteenth Army had good reason to be apprehensive about what Peta units might do once the news of Japan's collapse percolated through to the provinces. Elementary prudence demanded that these uncertain troops be disbanded and the Japanese resume their full monopoly of military force. Accordingly, as early as August 17, General Nagano decided on the dissolution of the Peta and Heihō throughout Java and Bali.[31]

Secret orders were issued to all Japanese non-commissioned officers attached to local Peta units to demobilize the units they were training and collect their arms in central dumps where they could be easily guarded. The orders were carried out with remarkable success, considering the psychological state of the Japanese officer corps at the time. The Peta youths were disarmed on a variety of pretexts, sometimes that they were to be issued new arms, sometimes that all weapons were to be inspected, sometimes that a new training program was about to be instituted. In areas close to Bandung and Djakarta, a few weapons seem to have been successfully concealed by men who were aware of the new political situation and brave enough to do so. In the interior of Java, where the surrender was not officially announced until August 21, battalions were disarmed without the arousal of any suspicion.[32] In many cases actual demobilization followed some time after the disarming. The men were paid six months' salary in advance as well as a large clothing bonus, and then sent quietly home. As General Nishimura later said, rather sardonically, "Luckily the rice-harvest that summer was the best in years." [33]

The disarmings of the Peta were naturally carried out first in the more sensitive areas near Bandung and Djakarta; disarmament was not completed in some outlying regions until Au-

[31] Pusat Sedjarah Militer Angkatan Darat, *Peranan TNI-Angkatan Darat*, p. 28.

[32] Even Bahsan, one of the heroes of the Sapu Mas and the Rengasdengklok Affair, admits that his Peta unit was disarmed without difficulty. *Tjatatan ringkas*, pp. 60–65.

[33] Nishimura, "Statement" of April 15, 1947, IC-RVO doc. no. 006808–11.

gust 20.[34] The Heihō troops were even more easily disposed of, since they were directly under the command of the Japanese, and in any case consisted of "other ranks," not officers. Heihō demobilization appears to have been wound up by August 25.[35]

The demobilization process was undoubtedly facilitated by two other factors: an all-Java conference of representatives of the 66 Peta battalions, which opened in Bandung on August 14, and the decisions made by the PPKI on the morning of August 19. On August 15, while the Bandung conference was still in progress, word of the Japanese surrender came through to some of the Indonesian delegates, who immediately asked for confirmation from the Japanese officers present.[36] Unconvinced by their denials that the war was over, a number of the delegates, led by Kasman Singodimedjo, gathered to discuss what their attitude toward the situation should be. The meeting proved inconclusive. While a small minority was evidently in favor of a more uncompromising stance, the majority supported the position of the elderly daidanchō of Banten, K. H. Sjam'oen, who urged that the Japanese be trusted to fulfill their promise of independence, and that discussions to this end be continued. It should not be forgotten that most of the daidanchō were politicians or religious leaders, rather than military men, and therefore less likely to be militant than their younger, more heavily trained subordinates.[37] Subsequently, the Japanese seem to have suc-

---

[34] Bahsan (*Tjatatan ringkas,* pp. 60–62) says that the disarming occurred in Rengasdengklok on August 19. The same date is given by Nishimura in his "Statement" of April 15, 1947, and can be found in "HQ Sixteenth Army Document on the Peta," IC-RVO doc. no. 005118. A. H. Nasution indicates that the disarmings in the Bandung area took place on the night of August 19–20. *Tentara Nasional Indonesia,* I (Djakarta, 1956), 66–67.

[35] According to "HQ Sixteenth Army Document on the Peta," Heihō units on Java were disbanded on August 23. Yanagawa, in his "Statement" of Oct. 14, 1945, says they were disbanded between August 20 and 25.

[36] Sidik Kertapati, *Sekitar proklamasi,* p. 103; Djèn Amar, *Bandung lautan api,* pp. 27–29.

[37] Interview with Kasman Singodimedjo, May 11, 1963.

cessfully headed off any second thoughts by reminding them that the Allies would probably regard them as guerrillas outside the protection of international military codes.[38] Significantly, the Peta leaders, though gathered together in Bandung at this critical juncture, could form no coherent policy for retaining their units. Indeed, their very presence at the meeting helped the Japanese demobilization effort by depriving local units of effective leadership.

Meanwhile, the hesitations of the PPKI leadership in Djakarta also aided the progress of Japanese policy. Meeting on the morning of August 19, the PPKI considered briefly the question of what to do about the Peta. Oto Iskandardinata, who was adviser to the Security Department (Chianbu) of the military administration and one of the Indonesians closest to the Japanese high command, urged the abolition of the Peta and the Heihō on the ground that their status in the eyes of the Allies was irreparably compromised. His argument was accepted, and the PPKI voted unanimously to ask the Japanese to dissolve both units. Subsequently, Sukarno appointed a subcommittee consisting of Oto and the two Peta men in the PPKI, Kasman and Abdul Kadir, to carry out this decision and at the same time to draw up plans for the eventual formation of a national defense force.[39] Later that day a meeting of pemuda and various underground figures was held at Prapatan 10; Sukarno, Subardjo, and Sjahrir also attended. At this meeting objections were raised to the steps taken by the PPKI. Wikana and others urged that the Peta and Heihō be immediately reorganized to provide the basis of a national army, and that all troops and units be declared troops of the new republic. After some hesitation and resistance, Sukarno finally signed a decree to this effect, and copies were hurriedly made for distribution in the capital.[40] But it was too late. The process of dissolution had already been set in motion.

While it is clear that the Japanese would certainly have dis-

---

[38] This point is brought out by Sidik Kertapati.

[39] Yamin, ed., *Naskah persiapan*, p. 463.

[40] Sidik Kertapati, *Sekitar proklamasi*, pp. 103–4.

solved the Peta and Heihō in any event, the PPKI's apparently
eager concurrence was to have unpleasant political consequences.
Oto's insistence at the PPKI meeting that "the dissolution should
take effect this very day," [41] coupled with the undeniable fact that
the Peta was dissolved that very evening, aroused among the
pemuda an understandable suspicion of complicity with the
Japanese high command. For this and subsequent actions Oto
was eventually to pay with his life. More generally, as the implications of the breakup of the Peta became clear, the feeling
persisted that an opportunity had been foregone: had the Peta
immediately been declared a national army, retaining its cohesion and structure while changing its name, the republic's position would not have been as weak as it soon proved to be.

Though the Peta and Heihō were now gone for good, the
republic's leaders clearly did want to build up a security force
of their own, though they felt obliged to move with great caution
because of the attitude of the Japanese and the continuing uncertainty about Allied intentions. On August 20 the PPKI formed
a body called the Badan Penolong Keluarga Korban Perang
(Organization for Aid to Families of War Victims), or BPKKP,
as a reconstituted version of the wartime Badan Pembantu Pradjurit (Organization for Aid to Soldiers) and later the Badan
Pembantu Pembelaan (Organization for Defense Aid), which
had been set up under Oto Iskandardinata to assist Peta men and
their families. Oto continued as the head of the reconstituted
organization. Within the BPKKP the Badan Keamanan Rakjat
(People's Security Organization), or BKR, was formed.[42] This
was prudence indeed—a security force unobtrusively attached to
a charitable organization.

The official statement on the two organizations throws some
light on the atmosphere surrounding their establishment:

1. The BPKKP is set up to protect the welfare of society.

2. Since well-being and security are basically the same thing, a
BKR will be set up as part of the BPKKP.

[41] Yamin, ed., *Naskah persiapan,* p. 464.

[42] For a good discussion, see Smail, *Bandung,* pp. 30–31.

3. Heads of the [local] BKR are to be members of the day-to-day leadership of the [local] BPKKP.

4. However, the BKR must carry on their own work on a voluntary basis.

5. Volunteers will therefore be summoned by the local BPKKP to meet in each regency on August 24.

6. At each level of administration of the BKR, the local (civilian) administrative chief will have authority over it. At the tonarigumi level the work should be carried out by 5 capable pemuda. The appropriate levels will be shū, ken, son, and ku.[43]

7. Chiefs of the local BKR are to be recommended by the local head of the BPKKP and approved by the BPKKP leader at the next higher level.

8. The task of the BKR is to maintain security with the help of the people and the relevant government bodies.

9. Both BKR and BPKKP are to work under the supervision and leadership of the local KN[I].[44]

The formation of the BKR seems to have been the result of a compromise between two groups. On the one hand, there was the Oto group in the PPKI and a number of high civilian officials who were anxious to remain on good terms with the Japanese and to prevent a repetition of the looting, murder, and sporadic anarchy that had broken out in some areas following the collapse of Dutch rule in 1942. For these men the BKR's prime function was to reinforce the police in maintaining law and order and bolstering the authority of the government. On the other hand, there was a group of former officers from both the Peta and the prewar Dutch colonial army (Koninklijk Nederlands Indisch Leger, or KNIL) who wanted to start a national army right away. Shortly after the dissolution of the Peta, a delegation led by a retired KNIL officer, Maj. Urip Sumohardjo, approached Sukarno and Hatta with this idea. Sukarno reportedly told Urip "after some days of hesitation" that he "had been thinking the

[43] The Japanese designations for residency, regency, subdistrict, and village.
[44] As reported in *Soeara Asia,* Aug. 25, 1945.

whole thing over very carefully—Indonesia's situation in the international world. We must immediately have some means of maintaining public security aside from the police, but not an army." [45] Nonetheless, in his first major radio address, on August 23, Sukarno urged all former members of the Peta and Heihō to unite their strength in the BKR, stressing that "the time will come when you will be called on to become soldiers in the Indonesian National Army." [46]

The actual outcome of the compromise, however—the formation of a police-style organization—reflected the arguments of the first group, probably because they were closer to the realities of the situation. There was as yet no question of resisting the anticipated Allied landing, and moreover, as a result of the disarming of the Peta and Heihō, there were simply no arms available for a national army. However, Sukarno's specific appeal to the Peta and Heihō, rather than to the more numerous Seinendan and Keibōdan, was clearly intended to reassure those who wanted a national army that that objective had not been abandoned. After all, the Peta and Heihō were trained as military units, not as police.

The development of the Indonesian national army presaged by Sukarno's speech will be dealt with later. It is only necessary here to stress one major consequence of the dissolution of the Peta that was not foreseen either by the Japanese or by the political elite in Djakarta. The structure of the Peta officer corps was, as already noted, highly paradoxical: in general the senior officers were men with less military skill and education than their subordinates. They were also, as a rule, older men who neither sympathized with the pemuda psychology prevalent among their younger colleagues nor shared their isolated barracks existence. Even in the Japanese period there had been tensions between the two groups. In the weeks following the dissolution of the Peta, this military hierarchy, which had subordinated the younger officers, was replaced by a natural hierarchy of ability.

[45] *Fakta dan dokumen2*, pp. 87f.   [46] *Ibid.*, pp. 4–10.

The younger officers returned to their home areas and began to recruit local pemuda, whether from the Peta or the Heihō, or from the Seinendan and other paramilitary youth organizations, on the basis of their own personal charisma and skills.[47] Subsequently, the national army began to build itself up in slow, local accumulations outside the control of Djakarta, or indeed any other external control, and army hierarchies came to be defined by personal relationships between commanders and by the relative firepower over which they disposed. The history of Indonesia's independence struggle was from then on to be marked by a long battle to impose central command and authority over a swarming mass of heterogeneous armed groups that grew up from the bottom on the basis of personal loyalties and fighting experience. With the breakup of the Peta, Indonesia lost for many years to come any chance of molding a national army as an instrument of state policy under the authority of a central civilian leadership.[48]

By the end of August 1945, the political situation in Java was marked by great instability and ambiguity. The policy of the Sukarno-Hatta leadership was to maintain the impetus and logic of developments in the later period of the occupation, appropriating, where possible, the instruments of power created by the Japanese and trying to adapt them to their own purposes. But in the new context of the Japanese defeat and uncertainty about Allied intentions, this policy of continuity was to prove increasingly difficult to pursue. The PPKI had indeed been transformed

[47] See Gorō Taniguchi, *Indoneshia to tomo ni ikite* [To Live Together with Indonesia], Vol. VI in *Hiroku Dai-Tōa Sen Shi* [Secret history of the War for Greater East Asia] (Tokyo, 1954), in a mimeographed translation in my possession prepared by Y. Sasaki, pp. 537ff.

[48] See Henri Alers, *Om een rode of groene Merdeka: Tien jaren binnenlandse politiek, Indonesië, 1943–1953* (Eindhoven, 1956), *passim,* for an intriguing analysis of Indonesian political developments on the basis of an opposition between "green" elements (hierarchic, elitist, authoritarian, and disciplinary) and "red" (popular, localist, anarchic, and communal). The Indonesian army contained from the start a powerful "red" element.

into the KNIP. But the PNI had been stillborn from the womb of the Hōkōkai, and the Peta and Heihō had disintegrated in a matter of days after the proclamation of independence. It became increasingly clear that virtually all of the institutions and organizations of the occupation era depended for their integrity and vitality on the backbone provided by Japanese military power in the cities and the countryside. Once that backbone was weakened and eventually removed, the structure of post-independence government began slowly to crumble away. The new leadership found that it had few autonomous political structures through which to work, little natural authority with which to impose its will on the population, and no sanctional weapons for maintaining political discipline and control.

The proclamation crisis had shown that so long as politics in Java were confined to high-level negotiations between the metropolitan elite and an external power, the older leadership could maintain, with some difficulty, its grip on the situation. Indeed, the fragile ascendancy of the older leadership in this period (quite comparable to Sjahrir's ascendancy somewhat later on) depended on its acceptability to external power. On August 23, Sukarno said to the nation:

To proclaim Independence is easy. To make a Constitution is not difficult. To elect a President and a Vice-President is easier still. But to form the bodies and posts of authority and administration of the State, as well as to seek international recognition, especially under conditions such as the present, where the Japanese Government is still obliged by the international status quo to remain in this country to run the administration and maintain public order—these tasks are not easy! [49]

Ironically, it was precisely the Japanese presence on Java that had permitted the formation of the first republican government, and it was precisely the Japanese withdrawal that would seal its fate.

[49] Sukarno, "The Change of the Times and Our Duty," *Fakta dan dokumen2*, pp. 4–10.

Outside the major metropolitan areas the forces aroused by the wartime experience and by the great changes instituted under Japanese rule were already beginning to break through the structures the Japanese had erected to contain them. Above all, the mass of rural and urban pemuda who had been mobilized in the Barisan Pelopor, Seinendan, Keibōdan, Hizbullah, Peta, Heihō, and other organizations started to flow out over the dykes these structures had once formed. Since these organizations owed their hierarchy and discipline to the military government that had instituted them, the decline of this military power brought about their dispersion into myriads of smaller or greater pools of militarized and semipoliticized youths. While the economic deterioration brought about by the military government's policies and the war had swelled the already large numbers of unemployed, the political organizations of the war years had absorbed them to some extent. Now they were released into society without aim or direction. The authority of the traditional ruling class, particularly the pangrèh pradja, had been gravely undermined by the complicity imposed on it for the more repressive aspects of occupation policy. In any case the pangrèh pradja, by outlook and training, was created for administrative functions, not to give political leadership. It was a sophisticated servant of any well integrated, militarily powerful government, but no substitute for one. Both in the later Dutch period and in the Japanese years, the pangrèh pradja's authority ultimately depended on the repressive apparatus above it.

The apocalyptic aspects of Japanese propaganda, the Javanese messianic tradition, and the dramatic, conspiratorial, crisis psychology imposed by war had built up an atmosphere of acute tension and vague but immense anticipation—partly an expectation and partly a fear of some astonishing transformation. As the consciousness of the reality of the Japanese surrender and of Indonesia Merdeka (Free Indonesia) seeped through Java, this apocalyptic sense increased. As it increased, the normalcy politique being pursued by the leaders in Djakarta seemed increasingly irrelevant, a relic from another age.

Moreover, the pulverization of indigenous political organizations the Japanese had carried out meant that at the close of the occupation there was no alternative leadership prepared, ideologically or organizationally, to lead the population in new directions. The underground, such as it was, had been confined to the Western-educated intelligentsia of the larger cities, far closer by ties of common experience, family connections, and education to the collaborationist elite than it was to the pemuda masses of the war years. While certain underground leaders were subsequently able to ride a pemuda wave to power, they were no more capable of giving it a satisfying organization and role than the men they supplanted.

The mutual frustration of the pemuda, who had revolutionary expectations but no revolutionary leadership, and the middle-class metropolitan intelligentsia, both collaborationist and underground, who were in a position to lead but totally inexperienced in doing so without external support, was to provide the leitmotif of the Indonesian Revolution.

Chapter 6

The Buchō Cabinet and Its Audiences

On September 4, 1945, Indonesia's first republican cabinet was formed, under President Sukarno's leadership.[1] Its membership was as follows:

Foreign Affairs: Mr. R. A. Subardjo (adviser to the Bukanfu)

Interior: R. A. A. Wiranatakusumah (chief of the Internal Affairs Department)

Justice: Prof. Mr. Dr. R. Soepomo (chief of the Justice Department)

Health: Dr. R. Buntaran Martoatmodjo (adviser to the Health Bureau of the Internal Affairs Department)

Education: Ki Hadjar Dewantoro (adviser to the Education Bureau of the Internal Affairs Department)

Information: Mr. Amir Sjarifuddin

Finance: Dr. Samsi Sastrawidagda (adviser to the Finance Department)

Social Affairs: Mr. R. Iwa Kusumasumantri (chief of the Labor Bureau of the Internal Affairs Department)

Communications and Public Works: R. Abikusno Tjokrosujoso (chief of the Bureau of Public Works)

Without portfolio: K. H. Wachid Hasjim (adviser to the Depart-

---

[1] According to the 1945 Constitution, articles 4 and 17, the president holds full executive power as head of the government. Ministers are his assistants, and are appointed and dismissed at his will. See Raliby, *Documenta Historica*, app. 1, pp. 489, 491.

ment of Religion); Mr. R. M. Sartono (adviser to the Internal Affairs Department); Mr. A. A. Maramis (adviser to the Bukanfu); R. Oto Iskandardinata (adviser to the Security Department); Dr. Amir (adviser to the military administration in Sumatra).[2]

The post of minister responsible for defense was left temporarily vacant. Only on October 6, more than a month later, was it to be filled—by the legendary Suprijadi, who had led the Blitar uprising of February 1945, and who was generally assumed to be dead.[3] Mr. Ali Sastroamidjojo, who had been head of the Savings Bureau of the Postal Department, temporarily took over Amir Sjarifuddin's functions until the latter returned from prison in East Java. At the same time various other cabinet-level positions were also filled: R. Sukardjo Wirjopranoto (adviser to the Sendenbu) became state spokesman, Mr. A. G. Pringgodigdo, ex-secretary of the Investigating Committee, became state secretary, and Mr. Gatot, previously head of the Purwokerto district court, became the first attorney-general.[4]

As one observer was to write much later: "There is no reason to conceal the fact that although ministers had been appointed by this time, there were still many of them who acted as Japanese officials, and, so to speak, had a dual role. On the one hand, they were officials for the Japanese, who still exercised real power; on the other hand, they were also appointed ministers of the Indonesian republic which had just been proclaimed." [5] Hatta stated the same idea in his own inimitable way, recalling that

[2] The average age of this cabinet was 46.8 years. Biographical details on these cabinet officers can be found in the Appendix.

[3] Suprijadi disappeared during the revolt, and his death was never announced. He therefore became a figure of legend, many believing that he would come back to help Indonesia when she needed it.

[4] The cabinet list can be found in Susan Finch and Daniel S. Lev, *Republic of Indonesia Cabinets, 1945–1965* (Ithaca, N.Y., 1965), p. 2. The additional appointments can be found in Raliby, *Documenta Historica,* p. 34.

[5] Nawawi Dusky, "Hari proklamasi."

"to hasten the seizure of power from within, the greater part of the ministers of the first presidential cabinet were selected from those men who were already placed at the top of the departmental hierarchies as *buchō* [chiefs] or *sanyō* [advisers]. In this way, the *downward* channels of command could be controlled and the Japanese could be easily set aside." [6] The major exceptions to this rule were, as in the case of the abortive PNI, certain members of the Kaigun group—Subardjo, Iwa, Maramis, and Gatot—who had not held high bureaucratic posts within the Japanese military administration but who now, through their connections with Maeda and their close personal relations with Sukarno, Hatta, and others with prominent positions, began to make their influence felt.

The perspective of what was to be known to its enemies as the Buchō Cabinet was well expressed by Hatta in these archetypal terms:

There was another way [i.e., than the one chosen by Hatta and Sukarno]—the seizure of power from the Japanese by building up a national governmental administrative arm alongside [the one controlled by the Japanese]. This way might seem to be revolutionary—but it would not be rational. *And what is not rational in a revolution is not revolutionary.* This second method would only have created difficulties and slowed down the transfer of power into our hands. It is very probable that it would have caused a violent struggle and the victory would not certainly have been ours. It would have created two different government administrations side by side. As a result the new national government administration, just set up, would not have been able to work effectively, while the administrative structure capable of working effectively would have been allowed to fall into the hands of the Japanese, to be then handed over to the Allies. And from the Allies it would have been transferred to the control of Holland. [7]

Given this perspective, it was natural that Sukarno and Hatta very early on devoted themselves to the task of assuming control

[6] Hatta, "Isi proklamasi," in *Fakta dan dokumen2,* Supp. I, p. 2; italics mine.
[7] *Ibid.,* p. 4; italics mine.

over the existing instruments of state power. With the disintegration of the armed units of the Peta and Heihō, this meant securing the loyalty and support of the pangrèh pradja, indeed of the whole administrative apparatus of the government.

On August 30, therefore, even before the official formation of the cabinet, an all-Java and Madura conference of the pangrèh pradja was opened in Djakarta at the joint suggestion of Sukarno and Soetardjo Kartohadikoesoemo, who was generally acknowledged as the chief spokesman for pangrèh pradja interests. On September 2 Sukarno gave a major address that expressed very clearly the intention behind the conference. He said in part:

This was an extremely difficult problem, since it appeared that we would be compelled to have two governmental systems, or a *dubbelregeering,* i.e., (1) a government of the Japanese army, obliged to maintain public security; (2) a government of the Republic of Indonesia, set up by the Indonesian people themselves. . . . [The solution therefore was that] as much real power and activity as possible be turned over to the Indonesian people—this was the result of a gentlemen's agreement between the Japanese authorities and the two of us. You can see this procedure working in the appointments of buchō, kyokuchō [bureau chiefs]. . . . The policy now adopted by the Indonesian republic must be oriented to the international world. For this the prime condition is *diplomacy.* Yet no nation can enter the international arena by diplomacy alone. Behind that diplomacy, indeed the very basis of that diplomacy, must be a power-force [*suatu tenaga kekuatan*]. For this reason we are now organizing a *collectieve opgehoopte volkswil*—an aggregate collective will of the people—in other words, a will to feel themselves independent, and to demand that they remain independent. That is why we are concentrating on forming national committees down to the village level, which will draw their life from the widest possible national foundations. . . . This being the case, the pangrèh pradja should not for a moment think that the policy of the leadership of the Indonesian republic is to regard the pangrèh pradja simply as secretaries, clerks or petty foremen. We are not going to degrade, we are not going to lower the pangrèh pradja. We are going to give it the proper place it deserves.[8]

8 *Antara-Dōmei* (Djakarta), Sept. 3, 1945.

The President went on to say that he was delighted to hear all the expressions of loyalty to the republic the conference had called forth. They would help show the world that the whole population was united behind the republic's leadership. Wiranatakusumah, shortly to become the first minister of the interior, also spoke, urging the pangrèh pradja to get close to the people and the national committees, and to avoid regarding themselves as above the people. He assured them that there would be no recriminations over the past, or interference with their positions. The situation demanded maximum unity.[9]

Meanwhile, Soetardjo had met with Sukarno and Hatta in private and had assured them of support from the pangrèh pradja, provided that its status was guaranteed.[10] In all probability one part of the bargain was that pangrèh pradja leaders would be given high positions in the provinces as an indication of the new government's confidence in them. In any case, on September 6 it was announced that in accordance with PPKI-KNIP decisions, Java would be divided into three provinces, West, Central, and East Java, headed by three governors working directly under the cabinet. Appointed to these three positions were Soetardjo himself, as governor of West Java, R. P. Soeroso as governor of Central Java, and R. M. T. A. Soerjo, as governor of East Java.[11] All three were prominent conservative prijaji leaders from before the war, and during the occupation they had been among those most rapidly promoted for their administrative competence and cooperativeness with the military government.[12] On September 5 all the existing vice-residents in Java and Madura, with the ex-

---

[9] *Soeara Asia,* Sept. 6, 1945.

[10] Interview with M. Soetardjo Kartohadikoesoemo, Jan. 31, 1962.

[11] *Soeara Asia,* Sept. 6, 1945.

[12] These three men were the only Indonesians to attain the position of resident during the occupation period—Soetardjo in Djakarta, Soeroso in Magelang, and Soerjo in Bodjonegoro. Soetardjo and Soerjo were appointed on November 10, 1943, and Soeroso on December 12, 1944. See *Kan Pō,* no. 31 (Nov. 25, 1943); and *Pandji Poestaka* (Djakarta), XXIII, no. 2 (Jan. 15, 1945), 57.

ception of the vice-resident of Pekalongan, were promoted to succeed their former superiors, the Japanese residents.[13]

The government also secured the other major source of traditional authority, the four principalities of Central Java: the Sunanate and the Mangkunegaran in Surakarta, and the Sultanate and the Pakualaman in Jogjakarta.[14] On August 19 Sukarno had already drawn up "establishing charters" (*piagam penetapan*) confirming the four rulers in their positions with the understanding that they would devote all their energies to the service of the republic.[15] On September 1 the Susuhunan and the Mangkunegoro proclaimed their respective territories to be part of the Indonesian republic, and nine days later the Sultan of Jogjakarta and the Pakualam followed suit.[16] In the meantime Sartono and Maramis had gone to Central Java to convey personally Sukarno's and Hatta's assurances that the rulers would be allowed to retain their status in payment for their loyalty to the republic.[17]

The government pursued the same goals in trying to activate the national committees. As early as his August 23 speech, Sukarno had outlined the purposes of these committees as being: announcing the will of the Indonesian people to live as a free nation; uniting all strata and occupations so that everywhere throughout Indonesia the solidarity of complete and close na-

[13] A full list is given in *Antara-Dōmei*, Sept. 5, 1945.

[14] These four principalities were the surviving remnants of the once powerful empire of Mataram, which reached its apogee in the reign of Sultan Agung (1613–45). Though legally they were self-administered protectorates of the Dutch government, in practice they were completely under Dutch control. Nonetheless, the rulers of these principalities continued to command considerable prestige and authority, particularly in traditionalist milieux.

[15] Koesnodiprodjo, *Himpunan, 1945*, p. 43. These charters were dated August 19, 1945.

[16] *Soeara Asia*, Sept. 4, 1945; Koesnodiprodjo, *Himpunan, 1945*, pp. 273–75.

[17] *Antara-Dōmei*, Sept. 5, 1945; "Sedjarah TNI Komando Daerah VII Diponegoro" (Army Historical Center [Bandung], typescript), p. 19; Indonesia, Kementerian Penerangan, *Republik Indonesia Daerah Istimewa Jogjakarta* (Djakarta, 1953–54), p. 36.

tional unity would be achieved; assisting in calming the people and participating in protecting public security; and assisting the leaders in putting the ideals of the Indonesian nation into effect, and in the regions helping the local administration to promote the well-being of the public. At the same time he urged that there be no recriminations among the population.[18]

The stated objectives of the national committees scarcely amounted to a clear and considered program of action. But they did represent an appeal for solidarity and support for the Djakarta leadership in its time of trial. Sukarno's radio appeal was rapidly reinforced by a stream of telegrams, telephone calls, and pemuda couriers out of Djakarta. In the last days of August and the early days of September, national committees sprang up in virtually every large urban center, and often even in the villages. In some cases they were born out of the dying sangikai (residency councils) of the occupation years. Elsewhere, they grew up around a core of veterans of the Hōkōkai and Barisan Pelopor. In many places their membership was almost completely improvised, drawn from clusters of local notables, often with the addition of a few pemuda activists. In general, however, the predominant role was played by members of the prewar nationalist movement (the *pergerakan*), particularly its non-Islamic sector.[19]

Yet the composition of the national committees was much less significant than the process of their formation and the political meaning of their birth. For their appearance was not the result of the coherent expansion of a central organization or the extension of disciplined hierarchies. Neither elective nor appointive mechanisms linked the national committees at different levels. In many cases, in fact, the higher-level committees—for example, those at the provincial level—rapidly vanished, since they pre-

---

[18] Sukarno, "The Change of the Times and Our Duty," *Fakta dan dokumen2,* pp. 4–10.

[19] For a good account of the formation and activities of the KNI in the Priangan, see Smail, *Bandung,* pp. 39–44.

sided over essentially administrative jurisdictions that by no means corresponded to natural political and ecological communities. Spontaneous, self-appointed, and local in character, the committees marked the disintegration of former hierarchies and the urgency of liberation. At heart, the formation of each committee was a local proclamation of independence, similar to, rather than an extension of, the Djakarta proclamation of August 17. Animating these myriad proclamations of independence were the ideas of *merdeka* (freedom) and of the formless solidarity of the nation, not the controlling, organized authority of the center.

While the cabinet had now secured the support of the traditional authorities in Java, and received a continuing flood of messages of support from the national committees, it found itself in an impasse in Djakarta. Sukarno, Hatta, and the cabinet were paralyzed both by the imminence of Allied landings and by their uncertainty and anxiety about Allied intentions in Indonesia. Though they were aware of the promises made in the Atlantic Charter (largely because these had been repeatedly denounced by the Japanese as a fraud), and though the San Francisco conference, which had been extensively discussed in the PPKI, seemed to offer a somewhat hopeful prospect, Dutch radio broadcasts had been extremely hostile toward the "collaborators." Colonel Abdulkadir had repeatedly warned that they would be shown no mercy. General van Oyen, deputy commander of the Dutch Armed Forces in the Far East, had spoken in only slightly less ominous terms when he expressed the opinion that all but a few dissidents would welcome the return of the Dutch; trials of collaborators would be held, but they would probably be few in number.[20] To the cabinet ministers, therefore, it seemed prudent to avoid any risk of jeopardizing themselves further by provocative actions. Caution was the better part of valor.

But while their elders were thus marking time, the Djakarta

[20] United States, Office of Strategic Services, Research and Analysis Branch, "Report No. 3250" [Pre-liberation Developments in the Netherlands East Indies], citing an *Aneta* (Manila) bulletin of Aug. 25, 1945.

pemuda seized the initiative. On September 1 the Angkatan Pemuda Indonesia (Younger Generation of Indonesia), or API, had been set up, with headquarters at the former Menteng 31 asrama. Its purpose was to coordinate the efforts of all the various pemuda groups in the capital. Wikana (Asrama Indonesia Merdeka) was elected chairman, with Chaerul Saleh (Menteng 31) as vice-chairman and secretary, and Darwis (Prapatan 10) as treasurer. Other members of the API leadership included Aidit, Pardjono, Hanafi, Kusnandar, Djohar Nur, and Chalid Rasjidi.[21] According to Malik at least, the API was planned as an armed sub-organization within a larger, looser Komité van Aksi (Action Committee). The formation of the API was rapidly followed by the establishment of the Barisan Rakjat (People's Front), a peasant organization led by Sidik Kertapati, Lukman, Maruto Nitimihardjo, and Sjamsuddin Tjan, and the Barisan Buruh (Workers' Front), a labor action group headed by Njono and Pandu Kartawiguna. All three organizations were nominally under the direction of the Komité van Aksi's headquarters at Menteng 31.[22]

In its first broadsheet, the Komité van Aksi issued a Manifesto that makes an interesting comparison with the statement of aims of the national committees issued by Sukarno the previous week. The Manifesto ran:

1. The unitary state of the Republic of Indonesia came into being on August 17, 1945, and the people are now independent, free from foreign rule.

2. All power must be placed in the hands of the state and the people of Indonesia.

[21] *Dokumentasi pemuda*, p. 24; Sidik Kertapati, *Sekitar proklamasi*, p. 111. This listing is confirmed by IC-RVO doc. no. 006566-7 (untitled), which appears to be a contemporary Dutch note on an API announcement. The list given differs considerably from that given by Malik in *Riwajat*, p. 69.

[22] Sidik Kertapati, *Sekitar proklamasi*, p. 111. Additional, less well-known names are also given for the leadership of these organizations. Malik lists the organizations but makes no mention of their leaders (*Riwajat*, p. 70).

3. Japan is now defeated, and has no more right to exercise authority over Indonesian territory.

4. The people of Indonesia must seize arms from the hands of the Japanese.

5. All enterprises (offices, factories, mines, plantations, etc.) must be seized from the Japanese, and controlled by the people of Indonesia.[23]

The crucial points in the Manifesto were the fourth and fifth. On these the pemuda leaders proceeded immediately to act. On September 3, at the instigation of emissaries from Menteng 31, workers took over the Manggarai and Djatinegara railway stations and declared them the property of the Indonesian republic. Within hours the movement began to spread until eventually the entire railway system in the Djakarta area was removed from Japanese control. On September 4, the day the cabinet was formed, the tram workers followed suit and seized control of the city's tram system.[24] On September 5 Radio Djakarta's employees began moving to oust the Japanese, and by September 11 the central radio station was fully in their hands.[25]

So far these pemuda-spurred actions, serious as they were, did not involve a direct confrontation with the Japanese high command or an explicit challenge of its public orders. But now, possibly stirred by news of demonstrations that occurred in Surabaja on September 11, the pemuda at Menteng 31 decided to try to organize a massive popular demonstration of support for the republic, at least partly in order to push the cabinet into taking a line more clearly independent of Nagano and Yamamoto. Preliminary negotiations were opened with Suwirjo, the mayor of Djakarta; and on September 18, the City National Committee,

[23] Malik, *Riwajat,* pp. 69–70. Malik's version has the words "(especially by the workers)" at the end of Point 5. These words do not occur in the version appearing in *Fakta dan dokumen2,* p. 156.

[24] Malik, *Riwajat,* pp. 69–73. Sidik Kertapati lists the central Telegraph and Telephone, the Gas and Electricity Corporation, and various large former Dutch enterprises as also having been seized (*Sekitar proklamasi,* p. 114).

[25] *Antara-Dōmei,* Sept. 5, 1945; *Fakta dan dokumen2,* p. 1.

headed by Suwirjo, announced that at six o'clock the following evening the national government would speak to the people in Ikada Square. "All chiefs of offices, groups, movements and other corps must take action to mobilize the entire Indonesian people to flood [*membandjiri*] this meeting, in orderly groupings." The population was urged to bring flags and painted slogans as well.[26]

General Nagano immediately countered with a special proclamation that same day, strictly forbidding the population to carry guns, bamboo spears, or krisses, or to hold any sort of assembly or parade, and adding:

In general, although the situation is now transitional, requiring a change from attitudes appropriate to a time of war to those of a time of peace, security in Java is excellent. This demonstrates that the entire population supports the army's efforts to maintain public order by utilizing the results of their continuous training and by heeding the requirements of order and discipline in order to realize their national aspirations in a peaceful atmosphere, conscious of the new situation. Nonetheless we strongly regret that just recently a part of the population with extreme desires for national independence has been acting in ways that may endanger the nation's future, namely by spreading mistaken notions among government officials and the people in general. From the depths of its heart Japan wants a healthy Indonesian independence, and up until now has helped it to be born, but we deeply regret that just as this aim was about to be achieved, Japan could no longer offer her assistance, because of the present situation. Since the wise leaders of Indonesia understand that changing international conditions require new approaches, they are doing their best to realize their nation's aspirations by appealing to world opinion in a peaceful way. In spite of this, there are groups who have forgotten the wide opportunities that exist for helping the people: increasing agricultural production, assisting the unemployed, teaching, and providing medical care. All they have done is to commit extremist acts which have seriously disturbed the public's security, ignoring the law and the orders of the Allied army: for example, they have been totally carried away in their efforts to complete the formal

[26] *Antara-Dōmei*, Sept. 18, 1945.

structure and character of the state, or to fly the national flag; with even less rationality, they have demanded the transfer of governmental power, have made illegal radio broadcasts and issued secret publications and other writings. Such actions as these are a matter of shame to civilized men, and will cause grief to the Indonesian people, for they will result in the loss of world sympathy for Indonesia's cause.

To make sure this does not happen, the authorities will take action against any ill-intentioned activities which may harm the public interest. Furthermore, the authorities have made repeated efforts to persuade these people to improve their behavior, to behave calmly in line with the wishes of their wise leaders, since this would be far better than for the government to have to use naked force. Yet these groups have recently shown that they can not be trusted to maintain public order—indeed some have even flouted international justice. If this situation continues to the danger point, the government will be compelled to take drastic action on a large scale.[27]

Although many of the younger generation reacted with hostility to General Nagano's words, there was a vast difference in tone between this proclamation and those of the war years. The General had made the conflict between his sympathy for the Indonesians and his responsibility toward the Allies quite explicit. On September 15 Rear Admiral Patterson of the Fifth Royal Cruiser Squadron had appeared in Tandjung Priok harbor with the H.M.S. *Cumberland,* accompanied by Dr. Charles van der Plas, former governor of East Java and now representative of the Netherlands Indies Civil Administration (NICA).[28] Talks had already taken place between Nagano and the Admiral, and

[27] *Berita Gunseikanboe* (Djakarta), Sept. 19, 1945. The text is written in very stiff and awkward Japanese-style Indonesian, and I have taken some mild liberties in translating it to bring out the General's meaning more clearly.

[28] F. S. V. Donnison, *British Military Administration in the Far East, 1943–1946* (London, 1956), pp. 423f. An advance group of British intelligence officers, led by Major Greenhalgh, had been parachuted into Djakarta as early as September 8. It is probable that Greenhalgh had already urged Nagano to preserve the status quo more strictly.

the Japanese were under heavy pressure to begin taking a much stronger line against the Indonesians.

While the official appeal for the Ikada rally was issued by the Djakarta City National Committee, we have seen that the prime movers behind it were the pemuda groups loosely clustered around Menteng 31. Couriers urging attendance rapidly fanned out to the kabupatèn in the vicinity of Djakarta. In this effort, Muwardi, who had excellent contacts with traditionalist kjai and djago of Banten and Bogor, played a major role. And at first the cabinet seemed quite willing to go along with the proposed rally. Following Nagano's proclamation, however, opinions in the cabinet were divided. Tan Malaka avers that Sukarno, Hatta, and Soepomo were strongly opposed, while Iwa, Gatot, and Subardjo, together with Ki Hadjar Dewantoro and Abikusno, were in favor.[29] The negative opinion prevailed, however, and at two o'clock on the afternoon of September 19, four hours before the rally was scheduled to begin, the cabinet sent a note to Menteng 31 threatening Sukarno's and Hatta's resignation unless all plans were canceled. The pemuda refused to yield and sent Malik himself, in his capacity as third vice-chairman of the KNIP, to persuade the cabinet to change its mind. He was finally able to convince them that popular expectations had reached a point where more trouble was likely to ensue if the rally was put off than if it was held.[30] A message to this effect was then sent by Sukarno and Hatta to Nagano; they added that they had decided to go ahead with the rally, and that the republic would take responsibility for the consequences.

Tension mounted steadily in Djakarta as the afternoon wore on, since the Kenpeitai guarded all the entrances to Ikada with tanks and machine guns, not so much to prevent the population from entering the huge square, as to make sure that outbreaks of

[29] Tan Malaka, *Dari pendjara,* III, 62f. Tan Malaka is not a wholly unbiased witness, so that his version should be approached with some caution.

[30] Malik, *Riwajat,* p. 75.

violence or disturbances of public order did not occur. Finally, in considerable trepidation, Sukarno and Hatta arrived at Ikada, together with members of the cabinet and some of the more prominent pemuda. Sukarno spoke:

As a matter of fact, the government of the Republic of Indonesia has given orders to cancel this meeting, but since you, my brothers, have compelled me, I have come here, together with all the ministers of the government of the Republic of Indonesia [crowd roars "Hurrah!"]. I am now speaking as your brother, Bung Karno. I ask you all to remain calm and to comprehend the leadership which is being given by the government of the Republic of Indonesia. Believe in this government! ["We believe!"] Brothers, I as the president, Bung Hatta as vice-president, the ministers, all of us are ready to accept responsibility toward the entire people of Indonesia. In return we ask the trust of the Indonesian people! ["We trust you! We trust you!"] We have proclaimed Indonesia's independence. And we are maintaining that proclamation, we are not withdrawing a single word of it. But in the meantime, we have been preparing a plan. Therefore submit to this plan of ours. Be calm, serene, but always ready to receive the orders which we give. If you, my brothers, really believe in the government of the Republic of Indonesia—which will defend the Proclamation of Independence, even if our breasts are rent asunder in the process—then give us your confidence, by obeying our orders and maintaining discipline. Can you do this, my brothers? ["We can! We can!"] Then our order for today is: Let us all go home now, calmly and serenely; obey the command of your president, but remain on the alert. Will you obey, my brothers? ["We will! We will!"] Once again then, my brothers, our order is: Let us all go home now, calmly and serenely, but maintain our vigilance. I close this meeting with our national salute—Merdeka! [31]

Though there were evidently many in the huge crowd (estimated by Tan Malaka to number 200,000) who were disappointed by the speech, the rally dispersed in quiet and orderly fashion.[32]

[31] *Antara-Dōmei*, Sept. 20, 1945.

[32] The Japanese retaliated against the pemuda the next day. Menteng 31 was raided, and a number of its habitués, such as Darwis, Aidit,

The Ikada rally gave the urban masses in the capital their first opportunity to participate in the independence drama, and both to feel and to express their solidarity. It marked (as had similar demonstrations in Surabaja and Semarang) their emergence from the psychological cocoon created by the Japanese aura of omnipotence. Although the Japanese tanks and machine guns were intended simply to prevent disorders, their forbidding presence was taken by the Indonesian participants in a much more hostile sense. The feeling, therefore, of having outfaced the Kenpeitai by holding the rally at all created a heightened sense of confidence and hope.

Moreover, Sukarno's demonstration of his undiminished charismatic hold over the masses was no less significant. His audiences were perhaps never of greater political value to him than in these early months of independence. At a time when to the Western world he was still very much the arch collaborator, his political future essentially depended on his capacity to keep a firm grip on the nation's imagination. Not only would this prove the best way of reestablishing his credentials in Allied eyes, but it would also demonstrate his irreplaceability to those figures from the underground who were waiting in the wings with shadowy hopes of seizing center stage. While intellectually Sukarno shared the cautious political strategy being pursued by the cabinet, instinctively he had already sensed that where the power of administrative hierarchies was in decline, the power of images and promises would grow, and in a time of confusion and liberation would represent an order and coherence of their own. In the months to come, while most of his colleagues stayed in the large metropolitan centers, he was constantly to be touring the Javanese hinterland, consolidating the mass support that would subsequently maintain him in power for a generation.

Lukman, Hanafi, and Sidik Kertapati were arrested. Malik himself was jailed two days later. See *Warta Indonesia* (Semarang), Oct. 1, 1945; Malik, *Riwajat,* pp. 77f.; and Sidik Kertapati, *Sekitar proklamasi,* pp. 118–19.

Chapter 7 ·

Pemuda in Arms

We have seen how the Proclamation of Independence in Djakarta on August 17 was echoed by scores of local declarations of independence in provincial capitals, in smaller inland towns, and even in many villages. We have watched the spontaneous mushrooming of national committees throughout the hinterland of Java as the PPKI gradually transformed itself into the KNIP. It was as if a hidden impulse emanating from Djakarta spread across the island, creating a rhythm linking locality to locality where organization, planning, programs, and ideology as yet scarcely existed. As the tempo of this rhythm accelerated in Djakarta from the days of the PPKI debates to the mass meeting in Ikada, so did the merdeka movement pick up speed in the interior. Everywhere, as in Djakarta, it was the pemuda who set the pace. There was a kind of natural progression in this movement during September, before the arrival of the Allies in some military force decisively transformed its thrust.

In many of the smaller towns and even in some provincial capitals, the spell of the Japanese occupation persisted long after the actual surrender took place. Like invalids unaccustomed to walking, only half believing that each faster, suppler step is really possible, the pemuda gropingly explored the extent of their merdeka. The first actions were almost always symbolic, such as hoisting the Indonesian flag over public buildings where the Hinomaru had long flown. And as the Japanese put up only nominal resistance, so at an increasing pace the pemuda grew

125

more and more confident. Posters were pasted up. Chalked or painted exclamations and appeals appeared on vacant walls. Japanese cars vanished from their owners' yards. Jails were broken open. Yet these were still the actions of individuals or tiny groups of pemuda friends. The breakthrough ending the spell of Japanese power came only with the first public manifestations of popular solidarity in the face of the occupation forces. This solidarity was typically expressed by a mass meeting held in defiance of Japanese orders to which pemuda of all social classes—pedicab drivers, tradesmen's apprentices, and pickpockets, as well as students and schoolchildren—swarmed in response to the magic summons of merdeka.

This pattern was first significantly manifested not in Djakarta but in the East Java port of Surabaja, a large industrial city with a long history of urban radicalism. Already on August 21 the workers in the city's oil refineries had formed their own organization, and on August 25 a subsidiary Angkatan Muda was created, led by Sumarsono and Ruslan Widjaja, both of whom seem to have had prewar connections with Amir Sjarifuddin.[1] Pemuda in various other institutions quickly followed suit, forming their own office- or factory-based organizations. As the days passed, these small ad hoc groups began to solidify and link up with one another through meetings of their leaders. By the second week of September the situation had developed far enough that the pemuda were able to issue a city-wide call for a mass meeting in Tambaksari Square. Posters appeared on the city's walls urging the population to summon each other to the rally with the shout

---

[1] *Dokumentasi pemuda,* p. 49. According to an anonymous article, "Njala api 10 Nopember—Mengenal orang dibalik lajar" (*Sinar Harapan* [Djakarta], Nov. 9, 1968), a major factor in the rapid initiative taken by the oil workers was the preparatory role played by Djohan Sjahroezah, a close friend of Sjahrir and a key figure linking various underground groups in Djakarta and the provinces. During the occupation he had entered the former Shell works and had succeeded in drawing in with him a number of trusted pemuda activists, such as Sumarsono, Ruslan Widjaja, Dimjati, E. M. Rambe, and others.

"Merdeka!" On September 11, eight days before the Ikada rally in Djakarta, the meeting took place under heavy Japanese guard. After R. Sudirman and Doel Arnowo, the resident of Surabaja and the head of the East Java KNI, had addressed the crowd in cautious, prudent tones, Sumarsono, then the most prominent pemuda leader in the city, made his own more radical appeal to the mass of assembled youth. On September 17, in defiance of a Kenpeitai ban on meetings and demonstrations, the oil workers' youth organization held a similar meeting at the Pasarturi Square in downtown Surabaja, at which demands for the immediate take-over of buildings and offices were insistently voiced.[2]

To understand the next stage of the pemuda movement it should be recalled that following the Japanese surrender there was a gradual disintegration of the armed guard at many of the concentration camps across Java where Dutch and Eurasian prisoners had been detained during the war. In late August and early September, while the spell of Japan's omnipotence still lingered in the hinterland, many of these prisoners had either bought their way out or simply left, usually returning to their prewar homes in the hope of starting up life again where they had left off in 1942. Many were in a deep state of shock as a result of the sufferings they had endured, and were not in the least prepared for what they discovered on their release. Their property in many cases had been confiscated by the Japanese, bought up by the Chinese, or requisitioned by the Indonesians. Nonetheless, it was rare in this period for any violence to break out. Many Dutch people reported being treated kindly and gently by Indonesians they had known before the war.[3] But as time passed the atmosphere began

[2] *Dokumentasi pemuda,* pp. 49–51; "Njala api 10 Nopember"; Pusat Sedjarah Militer Angkatan Darat, *Kronologi sedjarah TNI 1945* (Bandung, n.d.), pp. 26–27. Aside from the oil workers' organization, other key participants were the Angkatan Muda Kantor (Office Youth), Angkatan Muda Kereta Api (Railway Youth) and Angkatan Muda Gas dan Listrik (Gas and Electricity Youth).

[3] Smail (*Bandung,* p. 39) makes this point, and it has been confirmed by a number of former prisoners with whom I have talked.

to change. Not a few former prisoners now attempted to recoup their losses, and when they did so tensions rapidly built up. These tensions were heightened further as the more imminent arrival of the Allies encouraged the Dutch to hope for an immediate restoration and increased the fears of the Indonesians, who came to see these Dutchmen less and less as former prisoners and more and more as the vanguard of a returning Bourbon colonial order.[4] Not unexpectedly, perhaps, the first clashes between the more energetic former prisoners and the pemuda arose not over property or power, but over the symbols of their respective hopes. Many early incidents of violence were precipitated by the flying of either the Dutch or the Indonesian flag over government or other politically significant buildings.

The first serious violence in Java erupted in Surabaja on September 19, when a group of recently released prisoners hoisted the Dutch flag over the Hotel Yamato (once the Hotel Oranje) in Tundjungan. A crowd of pemuda and kampung dwellers rapidly gathered. In spite of a Kenpeitai guard round the building, one of the pemuda managed to scramble up the flagpole and rip the blue horizontal stripe off the Dutch pennant, leaving the remaining red and white stripes as an improvised Indonesian flag. The situation grew rapidly worse, with brawls breaking out between Dutch, Eurasian, and Indonesian pemuda, and ended in the death of a Dutch captain called Ploegman.[5] On September 20 a gigantic procession marched round the center of the town after a mass rally in Tambaksari Square. The pemuda ignored Japanese orders banning the carrying of bambu runtjing (sharpened bamboo spears), and these ominous weapons began to appear in all quarters of the city.

----

[4] Tjamboek Berdoeri, Indonesia dalem api, pp. 167–68. But he notes (p. 166) that in the villages outside Malang, it was still common up to this time to hear peasants saying "Sing bakal koeoso manèh Ratoe sing bijèn" ("The former ruler will rule once again").

[5] Sidik Kertapati, Sekitar proklamasi, p. 126. See also Antara-Dōmei, Sept. 22, 1945; Dokumentasi pemuda, p. 50; and "Njala api 10 Nopember."

On September 23 a new action organization was formed, the Pemuda Republik Indonesia (Youth of the Republic of Indonesia), or PRI, in which the leading roles were taken by Sumarsono, Kaslan, Krissubanu, Ruslan Widjaja, Kusnadi, Supardi, Supijah, and Soetomo, soon to achieve fame as Bung Tomo.[6] On the same day the Kenpeitai headquarters in Surabaja were surrounded by large masses of city workers, kampung dwellers, and pemuda. The Japanese, faced with huge urban crowds, were in an acute dilemma. Their heavy weapons would allow them to kill a great many people—but, with the war over, for what purpose? The risk of being overrun by sheer numbers and meeting their deaths at the hands of enraged mobs was not lightly to be ignored. Accordingly, resistance was nominal and the building passed into Indonesian hands.[7] Such withdrawals would become a frequently recurring pattern. The Japanese preferred to evacuate contested buildings and retire, where possible, to less provocative strongholds outside the urban areas.

Surabaja's example was soon followed in other cities. In every case the pemuda led the way and the urban masses followed in their wake. Jogjakarta was largely in Indonesian hands by September 25.[8] On September 28 Bandung began to be taken over.[9] By September 30 Malang and Surakarta were, at least as regards the main administrative offices and public buildings, no longer under Japanese control.[10]

It is notable that up to the end of the month pemuda activity was concentrated in urban areas and focused primarily on civilian installations, and that with a few exceptions the level of violence was low. The Japanese, now thinking mainly of their own

[6] *Dokumentasi pemuda,* p. 49. According to "Njala api 10 Nopember," the PRI's initial headquarters were in the Wilhelminalaan (Djl. Merdeka), but it soon moved to the former Dutch clubhouse, the Simpang Societeit.

[7] Pusat Sedjarah Militer Angkatan Darat, *Kronologi,* p. 29.

[8] "Sedjarah TNI, Diponegoro," p. 21; Indonesia, Kementerian Penerangan, *Republik Indonesia Daerah Istimewa Jogjakarta,* p. 40.

[9] Djèn Amar, *Bandung lautan api,* pp. 73–75; Smail, *Bandung,* p. 56.

[10] *Antara,* Oct. 4, 1945; "Sedjarah TNI, Diponegoro," p. 22.

repatriation and hoping to avoid trouble until then, were usually willing to yield such installations in order to lower tensions. The injunction given them by the Allies to preserve law and order could be reasonably stretched this far. Moreover, it could be argued that one of the Allies' major goals—to protect and rehabilitate the prisoners in the concentration camps—could be more easily achieved if Japanese military personnel were free to concentrate on this assignment. The pangrèh pradja and older-generation politicians in the KNI still served a buffer function between the pemuda-led crowds and the Japanese. It was usually to them that the liberated installations were transferred. Since the pemuda were at this stage still primarily concerned with the symbols of independence—with the physical seizure of state buildings rather than with actual control over the power apparatus they housed—they were for the moment satisfied once these symbols passed to Indonesian hands, even to those of the older generation.

But this pattern, which was predicated on a relatively uncomplicated relationship between the Japanese and the Indonesians, was disrupted at the end of September by the arrival of the first Allied military units, and with them the first considerable group of Dutch governmental personnel. The appearance of the Allied forces, more particularly of the Dutch elements within them, changed the situation in two ways. On the one hand, it made the government at the center even more anxious than before for Indonesia to be on its best behavior vis-à-vis the Allies. On the other hand, it broke up the existing gentlemen's agreements between the Japanese and the Indonesians. The policy of seeping eviction of Japanese authorities could be pursued no further. With the Allies present, the Japanese were forced to stiffen their backs, and in some cases even to take military action against the Indonesians. In their turn the pemuda and other groups began to look for arms to defend their merdeka against the returning colonial power. Thus pemuda and Japanese interests came increasingly into sharper contradiction, and the relative peacefulness of September passed into the bloodshed, violence, and terror of October and November.

It was only on September 29, 43 days after the Proclamation of Independence, that the first British troops landed at Djakarta. Even then they consisted of no more than one battalion of Seaforth Highlanders, from the First Brigade of Major General Hawthorn's Twenty-third (Indian) Division.[11] The full story behind the belated arrival of the Allies in Java, and the very small numbers in which they initially came, lies outside the scope of this study. The single most important factor was a decision made at the Potsdam conference to transfer the war theater into which Java fell from MacArthur's Southwest Pacific Command to Mountbatten's Southeast Asia Command (SEAC).[12] The decision found the SEAC lacking the necessary men, ships, communications, and intelligence files to handle the huge task with which it was faced. Half a million square miles of land were now suddenly added to the million already under its jurisdiction. Eighty million people were added to the forty-five million for which it was already responsible. Two thousand miles were added to an already grossly overextended communications system.[13] The confusion was increased by the fact that the transfer of jurisdiction was legally effected only on the day the Japanese made their unexpectedly rapid surrender. Indeed, it was not until

[11] Wehl, *Birth of Indonesia*, p. 39; A. J. F. Doulton, *The Fighting Cock: Being the History of the Twenty-third Indian Division, 1942–1947* (Aldershot, 1951), pp. 228, 230.

[12] Though the decision was finally made only at Potsdam, the question of the respective jurisdictions of the SWPC and SEAC had been the subject of intensifying lobbying and intrigue among various Allied military commanders and their respective political backers in Washington, London, and The Hague at least since late 1944. For a good account of the maneuverings involved, see Idrus Nasir Djajadiningrat, *The Beginnings of the Indonesian-Dutch Negotiations and the Hoge Veluwe Talks* (Ithaca, N.Y., 1958), pp. 7–16. Cf. also Donnison, *British Military Administration*, pp. 415–17.

[13] Donnison, *British Military Administration*, pp. 420ff.; Rajendra Singh, *Post-War Occupation Forces: Japan and Southeast Asia* (New Delhi, 1958), p. 220.

August 24 that the British and Dutch renegotiated and signed an agreement on their cooperation in reoccupying the areas previously scheduled to be American responsibilities.[14]

The delays were enhanced by MacArthur's insistence that no Japanese surrenders be permitted anywhere until after the formal signing of a general surrender in Tokyo, which did not take place until September 2. Even then it was thought necessary, to ensure the compliance of local Japanese commanders, to arrange the surrenders in Southeast Asia in sequence down the chain of the Japanese army command, from Marshal Terauchi in Saigon, through General Itagaki in Singapore, to General Nagano in Djakarta.

To add to Mountbatten's troubles, he was extremely poorly informed about the situation in Java, since neither the Dutch nor MacArthur had turned over to him the existing Allied intelligence files, whatever value these might have had. Mountbatten himself observed:

It was known, of course, that an Indonesian Independence Movement had been in existence before the war; and that it had been supported by prominent intellectuals, some of whom had suffered banishment for their participation in nationalist propaganda—but no information had been made available to me as to the fate of this movement under the Japanese occupation. Dr. H. J. van Mook, Lieutenant-Governor-General of the Netherlands East Indies, who had come to Kandy on the 1st September, had given me no reason to suppose that the re-

[14] The terms of this agreement specified that the reoccupation of the Netherlands East Indies would be a two-stage operation. In the first stage, Mountbatten would have plenary powers to take whatever measures he thought fit to end fighting in the islands. The Netherlands Indies Civil Administration (NICA) would, in this initial period, be unconditionally subordinate to the Allied command. In return, the SEAC would make no formal, legal assumption of authority and would see to it that the NICA was given as much support as the circumstances permitted. In the second stage, powers would be handed over to the Dutch. The text of the agreement can be found in Netherlands, Staten-Generaal, Tweede Kamer, *Enquête-commissie regeringsbeleid 1940–1945, militair beleid, terugkeer naar Nederlandsch-Indië, (8A en B)* (The Hague, 1956), pp. 650f.

occupation of Java would present any operational problem, beyond that of rounding-up the Japanese. . . . The seriousness of the position was not suspected, and the picture only started to emerge as the Allied Forces moved in to occupy key-points in Java.[15]

The SEAC had evidently expected to find the situation in Java quite comparable to that it had found in Malaya, where the reestablishment of Allied authority was achieved with little difficulty. Indeed, Mountbatten's original reoccupation plans envisaged that the Twenty-third Division alone, landing its three brigades in Djakarta, Surabaja, and Sumatra, would be able to restore Dutch authority single-handedly. Yet, as one participant in these events noted, "In the end it was necessary to have three Divisions, and they only held a few coastal cities." [16]

Yet even had SEAC been more adequately briefed, its options were circumscribed by an acute shortage of reliable military forces. There was only one ethnic English division in the Far East, and that was already committed in India and Burma, where British interests were more directly concerned. Mountbatten was therefore compelled to rely on Indian and Gurkha troops. David Wehl, one of his trusted intelligence officers, later stated that given the political situation in India, Mountbatten realized that he had about seven months to carry out his task of rescuing European prisoners, repatriating the Japanese, and restoring law and order, before irresistible political pressures would compel the withdrawal of these troops.[17]

The combination of these factors forced Mountbatten to alter his policy priorities quite drastically. He realized that while London was anxious to do what it could for its Dutch allies, diverting major military and other resources to a vast area peripheral to Britain's prime interests in Southeast Asia would not sit well with

[15] Vice-Admiral the Earl Mountbatten of Burma, *Post-Surrender Tasks: Section E of the Report to the Combined Chiefs of Staff by the Supreme Allied Commander, Southeast Asia, 1943–1945* (London, 1969), pp. 289f.

[16] Doulton, *Fighting Cock,* p. 235.

[17] Wehl, *Birth of Indonesia,* pp. 43–45.

his superiors. Moreover, two major tasks that he had been assigned, the repatriation of an estimated 73,000 Japanese troops from Java, and the rescue of over a hundred thousand European prisoners in the concentration camps in the interior of the island, might be rendered difficult, if not impossible, if he overplayed his hand.[18] The obedience of the Japanese to their commanders was by no means guaranteed. The strength of popular support for the new Indonesian republic was clearly considerable, but the control of the leaders in Djakarta over the small towns and rural areas of Java was quite uncertain. Any attempt to reimpose Dutch authority on the island forcibly with inadequate manpower might break the discipline of the Japanese military hierarchy and irrevocably jeopardize the lives of the internees. Last, but not least, the Dutch had neither the military nor the administrative personnel at hand to bear a major part of the burden of pursuing a tough policy—nor was there any prospect that they would be able to do so for many months. Mountbatten's liberal attitude on colonial questions and his considerable personal success in dealing with Aung San and the independence movement in Burma undoubtedly reinforced the judgment to which his assessment of the balance of forces in Java led.

It was essential, in his view, to secure the cooperation of the Indonesian leaders in Djakarta, if necessary by making significant political concessions. To some degree these concessions could be made by the British themselves, but ultimately they would have to come from the Dutch, since the British were obliged by the terms of the August 24 agreement to help the Dutch reestablish their authority in Indonesia. A liberal Dutch attitude would enormously alleviate his problems, and he was determined to use all the influence at his disposal to persuade his

---

[18] Mountbatten (*Post-Surrender Tasks,* p. 282) gives the 73,000 estimate. A later, more realistic total of 55,000 is offered by Doulton, *Fighting Cock,* p. 238. What is important here, however, is the SEAC's assumptions. The figure on internees is drawn from Wehl, *Birth of Indonesia,* p. 76.

Dutch associates to accept his views.[19] He expressed his new policy in succinct, if to Dutch ears grotesque terms, when he stated: "Our one idea is to get the Dutch and Indonesians to kiss and make friends and then pull out." [20]

It was quite consistent with the SEAC's reassessment of the situation that on September 29, just as the Seaforth Highlanders began landing in the harbor of Djakarta, Lieutenant General Sir Philip Christison, former commander in Arakan and now commander of the Allied Forces–Netherlands East Indies (AFNEI), made a controversial statement to the press that was immediately broadcast over Radio SEAC in Singapore.[21] In it he stated that the British had three objectives in Indonesia: to protect and evacuate Allied prisoners of war and other internees; to disarm and repatriate the Japanese; to maintain law and order. The Sixteenth Army would be held responsible for internal security in the non-occupied areas until "arrangements are reached for the local authorities to take over. Then the Japanese will be disarmed. . . . The British have no intention of meddling in Indonesian internal affairs, but only to ensure law and order." Pending a Dutch-Indonesian agreement, the General stated that he intended to ask present party leaders to treat him and his troops as guests, and to tell the Indonesians that they must support temporary British administration. He added, "British forces will not move outside the designated occupation areas of Batavia [Djakarta], Surabaja, Medan and Padang for any purpose." [22]

[19] This analysis of the changes in Mountbatten's thinking and his attempts to persuade the Dutch to liberalize their policy is largely based on his own account; see *Post-Surrender Tasks,* pp. 290–91.

[20] Quoted in Geoffrey Sawer, "Allied Policy in Indonesia," *Australian Asiatic Bulletin* (Melbourne), April 1946, p. 4. It should perhaps be noted that no more than a handful of Indonesians could have had any idea at this point of the SEAC's perplexities.

[21] Christison was appointed to this position only on August 30, replacing Admiral Patterson.

[22] This broadcast was long a matter of bitter controversy. No official transcript was ever released, probably because of the immediate and violent Dutch reaction. The SEAC tried subsequently to play it down,

The consequences of this broadcast were of major importance. It caused such an uproar in leading political circles in Holland that the British felt compelled to issue an official denial that they had gone back on the Civil Affairs Agreement of August 24. Tentative overtures being made by van der Plas to the Indonesian leaders in Djakarta were rendered abortive. And the position of Lieutenant-Governor General van Mook, who at Mountbatten's urging had been preparing for a meeting with Sukarno and Hatta, was made extremely difficult by an explicit repudiation of any such meeting by The Hague.[23] The effect of the broadcast among the Dutch population inside and outside the internment camps was no less devastating. They had endured considerable hardship at the hands of the Japanese and Indonesians during the war years, and emerged to find the Allies using a combination of Japanese and Indonesian power to maintain law and order, with the Dutch government representatives in the humiliating position of hangers-on of the British high com-

---

insisting that Christison had been misquoted and his intentions distorted (see Mountbatten, *Post-Surrender Tasks,* p. 290, for a sample of this). Accordingly, the precise wording is still not clear. Slightly differing versions can be found in *Enquête-commissie,* p. 657 (testimony of van der Plas, who gives the British Information Service paraphrase of the broadcast); *Fakta dan dokumen2,* p. 93; Raliby, *Documenta Historica,* pp. 36, 43; and an untitled bundle of documents, IC-RVO doc. no. 014235–42, which appear to have come from British Intelligence files, since they include memoranda of secret conversations between Mountbatten and his staff members. The quotations here are drawn from the last source, which gives the fullest and clearest version of the broadcast.

[23] The Governor-General himself, Tjarda van Starkenborgh Stachouwer, who had been a prisoner of war in China, resigned his post in mid-October 1945 in protest against any thought of major postwar concessions to Indonesian nationalism. From this time until he was forced to resign in 1948, van Mook was the main architect of Dutch policy in Indonesia. Because he was suspected of being a liberal and because his formidable intelligence and personality made conservatives in Holland jealous, he was never promoted to governor-general. In fact, this office was never again filled.

mand.[24] Moreover Sukarno, who in their eyes was the epitome of the worst type of pro-Japanese collaborator, was now being treated with respect as a political equal by the commander of the Allied forces.

On the other side, the effect was no less significant. The broadcast made it clear that the British had no intention of punishing Indonesian leaders or of allowing anyone else to do so. The danger of war crimes trials or other penal action against Sukarno and Hatta was thus effectively, if not explicitly, removed. Van Mook was perfectly correct when he said that the Christison broadcast amounted to a virtual British recognition of the new Indonesian regime.[25]

While embarrassed and concerned by the repercussions of the Christison affair, the SEAC was convinced that the military and political realities were unaltered. Public opinion in London and The Hague demanded that the internees be fed, medically treated, and evacuated as quickly as possible. Yet the prisoners remained in territory held by the Republic, where they were, willy-nilly, hostages for the Allies' good behavior. To be sure, the cabinet gave no particular indication that it would play this card to secure concessions from the Dutch and British; but a general fear prevailed that if political tensions rose, the Djakarta leaders would be unable to prevent massacres in the interior, where their bureaucratic and police authority would scarcely hold.

[24] Van der Plas sent a desperate wire to The Hague on September 30, informing the government of the broadcast's disastrous effects on local Dutch morale. *Enquête-commissie,* p. 657.

[25] H. J. van Mook, *Indonesië, Nederland en de wereld* (Batavia [Djakarta], 1949), p. 90; Wehl, *Birth of Indonesia,* p. 42. Doulton says that from the British perspective, "for better or for worse, the Indonesian Republic existed and could not be disregarded." *Fighting Cock,* p. 237. The Dutch, however, did have their revenge in part. Though Christison, a nonpolitical soldier's soldier, clearly acted for Mountbatten, and though his statement reflected the thrust of Mountbatten's new policy, the SEAC was forced to sacrifice him. He was retired from his job in January 1946, as soon as the immediate furor had died down.

Recognizing this political disadvantage and his own very limited military resources, Mountbatten decided to concentrate British power in the three major coastal cities of Djakarta, Semarang, and Surabaja; the hill towns immediately behind these ports, where many of the internees were concentrated, were also to be occupied if possible. This meant Bandung in West, Magelang and Ambarawa in Central, and Malang in East Java. Since troop shortages and temporary logistical difficulties made it impracticable to secure all these objectives at once, Mountbatten decided at a British-Dutch conference held in Singapore on October 10 to concentrate first on reoccupying the Djakarta-Bogor-Bandung road and securing Bandung itself.[26] This concentration of the initial Allied military effort in West Java, and its much slower spread to Central and East Java, was a major reason why the Indonesians were to respond so differently in these regions.

Word of the Allied landings at Djakarta on September 29 had in the meantime traveled rapidly through the towns of Java, leaving a new sense of urgency and crisis in its wake. As we have seen, in most of the larger urban centers, the process of assuming control of civilian installations and the quasi-institutionalization of independence had already taken place. There was now much to cherish and defend. In any event the thrust of the merdeka spirit would have soon demanded a move against Japanese military installations. But this movement was accelerated by reports and rumors of events unfolding in Djakarta. It became ever more important to secure not only the symbols but the living instruments of power and liberation—the guns in Japanese arsenals and barracks. The increasing sense of urgency was reciprocated in many places by the Japanese, for the question of arms faced them with an unprecedented dilemma. If the independence movement was to be helped, here was the last opportunity to do so in an effective way. On the other hand, yielding arms to the

[26] *Enquête-commissie,* pp. 658–59 (testimony of Admiral Helfrich).

pemuda involved not only the certainty of Allied punishment but also the real possibility that the arms would be turned against the Japanese themselves.

As we shall see, in different areas the way the Japanese resolved their dilemma and the timing of Allied arrivals as they impinged on the growing tide of pemuda militancy affected the development of the merdeka movement in strikingly dissimilar ways. By the end of October, Bandung was an island of occupied tranquillity, Central Java an armed and anxious fortress, and Surabaja a sea of fire.

Bandung

Political developments in Bandung in the weeks following the Proclamation of Independence have been admirably described by John Smail.[27] The general seizure of administrative buildings was completed by the end of September. Shortly afterward negotiations were opened between Major General Mabuchi, the Japanese commander in West Java, and leading members of the Bandung political elite, primarily over the increasingly urgent question of arms. On October 4 a secret agreement was signed between Mabuchi and the aristocratic Sundanese Resident of the Priangan, R. Puradiredja. The essential parts of the agreement were that the Indonesian flag would be flown over Japanese military magazines and dumps. Joint Japanese-Indonesian patrols would guard these installations with the Indonesians placed conspicuously and the Japanese inconspicuously. The Japanese would retain full responsibility (presumably vis-à-vis the Allies), while the Resident would undertake to ensure that nothing was damaged or destroyed. Puradiredja, Mabuchi, and the local BKR, together with representatives of the KNI, would arrange for the eventual transport and disposal of the goods (mainly weapons) inside. This document was signed in the presence of Oto Iskandardinata (chairman of the West Java KNI), R. Niti-

[27] *Bandung,* chap. 3.

sumantri (chairman of the KNI for the Priangan residency), R. Soehari (chairman of the Bandung City BKR), and R. Jusuf (the residency police chief).[28]

It is clear that the agreement did not involve the actual transfer of arms into the hands of even the BKR. Rather, a public façade of Indonesian control over the arms depots would be arranged, while the arms themselves would continue to remain at Mabuchi's disposition. Mabuchi's motives seem quite straightforward. The agreement meant that he secured the cooperation of the Bandung leaders in a ruse to reduce pemuda pressures for arming the population, hopefully gaining time until the imminently expected arrival of Allied troops acquitted him of his responsibilities. The motives of the Oto-Puradiredja group are harder to disentangle. It is likely that once again, as in the affair of the disbanding of the Peta, Oto was the victim of excessive trust in Japanese good intentions. He may have believed that the vague language of the last part of the agreement presaged an eventual delivery of arms to elements he and his friends trusted. Whatever his reasons, it is certain that he and the other Bandung leaders were party to Mabuchi's ruse to prevent arms from going to the city's pemuda. When this became clear to the pemuda, he was not to be forgiven.

It may be that the pemuda got wind of the agreement very soon after it was concluded, or it may be that they were irritated because the situation in Bandung was not changing as rapidly as they would have liked. In any event, on October 6 they organized a boycott of the Dutch in Bandung's markets. No one would now sell their produce to the former internees. Two days later a pemuda-led mass invasion of the Andir airfield to the west of the city led to its surrender by Japanese guards almost without a struggle.[29] By October 9 the wave temporarily dammed

[28] "Puradiredja-Mabuchi Agreement," IC-RVO doc. no. 006626–30. This document had not yet come to light at the time Smail's monograph was written, but he indicated his suspicion that some such agreement had been reached. *Bandung*, p. 58.

[29] *Soeara Merdeka* (Bandung), Oct. 9, 1945.

by the Puradiredja-Mabuchi agreement reached its peak. Hetero-geneous groups of pemuda and kampung dwellers, stiffened by some well-armed members of the Tokubetsu Keisatsutai (Special Police Force), broke into and seized the Kiaratjondong arms factory.[30] There was little fighting. The appearance of large crowds seems once again to have cowed the Japanese guards into rapid surrender.[31]

By the evening of October 9 it appeared that Mabuchi's de-laying ruse had failed and that the pemuda might secure military as well as political ascendancy in Bandung and its environs. But within twenty-four hours the situation changed quite suddenly. Whether the Japanese felt that the Puradiredja-Mabuchi agree-ment had been dangerously violated by the events of October 9, whether they were alarmed by a disorderly crowd attack on the Kenpeitai headquarters, or whether, as a Dutch source sardon-ically hints, they were enraged because on the previous day Ma-buchi had been unceremoniously shoved out of his car near the An-dir airfield by a small pemuda group, they reacted with precision and speed.[32] The local BKR leaders were summoned for a parley,

[30] The Tokubetsu Keisatsutai was a highly trained, heavily armed mobile police force established in 1944 with units in each residency on Java and Madura. It was under the control of the residency Security Bureau chief. See M. Oudang, *Perkembangan kepolisian di Indonesia* (Djakarta, 1952), pp. 46–47. Smail notes that the Tokubetsu Keisatsutai had unusual importance, since it was the one heavily armed Indonesian force remaining after the dissolution of the Peta and the Heihō. *Bandung,* p. 60, n. 12.

[31] Smail (*Bandung,* p. 60, n. 12) gives October 2 as the date of the seizure of Kiaratjondong, citing *Soeara Merdeka,* Oct. 3, 1945. Djèn Amar (*Bandung lautan api,* p. 75) and *Antara* (Oct. 10, 1945) both give October 9. The discrepancy is puzzling. As described by Smail, the October 2 seizure was "made to sound like a typical office takeover, with control passing to a 'leadership council' of its own civil servants." Pos-sibly, then, the Puradiredja-Mabuchi agreement of October 4 represented an attempt to maintain this situation—formal Indonesian authority and informal Japanese control—and therefore a second, serious takeover was required on October 9, when the pemuda realized what was going on.

[32] Smail, *Bandung,* p. 62; Anonymous Dutch annotation to "Pura-diredja-Mabuchi Agreement." Smail also raises the possibility that the

arrested, and later forced to make a humiliating round of the city
on army tanks telling the population to stop attacking the Japanese. At the same time Mabuchi's troops seized the BKR headquarters and all other important buildings. By the next morning,
with the erection of strong barricades at all entrances to the city,
and with a series of razzias through the main streets, the Japanese had regained complete control of Bandung, scattering the
pemuda and their followers, and confiscating most of what few
arms the Indonesians had so far managed to secure.[33] The humiliation was complete when Sutoko, the leading Bandung pemuda of the period, received an ironic present of lipstick from
the pemuda of East Java.[34] By the time Brigadier General Mac-
Donald arrived a few days later with part of the Thirty-seventh

---

Japanese may have been responding to pressure from Major Gray, the
RAPWI (Recovery of Allied Prisoners of War and Internees) representative in Bandung, whose task was made very difficult by the boycott of
October 6 and growing pemuda control over the city. The RAPWI was an
organization improvised after the Japanese surrender to provide emergency relief for prisoners of war and internees in Sumatra and Java. Its
members were a heterogeneous group, consisting in large degree, however, of military men who had been trained for parachute drops behind
Japanese lines in the event of an Allied invasion. In most cases RAPWI
officers were the first Allied personnel to be seen by the Indonesians,
and their behavior was watched very closely for indications of future
Allied policy. Their mission was primarily one of mercy (though they
did collect intelligence on the side), but it was bound to have a political
impact. Collecting food and supplies for the suspect Dutch and Eurasians was in itself likely to be met with hostility from the more militant
pemuda. When the pemuda instituted boycotts, they came into direct conflict with RAPWI. Gray had been parachuted into Bandung on September 17. See Smail, *Bandung*, pp. 64–65; and Donnison, *British Military
Administration*, pp. 283–85.

[33] For accounts of the October 10 *coup de force*, see Smail, *Bandung*,
pp. 62–63; Djèn Amar, *Bandung lautan api*, pp. 82–84; and Indonesia,
Kementerian Penerangan, *Republik Indonesia Propinsi Djawa Barat*
(Djakarta, 1953–54), pp. 181–83.

[34] Djèn Amar, *Bandung lautan api*, p. 97. October 10 was long to be
remembered as the Day of Peujeum Bol, *peujeum* being a Sundanese
word for a sweet, sticky dish of fermented cassava. The word was used,
especially by Javanese, to indicate scorn for what they considered the
softness of the Sundanese pemuda in this crisis.

(Gurkha) Brigade, in fulfillment of Mountbatten's plans, all was quiet. It was to be a whole month before the revolutionary impetus was felt again in the City of Flowers.

Central Java and Semarang

The course of events in Central Java differed strikingly from that in Bandung. In part this was because the Allies arrived there later and in smaller numbers. In part, too, it was because the local Japanese commander, Gen. Junji Nakamura, was decidedly more sympathetic to the nationalist movement than Mabuchi, had considerably fewer men under his authority, and had his headquarters neither in the great port city of Semarang nor in the old royal capitals of Surakarta and Jogjakarta, but in the small hill town of Magelang. But the situation was also affected by the fact that the province contained the Javanese principalities, in strong traditional rivalry with each other, yet at the same time forming powerful foci of Javanese nationalism. Thus when Semarang fell to a Japanese *coup de force,* the disaster did not have the same devastating consequences that Mabuchi's recapture of power had had in Bandung. Beyond the hills above Semarang the revolutionary movement continued to build up momentum almost without interruption.

In the ancient royal city of Surakarta, the process of taking over the installations of civil power had proceeded at an accelerating pace through the last days of September. The movement had not been confined to the usual targets of pemuda attention, such as the radio station, the telecommunications center, banks, and government buildings. It had also spread out beyond the city limits to the great sugar plantations in Klaten and Sragen. Leadership was assumed by a variety of pemuda groups, some from the Barisan Pelopor, others from the nucleus of Angkatan Muda members who had attended the Villa Isola Congress and maintained contacts with the API group in Djakarta, and still others from the disbanded Peta.[35] By the end of September the

[35] An excellent detailed account of the revolutionary movement in Surakarta is contained in an unpublished manuscript entitled "Surakarta

seizure of civil power was complete, and on October 1 a massive parade was held around the city to celebrate Surakarta's independence. Formally the head of government in the city was Mr. K. R. T. Sumodiningrat, chairman of the local KNI, but he was essentially only a figurehead.[36]

Thereafter, pemuda attention turned to the military, and to the question of arms. Negotiations led by former members of the Peta, such as Suadi, Sunarto, and Iskandar, with the Japanese commander, Lieutenant Colonel Mase, resulted on October 3 in an agreement that most of the Japanese troops would retire to extemporized relocation camps near Bojolali and Tampir.[37] By October 6 the relocation process was well advanced, few Japanese were left in the city, and a considerable number of arms had passed into pemuda possession. The last center of resistance was the headquarters of the hated Kenpeitai. But even here further negotiations, reinforced by the visible threat of a mass attack by pemuda, police, and BKR, ensured a virtually bloodless surrender on October 13.[38] The youthful Susuhunan Pakubuwono XII emerged briefly from his palace to make a tour of the city, praising the bravery of its population, though the British RAPWI representative, Wing Commander Tull, reported to his superiors in Djakarta that he seemed to be merely a puppet in his capital, hardly daring to speak to Tull for fear of being charged with pro-Allied sympathies.[39]

In the rival city of Jogjakarta, the process was similar, except

---

Hadiningrat dalam baranja api revolusi," compiled by Toekiran Notowardojo, Sujatno Josodipuro, Sadjimin Surobusono and Mardjio, dated November 10, 1963. An official, if less complete account, may be found in Surakarta, Djawatan Penerangan Kota Besar Surakarta, *Kenang-Kenangan Kota Besar Surakarta, 1945–1953* (Surakarta, 1953), pp. 3–4.

[36] *Warta Indonesia,* Oct. 2, 1945; "Surakarta Hadiningrat."

[37] "Sedjarah TNI, Diponegoro," p. 31. Mase commanded Battalion 155, the garrison troops for the city.

[38] *Antara,* Oct. 15, 1945. For details, see Surakarta, Djawatan Penerangan Kota Besar Surakarta, *Kenang-Kenangan,* p. 3.

[39] *Antara,* Oct. 15, 1945. See also "Tull Report," IC-RVO doc. no. 007414–53. Wing Commander Tull, originally trained for parachute operations against the Japanese on Java, was reassigned for RAPWI duty in

that here the traditional ruler played an active leading role. On October 5 Sultan Hamengkubuwono IX issued a proclamation establishing the Special District of Jogjakarta as a single unit within the Republic of Indonesia, while the Japanese Resident was arrested by pemuda led by the local police.[40] Tension increased on October 6, when open fighting broke out between the Kenpeitai, aided by elements from the elite Kidōbutai (Armored Corps), and the local BKR.[41] After some casualties, mainly on the Indonesian side (the press reported 18 dead and 42 wounded), the Japanese surrendered on October 7. At the same time Kaigun personnel at the Maguwo airfield handed over their equipment virtually intact to local pemuda trainees.[42]

In Magelang, General Nakamura began turning over considerable quantities of arms as early as October 5. In spite of Commander Tull's protests the process continued on the following day. Later that night, under cover of darkness, the bulk of the Japanese abandoned the city to the Indonesians, moving down to the strategic junction at Ambarawa on the road to Semarang.[43]

Central Java at the end of the war. He landed by parachute in Magelang on September 18. His minutely detailed notes and generally humane and objective viewpoint make the "Tull Report" an invaluable source for understanding the fast changing situation in Central Java from September to December 1945.

[40] Indonesia, Kementerian Penerangan, *Republik Indonesia Daerah Istimewa Jogjakarta*, p. 36. The administrative unification of the two royal courts in Jogjakarta, the Sultanate and the Pakualaman, thereby achieved, was never to be paralleled in Surakarta. See below, Chapter 15. For the pemuda attack on the Japanese Resident, see "Sedjarah TNI, Diponegoro," p. 21.

[41] *Antara,* Oct. 8, 1945; *Dokumentasi pemuda,* p. 38; Pusat Sedjarah Militer Angkatan Darat, *Peranan TNI-Angkatan Darat,* pp. 55–57.

[42] Interview with Mohammed Saleh Werdisastro, Jan. 3, 1963; for biographical details on Saleh, see the Appendix. In an interview granted on September 19, 1962, Sajuti Melik remarked that one of the reasons why the Japanese surrendered considerable quantities of arms to the pemuda in the Jogjakarta-Surakarta area was that Maeda had made a series of telephone calls urging local commanders to do so.

[43] "Tull Report." According to "Sedjarah TNI, Diponegoro," p. 29, and Indonesia, Kementerian Penerangan, *Republik Indonesia Propinsi Djawa Tengah* (Djakarta, 1953–54), p. 25, the exodus from Magelang took

In Semarang itself, however, the situation evolved very differently. As early as September 14, at the initiative of prominent local pemuda like S. Karno and Ibnu Parna, government buildings had begun to fly the Indonesian flag without the Hinomaru, while that very evening, a reported 10,000 people gathered to hear a "calming" speech by the Resident of Semarang, Mr. Wongsonagoro.[44] Thereafter the typical pattern of takeovers was set in motion. By October 1 most of the civilian installations in the port city had fallen into the hands of the local pemuda. Plantations and factories in the immediate vicinity were spontaneously seized by the workers employed there.[45] On October 12 Wongsonagoro, who had cultivated good relations with the pemuda and had already conducted successful, if minor, negotiations with both Commander Tull and the Japanese, was appointed governor of Central Java, replacing R. P. Soeroso, whose leadership up to this point had been less than decisive.[46] Although Wongsonagoro had managed to have a considerable amount of arms transferred and had secured the surrender of the Kenpeitai without difficulty, there remained the problem of the Kidōbutai. These elite troops refused to yield any of their weapons and remained on guard at their barracks in Djatingaleh, on the hills immediately behind Semarang, where they were strategically placed to cover all entrances into the city.

The atmosphere in Semarang began to deteriorate rapidly from October 12 onward, as news of the Mabuchi coup in Bandung and of the growing British presence in West Java

place on October 7. Tull, on the other hand, gives the date October 13. It appears that the main forces in Magelang left on the earlier date, while Nakamura himself stayed until the later date, when he surrendered the few weapons remaining.

[44] Kenpeitai (Semarang), "Daily Reports," IC-RVO doc. no. 006743–61.

[45] *Antara*, Oct. 4, 1945.

[46] *Ibid.*, Oct. 13, 1945. Soeroso became government high commissioner to the Central Java Principalities. Wongsonagoro was relieved as resident of Semarang by Mr. Besar on October 13, 1945 (*Warta Indonesia*, Oct. 13, 1945).

spread across the island. Pemuda suspicions about Japanese intentions were further heightened when General Nakamura provided armed escorts to help Commander Tull move prisoners from the great internment camps near Magelang and Ambarawa down into Semarang. The shift of Japanese forces toward the coast as a result of the evacuation of Magelang did nothing to allay their fears. Incidents in which small groups of pemuda clashed with individual Japanese soldiers grew more frequent, and the intimidation of Chinese and Eurasian elements thought to be preparing for the arrival of the Allies became common. On the morning of October 14 armed pemuda began arresting members of Tull's improvised staff, particularly Eurasians and Japanese. By dusk Semarang was a tinderbox, with scattered groups of pemuda circulating through the city streets, fearful of a Mabuchi-style coup and prepared to credit the most sinister rumors of Japanese intentions. When Japanese units moved to take control of the tower that supplied most of Semarang's water, word sped from mouth to mouth that the city reservoir was being poisoned.[47] Later that evening a group of students from the Taman Siswa commercial school invaded the Japanese officers' mess in Tjandi Baru, not far below the Kidōbutai barracks.

Perhaps because they sensed that a crisis was imminent, the Japanese now took the offensive. During the night the Kidōbutai began moving northward down into the city, clearing out pemuda clustered in Djatingaleh and Tjandi Baru and killing a considerable number of them. It promised to be Bandung all over again, and the pemuda reaction was instinctive and terrible. The previous evening a group of civilian Japanese, variously estimated at between 250 and 400 in all, employed at the Tjepiring steel plant about 25 miles west of Semarang, had been arrested and brought to the old Bulu Prison in the city. Now, late in the evening of

[47] *Warta Indonesia*, Oct. 23, 1945; "Sedjarah TNI, Diponegoro," p. 46. Such rumors were common during the months of October and November, and often had the most devastating consequences. Cf. Smail, *Bandung*, pp. 105–9.

October 15, these prisoners became the victims of the pemuda's fear and desire for revenge. At least 130 were horribly murdered, and 60 more vanished. In other parts of the city isolated Japanese were also murdered. Subsequently the Japanese estimated that at least 250 died.[48]

When the Kidōbutai discovered what had happened, they reacted with unrestrained fury. Although the Kidōbutai nucleus was only 500 men, other Japanese were given arms, bringing the force up to 1,100. In a massive body they swept down through the city. No prisoners were taken. Those with arms or suspected of carrying arms were killed on the spot. Truckloads of Indonesians were driven off into the countryside and never seen or heard of again.[49] Wongsonagoro was arrested in his gubernatorial mansion and taken down to the blood-wet Bulu jail. Only the knowledge that there were still 300 Japanese hostages in Ambarawa and about 75 on the east side of Semarang prevented the enraged Japanese from executing him then and there. Eventually he was sent off to negotiate their release, and managed to get at least the Ambarawa pemuda to release their prisoners, on the condition that the Japanese retire again to Djatingaleh. In the meantime, however, reports of bitter fighting in Semarang drew hundreds of pemuda into the city from nearby towns and villages, and in the despair that followed the Japanese sweep, the 75 hostages in East Semarang were murdered.[50]

It took the Japanese until October 19 to clear the city completely. An estimated 2,000 Indonesians had died in the six-day battle, and possibly 500 Japanese.[51] And the bloodshed was not over. In reprisal for the slaughter of the Semarang pemuda, 86

[48] "Report on the Semarang Incident," prepared by the officer commanding the Fifth Guard Unit, IC-RVO doc. no. 006762–3; cf. Pusat Sedjarah Militer Angkatan Darat, *Peranan TNI,* pp. 60–62.

[49] "Tull Report."

[50] Interview with Mr. Wongsonagoro, March 31, 1964. He and a number of pemuda leaders were briefly rearrested.

[51] *Merdeka,* Oct. 20, 1945. "Sedjarah TNI, Diponegoro" (p. 47) estimates that 850 Japanese and 2,000 Indonesians died.

of Maeda's naval personnel, traveling by train from Semarang to Djakarta, were stopped at Pegaden Baru near Tjikampek and hauled away to be tortured to death.[52] On October 20 Brigadier General Bethell, commander of the Forty-ninth Brigade, arrived to take control of a silent, devastated city.

Bethell now contacted Wongsonagoro, and an agreement was reached whereby the Indonesians would fulfill the supply needs of the Allied troops and not hinder their rescue operations, while the British would not tamper with Indonesian sovereignty.[53] Small units of Gurkhas pushed south to Ambarawa and Magelang, where well over 10,000 internees, mainly women and children, were being held. Reaching Magelang on October 26, the Allied troops took over the town. Almost at once conflict developed over the behavior of certain Dutchmen attached to RAPWI, and a boycott was organized in reprisal by local pemuda. On October 30, under the influence of events in Surabaja, fighting broke out in Semarang and spread rapidly to Magelang.[54] Fearing the possibility of an Allied strike into the heartland of the Jogjakarta-Surakarta plain, armed Indonesian bands began pouring into the outskirts of Magelang from the south.[55] Only repeated air strikes from Semarang prevented the Gurkhas from being overwhelmed.

In this emergency the British felt they had no recourse but to

[52] The "Report on the Semarang Incident" says that the group was under the command of Captain Takeshita and was on its way to an internment camp prior to repatriation. Maeda later said that he almost committed suicide when he heard the news ("Statement," April 20, 1946). He cannot have been consoled by the very abrupt tone of Sukarno's official letter to him, which expressed regret at what had happened but accused the dead men of having traveled with concealed weapons (Sukarno, "Letter to Maeda," Nov. 26, 1945, IC-RVO doc. no. 011240).

[53] Santosa, "Serangan di Ambarawa, 1945" (B.A. thesis, University of Gadjah Mada, 1967), p. 10.

[54] Doulton, *Fighting Cock*, p. 268.

[55] Santosa ("Serangan di Ambarawa, 1945," pp. 13–15) gives excellent details on Indonesian activities in and around Magelang. Reinforcements poured in especially from Kedu, Jogjakarta, and Banjumas.

turn to Sukarno (as we shall see, they had just done so in
Surabaja). On November 1 Sukarno and Amir Sjarifuddin flew
to Semarang. After failing initially to arrange a truce there they
proceeded south via Magelang to discuss the situation with military leaders in Jogjakarta. By the next morning a cease-fire was
arranged and an agreement drawn up whereby the Allies would
be permitted to retain whatever troops they felt necessary to
protect the internees in Magelang, the Magelang-Semarang road
would be kept open for rescue convoys, and NICA personnel
would be forbidden to carry out any activities on pain of instant
removal. So-called contact bodies for liaison were set up in
Semarang, Ambarawa, and Magelang to head off possible trouble.[56]

The agreement was kept by both sides until the news of the
Allied assault on Surabaja broke on November 10. Thereafter
suspicion and fear mounted rapidly. On November 18 Bethell
arrested Wongsonagoro in reprisal for the murder of three of
his officers the previous day. An attempt to capture pemuda headquarters failed, and as a consequence of an Indonesian counter-
attack, the British lost control of the center of the city. Only after
reinforcements arrived from Surabaja and heavy strafing and
bombing were carried out did Bethell regain the upper hand.
Some of the reinforcements were then sent to the relief of Ambarawa and Magelang. In the case of Magelang they were too
late. Early on the morning of November 21, the Gurkhas were
forced to abandon Magelang, leaving behind some 3,000 Eurasians who had fled from the interior in fear of their lives. The
same day the siege of Ambarawa began. The Allies found themselves in a difficult position. Pemuda had barricaded themselves
into the town jail, and resisted the assaults of tanks and shelling
by antitank guns. It was only when Royal Air Force Thunder-
bolts were summoned for air strikes and heavy artillery was

[56] Doulton, *Fighting Cock,* pp. 270–71; Santosa, "Serangan di Ambarawa, 1945," pp. 16–18. The text of the agreement can be found in
Kedaulatan Rakjat (Jogjakarta), Nov. 3, 1945.

brought into action that a breach was cleared through which the
Gurkhas could attack. In the meantime at least one of the internment camps was grenaded and burned by angry bands of Indonesians. Constant raids from the hills above the town kept the
Allied units under heavy pressure.[57] By the end of the month it
was decided to withdraw from Ambarawa. Though the cruiser
H.M.S. *Sussex* had been brought in to shell the heights of
Ungaran to keep the Ambarawa-Semarang road open, the position of the Allied troops was increasingly untenable. And with
the last internees successfully evacuated to the port city, Ambarawa was abandoned. Bethell had completed his major assignment, but the Allied presence was now confined to Semarang
alone, and the rest of Central Java was left completely in the
hands of the Republic.[58] The Indonesians were overjoyed, and
with no small justification regarded the Allied retreat as a strategic military victory, all the more to be savored after the blood-
bath in Surabaja.

Surabaja

The coup in Bandung had been an almost bloodless affair, the
local pemuda being inadequately prepared to make any effective
resistance. The bloodshed in Semarang had shown for the first
time the potential ferocity of the pemuda movement in the face
of the enemies of merdeka; the subsequent battle for Magelang
and Ambarawa proved how militarily effective this ferocity could
be when combined with favorable terrain and capable leadership.
But it was in Surabaja that the character of the pemuda consciousness would be revealed most memorably.

On the evening of October 1 bitter clashes between Indonesian
and Dutch youths rapidly grew into mass actions across the city,
with swarms of pemuda invading Morokrembangan airfield

[57] Doulton, *Fighting Cock*, pp. 271–75. For a detailed account of
Indonesian military operations during the siege of Ambarawa, see Santosa,
"Serangan di Ambarawa, 1945," chap. 3.

[58] Doulton, *Fighting Cock*, p. 275. Cf. Mountbatten, *Post-Surrender
Tasks*, p. 293.

(which fell into their hands about midnight) and the large internment camp located in the Darmo residential area.[59] Early in the afternoon of the following day a major attack was launched on the Kenpeitai building, while both the army and the navy headquarters were surrounded by crowds of rioters armed with everything from machine guns to bamboo spears. Before night came both the Kenpeitai headquarters and the naval barracks at Udjung had fallen.[60]

As in other parts of Java, the situation in Surabaja was decisively affected by the attitudes of the local Japanese authorities. The 56-year-old Vice-Adm. Yaichirō Shibata scarcely concealed his support of Indonesian independence. As early as the end of August he had begun to give arms to certain pemuda elements. Now, though he was anxious to protect the lives of his own men, he had no inclination to play the role of a Mabuchi.[61] The local army commander, Major General Iwabe, evidently not a man of strong character, was willing to follow Shibata's lead.

A second factor of major importance was that the initial Allied representative in Surabaja was not British, but Dutch, namely a certain Captain Huijer of the Royal Dutch Navy. Huijer's presence in Surabaja was the result of a private war being conducted against the British high command by Admiral Helf-

[59] Vice-Adm. Yaichirō Shibata, "Statement" of July 31, Aug. 1, 3, 19, 1946, IC-RVO doc. no. 006948–67; Capt. P. J. G. Huyer [Huijer], "Report on the Surabaja Affair," IC-RVO doc. no. 007177–9.

[60] *Warta Indonesia,* Oct. 4, 1945; Huyer [Huijer], "Report on the Surabaja Affair." See also Shibata, "Report" (IC-RVO doc. no. 059331) for some graphic details of the events of October 2.

[61] Shibata's sympathies with Southeast Asian nationalism were not new. In October 1935 he was among a group of prominent Japanese who welcomed the Filipino Sakdalista leader, Benigno Ramos, to Tokyo. Shibata told Ramos that after visiting the Philippines twice he was convinced that the Japanese and the Filipinos were of the same color and looked enough alike to be mistaken for one another, and that more Filipino students should be sent to Japan to increase the spiritual amity between the two peoples. For details, see Grant K. Goodman, *Four Aspects of Philippine-Japanese Relations, 1930–1940* (New Haven, Conn., 1967), pp. 153–56.

rich, the commander-in-chief of the Dutch forces attached to SEAC, who was determined that whatever mistakes had been made in Djakarta and Semarang, the Dutch would be the first to take control of the huge naval base in Surabaja. Huijer had flown into the city on September 23 for a preliminary inspection of the situation and five days later returned with orders from Rear Admiral Patterson simply to "prepare for the re-occupation of Surabaja." [62] But mindful of Helfrich's private instructions and at the same time bewildered by the apparent chaos and anarchy prevailing in the city, Huijer proceeded on October 3 to make the mistake that precipitated the Surabaja crisis.

At 6:30 P.M. that day, after talking to the KNI leaders in the city, Huijer appeared at Shibata's headquarters, escorted by a contingent of the Indonesian Special Police (the former Tokubetsu Keisatsutai). He warned the Admiral that attacks were being planned by Indonesian "extremists" on all three major naval installations in the city that night, and suggested that Shibata surrender everything under his command to Huijer *pro forma*. It would then become Allied property; the KNI had undertaken to guard these supplies and weapons until the arrival of Allied troops.[63] To Shibata this offer must have seemed a godsend. With calm irony he surrendered his ceremonial sword to the agitated Captain. The Admiral was not only fully acquitted by this action of any responsibility for further developments in the city; he was also well aware that neither Huijer nor very probably the KNI was in a position to make the second part of the agreement stick. Huijer had proposed the arrangement because he felt that the KNI, which in his eyes was composed of moderates like Sudirman and Doel Arnowo, would be preferable as guardians of the weapons to the Japanese, who might allow

[62] Wehl, *Birth of Indonesia*, p. 51. This was confirmed by Colonel A. G. Vromans in talks with the author at the Rijksinstituut voor Oorlogsdocumentatie, Amsterdam, in July 1964.

[63] Shibata, "Statement"; Rear Adm. Takeo Mori, officer in charge of the naval repair yard in Surabaja, "Statement" of Aug. 2, 1946, IC-RVO doc. no. 006969–72.

them to be taken by "extremist" groups that could not be controlled by anyone.[64] In the event, of course, the KNI had neither
the power nor the inclination to keep the agreement. Virtually all
the guns and ammunition belonging to the naval command in
Surabaja fell nominally to the KNI and the Special Police, but in
practice to the BKR, pemuda groups, police squads, and still less
organized bands.

By October 4 Surabaja was an armed camp completely in
Indonesian hands. The prisons had by now all been opened up,
and the inmates, whether they had been confined on political or
criminal charges, had joined the city crowds.[65] On that day
Shibata informed his subordinates that Huijer was now responsible for security in the city. Weapons still in Japanese hands
should be handed over to the Indonesians, provided a receipt for
them was given. The Indonesians would be responsible for turning them over to the Allies! [66] The same day Iwabe turned over
many of his arms to the Indonesian police to help them "keep
order." [67]

By October 8, Shibata noted, the Governor, the BKR, and
the police were gradually losing their remaining grip on the city,
which was drifting into virtually complete "anarchy." [68] The

[64] Probably the arrangement also salvaged Dutch pride, for here at least
one Japanese officer surrendered to a Dutchman, and not to an English-
man. It should be noted that elsewhere RAPWI officers were not
empowered to accept Japanese surrenders, since the British command
understood the dangers of relieving the Japanese of their law-and-order
responsibilities before it could muster sufficient forces to assume them
itself.

[65] Among them were two pemuda, Sudisman and Tjugito, who were
to play important parts in the Surabaja drama and later in the left wing
of the revolutionary independence movement. *Dokumentasi pemuda,*
p. 45. In the 1950's and 1960's they became top figures in the Indonesian
Communist Party. For biographical details, see the Appendix.

[66] Shibata, "Statement"; Mori, "Statement."

[67] Hiroshi Watanabe (governor of Surakarta, March 1943 to Oct.
1945), "Statement" of May 23, 1946, IC-RVO doc. no. 005809–11. Cf.
Warta Indonesia, Oct. 5, 1945.

[68] Shibata, "Statement"; cf. the "Addendum on the East Java Situation,"
IC-RVO doc. no. 005877–8.

long suppressed hostility to the Japanese among the pemuda, already intensified by the release of Kenpeitai prisoners, was further heightened by suspicion of the Eurasians and Dutch internees who were reappearing in the city in great numbers, either fleeing from an increasingly dangerous situation in the interior or seeking food, shelter, and their old homes in the great city. Many were murdered as NICA spies. The Bubutan Prison in the heart of Surabaja was the scene of executions of Japanese prisoners, performed in some cases by pemuda in a state of almost religious ecstasy.[69]

Meanwhile, certain pemuda leaders were attempting to impose some coherence on the revolutionary elements in the city. The earlier PRI, formed around the nucleus of Sumarsono, Ruslan Widjaja, Krissubanu, and Kaslan, found itself increasingly pushed out of the limelight after the arrival in Surabaja on October 12 of the 25-year-old Soetomo, soon to be known all over Java as Bung Tomo. Bung Tomo was at first glance an odd man to become the prime symbol of the pemuda movement in Java at this time. As we have already seen, in the prewar period he had managed to get a good secondary Dutch education, and had been prominent in the scout movement in East Java. He had then worked as a journalist, and in the Japanese period was employed by the Dōmei news agency in Surabaja. Nothing seemed to indicate the role he was about to play.

When he returned from Djakarta on October 12, he brought with him the idea that was to make him famous—the idea of setting up a radio station, which he called Radio Pemberontakan (Radio Rebellion), as a means of creating mass solidarity and intensifying pemuda fighting spirit. The unique authority Bung Tomo rapidly achieved, however, would perhaps have been im-

---

[69] Doel Arnowo related that when he arrived on the scene with Dr. Mustopo, the head of the Surabaja BKR, he found pemuda ceremonially drinking Japanese blood from the samurai swords with which the executions had been carried out. Questioned by the two leaders, the pemuda answered that they were imbibing the courage and bravery of the Japanese who had died at their hands. Interview with Doel Arnowo, August 13, 1962. Cf. *Dokumentasi pemuda,* p. 54.

possible had it not been that throughout October the normal, organized structure of authority in Surabaja gradually disintegrated, with KNI, BKR, and pangrèh pradja leaders desperately trying to control the surging masses. In this situation, Bung Tomo's voice, carried over the hundreds of radio sets previously distributed by the Japanese to disseminate war propaganda in the urban kampung, focused revolutionary energies as nothing else could have done. This passionate, disembodied voice, summoning Allah's help and protection in a strong Surabaja accent, and calling on all Indonesians to defend their merdeka, provided leadership without imposing hierarchies, and inspiration without enforcing organizational controls.

On October 13, indeed, Bung Tomo also began the formation of the Barisan Pemberontakan Republik Indonesia (Insurgent Corps of the Republic of Indonesia), or BPRI, as a separate organization from the Sumarsono-led PRI. But it was typical both of Soetomo and of the period that the BPRI was less an organization as such than a jumble of spontaneously formed traditional-style bands owing loose loyalty to a radio transmitter and its chief. Soetomo's appeals were specifically aimed at groups outside or below the bureaucratic and political elite of the Dutch and Japanese colonial eras, groups growing up from the anonymous depths of society and expressing the thrust of a "red" merdeka (in Henri Alers' sense of the word). Thus Soetomo was among the first to summon the djago of the Surabaja kampung to mobilize the urban masses against the Japanese and the Allies.[70] The authority of the djago was intensely personal, resting on their *silat* (traditional art of self-defense) skills, their possession of the lore of invulnerability, their armature of amulets, charms, daggers, and the like, and the mingled fear and admiration with which the kampung dwellers regarded them.

[70] S. T. Tjarly, ed., *Gelanggang repolusi: Sepuluh tahun proklamasi* (Djakarta, 1955), p. 17. On djago, see Chapter 1 above; on their role in the revolution, see Smail, *Bandung*, p. 88. P. M. van Wulfften Palthe's *Over het bendewezen op Java* (Amsterdam, 1950) is also interesting on this subject, though the author's hand-me-down Freudianism tends to mar his argument.

Bung Tomo's broadcasts, always opening with the cry "Allahuakbar! Allahuakbar!" also did not fail to stir "red" leaders in the santri community in Surabaja, in lowland and coastal East Java, and in the devoutly Moslem island of Madura. From early October onward, rural kjai had begun moving into the harbor metropolis. In their wake came the inmates of their pesantrèn, drawn out of their isolated retreats by the general sense of impending crisis. On October 21 and 22 the Nahdatul Ulama of all Java and Madura held a gigantic meeting in Surabaja in which they demanded that "the government of the Republic of Indonesia express a clear attitude and take appropriate action against every effort to imperil the independence of religion and the Indonesian state, particularly towards the Dutch and their henchmen; and that the government order the continuance of a struggle with the character 'sabiloellah' [holy war] for the maintenance of the independent state of the Republic of Indonesia and the religion of Islam." [71]

But no less important than his mastery of radio communication and the skill with which he appealed to those hitherto neglected local leaders who could mobilize popular resistance was Bung Tomo's creation of a personal style and legend out of the pemuda tradition. His public promise that he would touch no woman until the Dutch were driven from the land might perhaps be harmonized with the ideals of austerity and commitment of the twentieth-century revolutionary. But his vow that his hair would remain unshorn until Indonesia was free was drawn straight from the djago tradition. [72] For many, certainly, Bung

[71] *Antara,* Oct. 25, 1945; *Berita Indonesia* (Djakarta), Oct. 27, 1945. The Nahdatul Ulama, founded in 1926 as a rival to the modernist Muhammadijah, is the organization of Javanized Islam. It has always had its main strength in East Java and Madura. Because it was an explicitly religious and educational body, it was spared, as was the Muhammadijah, when the Japanese dissolved all political parties and associations.

[72] There is a fine evocative photograph of Bung Tomo making one of his famous radio speeches in Indonesia, Kementerian Penerangan, *Lukisan Revolusi, 1945–1950* (Djakarta, n.d.), p. 138. On page 108 there is a picture of an anonymous pemuda leader very much accoutred in the Bung Tomo style. Later on, when the revolutionary élan of 1945–46

Tomo's style, which was imitated all over Java, seemed the quintessence of revolutionary self-abnegation and courage. But for many others this style, based on negations of ordinary Javanese values, had a classical quality, appropriate to a society that was in a state of *kegelisahan* as it moved inexorably from one epoch to another.

The British finally made their appearance in the harbor of Tandjung Perak on October 25. Brigadier General Mallaby, commander of the Forty-ninth (Indian) Brigade, began moving his three thousand men into Surabaja as fast as the limited transportation available permitted. He was faced with a difficult situation, for while the main area of British encampment was to be at the north end of the town, in the working-class districts adjoining the docks, the camps where the internees were awaiting evacuation stood in the residential suburb of Darmo, at least seven miles farther south, with the business district, indeed the main area of the city, lying in between. It was only too likely that under the disturbed conditions prevailing in Surabaja, British efforts to establish regular communications between the docks and Darmo and the regular flow of white-skinned people through the city would arouse suspicion among the anxious population.

Mallaby himself and his deputy, Colonel Pugh, were greeted cordially at first by Mustopo, the 32-year-old former dentist acting as head of the city BKR, and by Atmadji, a former Gerindo activist in charge of the naval arm of the BKR in the dock areas. After talks with Mustopo, who was given to understand that "Allied troops would not smuggle in Dutch troops and NICA when they came," the British began moving troops down to Darmo across the heart of the city.[73] The Indonesians

---

ebbed, and Bung Tomo's reputation went into eclipse, the style he exemplified drew criticism from some quarters. There is a bitingly satirical portrait of him in Idrus' classic long short-story "Surabaja," which can be found translated into English in *Indonesia*, no. 5 (April 1968), pp. 1–28 (see esp. pp. 24–25).

[73] Doulton, *Fighting Cock*, p. 250; Pusat Sedjarah Militer Angkatan Darat, *Kronologi*, p. 61; *Antara*, Oct. 31, 1945. The quotation is from Raliby, *Documenta Historica*, p. 36.

were informed that the Allied soldiers were there simply to evacuate Japanese troops and internees.[74] The Gurkha commander, Major Indarjit Singh, reportedly told the Surabajans, "We respect the sentiment of the Indonesians for their struggle for independence." [75] In response to this encouraging atmosphere, the PRI even organized a reception for the Allied officers with bouquets of flowers and entertainment for the troops.

It is possible that Mallaby, who was without effective intelligence on the real situation in Surabaja, was misled by the initial greeting he received.[76] In any case that night he made the mistake of sending a platoon of his Field Security Section 611 under Captain Shaw to rescue Captain Huijer and his friends, who had been arrested (for their own safety) at Sudirman's orders two weeks before. David Wehl reports that Mustopo himself was compelled to join the rescue party, and thus lost considerable prestige.[77] In any case this British intervention on behalf of a man generally regarded as a NICA provocateur immediately dispelled the mood of October 26. The situation deteriorated further the next afternoon, when there was an apparently unexpected airdrop of pamphlets over the city on the orders of Major General Hawthorn, the Allied commander in Djakarta. These pamphlets, of which Mallaby knew nothing, gave the Indonesians 48 hours to surrender their arms. The pamphlets also called for the immediate clearing of the harbor area and the end of a pemuda-led food boycott against the Dutch and Eurasians. Such demands, which in effect abrogated the Mallaby-Mustopo entente, undercut what trust remained on the Indonesian side. Mallaby asked Mustopo to broadcast to the population explaining the new situation, but Mustopo had lost all confidence in British intentions and refused to comply. The city's mood was changing rapidly:

[74] A full text of the agreement is given in *Dokumentasi pemuda,* p. 56.
[75] *Antara,* Oct. 27, 1945.
[76] Wehl, *Birth of Indonesia,* p. 52.
[77] Indonesian silence on this affair, indeed the complete blackout on Mustopo at this time in the press, is perhaps an indirect indication of the story's truth.

Everywhere one could sense uneasiness: in the people, in the cars roaring past along the streets, in the printing presses, and in the dogs. The dogs barked themselves hoarse till their voices were gone and their bellies collapsed like flat bicycle tires; no one remembered to feed them. Everywhere people were saying the same thing: "Of course, the Allies aren't our enemies, but still they're killing and kidnapping people in Djakarta." And like a badly-trained choir they shouted: "We won't be treated like the people in Djakarta! We refuse such treatment! We'll fight! We've got revolvers and knives!"

These shouts rent the sky. But the Indonesian leaders were also rending the hearts of the people: they were trying with all their might to explain to the people that the Allies would not act as they had done in Djakarta. The Allies would only take away their prisoners of war and the Japanese. The hearts of the people were torn in two: one half believed what the leaders said, but the other half was still suspicious of the Allied forces. Nonetheless they restrained themselves and watched with resentment the Allies land. The Allied soldiers, black as locomotives, were suspected by the cowboys of being bandits who had been given permission to run loose and wreak their will. And when the bandits did run loose, like birds in the air, and wreaked their will, like the late lamented Hitler, the whole community became very upset. Nothing was safe: cattle, girls, gold, not even the revolvers and knives of the cowboys. Along the streets the cowboys were stopped by the bandits and forced to surrender their weapons. The bandits shouted, as they raised their bayonets: "Your gun or your life!" The cowboys did not put up their hands, nor were they prepared to surrender their weapons. They shouted back: "Take our lives!" And as they shouted these words, they began to fire. The bandits too opened fire and a fierce fight ensued.[78]

By the morning of October 28 "doom was in the air." [79] As Mountbatten recalled:

Our forces put up road-blocks, and seized about 30 civilian-owned motor vehicles: many of these motor-cars were found to contain arms,

[78] Idrus, "Surabaja," pp. 2–3. The reason that the Allied "bandit" forces are described as "black as locomotives" is, of course, that most of them were dark-skinned Indians or Gurkhas.

[79] Doulton, *Fighting Cock,* p. 252.

which our troops confiscated. The anger of the Indonesians on having their mobility limited was aggravated by the removal by the troops of the Indonesian flag from some of the vehicles; moreover, the Indonesians complained that the confiscation of arms found in the cars was contrary to the terms of the leaflets, which had stipulated a 48-hour limit.[80]

Indian troops arrived at Morokrembangan airfield and gave the Indonesians a four-hour ultimatum to abandon it. The municipal railway offices, the telephone and telegraph center, the Darmo hospital, and other key buildings were also occupied.[81] At eleven o'clock Mustopo came to PRI headquarters to warn that the British were about to disarm the population forcibly and that he was going to withdraw all units under his command outside the city limits to prevent this from happening.[82]

At 5 P.M. Sumarsono went on the air to expose the deceits of the Allies and to declare, "It is better that we die here than have the honor of our country and our people violated." [83] But even before he spoke clashes had started that spread across the whole city as darkness fell. The British had about 4,000 troops in the city, very well armed but divided between the RAPWI camps at one end of the town and the harbor base at the other. The Indonesians, estimated at over 120,000 pemuda, with various types of arms, attacked all British encampments. By midnight, after heavy losses on both sides, the situation was such that "this heroic resistance [of the British] could only end in the extermination of the 49th Brigade unless somebody could quell the passions of the mob. There was no such person in Surabaja and all hope rested on the influence of Sukarno." [84] As Mustopo's BKR units flooded back into the city, a desperate message was wired to Djakarta. At General Hawthorn's personal urging Sukarno agreed to fly to Surabaja to try to stop the impending massacre of the Forty-ninth Brigade. Arriving on the morning of October 29

[80] *Post-Surrender Tasks,* p. 292.   [81] *Warta Indonesia,* Oct. 31, 1945.
[82] *Dokumentasi pemuda,* p. 57.   [83] *Ibid.,* p. 58.
[84] Doulton, *Fighting Cock,* p. 257.

with Hatta and Amir Sjarifuddin, he immediately went on the air to announce that he had come to stop the fighting.[85]

Negotiations opened formally the next morning between the British, represented by Mallaby and Hawthorn with the aid of Sukarno, Hatta, and Amir, and the Surabaja group, represented by Sudirman, Muhammad, and Soerjo as older leaders, and Sungkono, Bung Tomo, and a PRI representative as pemuda. In spite of strong resistance by the pemuda leaders, an agreement was finally reached, though firing continued in many parts of the city.[86] By the terms of the agreement the Allies would withdraw to Tandjung Perak and Darmo, while the Indonesians would permit free passage of internees between the two sectors. Both sides would exchange prisoners, and the Contact Bureau, originally formed when Mallaby landed, would be resuscitated and obeyed. Joint patrols would be instituted in sensitive areas. Most important, the Hawthorn ultimatum was effectively canceled and the Indonesian masses' right to bear arms was tacitly accepted.

The Djakarta leaders, assuming that the violence was now largely over, flew back to Djakarta in the afternoon. By 4:30 P.M., however, as the joint patrols were trying to reestablish order, firing broke out once again, and in a scene of inextricable confusion, Mallaby was killed.[87]

[85] Dokumentasi pemuda, p. 60.

[86] There is an acute description of these negotiations in Doulton, Fighting Cock, pp. 259–61. Doulton felt that actually Hawthorn alone realized how desperate the situation was for the British forces. See also Enquête-commissie (p. 712), where the commission concluded that if the British had not persuaded Sukarno to go to Surabaja, an entire brigade would have been wiped out. (The commission forbore to state that the same visit cost the lives of probably twice as many of Sukarno's fellow Indonesians in the long run.) Muhammad was secretary of the Surabaja KNI and former daidanchō in Buduran. Warta Indonesia, Oct. 5, 1945. Sungkono was also from the Peta, but held a junior rank.

[87] For different versions of how Mallaby was killed, see Wehl, Birth of Indonesia, pp. 60–61; Doulton, Fighting Cock, p. 262; Dokumentasi pemuda, p. 60; and "Official Statement of the Surabaya Contactbureau on the Death of Brigadier Mallaby," Nov. 1, 1945, IC-RVO doc. no. 056029. Doel Arnowo, who was head of the Contact Bureau and of the Surabaja

The death of the British general set the stage for the even more violent events that were to follow. British sympathies, hitherto somewhat on the Indonesian side, began to swing markedly toward the Dutch. The blow to Allied prestige, and the fear of what would happen if the example of Surabaja were followed elsewhere, especially in Central Java, where the situation was extremely tense, impelled the British to take drastic action. In Djakarta Christison issued a special proclamation in which he warned the Indonesians:

These direct and unprovoked attacks upon British forces cannot in any circumstances be permitted and unless the Indonesians who have committed these attacks surrender to my forces, I intend to bring the whole weight of my sea, land and air forces and all the weapons of modern war against them until they are crushed. If in this process Indonesians should be killed or wounded, the sole responsibility will rest with those Indonesians who have committed the crimes that I have named. . . . I am determined to maintain law and order and I look to all good Indonesians to support me in this task.[88]

At the same time Christison informed Sukarno and Hatta that Major General Mansergh would shortly arrive in Surabaja with the entire Fifth Indian Infantry Division and a full equipment of tanks.

It was in response to the anger of the British and the threat of massive bloodshed that on October 31 Sukarno made one of the most remarkable radio addresses of his life:

We know that the Indonesian army was well organized there; that the pemuda and workers had already formed well-knit units. But because of abuses of this strength of ours, and because we did not base our struggle on a strategy of cooperation with other parts of Indonesia nor on a strategy of long-term struggle, a situation has now arisen which has weakened our strength in Surabaja and in Indonesia.

KNI at the time, said he was convinced that Mallaby had been accidentally shot by his own men. Interview, Aug. 13, 1962.

[88] Wehl, *Birth of Indonesia,* p. 62; cf. Mountbatten, *Post-Surrender Tasks,* p. 292.

. . . As a result of these considerations I have ordered all fighting against the Allies to cease, not only in Surabaja but also in Magelang. . . . Only NICA profits by the struggle we have been carrying on against the Allies, while we have been weakened by using up no little part of our military resources. . . . NICA spreads the word that we are anti-Allied. . . . NICA says that the Indonesian government can not control its people. . . . When certain difficulties have arisen our people have acted so that the principles of humanity have been violated. Cruelty towards Dutchmen, looting of their property, are some examples of this. We know the reason why: the rage of the people at the actions and behavior of NICA. But there is no reason yet for groups among the people to take the law into their own hands. . . . You all know that a tiny grain of arsenic is enough to ruin a glass of water—so also in a nation. One incorrect action, even one incorrect action by an individual can ruin the whole upbuilding of the nation. . . . Don't let us be forced to face alone the whole military power of England and all the Allies. . . . If there are problems, we must and shall follow the path of peace, since the Indonesians are a peace-loving people. . . . Once again, I order all fighting with the Allies to cease. Carry out my orders. Merdeka! [89]

The appeal had momentary effect. Calm descended again on Surabaja. Then on November 1 the H.M.S. *Sussex* appeared in the harbor of Tandjung Perak. For the next week the evacuation of somewhere between 6,000 and 8,000 internees proceeded steadily. By November 9 all who wanted to leave had done so.[90] With these hostages now safely withdrawn from Indonesian hands, the British began their counterstroke of revenge for Mallaby's death.[91] As Idrus described it: "For some days now the Allies had been landing more soldiers and giant tanks. These tanks rolled down from the ships like the Angel of Death himself descending from the sky: silently and secretly." [92]

On November 9 General Mansergh issued an ultimatum de-

[89] *Antara,* Nov. 1, 1945.

[90] Doulton, *Fighting Cock,* pp. 264–65.

[91] Since all the internees who wished to be evacuated had embarked, the British were unable convincingly to claim humanitarian objectives for their assault on Surabaja.

[92] "Surabaja," p. 3.

manding that all arms in Surabaja be turned in by six o'clock the next morning, and that those Indonesians responsible for the death of Mallaby be surrendered. The ultimatum was dropped from the sky over the city.[93] It is quite clear that Mansergh's main objective was to inflict punishment for what had occurred on October 31. The time allowed was quite insufficient to collect the arms so widely distributed throughout the pemuda population of Surabaja. There was little chance of apprehending the "murderers" of Mallaby; it was not even certain that he had not been shot by his own men. Moreover Mansergh explicitly warned that all women and children should leave the city by seven o'clock that night, showing his intention of capturing the city by force of arms. Death sentences were threatened for any Indonesians carrying weapons after 6 A.M. November tenth.[94]

The older leaders in Surabaja immediately telephoned Djakarta to get a national-level decision on what reply should be made to the Mansergh ultimatum. But neither Sukarno himself nor Subardjo, the Foreign Minister, would make a decisive answer: the matter was the local responsibility of Surabaja. A heated debate now took place between the older leaders and the pemuda, and ultimately the latter won the day. It was decided to reject the ultimatum, and at eleven o'clock that night Governor Soerjo went on the air to announce the decision that Surabaja would resist to the last.[95]

At 6:00 A.M. on November 10 the British attack started, while Bung Tomo summoned the people of the city to rise up against the invaders. Heavy naval and aerial bombardment rav-

[93] Its text can be found in Raliby, *Documenta Historica,* app. 17, p. 533.

[94] Wehl, *Birth of Indonesia,* pp. 63–64.

[95] *Berita Indonesia,* Nov. 10, 1945. Doel Arnowo related that he had repeatedly called Sukarno in Djakarta to get him to make a decision whether to resist or not, but every time was put off or referred to Subardjo, who told him to tell the people of Surabaja to decide for themselves; interview, Aug. 13, 1962. This is in part confirmed by Angkasa Darma in "Sebelas tahun nan lalu," where he recalls from the Djakarta end that Sukarno was "disturbed" until late in the evening by telephone calls from Doel Arnowo.

aged large sections of Surabaja. By evening the British had taken a third of the city, and by November 12 still another third.

In the centre of the city fighting was more severe, streets had to be occupied one by one, doorway by doorway. Bodies of men, horses and cats and dogs, lay in the gutters, broken glass, furniture, tangled telephone lines cluttered the roads, and the noise of battle echoed among the empty office buildings. . . . The Indonesian resistance went through two phases, firstly fanatical self-sacrifice, with men armed only with daggers charging Sherman tanks, and later in a better organized and effective manner, following closely Japanese military manuals.[96]

Savage fighting continued for more than three weeks, with the Indonesians at a heavy disadvantage and suffering huge losses. By the end of the month the city had fallen to the Allies, and the surviving Indonesians followed the thousands of refugees fleeing the city. The Allies did not pursue their successes further, and a relatively stationary perimeter was eventually established running from Modjokerto on the west around to Sidoardjo on the east.

The battle of Surabaja was intended as a punitive expedition, but the resistance that the British forces met astonished and appalled them. David Wehl, by no means an enthusiast for the Indonesian cause, summed up the battle's consequences very well:

Had similar risings taken place all over Java, millions would have died and the Republic of Indonesia and the Netherlands East Indies alike would have been drowned in blood. This possibility lay always before the eyes of the Allied commanders at the time, and considerably influenced their policy, an influence not always appreciated in Holland. The fanaticism and fury of Surabaja, however, were never repeated, and even when open war began between the Dutch and the Republicans there was no fighting in the Republican ranks to compare with Surabaja, either in courage or tenacity.[97]

[96] Wehl, *Birth of Indonesia*, p. 66.
[97] *Ibid.*, p. 67.

Chapter 8

A Silent Coup

For the ten weeks of the Sukarno cabinet's life, developments in Djakarta were overshadowed by the more dramatic events in Bandung, Semarang, and Surabaja. While there were sporadic armed clashes in the capital in the middle of October, there was never any serious possibility of a pemuda breakthrough such as had occurred in the provinces. The early arrival of the Allies had prevented the Djakarta pemuda from acquiring any considerable quantity of Japanese arms, whether by negotiations or by the threat of mass assault. Furthermore, the fact that General Christison's headquarters and the main body of General Mansergh's Twenty-third Division were in Djakarta gave the Allies a local military superiority that proved impossible to challenge effectively. In part, too, the greater degree of specifically political consciousness among the metropolitan pemuda, and the fact that the central leadership and institutions of the republic were located in the city, undoubtedly helped give pemuda activities there a less military and more political cast.

But the specific character of politics in Djakarta during October and November cannot be fully understood without taking into account the political, administrative, and even physical isolation of the metropolis. The heavy, if localized intrusion of Allied forces, the disintegration of wartime institutions, the regrouping of Japanese troops and civil servants, the chaotic communications system and continuing severe economic shortages all contributed to a growing paralysis of the routine functioning

167

of government. Under such conditions the ministers, whatever their formal powers, could scarcely execute any coherent or sustained policy. Provincial governments, insofar as they had any real authority, were absorbed in immediate local crises of which the center knew little and about which it could do less: we have seen how Djakarta relinquished all responsibility for the critical decision whether or not to resist in Surabaja on November 9. In many areas factories and plantations had been seized by the employees and their monetary and other assets parceled out. The government had no control over the money supply, and in the provinces huge stocks of Japanese currency fell into random hands.

Even in the immediate environs of the city, the cabinet's writ scarcely ran. Many of the more militant and less well-educated pemuda who were pushed out of Djakarta by the Allied forces established themselves in the outlying areas of Krawang, Bekasi, Depok, Bogor, and Tanggerang, gathering recruits among the village youth and carrying on their own revolutionary activities without any regard for the cabinet's wishes. Their efforts were all the more successful in that the lowland plain around Djakarta had been marked, even in Dutch times, by an unusually high degree of social dislocation and anomie, as a result of heavy migrations of Javanese, Sundanese, and Bantenese peasants and the presence of many of the infamous *particuliere landerijen* (private estates).

In origin the particuliere landerijen were lands sold, usually to individual Europeans and Chinese, first by the Dutch East India Company and subsequently by Thomas Stamford Raffles during the brief period of British rule in Java (1811–16). In the early days the owners of these lands enjoyed extensive and oppressive powers over their tenants, including the right to levy taxes and exact corvée labor. Though these powers were later gradually restricted by the colonial government, they were never wholly removed. Under the occupation, though the Japanese military administration confiscated the estates, administered them directly, and formally put an end to corvée labor, conditions were not appreciably improved for the tenantry.[1]

The area around Tanggerang, to the west of Djakarta, had long been dominated by these particuliere landerijen. It was not surprising, therefore, that here social disturbances were unusually severe as Japanese authority dwindled away after the arrival of the Allies. As early as October 8 widespread mass actions forced the resignation of virtually all of the local pangrèh pradja and police. On October 21 a Badan Direktorium Dewan Pusat (Central Directorate Council) was set up under Hadji Achmad Chairun, which proceeded to dissolve the local KNI, cut off all communications with the capital, and set up "popularly chosen" governments at all levels within the kabupatèn. The administrative head of the kabupatèn, the *bupati,* was forced to flee for his life. Hadji Chairun himself, living in a kampung near Tjurug, enjoyed the prestige of earlier involvement in the 1926 communist uprising in Banten, and had gained a wide local reputation as the head of an *ilmu kebathinan* movement in Tanggerang.[2] Supported by many of the pemuda who had studied under him, and working closely with a local Arab called Sjech Abdullah who headed a Lasjkar Hitam (Black Army), he established virtually complete power in an area less than fifteen miles from Djakarta.[3] A reign of terror began against the Dutch, Chinese, and Japanese who happened to be in the vicinity, which neither the Allies, nor, more important, the central government could quell until the following year.[4] Moreover, Hadji Chairun was not

[1] See Sutter, *Indonesianisasi,* pp. 25–27, 159. Most of these estates were located in the Djakarta and Bogor areas and in other parts of northern West Java. Considerable holdings also existed, however, in Pekalongan, Semarang, Surabaja, and Pasuruan.

[2] *Ilmu kebathinan* (science of the inner being) is the most common term for the magico-mystical beliefs that form the core of the religion of Java.

[3] Black is the color traditionally associated with the djago in Java (and also in parts of the Outer Islands).

[4] Most of this account is drawn from Indonesia, Kementerian Penerangan, *Republik Indonesia Propinsi Djawa Barat,* pp. 151–54.

alone. He was in fact only one of the better-known local charismatic insurgents in the rural hinterland of West Java. Hadji Darip in Tjikarang was another.[5] And in the later "social revolution" in Banten, many of their kind played central roles.

The growing internal weakness of the cabinet was not balanced by any marked increase in its external strength. While the Christison broadcast had removed the immediate threat of Allied reprisals against Sukarno and Hatta, and indeed had conferred some de facto recognition on the republican regime, the arrival of the British created new difficulties for the cabinet. We have seen that its early position of comparative strength had been based in large measure on the good relations it maintained with the Japanese. And while the British were willing to deal with the cabinet in the hope of exploiting its authority for their own purposes, it was obvious that the Dutch were deeply hostile to Sukarno, and in a wider sense, that the cloud of collaboration hung over the government.

To the pemuda of Djakarta the government seemed increasingly unsatisfactory. The bitterness of the clashes with the Japanese in Bandung and Semarang made the cabinet leaders' good relations with the Japanese an increasing liability. There was dissatisfaction with the government's pusillanimity in the denouement of the Ikada meeting and with its apparent inertia following the arrival of the Allies. The feeling began to spread that the government was also not overly enthusiastic about the activities of the militant pemuda in the provincial capitals. By early October there was widespread consensus in politically conscious circles in Djakarta that the period of drift and inertia must be brought to an end, and that it could only be ended by changing the government to adapt it to the rapidly changing situation.

The man who stepped forward at this juncture to voice the general discontent and to give leadership to pemuda pressures for change was Sutan Sjahrir. For this role, at this particular

[5] See *NEFIS Periodiek* (Djakarta), no. 1 (Feb. 1946), pp. 2–3, 5.

juncture, he was particularly well-suited. To the older political leaders he was a familiar figure, with considerable standing as a hard-headed and thoughtful nationalist intellectual and the added prestige of long exile under the Dutch. While by no means universally popular in these circles, he was widely respected, and above all, as a veteran of the pergerakan, he was felt to be one of them. Among the pemuda, on the other hand, his role in the occupation years had given him, in Djakarta at least, a high reputation for courage and principle. Moreover, the fact that he was at this time still only 36 years old made him seem spiritually closer to the generation of the pemuda than the men around Sukarno and Hatta, almost all of whom were in their midforties. To the Djakarta pemuda, then, he was at once one of them and a "national" politician who could express and realize their aspirations at the highest levels of state.

To Sjahrir's cool mind the logical starting point for change was the KNIP. With the demise of the PNI, the KNIP was the one functioning governmental institution in which the pemuda and the rest of the underground had significant representation, and through which leverage could be exerted on the cabinet and the president. In addition, its status was sufficiently ambiguous that radical changes could be made in its real powers without crudely violating or overturning the Constitution itself. The only mention of the KNIP in the Constitution was in Article Four of the Provisional Regulations, which stated: "Prior to the formation of the People's Consultative Assembly [MPR], the People's Representative Council [DPR] and the Supreme Advisory Council, in accordance with the terms of this Constitution, their several powers shall be exercised by the president with the assistance of a National Committee." [6] Neither the composition of this National Committee nor its powers were specified. The Indonesian phrase *dengan bantuan* (with the assistance) was vague enough to denote almost any role from that of a purely advisory council to that of an assembly with legislative powers, such as the main

[6] See, e.g., Yamin, ed., *Naskah persiapan,* p. 34.

body of the Constitution envisioned for the MPR and DPR themselves. The reason for this ambiguous language was partly haste, but also an unwillingness at the time to develop and formalize new government bodies that clearly lay outside the structures of the state as they existed before the Japanese surrender.

On October 7 Sjahrir made his first open move. On that day fifty members of the KNIP signed a petition directed to Sukarno and Hatta urging that the key words *dengan bantuan* be explicitly interpreted to give the KNIP the status of the MPR, the highest permanent constitutional body.[7] Whatever private reservations Sukarno and his cabinet may have had about this proposal, it was difficult to resist. Many felt that the lack of a parliamentary type of legislature opened the republic to defamation by the Dutch. While the Constitution was not in fact modeled on Japanese lines, the exceedingly wide powers it granted the president made it vulnerable at this time to charges of being "made in Japan." The need to give the government a more democratic image was strongly voiced not only by Sjahrir and the pemuda but also by a considerable body of the older politicians who were concerned about securing rapid international recognition for Indonesia and felt that no minor constitutional obstacles should be allowed to stand in the way of achieving this goal. Sjahrir also relied on most of the KNIP members to support a measure that would enlarge their own powers and prestige. And indeed, opposition to the move finally came from only a few individuals, who either presciently saw it as the start of a move away from a presidential to a parliamentary form of government along Dutch lines, or were worried that the effective authority of the state would be divided if the KNIP assumed equal status with the president.

By the time the KNIP met for its second plenary session on October 16 and 17 (as the fighting in Semarang was at its height), an informal decision had already been made to accept

[7] Kahin, *Nationalism and Revolution*, p. 152; Pringgodigdo, *Perubahan*, p. 27.

the new status of the KNIP. At the opening meeting Hatta stepped forward to read what was subsequently to attain ambiguous fame as Proclamation X:

The President of the Republic of Indonesia, after listening to the discussions of the Central National Committee with regard to the proposal that pending the formation of the MPR and DPR, their powers, hitherto exercised by the President with the assistance of a National Committee in accordance with Article 4 of the Provisional Regulations of the Constitution, should be exercised by the Central National Committee, and that the day-to-day work of the Central National Committee should, in view of the critical situation, be carried on by a body called the Working Committee, which should be responsible to the Central National Committee; considering that in the present critical situation it is necessary to have a body which can share responsibility for the fate of the Indonesian people beside the Government; considering further that this proposal is based on the concept of popular sovereignty; has decided: that prior to the formation of the MPR and the DPR, legislative power will be transferred to the Central National Committee, which will share in establishing the broad outlines of the aims of the state [*haluan Negara*]; and agrees that the day-to-day work of the Central National Committee shall, in view of the critical situation, be exercised by a Working Committee to be chosen from among its members and responsible to the Central National Committee as a whole.[8]

It was thereupon decided, probably by previous agreement, that Sjahrir and Amir Sjarifuddin would be made *formateurs* of the new Working Committee (Badan Pekerdja, or BP).[9] Fol-

---

[8] The title of the proclamation has caused a good deal of confusion, since "X" has been understood to stand for the Roman numeral X. In fact, according to Pringgodigdo, at the moment the proclamation was to be signed by Hatta, it turned out that the state secretary (Pringgodigdo himself) had forgotten to bring along his archives, which gave the proper system for numbering government proclamations. Thus it was decided to improvise, using the letter "X" for "number unknown." Pringgodigdo, *Perubahan*, p. 32. The text is drawn from Koesnodiprodjo, ed., *Himpunan, 1945*, p. 58.

[9] It was only one among the many legal and constitutional anomalies of the situation that Amir, who was still minister of information in

lowing this decision debate was opened to the floor, and a very unruly atmosphere rapidly developed, with the pemuda representatives strongly criticizing the government for its hesitations and lack of rapport with the pemuda in the streets. The meeting finally became so heated that Kasman, the chairman, was removed from his position, and his place taken temporarily by Adam Malik.[10]

The following day the discussion turned to a Sukarni-sponsored motion demanding a "radical change in the leadership of the KNIP to speed up the struggle of the Indonesian republic. . . . Our revolutionary people must have a revolutionary leadership. The leadership of the KNIP must be in harmony with the will of the people and its pemuda, in other words, it must be revolutionary. The KNIP must have a leadership which can take responsibility. Bureaucracy must be completely eliminated from the workings of the KNIP."[11] Sartono and Latuharhary defended the older leadership and the government in general, but to little effect. Shortly afterward it was agreed that the Sukarni motion would be withdrawn, but the previous leadership of the KNIP would immediately resign and make way for a new leadership selected by Sjahrir and Amir Sjarifuddin, with the confidence of the majority of the KNIP behind it. Sjahrir and Amir thereupon produced their list of fifteen members for the Working Committee: chairman, Sutan Sjahrir; vice-chairman, Mr. Amir Sjarifuddin; secretary, Mr. R. Soewandi; members, Mr. R. Sjafrudin Prawiranegara, A. Wachid Hasjim, Mr. R. Hindromartono, Mr. R. M. Sunario Kolopaking, Dr. Abdul Halim, Subadio Sastro-

---

Sukarno's cabinet, should act here as a *formateur* of the leadership of the insurgent KNIP. The idea of the Working Committee was evidently drawn from the example of the Indian National Congress. See Kahin, *Nationalism and Revolution*, p. 152.

[10] It will be recalled that Malik had been elected third deputy chairman of the KNIP at its August 27 session. For these events, see *Berita Indonesia*, Oct. 18, 1945.

[11] *Ibid.; Merdeka*, Oct. 19, 1945.

satomo, Tan Ling Djie, Supeno, Sarmidi Mangunsarkoro, Adam Malik, Tadjuludin, and Dr. Sudarsono.[12]

The average age of the Working Committee, 34.6 years, was considerably lower than that of the Sukarno cabinet itself, which was 46.4. The new body thus represented a different generation from the cabinet, and with at least three members still in their twenties, it gave the pemuda a powerful voice. Moreover, only two of the members (Soewandi and Wachid Hasjim) had held high positions under the Japanese. Shortly after the Working Committee was formed, Sjahrir was able to secure the addition of 38 new members to the KNIP, most of whom strongly supported him. In this enlarged legislative body he was assured, for the time being at least, of an effective majority.[13]

The second stage in the drive to shift power decisively away from the presidency, and to give the Indonesian government a format more consonant with Western European conceptions, was to press toward making the cabinet responsible to the legislature. To justify such a change, however, the establishment of some form of party system appeared essential. Once again, the vagueness and ambiguity of the Constitution was helpful to the proponents of reform. The second Additional Regulation, which stated that "for a period of six months following the end of the Greater East Asian War, the president of Indonesia regulates and implements everything laid down in this Constitution," could readily be interpreted to require the election of an MPR and a DPR at the end of that period.[14] Sjahrir was able to use

[12] For biographical details on these figures (except Tadjuludin), see the Appendix. According to Subadio Sastrosatomo, Tadjuludin was a medical student involved in the underground and close to Sjahrir. Interview with Subadio, June 4, 1967. In the 1950's he was to become a leading figure in Sjahrir's Indonesian Socialist Party (Partai Sosialis Indonesia, or PSI).

[13] Kahin, *Nationalism and Revolution,* p. 153. Sukarno and Hatta evidently appointed the new members without putting up any resistance.

[14] Yamin, ed., *Naskah persiapan,* p. 34.

the promise of these elections to urge the public acknowledgment of the right to form parties, on the ground that for such elections to be meaningful and democratic, participation by political parties was imperative. His argument received Amir Sjarifuddin's strong support.[15]

Whether it was persuaded by the logic of these arguments or by the pressure exerted by Sjahrir's supporters in the KNIP, the government finally approved these proposals. On October 30, while Sukarno, Hatta, and Amir Sjarifuddin were struggling to preserve the peace in Surabaja, Sjahrir and the Working Committee issued the Announcement on Parties, which said in part:

The original establishment of the National Committee was accompanied by the formation of a party, namely the PNI. Both were set up with the same purpose, namely the defense of our nation's independence. Since what was needed at that time was the unity of all aliran and strata of our society, and it proved that the National Committee could fulfill this need, whereas the formation of a Nationalist Party could cause the establishment of other parties—which would mean weakening the unity which was required at that time—endeavors to form the party were put off temporarily. . . . [Now, however,] in accordance with our Constitution, which contains specifications for the freedoms of session and assembly, the Working Committee considers the time has come to organize the popular movement systematically, . . . and since we hold high the principle of democracy, naturally we cannot possibly permit only one party to be established. Furthermore, with the establishment of these parties, it will be easier for us to estimate the strength of our struggle; and for the government, too, it will be easier to demand responsibility from the leaders of the struggle organizations. . . . In conclusion, the formation of parties may now be begun quite freely, provided that the formation of these parties strengthens our struggle, defends our liberty, and guarantees the security of the community, which is now seriously disturbed in several places.[16]

[15] Kahin, *Nationalism and Revolution,* pp. 154–55.
[16] *Merdeka,* Nov. 2, 1945, has the full text.

In the acrimonious disputes of later years, the multiparty system, so much denounced as the cause of Indonesia's political instability, was commonly attributed to the imprudence of the authors of this announcement. It was often assumed that had Sjahrir and his associates not been so firmly committed to establishing a political system along Western liberal-democratic lines, the evils of parties and party government need never have emerged to trouble the nation. While Sjahrir was certainly led by his ideological persuasion and political circumstances to urge the legitimation of political parties, the immediate effects of the announcement were confined to Djakarta, where they helped tip the balance in the power struggle between the Working Committee and the Sukarno cabinet. Outside the capital political parties were already germinating, prior to and heedless of Djakarta's permission for them to do so. In the provinces, therefore, the announcement was not so much an authorization as a recognition.

As early as October 11, for example, a group of older Islamic leaders met in Jogjakarta to plan a congress and work out a new organizational format and constitution to convert the wartime Masjumi into a political party. The congress itself opened on November 7 in Jogjakarta, scarcely a week after the Working Committee's announcement had been issued.[17] On October 21 the Indonesian Communist Party (PKI) was reconstituted as a public organization for the first time since the uprisings of 1926–27 had been crushed by the colonial authorities.[18] On November 1 it was announced that "after discussions among revolutionary circles in Jogjakarta," the Partai Sosialis Indonesia (Indonesian Socialist Party), or "Parsi," was being set up to lead the peasants, workers, soldiers, and pemuda toward a socialist society.[19] Thus by November 3, when Vice-President Hatta signed the official

[17] For a full discussion, see Chapter 10 below.
[18] See Chapter 10 below.
[19] *Berita Indonesia,* Nov. 1, 1945.

government decree permitting parties to operate and promising elections by January of the following year, at least three important parties were already being formed.[20] It was only a matter of time before others followed.

Though parties were beginning to germinate, they did not exert any influence as yet. But the official sanction given to their formation and the prospect of elections was a decisive step in the transformation of the presidential system of government specified by the Constitution into a quasi-parliamentary system, with the cabinet responsible to the legislature and more or less based on party strength. It was hard to deny the argument that political parties would be meaningless unless they ultimately found representation in the government itself.

It came as no surprise, therefore, when on November 11 the Working Committee announced that it had urged on the President the need for shifting ministerial responsibility to the legislature and that the President had agreed to changes in the structure of government on the basis of Article Four of the Constitution's Provisional Regulations.[21] The Working Committee had decided to entrust the formation of a new cabinet to its chairman and vice-chairman, Sjahrir and Amir Sjarifuddin, and Sukarno had consented to appoint Sjahrir *formateur*.[22] The following day a spokesman for Amir's Ministry of Information candidly noted that the new system of ministerial responsibility was not exactly in accordance with the Constitution; nonetheless, in view of the provisional character of "our institutions," it could, and would, be made a "convention," along British lines.[23] On November 14 the first Sjahrir cabinet was announced.

[20] The text can be found in Raliby, *Documenta Historica,* app. 15, p. 529.

[21] Pengumuman BP-KNIP no. 5, Nov. 11, 1945, as reported in *Berita Indonesia,* Nov. 12, 1945.

[22] Raliby, *Documenta Historica,* app. 23, pp. 547–48.

[23] *Berita Indonesia,* Nov. 14, 1945. For a full discussion of this change from the perspective of constitutional law, see Pringgodigdo, *Perubahan,* section 7.

It should not be supposed that the localized pressure exerted by Sjahrir's supporters could in itself have brought about the downfall of the Sukarno cabinet. What sapped the cabinet's morale and paralyzed its energies was the increasingly obvious fact that it was unable to make itself acceptable either to the outside world or to the inchoate revolutionary forces represented by the pemuda in the provinces. It was not that the government had not tried to achieve these incompatible ends. From the very beginning it had struggled to win what international sympathy it could. As early as October 8 Sukarno had issued invitations on the radio to Jawaharlal Nehru, Chiang Kai-shek, Carlos Romulo, and Herbert Evatt to come to Indonesia to see the republic for themselves.[24] Foreign Minister Subardjo had repeatedly briefed Western reporters, sent telegrams and arranged for broadcasts stating Indonesia's position to the United States, England, Australia, and India, and begun seeking direct diplomatic relations with the Chinese government's representative in Djakarta as well as with the Soviet Union.[25] In an attempt to give the Allies the most concrete reassurance, Sukarno released on October 12 the Government Proclamation on Foreign Property, which read in part:

The state of the Indonesian republic, as a state based on popular sovereignty and humanitarianism, naturally respects the property of private foreigners. The property of foreigners, formerly held by the Japanese, is now in Indonesian hands. This does not mean that the Indonesian republic is going to confiscate this property. This property is merely going to be handled as satisfactorily as possible by Indonesians as managers [sebagai pengurus] until the time comes for it to be surrendered to its owners. The Indonesian government is ready to set up a committee to handle the property of foreigners with representatives of the Allies.[26]

[24] Raliby, *Documenta Historica*, p. 52.
[25] See Amir's speech to the KNIP, as reported in *Berita Indonesia*, Oct. 20, 1945.
[26] Koesnodiprodjo, ed., *Himpunan, 1945*, p. 57.

But the violent reaction in Holland to van Mook's first discussions with Sukarno and Hatta on October 23, including the Dutch government's public disavowal of the talks, showed very clearly how difficult it would be for men still marked with the stigma of collaboration to achieve respectability.[27]

Intensely aware that pemuda violence and mass action were continually eroding the credibility of their external stance of peaceable moderation, Sukarno and Hatta struggled to stem the rising tide of revolutionary militancy. On October 27 they issued a joint proclamation warning against those who, perhaps understandably, kidnapped Dutchmen, declared the Holy War, and set up courts to punish anyone they disliked.

We understand the rage of the people . . . but we cannot permit the people to act on their own, according to their own ideas. These anarchic actions are giving rise to chaos which may end in the collapse of our republic. . . . Everyone, native Indonesians and foreigners alike, should feel able to live in security in our country. . . . Our unity must be strengthened by respecting differences among ourselves. . . . These differences cannot justify one group's arresting and imprisoning its opponents in unknown places, since such actions will cause divisions among us and possibly lead to civil war. . . . No group may put forward its demands by threats, or by forcing or deposing people it does not like, because actions of this kind destroy the sense of security of our government officials and of those who are performing some task of responsibility. No function can be carried on properly so long as those who perform them are in constant fear for their own safety. All actions of a Nazi or Fascist type must be abandoned, since they are in contradiction to our people's sovereignty.[28]

The culmination of the attempt to find a public stance that would command the sympathy and support of the cabinet's

[27] It should be noted that, according to van Mook, the Dutch government secretly approved these talks though it felt compelled to disown them publicly. See van Mook, *Indonesië*, pp. 100–104.

[28] Raliby, *Documenta Historica*, app. 12, pp. 519–20. Long-time observers of the Indonesian scene will appreciate the ironies of this proclamation.

audiences, both outside and inside the country, was the pro-
mulgation of the Political Manifesto of November 1, over Vice-
President Hatta's signature.[29] Bitterly attacking the rapacity of
the Japanese and Indonesia's abandonment to its fate by the
Dutch, the opening section of this manifesto strongly defended
the roles of all Indonesian groups during the occupation years:

For three and a half years our people have suffered from the oppression and cruelty of the Japanese, unprecedented in the previous decades of Dutch colonial rule. Our entire population was treated like
the cheapest goods to be wasted in the war effort. From the common
people, who were enslaved into forced labor and whose crops were
seized, up to the intellectuals, who were forced to lie and deceive the
people, all have experienced the iron grip of militarism. The physical
and spiritual suffering of our people for these three and a half years
has been virtually unlimited. . . . Yet in this period there has developed among our people a new consciousness, a fiercer national
feeling than ever before. . . . This development of our nationalism
in part took the form of resistance to Japanese military force, in secret
and also in uprisings, sabotage, etc., as can be proved by thousands
of our leftists who were sentenced, tortured, murdered, and hunted
down. The proofs of this are the uprisings in Tasikmalaja, Indramaju,
Blitar, Sumatra, West Borneo, and other places. . . . Another sector
of our nationalists, who organized our national consciousness by legal
means, was forced to cooperate with the Japanese, join in forming
ranks and shouting in the various corps formed by the Japanese for

[29] The text of the manifesto can be found in Raliby, *Documenta Historica,* app. 14, pp. 525–28. The manifesto was signed by Hatta because
Sukarno was at the time in Central Java trying to halt the fighting at
Ambarawa and Magelang. Who wrote it is not entirely clear. Kishi, et al.
(*Indoneshia ni okeru,* p. 501) aver that Sjahrir played a major role in
drafting the manifesto. This seems to me unlikely, since its theme of the
need for broad internal unity contrasts very strongly with the acid attacks
on the "collaborators" contained in Sjahrir's political pamphlet *Perdjuangan Kita,* which was issued at almost the same time. (For a discussion of this pamphlet, see Chapter 9 below.) My own inclination is to
assume that it was largely Hatta's work, since its substance accords well
with his general political orientation and his intermediary role between the
cabinet and the opposition during this period.

the needs of the war. The strength of our nationalism can also be seen among those nationalists who cooperated with the Japanese, who continually defended the ideals of democracy [*kerakjatan*] even though they were forced to march in the totalitarian ranks of the Japanese. The proof of this is the Constitution, which is clearly intended to be based on popular sovereignty, even though the Constitution itself was drafted in the period of Japanese colonial rule.

The second main section of the manifesto was a direct appeal for the sympathy and understanding of the outside world, especially the West. If Indonesia's claim to independence were not recognized, it said,

the world will not be able to take proper advantage of the riches of the state and people of Indonesia. This will be particularly saddening for Indonesia's neighbors, especially Australia, the Philippines, and the United States: above all the United States, which all of Asia and especially Indonesia is hoping will give the greatest possible assistance in the future to the efforts of the Indonesian people in making their country progress and raising the living standards of the population. For example, through the assistance of America's major industries, American credits, and the purchase of large quantities of raw materials. . . . For we know very well that in the next few years, for our country and people's needs, we shall need the assistance of foreign countries in building up our own, in the form of technicians, educated people (intellectuals), and also foreign capital.

This urgent plea for American support was coupled with promises that the new Indonesian state would fully compensate war victims, assume the debts of the Netherlands East Indies government, respect the rights of foreign enterprise, and fully adhere to all the principles of the United Nations Charter.[30]

[30] "All foreign property other than that which our state finds it necessary to operate itself will be returned to its legal owners, and as just compensation as possible will be paid for what is taken over by the state." As Sutter points out, "For the rest of the Revolutionary period, successive Indonesian governments would attempt to adhere to this statement of policy." *Indonesianisasi*, p. 312. For a full and warmly approving discussion of the conservative economic policies which these governments attempted to execute, see *ibid.*, pp. 274–455,

But while the manifesto was evidently received with some cordiality by the British, it aroused little enthusiasm among the pemuda and other radically inclined elements. Pemuda support for the government, never very strong, waned rapidly as the violence in the provinces increased. In many quarters Sukarno's intervention in Surabaja and Central Java was felt to be a betrayal of heroic pemuda resistance to the British and their NICA camp followers, since it seemed only to strengthen the Allied position. Pemuda hostility to Sukarno's October 31 radio speech urging a policy of appeasement toward the Allies was especially intense. Hatta later recalled that immediately after the broadcast, Sukarni came to see him, demanding that Sukarno resign from the presidency for his weakness and collaboration with the Allies.[31] Diah's *Merdeka* printed an outraged attack on Sukarno for an interview given on November 11, the day following Mansergh's massive assault on Surabaja, in which he expressed his regrets at anti-British feeling in that city and indicated his intention to do his best to "limit this incident." As *Merdeka* said, the crisis in Surabaja showed that diplomacy was a complete failure. The British had taken advantage of it to bring in their divisions. It was time to trust to the strength of the people, not the tricks of the Allies.[32] Most direct and poignant of all was Bung Tomo's bitter broadcast on the eve of the cabinet's fall:

Leaders of the Indonesian people! Listen to our demands, the leaders of the generation of the people in revolt. Why do you still trust the British and always act weakly toward them? . . . If you gentlemen negotiate with the British and Dutch, this means the possibility that our people will be stripped naked once again. . . . Our people are all ready; we have long been awaiting the order to attack those who are obstructing our efforts to defend our freedom. But we have not received this command. Nonetheless, our people have already begun

[31] Interview with Mohammed Hatta, Feb. 13, 1962. Cf. Raliby, *Documenta Historica,* p. 343.
[32] *Merdeka,* Nov. 12, 1945.

their struggle. . . . Do not remain silent! Act! Carry out your duties correctly! Here, we shall carry out ours—to defend the sovereignty of our country.[33]

Another pemuda spokesman on the same radio urged, "If the leadership in Djakarta is incapable [of defending the country], then surrender control of the government to those who will more bravely assume responsibility!"

The Buchō Cabinet had lasted little more than ten weeks. It had essentially been a holding operation, a government of transition between the period of Japanese rule and the period of confronting the British and the Dutch. In September it had negotiated with the Japanese for the gradual takeover of the administrative agencies of government, hoping to continue where the Sixteenth Army had left off. It had failed to realize that this very process would make its own demise inevitable. The indigenous bureaucracy, which had for so long relied on alien power as the ultimate enforcer of its authority, was now deprived of that external support by the withdrawal of the Japanese, and rapidly lost confidence, coherence, and capacity to exercise control. Insofar as the cabinet possessed no alternative instruments for exerting its will, it was condemned to impotence.

For a short time, while the spell of Japanese supremacy still lingered on, the government's authority was scarcely challenged. Later, the illusion of control was maintained because the initial phase of the pemuda movement was marked by the seizure of administrative buildings the officials were invited to occupy as servants of the new Indonesian state. But the illusion could not be sustained once the seizure of Japanese weapons began. The pemuda in arms rapidly developed into an uncoordinated force independent of the government. Nor was the plight of the central government unique. In the provinces, too, local officials and their counterparts, the local political leaders from the prewar period, having taken over the formal trappings of power from the Japanese, found themselves overwhelmed by the pemuda tide.

[33] *Ibid.*, Nov. 14, 1945.

For the pemuda it was a time of improvization and exhilaration. Underneath the anarchic spontaneity of their movement, giving it power and conviction, were the fundamental impulses of every revolution. Liberty was merdeka, not a political concept of independence or freedom, but an experience of personal liberation. For many it was a release from the disciplined structures of the occupation period—the youth organizations, the offices, and the factories—as these disintegrated in the October days. For others it was a liberation from the apparent fatality of their lives. It was a sense of vast and unexpected opportunities in a time when everything for a while seemed possible and permissible. The pemuda rode free on buses, trains, and trams. They forced Japanese soldiers to kneel before them in the dirt. They scrawled their terse slogans on doors and walls. They emptied the tills of unguarded banks, and opened warehouses to the people of the kampung. They attacked tanks with sharpened bamboo spears and homemade gasoline bombs. And they killed—Dutchmen, Englishmen, Japanese, Eurasians, Chinese, sometimes their fellow-Indonesians.

Equality was experienced in the crumbling of the existing structures of authority. In the process of disintegration officials, policemen, political leaders in established institutions, all were discovered to be without effective power. Stripped of the armature of hierarchy, law, legitimacy, and guns, they were no greater than those they ruled. Men were now defined by their actions, not by their office, rank, or status. The opacity of the social order no longer exercised its hegemonic hold.

Fraternity came out of equality. It was a community of shared experience, a solidarity not defined by the social structure, but growing at its dissolving margins. It was discovered in the unorganized and randomly assembled crowds that swarmed around Japanese offices and barracks. It was felt when the cry Siaaaaap! (Get ready!) was heard in the streets, and people streamed out of the kampung for whatever confrontation was awaiting them. It was there when Bung Tomo made his evening broadcasts and pedicab drivers, peddlers, clerks, and schoolboys stopped to listen to him together. In a larger sense it was an intuition of the unity of society—not an alliance between different aliran, ethnic groups, or social classes working for specific political goals, but a deeper solidarity that made these divisions irrelevant. This was clearly expressed in the constant calls for *kerakjatan* (people-ness), *kedaulatan rakjat* (sovereignty of the people), and *demokrasi*. These terms did not mean the ordered expression of differences among the population or popular majority rule, but an obscure sense of being in one flow. So it was that the anonymous heroisms and atrocities of those months were regarded within the pemuda movement not as individual acts to be lauded or condemned but as the expression of powerful, impersonal forces unleashed in society.

Perhaps it was because the pemuda movement was more revolutionary than political that it proved so difficult to control and so unpredictable in direction. In the larger cities, where there were concentrations of British and Japanese troops, the pemuda tide flowed against them as the most visible and powerful enemies of merdeka. In these places the older politicians, pangrèh pradja, and police were passed by, their authority largely ignored. Only if they were believed to have betrayed merdeka by ranging themselves alongside the enemy did the pemuda movement turn directly against them. The ill-fated Oto Iskandardinata paid with his life for the humiliation of Mabuchi's *coup de force*.[34] In

[34] The details of Oto's death are obscure. In 1959 a certain Mudjitaba bin Murkam was tried for the execution of Oto on December 20, 1945, near Mauk in the district of Tanggerang. At the time of Oto's murder Mudjitaba was a 27-year-old pemuda who was second in command of the Lasjkar Hitam and head of intelligence for Hadji Achmad Chairun's Direktorium in Tanggerang. The evidence produced at the trial was obscure and contradictory, and the prosecution's case was apparently dropped in the end, probably for political reasons. Mudjitaba himself claimed that he did not know of Oto's identity, and regarded him as simply one among a group of alleged NICA spies turned over to his charge by another unnamed pemuda group. Smail believes that Oto was first kidnapped in late October or early November, and was subsequently

smaller and remoter areas, where neither the Japanese nor the Allies maintained a significant presence, the pemuda movement found its targets in the remaining representatives of the old order —the police, the officials, and even the older politicians. This trend brought about "social revolutions," not only in Tanggerang, as we have already seen, but also in Banten, Bodjonegoro, Pati, Pekalongan, Tjirebon, and Surakarta.

Seen from this perspective, the political struggle in Djakarta that led to the downfall of the Sukarno cabinet appears as only one manifestation of a larger crisis. What Sjahrir's enemies were subsequently to call the "silent coup" of November 1945 was in many ways part of a general process going on all over Java in which the reliquary leadership and authority structures of the Dutch and Japanese periods were being swept aside. This process was often called democratization, but it had less to do with democracy than with the pemuda revolution.

At the same time, the crisis of the old order, as it manifested itself in Djakarta, was decisively affected by the particular conditions prevailing there. In the first place, Djakarta was largely isolated from the interior of the island, and in these months, events in Central and East Java engaged pemuda concern more deeply than developments in the capital. Thus in large degree the militancy of the revolutionary pemuda movement as a whole did not impinge directly on the struggle for power at the center. For the pemuda in the provinces the personalities in the national government were unimportant. Most of them did not know who Sjahrir was. What they asked for was simply a leadership that would express, as Bung Tomo did in Surabaja, the inflexible will of pemuda nationalism vis-à-vis the British and the Dutch. They did not expect the government to direct or control their activities. They expected it to be a symbolic reflection of themselves.

Second, the massive presence of the Allies in the capital made

---

moved from hand to hand until he met his death at Mauk in December. See Smail, *Bandung*, pp. 70–71; for good press coverage of the trial, see *Sin Po* (Djakarta), July 27, Aug. 2, Aug. 16 and Sept. 6, 1959.

it difficult to take drastic steps against the cabinet, even had the metropolitan pemuda wished to do so. Since the pemuda leaders in the capital had more Western education and were more politically conscious than their comrades in the provinces, it was easier to channel their energies into formal bodies like the KNIP and into the relative civility of the silent coup as opposed to the violence of, for example, the social revolutions in Banten and Pekalongan.

Third, the presence of men like Sjahrir and Amir Sjarifuddin, with the prestige of their wartime roles and the power of their radical and socialist language, gave the pemuda in the capital a sophisticated leadership that they could accept for a while at least because it felt like their own. Last, resistance to Sjahrir's rise among the older-generation politicians was relatively weak, since, like him, they were at heart committed to some form of dialogue or *diplomasi* with the Dutch, and many were persuaded that he was the man most fitted to pursue this commitment with success.

As we have seen, Sjahrir's rise to power did not depend on the development of political parties; although some parties were already germinating toward the end of the cabinet's life, they had no influence on its fall. Sjahrir's authority did not depend on any kind of organized political backing, but rather on the virtually unanimous support of the pemuda movement in the capital. Yet, although Sjahrir to a great extent rode to power on the wave of the pemuda movement, he did so without in any way sharing the pemuda consciousness or experience. Prominent pemuda who were subsequently to be violently hostile to him, such as Sukarni and Chaerul Saleh, were at this period among his strongest supporters. But their support rested on a fundamental misunderstanding—that Sjahrir was basically one of them, and that the political language they shared ("democracy," "popular sovereignty," "struggle," and "socialism") meant the same thing to both. The movement we have observed toward a quasi-parliamentary system of government, in which the fifteen

men on the Working Committee became the group that determined cabinet appointments, was to Sjahrir and those closest to
him both a means to satisfy their own political ambitions and a
movement away from the totalistic structures of Japanese rule
toward Western-style democratic government. But to many of
even the more politically conscious urban pemuda, the KNIP
was an expression of their own insurgency against the old order:
a cabinet chosen by, and answerable to, the KNIP would be a
cabinet "in the flow." So democratic forms seemed a logical extension of merdeka. As the illusion of congruity began to fade,
Sjahrir in his turn came to face the difficulties and dilemmas that
had brought the Sukarno cabinet to its knees.

Chapter 9

Perdjuangan Kita

On November 10 the Ministry of Information announced the publication of a political pamphlet written by Sjahrir entitled *Perdjuangan Kita* (Our Struggle).[1] Appearing just as news began to leak out that the author had been invited to form a government responsible to the KNIP, it seemed to presage fundamental changes in the composition and policies of the Indonesian government.

The heart of the pamphlet was a bitter inventory of the darkest features of the Japanese occupation: forced labor, compulsory rice deliveries, lawlessness, corruption, and brutality. But it focused particularly on what Sjahrir felt to be the two most permanently dangerous consequences of the war years: first, the rise of a considerable group of nationalists whom he regarded as having sold out to the Japanese; and second, what he saw as the corruption of Indonesian youth by the militarist and fascist attitudes inculcated through various Japanese-sponsored organizations. This corruption had resulted, after the surrender, in atrocities and terrorism against Dutchmen, Eurasians, and those Indonesian minorities popularly regarded as being pro-Dutch, such as the Christian Ambonese and Menadonese.

Sjahrir called for a complete purge of "collaborationist elements" and a massive effort to foster the principles of humani-

---

[1] *Merdeka,* Nov. 10, 1945. The quotations that follow are drawn from my translation of the original Indonesian, published as Sutan Sjahrir, *Our Struggle* (Ithaca, N.Y., 1968). The italics are in the original text.

tarian socialism in the minds of Indonesian youth. He insisted that:

We must never for a moment forget that we are creating a *democratic revolution*. Our *national revolution* is simply the "tail-end" of our *democratic revolution*. Top priority must be given, not to *nationalism,* but to democracy, even though it may seem easier to arouse the masses by encouraging their xenophobia. It is true, of course, that such methods can work for a while (see, for example, the successes of Mussolini, Hitler, Franco, Chiang Kai-shek, etc.) but in relation to the advancement of their societies, they are always *reactionary* and *conflict with progress* and the *social struggle* the world over. The men who urge such a course are always *enemies of the people,* even though they may, momentarily, be deified by the people, like Hitler and Mussolini.

The social-democratic struggle he envisaged should start by

purging itself of the *stains* of Japanese *fascism,* and curbing the views of those whose minds are still under the influence of Japanese propaganda and indoctrination. Those who have sold their *souls* and their *honor* to the Japanese fascists must be eliminated from the leadership of our revolution—those who have worked in the Japanese propaganda organizations, the secret police, and the Japanese fifth column in general. These men must be regarded as traitors to our struggle and must be sharply distinguished from ordinary people, who worked for the Japanese simply to earn their daily bread. Thus all such political collaborators with the Japanese fascists must be regarded as *fascists* themselves, or as the running-dogs and henchmen of the Japanese fascists, who, it goes without saying, are guilty of betraying the people's struggle and the people's revolution.[2]

[2] Arnold Brackman claims that the bitter words "running-dogs" were inserted in the text by the journalist M. Tabrani, who was then in charge of the state printing works, without the knowledge of Sjahrir himself. *Indonesian Communism* (New York, 1963), p. 41. This, however, was categorically denied by Tabrani in an interview with the author on November 14, 1963. Since Tabrani had been arrested and tortured by the Japanese, and was released only just before the surrender, he would have had reason to "sharpen" the text. On the other hand, he claims to have voted against Sjahrir in the KNIP during the constitutional crisis

Sjahrir openly and strongly attacked the first cabinet:

The people in control of the Republican Government are men without real character. Most of them are far too accustomed to kowtow or run errands for the Dutch and the Japanese. Psychologically they are irresolute and have proved quite incapable of acting decisively and assuming responsibility. . . . Many of them still feel morally obliged to the Japanese, who "bestowed" on them an opportunity to "prepare" Indonesian Independence. In their own eyes, they have become the government because they worked together with the Japanese.

It was for these reasons that when the power of the Japanese weakened and finally collapsed—and yet had still not been replaced by Allied military power—the Republic of Indonesia was unable to build up our nation's strength. The result was that we were a state and a nation without a government. The masses in their uncertainty were given no education or clear understanding of how to solve the problems of government administration. Thus was born the chaos which is now spreading contagiously everywhere. In this atmosphere nationalist agitation has had consequences which the nationalist agitators themselves neither wished for nor could control. Looting and murder of foreigners, which one can understand from the standpoint of the situation of the masses, nonetheless exposed the naked weakness of the Government of the Republic, which felt itself to be neither regarded nor respected by the people.

Turning his attention to the pemuda, Sjahrir wrote:

It cannot be denied that the remarkable surge of national consciousness that we are now experiencing appears to have been stimulated by the younger generation. It is as though it were they who determine the very rhythm of our struggle. It is as though the revolution we are now undergoing originated in the enthusiasm and stout-heartedness of our youth, in other words, that it has been driven forward by pure idealism alone. . . . [Nonetheless] their methods of agitation and

---

of October–November 1945, with the result that Chaerul Saleh and Sukarni threatened to shoot him, demanding to know, "Are you a fascist?" In view of Sjahrir's reputation for a biting tongue, I think it is safe to assume that the words are his own. In any case, he never publicly disowned them.

propaganda among the masses are those they have seen and learnt from the Japanese—in other words the methods of fascism. The present psychological condition of our youth is deeply tragic. In spite of their burning enthusiasm, they are full of confusion and indecision because they have no understanding of the potentialities and perspectives of the struggle they are waging. Thus their vision is necessarily very limited. Many of them simply cling to the slogan Freedom or Death. Whenever they sense that Freedom is still far from certain, and yet they themselves have not faced death, they are seized with doubt and hesitation. The remedy for these doubts is usually sought in constant uninterrupted action. Action thus becomes a psychological opiate. For our nation, our youths' intoxication with action is actually an inestimable advantage; their activism has been a powerful stimulus to our struggle at its beginning. Nevertheless, through lack of understanding, many of their actions have missed the mark, and have undermined and damaged our cause. . . . Agitation and violence against foreigners have seriously weakened the moral standing of our struggle in the eyes of the outside world.

Attacking the Constitution as "still far from fully democratic," Sjahrir urged its replacement by a *"wholly* democratic constitution, which will imprint on every organ of state administration the fundamental rights of the people." He also called for a revolutionary leadership that "must be like an army, fortified by ideology and scientific knowledge, and tightly organized in a revolutionary party." He warned the pemuda that they could "at the most become the advance guard of the party which leads the struggle," and attacked the misconception that "leadership of our revolution should devolve onto those youths who have been organized in military formations."

These last years we have felt only too deeply the impact of military rule. This, and the military training given to our youth and to our people in general, has encouraged the false idea that our struggle is primarily a military one, which should therefore be led by military men. Only a thorough understanding of the social basis of our present struggle can help us avoid this illusion. . . . Since our struggle is expressed in the form of an Indonesian State, and so must utilize the

power-instruments of the state, we are compelled to build up the
main instrument of state struggle, in other words, the Army. But
this certainly ought not to be taken to mean that we should become
the slaves of the state or the military—i.e., fascists and militarists.

Turning from Indonesia's domestic crisis to her international
position as he saw it, Sjahrir warned that "so long as the world
we live in is dominated by capital, we are forced to make sure
that we do not earn the enmity of capitalism. . . . Indonesia is
geographically situated within the sphere of influence of Anglo-
Saxon capitalism and imperialism. Accordingly, Indonesia's fate
depends ultimately on the fate of Anglo-Saxon capitalism and
imperialism." He noted, however, that British and American
ambitions in the Far East were considerably different, since "vis-
à-vis Britain's century-old politique in the Far East, the Americans feel themselves everywhere (also of course in Indonesia)
as reformers and innovators." Implicitly he suggested that it was
therefore in Indonesia's interest to work "in harmony with the
political ambitions of that Giant of the Pacific, the United States."

Fundamental to Sjahrir's analysis of the Indonesian situation
was the overwhelming contrast he saw between the vast power
of the Anglo-Saxon capitalist world and the critical weakness of
the young republic. In his view the ravages of the occupation
years, the decay of the bureaucracy, the absence of an effective
defense force, the corruption of the older nationalist leadership,
and the unorganized, anarchic character of the pemuda movement left Indonesia extremely vulnerable to the outside world.
The only recourse was a shrewd and flexible diplomacy to keep
the British and Americans from giving full support to the Dutch.
This in turn logically demanded a liberal policy toward foreign
capital; an end to pemuda-style violence, particularly against
white-skinned people; the establishment of political institutions
acceptable to the West; and a nationalist rhetoric without immediate radical components. At the same time, it should be noted,
the logic of his analysis harmonized very well with his own liberal-democratic political inclinations. It was clearly his hope that

the same basic policies would at once attract the sympathy of the dominant Western powers and begin to liberate Indonesian society from the institutional and psychological bondage of its feudal, colonial, and militarist past.

The immediate political impact of *Perdjuangan Kita* does not, in retrospect, seem to have been very widespread; where its influence was felt, in Djakarta, it probably won Sjahrir as many enemies as it did friends. Many of the older nationalists never forgave Sjahrir for his biting and scornful attacks on their character and motivation. His sharp and often abrasive analysis of the pemuda and his harsh criticism of the military wounded many sensitivities at a time when the battle for Surabaja was at its height. The real importance of the pamphlet lies in the light it sheds on the perspectives of Sjahrir and his closest associates at this critical juncture of Indonesia's history, and also in the fact that, with one exception that we shall encounter later, it was the only attempt made during the post-surrender years to analyze systematically the domestic and international forces affecting Indonesia and to provide a coherent perspective for the future of the independence movement.

Of far greater importance at the time were the decisions made by Sjahrir and Amir in forming the cabinet that would succeed the departing buchō. Sjahrir's designation as cabinet *formateur* was taken by many to presage the formation of an energetic and progressive government. As we have seen, many of the pemuda who had supported the campaign to establish the Working Committee and a cabinet responsible to the KNIP were motivated less by a considered commitment to these institutions as such than by confidence in Sjahrir and Amir and the feeling that the transformation of the constitutional order was probably necessary to bring a new leadership to the fore. There was a general expectation that from this point on things would be very different, indeed that the government and the pemuda movement would no longer be at loggerheads, but would be working together in the same flow.

On November 14 Sjahrir announced the composition of his cabinet: Prime Minister, Foreign Affairs, and Interior, Sutan Sjahrir; Information and People's Security, Mr. Amir Sjarifuddin; Finance, Mr. Sunario Kolopaking; Education, Mr. Dr. T. G. S. Moelia; Justice, Mr. Soewandi; Social Affairs, Dr. Adjidarmo Tjokronagoro; Prosperity, Ir. Darmawan Mangoenkoesoemo; Health, Dr. Darmasetiawan; Public Works, Ir. Putuhena; Communications, Ir. Abdul Karim; State (without portfolio), H. Rasjidi.[3] The press reaction to these appointments revealed very clearly that the great satisfaction with the Sukarno cabinet's fall was not matched by a proportional enthusiasm for its successor. *Berita Indonesia* observed:

The cabinet of buchō who became ministers has fallen. . . . The new ministers were not prominent in the Japanese period, so that for those who began their political life in that period, these new ministers are rather unfamiliar. But such people should understand who it was that stepped forward in the Japanese period, and who was deliberately left behind. Those who stepped forward were usually simply those who made speeches like claps of thunder: Live and Die together with Dai Nippon. Those who were prepared to lick the soles of the former fascist government were the ones who became prominent. The real nationalists . . . stayed in the background. . . . We still remember how it was the "fashion" for the "prominent people" to make rousing speeches, two or three hours long, even though the speeches were absolutely empty. . . . The new ministers are not willing to make speeches like that. They do not agree with imperialism of any sort. . . . These ministers are not the close friends of Yamamoto, Shimizu, or Maeda. They have not become ministers simply to become "puppet" ministers. These ministers have been appointed above all for their still unsullied nationalism and for their capability, which has been acknowledged through their actual practice. . . . We hope now that it will be "less talk, more work," . . . and may the Japanese

[3] See Raliby, *Documenta Historica*, pp. 94–95. For biographical details on these ministers, see the Appendix. The average age of this cabinet was just 40, about halfway between that of the presidential cabinet and that of the Working Committee.

bureaucracy be eliminated to its roots: henchmen of the Kenpeitai and Chianbu, who have tortured and murdered so many of our good nationalists; puppet journalists who have so often lied to our suffering people; leaders who were responsible for the miserable fate of so many Peta, Heihō, and rōmusha. We hope that all the playacting is now over. . . . This government does not depend on Tokyo. Nor on Moscow, nor on Amsterdam. . . . It depends on the confidence of the Indonesian people themselves.[4]

Ra'jat immediately attacked Sjahrir for claiming his government was popularly supported rather than simply a group of "technicians" like the first cabinet. In practice, it charged, half the new cabinet consisted of just such technicians. Sjahrir had boasted that it contained no collaborators, henchmen, or running-dogs of the Japanese, yet both Amir and Soewandi had been high officials before the war, and Moelia's politics had been very pro-Dutch. Should they not be considered henchmen of the Dutch?[5] Diah's *Merdeka,* while endorsing Sjahrir himself, attacked Moelia and Soewandi by name for their role in the Dutch colonial period, and warned that their "complete faith in the Dutch Ethical policy" could easily lead the new government astray.[6]

In response to these criticisms Sjahrir and Amir strongly defended their new cabinet, insisting that it was composed of non-collaborators and would be both tougher and more democratic than its predecessor, which had been unable to control the situation in Surabaja. They both promised elections in January 1946 and stressed that the new government was a government for the pemuda. Amir noted that only he and Sjahrir were "old-timers."[7]

Despite their disclaimers, however, much of the criticism was accurate, indeed possibly erred in the direction of understate-

[4] Nov. 14, 1945. *Berita Indonesia* was at this time under the editorship of S. Tahsin; see Sidik Kertapati, *Sekitar proklamasi,* p. 106.
[5] Nov. 14, 1945.   [6] Nov. 16, 1945.
[7] *Berita Indonesia,* Nov. 16, 1945.

ment. None of the ministers, aside from Sjahrir and Amir, had had distinguished nationalist records before the war. Nor had any but Sjahrir and Amir played a role in the underground. A sizable number had even held high positions under the Japanese, most notably Moelia, Soewandi, Sunario Kolopaking, and Darmawan. The presence of four Christians in the eleven-man cabinet heavily overrepresented the small Christian minority of the population. While their appointment was undoubtedly designed to reassure the Christians of their position in the republic and to prevent them from siding with the returning Dutch, it was bound to arouse criticism at a time when all Christians, and especially the formerly favored Menadonese and Ambonese, were regarded with deep suspicion by the pemuda and much of the public. Furthermore, the absence of any well-known Islamic representative not only revealed the cabinet's narrow social base, but also aroused the anger and resentment of santri leaders. (Indeed, Dr. Sukiman, chairman of the newly formed Masjumi, wired a strong protest to the President, accusing him of violating the Constitution by permitting such a cabinet to be formed.) [8] All the ministers except Sjahrir had university degrees, and over half had been educated in Holland. In spite of Amir's brave words, the pemuda were given no direct representation. It was notable that while Sjahrir and Amir Sjarifuddin took office as chairman and vice-chairman of the youthful Working Committee, of the remaining members of that body only the elderly Soewandi and Sunario Kolopaking were given ministerial posts. The cabinet contained not a single person, aside from its two leaders, who had played a prominent role in the proclamation crisis, or in the dramatic developments since that period. Moreover, it was unsettling that Sjahrir himself assumed three of the five key portfolios, and Amir was given temporary control of the other two. This arrangement probably reflected Sjahrir's feeling that there were few people who were capable, loyal, and politically accept-

[8] *Merdeka*, Nov. 16, 1945.

able, but to observers at the time it made the new government seem very much a two-man show.

It is hard to be sure why this cabinet was so oddly composed. To a considerable degree it consisted of long-time associates of its two leaders. Sunario, Darmasetiawan, Soewandi, and Abdul Karim were personal friends of Sjahrir; Moelia was Amir's cousin. Sukarno and Hatta may have intervened to oppose the inclusion of pemuda elements, but the views expressed in *Perdjuangan Kita* make it seem quite likely that Sjahrir himself was opposed to it. There is some reason to believe that Sjahrir was unwilling to have many people in his cabinet with powerful outside connections and loyalties; by giving preference to people who would be wholly dependent on him for their political survival, he gave himself maximum freedom of action within the government.

Whatever the reasons for the composition of the cabinet, it caused considerable disappointment to those who had supported Sjahrir up to this point, above all the pemuda. By the middle of November the main focus of pemuda hostility had begun to shift from the Japanese to the British and Dutch, and the presence in the cabinet of so many "Dutch-minded" men was taken badly. It was widely felt that they had been chosen because Sjahrir was anxious to conciliate the Allies and feared that the appointment of intransigent pemuda would either alarm the Dutch or be used by them as a pretext to reject negotiations. In other words, the composition of the cabinet was taken by many to be an implicit concession to the other side. This suspicion was not lessened by the haste with which Sjahrir opened discussions with van Mook on the day following his installation as prime minister.[9]

The sense of malaise deepened when on November 17 the cabinet's program was released to the press. Instead of the fiery document many had expected, the stated objectives of the new government were merely:

[9] *Ibid.*

1. To perfect the organization of regional government on the basis of popular sovereignty.

2. To attain coordination of all the energies of the people in the endeavor to build the state of the Indonesian republic and the development of a society based on justice and humanity.

3. To endeavor to improve the economic welfare of the people, in part by the [better] distribution of foodstuffs.

4. To endeavor to hasten a satisfactory solution to the question of issuing a national currency.[10]

In retrospect it is clear that the gradual alienation of important pemuda groups from Sjahrir's leadership began almost simultaneously with his installation as prime minister and the enunciation of his program. But this process was not directly manifested for some time. A more immediate consequence of the formation of the Sjahrir cabinet was that it accelerated the development of political parties and hastened the process of crystallizing hitherto largely latent ideological and other political antagonisms in the republic.

The members of the preceding cabinet were, naturally enough, very bitter about the way their downfall had been engineered, and deeply wounded by the savage attacks on their reputations in *Perdjuangan Kita* and in the press. Many of them had spent long years in the pergerakan and certainly did not feel that they had been traitors or "running-dogs" of the Japanese. This was particularly true of men like Ki Hadjar Dewantoro, Iwa, and Sartono, let alone Sukarno and Hatta. Certain passages in *Perdjuangan Kita* were clearly, if indirectly, aimed at Sukarno himself. Many who felt personally loyal to the President were deeply chagrined by the implications of Sjahrir's attacks, and it is safe to say that Sukarno himself, while outwardly agreeable to the political changes imposed on him, was far from happy in his heart.[11] All

---

[10] Koesnodiprodjo, ed., *Himpunan, 1945,* p. 80.

[11] In an interview on May 11, 1962, Subardjo said that at the time Sukarno had urged him to accept the changes, adding, "I shall bend, but I shall never break."

these men were anxious to reestablish their credentials and return to power.

In the context of the new constitutional system, in which control of the government now appeared to be in the hands of the legislature, their chances of making an effective comeback were clearly dependent on their ability to build political parties. Only the massing of such parties offered the possibility of challenging Sjahrir and Amir in the near future. Accordingly, it was to party formation that they turned. In this move they were joined by other political leaders from the prewar period who had been excluded from both Sukarno's and Sjahrir's governments. Nor were the cabinet leaders themselves unaware of the need to organize and concentrate their hitherto amorphous support within the framework of a political party. Accordingly, the three-month life of the first Sjahrir government was marked by the rapid proliferation of parties. The germination of these parties had, as we have seen, preceded the fall of the Sukarno cabinet, but the consequences of the silent coup were now to bring them rapidly to flower.

Chapter 10

Parties Are Born

The Socialist Party

Sjahrir's call in *Perdjuangan Kita* for the creation of a revolutionary party to lead the Indonesian revolution did not go unheeded. As we have already seen, it had been announced in Jogjakarta on November 1 that the Indonesian Socialist Party (Parsi) was being set up. On November 12 an initial congress was held in the same city, reportedly attended by representatives of 51 regions and 34 bodies, as well as by 750 observers. The assembly decided to urge the formation of a Popular Front to defend and strengthen the republic; to work toward the socialization of key enterprises, forests, and land; and to promote industrialization, transmigration, a cooperative economy and agricultural improvements, and the formation of unions. The Popular Front was to be the means of linking up workers, peasants, the army, and the pemuda. These objectives having been proclaimed, the congress elected Amir Sjarifuddin chairman and Soekindar vice-chairman.[1] Other leading figures at the congress, including Hindromartono and Usman Sastroamidjojo, indicated that the nucleus of the new party was to be formed by close associates of Amir Sjarifuddin in the prewar Gerindo and the labor groups associated with it.

Shortly thereafter, on November 19, the Partai Rakjat Sosialis (Socialist People's Party), or "Paras," was formed in Tjirebon, under Sjahrir's personal sponsorship.[2] From the composition of

[1] *Berita Indonesia,* Nov. 16, 1945.   [2] *Merdeka,* Nov. 22, 1945.

this party's leadership and from its program, it was clear that the ghost of the prewar Pendidikan Nasional Indonesia (Indonesia National Education Movement), the party of Hatta and Sjahrir, was being resurrected. The Paras' declared aims were to oppose capitalistic, *ningrat*,[3] and feudal mentalities; to eliminate autocracy and bureaucratism; to struggle toward a society of *sama rata sama rasa* (egalitarian collectivism); to enrich the spirit of the Indonesian people with a democratic outlook; and to urge the government to cooperate with all organizations at home and abroad to overthrow capitalism. But with Sjahrir and Amir in joint control of the cabinet after November 14, the continued existence of these parties as separate entities made little sense. Within four days of the Paras' formation, the two parties issued a joint statement urging everyone to support the Sjahrir-Amir government, in the name of its anticapitalist and anti-imperialist struggle,[4] and on December 3 the two parties announced that a "Fusion Congress" would be held in Tjirebon on December 16 and 17.[5] Later it was announced that only the respective party leaders would be permitted to attend.[6]

The Fusion Congress was held on schedule and attended by 57 members of the respective party boards. On December 17 the combined leadership of a Partai Sosialis (Socialist Party), or PS, was announced, reflecting the results of the bargaining between the two groups. The complicated structure of the new party was topped by a Leadership Council consisting of Mr. Amir Sjarifuddin, Mr. Hindromartono, Dr. Sudarsono, Supeno, and Oei Gie Hwat.[7] The Executive Committee of the party was subdivided as follows:

[3] *Ningrat*, or *kaum ningrat*, is a common word of abuse for people of aristocratic prijaji parentage. It derives from the fact that many aristocrats have *ningrat* at the end of their names: e.g., Djajadiningrat, Woerjaningrat, Hendraningrat. The suffix means "of the world" or "of the universe."

[4] *Antara*, Nov. 23, 1945.   [5] *Berita Indonesia*, Dec. 5, 1945.

[6] *Ibid.*, Dec. 11, 1945.

[7] The members of the Leadership Council and Executive Committee were listed in *Antara*, Dec. 18, with corrections listed in *ibid.*, Dec. 19.

Political Section: Mr. Abdulmadjid Djojoadiningrat, Mr. M. Tamzil, Mr. M. S. Moewaladi, Mr. Soemitro Reksodipoetro, Subadio Sastrosatomo, Soegondo Djojopoespito

Secretariat: Mr. Abdulmadjid Djojoadiningrat, Goenara, Soetrisno, Mr. R. Usman Sastroamidjojo, L. M. Sitoroes, Wijono, Soemartojo [8]

Information Section: Djohan Sjahroezah, Soebagio, I. Wangsawidjaja, Soewondo, Soedjono, Tan Ling Djie, Soenarno Sisworahardjo [9]

Education Section: Soekindar, Soekemi, Soekadi, Koesnaeni, Soegra, Djawoto [10]

Finance Section: Moenodo, Soekanda, H. Djunaedi [11]

Communications Section: Soebiantokoesoemo, Pramono, Abdul

See the Appendix for biographical details, except for those members mentioned below in notes 8–12, for whom little or no information is available.

[8] Biographical material on the members of the Secretariat is scarce except in the case of Usman, for whom see the Appendix. Goenara had been a member of the Indonesian student organization in Holland Perhimpunan Indonesia (Indonesian Association), or PI, before the war. Soetrisno was a top leader of the Barisan Pemuda Gerindo under Wikana. He became a member of the Illegal PKI, joined Amir's underground, and was sentenced to life imprisonment with him in 1944. Biro Pemuda, *Sedjarah perdjuangan pemuda Indonesia*, p. 84; *Dokumentasi pemuda*, p. 45. No information is available on the background of Sitoroes. Since he joined Sjahrir's Partai Sosialis Indonesia (Indonesian Socialist Party), or PSI, after 1948, it is possible he was associated with Sjahrir earlier, either in the Pendidikan Nasional Indonesia or in the underground. Wijono's background is also unclear, but his role in starting the Parsi and his founding of the Barisan Tani Indonesia (Indonesian Peasants' League), or BTI, suggest an earlier association with Amir. Subsequent to the Madiun Affair in 1948, however, he joined Sjahrir's PSI. Soemartojo was an associate of Wijono in Jogjakarta, and headed the pemuda section of the BTI under Wijono's leadership (*Antara*, Oct. 31, 1945). He subsequently followed his old chief into the PSI.

[9] I have no information on Soewondo, and little on Soenarno Sisworahardjo except that he was later a member of the PSI; see Indonesia, Kementerian Penerangan, *Kepartaian di Indonesia* (Tegal, 1950), p. 173.

[10] I have no information on Soekadi or Koesnaeni.

[11] I have no information on Moenodo.

Fatah, Ruslan, Noeroellah, Sardjono, Mohammed Tauchid, Soehadi.[12]

The leadership of what was to be Java's major left-wing party until its breakup in the spring of 1948 can be tentatively divided into five different clusters: a Surabaja group of former associates of Amir Sjarifuddin in the Illegal PKI and in his underground organization; a "Jogja" group centered around Wijono and Tauchid, who were involved with Amir in setting up the Parsi; a Tjirebon group with roots in the Pendidikan Nasional Indonesia and connections with Sjahrir's underground; a Djakarta group composed mainly of metropolitan pemuda and other close associates of the Prime Minister; and last, a small group of recent returnees from Holland, most of whom had been involved in the anti-Nazi underground.[13] The most prominent personality in this last group was Abdulmadjid Djojoadiningrat, who was a member of the Dutch Communist Party executive, though this was not generally known at the time.

Although the first four of these clusters were in essence localized groups of comrades and friends, they were more or less loosely attached either to Amir and the Parsi or to Sjahrir and the Paras. The fusion pronounced in December 1945 was never fully achieved in practice, and insofar as it was effective depended heavily on the trust between Sjahrir and Amir themselves. When the party finally split in 1948, the division took place largely along the original lines of fusion.

[12] Little is known of the first five members of the Communications Section. Soebiantokoesoemo and Abdul Fatah were members of Amir's underground, the latter receiving a life sentence in 1944. *Dokumentasi pemuda,* p. 45. I have no information on Pramono. Ruslan was a member of the PRI in Surabaja and regarded as a protégé of Amir's. Noeroellah sat in the KNIP as a representative of the city of Malang, and later joined Sjahrir's PSI. Indonesia, Kementerian Penerangan, *Kepartaian di Indonesia,* p. 173.

[13] These clusters derive in part from the biographical data referred to or contained above in notes 7–12, and in part from conversations with former members of the PS.

Amir's group was dominated by members of the Surabaja underground, many of whom had suffered severely under Japanese repression. Its political ancestry lay, like that of Amir himself, in the family of mass-oriented parties of the prewar period: the PKI of the twenties, Sukarno's PNI, the Partindo, and the Gerindo. In the main its members had humbler origins and less Western education than the followers of Sjahrir. Its Marxism was less sophisticated and less academic, and at the same time more populist and tinged with apocalyptic romanticism. Its radicalism was more experienced than read about. While the group lived with the bitter memory of imprisonment, torture, and execution at the hands of the Kenpeitai, it by no means wholly shared Sjahrir's perspective on the consequences of the occupation, particularly on the phenomenon of pemudaism. Indeed many of its members found themselves psychologically in tune with the veterans of the Seinendan, the Barisan Pelopor, and the metropolitan asrama, and took a fierce delight in the militant activism of the pemuda movement.

The group's cohesion, however, derived almost as much from the personality of its leader as from its common experience and outlook. Although he was to die before a firing squad within a mere four years, Amir was a man even his political adversaries found it difficult to hate. Though he participated in the campaign to overthrow the Sukarno cabinet, he remained friendly with many of its members and never aroused the bitterness among them that Sjahrir had. Highly intelligent, energetic, and ambitious, his personal warmth, humor, and emotional romanticism elicited an intense loyalty among his followers that was largely unaffected by the political line he took at any one time. His considerable oratorical talents, which some have recalled as being second only to Sukarno's, enabled him to generate confidence and affection among a much wider group than his immediate associates. Though a Sumatran Batak and a Protestant, he could communicate with the pemuda of Java as few other politicians of his generation. His wartime sufferings also gave him unusual credentials for assuming the leadership of the more radical left-wing elements who had survived the occupation, though it must be admitted that his assuming the leadership was facilitated by the absence of the top PKI leaders of the twenties, who were either dead or still in exile.

By contrast, Sjahrir's group within the Socialist Party was characterized by more elite origins and a higher level of Western-style education. Many of its members were former activists of the Pendidikan Nasional Indonesia, the organization in which Sjahrir had played a prominent role before his exile in the early thirties, and the group as a whole continued the political and intellectual tradition of the prewar organization. The Pendidikan Nasional Indonesia, in sharp conflict with the rival Partindo, had from the start stressed the need to develop disciplined, highly educated, and ideologically sophisticated cadres to give intelligent, purposeful leadership to the independence movement, rather than devoting itself to mass agitation and the propagation of populist nationalism.[14] For those who were by temperament or experience inclined toward this rationalist and elitist perspective, the personality of Sjahrir was naturally attractive. Cool, detached, sharp-tongued, and highly sophisticated, he was without question the leading intellectual figure of his generation. While by talent and temperament incapable of appealing to a mass public, he was able to draw around him a devoted circle of admirers, not least

---

[14] For an account of the split between the Pendidikan Nasional Indonesia and the Partindo, see Pluvier, *Overzicht,* pp. 47–52. Pluvier characterizes the two organizations very well when he says (p. 49) that "the Partindo was a real mass-party. It worked hard to increase its membership and to expand its organization. It attracted much public attention by its extensive propaganda among the masses and by its holding of mass gatherings. By contrast, the [Pendidikan Nasional Indonesia] worked in a smaller circle, particularly in the training of cadres which could spread ideas among the masses." There were also important ideological differences, since the Partindo wanted to unite all Indonesians into a single national front, regardless of social class. Their rivals found this a sociological monstrosity. Hatta later declared, for example, that it would bring about *persatéan* (dissension), not *persatuan* (unity).

among the university students in Djakarta and Bandung. Where Amir had affinities with Sukarno, Sjahrir was closer to the phlegmatic Hatta, with whom he shared not only their earlier comradeship in the Pendidikan Nasional Indonesia and in exile, but also a distaste for demagoguery and romanticism.

While the working relationship between Sjahrir and Amir at this time was excellent, the differences in their personal styles and outlooks tended from the start to be accentuated by their respective followings. Just below the surface, Sjahrir's men were inclined to view Amir's associates as somewhat provincial, romantic, and intellectually confused, while among the Amir group there was often a feeling that Sjahrir's followers were intellectually snobbish and unwilling to undertake the risks and hardships of working among the masses.

The temperament and interests of the two wings of the Socialist Party were reflected in the party's internal structure. It is interesting, for example, that it was Amir who actually headed the party, while Sjahrir was not even included in the roster of initial leaders. Whether this was a *quid pro quo* for Amir's deference to Sjahrir as leader of the government or not, it certainly reflected Amir's talent for organizational work and Sjahrir's well-known boredom with such matters. It is even more noticeable that Amir's men were concentrated in the Leadership Council, the Secretariat, and the Communications Section (the organizational heart of the party), while Sjahrir's group dominated the Information and Education sections.

Between these two wings, and for some time cementing them closer together, was the small group of returnees from Holland.[15] The influence of this group was less in matters of organization or program than in shaping the party's view of the outside world and of itself. It should not be forgotten that at this period the prestige and power of the Dutch left was at its height. Many of

[15] For an interesting discussion of this group and some of its leading personalities, see Soe Hok-gie, "Simpang kiri dari sebuah djalan" (M.A. thesis, University of Indonesia, 1969), pp. 23–27.

Abdulmadjid's former colleagues in the anti-Nazi resistance were in prominent positions in The Hague. Indeed, the Prime Minister himself, Prof. Schermerhorn, could be counted in this group. The experience of the resistance had created a genuine sense of solidarity between the Dutch and Indonesians who had joined it, and many months would pass before the diverging destinies of their two countries tore them apart. Given these circumstances, Abdulmadjid and his friends were naturally inclined to urge the path of diplomacy in dealing with Holland, and to rely, too optimistically as it proved, on the progressiveness and benevolence of public opinion in a country so recently freed from Nazi despotism. Abdulmadjid's encouraging reports on the political climate in Holland found ready listeners among the top leaders of the Socialist Party and the government. Both Sjahrir and Amir had spent part of their youth in Holland, and Sjahrir in particular had had extensive and relatively warm relations with sections of the Dutch left. This experience, now compounded with Abdulmadjid's evaluation, made it easier for them to envisage a reasonable accommodation with the Dutch government than for most other Indonesians, who had had little contact with the Dutch except in their forbidding colonial capacity.

In addition, the Abdulmadjid group served to strengthen the Socialist Party's self-definition as the party of the resistance.[16] It was widely assumed on the left, both in Holland and in Indonesia, that the undergrounds in both countries had been fighting essentially the same fight—against world fascism. There was little understanding of the radical differences between the Nazi and Japanese military regimes, or of the contrasting historical meanings of their respective conquests in Europe and Southeast Asia. (It was the denial of these differences implicit in *Perdjuangan Kita* that so embittered the members of Sukarno's cabinet, who felt that their being compared with the Dutch fascists, who col-

[16] It should be noted that virtually none of the PS leaders had held any official position of note in the Japanese period. The contrast with Sjahrir's cabinet is striking in this regard.

laborated with the Nazis to enslave a previously free country, was totally unjustified and malign.) Being identified as part of an international resistance movement appealed particularly to Amir's followers and was influential in persuading them to support the policy of diplomacy urged by Abdulmadjid, which they might otherwise have been inclined by temperament and prewar experience to reject.

The net effect, then, of the returnees was to encourage the party to pursue a policy of accommodation with Holland and at the same time to foster the party's inner cohesion by reinforcing its self-image as a party of resistance. In the short run this image was undoubtedly an advantage. But it was eventually to prove a weakness, since an image based on the past was likely to be vulnerable to changing events unless it was accompanied by a coherent and deeply shared program for the future.

The actual program drawn up by the PS reflected this self-image, and at the same time the inner dualism of the party's structure. On the one hand the political section of the program laid particular stress on the need for a democratization of administrative and political structures: seven of the ten points dealt with such matters as the need for broad popular participation in administration; for direct popular election of the head of state and regional heads of government; for the broadest democratic freedoms, especially the right to strike; and for the formation of elective councils at all important levels of government, to which the corresponding administrative organs would be responsible. On the other hand there were also calls for the formation of a general militia and for the creation of peasants' and workers' unions and paramilitary organizations.

The economic section of the program called for a collectivist economy based on cooperatives, with all basic industries, banks, and utilities to be in state hands. Furthermore, "land, water, and the natural resources contained in them should also be controlled by the state and used as far as possible for the people's welfare."

Stress was laid on the urgent need for transmigration, industrialization, and the rationalization of agricultural production. At the same time, the objectives of economic egalitarianism and social justice were to be kept in harmony with the technological transformation involved. Demands were made for the formation of workers' councils in state industries.

The social aspects of the program were perhaps the most interesting of all, since they specified "the end of class differences in society and the propagation of attitudes of *sama rata sama rasa*," with state-guaranteed minimum standards of living, progressive tax laws, labor legislation, free and compulsory education, and so on. A special clause was devoted to "ensuring that the army too should accept and practice the principles of *kerakjatan*." [17] These principles were also to be the basis for a socialist culture.[18]

Most of the program was thus unexceptionably "social democratic" in content, comparable to the programs of innumerable moderate socialist parties in Western Europe and elsewhere. A more authentic Marxist note was struck mainly in those sections concerned with the formation of popular military and paramilitary organizations alongside the army, which, it was strongly implied, was not yet properly democratic or revolutionary in its orientation. Yet the clause dealing with class conflict was perhaps the most revealing of all. Both Sjahrir and Amir regarded themselves as Marxists, yet the program carefully avoided stating that class conflict as such existed in Indonesia, merely urging that differences be removed. The idea of *sama rata sama rasa* seemed to be less an anticipation of a classless society achieved through the revolutionary process than of a tensionless community like

[17] *Kerakjatan* is almost impossible to translate, except by some neologism like "people-ness." *Rakjat,* technically meaning "the people," always has the sense of "common people." *Sama rata sama rasa* is a typically Indonesian expression meaning very roughly "everyone on the same level, feeling at one."

[18] The full program is given in *Ra'jat* (Djakarta), Jan. 5, 1946.

the idealized village societies of premodern times.[19] This was perhaps already an indication of how the Sjahrir-Amir government was to handle the whole problem of the social revolutions that would strongly influence Java's internal politics during its rule.

Whatever its internal differences, the Socialist Party represented in many ways the central tradition of left-wing intellectual nationalism as it had developed in the prewar period. But with the coming of the war, the placid years of the thirties were gone for good, and new forces were unleashed which this tradition and its carriers were only partly capable of encompassing. Accordingly, while the PS remained the dominant party of the left in the early years of the revolution, it was by no means the only one. In the Partai Buruh Indonesia (Indonesian Workers' Party), or PBI, and the Partai Komunis Indonesia (Indonesian Communist Party), or PKI, one can observe radical movements outside the central tradition, searching out some of the new political forces the occupation and its immediate aftermath had brought into being.

The Indonesian Workers' Party (PBI)

We have seen that as early as September 15, under the auspices of the Menteng 31 Komité van Aksi (Action Committee), the Barisan Buruh Indonesia (Indonesian Workers' League), or BBI, had been formed to organize workers in the environs of Djakarta. Shortly after its formation, the BBI demanded recognition by the KNIP as the sole legitimate representative of workers' interests, and urged that this recognition be endorsed by Iwa

[19] The same theme was to recur over and over in official Indonesian propaganda in the next twenty years, especially in the constant reference to *gotong-rojong* (mutual help) as the basis of Indonesian society and politics. For a sociological analysis of the hard reality of gotong-rojong practices, see the interesting study by Koentjaraningrat, *Some Social-Anthropological Observations on Gotong Rojong Practices in Two Villages of Central Java,* trans. Claire Holt (Ithaca, N.Y., 1961).

Kusumasumantri, then minister of social affairs.[20] It is very probable that Iwa himself unofficially promoted these demands. In any case the BBI, with his support, rapidly developed a significant following, particularly in the Surabaja area. There, on September 30, a local branch of the organization was set up under Sjamsu Harja Udaja, with a solid base in the workers of the dockyards and the public utilities.[21] On October 5 Iwa officially recognized the BBI as the sole representative of federated labor on Java, while the BBI itself began issuing instructions urging spontaneously formed local unions to begin developing horizontal coordination and closer contact with central headquarters.[22]

From November onward it began to become clear that there were two conflicting groups within the BBI. One group was largely concerned with building the BBI up as a powerful labor federation, independent of the political parties and ready to exert leverage on any government. The other group, led by Sjamsu, hoped to convert the BBI into a party that would be the political arm of the labor movement. The struggle first came out into the open at a Congress of Workers and Peasants held in Surakarta early in November, which was opened by Iwa in his capacity as minister.[23] Sjamsu's oratory and lobbying won the day, and it was decided that the BBI would be converted into the Indonesian Workers' Party, the PBI. The ascendancy of Sjamsu's group was further revealed when it was announced that the new party would for the time being have its headquarters in Surabaja and be led by Sjamsu himself.[24]

[20] *Berita Indonesia*, no. 1, undated, but probably printed on Sept. 31, 1945.

[21] *Warta Indonesia,* Oct. 4, 1945; *Dokumentasi pemuda,* p. 48. For biographical details on Sjamsu Harja Udaja, see the Appendix.

[22] *Merdeka,* Oct. 7, 1945.

[23] It was claimed that 3,000 people attended this congress representing 817 unions—104 of them from Surakarta!

[24] *Merdeka,* Nov. 10, 1945.

The first PBI congress opened in Madiun on December 15, and elected Sjamsu Harja Udaja its permanent chairman. Its program was in marked contrast to that of the Socialist Party, since it declared that the party "struggles on the basis of its understanding of the conflict between employers and workers, and endeavors by revolutionary methods to eliminate capitalism and progress toward socialism." Labor unions were to remain unchanged as the direct infrastructure of the PBI. While all Indonesian citizens who were "labor-minded" (*berhaluan buruh*) could join the party, no party discipline would be instituted, all members being quite free to join other parties.[25]

However, while the PBI leadership was able to make its will prevail at the congress and was strong in Sjamsu's home territory in East Java, it was unable to make itself obeyed in parts of Central and especially West Java. So many local sections of the BBI refused to accept the decision made in Surakarta and maintained their separate identity that on January 7 the PBI felt compelled to announce that it had decided to "revive" the BBI, which would not be in any way subordinate to it. The PBI would lead the workers' political struggle, but it was not necessary for all members of the BBI to join the party. The relationship between the two would consist primarily of spiritual solidarity.[26]

The reasons for the PBI's failure to command the loyalty of the unions associated with the BBI are not wholly clear. But it is certain that three interacting factors were at work. The first was the particular character of union organization itself at this period. The Japanese had not permitted any unions to exist and had exercised authoritarian control of the labor force through the Labor Bureau of the military administration. Nor was the prewar tradition of union organization strong enough to ensure the revival of unions of the thirties in their old form. The result was that in 1945, when labor organizations began to appear, they followed very much the pattern of the pemuda movement in general. They grew up on an ad hoc and localized basis as work-

[25] *Antara,* Dec. 18, 1945.   [26] *Berita Indonesia,* Jan. 8, 1946.

ers in individual enterprises and offices took these premises over and constituted themselves as unions. Thus from the start unions were organized on an essentially territorial basis rather than on the basis of particular industrial skills. While this largely spontaneous pattern of growth gave each local union considerable solidarity and cohesion, it tended to make any hierarchical union structure exceedingly difficult to achieve. Springing into existence as it were from the bottom up, and controlling their own enterprises and offices, these unions were unwilling to forego their newly found autonomy and freedom of action.

A second factor at work was the fact that especially in the Djakarta area, the BBI's original sponsor, Iwa Kusumasumantri, and the PBI's first elected chairman, Sjamsu, suffered from the Sjahrir campaign against the "collaborators." While such accusations were unjustified in Iwa's case, as we have seen, his association with the Sukarno cabinet weakened his position, and his fall as minister deprived Sjamsu of powerful backing. Sjamsu's own role in the occupation was evidently not one that gave him much credit in the eyes of the metropolitan underground. Thus the PBI's inability to attract leaders with unequivocal resistance backgrounds certainly contributed to its lack of authority.

A third factor was that the PS, seeing itself as the mainstream party of the left, was naturally unwilling to allow another party to assume the leadership of the working class' organizations. It was able to make its influence felt particularly in Djakarta and West Java, where its leaders, such as Njono, were former members of the Komité van Aksi and were close to the groups that had brought Sjahrir and Amir to power.

After January 1946 the PBI increasingly regarded itself as an opposition party and was treated as such. To mobilize political and financial resources for itself and against the party in power, it tried to make use of the spontaneous, localized radicalism among the workers that had earlier frustrated its consolidation. Accordingly, it began to propagate what might be called syndicalist ideas: the industrial installations seized by the workers should remain the property of the workers, not of the government, and control of the enterprises should be exercised by their former employees.

The PBI campaign rapidly aroused intense hostility from the government. Not only was the cabinet anxious to prevent the workers' support from going to a rival party, but, more important, it was alarmed by the political implications of the syndicalist ideas the PBI encouraged. Local control of the factories and plantations appeared, in the government's eyes, to threaten its hopes of achieving centralized control over the small but potentially productive modernized sector of the economy. And the government was convinced that without such control any coherent economic policy would be impossible to achieve. Still more important, the cabinet's determination to reach an accommodation with the Dutch and British meant that it had to reassure them that their economic interests would be safeguarded, or in other words, that much of their former property would be restored to them. Such assurances would be unconvincing so long as these properties remained in the workers' hands. Spurred, therefore, by its domestic political and diplomatic interests, the Sjahrir government moved as rapidly as it could to seize control of the enterprises and estates, establishing councils in which the workers were indeed represented, but which were thoroughly dominated by officials loyal to itself.[27]

In the face of unrelenting government pressure and hostility, and handicapped by its own weaknesses, the PBI was unable to develop much strength. In spite of its initial success in giving a political voice to the spontaneous radicalism of the working class, that class was too tiny a fraction of the whole population to provide an effective political base on its own.

The Indonesian Communist Party (PKI)

We have already seen that the PKI was the first political party to be formed after the Proclamation of Independence. An an-

[27] For a detailed account of the government's struggle to gain control over the estates and enterprises, see Sutter, *Indonesianisasi*, pp. 343–408.

nouncement in the Djakarta press on November 6 broke the news of its birth on October 21. The leaders of the party were two lawyers, Mr. Muhammad Jusuf and Mr. Soeprapto.[28] Neither had been a member of the Illegal PKI of the thirties or of Amir's underground. Jusuf, however, had been a middle-level cadre of the Gerindo, and on the eve of the occupation he had formed the so-called Djojobojo movement centered in Bandung and stretching down into the coastal plain around Indramaju and Tjirebon. This movement, in which radical socialist ideas and traditional mystical beliefs based on the putative prophecies of the legendary twelfth-century King Djojobojo of Kediri were inextricably mixed, survived the first year of the Japanese military administration, and if Sidik Kertapati is to be believed, its members engaged in small-scale sabotage before it was broken up by the Kenpeitai.[29] Jusuf was also attached for a time to Maeda's Asrama Indonesia Merdeka, and counted among his protégés the youthful D. N. Aidit. Soeprapto, too, formed a tiny underground group of his own, which apparently had close relations with the Djojobojo movement.[30]

On November 12, two days before Sjahrir was installed as prime minister, Jusuf's new party issued its program, which in some respects did not differ markedly from that of the PS.[31] It too demanded the fullest democratic rights, and guarantees of generous wages and reasonable hours of work. It promised the

---

The account is marred, however, by an uncritical bias in favor of free and foreign enterprise, and thus in favor of the government's activities.

[28] For the announcements on the formation of the PKI and its program, see *Berita Indonesia*, Nov. 6 and 13, 1945. For biographical details on Jusuf and Soeprapto, see the Appendix.

[29] Sidik Kertapati, *Sekitar proklamasi*, pp. 18–19. Cf. Kahin, *Nationalism and Revolution*, pp. 158–59; and Brackman, *Indonesian Communism*, p. 41.

[30] Sidik Kertapati (*Sekitar proklamasi*, pp. 18–19) describes Soeprapto's group and says that the sabotage activities included at least one train derailment. When the Kenpeitai destroyed the Djojobojo movement, some of its members were sentenced to death.

[31] *Antara*, Nov. 12, 1945.

nationalization of all important enterprises in the fields of production, distribution, and finance. The most interesting section of the program was that dealing with the peasantry, for here the demands of the PKI were in sharp contrast to those of the Socialist Party:

1. The PKI constantly struggles to achieve the free organization of the class of workers and peasants.

2. The PKI constantly makes clear the irreconcilable clash of interests between worker-peasants and bourgeois peasants.

3. All private estates and large-scale landholdings must be immediately confiscated.

4. All these lands must fall into the hands of the peasantry organized into soviets consisting of people's representatives.

5. Nationalization of all land.

The PKI warns the peasants not to be seduced in the direction of petty enterprise. This mode of production cannot abolish the misery of the masses [*rakjat djelata*]. Social revolution is the only way to eliminate and destroy the exploitation of the common people.

What is most striking about these words is not, as some later observers remarked, the degree to which they represented a deviation from the Popular Front line then prevailing in the international communist movement. It is probable that the PKI leaders knew little about international lines of any sort. Rather, what comes through most forcefully is the authentic voice of the spontaneous radicalism on Java in late 1945. The specific mention of the particuliere landerijen, which as we have seen were concentrated largely in the coastal plain of West Java, indicates how much the communism of Jusuf and his associates grew out of and reflected indigenous, localized social upheavals. For the PKI, as for the PBI, the immediate political problem was the internal domestic crisis in Java rather than, as for the PS, the international situation in which Indonesia found herself after the Japanese collapse. As in the case of the PBI, the PKI sought to give leadership to emerging revolutionary forces that the mainstream party of the left largely ignored or feared. But while the two parties shared the advantage of being based on the popular movements of the time among the workers and the peasantry, they also shared the weaknesses of lacking leadership of the first caliber and of rapidly incurring the hostility of the party in power. We shall see later how the PKI succumbed to these disabilities.

The Masjumi

If the PS, the PBI, and the PKI in their different ways represented the groups that had traditionally supplied the base for left-wing nationalism—the radical secular intelligentsia, the urban workers, and the abangan peasantry—the santri community, both urban and to a lesser extent rural, found its initial political expression in a Masjumi born in the war years but now transformed under the republic.[32]

Plans for this transformation were first formally broached at a meeting of older Islamic political leaders held in Jogjakarta on October 11.[33] Evidently the response in Islamic circles was

[32] The wartime Masjumi, set up by the Japanese on November 7, 1943, was the successor of the Madjlisul Islamil a'laa Indonesia (Great Islamic Council of Indonesia), or MIAI, a broad federation of Islamic organizations formed in the late Dutch colonial period. But whereas the MIAI had come increasingly to be dominated by politicians of the prewar Islamic political parties, the strength of the Masjumi was drawn primarily from the two major nonpolitical organizations of prewar Islam, the reformist Muhammadijah and the conservative Nahdatul Ulama. (Both were accorded legal recognition by the Japanese, while the parties were silently extinguished.) The leadership and policies of the wartime Masjumi were directly negotiated between representatives of these two large organizations. The *locus classicus* on this Masjumi is Benda's *The Crescent and the Rising Sun,* chap. 7.

[33] An interesting account of the negotiations preceding the Jogjakarta Congress can be found in Deliar Noer, "Masjumi: Its Organization, Ideology, and Political Role in Indonesia" (M.A. thesis, Cornell University, 1960), pp. 39–40. According to Noer, he was informed by Roem and Prawoto in March 1958 that the discussions about the political future of Islam that culminated in the Jogjakarta Congress were held in Djakarta in September 1945 by Roem, Wachid Hasjim, and K. H. Abdul Kahar Muzakkir. Feeling concern about Islam's lack of recognition in the Constitution and of representation in the government they decided to re-

favorable, since a heavily attended opening congress was successfully held a month later on November 7 and 8, also in Jogjakarta. By a narrow margin of 52 to 50, the assembled notables voted to retain the name Masjumi rather than the alternative proposal of Partai Rakjat Islam (Islamic People's Party).[34] Leaders were then elected as follows:

Chairman: Dr. H. Sukiman Wirjosandjojo
First vice-chairman: R. Abikusno Tjokrosujoso
Second vice-chairman: R. Wali al-Fatah
First secretary: S. M. Kartosoewirjo
Second secretary: M. Prawoto Mangkusasmito
Head of the Pemuda Section: R. M. Harsono Tjokroaminoto
Head of the Finance Section: Mr. R. A. Kasmat
Head of the Information Section: Gaffar Ismail
Head of the Hizbullah Section: H. Hasjim
Members: K. Dahlan, H. M. Faried Ma'ruf, K. H. Masjkoer, M. Joenoes Anies, K. H. Fakih Oesman, K. H. Fatoerrachman, Dr. Aboe Hanifah, M. Natsir, R. M. Anwar Tjokroaminoto, Mr. R. Samsoedin, Mr. Mohammed Roem.[35]

The degree to which this leadership reflected a real transformation of the wartime Masjumi can be judged from the fact that

---

activate and transform the wartime Masjumi. (The only fact tending to cast doubt on this version is that neither Wachid Hasjim nor Muzakkir was included in the new Masjumi's leadership roster, and Roem had no notably important role within it.)

[34] *Ibid.*, p. 43.

[35] *Merdeka*, Nov. 9, 1945; *Kedaulatan Rakjat*, Nov. 14, 1945. Biographical details on all of these figures except Anies and Hasjim can be found in the Appendix. According to Benda, M. Joenoes Anies was a Muhammadijah member as far back as 1932 and was enrolled in the Peta in 1943. (*The Crescent and the Rising Sun*, pp. 224, 253.) According to Alfian, he was a Jogjanese and the son of one of the founders of the Muhammadijah, Hadji Anies. ("Islamic Modernism in Indonesian Politics: The Muhammadijah Movement during the Dutch Colonial Period (1912–1942)" [Ph.D. thesis, University of Wisconsin, 1969], p. 261.) The only information obtained on Hasjim is that he was one of the five Muhammadijah representatives on the executive of the wartime Masjumi. (Benda, *The Crescent and the Rising Sun*, p. 263.)

only Faried Ma'ruf and Hasjim were carry-overs from the executive of the occupation period.[36] The central significance of the changes was that they brought to the fore once again the leaders of the prewar political parties and relegated the Muhammadijah and the Nahdatul Ulama to the background. Indeed, these two organizations between them could only claim a quarter of the Masjumi's new leadership.[37] Real power was held by former members of Sukiman's Partai Islam Indonesia (Indonesian Islamic Party), or PII, established as the result of a family quarrel in H.O.S. Tjokroaminoto's Partai Sarikat Islam Indonesia (Indonesian Islamic Union Party), or PSII. Not only was Sukiman chairman, but his associates and protégés controlled at least half of the executive positions. Three quarters of the leadership came from Central and East Java, and about half came from the Javanese lower prijaji or from upper-class Minangkabau from West Sumatra.

The Masjumi leadership thus by no means represented the broad mass of the santri community. Overwhelmingly urban and modernist in character, it offered little to the locally powerful rural kjai whom the Japanese had done much to politicize. Moreover, though they headed a potentially large and powerful Islamic organization, the leaders were mainly, by education and experience, party politicians who had been strongly affected by Western ideas and accustomed during the thirties to dealing with the secularly oriented nationalist intelligentsia.

The program adopted by the congress reflected clearly the thinking of this leadership. Declaring that its aims were to "establish the sovereignty of the Indonesian republic and the Islamic

---

[36] For a list of the wartime Masjumi's executive, see Benda, *The Crescent and the Rising Sun*, pp. 262–63.

[37] The Jogjakarta Congress did, however, make one important decision that seemed likely in the long run to increase the influence of the Muhammadijah and the Nahdatul Ulama. It was agreed that the Masjumi would admit both "ordinary" individual members and "extraordinary" collective members, such as the Muhammadijah and the Nahdatul Ulama. This decision ensured that the Masjumi would continue to have something of the federative character of the MIAI and the wartime Masjumi.

religion, and to put the ideals of Islam into practice in matters of state," the Masjumi pledged

to awaken the consciousness and broaden the knowledge and competence of Indonesians in the political struggle; to organize and solidify the ranks of the Islamic community for the struggle to defend religion and the sovereignty of the state; to put into practice a community way of life based on Iman and Taqwa [piety and Godfearingness], social humanitarianism, brotherhood, and equal rights according to the teachings of Islam; and to cooperate with other groups in the struggle to establish the sovereignty of the state.[38]

A month after the congress, the Masjumi leaders issued a more detailed and urgent Struggle Program that contrasts revealingly with the programs of the parties we have looked at so far.[39] The Struggle Program, as its name indicates, gave top priority to mobilizing and arming the santri community. It urged that the population be given military training while a people's army was developed and expanded. More specifically, it called for an acceleration in the organizing, training, and equipping of the Hizbullah and the Sabilillah everywhere, and a general mobilization among all Moslems of energy, property, and ideas to promote the interests of the Hizbullah and Sabilillah armies.[40]

[38] *Antara*, Nov. 16, 1945.
[39] *Ibid.*, Dec. 21, 1945, contains the full text.
[40] We have already seen the genesis of the Hizbullah (Army of Allah) as the proto-military arm of the wartime Masjumi in early 1945. In the fall of 1945 many of Yanagawa's pupils, who had in the meantime returned to their home areas, began passing on their knowledge and training to local santri youths. From these seeds a transformed Hizbullah based largely on urban Islamic pemuda grew; it was highly decentralized but an important power adjunct to the Masjumi. By a decision of the congress of November 7, the Hizbullah was made an "extraordinary" member of the party. The Barisan Sabilillah (Path of Allah Corps) had no formal antecedents in the Japanese period, had no formal military training, and was not organized in regular formations. It seems never to have become an integral organization, but was rather a generic name for the myriad rural kjai-led armed bands that sprang up during the period of the takeovers from the Japanese. For an excellent discussion of the two organizations in the Bandung area in 1945–46, see Smail, *Bandung*, pp. 91–92.

The economic section of the Struggle Program was decidedly conservative, even by comparison with the program of the Socialist Party. While opposing the "capitalist system" as being based purely on self-interest, the Masjumi insisted that the government's primary economic obligation was to create opportunities for its citizens. Private property rights must be fully recognized, limited only by the precepts of Islam.[41] There was no mention anywhere of socialism, or indeed of state control of even the major utilities and banks. It is not hard to see in all this the Sarekat Islam tradition of confining anticapitalist propaganda mainly to attacks on "sinful" (foreign) capitalism.[42]

The social program demanded a state ban on all forms of gambling, opium, alcohol, adultery, and usury, but at the same time urged extensive welfare and labor legislation. The party's political objectives were stated to be first, "an Indonesian state based on Islam"; second, "the general and direct right to elect and be elected"; and third, "the formation of electoral bodies with the duty of leading a propaganda drive to convince the people of the truth and perfection [kesempurnaan] of the demands in the Masjumi program."

The formation, leadership, and programs of the Masjumi presaged at once the party's weaknesses and its strengths. The weaknesses were perhaps the more obvious. The leadership, with a few exceptions, was not of the highest caliber, nor very representative of its constituency. The ideas contained in the program were rudimentary in the political section, traditionally puritanical in the social section, and oriented toward the status quo in the economic section. The emphasis on the sanctity of private property and the importance of individual enterprise reflected the sociological fact that political leadership in the santri community tended to be drawn from the prosperous merchants of the north

[41] This refers to the Moslem obligation to give zakat (religious tithes) and kurban (alms).

[42] Sutter (Indonesianisasi, pp. 115, 327) shows how closely the Masjumi economic program coincided with that of the prewar PII. The occupation does not seem to have affected the thinking of Sukiman and his associates in these matters.

coast ports, the pious, hard-working businessmen of the *kauman*
of the interior cities, and the landowning hadji and kjai of the
rural hinterland.[43] In such circles, if not among the peasants of
the santri community, the egalitarian collectivism of *sama rata
sama rasa* could arouse little enthusiasm. The Masjumi's potential strength derived in part from the fact that unlike the PS, it
had no real rival for its constituency. And the very vagueness of
its formal ideology made it easier for the party to focus the
loyalty of the santri community on itself. Moreover, the looseness
of its structure and the largely unpolitical character of many of
its demands left the pemuda of the pesantrèn to march as they
would under the banner of Islam.

The Serindo-PNI

While the leaders of the prewar left and of the undergrounds
moved with some rapidity into the PS, and to a lesser extent the
PKI and PBI, and many of the modernist prewar Islamic politicians coalesced quickly into the Masjumi, the considerable
group of political leaders from the thirties who saw themselves
primarily as nationalists pure and simple were slow to follow
these examples. The reasons for this delay and the surprising political weakness of the group as a whole are instructive.

In the first place many of the group, particularly its older
members, had been heavily involved in the official politics of the
Japanese occupation. In the immediate post-surrender days they
had tried rather halfheartedly to develop the PNI-Staatspartij,
but this effort, as we have seen, had rapidly proved abortive.
Considerable numbers felt sufficiently on the defensive as a result
of Sjahrir's attacks on "collaborationists" and the prevailing pop-

---

[43] The *kauman* is a typical feature of the larger towns of inland Java.
It is a residential area (often just one street) directly adjoining the main
mosque, which itself is usually located on the eastern side of the town
square (*alun-alun*). It is *par excellence* the home base of the devout
Moslem business class. The founders of the Muhammadijah, for example,
were almost exclusively drawn from the Kauman of Jogjakarta. Alfian,
Islamic Modernism, pp. 228, 241, 261–63, 277–78.

ular revulsion against the occupation, that they were reluctant to step rapidly to the fore. A few of the younger men, not particularly socialist in their thinking or way of life, even joined the PS because of its youth, its wartime record, and the personalities of Sjahrir and Amir. Others decided not to join any party for the time being.

There was also the problem of finding a constituency. The natural constituents of a nationalist party in Java, as in other parts of Southeast Asia, at that time, were the educated members of the traditional ruling class, government officials, professional people, and to some extent, village elites. In the case of Java, however, the experience of the later colonial period under the Dutch and Japanese had created antagonisms within this constituency that were to take some years of independence to heal.

In the Dutch period nationalist politicians had generally been hostile to Indonesian civil servants, even though the social origins of the two groups were almost identical. The nationalists had attacked the officials for supinely serving Dutch interests and acting as the henchmen of the Dutch in oppressing the people. In turn, many of the white-collar official class distrusted and resented the nationalists. With the coming of the Japanese, however, the two groups were drawn closer together, since the military government did its best to secure the support of both groups. Although rivalries persisted, the bitter antagonisms of the Dutch period began to diminish as the nationalists were given posts in the government administration and were included in innumerable organizations and councils alongside representatives of the colonial bureaucracy. The "cooperation" issue of the thirties became much less important than it had been, since both groups were now more or less cooperating with the Sixteenth Army.

In spite of this rapprochement, the populist ideology of the main prewar nationalist parties remained an important bar to further progress. Few of the bureaucrats in the government were really able to sympathize with this ideology or were cynical enough to disregard it. At the same time the nationalists who, whatever their actual behavior, saw themselves as antifeudal, revolutionary cadres, were ambivalent about openly and directly seeking support from the bureaucracy. Moreover, the immediate post-independence popular reaction against the administrative corps was so widespread that no group with claims to a revolutionary tradition would openly seek a constituency within it.

In spite of these difficulties, the example of the PS and Masjumi was eventually followed. On December 4 exploratory talks were held in Djakarta between Mr. Lukman Hakim, Mr. Wilopo, Osa Maliki, Sartono, and Suwirjo.[44] Sartono, Wilopo, and Suwirjo had all been members of the Partindo, and the first two at least had been prominent in the PNI-Staatspartij, Wilopo as head of the Djakarta branch. On December 13 a provisional central leadership was announced that was to hold office until the first congress of a projected Serikat Rakjat Indonesia (Union of the Indonesian People), or "Serindo," could be organized. This leadership formed a smaller Working Committee composed of Mr. R. Iwa Kusumasumantri, Mr. R. Lukman Hakim, Sarmidi Mangunsarkoro, Osa Maliki, Mr. Sunarjo, Sjamsuddin Sutan Makmur, E. Soegandi, Soepardjo, Suwirjo, and Nn. Setiati.[45]

Though the leadership of the Serindo at this initial stage of its development seems to have been somewhat randomly selected, consisting mainly of interlocking groups of friends who happened

[44] See the reminiscences of Soebagio Reksodipoero published in *Kedaulatan Rakjat*, Aug. 30, 1966. For biographical details on these leaders, see the Appendix.

[45] Biographical details on all these figures except Soepardjo and Soegandi can be found in the Appendix. Other members of the provisional leadership included Achmad Soeladji, Mr. Radèn Soendoro Boeddhyarto Martoatmodjo, A. M. Dasaad, Kakung Gunadi, Moekarto Notowidagdo, R. Mashoed Hardjokoesoemo, Mr. Maramis, Njonoprawoto, V. E. Paath, Sartono, Sabilal Rasad gelar Datuk Bendoro, Dr. Radèn Mas Slamet Sudibjo, Mr. Sumanang, Mr. Radèn Sudjono, Dr. Radèn Suharto, Soemosoediro, Soemali, Soediro Goentoer, Soedjadi, Ir. Soedibjo Tjokronolo, Wachid gelar Sutan Radjolelo, and Wilopo. Biographical details on some of these men are given in Benedict O'Gorman Anderson, "The Pemuda Revolution" (Ph. D. thesis, Cornell University, 1967), pp. 444–46.

to be living in Djakarta, it did have certain distinguishable characteristics. First, it was dominated by former members of the Partindo, and included not a single member of the Partindo's main rival, the Hatta-Sjahrir Pendidikan Nasional Indonesia—a striking indication of the stability of prewar lines of division within the nationalist intelligentsia. Second, there was a virtually even division between former members of the two prime successors of the Partindo, the more radical, noncooperating Gerindo, and the more conservative, cooperating, and mildly philonippon Parindra. Third, there was a small but identifiable cluster from the "Kaigun group." Few members of the leadership could have been classified as underground, whereas a significant minority had held high positions under the Japanese.

On December 16 it was announced that all preparations for the coming congress of the Serindo would be in the hands of the general secretary, Sarmidi Mangunsarkoro, assisted by Osa Maliki and Lukman Hakim.[46] Shortly afterward negotiations were opened with the leaders of a number of miniscule nationalist parties that had sprung up in various provincial towns, such as the Partai Kedaulatan Rakjat (People's Sovereignty Party), started by Sujono Hadinoto in Jogjakarta, and the Partai Republik Indonesia (Indonesian Republic Party), formed in Madiun by Soeradji, as well as with leaders of residual local fragments of the PNI-Staatspartij, such as the PNI Madiun, the PNI Pati, the PNI Palembang and the PNI Sulawesi. The upshot of these negotiations was that at the first Serindo congress, held from January 28 to February 1, it was agreed that all attending organizations should fuse into a new PNI, which was thus subsequently to date its founding from January 29.[47] A new leadership was then elected as follows:

Chairman: Sarmidi Mangunsarkoro
Vice-chairman and chairman of the Central Java Regional Party
    Council: Mr. Djody Gondokusumo

[46] *Antara,* Dec. 18, 1945.
[47] Indonesia, Kementerian Penerangan, *Kepartaian di Indonesia,* p. 74.

Vice-chairman and chairman of the East Java Regional Party
    Council: Sidik Djojosoekarto
Vice-chairman and chairman of the West Java Regional Party
    Council: Mr. Wilopo
Political Department: Mr. R. M. Sartono
Economic Department: Mr. Sumanang, assisted by Mr. Lukman
    Hakim
Social Affairs Department: Sudiro
Information Department: Sjamsuddin Sutan Makmur.

The daily execution of party affairs was entrusted to Sarmidi,
Djody, and Moerdjodo, who headed the General Affairs Department on an interim basis.[48]

Perhaps somewhat surprisingly, the transformation of the
Serindo into the PNI made its leadership much more coherent
and homogeneous than it had previously promised to be. The
inner core, composed of Sarmidi, Sidik, Sartono, and Wilopo,
were all veterans of the Partindo in the days when Sukarno had
led it, and had moved on into the Gerindo when the Partindo
disappeared. With the exception of Djody and Sjamsuddin Sutan
Makmur, the Parindra group had dropped out, and so, evidently,
had the "Kaigun group." Javanese dominance of the party was
now overwhelming, Sjamsuddin being the only outsider in the
central party council. Nonetheless there was a noticeable, if as
yet not politically significant, division based on level of education, residence, and previous association. Wilopo, Lukman
Hakim, and Sumanang had all graduated from the Law Faculty
within a year or so of each other. They were all living in Djakarta
and had participated in the Perguruan Rakjat (People's Education) nationalist school organization together before the war.

[48] Biographical details on these figures can be found in the Appendix.
Some of the leaders of the rudimentary PNI-Staatspartij branches in the
Outer Islands who joined the new PNI became leaders of its branches in
their respective areas: for example, Dr. A. K. Gani for Sumatra and
Manai Sophiaan for Sulawesi. Regional heads of the party in the Lesser
Sundas and Kalimantan were A. S. Pello and M. Gozali.

Sarmidi, Sidik, and Sudiro did not have university degrees, and had their prewar residences and political contacts primarily in Central and East Java. Sarmidi and Sudiro were both involved in the Taman Siswa nationalist school system founded by Ki Hadjar Dewantoro.

As far as can be discovered the new PNI issued no manifesto or program, merely demanding that the distribution of seats in the KNIP and in the regional councils be made to reflect more accurately the wishes of the population—in other words, that the PNI be given larger representation. The subdued role of this early PNI contrasts strongly with its later domination of the Indonesian political scene. Part of the explanation for this has already been suggested: the stigma of collaboration that hung over some of its potential and actual leaders; the ideological disorientation consequent on the occupation and the capture by the PS of the radical nationalist tradition of the 1930's; and the as yet unsolved problem of finding a political constituency. But one additional factor should also be mentioned—the idiosyncratic personality of the key figure in the PNI, Sarmidi Mangunsarkoro.

One of the very few top political leaders of the period who had no inhibitions about wearing simple Javanese clothing in public, his strong Javanese nationalism and cultural conservatism made him an attractive figure to many Javanese political activists who felt intimidated or looked down upon by those they regarded as the "Dutch-minded" intellectuals of the PS and Djakarta. This factor, combined with his long and honorable role in the Taman Siswa organization and his excellent record during the occupation, gave him high prestige and a considerable base of personal support. His genuinely radical nationalism, however, and his cool relationship with Sukarno created some discomfort among many potential PNI cadres. Sarmidi's difficulties with Sukarno were of real significance, since many prewar leaders continued to look to the President for guidance. But these difficulties were not simply the product of the contrast between Sarmidi's austere, puritanical character and Sukarno's flamboyant, self-indulgent personality. The two men were also moving in different directions in this period. Sarmidi had initially supported Sjahrir in his campaign against the Sukarno cabinet. After the Sjahrir cabinet was formed, however, Sukarno moved over to give it his full public support, while Sarmidi, increasingly alienated by what he re-garded as its weak policy of compromise with the Dutch, shifted into the ranks of the opposition.

In looking at the various parties that sprang up on Java at the end of 1945 and the beginning of 1946, it is essential to recognize that whatever their claimed ideological differences, they shared in most cases certain basic structural features. Virtually all of them were little more than clusters of small personal cliques originating in the politics of the prewar period. None, even the Masjumi, had as yet any organized base among the masses, even in the urban areas. It would scarcely be too much to say that party politics at this time could be defined in terms of the interaction between five key cliques (those of Sjahrir, Amir, Sukiman, Sar-midi, and the "Kaigun group"), none notably stronger than the others, but with the aftermath of the occupation, the international situation, and the backing of Sukarno and Hatta giving a decisive, if temporary, advantage to the first two.

The effective leverage of any of these parties was limited not only by their organizational immaturity but by the rise of power-ful political organizations outside the party complex. These organizations—the army and the so-called *badan perdjuangan* (literally, struggle organizations) emerged from the organiza-tional debris of the Japanese occupation and the high tide of the pemuda movement. The relationships between these organiza-tions and the parties were for a long time tenuous, where they were not hostile, and their spheres of activity were markedly different. Whereas the parties confined their attention to the larger towns and to the formal governmental institutions of the center, the army and the badan perdjuangan, less concerned with the acquisition of power at the center than with the realization of the merdeka for which they were striving, were mainly active at the fronts or in the areas immediately behind them. It was not until later, when the élan of the merdeka movement began to ebb, that alliances between certain parties and elements within the army and the badan perdjuangan were slowly forged.

Chapter 11

The Army and the Badan Perdjuangan

It had become clear toward the end of September that the BKR were no longer effective or useful organizations, if they had ever been. Formally subordinated to the local national committees, they were difficult for the central government to control or lead. Uncertainty about whether they were primarily police or military units sapped their élan and created tensions with the civilian leaders to whom they were formally subordinate. Moreover, the flow of Japanese weapons into the hands of pemuda, many of them not enrolled in the BKR, impelled the Sukarno cabinet to think seriously about superseding the BKR with a more hierarchical and purely military organization directly under its own control.

Accordingly, on October 5 Sukarno signed an official proclamation forming the Tentara Keamanan Rakjat (People's Security Army), or TKR, and the next day he appointed Suprijadi minister of people's security. The effect of both these acts was chiefly symbolic, since the cabinet was well aware that the hero of the Blitar uprising was dead, and no semblance of an army was yet in sight.[1] A more concrete step toward building a national army was the decision to entrust the task to Urip Sumohardjo. The 52-year-old Urip had been in the Royal Netherlands Indies Army (KNIL) since 1914, rising slowly until in 1935 he was promoted to major, at that time the highest rank achieved by a native

[1] *Berita Indonesia,* Oct. 10, 1945; Nasution, *Tentara Nasional Indonesia,* p. 84.

officer in the colonial army.[2] He was retired in 1939, but was recalled two years later to take a command position in the Native Militia near Bandung. With the surrender of the Dutch forces at Kalidjati in March 1942, he went into retirement and seemed to have finished his career. As a veteran of the KNIL, his life had been spent far away from the nationalist intelligentsia and he seems to have personally known only a few of them. That he was entrusted with the task of building a nationalist army seems to have been due to the intermediary role played by a young KNIL officer named Didi Kartasasmita.

Didi, not yet thirty at the time, had begun a promising career in the KNIL by graduating from the Royal Military Academy in Breda, the first native Sundanese to do so. By the time the war broke out, he had risen to the rank of lieutenant.[3] He fought against the Japanese in Ambon and was interned for ten months after the Dutch collapse. He then returned to Java and went to work as a civilian in the office of the resident of Bandung.[4] Being from an upper-class Sundanese family himself, he was in frequent contact with Oto Iskandardinata, to whom, as we have seen, the BKR had been entrusted. Through Didi, Urip was brought into close relations with the cabinet leaders. On October 14 he was appointed Chief of the General Staff.[5]

From the point of view of Urip and Didi, the immediate problem was to assemble the trained military personnel available and form an effective central organizational structure around which the national army could grow. Naturally enough, given their past careers, they initially turned not to the former cadres of the Peta, who, as we have seen, were trained for guerrilla warfare in very small units and had no experience in staff work at the officer level, but to their former comrades in the KNIL. In this endeavor

[2] *Orang Indonesia jang terkemoeka di Djawa* (Djakarta, 1944), p. 133. Urip was born in Bagelen, Central Java, on February 21, 1893.

[3] *Orang Indonesia,* p. 130. He was born in Tasikmalaja, West Java, on November 20, 1915.

[4] Interview with retired Maj. Gen. Didi Kartasasmita, July 2, 1962.

[5] Nasution, *Tentara Nasional Indonesia,* p. 85.

they received the full support of the government, which was concerned that the returning Dutch might reclaim the loyalty of former KNIL elements unless they were given a stake in the republic. The persuasive efforts of Urip and Didi were largely successful. On October 14 a significant group of former KNIL officers in Djakarta issued a public statement that they regarded the fall of the Dutch in 1942 as releasing them from their oath of allegiance to the Dutch queen, and that they were now ready to give their full loyalty and obedience to the government of the Republic.[6]

The former KNIL officers summoned by the new Chief of the General Staff were of two rather different types. First there was a small group of older men, recruited into the colonial army long before the war, who like Urip had little interest in politics but a strong career orientation. It was primarily this group that the cabinet had felt might be vulnerable to Dutch appeals. Second there was a group of younger men, some of whom, like Didi Kartasasmita, Suriadarma, Hidajat, and Soerjosoelarso, had graduated from Breda, but most of whom had been trained in a substitute for this academy established on an emergency basis in Bandung after the Nazi invasion of the Netherlands. The main figures in what was to be known as the Bandung group, class of 1940, were A. H. Nasution, Rachmat Kartakusumah, T. B. Simatupang, Askari, and Alex Kawilarang, all of whom were eventually to become important actors in the Indonesian political struggle.[7] The most significant characteristic of the core of the Bandung group was that by contrast with their elders, they were intellectuals who became army officers largely by accident due to the impending Pacific War. Almost all of them came from the Sundanese upper class or from well-to-do families in the Outer Islands.[8] With these family connections and good Dutch educa-

[6] *Antara,* Oct. 15, 1945.

[7] On this group see *Sinar Harapan,* Aug. 18, 1968. For biographical details, see the Appendix.

[8] It appears that the Javanese were proportionately underrepresented in this group. In the class of 1941, which graduated on the eve of the war, the most notable figures were such men as Mokoginta, Satari, and

tions, as well as the experience of studying in the relatively cosmopolitan atmosphere of Bandung, they had far better access to and sympathy with the Djakarta intelligentsia than either the older KNIL officers or, as we shall see, the bulk of the Peta.

But in spite of the former KNIL officers' rapport with high government leaders, in other respects their position was singularly weak. None of them, with the possible exception of Nasution, who had headed the Seinendan in Bandung, had a corps of men ready to serve under them. The KNIL rank and file had been scattered three years before and clearly could not be regrouped even partially. Lack of men also meant in most cases lack of weapons, and this, as we shall see, was an important factor in the struggle for control of the new army. Finally, their association with the KNIL, which was regarded by many nationalists, both young and old, as a mercenary colonial army trained to repress Indonesian nationalism, put them at a strong moral disadvantage vis-à-vis the Peta officers, who regarded themselves as the pioneers of an authentically Indonesian (and Indonesian-led) national army.

The task facing Urip and his associates was made even more formidable by the Japanese dissolution of the Peta and the rapid development of the armed pemuda movement. There was simply no effective central control agency through which Urip's plans could be immediately realized. The announcement of the formation of the TKR hardly had more effect than to rename the local BKR and other armed groups without changing their relationship to Djakarta. Nasution later described the situation vividly:

It is true that at that time the TKR already existed, but it would be more accurate to say that hundreds of TKR had sprung up locally, acting entirely on their own. The leadership of the central headquarters was not felt at all. All that was known was that [at central headquarters] there was a "sale of generals' stars," which made the people on the battlefronts very envious. Most of the regions paid for their own expenses, made use of what funds they could find in their own

Soerjosoemarno; they came into political prominence well after the class of 1940. (Information kindly supplied by Nugroho Notosusanto.)

localities, and took advantage of the materiel and equipment left behind by the Japanese. Some units were rich with materiel they had
either inherited [from the Japanese] or seized, others were poor. Some
were completely equipped, others were armed only with lances and
bamboo spears. They wore black, white, green, yellow uniforms according to what supplies they could find in their own areas. The truth
of it was that the TKR rose out of the revolution itself, from the lap
of the people themselves, growing up according to local conditions,
without planning, leadership, or equipment from the state. Each unit
worked for itself. Naturally no one knew how many there were, nor
how many men or arms they contained.

It was a time when the idea of "bapakism" and the individual
unit's sovereignty were widely accepted. Bapak who were clever at
leading their men, quick to satisfy their needs and their ideological
orientations, judicious in fulfilling their materiel requirements, assumed very strong positions, and were obeyed as fathers. Usually
they acted less as commanders giving orders than as bapak defending
the interests of their "children." In such circumstances the bapak
held a powerful position vis-à-vis his superiors. He could not be
transferred. Nor was he willing to carry out orders which he opposed.
Thus the army leadership could not control him. Moreover, in the
long run many such bapak simply became the executors of their subordinates' wishes. The command no longer went from above below,
but from bottom to top.[9]

But it was not simply that units formed on the basis of the
personal authority of individual commanders. The influx of non-
Peta people into the TKR, which was in theory open to any
pemuda who wished to enroll, meant that basic conceptions of
what the national army should be like were imported from many
of the Japanese-period youth organizations such as the Seinendan
and the Barisan Pelopor. As Nasution observed:

At that time in military circles there was contempt and even suspicion
for the viewpoint of those who wished to plan strategy, rationalize organization and other matters in the regular, normal fashion. Everything had to be done "extraordinarily." Military prowess was not a
matter of skill but of courage. The discipline which had been known

[9] Nasution, *Tentara Nasional Indonesia*, pp. 154–55.

in the colonial period was "cadaver discipline." Giving the military salute was thought to be out of keeping with the revolution, which demanded the clenched fist salute and the shout of "Merdeka," "Revolt," "Struggle on till the Colonialists are Destroyed," etc. Standardized, regular uniforms were considered inappropriate; rather one had to have an appearance and a uniform which expressed the Rebel —with long hair, belts full of bullets, etc. Ranks were not necessary, since we were not struggling for rank but for our tasks. Medals were not needed, since there were no "merits" [which they could reward] —everyone was simply carrying out a sacred duty.[10]

In the face of such conditions, for which nothing in their experience or training had prepared them, it was natural for the former KNIL men to gravitate to the embryonic General Staff and what was to become the Ministry of Defense, where their skills were most valued and their political weakness was least likely to cripple their performance.

The former Peta officers, who were by their very numbers bound to make up the bulk of the new national army's leadership cadres, had strengths and weaknesses that were more or less complementary to those of the former KNIL men. Their experience in the Peta had given them, particularly the section and company commanders, military skills peculiarly appropriate to the kind of warfare the republic would soon be called upon to wage: small-scale, localized guerrilla operations within a larger defensive strategy. Having so recently parted from their men, they were likely to find it relatively easy to reassemble them. This was even truer insofar as the Peta was explicitly organized on a regional basis, so that an officer's men normally came from his own district. By contrast the troops of the KNIL were not grouped together on a local basis, nor did a KNIL officer usually command men from his home area. And since former Peta men were closely involved in the movement to take over Japanese arms, their control of weapons made it relatively easy to gather followers and impose a local but largely effective authority.

No less important, at that time, were the ideological concep-

[10] *Ibid.*, p. 105.

tions instilled in many Peta officers by men like Yanagawa. In Soehoed's words,

Trainees were reminded of the importance of spiritual education, and that this could only be obtained by spiritual means. Thousands of words were of less value than one living example. Trainees destined to become Peta leaders must face every situation in a spirit of service. They must be willing to sacrifice themselves for the fatherland with a sincere and honest heart so that they can guide their subordinates in the same direction. . . . In every action they must be sincere, pure in spirit, and able to distinguish the common interest from personal advantage. Aside from all military obligations, they must lead their subordinates with a deep feeling that these men are their own flesh and blood, to develop leaders who are protectors of their anak buah.[11]

Aside from the intense nationalism inculcated by these conceptions, so different from the professional orientation of the KNIL, it is striking how close this vision of military leadership and military comradeship was to the spirit of the pemuda movement in general. Moreover, the bapak–anak buah relationship in many respects clearly paralleled the intimate ties between kjai and santri and between the djago and his apprentices. As a consequence the former Peta officers, most of whom were pemuda themselves, were more in tune than the former KNIL men with the pemuda movement as a whole, and to its armed expression, the badan perdjuangan.

On the other hand, the former Peta men, precisely because of their intensive field training and their lack of formal schooling in military history and strategy, and also because the Peta did not have any units above the battalion level or any central staff, was poorly equipped to man those echelons of the new army for which the KNIL veterans seemed so well adapted.

Among the men in arms in those days there was thus a kind of spectrum, ranging from the "green" KNIL veterans, depending for what authority they had on their education, their expertise in

[11] Soehoed, *Perlawanan bersendjata*, pp. 54–55.

staff organization and military theory, and their conventional professional training, to the "red" badan perdjuangan members, whose power rested on personal example, revolutionary visions, and the egalitarian solidarity of pemuda comradeship.[12] Between these two stood the former Peta men, who while sharing something of the KNIL's professionalism and strictly military outlook, tended in the initial stages of the revolution at least to feel a bond with the badan perdjuangan, since the two groups had grown out of a common experience and now shared the dangers and hardships of the front. It was not until much later, after severe defeats at the hands of the Dutch, that the former Peta and KNIL men began to abandon their mutual distrust and resentment, and to cooperate against the badan perdjuangan, disarming and disbanding them, or incorporating them into an increasingly hierarchical central military command structure. At the outset, however, the lines were primarily drawn between the former officers of the Peta and those of the KNIL. In Nasution's words, "It even happened that a former KNIL officer stated his doubts as to the expertise and military skills of the former Peta officers, who had only received a few months' military training." The Peta men were not slow to reply: "We don't need 'clever' officers, 'international' officers. It is enough for us to have officers from the *sekolah rakjat* [people's schools; elementary schools] who are sincerely committed and have the courage to struggle." [13]

As if the difficulties posed by the heterogeneity and rivalry of different groups of officer cadres were not enough, Urip was also faced with the fact that his embryo staff had no control over the distribution of weapons in the new army, which as Nasution said was growing in effect from the bottom up rather than from the top down. This single fact did more than anything else to influence the military politics of the period and determine the lines along which the TKR would develop.

If Nasution is to be relied on, there were at the time approxi-

---

[12] Again I am using the terminology of Alers; see Chap. 5, n. 48 above.
[13] Nasution, *Tentara Nasional Indonesia*, p. 181.

mately 150,000 people who had received some form of serious military training in the KNIL, Heihō, and Peta. There were tens of thousands more who had been given paramilitary training in such organizations as the Seinendan and Keibōdan. However, the number of weapons available, even after the successful seizures in East and Central Java, was not even remotely comparable to the number of men ready and anxious to be mobilized for military action. Nasution estimated that the arms available sufficed to equip fully only a dozen combat regiments (roughly 28,000 men), and less fully another dozen territorial regiments for local defense. There was thus from the start an intense competition for arms between spontaneously forming military units, and those units that for one reason or another acquired relatively large quantities of weapons wielded power quite out of proportion to their size. The degree of competition can be guessed by comparing the estimated 400 battalions officially formed in the fall of 1945 with the 96 battalions Nasution estimated the existing materiel could have equipped.[14]

Given the realities of this situation and the virtually random concentration of weapons in various places across the island, any centrally planned, logical hierarchy of command Urip could devise had only highly provisional status, since it constantly had to be adjusted to the real armed strength of particular local military units. One can watch this process at work in the fate of Urip's first attempt to create an all-Java military command structure. According to the plan three regional commands were to be established directly under the General Staff (located out of harm's way in Jogjakarta): Command I (West Java), under Maj. Gen. Didi Kartasasmita; Command II (Central Java), under Major General Suratman; and Command III (East Java), under Major General Muhammad. Under these three commanders were to come ten divisional commanders. In fact, however, the three regional commands never really had any operating effect. Didi Kartasasmita seems to have hung on the longest,

[14] *Ibid.*, pp. 114–15.

perhaps in part because Nasution served as his chief of staff, but it was for little more than a month. The KNIL veteran Suratman was never accepted by his Peta division commanders; and Muhammad, formerly daidanchō in Buduran, was even arrested by the military police of his subordinate, Jonosewojo. Both men had to be withdrawn rapidly to the security of General Staff headquarters.[15]

The position of the divisional commanders proved almost as fragile, and with one possible exception they were never able to develop their divisions into operational units. The commander of Division I (Banten-Bogor) was the former daidanchō of Banten, Col. K. H. Sjam'oen, an elderly kjai whose reputation and influence spread no farther than Banten's borders. He had no authority either in Bogor itself, which was economically and culturally attached to Djakarta, or in Sukabumi and Tjiandjur, which similarly belonged to the Priangan. Accordingly, these districts almost immediately broke off from his command, Sukabumi and Tjiandjur being added to Division III, and Bogor to Division II, which covered the West Java coastal plain.[16] It was originally intended that Didi Kartasasmita would hold command of Division II (Djakarta-Tjirebon) as well as the West Java Command, but the General Staff was compelled to give way and allow Colonel Asikin to take his place. In Division III (Priangan) the former daidanchō of Tjimahi, Col. Arudji Kartawinata, rapidly yielded his position to Colonel Nasution, the one former KNIL officer to take control of a divisional command successfully in this period. Division IV (Pekalongan-Semarang-Pati) remained relatively stable under the command of the Peta veteran Colonel Djatikusumo, who had the extra prestige of being the uncle of the Susuhunan of Surakarta to back his authority. Division V (Kedu-Banjumas) remained under former daidanchō Colonel Sudirman until his promotion to head of the army in November. Divisions VI (Madiun-Kediri), VIII (Malang-Besuki), and IX (Jogjakarta) remained for a while under former daidan-

---

[15] *Ibid.*, p. 139.   [16] *Ibid.*, p. 109.

chō: Colonel Soediro of Kediri; Maj. Gen. Imam Sudja'i of Malang; and Colonel Sudarsono of Jogjakarta. But the commander of Division VII (Bodjonegoro-Surabaja-Madura), Major General Jonosewojo was forced to yield to Colonel Sungkono, who had taken a major part in the Surabaja fighting.[17] The first man appointed to the command of Division X (Surakarta) was Maj. Gen. B. P. H. Purbonagoro, an elder brother of Djatikusumo, who had served as a captain in the KNIL after receiving a cavalry officer's education at Breda and St. Cyr. But shortly after his appointment he was replaced by Colonel Sutarto, a Peta veteran who, in Nasution's words, was the "strong man" in the Surakarta area for most of the early period of the revolution.[18]

But even when the initial division commanders were pushed aside, their replacements usually had little power. Their position remained very much like that of the daidanchō in the Peta. Formally the heads of the regional military hierarchy, they either became figureheads or were relegated to the role of arbiters between rival lower-level officers who were in real control of effective armed strength. Indeed, many of them were former daidanchō: Sjam'oen, Arudji, Sudarsono, Soediro, Djatikusumo, and Imam Sudja'i all fell into this category. When actual fighting took place, these men rarely had much control over the course of operations, which were usually uncoordinated, localized actions initiated by battalion commanders and even more junior officers. Moreover, in some cases their lack of any considerable military skill meant that when a military crisis arose, they failed to pass muster; thus, for example, Arudji was pushed aside by Nasution,

[17] In an interview on June 5, 1967, General Subijono stated that at least one reason for Jonosewojo's fall was his role in the pistol holdup of Muhammad.

[18] According to "Surakarta Hadiningrat," at a meeting held on about November 4, after a heated debate on whether the TKR was to be a military dictatorship army, a feudal army, or a people's army, an election was held for the position of division commander. The three candidates were Purbonagoro, Sutarto, and Sunarto, and Sutarto was the victor.

whose greater military skills were needed in the critical situation in Bandung.[19]

The dismemberment of Urip's regional command structure did not, however, mean simply that the General Staff had had to bow to the realities of local military politics. It also meant that virtually all the former KNIL men were swept from senior command positions. This in turn reflected the continuing conflict between the veterans of the Peta and the KNIL. From the start the government had done what it could to satisfy the competing interests of the two groups. When Urip had been appointed chief of staff, the cabinet had successively named Suprijadi, the missing hero of the Peta rebellion in Blitar, and Suljoadikusumo, a prewar leader of the PSII and PII who had become a daidanchō during the occupation, to the post of minister for people's security (the latter on a temporary basis).[20] But the silent rivalry continued, finally coming to a head at a conference of top military commanders held on November 12, 1945, in Jogjakarta, just at the time of the fall of the Sukarno cabinet.[21] The conference was dominated by members of Urip's staff and the divisional and regimental commanders of Central Java, since most of the officers in East Java were busy with the fighting in Surabaja and the situation around Bandung was so difficult that only Nasution and a few of his associates felt able to leave. At the same time the atmosphere of the meeting was heavily influenced by the bitter

[19] The official date of Arudji's replacement by Nasution is October 11, 1945. See Sedjarah Militer Kodam VI, *Siliwangi dari masa kemasa*, p. 62.

[20] Suljoadikusumo was appointed minister ad interim as of October 20; see Koesnodiprodjo, ed., *Himpunan, 1945*, p. 61. Shortly afterward, while on a visit to Surabaja, he was arrested by Mustopo; after his release he lost what little importance he had previously enjoyed. Following the arrest Mustopo proclaimed himself minister, but he was later persuaded to drop his claim. See *Warta Indonesia*, Oct. 22, 1945.

[21] Nasution, *Tentara Nasional Indonesia*, pp. 156, 169. Cf. also A. H. Nasution, *Tjatatan2 sekitar politik militer Indonesia* (Djakarta, 1955), p. 111. Sidik Kertapati gives the date of the conference as November 13; *Sekitar proklamasi*, p. 134.

fighting going on not only in Surabaja but in Semarang and Ambarawa.

The first problem before the conference was the choice of a *panglima besar*.[22] The KNIL and Peta men immediately clashed over who was to be elected to this position. Urip was the candidate of the former group and Sudirman, the commander of Division V, that of the latter. In the event Sudirman was the victor, though apparently by the margin of only a few votes.

Sudirman, who was probably only 30 years old when he was elected panglima besar in this fashion, had been in the Japanese period both a member of the Banjumas Residency sangikai and daidanchō in Kroja.[23] After the Japanese surrender he had been highly successful in arranging for a wholesale surrender of arms by the Japanese commandant in his area.[24] Thus from the start

[22] There is no exact translation of the title panglima besar. Panglima is an old Malay military title with rich historical connotations. Panglima besar literally means "big panglima." It is interesting that while all other offices in the national army were given Western-derived names, the topmost one was thus endowed with the aura of ancient glory. It is difficult to use the title commander-in-chief as a translation of panglima besar, since technically Sukarno, as president of the Republic, was commander-in-chief. In fact, however, the office of panglima besar conferred supreme authority over all troops and military operations.

[23] For biographical details on Sudirman, see the Appendix.

[24] According to "Sedjarah TNI, Diponegoro," pp. 29–30, Sudirman's daidan was virtually the only one that was effectively reconstructed after its dissolution, mainly because of the loyalty Sudirman inspired among his subordinates. Early in September he summoned all the former Peta officers in the Residency of Banjumas and held talks with them, with local political notables, and with the Resident, Mr. Iskaq Tjokroadisoerjo. It was decided that Sudirman, Iskaq, and Sutirto (Sudirman's chief of staff) should open negotiations with the Japanese. As the talks started, on October 8 in the town of Banjumas, the building where they were being held was surrounded by pemuda and townspeople. While the talks dragged on, five Japanese soldiers were seen coming out of the building. They were arrested, found to be carrying grenades, and killed on the spot. The Japanese in the city thereupon surrendered all their equipment to Sudirman's comrade Gatot Subroto, the former daidanchō of Banjumas, who had become the local chief of police. The result of this sweep was that Sudirman had one weapon for every two men in his six battalions—

he controlled the largest single supply of weapons in Central Java. He had also gained a high reputation by his role on the Semarang and Magelang front, not least by the good discipline he had managed to maintain among his men. But the support for his candidacy among the former Peta men was not only a recognition of his real military power and his combat record. It was also due to his unusual personal qualities. He was a man who was able to combine a calm asceticism and inward-looking piety with a quiet warmth and gentleness that won over most of the people he encountered. His simple manner, however, concealed both a powerful will and a passionate commitment to the nationalist cause. Intensely Javanese himself, he evoked, particularly in the Javanese milieu, the traditional image of the satria, the warrior devoted to the defense and glory of the kingdom, and endowed by his asceticism with supernatural power.[25]

Immediately upon his election, Sudirman moved with tact and skill to consolidate his position. Urip had resigned his position after his defeat, but Sudirman immediately asked him to resume his functions as chief of staff, and very soon developed a close rapport with the older man. Deferring to Urip on organizational and technical matters, he devoted himself primarily to the political problems of uniting the army and giving it a coherent vision of its role in the revolution. He also did his best to heal the wounds opened at the conference by assuring all present that henceforth he would refuse to take an officer's background into account, but would treat each one on the basis of his merits and service to the cause of independence. Within a short space of time he secured himself a virtually unassailable position within the

---

a uniquely high ratio for this period of the revolution. With some more fanciful additions, the same story is given in Pusat Sedjarah Militer Angkatan Darat, *Peranan TNI-Angkatan Darat*, pp. 63–65. An alternative date for this episode, September 24, given in Pusat Sedjarah Militer Angkatan Darat, *Kronologi*, p. 29, is also possible.

[25] For a detailed analysis of traditional Javanese ideas about power and its wielders, see Benedict O'Gorman Anderson, "The Idea of Power in Javanese Culture," in Holt, ed., *Culture and Politics*.

army, commanding the loyalty of former KNIL and Peta men alike.

The strength of Sudirman's new position did not, however, derive solely from his own record and personality, or from the fact that he was the elected choice of the senior military officers. It also derived from the way in which his office was regarded by the dominant Peta component of the army. The Peta had been nurtured in the Japanese tradition, and by that tradition, at least in the latter days of the Empire, the effective head of the army, the chief of staff, was chosen by consultations among the senior officers from which civilians were rigidly excluded. Moreover, the chief of staff was not subordinated to the Japanese cabinet but reported directly to the Emperor.[26] From the start Sudirman made every effort to live up to this tradition. He regarded himself as coequal to the cabinet leaders, not subordinate to them, and in this interpretation of his role received strong support from within the army. In effect, Sudirman strengthened his personal position within the military by emphasizing the special position of the army as a whole within the government and the revolutionary movement.

The influence of Japanese precedent was no less clear and important, however, when the Jogjakarta conference turned to the question of the Ministry of Defense. From the Meiji period onward the service ministers in the Japanese cabinet had always been military men; between 1900 and 1913, and again after 1936, these ministers had had to be officers on active duty. This practice had given the Japanese army and navy not only effective control of their respective ministries, but in many cases indirect control over the cabinet itself, since by withdrawing their ministers and refusing to appoint replacements they could usually bring about the fall of the government.[27]

For the former Peta officers, then, there was nothing peculiar

[26] Nasution (*Tentara Nasional Indonesia*, p. 169) brings out this point.
[27] See Edwin O. Reischauer, *Japan: The Story of a Nation* (New York, 1970), pp. 165, 195,

in taking up the question of their choice for the position of minister of people's security (defense). Almost unanimously they decided on the youthful sultan of Jogjakarta, Hamengkubuwono IX.[28] This choice was probably in part influenced by the great traditional prestige of the sultanate in western Central Java, particularly, of course, in Jogjakarta, where the conference was being held. But it was also clearly influenced by the stubborn and courageous role the Sultan had played during the Japanese occupation and his wholehearted participation in the independence movement.[29]

The Sultan's election as minister of people's security by the military two days before the formation of the Sjahrir cabinet was taken as a direct and personal challenge to the incoming prime minister, who declared his intention of appointing Amir Sjarifuddin to the post and made it plain that he would not accept what he regarded as a militaristic Japanese-style precedent. In the end the army backed down, though not before many heated words had been exchanged.[30] On Sudirman's position, however, the army was not to be budged, and finally, on December 18, nearly six weeks after the Jogjakarta conference, the Sjahrir government grudgingly proclaimed his official appointment as panglima besar.[31]

The installation of the Sjahrir cabinet in fact marked the open-

[28] Nasution, *Tentara Nasional Indonesia,* pp. 156–57; "Sedjarah TNI, Diponegoro," p. 66.

[29] On the Sultan's role, see Chapter 15 below. He was regarded by the military as a general officer and attended meetings with them in military uniform.

[30] Why the army backed down is not wholly clear. It is possible that the Sultan himself refused to serve against the cabinet's wishes. Probably Sukarno and Hatta also intervened on Sjahrir's behalf.

[31] See "Sedjarah TNI, Diponegoro," p. 66. The anonymous author avoids mentioning the date of the Jogjakarta conference but gives the date of Sudirman's official inauguration. Intentionally or unintentionally he thus tends to give the impression that the two events virtually coincided, and that the appointment of the panglima besar was not the outcome of a long, drawn out political struggle. Cf. also Raliby, *Documenta Historica,* pp. 156–57.

ing of a long period of conflict and rivalry between the government and the military high command. Neither side felt satisfied with the aftermath of the Jogjakarta conference. Sudirman and his associates resented the government's thinly veiled charges of militarism and fascism, and felt humiliated by the long delay in the confirmation of Sudirman as panglima besar. Sjahrir and Amir were intensely conscious of the independence and hostility of army headquarters and began almost at once to take steps to circumscribe and undermine Sudirman's authority. In time Sudirman became a natural magnet for a variety of political groups who opposed the cabinet leaders and hoped to use the young panglima besar to unseat them.

Behind these rivalries, however, there also loomed two different visions of what the character and role of the national army was to be. The cabinet's conception was largely formulated by Amir, and can perhaps best be seen in the first proclamation he made on becoming minister. Discussing the character of the TKR, Amir stressed the difference between the new army he saw emerging and the two previous "Indonesian" armies—the KNIL and the Peta. The KNIL he bitterly characterized as a mercenary army whose members were willing to be used by the Dutch government against their own countrymen, while the Peta was simply a device of the Japanese to forward their own colonial aims. On the other hand,

the Indonesian pemuda who enter the TKR have a political basis and conviction. This conviction is a desire to contribute everything they have to guarding the security of their country. It is obvious how great the difference is, compared to the two armies we have described before. The armies [created by] the Netherlands East Indies government and the Japanese were fundamentally empty of any political conviction.

Amir also drew a contrast between Nazi and Russian youth during the war, attributing Russian successes to the firm political convictions of the Red Army. "We believe," he said, "that the pemuda now entering the TKR have the same spirit as the Russian pemuda who joined the Red Army." [32]

We have already seen how the program of the PS had stressed the need for kerakjatan (people-ness) among the Indonesian armed forces. For those like Amir, who had suffered severely under the Japanese occupation and were hostile to the militarist colonial rule exerted by the Sixteenth Army, it seemed imperative to eradicate the psychological influences of Japanese training on the pemuda in the army. Mindful of the Japanese army's long-standing insistence on its autonomous political role, separate from or even above civilian authority, Amir was eager to prevent a similar development in Indonesia. He was therefore from the outset anxious to educate the army officer corps politically, both to "democratize" and to "socialize" their outlook, and also to build up his own authority as minister of people's security vis-à-vis army headquarters. The drive to give the army political convictions was conceived as an effort not merely to link the officer corps closely to the government in power, but also to give them an ideological orientation that would keep them permanently within the reach of the socialist-minded groups Amir represented. The example of the Red Army cited in Amir's proclamation was not idly chosen. Though he may have had little clear idea of how the Red Army was organized, Amir conceived it as a militant, patriotic army imbued with socialist goals and under the permanent political guidance of a powerful government party.

To Sudirman the charges made by many supporters of the Sjahrir cabinet that he and his fellow officers from the Peta had been indoctrinated by the Japanese with fascist ideas must have seemed either malicious or stupid. He had indeed acquired his military skills from the Japanese, but the models in his mind were not the samurai but the heroes of earlier rebellions against Dutch rule. If any group was influenced by alien models and

[32] Nasution, *Tentara Nasional Indonesia*, p. 81; Koesnodiprodjo, ed., *Himpunan, 1945*, p. 211.

conceptions, it was precisely the Dutch-speaking intellectuals of the capital, who seemed constantly to press for negotiations with the enemy and to find it easier to cooperate with like-minded Dutchmen than with the authentic patriots in the army.

As in Amir's case, Sudirman's conception of the character and role of a national army was at bottom the product of his own experience. Himself a man of the people, with only a very limited formal education, he saw the army less as an instrument of the Westernized center than as an organized expression of the popular will. He was also deeply aware that he had achieved his position by what might be called without excessive exaggeration an informal, tiered elective process, the basic electoral units of which were localized military groups with deep roots in the small towns and villages of the Javanese heartland. Furthermore, maintaining his position would depend on his capacity to continue commanding the loyalty and confidence of this base. From this perspective it was understandable that he viewed the national army as a people's army, both more democratic and more egalitarian than the political parties. Insofar as he conceived of the army as a revolutionary force, it was revolutionary primarily in the sense that the pemuda understood the word: committed wholeheartedly to the struggle for merdeka. It followed naturally that the political parties, perhaps especially the ruling Socialist Party, were regarded with suspicion, for their very existence seemed to threaten to divide the population and undermine the army's cohesion. Revolutionary élan was inseparable from national solidarity. For this élan to be sustained, it was essential that the army, at least, remain uncontaminated by partial creeds and political factions to be the unified guarantor of the national cause.

In the developing conflict between the proponents of these different conceptions, the first initiative was taken by the civilians in the government. Early in January 1946, Amir's ministry announced the impending formation of a Staf Pendidikan (Education Staff) within the TKR.[33] This step, the accompanying statement declared, was a response to the people's wish that

the army become an army with an ideology and a sufficient political foundation so that it will be certain of its duties and rights in this revolutionary age. . . . The content of this education will not be the political views of a political party or the opinions of a particular group, but the ideology already contained in the Constitution. The broad outlines of this ideology will be determined by a commission to ensure that all the materials given to members of the army will have an ideological base to be found in the Constitution. . . . Among the educators there will also be Islamic religious experts so that all propaganda for the army within the Staf Pendidikan can be harmonized with religious doctrine.[34]

After a month of discussion and negotiation, the Education Staff was inaugurated on February 19. An accompanying statement said in part: "It is strongly felt that Indonesian society must be swept clean of the evil influences introduced by the colonialists—the imperialist Dutch and the fascist Japanese. *Above all it is in the army that these evil characteristics must be wiped clean.*" [35] The Education Staff's job, the statement continued, was to make every soldier aware of his role as what the President had called an instrument of the state. Instruction would be given by the Education Staff in a wide variety of subjects, but it would be uniform for the entire army. All forms of communications media would be used to instill correct ideas, while cadets for the officer corps would be given special training as teachers. Significantly, it was announced at the same time that the Education Staff would be a part of the Ministry of Defense, not of the

[33] On January 1, 1946, the army's name was changed from Tentara Keamanan Rakjat to Tentara Keselamatan Rakjat; see Nasution, *Tentara Nasional Indonesia,* pp. 169–70. Since *keselamatan* (welfare, salvation) has a wider meaning than *keamanan* (security), it is perhaps legitimate to assume that the change reflected the army's growing importance in national life.

[34] *Antara,* Jan. 17, 1946.   [35] *Ibid.,* Feb. 19, 1946. Italics mine.

general headquarters of the army. The appointed leadership consisted of seven men: Sockono Djojopratiknjo, Anwar Tjokroaminoto, Wijono, Dr. Mustopo, Faried Ma'ruf, H. Abdul Mukti,
and Sumarsono.[36] In this group the PS and Masjumi were well
represented, and the other political organizations virtually not at
all. It was to be expected, therefore, that the Education Staff
would soon come under attack. This did not occur, however,
until after the fall of the first Sjahrir cabinet, when the issue was
subsumed in a much wider conflict within the republic's leadership.

But it was not only within the army that the last months of
1945 saw the beginning of efforts to develop greater organizational cohesion and more centralized leadership. The thousands
of pemuda unleashed on Java by the collapse of the structures
of the Japanese period could by no means be wholly absorbed
into the army. Many of them had acquired weapons in the course
of the takeovers from the Japanese; even larger numbers had
participated or were about to participate in the struggle for the
defense of merdeka against the Dutch and British. In September
and October a vast proliferation of small-scale, localized, and
fluid pemuda groups had sprung up that were in part military
and in part political in character—indeed, the two aspects could
not readily be separated from one another. As October wore on,
it became clear that both among various pemuda groupings themselves and among certain elements in the republican leadership,

[36] *Ibid.* According to Nasution (*Tentara Nasional Indonesia,* p. 186)
all seven were given high military ranks: Soekono became a lieutenant
general, and the others major generals. Nasution identifies their political
affiliations, with some accuracy, as follows: Soekono, a former official
in the Posts, Telegraph, and Telephone Service, was a member of the
PS, as was Wijono; Faried Ma'ruf and Anwar Tjokroaminoto were from
the Masjumi (Nasution actually labels Anwar a PSII member, but this
is an anachronism); and Sumarsono was a leader of the badan perdjuangan Pesindo (discussed below), which was under considerable PS
influence. Only the unique Dr. Mustopo stood unaffiliated. We have
already encountered Mustopo in the battle of Surabaja. For biographical
details, see the Appendix.

increasing thought was being given to concentrating and chan-
neling pemuda energies into new organizational formats, more
disciplined and more susceptible to central control. The need
was particularly evident to men like Amir Sjarifuddin and
Sjahrir, who perceived very clearly that without such control,
the pemuda movement was a threat to any republican government that wished to consolidate its authority and negotiate a
settlement with the Dutch. But the attempt to give a "green"
character to a movement so fundamentally "red" in nature was
to succeed only to a limited degree; and the consequences of the
attempt and its partial failure were initially to split the pemuda
movement, and ultimately to polarize it along lines parallel to the
divisions within the national elite itself.

Evidently at Amir's instigation in part, it was announced on
October 25 that a pemuda congress would be held in Jogjakarta
from November 10 to 11, sponsored by local pemuda leaders in
that city.[37] Six days later a preliminary congress was held in the
old *kraton* (royal palace) capital with two representatives each
from the API (Djakarta), Gerpri (Jogjakarta), Pelopor (Djakarta), and AMRI (Central Java), and one each from the PRI
(Surabaja), PRI (Bandung), IPI (Djakarta), and Staf Wartawan
Kementerian Penerangan.[38] It was decided that in addition to
these organizations those invited to the full congress should in-

[37] *Merdeka,* Oct. 25, 1945.

[38] The API Djakarta we have already encountered, as well as the
PRI. The Gerpri (Gerakan Pemuda Republik Indonesia, or Youth Move-
ment of the Republic of Indonesia) was the dominant youth organization
in Jogjakarta. Pelopor Djakarta was a portion of the old Barisan Pelopor
from occupation days. The IPI (Ikatan Peladjar Indonesia, or League of
Indonesian Students) was Djakarta-based, and the AMRI (Angkatan
Muda Republik Indonesia, or Younger Generation of the Republic of
Indonesia), though claiming to speak for Central Java, was essentially a
local Semarang group. The Staf Wartawan Kementerian Penerangan
(Journalists' Staff of the Ministry of Information) represented the subordinates of Amir, at that time still minister of information. The most
important of these groups were the API, PRI Surabaja, Gerpri, and
AMRI, and all were soon to merge into the Amir-backed Pesindo. Amir's
hand is thus very clear in the preparations for the congress.

clude the Pemuda Muhammadijah Mataram (Muhammadijah Youth, Mataram), Pemuda Nahdatul Ulama Surabaja (Nahdatul Ulama Youth, Surabaja), Pemuda Katolik (Catholic Youth), Pemuda Protestan (Protestant Youth), and Persatuan Pemuda Puteri Djakarta (Young Women's Union, Djakarta), and that the API (Djakarta), Gerpri (Jogjakarta), and PRI (Surabaja) would be responsible for determining the credentials and the representation of West, Central, and East Java at the congress. It was also agreed that the congress would be urged to create a "fusion of Indonesian youth on the basis of socialist principles for the establishment of an Indonesian republic founded on genuine popular sovereignty." The keynote speech would be delivered by Amir Sjarifuddin, while Adam Malik and Wikana would give more detailed statements in subsequent closed sessions.[39]

The decisions of the preliminary congress brought immediate and sharp reaction in some quarters. *Berita Indonesia,* for example, while agreeing in an editorial that socialism was the best system for Indonesia, warned against the idea of fusion, which would simply result in paper unity. All should be allowed their own views and not be forced into "opinions which may possibly conflict with their *djiwa* [spirit] and knowledge." The editorial also criticized the facts that only eleven organizations were to get a voice at the congress and that seven of these had already held caucuses to predetermine a common attitude at the plenary sessions.[40] After suggesting that the projected congress looked very much as if it would be run along the dictatorial lines of the Villa Isola meeting, the editorial urged far wider representation of different groups, claiming that many uninvited youth organizations were deeply humiliated at being left unrepresented, particularly when decisions were being made in their names.[41]

[39] *Berita Indonesia,* Nov. 5, 1945.

[40] In fact, fifteen organizations were invited, as is shown by Hardjito, ed., *Risalah gerakan pemuda* (Djakarta, 1952), p. 33.

[41] *Berita Indonesia,* Nov. 5, 1945.

Perhaps because of this criticism, representation was quite broad when the congress opened on the morning of November 10. A reported 580 delegates and 700 observers were on hand. Moreover, the political importance generally attached to the meeting was attested by the presence of Sukarno, Hatta, and six cabinet ministers.[42] Amir, who was widely understood to have been the main promoter of the assembly, gave a fiery address, culminating in the following appeal: "Pemuda! If you hold a rifle in your right hand, you must hold a hammer in your left. If you hold a sword in your right hand, then grasp a sickle in your left!" [43] The political lobbying that followed in the closed sessions was intense. Virtually all the discussion centered around the proposals made at the preliminary congress, which called both for a genuine fusion of differing youth groups into a single disciplined organization and for the acceptance of a socialist program.

In the event, in spite of pressure exerted by Amir and those supporting him, neither objective was attained. To compensate for this failure, late on the evening of November 10, just as the fighting in Surabaja was at its fiercest, seven of the 28 major organizations attending announced that they were fusing into a single organization, to be known as the Pemuda Sosialis Indonesia (Socialist Youth of Indonesia), or "Pesindo." Although only a quarter of the represented groups joined the Pesindo, its members were among the most sophisticated and best organized of all. They included the API of Djakarta under Wikana; the Gerpri, the dominant youth organization in Jogjakarta, under

[42] *Ibid.*, Nov. 10, 1945. For a full list of the delegations, see Biro Pemuda, *Sedjarah perdjuangan pemuda Indonesia*, p. 165. This source gives the number of delegates as 400, including 166 from Sumatra, 25 from the Moluccas, 18 from the Lesser Sundas, 11 from Kalimantan and 9 from Sulawesi. Hardjito (*Risalah,* p. 34) says there were 166 from Sumatra, 400 from Java, 25 from Madura, 18 from the Lesser Sundas, 11 from Kalimantan, and 9 from Sulawesi. Hardjito's version seems nearer the truth.

[43] Hardjito, ed., *Risalah,* p. 35. Sudisman, who was closely linked to Amir, was secretary to the congress.

Lagiono; the AMRI, the main pemuda group in Semarang; the PRI of Surabaja; and the Angkatan Muda Kereta Api, Angkatan Muda Gas dan Listrik, and Angkatan Muda Pos, Telegrap dan Telepon, three important associations of youthful employees in the railways, public utilities, and telegraph and telephone services.

In spite of its failure to fuse the attending youth organizations together, the congress did agree on November 11 to establish a loose federative structure to coordinate future pemuda activities. A Central Leadership Council was set up in which each of the main participating organizations would have a single voting representative; a two-thirds vote of this body would be necessary to validate any decision it made. Once made, however, any decision would be binding on all.[44] The council's members were thereupon elected, as follows: chairman, Chaerul Saleh; first vice-chairman, Soepardo; second vice-chairman, A. Boechari; and secretary, Moeljo. Also elected to the council were representatives of the IPI, Pemuda Protestan, Pemuda Katolik, Persatuan Pemuda Puteri Indonesia, Barisan Pelopor, Angkatan Muda Guru (Younger Generation Teachers), Pemuda Maluku, KRIS (Kebaktian Rakjat Indonesia Sulawesi, or Service of the Indonesian People of Sulawesi), and Pesindo, and of Andalas (Sumatra) and Kalimantan. The representatives of the two most powerful constituent units, the Barisan Pelopor and Pesindo, were Dr. Muwardi and Supeno.[45]

[44] *Ibid.*, pp. 43–44.

[45] By the terms of the constitution of the new body, the people elected to the four leadership offices were required to relinquish their seats in the council to other members of the organizations they represented, and they were not allowed to vote. Chaerul Saleh was a member of the API and Pesindo; Soepardo, who in the thirties had been a leader of the Persatuan Pemuda Taman Siswa (Union of Taman Siswa Youth) with Sjamsu Harja Udaja, represented the Gerakan Pegawai Angkatan Muda (Movement of Younger Generation Officials); Boechari represented the GPII (Gerakan Pemuda Islam Indonesia, or Indonesian Islamic Youth Movement); and Moeljo represented the Masjarakat Peladjar Perguruan Tinggi (Society of Students in Higher Education).

The congress also voted to form two working committees to run the federative organization under the supervision of the Central Leadership Council: a Working Committee for Struggle (Dewan Pekerdja Perdjuangan) and a Working Committee for Construction (Dewan Pekerdja Pembangunan). The first committee was entrusted with full responsibility for the organization of all popular military units outside the regular army, including their mobilization, supply, and training, and for the formation of a Resistance Council (Dewan Perdjuangan) at each administrative level in the provinces. The second was put in charge of all political activities, including propagandizing among the masses for the independence struggle and representing the pemuda to the government and regional administrations. (Since the heads of these two committees and of the Central Leadership Council— Sumarsono, Wikana, and Chaerul Saleh respectively—were all three Pesindo men, this organization was compensated somewhat for its defeat on the fusion issue.)

On the question of a program, too, the proposals of the preliminary congress did not find general acceptance. The program finally adopted was extremely general, making no mention of any socialist objectives or economic strategies. The main emphasis was laid on urging strong measures against the Allies, particularly the barring of further penetration into the interior. Indonesia would be responsible for the internees' security until they could be transported to the Allied-held harbor enclaves. The congress also strongly protested the talks that had been held by Sukarno, Hatta, and van Mook, pressed for the creation of a special Youth Ministry, and warned the government against permitting the "disarming of the population." [46]

Starting on November 11, immediately following the congress, the Pesindo delegations held their own assembly under the temporary leadership of Chaerul Saleh.[47] Subsequently, however,

[46] *Berita Indonesia*, Nov. 14, 1945; Hardjito, ed., *Risalah*, p. 39.

[47] See the excellent account of the Pesindo congress given in *Kedaulatan Rakjat*, Nov. 16, 1945. The Pesindo claimed to have delegations from

Krissubanu (PRI Surabaja) was elected chairman; Wikana (API Djakarta), vice-chairman for Djakarta; and Ibnu Parna (AMRI Semarang), vice-chairman for Semarang.[48] The regional center of gravity was clearly indicated by the decision to place the Pesindo's general headquarters in Surabaja, with subordinate headquarters in Djakarta, Jogjakarta (Mataram), Semarang, Malang, Denpasar, Palembang, and Bandjarmasin. The prominence of the Surabaja delegation was undoubtedly momentarily enhanced by the role being played there by the PRI group under Sumarsono,[49] but the subsequent history of the Pesindo was to show that its main strength continued to lie in East Java, spilling over into the Madiun valley.[50]

The tone of the Pesindo program is exemplified by the clause dealing with aims: "Pesindo should make use of every opportunity to hasten the creation of a socialist society in Indonesia by radical revolutionary means." Unlike most of the other youth organizations of the period, the Pesindo also urged strengthening contacts with "like-minded [sepaham] friends overseas."[51] Later,

---

Djakarta, Bogor, Priangan, Banten, Tjirebon, Pekalongan, Semarang, Banjumas, Kedu, Mataram, Surakarta, Pati, Bodjonegoro, Madiun, Kediri, Surabaja, Malang, Besuki, Madura, Sunda Ketjil, Palembang, Bengkulu, Lampung, and Kalimantan.

[48] For biographical details on Krissubanu, see the Appendix. A rather different listing of the Pesindo leadership, presumably for late 1945, is given in Biro Pemuda, Sedjarah perdjuangan pemuda Indonesia, p. 168: Ruslan Widjajasastra, Krissubanu, Sudisman, D. J. Nasution, Subroto, Tjugito, Wikana, Sukarno (S. Karno?), Sudjono, and Jetty Zain.

[49] According to Dokumentasi pemuda (p. 62), Krissubanu and Kaslan led their delegation straight back to Surabaja when the news came that the fighting had broken out. Sumarsono had gone back a day earlier. It was fortunate for Krissubanu that he had time to be elected chairman before he left.

[50] Antara (Feb. 13, 1946) reported that at a recent East Java Pesindo conference in Djember, the head of the Besuki residency Pesindo boasted of having 79,000 members in his area alone. These figures should not be taken seriously, but they are an indication of where the power of the Pesindo lay.

[51] Kedaulatan Rakjat, Nov. 16, 1945.

on December 15, the Pesindo leadership issued a detailed program, of which perhaps the most important features were its
general support for the government and its specific demands for
the creation of an army with a "people's ideology" and the elimination of military "methods" that might separate the army from
the people.[52]

The power of the Pesindo rested from the start on two quite
separate bases. The first was its ability to attract wide pemuda
support by appealing to the prevalent hostility to the Japanese
and by making use of the underground associations and organizational experience of many of its leaders. The second was its association with Amir Sjarifuddin, particularly when he became
minister of defense in the Sjahrir government. While there is no
direct evidence to prove it, the widely held belief that he was
instrumental in providing the organization with a considerable
variety of facilities, including money and guns, seems hard not
to accept.

The Pesindo's position vis-à-vis the government was made
strikingly clear on January 7, when the cabinet held an unprecedented special session in Jogjakarta for the specific purpose of
discussing the Pesindo program with top Pesindo leaders.[53] The

---

[52] *Antara*, Dec. 27, 1945. Though the Pesindo was in many ways a
genuine fusion of existing organizations, it also showed clear signs of
continuity with the past. For example, no effective Central Java organization was created, since the older Semarang and Jogjakarta groups continued in their rivalry. In *Antara* (Nov. 28, 1945) details are given of
a "South Central Java" Pesindo leadership (with no clear connection to
Ibnu Parna in Semarang), consisting of B. R. M. Hertog (a member of
the Sultan of Jogjakarta's family and a prewar leader of Sangkoro Mudo,
an organization committed, *inter alia*, to "strengthening the descendants of
Hamengkubuwono I," founder of the Jogjakarta dynasty); Lagiono
(former head of Gerpri); Mantoro Tirtonegoro (a prewar leader of the
Perpri [Persatuan Pemuda Rakjat Indonesia, or Union of the Youth of
the Indonesian People] in Jogjakarta); and Djalaludin Jusuf Nasution,
who in the early sixties was to become secretary of the North Sumatra
PKI. (See *Kedaulatan Rakjat,* Nov. 20, 1945; Biro Pemuda, *Sedjarah
perdjuangan pemuda Indonesia,* pp. 75, 84.)

[53] *Antara*, Jan. 9, 1946.

satisfactory nature of these talks was shown at the Pesindo conference held in Jogjakarta two days later, where it was decided
to devote all efforts to helping the government in social, economic, security, and political matters, and to educate cadres
specifically for this function. The conference forged even closer
links with the government by forming a new Council of Advisers
to the Pesindo leadership, to be headed by Amir himself and
including Djokosoejono, Chaerul Saleh, S. K. Trimurti, Sitoroes,
Mantoro Tirtonegoro, Soegiono, and S. Widagdo.[54]

In later years it was common for people of many different
groups to look back at the Youth Congress as a turning point in
post-independence political history—one at least as important as
the formation of the Sjahrir cabinet four days later. Those who
subsequently felt hostile to the personalities and policies of Amir
and Sjahrir accused them of having begun the breakup of pemuda
solidarity by trying to dominate this congress through the formation of the Pesindo and the attempt to impose Pesindo programs
as congress decisions. It was claimed that these actions in themselves forced other groups into a much sharper self-awareness
and a wider consciousness of latent ideological divisions within
Indonesian society. Unquestionably there is an element of truth
in these charges. Certainly the combination of Sjahrir's rise to
power and Amir's activities before and after the Youth Congress
contributed to the disintegration of the sense of solidarity that
had generally prevailed among the pemuda up to that time, however unorganized that solidarity may have been. But it would be
unwise to overlook the fact that signs of fissures already existed,
which, though they were to be exploited by differing segments
of the political elite, were by no means created by them.

[54] Some of these figures we have already encountered. The most interesting in this context, since his appearance signified that the Pesindo
would get serious military training, was Djokosoejono, a former shōdanchō in the Peta (Madiun) with radical tendencies. A good character
sketch is contained in Tahi Bonar Simatupang, *Laporan dari Banaran*
(Djakarta, 1960), pp. 90–91. He was a relative of Sukarni's and was
staying at his house at the time of the Rengasdengklok affair, though he
seems to have taken no part in it. Tjarly, ed., *Gelanggang repolusi,* p. 111.

The armed Islamic youth groups loosely subsumed under the name Hizbullah did not even appear at the Youth Congress, and organizationally they were already a key part of the federative structure of the Masjumi. Conflict had existed almost from the start between the PRI of Sumarsono and Ruslan and the Barisan Pemberontakan Republik Indonesia of Bung Tomo in Surabaja. Bung Tomo did not appear in Jogjakarta, and "branches" of his organization, many of them without real organizational links to Surabaja, had begun springing up in a considerable number of towns, particularly in East and Central Java. The Surabaja rivalry thus spread to different areas of the island. Five weeks before the convening of the Youth Congress, the KRIS had been formed (and armed) to express, within a general national framework, the solidarity of youths from the island of Sulawesi.[55] (In

[55] The KRIS was founded on October 8, 1945. Hardjito, ed., *Risalah*, p. 126; B. C. J. Waardeburg, "KRIS," *NEFIS Publikatie*, no. 16 (July 23, 1946). It seems to have grown out of the Choku-eitai, a semi-military organization formed by Maeda for a variety of purposes, including counterintelligence, sabotage, and coast-watching duties in the event of Allied landings. At least some members of this organization were recruited from among Menadonese stranded in Java by the war, whom Maeda had been instructed to keep an eye on by the naval authorities in Makasar. A fair number of them seem to have been former KNIL soldiers who were out of work and separated from their families. (For Maeda's own account of this organization, which may also have been used as a bodyguard for him, see Maeda, "Statement" of Aug. 26, 1946 [IC-RVO doc. no. 006825–9]; cf. Nishijima, "Verklaring," March 10–13, 1947.) Since naval personnel in Java were concentrated mainly in Djakarta and Surabaja, it is not surprising that when the KRIS was formed, its main centers of strength were in these two cities. In Surabaja the organization seems to have confined itself to strictly military activities and was dominated by Menadonese. In Djakarta it was less exclusively Menadonese in character, and came to represent most of the major ethnic groups of Sulawesi. It contained a number of well-educated students from the Djakarta faculties, and was active in relief work as well as propaganda activities to counter the widespread suspicion of pro-Dutch leanings among the once-favored Menadonese. Incorporated into this branch of the KRIS was a smaller group called the API Sulawesi, led by a well-known djago, J. Rappar. Under his direction the KRIS built up a powerful, cohesive, and well-armed paramilitary organization operating on the eastern fringes of Djakarta. Among the better known leaders of

Jogjakarta, the KRIS was among the most effective opponents of the Pesindo group.) The example of the KRIS was followed by a considerable number of groups representing various ethnic and religious minorities that were pushed into increasing self-awareness by each other's growing solidarity.

But of all the badan perdjuangan that began to define themselves vis-à-vis the Pesindo after the Youth Congress, the most significant politically was the Barisan Banteng (Wild Buffalo Corps), which grew out of Muwardi's wartime Barisan Pelopor. What Muwardi represented at Jogjakarta was still a residual rump of the Barisan Pelopor. At a conference held in Surakarta on December 14 and 15, however, it was decided to change the organization's name to Barisan Banteng and to establish its headquarters in that city under the continuing leadership of Muwardi and Sudiro.[56] But whereas the Barisan Pelopor had had branches in most parts of Java during the Japanese period, the Barisan Banteng proved unable to match its ancestor in this regard. During the three months since independence, much of the former membership had melted away, joining other badan perdjuangan or the army. From the start the Barisan Banteng's strength was centered in Surakarta and was largely based on the personal followings of Muwardi and Sudiro and their intimates.[57] In time, indeed, it was

---

the Djakarta KRIS were the daughter of the prominent prewar nationalist leader Dr. Ratulangie and the future leader of the Darul Islam rebellion in South Sulawesi, Kahar Muzakkar. (See *Antara*, Oct. 25, 1945.) It was typical of the times that the name chosen by the organizers of the movement meant in acronym form the short dagger found all over the Malay archipelago and commonly regarded as a repository of magical power.

[56] *Merdeka*, Dec. 16, 1945; *Menara* (Surakarta), Dec. 18, 1945.

[57] According to Major Jusuf, formerly Muwardi's right-hand man in the Barisan Banteng, the organization had branches in Purwokerto, Tjirebon, Bandung, Purwakarta, Pekalongan, Jogjakarta, and Bodjonegoro, but these were relatively small compared with the branches in Madiun (where Sudiro had many relatives), Kediri (where Sidik Djojosoekarto's political skills drew a large following), and Surakarta, which alone boasted ten thousand members. Interview of July 11, 1967. In early February 1946 the Barisan Banteng announced that it had accredited delegates for a conference from Pati, Purwakarta, Demak, Djepara,

to become the most powerful armed paramilitary force in that city.

Like so many other organizations in this period, the Barisan Banteng was decisively marked by the personality of its leader.[58] Though he was a dedicated, well-trained medical practitioner, Dr. Muwardi scarcely fitted the stereotype of the Western-educated Javanese doctor. A strong-willed, hot-tempered, puritanical, and intensely courageous man in spite of his small size, he had long been active in the prewar nationalist scouting movement, practiced silat skills, kept close contacts with various djago, and was a devotee of ilmu kebathinan. His nationalism had an intensely Javanese character, in some respects parallel to that of Sarmidi Mangunsarkoro. Yet it was typical of his view of himself as a *pedjuang* (fighter), not a politician, that he did not join Sarmidi's PNI, though, as we have seen, his subordinate Sudiro did. While the Barisan Banteng was often identified with the PNI, it was in many ways closer to the Central Java Peta group, and because of Muwardi's attachment to the President, to Sukarno. Given Muwardi's personality, the Barisan Banteng was from the beginning somewhat suspicious of the cosmopolitan membership of the Sjahrir cabinet, and thus tended in time to attract to its ranks a variety of men who shared these suspicions. It was soon therefore to become a leading component of the opposition.

In retrospect it seems indisputable that the failure of the Youth Congress and the formation of the Sjahrir cabinet in the second week of November accelerated the breakup of the pemuda solidarity that had generally prevailed up to that time. To understand the dynamics of the process in full, it must be recognized that the youth organizations were in most cases larger and more powerful than the political parties and in some cases preceded

---

Purwodadi, and Kroja. (*Antara*, Feb. 6, 1946.) This confirms the impression that its operations were almost completely confined to Central Java.

[58] For biographical details on Muwardi, see the Appendix.

their formation. Thus the Pesindo was formed before the Socialist Party and for a long time overshadowed it. The Barisan Banteng was a more formidable opponent of the government than the embryonic PNI. And the Hizbullah was from the start a major factor in the political power of Islam. The parties, as such, could exercise leverage only at the rare meetings of the KNIP. They were poorly organized, composed largely of older men accustomed to a pacific style of politics, and unarmed. The badan perdjuangan, operating outside the parliamentary context, enlisted the energies of the pemuda, participated in the day-to-day physical defense of the republic, and above all were armed in various ways. Under these conditions it was natural that in the struggle for power the politicians turned for support to the badan perdjuangan. For the leaders of the youth organizations themselves, once the military front began to stabilize itself and the feverish days of the Siap period passed it was difficult to avoid being drawn into the competition among the elite. In many cases without clear *political* philosophies and goals, the young leaders were vulnerable to the influence of the older politicians, not so much in terms of their character as in terms of the political currents they represented and articulated.

The difficulties of the situation were compounded by the fact that the badan perdjuangan were not strictly political organizations. They could be, and often were, important military groups. Their existence therefore affected the calculations of the army no less than those of the politicians, and they were gradually involved in the competition both within the army itself, and between the army and the government. In addition there were some basic problems that embittered the relations between the army and the badan perdjuangan as a whole.

These problems arose in part from the struggle for resources and in part from inherent differences in organization, recruitment, and outlook. The scarcity of arms in Java generated keen rivalry among all armed groups. Since the army felt that its needs should have top priority, it was constantly tempted to try either to disarm the badan perdjuangan or to incorporate them within itself—a tendency the badan perdjuangan resented and resisted. Moreover, since the budgetary resources of the state were minuscule, all armed groups had to a greater or lesser extent to live off the local population, and competition for control of the economic surplus was intense. While the army was better armed, and often better disciplined, the populist radicalism of the pemuda groups often made it easier for them to win popular support. There was a natural tendency—and it was encouraged by various party leaders, especially in the government—for the badan perdjuangan to characterize themselves as a democratic alternative to the army, which was, as we have seen, frequently stigmatized as authoritarian, fascist, and likely to form a caste. Although the army could claim that it was born from the people and the revolution, the badan perdjuangan seemed the very symbol of the people in arms. The popular legitimacy of many of the various badan perdjuangan and of the even more numerous, ill-defined local resistance groups collectively known in this period as *lasjkar rakjat* (People's Militias), as well as the prevailing military weakness and fragile internal articulation of the army necessitated a sharing of power and functions. Accordingly, the army high command felt compelled very early on to define its own role and tasks vis-à-vis the lasjkar, in an attempt to limit friction and competition and develop a modus vivendi. On December 6 Urip Sumohardjo issued a special proclamation on the relationship between the TKR and the lasjkar. Since this proclamation goes to the heart of a debate that has continued to reverberate up to recent times, it is perhaps worth quoting at some length:

> To avoid misunderstandings and doubts that are now arising between the popular armed groups and the TKR and vice versa, . . . [it is declared that] the TKR is a part of society which is given the duty of defending the integrity of the Indonesian republic; to be able to carry out this duty as well as possible, the army is released from all other work aside from national defense, and its livelihood is guar-

anteed by society. Thus the army is not a group apart from society; it is not a "caste" standing above the community. The army is nothing more than a part of the community with its own specific duties, just like other parts of the community, such as peasants, workers, etc.

The right and duty to maintain internal and external security is not the monopoly of the army. In fact in every effort to defend the state, the whole community struggles alongside the army, through its efforts in the fields of production and transportation, and in its willingness to make sacrifices. . . . But there are also many of our people who are not content with carrying out these everyday tasks; besides their ordinary work, they are forming lasjkar, barisan, and badan perdjuangan, all of which demonstrate their desire to participate actively in ensuring the integrity of the Indonesian state. This development is very gratifying and indeed the formation of these lasjkar rakjat has even been urged by the TKR, . . . for it is obvious that if we must resist colonialism, it is not enough to advance our army by itself; the whole population must join the struggle, with the army as its backbone. But this type of struggle will result in many unnecessary victims, if the most careful preparations are not made. Such preparations concern: (a) the formation of disciplined barisan with tight-knit leadership; (b) training and armaments; (c) planning and coordination between all groups in the struggle.

The lasjkar rakjat must remain people's organizations. The TKR will not interfere in the selection of their leaders or in their internal regulations. The TKR will not disarm the people; in fact, if it proves possible, the TKR will arm the people. . . . Nonetheless for the present the TKR is not in a position to do this. Training [of the lasjkar] may be given by the TKR through consultations with the local TKR headquarters in the regions.[59]

In spite of this proclamation, however, tension and competition persisted owing to continuing political manipulations and the basic struggle for scarce resources. In a number of areas various local badan perdjuangan developed sufficient awareness of their common interests that they were able to form loose overcapping leadership structures that coordinated their activities

[59] *Merdeka,* Dec. 14, 1945.

and helped them develop into effective counterweights to the local army units, which were themselves none too tightly organized. The actual relationship between the badan perdjuangan and the army in each area tended in the long run to vary according to the ideological and organizational coherence of the local military themselves, and the strengths and weaknesses of their competitors.

In West Java Nasution was able to incorporate large sections of the armed pemuda groups from the Priangan into the division he was building, through negotiations with congenial educated pemuda leaders such as Sutoko. Where negotiations failed, he used force. (The radical API organization in Bandung was violently suppressed.) [60] Between 1945 and 1947 he succeeded largely in disarming and liquidating the so-called West Java Lasjkar Rakjat, which grew out of the various armed pemuda groups forced out of Djakarta by the expanding power of the Allies, and which for a while dominated the lowland coastal plain between Bekasi and Tjirebon.

In East Java the army was more dispersed and was dominated by former Peta men, who came closer than the KNIL veterans to sharing the populist ideology of the pemuda groups. It was also the area where the Pesindo and Hizbullah both developed considerable strength, far more than in West Java. The Pesindo was in fact able to dominate the Dewan Perdjuangan Djawa Timur (East Java Resistance Council), which coordinated the various lasjkar in the area, and by its capable leadership to command the respect of the army. East Java's remoteness from the center of political competition encouraged both army and lasjkar to focus primarily on military problems, and a relatively high degree of cooperation and tolerance was achieved.

In Central Java the situation was more complex. Early in January 1946 the government found it advisable to move away from exposed Djakarta to the relative security of Jogjakarta,

[60] Smail (*Bandung,* pp. 129–37) gives an excellent description of this process.

where the army General Staff was already located. The result was that Central Java became the main arena for the struggle for power within the national elite. This competition made the cooperation prevailing in East Java difficult to attain in Central Java, and pitted the badan perdjuangan against the military and each other, with no single group achieving a dominant position. Furthermore, the Sultan of Jogjakarta had very early had the foresight to form his own lasjkar rakjat, which was tightly linked with, indeed formed a completely loyal appendage of the administrative apparatus of the Sultanate.[61] Although somewhat later a Central Java Lasjkar Rakjat was formed under the guidance of Ir. Sakirman and Sajuti Melik, it was neither well-armed nor well-organized, and was in no position to incorporate or even to compete with the Sultan's organization. The situation in the province was thus fragmented, fluid, and tense, in marked contrast to that prevailing to the west and east.

[61] See Nasution, *Tentara Nasional Indonesia*, pp. 97–100. The Sultan issued his proclamation on the formation of the Jogjakarta Lasjkar Rakjat on October 26, 1945. The text is given in *ibid.*, pp. 97–98.

Chapter 12

Tan Malaka and the Rise of the Persatuan Perdjuangan

It was only one of the many paradoxes of the early revolution that the factors and forces behind Sjahrir's and Amir's rise to power in November 1945 created within a matter of a few weeks a powerful opposition to their continued rule. The exploitation of the collaboration issue, while useful prior to the downfall of the Sukarno cabinet, sharply divided the elite and helped frustrate the effort to build a strong government of national unity. The legitimation of parliamentary government of a sort and the development of a government political party, the Socialist Party, accelerated the proliferation of party groupings outside the government, which were naturally eager to displace the PS. The attempt to harness the revolutionary energies of the pemuda through the Youth Congress, perhaps largely because of its relative failure, set an example the government's enemies were quick to follow. The result was a growing fragmentation within the pemuda movement. Furthermore, the government's only partial success in subjecting the TKR to its will made the TKR leadership all the more determined to defend its autonomy and to seek allies among the politicians and pemuda organizations.

Almost from the start of the Sjahrir cabinet's life, then, the elements of a formidable opposition were already in existence. The cabinet was especially vulnerable on two counts. First, it was clearly unrepresentative, dominated as it was by the Socialist Party leaders and largely apolitical professional men. So constituted, the cabinet could hardly claim to be a government of national unity, particularly since the number of organized groups outside the government grew by the day. In the second place, the cabinet had demonstrated by the character of its program and the speed with which it opened talks with the Dutch that it favored diplomacy over armed resistance. During its months of office the suspicion grew that the cabinet feared dissatisfied pemuda at least as much as it feared the Dutch and British armed forces.

Given the proliferation of opposition groups and the government's own weaknesses, only a personality and a program were needed to focus the opposition and precipitate a governmental crisis. The man who came forward to fill this role was the enigmatic and legendary Tan Malaka.

Sutan Ibrahim gelar Datuk Tan Malaka was born in Suliki, West Sumatra, probably in 1897, of local Minangkabau nobility.[1] He was among the tiny group who were able to enter the Teacher Training School in Bukittinggi (then Fort de Kock), which was known popularly as the Sekolah Radja (Kings' School) because only the sons of the local upper class had access to it. The Dutch principal of the school was impressed enough with the boy that he persuaded the leading families in Suliki to establish a fund to finance his further education in Holland.[2] He spent six rather miserable years in Holland from 1913 to 1919, often ill and lonely. Already impressed by the stoicism and self-reliance of a working-class family with whom he lodged, he was immediately

---

[1] The various dates given for Tan Malaka's birth are listed in Ruth T. McVey, *The Rise of Indonesian Communism* (Ithaca, N.Y., 1965), p. 398, n. 35. Professor McVey appears to prefer the year 1897, which is also given by Budiman Djaja in "Mengenang seorang pahlawan: Tan Malaka, sepandjang hidup dan sepandjang perdjuangannja," *Tempo* (Semarang), March 28, 1963—an excellent and sympathetic short biography.

[2] McVey, *The Rise*, p. 117; Tan Malaka, *Dari pendjara ke pendjara*, I (Djakarta, n.d.), 21–22.

attracted by the success of the October Revolution, and read avidly in Marxist literature thereafter.[3]

In November 1919 he returned to the Indies to take up a position teaching coolies contracted to the Senembah Corporation in East Sumatra. The experience was a traumatic one. Trapped between a colonial elite that despised educated natives and a coolie population that distrusted them, he found little outlet for his new political views, which were only confirmed by the realities of the life he observed.[4] The freedom he had enjoyed as a student in Holland was gone for good. In June 1921 he moved to Java, where he was at once taken up by the growing radical movement. He was brought to Semarang by Semaun, the chairman of the PKI, and asked to start a school there.[5] His success in developing the school—the first clear sign of the passion for education and for the young that was to mark the rest of his life —was a major factor in his elevation to the chairmanship of the PKI at the party's eighth congress in December that same year.[6] Although still only 25 years old, he led the party vigorously enough to draw rapid repressive action from the colonial government. In March 1922 he was exiled from the Indies.[7] It was to be twenty years before he again set foot on his native soil.

He made his way to Holland, where he was greeted with some warmth by the Dutch Communist Party, and placed third on the party ticket in the parliamentary elections to be held in the fall of that year. Campaigning vigorously, he outpolled the second man, van Ravestyn, the party's leading theoretician and parliamentary spokesman. Since the Dutch Communist Party had succeeded in obtaining only two seats in the legislature, it was put in an awkward position from which it was extricated only when it was discovered that Tan Malaka was too young to

[3] Tan Malaka, *Dari pendjara*, I, 24–39, esp. pp. 27–28.
[4] *Ibid.*, pp. 47–65. [5] *Ibid.*, pp. 66, 68.
[6] *Ibid.*, p. 74; cf. McVey, *The Rise*, p. 107.
[7] *Ibid.*, p. 76; cf. McVey, *The Rise*, p. 123.

be a member of parliament.[8] The young revolutionary then proceeded to Moscow to attend the Fourth Comintern Congress,
where he made some impression by his outspoken opposition to
the Comintern's hostility to Pan-Islamism as an untrustworthy,
bourgeois force. On this occasion and consistently throughout
his life, Tan Malaka stressed the revolutionary potential of Islam
in the colonized territories and the need for communist parties
to cooperate with radical Islamic groups. Without gaining much
credence with his European colleagues, he insisted that most
Moslems were poor and oppressed workers and peasants who
wanted national liberation from European colonial rule.[9]

In spite of his oppositionist role, Tan Malaka was appointed
Comintern representative in Southeast Asia in the middle of
1923.[10] In December 1923 he set up his headquarters in Canton,
where he met Sun Yat-sen and a number of other top Kuomintang leaders. He attempted without much success to build a Red
Eastern Labor Bureau that would keep transport workers in the
Far East *au courant* with the revolutionary movement in the
West and strengthen the Comintern's communications network
in the area.[11] Discouragement, the loneliness of living in a vast
country whose language he could not speak, and deteriorating
health led him to move in June 1925 to Manila. In the Philippines
he made contact with a number of prominent Filipino leaders,
particularly José Abad Santos and Manuel Quezon, and maintained connections with the PKI leadership in Java.[12]

During his stay in Manila, however, Tan Malaka came into increasing conflict with his party comrades. While still chairman of

[8] McVey, *The Rise*, pp. 237–38.
[9] See *ibid.*, pp. 159–63, for full details on the congress and Tan
Malaka's role within it.
[10] *Ibid.*, pp. 206–7; Tan Malaka, *Dari pendjara*, I, 104–5.
[11] McVey, *The Rise*, pp. 207–10. For Tan Malaka's sympathetic
observations on Sun Yat-sen, see *Dari pendjara*, I, 106–10.
[12] Tan Malaka, *Dari pendjara*, I, 159–61. Tan Malaka's extended
analysis of American imperialism in the Philippines is contained on pp.
124–42.

the party, he had tried to heal the breach between the PKI and the Sarekat Islam, led by Tjokroaminoto and Hadji Agus Salim. As the breach widened, and as the PKI, weakened by internal schisms and government repression, moved toward insurrection, he became increasingly alarmed. In 1925 he had warned the party against sectarianism and against a program that would alienate the party from the broad masses of the people, who were national-socialist rather than proletarian-socialist in their orientation. He was convinced that the lack of an indigenous Indonesian bourgeoisie and the presence of a strong communist movement would guarantee proletarian leadership of the revolution when it came.[13] When he learned that the Executive Committee of the party had decided, at a meeting at the Prambanan temple-complex in Central Java in October 1925, to launch an insurrection against the colonial government, he tried to use his Comintern status to countermand the decision. Convinced that a desperate putsch launched without adequate training, preparation, and organization and without any relation to the real balance of forces in Indonesia would be a total disaster for the party and the population, and furious that the top PKI leadership ignored his remonstrations and tried to prevent the dissemination of his theses, he moved to Singapore and started a letter-writing campaign to convince the party's provincial cadres not to go along with the leadership's plans. To the extent that this campaign was successful, the insurrection, already doomed to failure, was further weakened. When it broke out in West Java in November 1926 and in West Sumatra in January 1927, it was summarily crushed. Tan Malaka's analysis had proven correct, but his activities had thoroughly embittered the party leaders, who never forgave him and were able in part to lay the blame for their own failure on his intervention.[14]

[13] McVey, *The Rise,* p. 316.

[14] For full details on the PKI uprising and Tan Malaka's relationship to it, see McVey, *The Rise,* chap. 11; and Kahin, *Nationalism and Revolution,* pp. 80–85.

From this time onward Tan Malaka increasingly went his own way. In 1927, aided by two loyal comrades, Djamaludin Tamin and Subakat, he formed the Partai Republik Indonesia (Republic of Indonesia Party), or "Pari," in Bangkok, with the intention of training underground cadres to be smuggled back into Indonesia, where they would attempt to pick up the pieces left by the destruction of the PKI. But this project met with little success. The PKI was too shattered and demoralized to be resuscitated, particularly by a man who had become so controversial in the movement. In 1928 he attended the Sixth Comintern Congress and again appeared in an oppositionist role. He attacked Bukharin's theses calling for cooperation between the nationalist bourgeoisie and the communists, citing the tragedy such a policy had brought to the Chinese left.[15]

Thereafter he seems to have led an increasingly lonely and isolated life, largely in the coastal cities of China. In 1932 he was briefly arrested by the British authorities in Hong Kong; on his release he settled near Amoy, living with Chinese friends, and eventually returned to his favorite occupation as a teacher.[16] When the Sino-Japanese War broke out, he felt compelled to flee southward. He settled in Singapore in September 1937, where his friends in the Chinese community provided him with a teaching job in the Chinese school system.[17] When Singapore fell to the Japanese,

[15] Kahin, *Nationalism and Revolution*, pp. 85–86. Tan Malaka himself touches only briefly on the Pari and makes no mention at all of the Sixth Comintern Congress in his autobiography.

[16] For Tan Malaka's arrest and interrogation by the British, see *Dari pendjara*, II, 31–50; and for his long residence in and near Amoy, *ibid.*, pp. 51–86.

[17] *Ibid.*, pp. 100–106. Tan Malaka, now fluent in Hokkien, evidently found it easier to conceal his presence in the Chinese than in the Malay residential area. In reading his autobiography one is struck by how warm Tan Malaka's personal relationships with Chinese of virtually all social classes were. He gives a multitude of examples where he was saved from arrest, illness, or destitution by Chinese businessmen, students, schoolboys, clerks, and so on. I can think of no other Indonesian leader of stature so willing to be publicly indebted to the Chinese, or so genuinely free of racial prejudice.

the same friends arranged for him to be smuggled to Medan. He then headed for Djakarta, which he reached in July 1942.[18] For more than a year he lived in anonymous poverty in a slum area on the southern fringes of the city, primarily reading, writing, and talking with his neighbors. Probably late in 1943, as life became increasingly hard, he found a job as a clerk in the Bajah Kōzan, a coal-mining enterprise in South Banten controlled by the Sumitomo interests.[19] Much of the labor for this enterprise was provided by the rōmusha program, and Tan Malaka's passionate descriptions of his experiences in Bajah show how deeply he was moved by the suffering he witnessed.[20] A friend of his who did not, however, then know his real identity, later described him as follows:

He already looked very old. But I could tell from the way he behaved that he was someone extraordinary. He spoke of the international situation as a real intellectual would have. In that environment he stood out a great deal. We all talked and spoke of nothing but Japan, and complained bitterly. But occasionally he would tell us that Japan was not the real problem—the real problem was America and Britain, and how they were to be dealt with when Japan was finished. . . . You could tell he had been abroad for a long time from the fact that he never washed, except his face and hands, in the European way, not like us who have to wash fully twice a day. He couldn't speak a word of Japanese and his Indonesian was a bit bookish, intellectual. . . . The local workers couldn't understand his ideas at all. He liked to take long walks by himself and you could see he was

18 For his adventures along the way see *ibid.*, pp. 118–32.

19 For his life in Djakarta see *ibid.*, pp. 133–46; for his days in Bajah, pp. 146–83.

20 *Ibid.*, pp. 156–58, and esp. pp. 166–67. Tan Malaka's bitter, detailed description of the rōmusha system, as well as his account earlier in the same volume of Japanese atrocities in China and Singapore and corruption in Djakarta, should suffice to dispel the stories put about after his murder that he was pro-Japanese. What does come out of his description of the Bajah Kōzan is his capacity to pick out the humane Japanese individuals within the machinery of militarist exploitation and give that humanity its due. See esp. pp. 158–59.

a man who talked and thought a lot, unlike the rest of us Indonesians. To keep us all amused I used to write plays and dramatic pieces for the boys; he used to be given the *pendeta* [priestly] parts. I especially remember that we made him Kjai Madja in my version of Diponegoro. He never had any sex and I think he was well past it. He liked to have young people about him and to have them hanging on his words. He usually had such pemuda with him wherever he went.[21]

His work allowed him to travel periodically to various parts of Java; by his own account he went on several occasions to Djakarta as the summer of 1945 wore on, and he was in fact deputed by local groups in Rangkasbitung to attend the conference of pemuda scheduled to be held in early August. He arrived in Djakarta only to find that this conference had been canceled by the military authorities. Though he tried to make contact with Wikana and Pandu Kartawiguna, whose names he had heard before, he succeeded only in reaching the Tjokroaminoto brothers and Chaerul Saleh, but did not reveal his identity to them.[22] He seems also to have been staying at the house of Sukarni in Djakarta during the period of the Rengasdengklok kidnapping—still under an alias. But he took no part in that affair, evidently to his later regret.[23]

Though there can be no certainty about it, some circumstantial evidence suggests that at the very end of the occupation, Tan Malaka came into contact with the Maeda group. Nishijima sub-

[21] Interview with Soeharto, Sept. 4, 1963. Cf. Budiman Djaja ("Mengenang seorang pahlawan"): "Compared with many of our popular leaders, Tan Malaka belonged to that group of leaders who rarely step into the limelight. But when he did, he could talk passionately without ever repeating himself for an hour, two hours . . . even six hours at a stretch. In everyday life, Tan Malaka was never a dandy, but he wasn't too shabby either. In the whole of his life he never managed to start a family of his own. In fact, Mrs. S. K. Trimurti once assured me that one unique thing about Tan Malaka was that he never discussed women in a sexual context. In that respect he was pure, she said."

[22] Tan Malaka, *Dari pendjara,* III, 53.

[23] *Ibid.,* p. 55. As he noted: "I regretted it very much. But history pays no heed to the regrets of a human being, or even of a group of human beings."

sequently stated that the Bukanfu was informed about Tan Malaka's whereabouts through Subardjo, and that he himself had made a special trip to Bajah to seek him out.[24] Another source asserted that he was seen in conversation with high naval officers.[25] On the other hand, Tan Malaka himself relates that he saw Subardjo on August 25 for the first time since they had parted in Holland in 1922, and this version of their encounter has been corroborated by Subardjo.[26] In any event, after August 25 he moved in with the Subardjo family, and was soon introduced under his real name to the more prominent members of the Djakarta elite, particularly to Sukarno, Hatta, Sjahrir, Iwa Kusumasumantri, Sajuti Melik, and others, all of whom had become prominent only after his exile from Indonesia 23 years before.[27]

To understand the situation Tan Malaka found himself in and the role he attempted to play in the earliest days of the republic, it is essential to recall that he was both a stranger and a legend. He had few if any real friends in Djakarta, knew little of the political relationships within the Djakarta intelligentsia, and had neither "collaborated" nor been a member of the "underground." Whereas virtually all the leaders with whom he had now to deal were men who had experienced the occupation in the capital city, he had seen it in the remote coal town of Bajah. Since he had never been faced with the choices confronting the nationalist intelligentsia in Djakarta—whether to cooperate with the Japanese or not—he was in part removed from the struggle over the collaboration issue. Moreover, distance and isolation seem to have given him a perspective difficult to achieve in the metropolis: in this perspective relationships with the vanquished Japa-

[24] Interview given by Nishijima at Cornell University, Sept. 26, 1958.
[25] Interview with Soeharto, Sept. 4, 1963.
[26] Tan Malaka, *Dari pendjara,* III, 61. Subardjo recalled that he was astounded when Tan Malaka revealed his identity, for he had been convinced that his old acquaintance was long since dead. Interview, Jan. 29, 1962.
[27] Tan Malaka, *Dari pendjara,* III, 61.

nese were far less important than the impending relationships with the Dutch, and behind them, the Anglo-Saxon powers.

At the same time his spectacular role in the 1920's and his shadowy career thereafter gave him a legendary aura, which as we shall see, different groups were tempted to exploit. Few people in Djakarta knew him, aside from Subardjo and some others who had been in Holland in 1922, and their uncertainty about his character, capacities, and views helps to account for their confused and perplexing relationships with him in the immediate post-independence period.

It is important to bear in mind that Tan Malaka appeared in Djakarta precisely at the time when the republican leadership was experiencing the greatest anxiety about its future. It was a period when there was real reason to believe that Sukarno and Hatta would be arrested and tried for collaboration by the Allies, and when there was as yet no real sign of the coming pemuda tide. In late August and early September the future of the republic was completely problematic. This atmosphere explains why Sukarno and Hatta offered Tan Malaka a "non-buchō" post in the first republican cabinet, and also why the offer was refused.[28] Like Sjahrir, Tan Malaka was not eager to associate himself with a government in which he would have no decisive voice and whose life-expectancy seemed so limited. The same atmosphere does much to illuminate the curious Testament Affair, which was subsequently used with great skill by his enemies to blacken Tan Malaka's reputation.

Early in September, shortly after the cabinet was formed, Tan Malaka visited Sukarno at the house of the latter's physician, Dr. Suharto. In the ensuing conversation, which Sajuti Melik witnessed,[29] Tan Malaka urged the President to retreat into the interior and suggested various methods for organizing effective resistance. Evidently impressed, Sukarno responded that if anything happened to him personally, he hoped Tan Malaka would take over. Subsequently Tan Malaka told Subardjo what Sukarno

[28] Interview with Hatta, June 5, 1960.
[29] Interview with Sajuti Melik, Sept. 24, 1962,

had said, and between the two of them the idea of a formal testament bequeathing the leadership of the new state to Tan Malaka was conceived. Finally, Tan Malaka asked Subardjo to invite Sukarno to his house, where a draft testament was presented to him. Hatta joined them shortly thereafter, and it was evidently on his insistence that not one but four men were finally named as political legatees. These four were Tan Malaka; Sjahrir; Mr. Wongsonagoro, the resident of Semarang, who was regarded as influential in older nationalist and pangrèh pradja circles; and Dr. Sukiman, the prominent prewar leader of the modernist Islamic party PII.[30] In the course of the discussions, however, the fact was brought up that Sukiman was resident in Jogjakarta and therefore not immediately available. At this point the appearance of Iwa, whether by chance or not, led Subardjo to suggest that since as a Sundanese Iwa had clear Islamic credentials, his name should be substituted for that of Sukiman. This proposal was accepted without more ado.[31]

It was subsequently to be charged that the whole Testament Affair was a plot engineered by Tan Malaka and Subardjo to lay the groundwork for a seizure of power from Sukarno and Hatta. Tan Malaka's enemies, particularly Sjahrir and his associates, alleged that Subardjo never informed Sjahrir and Wongsonagoro about the document, and that Tan Malaka tried to exploit it to give himself political legitimacy on his subsequent travels through Java.[32] There is good reason to doubt the accuracy of these alle-

[30] This account is based on interviews with Hatta, Feb. 13, 1962, and with Subardjo, May 11, 1962. For biographical details on Wongsonagoro, see the Appendix. Sukiman was probably chosen because of his close personal relationships with Sukarno and Subardjo, and also because he had cooperated relatively little with the occupation authorities.

[31] Interview with Sajuti Melik, Sept. 24, 1962; also the interviews cited in the previous note. Sajuti observed, "It was simply playing games with the revolution. It showed that all these people were still not taking the revolution seriously as a social transformation, but were only thinking in elite political terms."

[32] See Kahin (*Nationalism and Revolution*, pp. 148–50) for a detailing of these charges and an analysis of the Testament Affair based on sources hostile to Tan Malaka. The date given there for the signing of the Testa-

gations. Wongsonagoro was deeply involved in the drama of Semarang and did not come to Djakarta until much later in the year. And it is inconceivable that Sjahrir was not informed about the document by Hatta, who, after all, had proposed that Sjahrir's name be included in it. Clearly, the real reason for the disappearance of the Testament as an issue of any importance was the plain fact that the premises that had led to its being drafted were almost immediately rendered obsolete by the Christison proclamation, which guaranteed British respect for the Sukarno government, and by the opening on October 23 of the first Sukarno–van Mook talks. Far from being suppressed, the Testament simply became irrelevant.

However unimportant it basically was, the Testament Affair does throw some momentary light on the attitudes and perspectives of Sukarno and Tan Malaka at the time. Given the intense egocentricity and sense of personal mission that marked the whole of Sukarno's life, nothing more pointedly illustrates his fears and consciousness of weakness at this juncture than his willingness to sign such a document at all. For Tan Malaka's part, his willingness to take such a testament seriously suggests that he was deeply afraid that a critical historical juncture would pass (or in more practical terms, that the Allies would consolidate their control) before he had time to develop an organization or promote a program on his own account; hence the need to tap some of the legitimacy Sukarno already held. The episode also suggests that Tan Malaka, along with many others in Djakarta, had certain illusions about the real importance of formal institutions in the developing revolutionary process.[33]

Shortly after the Christison proclamation and the Allied landings in Djakarta, Tan Malaka moved out of the city to watch the developing situation from the coolness and security of Bogor.

---

ment, October 1, is too late, coming after the date of the Christison broadcast which made it obsolete.

[33] Nonetheless, it is difficult to avoid seeing a certain parallel with Bao Dai's delivering the Great Imperial Seal of Hué to Ho Chi Minh's representatives on August 26, 1945.

It seems to have been at this point that he came into closer contact with Sjahrir and the group of pemuda who were then looking to Sjahrir for leadership. The precise nature of the relationship is still unclear, the subsequent political histories of the two men having led to quite different versions of what took place.

According to the first version Tan Malaka approached Sjahrir early in October and urged an alliance to set aside the Sukarno-Hatta government by some sort of coup d'état and to pursue a far more radical policy vis-à-vis the Allies than the cabinet had so far conducted. Sjahrir was offered either the post of prime minister or the presidency, with Tan Malaka taking either the presidency or some ministries like those of Labor and the Interior.[34] Gradually, however, the deviousness of Tan Malaka's advances dawned on Sjahrir, and he refused to have anything to do with the plot. He also advised Tan Malaka to go to the provinces and see for himself whether it was he or Sukarno who had the real support of the population.[35]

In the second version the crucial conference between Sjahrir and Tan Malaka occurred early in October at Serang, where a whole group of the leading pemuda in Djakarta, including Sukarni, Maruto Nitimihardjo, Adam Malik, Pandu Kartawiguna, Soegra, Djalil, Kartamuhari, Djohan Sjahroezah, and Dr. Sudarsono, came to talk to Tan Malaka, with Sjahrir at their head.[36] The delegation questioned Tan Malaka about his views on the

[34] The two versions of what Sjahrir was offered are given in Kahin, *Nationalism and Revolution*, pp. 149, 167.

[35] For this interpretation, see the account given in *ibid.*, pp. 147–49.

[36] In an interview on June 4, 1967, Subadio Sastrosatomo dated the Serang meeting just after the establishment of the Working Committee of the KNIP, or about October 18. This date seems plausible in that it coincides with the start of the so-called silent coup against the Sukarno cabinet. If it is correct, then it suggests that the initiative for the meeting may have come from Sjahrir and the Djakarta pemuda rather than from Tan Malaka, and that the meeting's objective was to obtain Tan Malaka's endorsement for the campaign under way in the capital. That this was the case is further suggested by Subadio's interesting observation that Tan Malaka "opposed changing the Constitution"—precisely what Sjahrir and his friends were doing.

situation and his willingness to join in the leadership of a socialist party to be set up shortly in Jogjakarta.[37] Tan Malaka replied that he was opposed to the formation of any party at this point, since it was still uncertain that the British-Dutch forces would not eventually undertake drastic military action against the republic. In such a situation the formation of a party would be a mistake, since "others would immediately spring up like mushrooms after rain." Once they had been set up it would be extremely hard to coordinate different parties against the imperialist forces. The best strategy would be to try to strengthen the existing government by bringing in revolutionary leaders from the outside.[38]

While both versions reflect the later interests of the two parties, the second, Tan Malaka's, seems closer to the truth. The testimony of observers identified with neither group in their subsequent clashes indicates that the break between them came only after Sjahrir's rise to power, and that while the Sukarno cabinet survived in office, there were no fundamental disagreements. This testimony is confirmed by two other clear indications of relative harmony between Sjahrir and Tan Malaka in this period. First, there is the complete silence in the Djakarta press about Tan Malaka for the duration of the first cabinet, and indeed for some weeks after the Sjahrir government's installation. Since the Djakarta elite, and such pemuda press leaders as Diah, the editor of *Merdeka,* were clearly well aware of his existence, this silence is suggestive. Had Sjahrir and his pemuda following really believed at this time that Tan Malaka was playing the sinister role later attributed to him, it is incomprehensible that he would not

[37] Tan Malaka, *Dari pendjara,* III, 68. This possibly checks with the fact that Parsi was shortly to be formed in Jogjakarta.

[38] *Ibid.* Tan Malaka also noted that later on, in early November, when he was in Jogjakarta, he was approached by a group headed by Wijono (who were in fact the organizers of Parsi) and asked to lead a projected socialist party. But he again refused, feeling that the time had "not yet come for me clearly to emerge as the leader of a party." It is instructive that here again the initiative in contacts between Tan Malaka and the Socialist leaders seem to have come from the latter.

have been publicly attacked. It seems plausible to assume that the press silence, which was not broken until December, was the result of a general respect in Djakarta circles for Tan Malaka's wish to remain in the background until the time seemed ripe for him to emerge. Second, when Tan Malaka traveled to Surabaja early in November, he was apparently accompanied by Djohan Sjahroezah, one of Sjahrir's closest and most trusted associates.[39]

In retrospect, it seems probable that the battle of Surabaja marked a turning point in the relations between Sjahrir and Tan Malaka. The heavy casualties among the Indonesian masses and the violent, anarchic character of their resistance seem to have convinced Sjahrir that prompt negotiations with the British and the Dutch were essential to avoid useless sacrifices and further deterioration of the political situation. As we have seen, no sooner was the Sjahrir cabinet formed than negotiations were instituted.

From the same sacrifices and the same "fanaticism" Tan Malaka drew quite opposite conclusions. The will to resist the British and the Dutch was clearly revealed by the fighting he

[39] According to his own account Tan Malaka was in Jogjakarta when he heard over Bung Tomo's Radio Pemberontakan that "Tan Malaka is in Surabaja leading the resistance." Realizing that the Surabaja Tan Malaka must be an impostor, he hurried off to expose the fraud. When he reached the embattled city, however, he was promptly arrested as an impostor himself, and 24 hours passed before he was released. *Ibid.*, pp. 68–69. Since this radio broadcast was recorded in *Merdeka* on November 9, the real Tan Malaka probably reached the harbor city by the evening of that day at the latest. His own account makes no mention of Djohan Sjahroezah. (In the preface to his pamphlet *Politik* [Jogjakarta, 1945] Tan Malaka says he was in Surabaja from November 17 to 24, but this seems too late.) On the other hand, A. M. Chandra ("10 Nopember dan obor mental generasi muda," *Sinar Harapan,* Nov. 9, 1968), while confirming the story of Tan Malaka's arrest on or about November 10, asserts that he and Djohan Sjahroezah were the guiding spirits behind the Surabaja resistance. According to the very anti–Tan Malaka *Dokumentasi pemuda* (pp. 60–61), the two men arrived together in Surabaja for the first time in mid-October, and Tan Malaka was arrested for carrying a copy of the notorious Testament. (This detail seems implausible for the reasons given earlier.)

observed around him; what was lacking was organization and leadership. It was not negotiations that were needed to prevent a vain repetition of Surabaja, but the creation of a massive, coordinated, armed resistance movement. It seems no accident that the first major public elaboration of his views on the course of the revolution was issued from Surabaja, and that it appeared on December 2, three weeks after the publication of *Perdjuangan Kita,* to which in effect it was a radical rejoinder. Nor was it inappropriate that Tan Malaka entitled this pamphlet *Muslihat* —Strategy.[40]

Muslihat is dramatically cast in the form of a discussion between symbolic representatives of all the groups Tan Malaka hoped to weld into the popular resistance movement: Mr. Apal (the Western-educated urban intelligentsia), Dènmas (enlightened members of the traditional upper class), Toké (patriotic businessmen and merchants), Patjul (the peasantry), and Godam (the workers).[41] In response to the opening remarks of Mr. Apal and Dènmas that Indonesia's weakness requires a strategy of conciliation, enlisting the sympathy of the Allies by strictly conforming to international law and adopting parliamentary institutions copied from the West, Godam strongly criticizes their defeatism and attacks the idea that gaining recognition for the republic is the prime aim of the revolutionary struggle: "Recognition is no condition for life." The real aim of the struggle is freedom—and ultimately a socialist society based on heavy industry. He insists that "provided all the conditions of resistance are understood and carried out, seventy million human beings

[40] Tan Malaka, *Moeslihat* (Jogjakarta, 1945). It seems that his pamphlet *Politik* was written and possibly published earlier, but its contents are quite general, with little specific reference to Indonesia.

[41] All quotations in the following pages are drawn from *Moeslihat.* The name Mr. Apal is slightly sardonic, "Mr." referring to the holder of a law degree and *apal* meaning "to learn" with the connotation of learning by rote. Dènmas is short for the Javanese aristocratic title Radèn Mas. Toké (*tauké*) is a faintly derogatory word for "businessman." Patjul means "hoe," and Godam "hammer."

cannot be colonized once again." The essential conditions are that Indonesians have no illusions about imperialism, which understands only force and power, and that the entire population be involved in the struggle for freedom.

Godam lists nine factors that will determine the character of the coming struggle. Geographical conditions are clearly in Indonesia's favor. Her natural fertility and tropical climate mean that the resistance can easily obtain the food and the little clothing it will require. Indonesians will be fighting on their own soil, while the enemy will be far from home, unaccustomed to local conditions and dependent on extended supply lines. The international situation is also advantageous. The world is divided between the Anglo-Saxons, together with their camp followers, the French and the Dutch, and the Soviet Union, together with the oppressed colored people of Asia and Africa. But the Anglo-Saxon bloc is internally divided along class lines, and Indonesia's struggle will only exacerbate these divisions further. In sheer numbers, too, Indonesia holds the upper hand. The enemy cannot conceivably muster more than 200,000 troops, while the resistance can mobilize many times that figure. And clearly, with regard to morale, popular enthusiasm for independence has never been more fiercely aroused. On the other hand, the factors of weakness are not to be ignored. The republic has few officers with real military understanding; arms are in short supply, and there are virtually no munitions factories; the enemy controls the sea and the air. Thus for the moment the resistance is weak in sheer military terms; but these weaknesses are far from insurmountable. What is more important is that the experience of the last months has shown that the republic seriously lacks discipline, organizational strength, political and administrative unity, and coordinated and intelligent planning.

Given this balance sheet of strengths and weaknesses, the proper strategy is to proclaim a minimum program behind which the entire population can unite, and at the same time to build a popular front organization that can channel the population's energies, talents, and hopes to carry out that program effectively. In Godam's view the minimum program should call for the creation of a fighting regime by the fighting people; the formation of a Lasjkar Rakjat; the division of land to poor peasants; the realization of the workers' right to control production; the realization of an economic "struggle-plan"; the ousting of all foreign troops from Indonesian soil; and the disarming of the Japanese.

Replying to alarmed murmurs from Dènmas, Godam assures him that the land to be divided among the peasants will be confined to the property of hostile aliens and aristocratic parasites of the Dutch. No one will be deprived of any land he needs for his own subsistence, but anything over that will be given to the poor and landless. Workers' control will help to increase production and develop political support for the revolutionary regime; but the workers will also be involved in a coordinating political organization so that their activities will be directly related to the economic "struggle-plan."

Turning to the question of the formation of the popular front, Godam proposes that it be divided organizationally into three sections. The first and highest in status will be the political section, responsible for devising the front's overall strategy and determining day-to-day tactics, coping with organizational problems, and preparing and disseminating propaganda. He emphasizes that leadership should not be taken by military men but should stay in civilian hands.[42] The second section will handle military and police training, the creation of cadres, and the organization and supplying of the fighting pemuda.[43] The third section will be re-

[42] Godam warns against the danger of military dictatorship and warlordism in the Outer Islands if firm civilian leadership at the center is not guaranteed. Here one can see the impact of the Chinese experience in the 1920's and 1930's on Tan Malaka's thinking. The history of the Kuomintang was an object lesson in the failure of a revolutionary movement.

[43] Patjul notes that "in the era of Dutch imperialism, there was one group of Indonesians with free blood in their veins, ready to give leadership. They refused to be bound by the institutions created by Dutch im-

sponsible for economic matters insofar as they related to the armed resistance. All other matters, such as education, welfare, and so on, could be left to the government[!]. Godam stresses that the front will not be a government as such, but rather an organization to mobilize energies for winning the war. It should include the widest possible range of groups and be organized on the most democratic, centralized basis, with maximum opportunity for criticisms and proposals from the various participants.

In conclusion Godam spells out the classic rules of guerrilla warfare for the armed struggle he sees as imminent. He urges his listeners to remember that *Muslihat* is above all a political and economic rather than a military concept. Time is on Indonesia's side. Even if the enemy occupies the cities of the coastal perimeter, the strength of the resistance, deep in the villages of the interior, will be unaffected. In the long run the patience of the outside world will wear thin. "The Strategy of the Indonesian people is long-term resistance, avoiding all actions which are rash, taken in haste, fanatical or adventurist. With hearts serene, but strong as steel, minds cool and calculating, and finally with an invincible determination and conviction, the people of Indonesia will wait for the dawn of freedom."

Although *Muslihat* contained the first reasoned alternative to

---

perialism, whether political or economic. They would have 500 to 1,000 men behind them, followers who obeyed their orders without calculating loss or gain, life or death. In the era of Dutch imperialism they were regarded as enemies of the social order, which was indeed rotten to the core. And now they have no desire for the restoration of that order. Everywhere they are taking action on their own, facing an aggressive and heavily armed foe. Where they receive the trust of the common people [*rakjat murba*] and responsibilities, they undergo a great change for the good. These men who were formed by the old colonial society, the paréwa, with their undying spirit of rebellion, must be brought under healthy leadership and supervision. If not, they will act on their own, and perhaps will harm our struggle." In some ways, Tan Malaka was the paréwa type himself, so it was fitting that he devoted some space to this group.

the strategy pursued by the republican governments to date, it does not appear to have received wide circulation at the time. And Tan Malaka's name was not brought before the general public until late in December, when extended articles about him appeared in the Djakarta press, penned by another unusual Minangkabau, Mr. Muhammad Yamin.[44] In these articles Yamin described Tan Malaka's twenty years of service to Indonesian liberation and noted that the public was "overjoyed" to hear now of his reappearance in their midst. Readers were informed that he had been "dynamite" outside the sessions of the Youth Congress in Jogjakarta and had been deeply involved in the fighting at Surabaja.[45]

The timing of the articles was excellent, for disillusionment with the Sjahrir-Amir government had already set in when they appeared. Though Tan Malaka was publicly introduced only on December 22, he was the leader and main speaker at a large congress that opened less than two weeks later, on January 3, at Purwokerto in Central Java.[46] The tone of this congress was set

[44] Mr. Muhammad Yamin was Indonesia's best-known political eccentric so long as he lived. It was said of him, not altogether unkindly, that he was like a horse: if you were in front of him, you were likely to get nipped; if behind him, to get kicked; and if under him, to be trampled on. But if you were on top of him, with the reins in your hands, he would carry you fast and far. For biographical details, see the Appendix.

[45] Ra'jat, Dec. 22, 1945; Berita Indonesia, Dec. 26, 1945. See also Muhammad Yamin, Tan Malacca: Bapak Republik Indonesia (Djakarta, n.d.), a booklet issued at the end of December or early in January, according to internal evidence.

[46] Tan Malaka later wrote that the idea of a massive people's congress was born in December, after the fall of Surabaja. Originally the congress had been planned for Malang. Organizational difficulties had intervened, and it was only at a meeting on January 1 in Demakidjo, a small village near Klaten, that final plans for the Purwokerto gathering were settled. Dari pendjara, III, 71. Sajuti Melik subsequently gave a rather different account. He said that late in December 1945 in a village to the west of Jogjakarta, there was a get-together to introduce Tan Malaka to old friends in the nationalist movement. This happened about a week before the Purwokerto meeting. The initiative for the conference was taken not by Tan Malaka but by a committee consisting of Sukarni and some of

at the start by Sajuti Melik, who attributed the confused situation on the Semarang front to a lack of internal unity and strongly urged the formation of an all-Indonesia coordinating body to direct resistance against the perfidious British. Speeches by such well-known pemuda as Armunanto and Ismail echoed these themes, and a sympathetic message from General Sudirman was read before the assembled delegates. Finally Tan Malaka appeared on the stage to give his first public address in Indonesia since 1922. Pointing to the growing internal tensions between different groups of Indonesians, he urged the formulation of a minimum program as short and concrete as possible behind which all groups could consolidate. Reminding his listeners of the sad example of Diponegoro, betrayed by his own followers, and the fatal divisions between the PKI and the Sarekat Islam in the early twenties, he warned that only the enemy would profit from further splits in national unity. In a fine anticipation of a later period, he urged that socialists, religious people, and nationalists all unite in a popular front behind a program cen-

---

his friends. Sajuti himself did not join, and he questioned Tan Malaka's wisdom in bringing forward a program of his own at this point, since many people were hostile to him from prewar days and might oppose his program for this reason. Tan Malaka rejected this advice, saying that once the program was made public, old comrades would see that he was right. Sajuti felt that Tan Malaka still did not "understand the real situation," and that the consequences would be those he, Sajuti, feared. See "Stenographisch verslag: Sidang Mahkamah Tentara Agung, dalam pemeriksaan proces Sudarsono cs., Maret 1948" (hereinafter referred to as "SV"), p. 230 (testimony of Sajuti Melik). The mention of Sukarni as the initiator of the committee to set up the conference, whether true or not, is the first indication that Sjahrir's pemuda following was breaking away. Another indication is that on December 31, 1945, *Kedaulatan Rakjat* announced that Tan Malaka's book *Politik,* "as big as Sjahrir's *Perdjuangan Kita,*" was on the stands, issued by the publishers of *Kedaulatan Rakjat* itself, the Badan Usaha Penerbitan Nasional. This body had been founded by Adam Malik in early September, in association with Anwar Tjokroaminoto, R. H. O. Djoenaedi, Mashoed Hardjokoesoemo, Soebrata, Sumanang, and Winarno Danuatmodjo. (See *Soeara Asia,* Sept. 11, 1945.) At the very least Malik must have approved this publication, a clear sign of his disenchantment with Sjahrir.

tering on "100% Merdeka" and the expulsion of all foreign troops from Indonesian shores. Tan Malaka's speech appears to have been very warmly received. He was tactful enough not to attack the government himself, though Ismail, for example, openly charged that the cabinet's policy of long, drawn out diplomacy was simply giving the Allies time to build up their forces.

After his address Tan Malaka unveiled his seven-point Minimum Program, which was to become the subject of bitter controversy in the months to follow:

1. The state should be based on the acknowledgment of 100 per cent sovereignty and all foreign troops should leave the shores and waters of Indonesia.
2. [The formation of] a people's government.
3. [The formation of] a people's army.
4. The disarming of all Japanese troops.
5. The taking charge of [*mengurus*] all European internees.
6. The confiscation and control of plantations.
7. The confiscation and control of industrial installations.

He added that the program contained the basis for an anticapitalist and anti-imperialist struggle that could be easily understood and fought for by the common people.[47]

Though Tan Malaka himself made no direct mention of the program of the Sjahrir cabinet, the contrast between the two was immediate and striking. While points two, three, and four were either uncontroversial or vague enough not to be disturbing, all of the others ran directly counter to the government's stated or unstated policies. Point one challenged the policy of conciliating the British and trying to win their support in negotiations with the Dutch. Points six and seven were a direct contradiction of key sections of the Political Manifesto, which explicitly rejected the confiscation of Dutch and other foreign-held property, and indeed promised to return confiscated property to its original owners. Point five was ambiguous, but seemed to imply that the European internees should be used as hostages until the British

[47] *Kedaulatan Rakjat,* Jan. 10, 1946; *Merdeka,* Jan. 10, 1946.

and Dutch gave concrete guarantees that they would accept Indonesia's independence. Coming at a time when the Sjahrir-Amir cabinet was trying to reassure the Allies on precisely this matter, point five seemed likely to cause the cabinet political embarrassment.

The cabinet leaders immediately understood the challenge that had been laid down by the caucus at Purwokerto and tried to head off the threat it seemed to portend. On January 11 *Kedaulatan Rakjat,* the most important newspaper in the new republican capital of Jogjakarta, published an open letter from the Socialist Party urging all parties and organizations to join a projected Barisan Nasional (National League) with a common program. The Barisan would have a ruling directorate in which all constituent organizations would have a voice, and which would settle differences in a comradely way. The proposed political program would aim at extending democracy at home and defending merdeka abroad; the economic program would aim at increasing the production and distribution of goods and stepping up educational efforts.[48] There was no reference anywhere in the program to any of the controversial matters raised by Tan Malaka. While the Barisan Nasional never got off the ground, perhaps because it was so obviously intended to preempt the plans laid at Purwokerto, the open letter was a clear public indication that the government felt alarmed.

Tension began to build up from this time on between the cabinet and the crystallizing opposition over which Tan Malaka was seen to preside. On January 14 Sajuti Melik wrote a lengthy article warmly praising the popular front projected at Purwokerto, but very frankly describing the private reactions of government politicians toward it. He warned that the front could be obstructed by mutual suspicions, prejudices, and private ambitions. "Don't let the idea develop that [the slogan] 'people's unity' is [designed] to overthrow the government, or that 'government authority' is really aimed at crushing the popular move-

[48] *Kedaulatan Rakjat,* Jan. 11, 1946.

ment." Trust and unity should be given priority over all considerations of strategy.[49]

But Sajuti's warnings were in vain. The cabinet leaders assumed from the start that the embryonic popular front was in fact designed to bring about their downfall. Since it seemed difficult to attack the front's program directly without risking a serious loss of political support, it was decided that the only way to counter the front was to join it, and either take control of it or wreck it from within.

The drawing power of Tan Malaka's presence and program, and the tactical decision taken by the Socialist leaders to participate, led to the attendance of at least 133 organizations at the second popular front conference held in Surakarta on January 15 and 16.[50] But the degree to which the conference was regarded as oppositionist is clearly revealed by the fact that although Sukarno, Hatta, and all the ministers had been invited, none of them came. The Panglima Besar, General Sudirman, did attend, and made his own opposition to the cabinet quite explicit when he told his audience, "It would be better for us to be atom-bombed [diatom] than to win less than 100 per cent merdeka." [51]

The final speaker was again Tan Malaka. He spoke of the great overriding need for organization, criticizing the mushrooming parties as being divisive and very difficult to control. He urged a return to unity, a unity for resistance [persatuan untuk perdjuangan]. He explained again his concept of the popular front and his Minimum Program, strongly defending the sections dealing with the confiscation of enemy property. With this property in their hands the people's fighting spirit would be greatly enhanced, since what they were defending would now be their own; moreover, only Dutch and possibly British property would be confiscated. In fact, in case of shortages and difficulties, Tan

[49] *Ibid.*, Jan. 14, 1946.

[50] *Ibid.*, Jan. 16, 1946, lists 133 organizations, while Tan Malaka (*Dari pendjara*, III, 71) gives 141.

[51] *Antara*, Jan. 17, 1946.

Malaka averred that it should be possible to get expert help from "countries which have not colonized us, like Germany, America, Switzerland, Sweden, etc." [52]

Following Tan Malaka's address it was agreed that the popular front's name should be drawn from his speech: Persatuan Perdjuangan (Struggle Union; Union of Resistance), or PP. A subcommittee of eleven members was formed to make concrete proposals for the internal organization of the new body. The membership of this subcommittee reflects the groupings assembled at this point within Tan Malaka's germinating coalition: Ibnu Parna, from the Pesindo; Wali al-Fatah, Masjumi; Sakirman, Dewan Perdjuangan (Resistance Council) of Central Java; Abdulmadjid, PS; General Sudirman, TKR; Atmadji, TKR (naval branch); Soejono, KNI-Surakarta; Tan Malaka; an unnamed member from the congress committee; Usman, PRI Surabaja; and Mrs. Mangoenkoesoemo, Perwani.[53]

On the second day of the congress the subcommittee presented its recommendations. In general Tan Malaka's Purwokerto proposals were accepted *in toto,* especially the Minimum Program. Political, economic, social, and military subsections were to be instituted under a leadership partly elected by the congress, and partly consisting of coopted experts. The leadership would have a secretariat under it, formed out of its own membership. All members of the PP were obliged to carry out decisions of the congress. At the same time a special conciliation body would be set up to handle disagreements between constituent elements; if a dispute could not be resolved by this body, it might be referred to the secretariat and ultimately to the congress of the PP itself. Having approved these proposals, the congress urged the government to take immediate steps to put them into action.[54]

[52] *Ibid.,* Jan. 19, 1946.
[53] *Ibid.,* Jan. 18, 1946. The Perwani (Persatuan Wanita Indonesia, or Indonesian Women's Union) was a leading women's organization of the time.
[54] *Ibid.; Kedaulatan Rakjat,* Jan. 17, 1946.

The government, meantime, acutely aware of the growing popularity of the PP and determined to avoid being outmaneuvered, tried to take the offensive. On the opening day of the Surakarta meeting it issued a major proclamation through the KNIP Working Committee, which it still controlled, urging maximum unity and attacking unnamed groups for trying to divide the government against itself by disrupting relationships between the central and regional governments and between the government and the population. Rather defensively the proclamation cited examples of the government's willingness to listen to popular demands: the President and Vice-President had moved on January 4 from Djakarta to Jogjakarta; a Ministry of Religion had been created and a minister appointed; a new minister of information had been installed; and a Balai Pemuda (Youth Institute) had been set up within the Ministry of Social Affairs to take special care of the needs of youth.[55]

But the impetus of the PP continued to develop. On January 25 its steering committee announced that a further assembly would be held in Surakarta on January 27 and that the PKI of Mr. Jusuf, Bung Tomo's BPRI, the PBI, and various other parties had meantime joined the central leadership.[56] As Sajuti Melik put it, all the major organizations had now joined the PP; only the biggest and most powerful remained outside—the government itself. He urged the government to join the PP, indeed to assume a leadership role within it. The Minimum Program was actually the government's responsibility; the population at large could only help. He warned that unless the government accepted

[55] The proclamation, Pengumuman BP-KNIP no. 20, is contained in *Antara*, Jan. 22, 1946. The minister of religion was H. Rasjidi of the Masjumi, whose appointment dated from January 4; see *Antara*, Jan. 5. The new minister of information was Mohammad Natsir, also of the Masjumi, whose appointment dated from the same day. The Balai Pemuda was to be headed by Supeno, who remained a member of the KNIP's Working Committee and a powerful influence within the PS and Pesindo.
[56] *Antara*, Jan. 25, 1946.

this responsibility the PP would fail, for it could not by itself implement the key points in the program.[57]

At the Surakarta meeting at the end of January, the PP's ranks were further swelled by the addition of the BKPRI [58] and some major badan perdjuangan: the Barisan Banteng and the Dewan Perdjuangan of Central, East, and West Java. An election was held for the five members of the central secretariat, in which representation was given to Bung Tomo's BPRI, the Masjumi, the Pesindo, the PBI, and the BKPRI.[59]

By the end of January, then, the campaign launched by Tan Malaka seemed to have reached a highly successful climax. A large number of different groups, whether for reasons of conviction, of tactics, or of political opportunism, had decided to join the PP, and the government appeared to be increasingly isolated. Significantly, voices were beginning to be heard declaring that the PP was fundamentally a more genuinely representative body than the KNIP, let alone the Working Committee. And in fact a number of the top leaders of the PP, most notably Tan Malaka and General Sudirman, did not sit in the KNIP, while many of the PP's component organizations, because they were formed after the KNIP and were based in the provinces rather than the capital, were seriously underrepresented in it. Under these conditions, it seemed improbable that the government could long survive.

[57] See his thoughtful article in *Kedaulatan Rakjat,* Jan. 23, 1946.

[58] Badan Kongres Pemuda Republik Indonesia (Council of the Youth Congress of the Republic of Indonesia)—the organization set up to coordinate pemuda activities after the Youth Congress of November 10, 1945.

[59] *Merdeka,* Feb. 1, 1946.

Chapter 13

The Cabinet Falls

The rapidly growing popularity of the Persatuan Perdjuangan was certainly in considerable measure a tribute to the personality of Tan Malaka and to the strategy of resistance he had consistently advocated. But no less important were the difficulties the government itself faced and the malaise engendered by its evident failure to overcome them.

After Sudirman's successes at Ambarawa, the military situation steadily worsened. By the end of November, Surabaja was completely in Allied hands, and the Indonesians had suffered enormous losses. Heavy fighting flared up in Bandung on November 25 and 26, and on November 27 General MacDonald issued an ultimatum demanding that the northern half of the city be cleared of all Indonesians within 48 hours.[1] In spite of the efforts of Amir, Natsir, and Soetardjo Kartohadikoesoemo and Datuk Djamin (the governor and vice-governor of West Java) to mediate, the ultimatum was put into effect, causing a massive migration of Indonesians into the poor southern half of the city.[2] Once again, as in the period of the Sukarno cabinet, the government was put in the position of appearing to help the Allied forces establish a position of strength at the expense of the local lasjkar and badan perdjuangan.[3] On December 8 the British seized the

[1] The text is given in Smail, *Bandung*, p. 110.

[2] For an excellent description of these events see *ibid.*, pp. 111–16.

[3] *Antara* (Dec. 10, 1945) makes this point quite clearly in its account of Amir's mission to settle the Bandung crisis.

former governor-general's palace in Bogor, and in the days that followed they drove the existing republican military units out of the town.[4] The government had earlier been forced to accede to Allied pressure in the capital, and on November 19 had ordered all army units in and around Djakarta to move outside the city limits.[5] On December 13 British units made brutal air and ground attacks on the area round Bekasi in reprisal for the murder by local peasantry of British and Indian airmen who had crashed there on November 23.[6]

Sjahrir, Hatta, and Amir in these days made constant appeals over the radio, urging the population to remain calm and disciplined, and to refrain from acts of violence toward the minorities and the Allies. But to little effect. The losses suffered in frontal clashes with the British and Indian troops in no way stemmed the tide of violence sweeping across the island. On December 11 *Merdeka* reported heavy fighting in Sukabumi, Bogor, Ambarawa, Semarang, and East Java.[7] In the meantime, outside Java, the Dutch and Australians were strengthening their grip over East Indonesia and Kalimantan, while the British pressed forward around the main urban enclaves in Sumatra.[8] And Djakarta itself was becoming increasingly unsafe for the government. With the removal of Indonesian troops from the area, undisciplined KNIL soldiers began running wild. On December 26 and 28, trigger-happy squads made separate attempts on the lives of Sjahrir and Amir Sjarifuddin.[9]

[4] Indonesia, Kementerian Penerangan, *Republik Indonesia Propinsi Djawa Barat*, p. 148.

[5] Pusat Sedjarah Militer Angkatan Darat, *Kronologi*, p. 85, gives the text of this order.

[6] *Antara,* Dec. 14 and 17, 1945. *Antara* reported that 600 houses were deliberately burnt to the ground. The Indonesian government did not protest the action until six days later. Cf. Koesnodiprodjo, ed., *Himpunan, 1945,* p. 96.

[7] *Merdeka,* Dec. 11, 1945.

[8] C. Smit, *De liquidatie van een imperium: Nederland en Indonesië, 1945–1962* (Amsterdam, 1962), pp. 24–25.

[9] *Antara,* Dec. 27 and 29, 1945.

If the military situation was difficult for the government to cope with, the diplomatic problem seemed no less intractable. After a few weeks of desultory and inconclusive talks with republican representatives, van Mook left for Holland on December 15 to gain a better understanding of the political climate prevailing there and to discuss developments in Indonesia with the Dutch cabinet. He did not return until early in February 1946, and in the meantime nothing could be done to demonstrate to the Indonesian public that the Sjahrir-Amir policy of diplomacy was achieving any useful results. Indeed, the Allies seemed to be consolidating their power with every week that passed.

Even among supporters of the cabinet, there were signs of dissension and discontent. When the KNIP met for its third plenary session from November 25 to 27, Sjahrir's government was indeed approved by a vote of eighty-four to eight, with fifteen abstentions.[10] But the government was forced to accept the principle that simultaneous membership in the cabinet and the Working Committee would no longer be permitted. There was some unpleasant wrangling over the new membership of the Working Committee itself, which was expanded to number twenty-five people, seventeen of whom would represent political groups, while eight would be defined as "regional representatives." [11] Evidence of disaffection among the leading pemuda was

[10] *Berita Indonesia*, Nov. 28, 1945.

[11] *Antara* (Nov. 27, 1945) noted that though the total number of KNIP members was 232, only 132 actually showed up for the session. The new Working Committee was eventually composed as follows (new members indicated by an asterisk): worker-peasant-pemuda bloc, Dr. Sudarsono, Subadio Sastrosatomo, Supeno, Dr. Abdul Halim, Adam Malik, Sjafrudin Prawiranegara, *Miss Soesilowati, *Sukarni, *Mr. Assaat gelar Datuk Mudo; national-democratic bloc, Sarmidi Mangunsarkoro, *Sjamsuddin Sutan Makmur, *Mr. R. Sunarjo, *Pardi; Islamic bloc, *Mohammad Natsir, *Jusuf Wibisono; Christians, *Mr. Tambunan; Chinese minority, Tan Ling Djie; regional representatives: *Awibowo (West Java), *Wijono (Central Java), *Doel Arnowo (East Java), *Mohammad Zain Djambek (Sumatra), *V. E. Maramis (Sulawesi), *P. de Queljoe (Maluku), *Dr. W. Z. Johannes (Sunda Ketjil), and a new, unnamed representative from Kalimantan. Dr. Johannes was originally elected as

beginning to emerge. Chaerul Saleh, for example, warned that among the new ministers there were "men who have connections with the Dutch, are under Dutch influence, and do not support the ideals of Indonesia Merdeka." To heavy applause, he added that "the pemuda cannot accept people who still 'smell Dutch' just like that." (One recalls his similar concern in the proclamation crisis.) The attack was sharp enough that Sjahrir himself was forced to step forward and declare that though members of his cabinet had once held "rightist" views, "now they are able to recognize the validity of our ideals, so that they can be regarded as already in our circle." Two small changes in cabinet personnel instituted on December 5, when the capable Dr. Sudarsono replaced Sunario Kolopaking as minister for social affairs, and Adjidarmo was relieved as minister of finance by Ir. Soerachman, a leading "collaborator" and prominent member of the Sukarno cabinet, did little to allay the growing malaise.[12]

Another blow to the prestige and authority of the government was a decision precipitated by the *attentats* against Amir and Sjahrir, but necessitated by the consolidation of Dutch and British

---

representative of the Christian group, but was replaced by Tambunan in this capacity. Johannes' name is contained in the list of seventeen political representatives given in *Berita Indonesia* (Nov. 28, 1945). The names of the regional representatives were not settled until December 20 (*Berita Indonesia,* Dec. 31, 1945). For full details of the wrangles over regional representation, see "Pemberitaan BP-KNIP tentang pekerdjaan dalam masa 27 Nopember 1945–28 Februari 1946," IC-RVO doc. no. 008985–91. Much of the wrangling arose because the so-called regional candidates were in fact selected on the basis of their attitude toward the cabinet. For example, Wijono was chosen because he was a top leader of Parsi and later of the PS rather than because he came from Central Java. Tan Ling Djie was less a spokesman for the Chinese minority than a close associate of Amir Sjarifuddin and Sjahrir. Of the earlier members of the Working Committee, Sjahrir, Amir, Soewandi, and Sunario Kolopaking had become ministers. Wachid Hasjim had yielded place to Natsir and Jusuf Wibisono. Tadjuludin was not reelected, for reasons unknown. And Hindromartono had left to become resident of the disturbed Residency of Bodjonegoro in East Java.

[12] *Merdeka,* Dec. 8, 1945.

power in Djakarta, to move the republic's capital to Jogjakarta. This was done on January 4, 1946.[13] The move was not only a signal admission of the government's weakness but had important consequences for the distribution of power between the cabinet and its enemies.

Since Sjahrir served as foreign minister as well as prime minister, he felt compelled to retain his residence in Djakarta when the rest of the government, including the President and Vice-President, moved into the interior. This physical separation tended to accentuate and reinforce the psychological and political gap between the cabinet and its enemies, for Djakarta and Jogjakarta were two different worlds. In the Allied-occupied harbor city there was little room for the pemuda, the badan perdjuangan, the army, or even the President to participate in the republic's politics. The men who counted there were the small group of Dutch-trained and Dutch-speaking intellectuals who conducted the delicate game of diplomatic maneuver and tried to run the municipal administration. In the old royal city of Jogjakarta, where not a single Allied soldier could be found, and where the exhilaration of merdeka could be freely experienced, all the variegated forces of the independence movement were gathered. Here the headquarters of the military had long been established. Here the Hizbullah and the Sultan's Lasjkar Rakjat were centered. The troops on the South Semarang front were only a short distance away, and in neighboring Surakarta the Barisan Banteng had its base. In Jogjakarta almost everyone who wished could participate in politics, and the men who counted were those who had armed units behind them or could command the support of the population through oratory and organization. Groups that had little influence on the central government so long as it was still in Djakarta could now bring their demands and hopes directly to bear on the leaders of the republic.[14] From

[13] The move was publicly announced only after it had taken place. See *Antara*, Jan. 5, 1946.

[14] Many opponents of the cabinet, including a nucleus of the fallen Sukarno government, preceded it to Central Java and began cultivating

a larger perspective Djakarta and Jogjakarta came to symbolize the opposition between *diplomasi* and *perdjuangan,* diplomacy and resistance. If one lived in occupied, cosmopolitan Djakarta, it was hard not to become convinced of the imperative need for diplomacy. But if one lived in unoccupied, traditional Jogjakarta, where scarcely a white face was to be seen, how could one not believe, watching and experiencing the city's turbulent vitality, that resistance was possible and necessary?

It was in Jogjakarta that Sukarno came into his own, after the anxieties and defeats of October and November. He was now in his native Javanese milieu, where his proleptic oratory stirred its deepest resonances, and where none could match him in firing the imagination and devotion of the people. In his own way he understood the lesson Bung Tomo had learned in Surabaja, that in a time of revolution, a voice could be worth more than a ministry. It is ironic that it was precisely the silent coup against his cabinet that freed him from the direct burdens of government and allowed him to increase his power in the way that he knew best. After November he was incessantly on the move, criss-crossing Java and speaking wherever he went. From December 9 to 11, he traveled with Hatta into Banten, penetrating as far as Serang and Rangkasbitung.[15] On December 16 he was off again to East and Central Java, reaching Jogjakarta on the eighteenth, in time to announce Sudirman's appointment as Panglima Besar.[16] From there, with Sjahrir now in his company, he passed through Madiun and Kediri on the nineteenth, and Blitar and Malang on the twentieth.[17] By the twenty-second he was traveling through Purwokerto, and from there he spoke in Pekalongan, Tegal, and Tjirebon before returning to Djakarta.[18] On January 4 he led the exodus to Jogjakarta, but by the fifteenth he was moving again, this time to Demak, Kudus, Djepara, Pati, Rembang, and Blora, the main towns of the central north coast, before returning to

---

local support in the region. It was no accident that the first popular front conference was held in Central Java.

[15] *Merdeka,* Dec. 13, 1945.   [16] *Antara,* Dec. 19, 1945.
[17] *Ibid.,* Dec. 21, 1945.   [18] *Ibid.,* Dec. 26, 1945.

Jogjakarta through Surakarta on about the twenty-first.[19] By the end of January, with the exception of the Priangan, there was not one important area of Java in which he had not made his presence felt. Everywhere the news that he was coming brought villagers and townspeople flocking from miles around. At a time when authority on Java seemed so fragile and uncertain, these tangible evidences of popularity seemed all the more impressive, not least to political leaders. It was quite clear that whatever his status in the eyes of the Allies, Sukarno's personal authority over the people remained undiminished. If it had been doubted before, his indispensability to the nation grew ever harder to dispute.

Freed from direct responsibility for government policy, he was able, gently and subtly, to separate himself from its shortcomings. It was not that Sukarno failed to give Sjahrir the fullest public support—quite the contrary. But it is clear from the tone and manner of his speeches in this period that he was presenting himself to his listeners as the embodiment of Indonesian nationalism, permanent and unchanging, while cabinets might come and go. If, like the cabinet, he called for calm and discipline at every place he visited, his speeches were always tinged with the messianic imagery that appeals so deeply to the Javanese.

Early in February the cabinet's long wait came to an end. Van Mook returned to Djakarta at last, bringing with him the proposals the authorities in The Hague felt in a position to make. Given the political situation in Holland, it was scarcely surprising that these proposals, which were first officially announced on February 10, were far less accommodating than might have been expected from a socialist-led cabinet. For the Schermerhorn ministry was essentially a caretaker administration, holding power only until normal parliamentary government could be restored with the holding of the first post-occupation elections, scheduled for May. Without a clear electoral mandate the ministry was unwilling to initiate any far-reaching change in the status of the Indies. Furthermore, it was badly informed about political condi-

[19] *Ibid.*, Jan. 22 and 23, 1946.

tions in Indonesia, and its awareness of this deficiency, as well as a certain mistrust for the formidable and independent van Mook himself, reinforced the ministers' inclination toward caution. The Dutch public was also confused, irritable, and anxious about developments in Indonesia. The fate of many internees was still in doubt. After the humiliation of the Nazi occupation, Dutch pride was highly sensitive to the idea of losing the vast colony in the East. Powerful economic interests and conservative political groups were determined to prevent what they regarded as a capitulation to Indonesian extremists, and with some success these groups accused the cabinet of keeping the public in the dark about its intentions toward and dealings with the republic's leaders.[20]

The proposals offered by van Mook stipulated that "after a limited period of preparation," the Indonesian people should have the freedom to decide on their "constitutional destiny." During the period of preparation the Netherlands East Indies government would create a United States of Indonesia under the Dutch crown, consisting of "units" with graduated degrees of self-rule.[21] In a clarification issued on February 22, van Mook stated that the "United States" was a constitutional form chosen to preserve a balance between regional autonomy and central authority, but that everything would be done to strengthen the unity of Indonesia as a nation. It was notable that neither in the proposals themselves nor in the clarification was any mention made of the republic.[22]

While the plan for a federal state of Indonesia reflected long-standing preoccupations of van Mook himself, in the context of early 1946 the official justification for it was clearly disingenuous

[20] For details on the political conditions prevailing in Holland at this time and their impact on The Hague's policy toward the republic, see Smit, *De liquidatie*, pp. 26–32; and Djajadiningrat, *Beginnings of Indonesian-Dutch Negotiations*, pp. 50–51.

[21] Smit, *De liquidatie*, p. 28. For fuller details, see *Voice of Free Indonesia* (Djakarta), Feb. 5, 1946, pp. 1–2.

[22] Van Mook, *Indonesië*, p. 117.

and was immediately seen to be so in Djakarta. As early as November 1945 the Dutch government had calculated that until October 1946 at least, no more than 30,000 troops would be available for duty in the Indies. Nor could The Hague rely indefinitely on the British, who were clearly anxious to pull out as soon as possible. At van Mook's urging the Dutch government adopted the policy of giving first priority to repossessing the Outer Islands, with their rich resources and sparse populations, isolating revolutionary Java as far as possible in the expectation that the republic would eventually be compelled to come to satisfactory terms.[23]

From the point of view of the Sjahrir cabinet, the proposals were scarcely attractive. But it was assured by Sir Archibald Clark Kerr, the senior diplomat sent from London to "assist" the negotiations between the Indonesians and the Dutch, that there was absolutely no chance of the republic's being recognized either by the British or by any of the other major powers.[24] Accordingly the cabinet felt that it had no choice but to respond to the Dutch proposals. At the same time it hesitated to take any steps before ensuring that they would command effective support in Jogjakarta.

On February 6 Sjahrir and Amir arrived in the republican capital to lead a plenary cabinet session and hold conversations with leaders of the Persatuan Perdjuangan.[25] What precisely transpired at these talks has never been made public.[26] But it seems evident from other moves the government made that Sjahrir and Amir did their utmost to convince the opposition that

[23] Smit, *De liquidatie,* pp. 26–29; Djajadiningrat, *Beginnings of Indonesian-Dutch Negotiations,* pp. 42–43.

[24] Smit, *De liquidatie,* pp. 28–29. Kerr arrived in Djakarta on February 1 and immediately opened informal discussions with Sjahrir.

[25] *Antara,* Feb. 9, 1946; *Kedaulatan Rakjat,* Feb. 9, 1946.

[26] It seems doubtful that Tan Malaka attended these talks. In any case his usually candid account makes no mention of any meeting with government leaders.

in view of Allied strength and British attitudes, there was no realistic alternative to immediate negotiations with the Dutch. They must have tried also to rally support for their own leadership. On February 7 Sjahrir spoke to an all-Java assembly of pangrèh pradja and regional government functionaries in highly conciliatory terms. While mildly criticizing remnants of feudalism in the administration, he suggested no concrete steps toward their removal. The main theme of his address was a strong appeal to capable officials of both the Dutch and the Japanese period to cooperate with the government in its plans for reconstruction.[27] More generally, it was noticeable that since November, attacks on Japanese-minded people in the bureaucracy had largely vanished from his and Amir's public statements.

But in spite of the cabinet leaders' conciliatory moves, the opposition was not appeased. Speaking at a meeting in the Priangan, Wali al-Fatah, who represented the Masjumi in the directorate of the PP, insisted that "diplomacy between the goat and the tiger must become diplomacy between the horned buffalo and the tiger!" On February 6 the Masjumi executive wired the President that as a result of British massacres of pemuda in Tanggerang, Djakarta, Bogor, and elsewhere, "the confidence and hope of the people in the Sjahrir-Sjarifuddin cabinet has completely vanished"; the government was held to be "morally and politically responsible" for these deaths.[28] And when the Dutch proposals were formally announced on February 10, public pressure on the cabinet became even more intense. Sjahrir was deluged with telegrams and letters from organizations all over Java and the Outer Islands which, while frequently expressing confidence in him personally, demanded that he make no concessions to the Dutch and only negotiate on the basis of 100 per cent merdeka. When the Masjumi held a major conference in Surakarta on February 11 to 13, it explicitly approved

[27] This is reported in *NEFIS Periodiek*, no. 6 (May 1, 1946), p. 23.
[28] *Antara*, Feb. 6, 1946.

the contents of the wire of February 6 and demanded the formation of a genuine national coalition government to face the Dutch challenge.[29]

The cabinet was finally forced to bow to this pressure. On February 16 the Working Committee, on which the cabinet's tenure depended, convened in an atmosphere of crisis. Its prestige had been steadily declining since the rise of the Persatuan Perdjuangan; and its morale had been sapped by the disillusioned refusal of Adam Malik and Sukarni to attend any of its meetings after early January, and their subsequent active role in the PP. Accordingly the Working Committee decided to urge the President to take immediate action to alter the composition of the government and the membership of the KNIP on the basis of resolutions passed at recent party conferences of the Masjumi, PNI, and PKI.[30] The Working Committee's decision made the cabinet automatically demissionary. On February 23 Sjahrir sent Sukarno a secret letter of resignation.[31] Although the President did not accept it formally until February 28, by the time the KNIP met in plenary session that day, the government had already fallen.

The cabinet had lasted a bare three months. But its brief tenure had set in motion forces that were difficult to reverse, had sharpened antagonisms that were difficult to heal, and had clarified perspectives that were difficult to combine or synthesize.

Out of the administrative and organizational debris left by the crumbling of the colonial power structure, there had germinated with ever increasing rapidity a plethora of civilian, military, and paramilitary groups. The growth of each focused the self-awareness of the others, and from these reciprocal definitions organizational entities began to solidify. When Sjahrir came to power in November 1945, scarcely any organizations existed, but

[29] *Ibid.*, Feb. 14, 1946.   [30] *Ibid.*, Feb. 20, 1946.

[31] See the article by Tabrani in *Kedaulatan Rakjat,* March 6, 1946. See also *Merdeka,* March 6, 1946; and Tan Malaka, *Dari pendjara,* III, 80.

by February 1946, Tan Malaka's Persatuan Perdjuangan encompassed dozens.

The Socialists had attempted to provide a unifying leadership for the revolutionary forces, but their failure in practice to create a political structure through which Indonesia's abundant revolutionary energies could be channeled and mobilized stirred mistrust and competition. And once the vicious circle of mutual reinforcing suspicion was established, it proved virtually impossible to break. To form the Pesindo, but to fail to encompass the pemuda in a larger and effective whole; to create a Socialist cabinet without designing a popular, institutionalized national front; to meddle with the military forces without being able to bind them tightly to a revolutionary government: all tended to accelerate the fissiparous processes they were intended to counteract and overcome.

In another sense, too, the cabinet's life marked a parting of the ways, for it was during these months that the fundamental choice before the national movement was consciously formulated: diplomasi or perdjuangan. Each choice had a logic of its own. As we have seen, the decision to take the road of diplomasi, latent under Sukarno and manifest under Sjahrir and Amir Sjarifuddin, was based on a pessimistic view of the world balance of power and of the strength of Indonesia's revolutionary forces. The organizational, military, and ideological weakness of the republic dominated the imagination of those who espoused this view. For them diplomacy in its widest sense was the key to the republic's survival. Given this premise it was logical to subordinate everything else to the achieving of a settlement with the Dutch guaranteed by the great powers. Once this settlement had been made, the tasks of renovating, democratizing, and transforming society could be undertaken. Yet the external policy of diplomasi, of seeking an accommodation with the Dutch, required an internal policy that in the long run was likely to render those tasks more difficult to fulfill. The logic of diplomasi demanded that the pemuda be restrained, that foreign property be protected, and that spontaneous revolutionary action among the people be suppressed. Conversely, it encouraged reliance on and coalitions with precisely those groups against whom the process of renovation would eventually have to be directed: the discredited pangrèh pradja, traditionalist local notables, older politicians with more interest in the fruits of office than in the possibilities of change, former colonial officers who distrusted and feared the visionary energy of the merdeka spirit. At bottom, diplomasi was a gamble that one step forward to an international recognition of Indonesia's independence would not mean two steps backward from the goal of a society renewed.

The logic of perdjuangan pointed in a quite different direction, premised as it was on an undaunted optimism about the strength of a national revolutionary movement adeptly led and backed up by the full mobilized force of popular hopes and energies. For its more politically conscious proponents, perdjuangan rested on the conviction that armed struggle was inevitable. Only through the experience of conflict, it was believed, could the bases of Indonesian society be transformed and a cohesive, organized sense of purpose be created out of the apolitical exaltation of the pemuda movement. For many others who were less self-conscious, perdjuangan, like merdeka, was less a goal than a state of being. Independence was not an international transaction, but an inner experience.

In its own way, perdjuangan was no less a gamble than diplomasi. It was a wager that given the fragmentation of Indonesia's physical and social geography, given the ideological and organizational confusion left behind by the Japanese, and given the shortages of arms and trained cadres, a coherent movement could still be built. The Persatuan Perdjuangan was a logical step in this direction, but it was really logical only *faute de mieux*, attempting as it did to substitute a unity between organizations for the lacking unity of organization. Because of Tan Malaka's long isolation and because he had no cadre of capable lieutenants, he was compelled to rely, in building his coalition, on oppositionist political leaders whose real commitment to perdjuangan was in many cases small. He was soon to realize that many of these leaders had helped bring down Sjahrir's cabinet not so much because they rejected its policies as because they resented its composition.

Chapter 14

The March Crisis

In the last half of February the tide seemed to be running irresistibly in favor of the Persatuan Perdjuangan. The PP successfully organized massive demonstrations in Jogjakarta on February 17 to commemorate six months of independence. A vast procession, reportedly eight kilometers long, marched through the city, with General Sudirman taking pride of place. The theme of the procession was the demand for a sterner attitude toward the Dutch: the government was urged to carry on its diplomacy like a *bantèng* (wild buffalo) with its horns down. Sudirman himself gave an extremely militant speech to the effect that though short of weapons, Indonesia was strong in *semangat* (fighting spirit). Provided real national unity existed, he said, as in the Persatuan Perdjuangan, the resistance would be victorious; the army would live and die with the republic.[1]

---

[1] *Antara,* Feb. 19, 1946; *Merdeka,* Feb. 20, 1946. The whole political orientation represented by Sudirman's remarks was strongly criticized by the secretary of the Working Committee, Sjafrudin Prawiranegara, in an important article comparing the Indonesian and Russian revolutions that appeared in *Berita Indonesia* on February 5, 1946. In this article Sjafrudin urged the fullest support for Sjahrir's realpolitik and warned that too many people were completely unaware of Indonesia's weaknesses. "Japanese flattery has exaggerated the importance of semangat beyond all limits, and has derided and aroused hatred for *akal* [reason], as though akal were simply a Western invention—an invention of the imperialists and capitalists, which has had an evil influence among our people, both old and young." The result of this Japanese flattery had been that no attention was being paid to history. Excessive and unrealistic demands were

On February 25 a general congress of lasjkar rakjat was held in Magelang and attended by Sudirman; Tan Malaka; the Dewan Perdjuangan of West, Central, and East Java; the governor of Central Java; the PP secretariat; and many other leaders. Once again Sudirman made the key address, in reply to a motion offered to the congress by Sajuti Melik and Sakirman that war should be declared on the British: "This is something which has become the will of the people and cannot be withdrawn; this motion is to be considered as a motion supported by the whole people. . . . Come, come, let all the barisan, all the armed organizations struggle sincerely—don't let our people be made victims in vain." [2] And these militant demands were echoed by Bung Tomo's BPRI, the BKPRI, and many other organizations.[3]

Accordingly, when Sjahrir arrived in Jogjakarta on February 26, having already secretly tendered his resignation to Sukarno, there was a widespread feeling that the republic had come to a crossroads, and that the struggle between the forces backing Sjahrir and Amir and those backing Tan Malaka and Sudirman would soon be decisively resolved.

In the maneuvering that followed, the strategies employed by the protagonists were clear from the outset. In spite of their defensive public stance, the cabinet leaders had two trump cards in their hands. In the first place, among the backers of the PP there were a number of leaders who, whatever their formal rhetoric, were by no means as convinced as Tan Malaka and Sudirman that a strategy of radical opposition to the Allied presence was feasible or likely to be fruitful. In the second place, some of

---

being made on the government, particularly by well-meaning pemuda who criticized the government for certain objective realities that no government could change. Sjafrudin, a devout Moslem, went on to praise Lenin and Stalin as great realists, often attacked by their own less clear-sighted juniors. Denouncing many self-styled socialists in Indonesia for failing to understand socialism, he declared that the semangat people, who advocated sending pemuda armed with bamboo spears against Allied troops with machine guns, were stupid, if not criminal.

[2] *Antara*, Feb. 26, 1946.   [3] *Ibid.*, Feb. 27, 1946.

the opposition leaders were anxious enough to enter the government that they were open to bargaining on matters of policy and principle. The strategy of Sjahrir and Amir was therefore to try to define the issue at stake in the Jogjakarta maneuverings as broadening the basis of the government rather than as changing its policy. Their expectation was that the bait of office would attract enough PP leaders to break the solidarity of the PP, thus isolating Tan Malaka and his closest supporters.[4] To reinforce this aim a whispering campaign began against Tan Malaka, drawing attention to his "divisive" role in 1926–27 and suggesting that the PP was simply an instrument designed to serve Tan Malaka's selfish ambitions to overthrow the government and install himself as dictator.

On the other side, the prime cards in Tan Malaka's hand were the widespread feeling that the PP was more genuinely representative than the KNIP and the government and the great appeal the militant Minimum Program had among the pemuda and the public at large. A lesser but still important card was the dislike Sjahrir in particular had aroused in various circles as a result of *Perdjuangan Kita*. Tan Malaka's strategy was naturally a counterpart to that of his opponents. The issue involved in the cabinet crisis had to be defined as the acceptance or rejection of the Minimum Program rather than as changing the composition of the new government. Above all, the discipline of the PP had to be maintained, since defections for the sake of cabinet posts would undermine its credibility.

Given their strategies, it was obvious that Tan Malaka and Sjahrir did not have equal room to maneuver. While it was relatively easy for Sjahrir to prove his flexibility by offering cabinet posts to some of the opposition leaders, Tan Malaka could not afford to be flexible about the Minimum Program, since its moral

---

[4] On February 26 it was announced that the membership of the KNIP had been expanded to 294. *Kedaulatan Rakjat* (Feb. 26, 1946) has a full listing of the enlarged membership. It was certainly expected that this change would enhance the legitimacy of the KNIP in the eyes of PP leaders, who would thus be encouraged to accept the legislature as the primary arena of political activity.

and political value lay precisely in its militant sternness. As the parties maneuvered for position, it became clear that the decisive factor would be the attitude of Sukarno, and to a lesser extent, of Hatta. Not only did his position as president give Sukarno constitutional power to play a decisive role, but as we have seen, the enormous success of his travels through Java demonstrated that he had a legitimacy in the eyes of the Javanese masses unequaled by either the cabinet leaders or their opponents.

On February 17 the President had given a major address in Malang in which he declared: "Be confident that our prime minister will not swerve in his determination to maintain the demand for 100 per cent independence. But if it should ever turn out that Sjahrir is not maintaining the demand for 100 per cent independence that all of you, my brothers, want, then I have the right to dismiss him." [5] These words—greeted, incidentally, by wild applause—very plainly showed Sukarno's understanding that he had regained the middle ground in domestic politics that he had lost in October, when his role in the late Japanese period and his official position as head of the "Buchō" cabinet had put him at the opposite pole from the pemuda and the underground. Now he was in a position to arbitrate between the Sjahrir-Amir group and their adversaries, among whom he counted many friends and admirers; and to a considerable extent, he was also in a position to bend both to his will.

When the KNIP sessions opened in Surakarta on February 28, Sukarno spoke first to announce that he had accepted the resignation of Sjahrir. Sjahrir himself then followed, giving an account of his cabinet's activities and urging again the central line of his policy—that Indonesia had no choice but to try the road of peace and negotiations.[6] Later the report of the Working Committee, including its proposals for the formation of a new coalition cabinet, was discussed and approved by a vote of 140 to 67, with 18 abstentions.[7] After several strongly worded speeches, including one by Chaerul Saleh, representative of the PP execu-

[5] *Antara*, Feb. 20, 1946.   [6] Tan Malaka, *Dari pendjara*, III, 80–81.
[7] *Kedaulatan Rakjat*, March 2, 1946.

tive, and a "communication" by General Sudirman, a Sukarno invitation that the KNIP form an eleven-man committee to assist him in forming a new cabinet was accepted.[8] This committee, fairly evenly divided between supporters of Sjahrir and Tan Malaka, but including neither of the protagonists themselves, appears to have convened for the first time on the afternoon of February 28.[9] Sukarno immediately took charge and made it plain that he was supporting the Socialist leaders. He indicated that he wanted to see a broad coalition cabinet representing all major political groups but nonetheless pursuing policies consistent with the line of the Sjahrir government. In other words the government's membership should be changed, but not its perspectives. His first proposal was for an enlarged cabinet in which Sjahrir and Amir would retain the two key posts of foreign minister and minister of defense, while the remaining portfolios would be apportioned among the various party factions. He asked the PP leaders present to return later with their list of candidates for these ministerial posts and their decision whether they would be willing to participate on this basis or not.

At nine o'clock that night the PP leaders met in the KNIP building for an intense debate.[10] Those closest to Tan Malaka

[8] "SV," p. 146 (testimony of Yamin) and p. 253 (testimony of Pandu Kartawiguna). Cf. Tan Malaka, *Dari pendjara*, III, 81. According to *Antara* (Feb. 13, 1946), the PP executive was reorganized at a meeting in Jogjakarta on February 12 as follows: promoter, Tan Malaka; Section for Settling Disputes, Wali al-Fatah; Political Section, Chaerul Saleh; Economic Section, S. K. Trimurti; Defense Section, Ir. Sakirman; General Secretary, Sukarni. In this new executive there were no PS members, and all but Tan Malaka and Wali al-Fatah were prominent pemuda from Djakarta.

[9] The membership seems to have included Chaerul Saleh, Wali al-Fatah, Trimurti, Sukiman, and Sarmidi, for the PP; and Amir Sjarifuddin, Abdulmadjid, Kasimo (from the small Catholic party), and Pellaupessy (representing the Protestant minority) for the groups backing Sjahrir. Sukarni may also have attended.

[10] Among the groups represented were the Masjumi, the PBI, the PNI, the Dewan Perdjuangan of East and Central Java, the Pesindo, and Bung Tomo's BPRI. See Tan Malaka, *Dari pendjara*, III, 82.

argued that no bargaining should be entertained with respect to the PP's candidates for cabinet positions until the principle of the Minimum Program was accepted. For if the Minimum Program were accepted, the PP was bound to have a dominant position in any cabinet to be formed; otherwise the Sjahrir-Amir group, as the most powerful advocates of negotiations, would be in a position to silence their critics once they had drawn them into the government. This view seems to have prevailed, and the meeting decided to press for the acceptance of the Minimum Program, with the formation of the cabinet a secondary matter. If, however, the program was rejected, the leaders of the PP would "then determine their own attitude." But even as the debate was in progress, Sukarno's maneuvering continued: Sukarni brought Tan Malaka a message from Sukarno asking whether he personally would be willing to accept a cabinet post. Tan Malaka replied that he did not rule out such a position but would serve only if the Minimum Program was accepted.[11]

Throughout the next day the negotiations continued, but no agreement was reached.[12] It was now clear that the original Sukarno solution was not going to prove possible. While there were signs of division within the PP, these were not serious enough to break its discipline and permit the formation of a widely based coalition cabinet. Since Sukarno himself, like Hatta, was strongly opposed to the Minimum Program and was convinced that the KNIP, which was still clearly weighted in favor of the supporters of the previous government, would not accept it either, there now appeared to be no alternative to renewing Sjahrir's mandate, and trusting to the lure of office to rally as

[11] *Ibid.*

[12] *Ibid.*, p. 83. According to Tan Malaka, Hatta now joined the committee's discussions, alternating with Sukarno as chairman. The highlight of the day was a violent dispute between the Vice-President and Chaerul Saleh. When the former insisted that the Minimum Program would "unite all the imperialists against Indonesia," the latter replied that the Proclamation of Independence itself had already performed this function.

much scattered individual support as possible to a new cabinet under his leadership.

Accordingly, when the KNIP reconvened on March 2, Hatta announced that Sjahrir had been chosen *formateur* of a new cabinet, hopefully designated a coalition government.[13] Later in the afternoon the KNIP was informed that this coalition government would work on the basis of a new Five-Point Program:

1. Negotiate on the basis of recognition of 100 per cent merdeka.

2. Prepare the people in the political, military, economic, and social fields to defend the Republic of Indonesia.

3. Achieve the democratization of the central and regional governments.

4. Make great efforts to improve production and distribution, especially of food and clothing.

5. Take all necessary action with regard to the more important enterprises and plantations, to accomplish the purposes outlined in Article 33 of the Constitution.[14]

As Tan Malaka was bitterly to point out, the program was vague to the point of evasiveness. Point One was deliberately ambiguous as to whether "basis" meant the required result of or an initial bargaining position for diplomatic negotiations. Point Two was quite imprecise as to the *content* of the preparations to be made, and what form and direction they would take. Point Three was no less imprecise, since it was by now clear that no national-level elections would be held in the near future. The suspicion readily arose that "democratization" meant the substitution of government supporters in provincial and central administrative positions for those regarded as hostile to the cabinet leaders. Point Four was good as far as it went; but, as Tan Malaka noted, it said nothing about the production and distribution of arms, nothing about the methods of production and distribution, and

[13] *Menara,* March 5, 1946. According to *Merdeka,* March 6, 1946, Sjahrir had already promised to include both PNI and Masjumi members in his new cabinet.

[14] *Antara,* March 5, 1946.

nothing about who was to receive the goods produced and distributed. Point Five evaded the Minimum Program demand for the confiscation of Dutch assets and made no commitment to any concrete policy on the advanced sector of the economy.[15] In sum, the Five-Point Program clearly rejected Tan Malaka's urging of a war economy, direct barter between peasants and workers, the seizure of enemy property, and the arming of the population.[16]

Once the Five-Point Program had been announced, the lines of division were even more sharply drawn. Under pressure from his old API comrades, Chaerul Saleh and Sukarni, Wikana, then the leading pemuda in the Pesindo, announced to the closing session of the KNIP that in view of the government's (in other words, Sukarno and Hatta's) refusal to entertain the Minimum Program, the PP had decided to forbid all its member organizations from sitting in the new cabinet, since "the PP cannot accept a cabinet which does not carry out the Minimum Program." [17] At the same time Sjahrir announced that he had agreed to try to form a new coalition cabinet on the basis of what he

[15] Article 33 of the Constitution said: "1) The economy shall be based on common endeavor according to the family principle; 2) Branches of production important to the state and which dominate the lives of many people shall be controlled by the state; 3) Land and water and the natural wealth therein shall be controlled by the state and shall be exploited for the greatest possible welfare of the people." Yamin, ed., *Naskah persiapan*, p. 33.

[16] See Tan Malaka, *Dari pendjara*, III, 85–93, for his sharp critique of the Five-Point Program. It is very noticeable that in this critique Tan Malaka makes almost no mention of Sjahrir, but constantly refers to the "Sukarno-Hatta government," in effect attributing the program to these two men. He remarked at the end of his evaluation that he and the government differed on four fundamental questions: whether the interests of Dutch capitalism and the Indonesian people were radically opposed; what was the balance of power between the two sides; what was the international balance of power, and how far this could be exploited by Indonesia; and whether it was better to play to the good will and humanity of the Dutch or to use guerrilla warfare and economic boycott against them.

[17] *Antara*, March 8, 1946. A special meeting of the PP on March 4 confirmed this decision.

called, significantly, "Sukarno's five points." [18] Now the crucial test of strength had come, since if the solidarity of the PP held, there was no possibility of forming the broad coalition cabinet that Sjahrir's mandate required. Accordingly, the ten days between the naming of Sjahrir as *formateur* and the announcement of the membership of a new cabinet on March 12 saw an intensive effort to break up the PP from within.

On March 1 Sarmidi announced that the PNI was now formally a full member of the PP, and urged all party branches to sign up with local subsidiaries of the PP's central secretariat.[19] But this was the last accretion to PP strength. That same day the BTI (Barisan Tani Indonesia, or Indonesian Peasants' League), under the leadership of two PS members, Wijono and Tauchid, officially rejected the PP while still agreeing in principle to the popular front idea.[20] On March 4 the top leaders of the Pesindo, meeting in Madiun, criticized the PP leadership for its hostile attitude toward the government. Since in their view the government's Five-Point Program and the PP's Minimum Program were not basically in conflict, they had decided to support the former.[21] Two days later the Pesindo announced the removal of its representative in the PP, Ibnu Parna, and demanded that the PP refrain from any further overt actions against the government now being formed. The same day, owing to the dominant influence of the Pesindo within it, the Dewan Perdjuangan of East Java withdrew from the PP.[22] On March 7 the Koperasi Rakjat Indonesia (Indonesian People's Cooperative) in Tjirebon, (a cooperative association dating from the Japanese period led by friends of Sjahrir), which had held a seat on the secretariat of the PP, left the organization and announced its full support for Sjahrir and

[18] *Antara*, March 5, 1946.   [19] *Ibid.*
[20] *Kedaulatan Rakjat*, March 1, 1946. The BTI also denounced the PBI for interfering in its affairs and claiming to act as its representative and supervisor. Evidently the PBI's difficulties with the labor unions had not discouraged it from trying to control germinating peasant organizations such as the BTI.
[21] *Ibid.*, March 9, 1946.   [22] *Ibid.*, March 6, 1946.

his program.[23] On the same day the BTI in Jogjakarta; the Partai Kedaulatan Rakjat Indonesia (Indonesian People's Sovereignty Party) in Jogjakarta; the Partai Indonesia Maluku (an Ambonese political group); the Protestant "Parkindo" (Partai Keristen Indonesia, or Indonesian Christian Party) and the PS in Djakarta; and the Catholic Party and the Gerakan Rakjat Indonesia (Movement of the Indonesian People) in Surakarta all expressed full confidence in the Prime Minister and his program.[24] Strong pressure was also exerted within the Masjumi. On March 11 the party leadership felt compelled to issue a special statement denying reports of a cabinet composed of Masjumi members, nationalists, and Socialists, and declaring that "after weighing up everything in connection with the formation of a new cabinet under the leadership of Mr. Sutan Sjahrir, Masjumi has determined its attitude as being in accordance with the decision of the PP, and will not take part in the forthcoming cabinet." [25] The fact that the Masjumi took ten days to make up its mind and openly admitted that the possibility of breaking PP discipline had been considered indicates how divided its ranks were.

On March 12 Sjahrir was finally able to announce the composition of his new cabinet (new members are marked by an asterisk):

Prime Minister: Sutan Sjahrir

Foreign Affairs: Sutan Sjahrir; deputy minister, *Hadji Agus Salim

Interior: Dr. Sudarsono (PS); deputy minister, *R. Samadikun

Health: Dr. Darmasetiawan; deputy minister, *Dr. Johannes Leimena (Parkindo)

Finance: Ir. R. M. P. Soerachman Tjokroadisoerjo; deputy minister, *Mr. R. Sjafrudin Prawiranegara (Masjumi)

Trade and Industry: Ir. Darmawan Mangoenkoesoemo; deputy minister, *Sjamsu Harja Udaja (PBI)

[23] *Ibid.*, March 12, 1946.   [24] *Ibid.*, March 7, 1946.
[25] *Antara*, March 11, 1946.

Agriculture and Supply: *Ir. Baginda Zainuddin Rasad; deputy minister, *Ir. R. Saksono Prawirohardjo

Defense: Mr. Amir Sjarifuddin (PS); deputy minister, *Arudji Kartawinata (Masjumi)

Justice: Mr. R. Soewandi; deputy minister, *Mr. R. Hadi

Education: *Mohammad Sjafe'i; deputy minister, Mr. Dr. Todoeng gelar Soetan Goenoeng Moelia (Parkindo)

Information (ad interim): Mohammad Natsir (Masjumi)

Social Affairs: *Mr. Radèn Aju Maria Ulfah Santoso Wirodihardjo; deputy minister, *Mr. Abdulmadjid Djojoadiningrat (PS)

Religion (ad interim): H. Rasjidi (Masjumi)

Communications: Ir. Abdul Karim; deputy minister, *Ir. R. Djuanda

Public Works: Ir. Putuhena (Parkindo); deputy minister, *Ir. Herling Laoh (PNI)

Minister of State (for Pemuda Affairs): *Wikana (BKPRI).[26]

The list showed clearly how far the cabinet was from fulfilling the criteria of a national coalition government, despite the best efforts of Sukarno, Sjahrir, and Amir Sjarifuddin. It was still dominated by leaders of the PS and nonparty personalities sympathetic to their ideas or related to them by family. Moreover, like the previous cabinet it had an extremely large professional contingent: eighteen of the twenty-seven ministers had Western-style university degrees.

Of the more important political parties associated with the PP, only the Masjumi was unable to maintain internal discipline. The PBI representative, Sjamsu Harja Udaja, refused the position offered him, as did Samadikun and Sjafe'i. The sole PNI minister, Laoh, while a respected professional, carried no weight in party circles.[27] In the case of the Masjumi, the formers of the

[26] *Ibid.*, March 13, 1946. For biographical details, see the Appendix.

[27] Sarmidi's reaction to the cabinet list was, however, quite conciliatory: "In the present situation the composition of this cabinet gives us confidence that it will be able to continue the work and ideals of our government effectively." *Merdeka,* March 13, 1946.

cabinet were able to get significant representation by playing on personal friendships (as between Sjahrir and Natsir) and long-standing animosities within the party leadership. Arudji had been an important member of the prewar PSII from which Sukiman had broken away. Sjafrudin, Natsir, and Rasjidi were all intimates of Sjahrir and not very friendly to the Masjumi chairman. Salim (a relative of Sjahrir), while not a formal member of Masjumi, was widely influential in Moslem circles and had been a bitter enemy of Sukiman since the early thirties. It was not surprising, therefore, that Sukiman strongly criticized the composition of the cabinet, asserting that there was still no "unity of government and the people." [28]

Perhaps the most unexpected addition to the cabinet was Wikana, who had presented the KNIP with the PP's decision not to accept seats in a cabinet that was not committed to the Minimum Program. He had been under heavy pressure both from his old comrades Sukarni and Chaerul Saleh, who were in the PP executive, and from the Socialists and the dominant faction in the Pesindo, of which he was a leading member. It is possible that he agreed to take a ministerial position in the hope of being able to influence the cabinet to move in a more militant direction.[29]

The situation was fairly summed up by an editorial in *Merdeka,* which observed that while Sjahrir had failed to carry out the President's mandate to form a real coalition cabinet, the fact that Sukarno had agreed to the new government indicated his

[28] *Kedaulatan Rakjat,* March 13, 1946. Sukiman added that the Masjumi would remain in opposition until a genuine coalition cabinet was formed. He refused to commit himself on the party status of those Masjumi members who joined the government. The difficulties of Sukiman's position were intensified by some biting attacks on him in the press, such as the article by Umar Ali [pseud.?] in *Merdeka,* March 15, 1946. It is possible that Natsir's and Rasjidi's appointments were made temporary in order to take the edge off the violation of party discipline.

[29] Subardjo told me he thought Wikana had been suspicious of Tan Malaka from the start, for Wikana had been much influenced by an older relative who had been imprisoned in Boven Digul and blamed the disaster of 1926–27 on the Minangkabau revolutionary.

confidence in the Prime Minister. It was somewhat disturbing
that the key portfolios of Foreign Affairs, Defense, and the Interior were all in PS hands, and that many of the new ministers
were unknown, but there were good grounds for believing that
Sjahrir's toughness and competence would bring success. Noting
that the reason for the PP's failure to form a government had
been "the President's rejection of the Minimum Program," *Merdeka* revealed that Sukarno had explicitly requested Sjahrir to
make immediate preparations for further talks with the Dutch.[30]

The day after his new cabinet was formed, Sjahrir offered his
counterproposals to van Mook. He declared Indonesia's willingness to accept Dutch economic help and leadership and to participate in a Union relationship with Holland; but he insisted
that in this relationship Indonesia be represented as an indivis-
ible whole by the republican government.[31] Van Mook immediately rejected these counterproposals. Instead, drawing inspiration from the Franco-Vietnamese accords of March 6, he urged
the formation of an independent but federated Indonesian state
in a Union with the Netherlands. He told Sjahrir that in such a
federated state, the republic could not expect to represent more
than the island of Java.[32]

Possibly, as has been suggested, Sjahrir was impressed by the
strategy of Ho Chi Minh.[33] More probably he was convinced by
Kerr that he could expect no assistance in the negotiations with
the Dutch unless he made important concessions, and realized
that in any case the Dutch had already reconquered virtually
the whole of the eastern half of the archipelago. Whatever the
precise reason, the secret proposals he eventually presented to
van Mook on March 27 were a marked retreat from those advanced two weeks before. In these new proposals he asked for
de facto acknowledgment by the Dutch of the republic's author-

[30] *Merdeka,* March 12, 1946.

[31] Smit, *De liquidatie,* p. 29; Indonesia, Kementerian Penerangan,
Lembaran sedjarah (Djakarta, 1951), p. 50.

[32] Smit, *De liquidatie,* p. 29.

[33] Subadio Sastrosatomo, in an interview on June 4, 1967.

ity in Java, Madura, and Sumatra in exchange for concessions on the issue of the federated state and participation in the Union.[34]

In deciding to make these concessions, Sjahrir understood very well the risks he was running. While the Dutch would probably respect his confidence, it was inevitable that sooner or later the substance of his proposals would leak out. Since he was in effect offering to concede Dutch authority over Sulawesi, Kalimantan, and East Indonesia, a step that appeared to abandon the first principle of even Sukarno's Five-Point Program, he could well expect a storm of indignation that the Persatuan Perdjuangan could capitalize on to bring down the government. It was therefore essential to destroy the opposition.

Accordingly, some time between March 13 and March 16 a secret letter was sent to Jogjakarta ordering the arrest of the top leaders of the Persatuan Perdjuangan.[35] Since Sukarno, Hatta, and Amir had already committed themselves to rejecting the Minimum Program and fully supporting Sjahrir's diplomacy, they felt they had no choice but to accept the PP's destruction as a logical concomitant. It remained only to act.

The first step was to try to neutralize some of the pemuda support available to the opposition. In anticipation of a PP Congress to be held on March 15 in Madiun, the top Pesindo leadership met in the same city on March 13 and decided to leave the PP as of the fourteenth.[36] On March 14 a meeting of the BKPRI top leadership was held, also in Madiun, at which twelve of the fourteen organizations represented on this body

[34] Smit, *De liquidatie*, p. 30.

[35] Muhammad Dimyati, *Sedjarah perdjuangan Indonesia* (Djakarta, 1951), p. 129. Tan Malaka (*Dari pendjara*, III, 120) says that Amir admitted the existence of the letter when he appeared as a witness at the 1948 trials of the PP leaders. Since "Stenographisch verslag" is heavily censored, the absence in it of such testimony by Amir does not contradict Tan Malaka's statement. In an interview on June 4, 1967, Subadio Sastrosatomo recalled that he had been one of the couriers bringing the arrest orders to Jogjakarta. But he stated that the message was oral, not written.

[36] *Antara*, March 16, 1946; *Kedaulatan Rakjat*, March 19, 1946.

appeared. Again the powerful influence of the Pesindo was felt, even though this organization was having trouble with its unruly vice-chairman, Ibnu Parna. It was decided that the BKPRI would leave the Persatuan Perdjuangan, on the ground that the BKPRI was a federated body and should confine itself to coordinating youth activities, leaving individual member organizations to join the PP or not as they liked. This effectively undercut the position of Chaerul Saleh, who as we have seen was the chairman of the BPKRI and its representative within the PP leadership.[37] Chaerul Saleh thereupon resigned his position.[38] Stresses within the Pesindo itself were revealed when the AMKA, AMPT&T, and AMG&L, three of its constituent units, withdrew and asked to join the BKPRI as autonomous bodies.[39]

With the pemuda groups now badly divided, and the party leaders at odds as a result of the long cabinet crisis, attendance at the opening session of the PP Congress on March 15 was a bare fraction of what it had been a month before. According to one report, scarcely 40 of the original 141 organizations were represented.[40] The atmosphere of the congress was tense from the start. There were still considerable numbers of heavily armed Pesindo elements in the town. On the other hand, General Sudirman had ordered a special guard sent to protect the congress— presumably from intimidation.[41] The first day was devoted to speeches by the leading figures present: Mohammed Saleh for the lasjkar rakjat, Muljadi Djojomartono for the Barisan Banteng, and a representative of army headquarters who hoped that "the PP would become the dynamo of unity between the government, the army, and the people." [42] Tan Malaka and Yamin both gave keynote addresses, Yamin in his most flamboyant vein.

On March 16 Sukarno spoke in Magelang in strong support

---

[37] *Antara,* March 15, 1946; Hardjito, ed., *Risalah,* p. 46.

[38] *Antara,* March 17, 1946; *Kedaulatan Rakjat,* March 19, 1946.

[39] *Merdeka,* March 19, 1946.   [40] *Antara,* March 17, 1946.

[41] This comes out in the prosecution address of Attorney-General Tirtawinata in "SV," p. 286.

[42] *Kedaulatan Rakjat,* March 16, 1946.

of the government, telling his audience that diplomacy was one of the two main props of Indonesia's struggle. He warned them against paying attention to accusations against the government's diplomatic tactics.[43] By sharp contrast, when the PP formulated its own decisions that same day, it not only called for a general mobilization of the population but addressed eight statements to the outside world, of which perhaps the most striking was the second—a demand that Indonesia's territory be recognized as extending to Malaya, North Borneo, Timor, and all of Papua. Here clearly the Yamin touch was to be seen! [44] The remaining statements expressed a willingness to enter the United Nations and to make trade and cultural pacts with "progressive" countries, while threatening to confiscate all property held by aliens of countries hostile to Indonesian independence.[45]

On the Sunday morning, March 17, the congress was preparing to hold a parade and closing rally when Pesindo units appeared and demanded to participate in the parade for the sake of "security." Apparently the PP leadership acquiesced, and as a result about 7,000 people marched through the small provincial town, led by Wali al-Fatah, Soerjo, the governor of East Java, Tan Malaka, Sukarni, and others; units participating in the parade included Bung Tomo's BPRI, the Hizbullah, the Lasjkar Rakjat, and the Special Police.[46] In spite of the considerable tension the rally took place without serious incident and the congress adjourned. Most of the armed units involved in the congress then moved out of the town. Now came the moment for which the

[43] *Ibid.,* March 18, 1946.

[44] At the first session of the Investigating Committee, Yamin had given a lengthy address urging the adoption of this concept and giving an elaborate historical and cultural justification for it. When the Investigating Committee came to vote on its preference for the future territorial limits of Indonesia, Yamin's proposal received 39 out of the 66 votes cast. See Yamin, ed., *Naskah persiapan,* pp. 125–41, 214.

[45] *Antara,* March 17 and 19, 1946, gives a full account of the congress proceedings.

[46] *Kedaulatan Rakjat,* March 18, 1946; Tan Malaka, *Dari pendjara,* III, 120.

government was waiting. Not only had the congress made the mistake of passing resolutions of a needlessly provocative character, but the mere holding of the congress itself, by gathering the opposition leaders together, had greatly facilitated their apprehension.

At 4 P.M., when Tan Malaka was about to go up to rest at Magetan on the Gunung Lawu, he was told that the road was barred by Pesindo units; soon word came that all the main exits to the town were closed and that the Hizbullah groups which might have protected him had been surrounded. Shortly thereafter, the Pesindo and the Polisi Tentara (Military Police) closed in. By 8 P.M. Tan Malaka, Abikusno Tjokrosujoso, Yamin, and Sukarni had all been picked up and taken to the Military Police headquarters in Madiun.[47] At the same time Sajuti Melik, the outspoken political commentator of Kedaulatan Rakjat, was arrested by the Military Police while sick in bed in a hotel in Surakarta.[48]

At this point Major General Djokosoejono, an intimate of Amir Sjarifuddin and an adviser to the Pesindo, arrived to take charge.[49] Although a polite pretense was made that the arrestees were being taken to Jogjakarta to see the President, it was clear that they were under preventive detention. They were taken from Madiun through heavily guarded Pesindo roadblocks to Kadipolo in Surakarta, arriving there at dawn.[50] There they were held until March 22, when they were moved to Djetis, a small village south-

[47] There is some reason to think that the Military Police answered to the minister of defense rather than to army headquarters.

[48] "SV," p. 234 (testimony of Sajuti Melik). According to Yamin and Sumantoro, their arrests were announced as early as March 16 by Radio Hilversum and at 5 P.M. on March 17 by the Dutch-controlled Radio Djakarta and Radio Surabaja, indicating, if true, that Sjahrir had forewarned the Dutch of the action he intended to take against the PP. "SV," p. 148 (testimony of Yarmin) and p. 246 (testimony of Sumantoro).

[49] It was ironic, but typical of the times, that Djokosoejono was a close relative of Sukarni.

[50] "SV," p. 148 (testimony of Yamin); Tan Malaka, Dari pendjara, III, 121–22.

east of Surakarta, where they were guarded by Military Police and lasjkar rakjat loyal to Amir. Chaerul Saleh was not picked up until March 20.[51] Six days later Gatot, the former attorney-general, was arrested while he was driving from Purwokerto to Jogjakarta and taken to Military Police headquarters in Magelang.[52]

Not until March 22 did the government announce the arrests (and that the prisoners were being held in Surakarta). It stated that the arrests had been carried out by responsible authorities and were legally based on a joint Amir-Sudarsono warning issued on March 18 to the effect that the government would take strong action in the critical situation against anyone acting or speaking to agitate (*menggelisahkan*) or to disturb (*mengatjaukan*) society, or "designing to create splits" or to hinder the completion of defense work.[53] The facts that the warning was issued subsequent to the arrests and that the detentions violated the freedoms of speech and assembly for which government leaders had spoken so strongly since November seem to have caused few qualms.[54]

It was not until April 1 that a full official explanation of the arrests was given:

The purpose and aim of these arrests, based exclusively on the government's full responsibility, was to avoid the possibility of still graver dangers to the security and well-being of the state, since the actions of these political leaders threatened to weaken, disrupt and/or break up the firm solidarity between the government and the people. For this strong and compact unity of effort and endeavor between the government and the people is an essential condition for the state leadership to overcome the difficulties facing the state in this critical period.

The actions of these leaders in opposing the government prove con-

[51] *Antara,* March 22, 1946.

[52] *Ibid.,* March 29, 1946. He was released on April 24, 1946, according to *Bulan Sabit* (Surakarta), May 3, 1946.

[53] *Antara,* March 22 and 30, 1946.

[54] Still another irony of modern Indonesian history is that Sjahrir was to become the victim in 1962 of just such a violation of basic freedoms.

clusively that their opposition was disloyal or at least insufficiently [*kurang*] loyal, and was, as it were, aimed at weakening the position of the government, quite irresponsibly, as was demonstrated during the recent cabinet crisis.

The government has in its possession proofs that indicate that the activities of some of these leaders were aimed at altering the structure of the central government by means outside the terms of the Constitution.

For these reasons the government considered it necessary to act as it did. Meanwhile the government is convinced that there are still ways of settling this affair by purely political means, so as to strengthen the power of our struggle. . . .[55]

But even before the government had issued its first explanation of the arrests, army headquarters issued an emergency statement: "To avoid misunderstanding and false conceptions with regard to the recent arrests of various leaders and important people, the Supreme Headquarters of the Armed Forces announces that these arrests were absolutely not [*sekali-kali bukan*] done on the orders of the army leadership." [56] And on March 23 *Kedaulatan Rakjat* published an article strongly critical of the government, saying that its actions were reminiscent of the Kenpeitai and the PID (Dutch colonial political police). In an open thrust at Amir the article complained that Tan Malaka had been arrested by people who had previously accepted money and jobs from van der Plas. Did anyone really believe that Tan Malaka wanted to betray Indonesia to the Dutch? Why had the proclamation on the arrests not been signed by Sukarno? [57]

The government had selected its targets with some care. Tan Malaka, Yamin, Sajuti, Chaerul Saleh, Sukarni, Gatot—none had large parties or *badan perdjuangan* of their own. While Abikusno was a prominent Masjumi figure, he was known to be personally at odds with Sukiman. None of the leaders with direct

---

[55] *Antara*, April 1, 1946.   [56] *Ibid.*, March 21, 1946.
[57] The article was signed "Am"—possibly the initials of Adam Malik.

and powerful organized backing were touched. (This was all the more noticeable since Wali al-Fatah, Sukiman, and even Sarmidi had played important roles in the cabinet crisis.) And clearly the government felt unable to do or say anything directly against General Sudirman.

In spite of the shock created by the arrests, negotiations opened almost immediately for some sort of compromise. On both March 22 and March 27, the PP leaders who were still at large sent a delegation to the presidential palace to ask for explanations and to urge the release of the prisoners.[58] On March 23 Amir sent Djokosoejono to see Tan Malaka and Sukarni in Djetis to explore the possibility of a settlement, but the prisoners demanded their release as a preliminary condition to any further discussions.[59] At this Amir and Sudarsono stood firm, and the President and Hatta sided with them. Sukarno reportedly stressed that the arrests were not aimed at any political party and promised to do his best to solve the problem. He said he hoped the arrests would not be misunderstood, and urged that maximum unity be maintained while the most rapid possible solution of political difficulties was sought.[60] Amir himself stated that he had talked witih the prisoners to exchange views, and promised that they would be brought before a court in the normal way. Asked by Western reporters in Djakarta whether a general purge was under way, he replied in part, "We Easterners have a different philosophy of life than people in the West." [61]

With the at least temporary success of its measures against the opposition now assured, the government could proceed with the next step in its negotiations with the Dutch. On March 29 an Indonesian delegation was named to continue talks with the

[58] *Antara,* March 30, 1946. General Sudirman also tried to arrange a compromise without success.

[59] Tan Malaka, *Dari pendjara,* III, 122; "SV," p. 149 (testimony of Yamin).

[60] *Merdeka,* March 29, 1946, citing *Al Djihad* (Jogjakarta).

[61] *Merdeka,* April 4, 1946.

Dutch government, this time in Holland itself.[62] On April 4 the Indonesian representatives left Djakarta in the company of van Mook and Sir Archibald Clark Kerr.[63] Three days earlier Sjahrir had signed an agreement for the evacuation of the internees whereby the Indonesian government would assume full responsibility for their immediate care and transport.[64] While this agreement represented a considerable success for Sjahrir, in that it forestalled any further Allied military moves in Central and East Java, it was counterbalanced by the loss of Bandung to the British. On March 24 the city had to be evacuated by republican forces, who put the areas hitherto under their control to the torch.[65]

The fall of Bandung was a serious military and psychological blow to the government. It was also a portent of things to come.

[62] Indonesia, Kementerian Penerangan, *Lembaran sedjarah,* p. 50. Van Mook later wrote that at this time he felt that everything should be done to keep Sjahrir in power, and therefore made "maximal concessions." Van Mook, *Indonesië,* p. 131.

[63] *Merdeka,* April 4, 1946.

[64] The agreement specified that the Japanese would not be rearmed. Malang and Surakarta would be the main transshipment centers. The Allies would provide food, trains, and supplies, but their troops would not be permitted to interfere in anything else. The evacuation of the internees was assigned to a new organization known as the POPDA (Panitia Oentoek Pengembalian Bangsa Djepang dan Asing, or Committee for the Return of Japanese and Other Foreigners) under the former KNIL officer Major General Sudibjo. "Sedjarah TNI, Diponegoro," pp. 89–91.

[65] For an excellent description of the fall of Bandung, see Smail, *Bandung,* chap. 6. The Dutch army intelligence service reported that it had learned on good authority that Sukarno, Hatta, Sudirman, and Urip all urged Sjahrir not to permit the evacuation of the city, on the grounds that it was the key to the whole of the Priangan and its surrender would encourage the British to make further demands. They urged him at least to encourage the lasjkar units to fight on, even if the army had to abandon the city. The report also revealed that Nasution had induced the British to give him 50 trucks to move his supplies into the countryside by threatening otherwise to turn them over to the Hizbullah. *Militair overzicht* (week of March 28), to be found in the files of the Rijksinstituut voor Oorlogsdocumentatie, Amsterdam.

By April 17 the British had turned the city over to the Dutch, and in the meantime General Spoor, head of the Dutch forces in the archipelago, announced that there were already 30,000 troops under his command.[66] In effect, from this point on the British began to withdraw their forces, a process completed by October 1946, and the Indonesians were increasingly left to confront their former colonial rulers on their own. It would be less and less possible for the Indonesians to use the British against van Mook and his colleagues.

While the opposition had been silenced for the time being, the position of the government thus continued to be uncertain. The cabinet's uneasiness was well reflected in Sjahrir's public denial on April 2 that an agreement had been made with the Dutch whereby Holland would recognize de facto republican authority over Java and Sumatra alone; for precisely these terms were the core of the proposals he had presented to van Mook on March 27.[67]

[66] *Kedaulatan Rakjat,* April 17, 1946; *Antara,* April 15, 1946.
[67] *Merdeka,* April 2, 1946.

Chapter 15

Socialists and
Social Revolution

While it is understandable that in retrospect, and from perspectives that consciously or unconsciously focus almost exclusively on national leaders, national movements, and national destinies, the drama of the early revolution is conceived as the struggle between the Indonesians and the Dutch, and between the government and the Persatuan Perdjuangan, such a frame of reference scarcely does justice to the richness and density of the revolutionary process as it was experienced in Java in those days. In many parts of Java revolutionary upheavals were taking place throughout the life of the Sukarno and Sjahrir cabinets, developing largely outside the ken or control of these governments. If the politics of Jogjakarta were dominated by the elite veterans of the pergerakan, the military high command, and certain of the badan perdjuangan, in Banten, Bogor, Tjirebon, Pekalongan, Bodjonegoro, and other localities the common people came for a while into their own, in movements which were referred to generically as the *revolusi sosial* (social revolutions). And if at the national level the flood tide of pemudaism was in the long run dissipated in diplomacy, intrigue, and realpolitik, in the social revolutions it flowed on relatively unchecked. Nothing strikes the observer of the early revolution more painfully than this disjuncture between the social revolutions and the so-called national revolution. For all the intense conflict between the government and the Persatuan Perdjuangan, in one thing, at least, they were alike: neither was able to comprehend fully the significance of the social revolutions or to build coherent links to them.

In the case of the government leaders, this failure should not, perhaps, be any cause for surprise. Primarily professional men and prominent members of the prewar intelligentsia, who for most of their lives had lived far from the common people, it was difficult for them, except possibly in the abstract, to sympathize deeply with the inchoate hopes to which pemudaism gave expression. Moreover, there was a fundamental logic to their policy of diplomasi that necessarily subordinated everything else to the goal of international recognition of Indonesian sovereignty. As we have already seen, the Five-Point Program, the policy on foreign assets, and the official attitude toward worker and peasant control of enterprises and plantations followed inexorably from this hierarchy of priorities.

In the case of the Persatuan Perdjuangan, there may be more room for puzzlement. For there were certainly socially revolutionary aspects to the Minimum Program, and within Tan Malaka's coalition there were groups who in various ways participated in the social revolutions. And Tan Malaka himself was certainly aware of the potentialities of pemudaism. But on the other hand, he was also the victim of the circumstances in which he started to build his coalition. Without an organizational apparatus strictly loyal to him and his ideas, his united front was always at the mercy of its constituent organized units, and his leverage was never very great. Since many of these units were no more radical at heart than the groups behind the government, there was no guarantee that a real commitment to the social revolutions would not break up that united front from within. In its own way perdjuangan imposed a logic no less compelling than diplomasi, given the situation in which Tan Malaka found himself. Without the cadres available, say, to a Ho Chi Minh, Tan Malaka was exposed to the danger—which faced Sukarno two decades later—that a national unity front not under the tight control of a single, disciplined radical party was more likely to postpone than to promote revolutionary social change. And, as in later years, there was always the temptation to accentuate a violent external radicalism vis-à-vis the Dutch or the British to compensate for an inability to develop a coherent internal radicalism vis-à-vis the residual components of the colonial order.

So it was that the social revolutions largely went their own way, except in the case of Surakarta, where as we shall see, local crisis and national crisis became inextricably entangled in the debacle of the so-called July Third Affair. Everywhere they occurred the social revolutions expressed old hatreds of the collaborationist pangrèh pradja, the police, and other instruments of the two periods of colonial rule; their severity tended to vary according to the degree of social dislocation during the Dutch and Japanese periods, their distance from centers of Allied power, and the presence of organized groups ready to provide leadership.

In their political style the social revolutions exhibited many of the features of the pemuda movement—indeed it is hard to separate one from the other, since most of the former were led by representatives of the latter. The nexus between the two is probably most clearly expressed in the language of the time. For the older word *kedaulatan* (sovereignty or authority), so often, in this time of revolution, married to *rakjat* (the people), gave birth to the new word *mendaulat*, which acquired rapid currency all over Java, and which meant the deposition, humiliation, kidnapping, or murder of hated officials or other representatives of authority, usually carried out by groups of armed pemuda.

Most of the daulat actions mirrored the example set in the Rengasdengklok Affair, in which the pemuda had kidnapped older leaders to compel them to make a political decision they had previously evaded through caution or fear. Though some ended in murder, the great majority did not. Indeed, the degree to which they were removed from the strictly political realm is indicated by the frequency with which they were conceived by their pemuda promoters as a way of changing the attitudes of the kidnapped leaders by demonstrating their own daring and sincerity.

It was as if the official could be brought to understand the revolutionary process by the example of commitment and selflessness displayed by his kidnappers. When this change of heart seemed to be effected, it was not uncommon for the official to be released and even, on occasion, reinstated.

In the wake of such *daulat* actions, improvised local governments were often formed under the loose control of the social revolutionaries, typically heterogeneous clusters of religious, military, and pemuda elements, frequently bearing romantic traditional or radical names. Such local governments rarely created new social structures on their own, partly because of their composition and partly because their goals were scarcely political. Social change tended to flow out of their actions, as the authorities fled before them and peasants moved in behind them to squat on lands abandoned by their former Chinese and prijaji masters. Nor were these governments very durable. Their horizons were bounded by the local landscape; they frequently were divided among themselves; and higher authorities, whether Allied or Indonesian, would eventually move to deal with them once the opportunity and the necessary military resources could be accumulated. Yet however ephemeral their existence, they left their mark on the times, giving the early revolution its special character and forming an essential link between the old tradition of agrarian insurrection in Java and the organized radicalism of a later generation.

Most of these features of the social revolutions are clearly revealed in the upheavals that took place in Banten shortly after the Proclamation of Independence. The area had been the scene of repeated insurrections in the nineteenth century, culminating in the Tjilegon rising in 1888.[1] It was in Banten, too, that the PKI had started the unsuccessful insurrection of 1926.[2] Conflict

---

[1] For a synoptic account of agrarian unrest in the nineteenth century, see Sartono Kartodirjo, *Peasants' Revolt*, pp. 112–39 and *passim*.

[2] See Harry J. Benda and Ruth T. McVey, *The Communist Uprisings of 1926–1927 in Indonesia: Key Documents* (Ithaca, N.Y., 1960), Part II ("The Bantam Report").

had long been high between the traditionalist kjai for whom the region was famous and the local prijaji who staffed the upper levels of the pangrèh pradja. For as the prijaji had increasingly become instruments of Dutch control and channels for the introduction of Western culture, so the "wild" kjai, outside the official hierarchy and bitterly opposed to the spread of the *kafir* (infidel) ideas that threatened to undermine their influence, became the prime movers of resistance to the alien rulers.[3] During the Japanese occupation the prestige of the kjai had been enhanced by the respectful treatment they received from the military administration. Some of their leaders, such as K. H. Sjam'oen, whom we have already encountered, were enlisted in the Peta and so acquired military authority in addition to their religious charisma. A further complication was the fact that northern Banten, with its dense, mixed population of migrant Javanese, Bantenese, and Lampung men, was well-known for its *djawara,* the local variant of the djago. In every earlier disturbance in Banten these men had played an important part. Habitually they were harassed, kept under surveillance, or even imprisoned by the authorities, who regarded them as perennial troublemakers; their hostility to the pangrèh pradja and the police was proverbial.[4]

As early as October 1945 serious disorders had broken out in the area around Serang. Armed pemuda bands formed their own extemporized police in place of the regular police force, which was regarded as the tool of the prijaji and the Japanese and was particularly blamed for its role in the recruitment of rōmusha. Led by Tje' Mamat, a djawara of Lampung origin who was closely related to the most famous djawara of the prewar period, these pemuda made a frontal assault on the authorities, culminating in the arrest of the bupati of Serang, R. Hilman Djajadiningrat, a leading member of the strongly pro-Dutch older generation of the celebrated Djajadiningrat family. Hilman was subsequently

[3] Sartono Kartodirjo, *Peasants' Revolt,* chap. 5.

[4] On the djawara, see Benda and McVey, *Communist Uprisings,* pp. 23, 30.

released and fled to the Priangan, and for a short time Tje' Mamat
and his men held power in Serang.

In the meantime the kjai were on the move farther south. With
the backing of their santri pupils, many of whom enrolled in the
Hizbullah, they swept out against the authorities. The bupati of
Lebak, R. Hardiwinangun, was murdered and his place eventually taken by Kjai Hadji Hasan. The bupati of Pandeglang, Mr.
Djumhana, was forced to flee for his life, and his position was
assumed by Kjai Hadji Tubagus Abdulhalim. The *wedana* (district officers) below the bupati were also killed or run out of the
area. In effect, the entire ruling class of Banten was overthrown
in a matter of weeks. Subsequently the kjai moved northward,
and clashes ensued with Tje' Mamat and his followers. By January 1946 the latter had been put to flight, and K. H. Sjam'oen
became the self-appointed bupati of Serang.

For a while the kjai maintained their positions, which were
largely symbolic in their eyes and those of their followers. But
having neither the administrative skills nor the political ambition
to create new bureaucratic structures, they were unlikely to survive long when the central government turned its attention to
them. Sukanda Bratamenggala was sent into the area by the TKR
leaders in the Priangan, and by a combination of military and
diplomatic skill he was eventually able to gain the upper hand.
Slowly younger, less compromised members of the old ruling
families were moved back into the bureaucratic positions their
elders had been forced to abandon, now with the authority of
the republican government's troops behind them.[5]

In the north-coast Residency of Pekalongan, a similar upheaval
took place that has gone down in national history as the Peristiwa
Tiga Daerah (Three Regions Affair). While many aspects of the
affair remain obscure, the main course of events can be briefly

[5] This account of the social revolution in Banten is drawn from Indonesia, Kementerian Penerangan, *Republik Indonesia Propinsi Djawa
Barat*, p. 150; Toebagoes Roeslan, *Sedjarah Tanah Banten* (n.p., 1954);
and an interview with Sukanda Bratamenggala, June 9, 1967.

outlined.[6] After the Japanese surrender the residency was left in a power vacuum. During the month of September the few Japanese troops in the area began to concentrate in the largest towns, leaving the rural hinterland without effective instruments of repression. It is reported that the government apparatus in the residency had been among the most extortionate in Java, and popular hatred was intensified by the fact that large numbers of rōmusha had been recruited locally for work in South Banten. After the surrender some of these men began to return to their homes, many of them in miserable physical and mental condition.[7] The local KNI, set up in September, consisted almost exclusively of persons who had held high rank in the Hōkōkai or in the pangrèh pradja. Since these groups were widely regarded as accomplices of the Japanese, their authority was highly vulnerable. It began to disintegrate rapidly when the local Barisan Pelopor pemuda began disarming the Japanese military in early October.

Possibly because the Japanese were aware of the hatred directed toward them, and possibly because of confusions in the process of negotiations such as had taken place elsewhere, serious clashes developed in Pekalongan on October 3 and 4.[8] An initial agreement worked out by the Resident, Mr. Besar, whereby the local Kenpeitai promised to surrender enough guns to ensure equal firepower between themselves and the city police, the guns being stored in a dump to which both Besar and the Kenpeitai chief had access, was rejected by pemuda leaders. Fighting then broke out in which a number of youths were shot dead and the rest forced to retreat. Great bitterness was caused by these events. The deaths of the pemuda were blamed on the Resident's indeci-

---

[6] The long-term historical background of the social conflict in the Pekalongan residency has yet to be studied. Nothing exists for this area comparable to Sartono's work on Banten.

[7] See Muhammad Nuh, "Peristiwa Tiga Daerah, I," *Penelitian Sedjarah*, III, 1 (March 1962), 31.

[8] *Merdeka*, Oct. 8, 1945.

sion and weakness.[9] His position rapidly became dangerous, and he was transferred to become Resident of Semarang on October 12.[10]

Following the debacle in the city of Pekalongan, similar incidents took place in other townships within the residency, in each case apparently initiated by members of the local Barisan Pelopor. Toward the end of the month there followed a virtually complete breakdown of authority. The movement began with daulat actions against the local pangrèh pradja, but soon involved attacks on all local groups regarded as pro-Japanese or "feudal." In some cases the property of pangrèh pradja families was distributed to the local peasantry.

The central government attempted to reassert its authority by installing R. M. Soeprapto in Besar's position on November 10, but the new resident proved just as powerless as his predecessor.[11] By mid-November the popular insurrectionary movements in the regencies of Tegal, Brebes, and Pemalang had joined in the so-called Gabungan Badan Perdjuangan Tiga Daerah (Federation of Resistance Organizations of the Three Regions), or GBP-3D, headed by Soekirman and Soewignjo.[12] Thereafter events moved with increasing speed. By the end of the month the entire upper-level pangrèh pradja in Brebes had been arrested along with their families, and a new, popularly chosen bupati, Kjai Satari, took office. In Tegal, especially in the district of Adiwerno, power fell into the hands of a local djago, Sachjani, also known as Kutil, who quickly won a reputation for cruelty and violence throughout the residency. The bupati of Tegal, R. M. Soenarjo, was forced to flee, while his family was caught and tortured. On November 28 Hadji Soedja'i, an associate of Kutil, was named bupati by the GBP-3D. In Pemalang the bupati, R. Rahardjo, was also arrested

[9] *Antara,* Oct. 6 and 8, 1945.

[10] *Warta Indonesia,* Oct. 13, 1945. Besar succeeded Wongsonagoro. For a month thereafter Pekalongan was without a resident.

[11] *Merdeka,* Nov. 13, 1945.

[12] "Sedjarah TNI, Diponegoro," pp. 32–33.

with his family, as well as the local wedana and *tjamat* (subdistrict officers), but none were harmed further. Local leadership was assumed by R. Soepangat, an old Gerindo activist who headed the Pemalang branch of the GBP-3D.[13]

By this time the authority of the central administrative apparatus was confined strictly to the eastern part of the residency—the city of Pekalongan and its environs. Attempts at mediation by Sajuti Melik, sent as the representative of Governor Wongsonagoro, and Lt. Col. Kjai Hadji Iskandar Idris, commander of Regiment Seventeen, were of no greater avail.[14] Early in December both were arrested by Kutil while on a mediation mission, and were almost murdered on the spot. They were later taken under heavy guard to the township of Slawi in the hills behind Tegal.[15]

There now appeared on the scene a certain Sardjio, who had been a member both of the prewar PNI and of the Illegal PKI. In the Japanese period he had kept his political affiliations hidden, and had risen to become the Kedu residency representative on the Central Advisory Council. But finally, in 1944, he was caught by the Kenpeitai and sentenced to thirteen years in prison as a member of the underground. In mid-September he was released from jail in Ambarawa, and after recovering from his prison experiences became a leader of the Kedu KNI Executive Board. On December 6 he visited Tegal at the request of the social revolutionaries.[16]

---

[13] *Ibid.;* Muhammad Nuh, "Peristiwa Tiga Daerah, II," *Penelitian Sedjarah,* III, 6 (June 1962), 34. For more details on developments in Tegal, see Suputro, *Tegal dari masa ke masa* (Djakarta, 1959), pp. 61–64.

[14] Iskandar Idris had been daidanchō in Pekalongan and head of the local BKR after the proclamation of independence. Sajuti had been responsible for the unsuccessful choice of Soeprapto as Besar's successor. See Indonesia, Kementerian Penerangan, *Republik Indonesia Propinsi Djawa Tengah,* p. 27.

[15] "Sedjarah TNI, Diponegoro," p. 33.

[16] See the detailed account given in *Antara,* Feb. 12, 1946. Sardjio is an excellent example of how lower-level political activists in the prewar pergerakan became involved in the social revolutions.

His arrival coincided with the arrest of Sajuti and Iskandar Idris and the mounting campaign against Soeprapto. On December 9 the GBP-3D confronted Soeprapto, demanding that he give way to a popularly chosen resident. The GBP-3D's first choice was a Jogjanese, Soemedi, but when he refused to accept the post, Sardjio stepped forward or was put forward by the movement's leadership. An ultimatum was then issued demanding the resignations of Soeprapto and all other senior pangrèh pradja officials within three days. On December 11, getting no satisfactory response, the GBP-3D marched on the resident's office, took control of all transport in Pekalongan, and held mass rallies, while Soeprapto fled to Semarang. Sardjio was then officially installed by the GBP-3D as the new resident.[17]

It seems that at first the central government was willing to accept his accession as a *fait accompli*.[18] But again local forces ignored official policy and proceeded to try to overthrow Sardjio. The Pekalongan military, already upset by Kutil's arrest of its commander, was further antagonized by the GBP-3D's decision not to recognize the TKR as the official security force in the area and by an embargo the GBP-3D placed on shipments of supplies to TKR units. By December 21 TKR soldiers marched against the social revolutionary regime and succeeded in recapturing Pekalongan. Soon afterward the other townships in the residency were also recaptured, evidently with little bloodshed. Idris and Sajuti were released in Slawi, and Kutil, Sardjio, and the others were put under military arrest.[19] There was little further open resistance, though conditions in the residency remained disturbed. There was no attempt to reappoint Soeprapto, and the ad interim resident installed by the central government, Sumitro Kolopaking,

---

[17] *Ibid.;* "Sedjarah TNI, Diponegoro," p. 33; Indonesia, Kementerian Penerangan, *Republik Indonesia Propinsi Djawa Tengah,* p. 27.

[18] At least according to G. W. Overdijkink, *Het Indonesische probleem* (Amsterdam, 1948), p. 34.

[19] The government dropped its charges against Sardjio in March 1946. Kutil, however, was tried for murder in October 1946, and was executed on May 5, 1951. "Sedjarah TNI, Diponegoro," pp. 33–34.

never enjoyed any real authority. He was ultimately replaced in May 1946 by Wali al-Fatah.[20]

The complexity of the situation was well illustrated by the line-up of personalities involved. Sardjio and Sajuti Melik were both members of the prewar Illegal PKI. Iskandar Idris, the santri commander of the local TKR, was arrayed against a variety of Islamic notables in the GBP-3D, such as Kjai Satari and Hadji Soedja'i. The choice of Wali al-Fatah, a top leader of the PP, to become the bulwark of government authority in the region as resident, added a final touch of irony.[21]

Commenting on the affair somewhat later, the journalist Rosihan Anwar, who was close to cabinet circles, agreed with Hatta's verdict that there was "too much popular sovereignty" in the Pekalongan residency, and accused Sardjio and his aides of "atrocious, fascistic" actions.[22] The judgment was typical of the government's outlook. Earlier the cry had been for the removal of "feudal" and "Japanese" elements in favor of popular forces, but when faced with spontaneous "red" movements they could neither control nor direct, the government turned to representatives of the traditional ruling class (as the successive appointments of Soeprapto and Sumitro Kolopaking demonstrated) and denounced the forces it had once invoked.

If the social revolutionary movements in Banten and Pekalongan were essentially expressions of local radicalism, and as

[20] Indonesia, Kementerian Penerangan, *Republik Indonesia Propinsi Djawa Tengah*, p. 27.

[21] The heterogeneity of the GBP-3D, consisting as it did of santri notables, djago like Kutil, and prewar radicals like Sardjio and Soepangat, illustrates both its popular support and its potential fragility. Wali al-Fatah was probably appointed primarily because he was a well-known santri leader likely to appeal to the predominantly santri population of Pekalongan. Three successive prijaji residents had been completely without authority. Sumitro Kolopaking could only be installed on January 23 with a major government display of force. *Antara*, Jan. 26, 1946. (In passing, it is probable that the cabinet was glad to see a top PP leader out of Jogjakarta.)

[22] *Merdeka*, Dec. 29 and Jan. 9, 1946.

such did not in the long run present a major challenge to the government, the same was not entirely the case with Mr. Jusuf's PKI, which, with some interesting variations, was disposed of in much the same fashion as the GBP-3D. After its formation in October 1945, the PKI speedily established regional branches in Sukabumi, Tjirebon, Surakarta, Pekalongan, Madiun, Malang, and Surabaja, and started publishing a journal of its own, the *Bintang Merah*.[23] On December 11 the party followed the example of its competitors in forming a Lasjkar Merah (Red Militia) under a certain Engkoen Coerdian.[24] Registration for this armed organization began at the end of the year, and Dutch intelligence sources reported that it quickly formed branches in Madiun, Purwokerto, Ambarawa, Magelang, Salatiga, and Jogjakarta, with headquarters in Surakarta.[25]

On February 8, 1946, the PKI held its first congress in Jusuf's home town of Tjirebon. From the very start the meeting took on a strongly social revolutionary tone. The delegate from Besuki, Lauw King Ho, reminded his listeners of the glories of Yenan and the Chinese people's valiant struggle against bourgeois capitalism and imperialism. Mr. Soeprapto was even more specific:

Nationalism in the colonial period, as led by Brother Sukarno, should indeed be honored, since it genuinely defended the interests of the poor and dispossessed [*rakjat djémbél*], but nationalism in the Japanese period behaved most regrettably, since the poor and dispossessed were offered glittering promises, which resulted in the delivery of

---

[23] *NEFIS Periodiek,* no. 7, p. 13.

[24] The proclamation announcing the formation of the Lasjkar Merah specifically stated that the organization would cooperate with the TKR, the lasjkar rakjat, the BPRI, and the Sabilillah. (See *Antara,* Dec. 28, 1945, for the full text of the party's proclamation no. 2.) It is a striking indication of the mood of the times and of the character of Jusuf's leadership that the party executive was invariably referred to as the Markas Besar PKI (PKI Headquarters), not the Politburo. For some biographical details on Coerdian, see Sutter, *Indonesianisasi,* p. 340.

[25] *NEFIS Periodiek,* no. 7, pp. 14–15. According to this source the Lasjkar Merah held a combined military and political training course in an asrama in Surakarta sometime in January 1946.

much rice and the mobilization of many rōmusha. After Indonesian independence was announced, a lot of noise was made once again about this "nationalism." After that, there emerged Socialism: but these Socialists do not differ from their ideological comrades overseas. They claim to be anti-imperialist and anticapitalist, but by their diplomatic tactics they have obstructed and weakened the struggle of the poor and dispossessed; and they will immediately cease the struggle, once they have obtained ministerial positions. At the present moment independence is still simply independence for the bourgeoisie—not yet for Si Djémbél.

Finally Jusuf himself addressed the congress. After detailing the Soviet Union's prowess and its emergence as one of the great world powers, he turned to representatives of the Hizbullah and BPRI, who attended as observers, and invited them to join the party members in singing the Internationale and shouting the slogan "Soviet!" In its final resolutions the congress demanded an end to the disarming of popular organizations and complete freedom for the formation of independent workers' and peasants' unions; and it concluded by warning the government to confer with the people before conferring with van Mook and his friends.[26]

So far all had gone smoothly. But while the congress was in session, incidents began to break out between the Lasjkar Merah and local units of the Military Police. By February 12 Tjirebon was in chaos, as Jusuf's men seized the barracks of the Military

[26] Full details on the congress are contained in *Antara*, Feb. 11, 12, and esp. 16, 1946. Just prior to the congress a large-scale East Java PKI conference had been held in Djember at which Soeprapto had been the main speaker. It appears that many small fragments of the prewar and wartime PKI, whose members had remained in isolation and concealment during the occupation, surfaced toward the end of 1945 and began contacting old friends and associates. They naturally gathered around the only effective leadership group that presented itself—that of Jusuf. (Interview of Ruth McVey with the late Njoto, second deputy chairman of the Aidit PKI, Feb. 23, 1965, kindly made available to the author. Njoto stated that the Besuki PKI was the largest constituent unit in Jusuf's organization.) Soeprapto came to the Tjirebon congress straight from Djember, bringing with him a number of heavily armed pemuda (*NEFIS Periodiek*, no. 7, pp. 14–15).

Police and drove the remaining TKR units out of town. The Resident of Tjirebon and the local chief of the civilian police were both arrested, since they were judged sympathetic to the military. An initial attempt to retake the city by units under Lieutenant Colonel Muffraeni was beaten off, but when reinforcements arrived from Tegal and Pekalongan, Jusuf could not hold out. After some bloodshed resistance collapsed, and Jusuf and Soeprapto were taken prisoner.[27]

But the fighting in Tjirebon is less instructive in following the fate of the social revolutions than the developments that took place after its suppression. For within two weeks a group of former internees in Boven Digul, recently returned from Australia, met in Jogjakarta to denounce Jusuf's claim to represent the tradition of the PKI of 1926–27. They called on all sections of the PKI and other units formed by Jusuf to contact a "Purge Committee" they had set up, so that a "purge" congress could be held as quickly as possible.[28] When the projected congress was

[27] The origin and nature of the clashes is unclear. The two chief sources give conflicting accounts. According to *NEFIS Periodiek* (no. 7, pp. 14–15), the Lasjkar Merah numbered barely 200, and the TKR, 1,750. The outbreaks were caused by banal disputes over hotel accommodations, food supplies, and girls. The report adds, rather interestingly, that after the TKR recapture of Tjirebon on February 18, a number of local kjai were arrested along with Jusuf and Soeprapto. According to the strongly anti-communist Sedjarah Militer Kodam VI (*Siliwangi dari masa kemasa*, pp. 99–100), the TKR was heavily outnumbered by the Lasjkar Merah, which acted provocatively by waving the Red Flag and shouting "Up the Soviets!" and unilaterally attacked the barracks of the Military Police. The city was recaptured by the TKR on February 14. The arrests of Jusuf and Soeprapto were kept from the public until early April, when Amir announced them lumped indiscriminately with the arrests of March 17. (See Amir's statement in *Merdeka*, April 4, 1946). This suggests that the cabinet saw the suppression of Jusuf's PKI as part of its strategy for dealing with the Persatuan Perdjuangan.

[28] For details see *Merdeka*, March 11, 1946. The former internees, most of whom had been confined in Australia during the latter part of the war, began returning to Java in small groups toward the end of 1945 and early in 1946. They were in general badly out of touch with developments in Indonesia, and were by no means united among themselves.

finally held on April 29, the returned exiles took full command. Sardjono, who had been party chairman at the time of the 1926 insurrection, was elected chairman with full discretion to choose other members of the party leadership as he saw fit.[29] Jusuf's original militant program was scrapped. In a manifesto issued on May 10, the Sardjono group stated that while the long-term aim of the PKI was the creation of a socialist society with the dictatorship of the proletariat as the first stage in building communism, the immediate task was to defend and strengthen the government of the Republic of Indonesia "as a democratic structure, through the formation of a national front to oppose fascist-reactionary colonialism." [30]

From this point on the purged PKI gave the Sjahrir-Amir cabinet its fullest support, and gradually subdued residual sections of Jusuf's organization to its will. What hand the govern-

---

Recriminations over the disaster of 1926–27 had never ceased, though the majority of internees agreed in blaming Tan Malaka for much of their suffering. A considerable number of them, including Sardjono, the party chairman at the time of the insurrection, were sufficiently persuaded of the reality of the world-wide struggle against fascism that, like their counterparts in the resistance against the Nazis, they voluntarily cooperated with the Dutch colonial authorities in Australia. This in turn gave rise to further passionate recriminations, for noncooperating internees remained in improvised detention camps where conditions were very far from agreeable. For details on the former internees, see Soe Hok-gie, "Simpang kiri," pp. 27–34; and Sudijono Djojoprajitno, *PKI-Sibar contra Tan Malaka* (Djakarta, 1962), *passim*. (The latter source is a pro-Tan Malaka and anti-Sardjono polemic.)

[29] *Antara*, April 30, 1946; *Merdeka*, May 2, 1946. The new leadership was eventually constituted as follows: chairman, Sardjono (PKI chairman, 1924–26); vice-chairman, Alibasah Winanta (PKI chairman, 1924; later treasurer under Sardjono); first secretary, Soeleiman (PKI leader in Tegal in the early 1920's); second secretary and treasurer, Ali Kasim (second secretary in Jusuf's PKI); assistant, Hadji Datuk Batuah (PKI leader in West Sumatra in the 1920's). It should be noted that while in Australia, Sardjono had served on the editorial staff of the Dutch Information Service's propaganda magazine, *Penjoeloeh*. See *Kedaulatan Rakjat*, May 4, 1946, and *Merdeka*, May 3, 1946, for these listings, and also for the PKI's Seven-Point Program.

[30] The manifesto can be found in *Merdeka*, May 11, 1946.

ment had in these developments remains obscure. But given the former internees' concentration in the republican capital of Jogjakarta and the association of many PS leaders with the prewar PKI, it seems unlikely that the government was not involved. Certainly the continued detention of Jusuf and Soeprapto made it easier to carry out the purge. Whatever the nature and degree of the intervention, the course of events ran decisively in the government's favor. For in the place of a socially radical PKI allied with the Persatuan Perdjuangan, it now had a relatively conservative party strongly loyal to itself.[31]

If the upheavals and armed clashes in Banten, Pekalongan, Tjirebon, and other outlying areas affected the struggle for power at the center only to a limited degree, the social revolution that broke out in Surakarta, while similarly local in origins, was to have a decisive impact on the republican government—indeed was a necessary precondition for the *crise de régime* later known as the July Third Affair. The seeds of the social revolution in Surakarta were sown toward the end of the nineteenth century, when the region was opened up for intensive exploitation by European corporate capitalism. By the end of the Dutch colonial period there were more than a hundred estate enterprises operat-

---

[31] Those former internees who had quarreled with Sardjono and who were sympathetic to Tan Malaka did not join the purged PKI, though they continued to regard themselves as communists. Led by Djamaludin Tamin, an old intimate of Tan Malaka, they met in Surakarta on May 26 to 27 and agreed to form a Partai Rakjat (People's Party) on their own. But this party never amounted to anything, probably because Tan Malaka himself was out of circulation. For details see *Merdeka,* May 28, 1946; *Kedaulatan Rakjat,* May 30, 1946; and Sudijono Djojoprajitno, *PKI-Sibar,* p. 27. There can be little doubt that the appearance of Sardjono and his followers, deeply committed to their long feud with Tan Malaka, served not only to strengthen the hand of the government but to spread the idea that the leader of the Persatuan Perdjuangan was an unreliable and ambitious adventurer. Tan Malaka was no longer the sole major figure from the insurrectionary generation on the scene, and the long sojourn of Sardjono and his friends in Boven Digul gave them credentials that were evidently not seriously diminished by their having cooperated with the Dutch in Australia.

ing in the area, particularly in the kabupatèn of Klaten and Sragen. The spread of these plantations, primarily devoted to the production of sugar, coffee, and tobacco, drastically altered the economy of the region and undermined the established relationship between the rulers of the Central Java principalities and their subjects.[32]

Traditionally the royal administration had been financed largely by an appanage system. Court functionaries were assigned rights not to land itself (which was theoretically in the hands of the rulers), but to the so-called *padjeg* and the limited corvée labor of particular clusters of peasants. The padjeg was essentially a tax on agricultural produce, paid mainly in kind, and collected for the appanage holders by specially appointed *bekel* (bailiffs) who took a percentage from what they collected. Since the padjeg was based on actual production, it fluctuated from season to season, and was usually adjusted to the real economic situation of the peasantry. When estates started to penetrate the area, the rulers and appanage holders began to turn over their traditional rights in exchange for cash payments. However, since the plantation managers had no interest in payments of the traditional kind, they developed the quasi-legal convention that the padjeg should be paid either in cash or in produce designed specifically for export.

With corporate interests in control the appanage system was manipulated to its limits, without any of the traditional restraints imposed by custom or seasonal fluctuations.[33] Labor services,

[32] The following account of economic and administrative changes in the principalities is drawn primarily from "Vorstenlanden" in the *Encyclopaedie van Nederlandsch-Indië* (2d ed.; The Hague and Leiden, 1917–39), pp. 626–36. See also the superb analysis contained in Clifford Geertz, *Agricultural Involution: The Processes of Ecological Change in Indonesia* (Berkeley, Calif., 1963), p. 55, n. 13, and pp. 85–103.

[33] Two striking examples may be cited. Where perennials like coffee were to be grown, a system called *béngkok* was devised, under which the peasant turned over a fixed half of his land to the estates and guaranteed to provide the labor necessary to work it. In the case of annuals, like sugar, the *glébagan* system was instituted, whereby the land turned over to the estates rotated seasonally, the peasant again providing the

formerly adjusted to the rice cycle and to the occasional needs of the ruling class, were now rigidly tied to the requirements of production for the international market. Tax payments were tightly enforced irrespective of the success or failure of the harvests. Furthermore, the royal bureaucracy became increasingly dependent for its economic well-being on the estates, which were now effectively interposed between the peasantry and their traditional rulers. Since the exactions of the plantations were enforced by the royal judiciary and police, the latter increasingly incurred the hatred of the rural population. Ancient habits of loyalty and deference were undermined, and the ruling class came more and more to be identified as an instrument of alien oppression. This process was accelerated by growing land-hunger as the population rose, and by the appearance in the hitherto isolated principalities of white faces, to whose owners the traditional overlords were ever more clearly subservient.

In the early years of the twentieth century, the colonial administration gradually abolished the appanage system, in part to remedy the obvious abuses to which it had led, and in part to rationalize the finances of the principalities. By 1918 the appanages were gone, giving way to modernized treasuries, annual budgets, and fixed civil lists.[34] Under the new system the bekel were dismissed, but were compensated with one-fifth of all the land reverting to the rulers with the liquidation of the appanages. The rest of the lands were turned over to newly created *kalurahan*

---

labor required to work it. Since the pattern of the sugar cycle meant that in any two-year period the estates held a given piece of land for sixteen months, leaving the peasant with eight months, further distortions and inequities were involved under glébagan. As for labor exactions, one finds the institution of *glidig*, whereby the peasant was required, in the event that he failed to supply the labor demanded of him, to make up the difference by paying the wages of "free labor" hired by the estates in his place. In all these cases there was virtually no legal protection for the peasants against exploitation by their new masters.

[34] The Mangkunegaran had begun ending its appanages in the nineteenth century. The Sultanate, the Pakualaman, and the Sunanate finally abolished their appanages in 1912, 1914, and 1918 respectively.

(administrative villages) as communal property.[35] The rulers were authorized to levy a direct land tax, amounting to about half the crop, on all land not assigned to the former bekel. While rationalizing the royal exchequers, these changes did nothing to narrow the growing gulf between the rulers and their subjects. As for the estates, they now contracted directly with the ex-bekel and the kalurahan authorities for land and with the individual peasant for labor, since the corvée had been abolished with the appanages. In practice these changes only accentuated peasant misery. The enormous economic power of the plantation managers made it easy for them to suborn and manipulate the village authorities in matters of land. Habitually the best land was contracted away. And the transition from the corvée to wage labor now pitted not the rural community but the individual peasant against the plantation, hastening the growth of a destitute rural proletariat.[36]

Under these conditions it was inevitable that the prestige and moral authority of the rulers in Central Java sharply declined, particularly in Surakarta, where the majority of the estates were located. The situation there was further aggravated by competition between the Sunanate and the Mangkunegaran, a rivalry that was at heart political but that was expressed in obtuse displays of pomp and ostentation. This opulence in the midst of misery did not go unmarked. It was commonly whispered, by the end of the Dutch period, that the Susuhunan and the Mangkunegoro were like the slender, feathery *tjemara* trees that line the streets of Surakarta—"They grow tall and beautiful, but they offer no shade to the people."

[35] The Dutch colonial government made some effort, by no means wholly successful, to ensure that those who had held working rights to particular lands under the old system retained them under the new.

[36] Again, the colonial government was in theory committed to supervising the contracts between the estates and the ex-bekel and kalurahan authorities, in order to prevent complicity at the expense of the peasantry, and also to ensuring that "free laborers" would receive a decent wage. In practice, however, the estates, many of which maintained their own private police forces, operated pretty much as they pleased.

During the Depression the bottom dropped out of the sugar market. Not only did this seriously reduce the income of the rulers in Surakarta, who by now owned sugar plantations of their own, but it persuaded the authorities in Djakarta to make drastic cuts in their civil lists. In the case of the Sunanate the government waited until the death in 1939 of the long-lived susuhunan Pakubuwono X to institute these cuts (amounting to 50 per cent), which were written into the contract signed with his successor, Pakubuwono XI. The financial crisis compelled the new ruler to pension off or dismiss many of his officials—a devastating admission of weakness to traditional Javanese ways of thinking, which deduced a king's power from the number of his courtiers and the munificence of his largesse. As one Javanese recalled later:

The feeling of respect and obedience, of awe and service to the ruler on the throne began to diminish. As a result things began to happen that had never occurred in the time of Pakubuwono X. One heard voices speaking disrespectfully of the rulers, especially each time the Susuhunan came to the residence of the [Dutch] Governor for a conference. *Kraton* [royal palace] people began to say: "He's not a real king any more. Just like the Mangkunegoro. Every day he goes visiting the Governor." In Pakubuwono X's day, the ruler never visited the Governor; the Governor always visited him and had to ask permission first. It began to be whispered that *"kraton wis kontjatan wahju"* ["the kraton has lost its magic power"].[37]

The Japanese occupation caused a further decline in the position of the kraton. The final collapse of the estate economy eliminated a major source of royal revenue. Many of the plantations were turned over by the Japanese to the local peasantry to grow rice and other food crops. The monetary salaries of kraton functionaries dropped catastrophically in value as inflation soared. The feeling of disintegration was enhanced by succession crises in both the Sunanate and the Mangkunegaran. In 1944 Pakubuwono XI died, and was succeeded by his teen-age son, Pakubu-

[37] Dwidjosugondo, *Peranan ramalan Djojobojo,* pp. 129–33.

wono XII. Entirely inexperienced, with little interest in political activity or indeed in anything beyond his own amusements, the young Susuhunan was easily dominated by the Queen Mother and her allies at the court, most notably the *papatih dalem* (grand vizier), Sosrodiningrat.[38] In the same year the celebrated Mangkunegoro VII died after a reign of 28 years, leaving a young son to succeed him, who, like the Susuhunan, was entirely without experience and totally in the hands of elderly and conservative court officials.

As if the situation was not already bad enough, it was further aggravated in the chaotic atmosphere prevailing after the Japanese surrender by the short-sighted behavior of the kraton authorities themselves. Intrigues within the Sunanate, for example, culminated in the kidnapping and eventual deposition of Sosrodiningrat by a rival court clique that accused him of collaboration with the occupation administration.[39] And the bitter rivalry between the Sunanate and the Mangkunegaran, almost two hundred years old, continued unabated. The Mangkunegaran, which controlled about one-third of the city of Surakarta, flatly refused to enter into any subordinate relationship with the Sunanate, in sharp contrast to developments in Jogjakarta, where from the

[38] The *papatih dalem,* or *patih,* was traditionally the chief minister of the ruler and carried out the ordinary administration of the kingdom. In the later Dutch colonial period, however, indirect rule was exercised through this official, who could not be appointed without Dutch consent and who was paid by the colonial government. In time the patih tended to become more loyal to the colonial authorities than to the ruler he was supposed to serve. There was often severe rivalry between the powerless but prestigious ruler and his powerful but less legitimate chief minister. The Queen Mother, the Kandjeng Ratu, came from the family which had long supplied the patih of the Sunanate. She was thus closely related to Sosrodiningrat. For biographical details on Sosrodiningrat, see the Appendix.

[39] The kidnapping seems to have taken place on or about October 23, 1945, at least judging from the Tull Report. The rival clique, hostile primarily to the Queen Mother, supported the bupati of Klaten, Kandjeng Radèn Mas Tumenggung Judonagoro, as its candidate for patih. But he does not seem to have been successfully installed until 1946.

start the Pakualaman willingly took second place to the Sultanate.[40]

While the courts quarreled, a vacuum of power rapidly developed. The Surakarta KNI, led by Mr. Sumodiningrat, a brother-in-law of the Susuhunan, proved completely ineffective, as arms in Surakarta passed out of its control into the hands of a variety of pemuda groups. On October 29 Sakirman arrived in the city to reorganize the local KNI along lines specified by the Working Committee of the KNIP in Djakarta. A new Working Committee for Surakarta was established on November 1, under the chairmanship of a veteran of the prewar PKI and dominated by a variety of radically-minded pemuda and old hands from the pergerakan.[41]

The same day the government's high commissioner for the principalities, R. P. Soeroso, intervened to halt the continuing deterioration. He announced that with the full agreement of the Susuhunan and the Mangkunegoro he was setting up a Directorate to coordinate governmental activities in the Surakarta region, since at present these were "very divided." [42] The Directorate would be headed by Soeroso (in a nonvoting capacity) and would consist of the rulers or their representatives and five mem-

[40] There were powerful historical reasons for this difference. The Mangkunegaran house, which dated back to 1757, had been founded as the result of a rebellion against the old kraton of Kartasura, regarded as too submissive to the Dutch. The Sultanate of Jogjakarta, formed by another rebel against Kartasura, was barely two years older, and owed its seniority only to the fact that its founder surrendered to the Dutch two years sooner. Accordingly, the Mangkunegaran's prestige was considerably higher than that of the Pakualaman, which was established during the British interregnum early in the nineteenth century as a reward to its founder for his services in the struggle against the strongly anti-British sultan of the time. To put it crudely, the Mangkunegaran was born from rebellion, the Pakualaman from collaboration.

[41] See "Surakarta Hadiningrat," which gives a complete list of the membership of the Surakarta Working Committee. Virtually none have aristocratic names, only two have academic titles, and at least three were former internees in Boven Digul.

[42] *Kedaulatan Rakjat,* Nov. 3, 1945.

bers of the KNI. It would act as the executive arm of the central
government and the Surakarta KNI. Officials in both courts
would be responsible to it for administration in their respective
domains.[43] But the Directorate was never able to function as
intended, partly because of Soeroso's cautious and bureaucratic
personality but mainly because the informal understanding on
which it was based—that while the Susuhunan and Mangkunegoro officially retained their powers, political control would pass
to the KNI majority—collapsed in the face of the systematic resistance of the senior court officials, who insisted on trying to retain their prewar authority.[44]

In the midst of these difficulties the high tide of pemudaism
that marked the end of 1945 swept over Surakarta. The atmo-

[43] The Directorate was originally constituted as follows: chairman,
R. P. Soeroso; members, Pakubuwono XII and Mangkunegoro VIII,
Mr. Mohammad Daljono (for general affairs), R. Ng. Prodjosudodo
(for pangrèh pradja affairs), Achmad Dasuki Siradj (for social affairs),
Ronomarsono (for economic affairs), and Djuwardi (for security affairs). See *Kedaulatan Rakjat*, Nov. 2, 1945. On November 8 it was an-
nounced that two high court officials, R. M. T. P. Atmodiningrat and
K. P. H. Soerjosoerardjo, would sit on the Directorate as representatives
of the Susuhunan and the Mangkunegoro respectively. (*Kedaulatan
Rakjat*, Nov. 8, 1945). Daljono was a close associate of Sjamsu Harja
Udaja in the PBI. Prodjosudodo was a progressive member of the pangrèh
pradja and had distinguished himself by the leading role he played, as
wedana of Kartasura, in the takeover of arms from the Japanese. Achmad
Dasuki Siradj had been involved in the Sarekat Islam and the PKI in
the 1920's and had been interned in Boven Digul from 1927 to 1933.
On his return he joined the Illegal PKI, and during the Japanese period
he was arrested and tortured by the Kenpeitai. (Indonesia, Departemen
Penerangan, unpublished biographic files; hereinafter referred to as
Deppen Files.) Djuwardi was also a former inmate of Boven Digul and
was active in the Surakarta Barisan Pelopor during the occupation. See
L. M. H. Jungschlaeger, "The Double Coup," *NEFIS Periodiek*, no. 13
(Aug. 14, 1946), p. 12. I have no information on Ronomarsono.

[44] Interview with Radèn Pandji Soeroso, Jan. 25, 1963; interview with
Mohammed Saleh Werdisastro, Jan. 3, 1963. According to Surakarta,
Djawatan Penerangan Kota Besar Surakarta, *Kenang-Kenangan*, p. 4,
the Sunanate and the Mangkunegaran in effect boycotted the Directorate,
since they did not control it.

sphere created by the bitter fighting in Surabaja and on the Semarang front exacerbated the already existing dislike of the rulers and their aristocratic entourages. Under other circumstances the young Susuhunan's affair with a Eurasian girl would probably have been passed off with a shrug in Surakarta, known all over Indonesia as "the city that never sleeps." But at a time when all Eurasians were under suspicion as spies or sympathizers of the Dutch, the affair was regarded as politically provocative. And many pemuda, imbued with the revolutionary ethos, felt incensed that in the middle of the national crisis the Susuhunan, their contemporary, appeared to put his private pleasures above the interests of the people.[45] Rumors also spread that within the high walls of the kraton a secret Comité van Ontvangst (Reception Committee) had been formed to hasten the return of the colonial masters, with its headquarters in the compound of Pangéran Soerjohamidjojo, an uncle of the Susuhunan.

The political power of the kraton was decisively weakened when Purbonagoro was overthrown as commander of the Tenth Division of the TKR and replaced by the radically-minded Colonel Sutarto. So it was that the court found itself literally defenseless when, early in January 1946, units of the Barisan Banteng, operating under orders from Dr. Muwardi, kidnapped the Susuhunan, the Queen Mother, and Soerjohamidjojo. The daulat operation was carried out in exemplary style, the three royal figures being treated with politeness but held incommunicado for several days to impress upon them the seriousness of popular displeasure.[46] When the lesson seemed to have been driven home, they were released. Shortly afterward, in a rather pathetic gesture of contrition, the Susuhunan had it announced that he wished to

[45] See "Surakarta Hadiningrat."

[46] *Ibid.* See also Jungschlaeger, "Double Coup," p. 11. It appears that the kidnapping must have taken place early in January, since *Soeara Moeda* (Surakarta) announced on January 11, 1946, "Because of the critical situation, for the time being Sri Paduka Ingkang Sinuhun Kandjeng Susuhunan will not come out to the audience hall as usual, except for emergencies."

be called Bung Pakubuwono (Brother Pakubuwono), obviously in imitation of the revolutionary names Bung Karno, Bung Sjahrir, Bung Hatta, and Bung Amir.[47]

The special character of events in Surakarta in these months can perhaps best be illustrated by the contrast with political developments in the other royal city of Java. For Jogjakarta's politics, though turbulent enough in their way, were always dominated by the young Sultan, Hamengkubuwono IX. Assisted by the wide disparity in prestige between the Sultanate and the Pakualaman, and the cooperativeness of the reigning Pakualam, Hamengkubuwono was wise enough, on the death of the last patih shortly before the Japanese surrender, to assume the vacant office himself.[48] He thereupon closed the kraton as a place for receiving high Japanese officials, politely forcing them to call on him at the Kepatihan. (The Solonese royalty made no such effort to distance themselves from the occupation authorities.) [49] The Sultan was also tactful in his relationship with the local KNI, and through the formation of the Jogjakarta Lasjkar Rakjat, strongly loyal to himself, was able to prevent any powerful movement against his authority.[50]

These initial advantages were compounded by the Sultan's shrewd decision in December to invite the central government to move to Jogjakarta, for the move created an association between himself and the new republican leadership that heightened the prestige of both. Since the government could not afford to permit unrest and disturbances at its own seat of power, its presence reinforced the authority of the Sultanate. Very soon Jogjakarta

[47] *Kedaulatan Rakjat,* Jan. 17, 1946. Since Pakubuwono means "Nail of the Universe," one can imagine how bizarre the name Bung Pakubuwono must have sounded to traditional ears.

[48] The old patih died on August 1, 1945. Indonesia, Kementerian Penerangan, *Republik Indonesia Daerah Istimewa Jogjakarta,* p. 30. For a detailed analysis of this decision and its consequences, see Selosoemardjan, *Social Changes in Jogjakarta* (Ithaca, N.Y., 1962), pp. 51–53.

[49] Interview with K. R. T. Honggowongso, Dec. 31, 1962; and interview with Mohammed Saleh Werdisastro, Jan. 3, 1963.

[50] For biographical details on Hamengkubuwono IX, see the Appendix.

came to be identified as the "city of the government." Conversely, Surakarta, which for two hundred years had been locked in bitter rivalry with Jogjakarta, became a natural gravitation point for groups hostile to the government. Near enough to Jogjakarta to exert an influence, and yet far enough away to form an independent center, Surakarta became in 1946 the "city of the opposition" *par excellence*. Inevitably the increasing presence in the city not only of local radicals but also of national-level oppositionists created a political atmosphere of great volatility and tension.

It is therefore scarcely surprising that the government's March razzias against the leaders of the Persatuan Perdjuangan were answered in April and May by increasingly militant oppositionist and social revolutionary activity in the region of Surakarta. On April 19 the Barisan Banteng and other pemuda elements forced their way into the kraton and compelled the Susuhunan to declare his readiness to surrender his authority to the people.[51] Three days later the Working Committee of the KNI of Klaten, the richest and most socially disturbed kabupatèn in the Sunanate domain, met with representatives of about sixty organizations, including the PBI, BTI, Lasjkar Rakjat, Lasjkar Buruh, Pesindo, Barisan Banteng, Masjumi, Hizbullah, GPII, Parkindo, and local pangrèh pradja, and issued the following declaration:

Bearing in mind that the Constitution demands a government of the people, while the government of the Special Region of Surakarta is not a government of the people; that in a unified state, there should be only one authority; that the whole people clearly looks toward the formation of a socialist society, while the Special Region in itself contradicts this; considering that almost all the people of Klaten dislike the Special Region; that the power of the government of the Special Region diminishes the right of the people to their own sovereignty; that the governments of the Sunanate and the Mangkunegaran are monarchies, and thus no longer in harmony with the aliran existing among the people; [the assembled parties] resolve: (1) to abolish

[51] *Merdeka,* May 2, 1946.

the Special Region as soon as possible; (2) to abolish feudal government; and (3) to [declare its] wish for a single popular government for the whole Surakarta region.[52]

By April 24 the anti-kraton movement had developed a powerful new impetus of its own. The Susuhunan was forced to receive leaders of the Barisan Banteng again and to reaffirm his earlier readiness to abdicate all political power. At the same time the administrative corps of the kabupatèn of Klaten broke off all relationships with the kraton—evidently as a result of pressures exerted by local party groups and paramilitary organizations.[53]

Three days later the Working Committee of the KNI of Sragen followed the example of Klaten, and broke off all relations with the Sunanate.[54] That same evening the pangrèh pradja of the urban kabupatèn of Surakarta met to demand that the central government change the Special Region of Surakarta into a normal residency with an executive body like any other, leaving the two rulers a staff of officials to manage internal palace affairs and maintain traditional culture and ceremonies. To preserve the honor and prestige of the rulers, however, the resident to be appointed should be given the rank of governor.[55] The following day a general meeting of PNI leaders for the whole of the Surakarta area decided to send a delegation to both the Susuhunan and the Mangkunegoro demanding the end of the Special Region and stating that the dualistic character of the existing regime, its aimlessness, and its antiquated feudal structure could no longer be tolerated by the democratic revolutionary spirit of the population.[56]

[52] *Antara,* April 27, 1946.

[53] *Kedaulatan Rakjat,* May 4, 1946. It is noticeable that four days later a new bupati of Klaten was appointed. See *Kedaulatan Rakjat,* April 28, 1946.

[54] *Merdeka,* May 2, 1946. Sragen and Klaten were the two largest and most prosperous kabupatèn within the Sunanate domain.

[55] *Ibid.,* May 6, 1946. At the same time the police refused to serve the courts any longer, and nine senior officials in the patih's office were kidnapped by younger subordinates. Surakarta, Djawatan Penerangan Kota Besar Surakarta, *Kenang-Kenangan,* p. 5.

[56] *Merdeka,* May 6, 1946; *Kedaulatan Rakjat,* May 4, 1946.

On April 30 the Susuhunan, against whom most of the pressure had been directed, yielded and issued a proclamation:

Mindful of the contents of Article 18 of our Constitution, and the charter of His Excellency the President on August 19, 1945, and taking cognizance of movements among the people in Our region concerning the abolishing or not of the Special Region of Surakarta Hadiningrat, We proclaim to Our people that if the abolition of the Special Region of Surakarta Hadiningrat is indeed clearly the sincere wish of the people, and has been established as such by the government of the Indonesian republic, then We do not object to the surrender of our authority to the central government.[57]

Dr. Muwardi answered the next day in the name of the headquarters of the Barisan Banteng. With typically Solonese politesse he thanked the Susuhunan for his generosity in being willing to sacrifice himself for the greater unity of the republic. At the same time he urged Sukarno to confirm the transfer of power to the central government.[58]

If the Susuhunan and his advisers had now capitulated almost completely, the Mangkunegoro put up longer resistance. On May 1 a special announcement was issued by the Mangkunegaran government, which, while applauding the popular desire for democracy and social justice, declared that for some months a new constitution for the Mangkunegaran territory had been drafted within the palace itself, and that this constitution would have long since been put into practice had there not been "obstructions." The planned constitution would have put the Mangkunegoro, as head of a Special Mangkunegaran District, directly under the President, governing in accordance with the stipulations of the republican Constitution. The Mangkunegoro was to have been assisted by a local representative council directly elected from the territory's population that would form its own executive council. The limits of the Mangkunegoro's own authority would be determined by the central government, and all his decrees would be brought into harmony with those of the

---

[57] *Merdeka,* May 3, 1946.

[58] The whole text appears in *Kedaulatan Rakjat,* May 4, 1946.

other three Central Javanese principalities. Urging the people to be calm and patient, the proclamation warned them not to let the problems of a small territory like the Mangkunegaran divide and weaken the national endeavor of Indonesia as a whole.[59] The Mangkunegoro's proclamation was considerably harder in tone than the Susuhunan's and clearly envisaged the retention both of his autonomy vis-à-vis the Sunanate and of a political position analogous to that of the Sultan in Jogjakarta. This tone reflected the Mangkunegoro's relatively stronger position: his personal life was less open to criticism than the Susuhunan's, and the territory of the Mangkunegaran was more traditional and less proletarianized than that of the Sunanate.

The most notable aspect, however, of both the Susuhunan's and the Mangkunegoro's proclamations was that they indirectly appealed for help and protection from Sukarno and the central government in Jogjakarta. As born Solonese, the rulers probably perceived very early the possibilities of mobilizing the cabinet and its supporters against the leaders of the anti-Swapradja (anti–Special Region) movement, many of whom were either former members of the Persatuan Perdjuangan or at least associated with oppositionist groups. It may also have occurred to them that the cabinet might be interested in protecting the financial interests of the courts for reasons of its own. There had already been insistent demands from anti-Swapradja groups that the factories and plantations owned by the Sunanate and Mangkunegaran be socialized, or in other words, turned over to the workers and laborers employed in them.[60] It was reasonable to suppose that the government would be unhappy to see these sources of revenue and patronage fall permanently into hostile hands.

Whether such calculations were in fact made or not, the rulers' appeals met with a gratifyingly rapid response. On May 5 Dr.

[59] *Ibid.*

[60] The Mangkunegoro's May 1 proclamation had specifically stated that these demands were unnecessary, since, it alleged, the enterprises had already been fully socialized.

Sudarsono, the minister of the interior, went to Surakarta to open discussions with both the pro- and the anti-Swapradja group, calling first on the rulers and subsequently on their antagonists.[61] According to at least one report he proposed the formation of an all-Surakarta executive council chaired by the Susuhunan, but was rebuffed by the groups behind Muwardi.[62] In any event Sudarsono issued a proclamation that within seven days a committee would be formed to plan and carry out general elections in the Surakarta area, and that the bodies elected by this process would have the right to settle the question of the Special Region. The Minister added that the Surakarta question must be settled by peaceful and democratic methods.[63] Although at first glance this appeared to be an unexceptionable idea, the anti-Swapradja groups were well aware that elections for the national KNIP, repeatedly promised from the time of the formation of the first Sjahrir cabinet, had in fact never been held. Indeed, no regular elections of any kind had so far been held within the territory of the republic. It was thus natural to suspect, rightly or wrongly, that the government was playing for time in the hope that it could destroy the opposition in the interim.

The anti-Swapradja movement's riposte was a huge rally convened by Muwardi in Surakarta on May 9 and attended by 36 political organizations. A resolution was unanimously passed demanding that the committee to prepare any election be selected from representatives of the political bodies, and that all of the members of the new democratic legislature be directly elected.[64] The aim was clearly to ensure that the government did not pack

[61] *Merdeka,* May 7, 1946.

[62] J. C. Smit, in an untitled article in *NEFIS Periodiek,* no. 9 (June 15, 1946), p. 15.

[63] The full text of the proclamation appears in *Merdeka,* May 7, 1946.

[64] Smit, in *NEFIS Periodiek,* no. 9 (June 15, 1946), 15. Muwardi was evidently confident of popular backing for his movement. In other areas, where government control was stronger, new, "democratized" legislatures had been created on a basis of appointment and indirect elections. (In other words, bodies at the lowest levels were appointed, and these appointees elected members of higher-level legislative bodies.)

the electoral committee or make arrangements for coopted kraton representatives to sit on the new body. Increased pressure was now exerted against the Mangkunegaran, which had hitherto been only sporadically attacked. Twelve of the thirteen members of the Working Committee of the urban kabupatèn Kota Mangkunegaran met and passed resolutions urging the central government to institute a genuinely democratic form of authority in Surakarta, and pointing to the sharp differences in tone between the Susuhunan's proclamation and that of the Mangkunegoro, clearly in criticism of the latter.[65]

On May 17 Sudarsono announced that he had formed an electoral commission for Surakarta and had wired its composition to Soeroso. Its chairman was Subadio Sastrosatomo, and its members were Siswosudarmo, Mr. Atmodiningrat, Soejono, Mr. Sumardi, Suhadi, and Mr. Suwidji.[66] That Subadio was appointed chairman clearly indicated the cabinet's determination to control the electoral committee's operations, for he was a prominent PS member of the KNIP's Working Committee and very close to Sjahrir and Amir.[67]

But regardless of Sudarsono, the social revolution rolled on.

[65] *Merdeka,* May 13, 1946. It is interesting to note the moderate tone of these resolutions by comparison with those of rebellious officials of the Sunanate. For example, the appeal to the central government was more in harmony with court policy than the demands of the more radical anti-Swapradja elements.

[66] *Ibid.,* May 23, 1946.

[67] Subadio was, as we have seen, a key member of the PS executive. Siswosudarmo represented the Masjumi. Atmodiningrat was the brother-in-law of the Susuhunan. He had married G. R. Adjeng Kusdurjatinah, Pakubuwono XII's sister, on December 3, 1945 (see *Soeara Moeda,* Dec. 1, 1945, for the announcement). Soejono, the chairman of the Surakarta KNI, had been imprisoned for six years for his connections with the Communist uprising of 1926, and on his release had worked in the Illegal PKI and the Gerindo. *Harian Rakjat,* July 2, 1962. Suwidji, a graduate of Leiden University, had worked during the Dutch period as an official of the Department of Economic Affairs and later became vice-chairman of the Perserikatan Kaum Keristen (Association of the Christian Community) in Surakarta. *Orang Indonesia,* p. 297. The affiliations of the other members are unknown to me.

The very same day mass meetings were held in Klaten, Sragen, and Bojolali, at which loud demands were voiced for the end of the Special Region; and teachers in the Mangkunegaran areas of Tawangmangu and Wonogiri declared their independence of the Mangkunegaran government, urging that Surakarta be among the first residencies to hold democratic general elections.[68] By May 23 the situation had become critical. All four kabupatèn governments had now broken off relations with the Sunanate. The Surakarta City Working Committee had decided unilaterally to centralize all administration, nominally under Soeroso, but effectively in its own hands. Still more significantly, powerful army leaders in the city, most notably Sutarto and Suadi, openly supported this move.[69]

Accordingly, on that day, the cabinet decided to remove Soeroso, who was felt to be too weak to handle the crisis, and replace him with Soerjo, the governor of East Java, believing that the prestige the latter had acquired in the Surabaja fighting would permit him to solve the crisis. Sudarsono announced that Soerjo would be given full powers to take all actions necessary to restore security in the Surakarta area, and expressed the hope that all groups and strata of society loyal to the republic would show a helpful and cooperative attitude toward the government's efforts.[70] To make doubly sure of their cooperativeness he ordered the arrest of Muwardi and eleven other prominent anti-Swapradja figures, including the core of the KNI.[71]

The detention of the widely respected Muwardi aroused a

[68] *Merdeka,* May 18, 1946.

[69] *Ibid.,* May 23, 1946; Smit, in *NEFIS Periodiek,* no. 9 (June 15, 1946), p. 16.

[70] *Merdeka,* May 25, 1946.

[71] *Bulan Sabit* (June 1, 1946) reported that aside from Muwardi, the key figures arrested included Mangkusudiono, Muljadi Djojomartono, and Hadisunarto, all associated with the Barisan Banteng. According to *Soeara Moeda* (May 26, 1946), the other men arrested were Prodjosu-dodo, Djuwardi, Ronomarsono, and five others, four of whom were chiefs of offices in the Kepatihan. In effect, the whole of the old KNI leadership was put behind bars.

storm in Surakarta. Angry demonstrations began immediately, culminating in a massive rally held jointly on May 28 by the Barisan Banteng, the Hizbullah, and the Special Police. Sudiro, the acting head of the Barisan Banteng, gave the cabinet a 48-hour deadline to release the prisoners; otherwise, he threatened to resign from the leadership of his organization—implying that he would no longer attempt to control his enraged followers.[72] Soerjo attempted to intervene and calm the passions aroused on both sides, but to no avail.

Sudiro's ultimatum had its effect. On May 31 the cabinet announced that Muwardi, Hadisunarto, and Muljadi Djojomartono had been released as a result of discussions between the Surakarta Special Police and Soerjo.[73] This public statement, however, seems to have been a face-saving device for the government. Evidently Barisan Banteng leaders had persuaded General Sudirman to order the prisoners' release.[74] The psychological blow the government had received was accentuated by massive victory parades held in Surakarta to celebrate the return of the political prisoners, and by Soerjo's announcement that "from now on it is absolutely forbidden to make arrests in the Surakarta area without my permission." [75] Thus not only did the anti-Swapradja people appear to be guaranteed immunity from further government interference, but Soerjo had disassociated himself from the original arrests.

Following the release of the Muwardi group, an urgent cabinet session was held, attended by the President, the Vice-President, General Sudirman, and other notables, in which an attempt was

[72] *Kedaulatan Rakjat,* May 29, 1946.

[73] *Merdeka,* May 31, 1946; according to *Bulan Sabit,* June 1, 1946, the prisoners were released on the evening of the 29th.

[74] "SV," p. 46 (testimony of General Sudarsono). Circumstantial evidence is provided by Sudirman's statement warning against unauthorized actions taken in the army's name (*Merdeka,* May 30, 1946), and by an announcement from army headquarters that it "knew nothing of and had nothing to do with the arrests of the evening of May 25" (*Bulan Sabit,* June 1, 1946).

[75] *Merdeka,* May 31, 1946.

made to disguise the government's humiliation. After these discussions a statement was issued that "with the agreement of the cabinet and General Sudirman," [76] a Pemerintah Daerah Rakjat dan Tentara (People's and Army Territorial Government), or PDR&T, would be established in Surakarta as of June 1. With its formation the former governments of the Sunanate, the Mangkunegaran, and the Directorate were to be abolished. Power would henceforth lie in the hands of a six-man Working Committee, consisting of four civilians and two military men, to whom all officials would be subordinated.[77] Soerjo was attached to this committee as "adviser," the "full powers" given to him by Sudarsono ten days before being thus withdrawn.[78] A legislative body headed by the local divisional commander, Colonel Sutarto, would be set up representing all political, economic, and social groups. Simultaneously, Sutarto announced in his own name the composition of the Working Committee. Its chairman was Sudiro (mBah), while its members were Sudiro, general affairs; Sumodihardjo, social affairs; Soejono, economic affairs; Djuwardi, pangrèh pradja affairs; and Sutarto, security. On June 2 Sutarto himself presided over the inauguration of the new regime.[79]

With the formation of the PDR&T, the anti-Swapradja movement had successfully completed its campaign against the Solo-

[76] *Merdeka,* June 3, 1946. Sudirman's virtual parity of status with the cabinet is well illustrated by this phrasing.

[77] *Bulan Sabit* (June 8, 1946) went even further, specifically attributing the appointment of the Working Committee to the army.

[78] "Surakarta Hadiningrat" notes that Soerjo was "in effect disavowed."

[79] *Merdeka,* June 3 and 4, 1946; *Bulan Sabit,* June 8, 1946. Sudiro (mBah) was an old associate of Subardjo at the Asrama Indonesia Merdeka. Sudiro was a top leader of the Barisan Banteng and influential in the PNI. Sumodihardjo was a member of the PBI. Soejono and Djuwardi represented the old KNI leadership. "Surakarta Hadiningrat" gives a different list: Sutarto, chairman; Lieutenant Colonel Fadjar (Sutarto's deputy), secretary; Sudiro (mBah), in charge of general affairs; Dr. Kartono, social affairs; Soejono, political affairs; Domopranoto, pangrèh pradja affairs; and Sutarto Pèjèk (from the Military Police), security. Whichever list is correct, both indicate a Working Committee dominated by anti-Swapradja and anti-government groups.

nese monarchies. In the face of the powerful Barisan Banteng, Sudirman, and the local military under Sutarto, the cabinet had proved impotent.[80] At the time of the March arrests, it had been able to justify its actions in part by denouncing the opposition as undermining the nation's legitimate government. Now, however, it had put itself in the awkward, if not embarrassing, position of attempting to prop up two largely discredited feudal institutions by taking repressive measures against groups with wide local support. The composition of the new regime in Surakarta completely excluded any representatives of kraton interests or even any strong supporters of the central government itself. Jogjakarta and Surakarta had now come into the hands of mutually hostile groups.

In an atmosphere of great tension, people waited anxiously for the cabinet's next move. Meeting in extraordinary session on June 5 in Purworedjo, the KNIP Working Committee accepted a draft law on the declaration of a State of Emergency.[81] The following day Hatta left for Surakarta to warn the local army and political leaders, as well as the rulers, that the President would that night declare a State of Emergency for the Surakarta area. Asked if the government's move was designed to "dissolve" what had been established by the population and the army, Hatta was quick to respond that it was intended simply to bring the local governmental structure into harmony with the law of the state.[82] Sukarno duly made the announcement in a radio address that same evening.

The terms of the new State of Emergency law need some clarification to allow a fuller understanding of the conflict between Surakarta and Jogjakarta. The law specified that in the event of a

[80] It is ironic that in the 1930's Sutarto was the leader of the Madiun branch of the SPI, the radical youth affiliate of Hatta's and Sjahrir's Pendidikan Nasional Indonesia. See Biro Pemuda, *Sedjarah perdjuangan pemuda Indonesia,* p. 73.

[81] *Merdeka,* June 8, 1946. The text may be found in Koesnodiprodjo, ed., *Himpunan undang2, peraturan2, penetapan2 pemerintah Republik Indonesia, 1946* (rev. ed.; Djakarta, 1951), pp. 29–34.

[82] *Kedaulatan Rakjat,* June 7, 1946.

general attack, the danger of such an attack, a rebellion or internal upheaval threatening the paralysis of civil government, or a natural disaster, the president could declare a State of Emergency for the area concerned. In the event of local troubles a Dewan Pertahanan Daerah (Regional Defense Council), or DPD, would be formed, consisting of the resident (as chairman), two members of the Executive Board of the local legislative body, the senior military commander in the area, and three representatives of popular organizations. The DPD would have virtually absolute powers to suspend civil liberties for a limited period, but would be answerable ultimately to the cabinet or, in the event of a national emergency, to the State Defense Council (Dewan Pertahanan Negara). If put into effect, this law would have done exactly what Hatta had promised not to do—dissolve the PDR&T. Accordingly, on June 7 a special Government Regulation was issued as a gloss to the original law, stating that in Surakarta a different arrangement would be made: the DPD chairman would be the senior military officer in the area, not the resident, while a member of the "civil government" would act as his deputy. Other members would be as specified in the main law.[83]

The day following the declaration of the State of Emergency in Surakarta, the government took advantage of severe fighting between Dutch and Indonesian troops in Tanggerang, which had resulted in an appalling pogrom against local Chinese, to declare a general State of Emergency for the whole of Java and Madura.[84] Supreme authority now passed, theoretically at least, into the hands of the projected State Defense Council.[85]

On June 10, in the presence of Hatta, Sudirman, Amir, the

[83] For the State of Emergency law (no. 6/1946) and the Government Regulation amending it, see Koesnodiprodjo, ed., *Himpunan, 1946*, pp. 81–82.

[84] Actually, both the fighting and the pogrom were over by June 4, or before the State of Emergency was declared. But it is possible the government did not know this. For a description of the massacres see the vivid reports of Rosihan Anwar in *Merdeka*, June 13 and 14, 1946; see also Mary Frances Ann Somers, "Peranakan Chinese Politics in Indonesia" (Ph.D. thesis, Cornell University, 1965), pp. 112–18.

[85] *Merdeka*, June 8, 1946.

Susuhunan, and the Mangkunegoro, the DPD-Surakarta was formally inaugurated, superseding the PDR&T, but headed by Sutarto, with Sudiro (mBah), Sudiro, Sumodihardjo, Siswosudarmo, Soejono, Djuwardi, and R. Sudirman as members.[86] None of these men belonged to groups supporting the cabinet. Two days later Sutarto organized all the different local lasjkar into a Joint Lasjkar of Surakarta (Gabungan Lasjkar Surakarta) under his own control.[87] Not long afterward Sudarsono was forced to announce that Soerjo would return to his old job as governor of East Java and that Soeroso would return as the central government's representative in Surakarta.[88]

Nothing the cabinet had managed to do since the failure of the May coup against Muwardi had improved its position. The declaration of the State of Emergency helped to conceal the defeat it had suffered, since all government in Java and Madura was now put on an emergency basis, superficially similar to the situation in Surakarta. But the special features of the government regulations on the governing body in that area, and the fact that the declaration of the State of Emergency was proclaimed there first, are clear evidence that it was in Surakarta, not in Tanggerang or in Djakarta, that the government found itself most severely challenged.

In retrospect the crisis in Surakarta, like the social revolutions in other parts of Java, clearly illustrates the ironies and complexities of the revolutionary process. The conspicuous discrepancy between the government's antifeudal public stance and its attempts to restrain or reverse the anti-Swapradja movement cannot simply be attributed to opportunism and hypocrisy. It is quite conceivable that under other circumstances, the cabinet would

[86] *Kedaulatan Rakjat,* June 11, 1946. All were members of the PDR&T except Siswosudarmo (from the Masjumi) and Sudirman, who had earlier been Soerjo's subordinate as Resident of Surabaja.

[87] *Ibid.,* June 13, 1946. In this new organization the Barisan Banteng was given charge of the key Lasjkar Section, while the Pesindo was awarded the Administration Section.

[88] *Merdeka,* June 26, 1946.

have endorsed, however cautiously, the end of aristocratic privilege in the principalities. But the logic of diplomasi led in quite opposite directions than the social revolutions. The overriding need to reach a diplomatic settlement with the Dutch pushed the cabinet leaders in an increasingly conservative direction, as the pattern of events in Banten and Pekalongan makes quite clear. In the case of Surakarta the same logic prevailed, its force compounded by the nexus between a local social revolutionary movement and the national opposition. The necessity of combating this opposition led the government into an alliance with traditional authorities; and the opposition, defeated in Jogjakarta, found new cause for hope in linking itself to the anti-Swapradja movement in Surakarta. After May 1946 local and national politics were inextricably entangled in Surakarta, and the resultant crisis culminated in the bizarre events that have gone down in history as the July Third Affair.

Chapter 16

The July Third Affair

While the oppositionist and social revolutionary movement in Surakarta was gathering momentum in April, May, and June of 1946, the government's political position was deteriorating in two other significant respects. A storm was brewing in the army, and the possibilities for a diplomatic settlement with the Dutch decreased sharply as a result of the elections held in the Netherlands on May 17. It was the increasing entanglement of these military and diplomatic problems with the imbroglio in Surakarta that finally precipitated the July Third Affair.

Ever since the conflict over the appointment of Sudirman as panglima besar, the relations between the cabinet (particularly the minister of defense, Amir Sjarifuddin) and army headquarters had been characterized by suspicion and mistrust. The antagonism had deepened as a consequence of the March razzias, to which Sudirman had been strongly opposed. Persistent rumors circulated that the government had a blacklist of high military officers marked for purging; there was no lack of counter-rumors that certain officers were planning some kind of action against the government. The atmosphere was one in which suspicion fed on suspicion, each side attempting to anticipate the other's moves, and attributing to the other the worst of motives.

The creation of the Education Staff, subsequently known as the Staf Pendidikan Politik Tentara, or "Pepolit," for the purpose of giving the army political education, was a sore point from the start. As we have seen earlier, this institution was dominated by members of the PS and Masjumi. Many officers who were unsympathetic to these two parties resented the Pepolit and regarded it as likely to split the army by accentuating political cleavages, encouraging cliques and favoritism, and presaging a system of promotions based on political criteria. It was easy to believe that the agency would be used to compile dossiers for the rumored blacklists. The Pepolit itself had encouraged such suspicions by taking a clear pro-cabinet stand during the March crisis. It had issued a statement on March 25 urging the population to look on the government as the "father of the whole people," not simply of one or two aliran. Furthermore, it insisted that the Ministry of Defense's "recent actions" had been necessary in an emergency situation; like a child learning to walk, the young republic needed "firm guidance." [1] Early in April it became evident that the government intended to enlarge the Pepolit and expand the scope of its activities. It was announced that a Pepolit training school was being established to produce "education officers" who would be attached to each divisional command.[2] Sudirman's response was quick. On April 20 he announced the formation of an Advisory Council to the Supreme Army Leadership, which, while including representation from the Pesindo, was heavily weighted with oppositionist figures.[3] Instructions were also issued to the divisional commanders to appoint comparable advisory bodies for themselves, though the Panglima Besar was

[1] Antara, March 25, 1946.   [2] Ibid., April 8, 1946.

[3] Ibid., April 23, 1946. The members were Sajuti Melok (Central Java Resistance Council and Pesindo); Dr. Muwardi (Barisan Banteng); Tirwan (West Java Resistance Council); Kusnandar (East Java Resistance Council and Pesindo), Wachid Hasjim (GPII), Bung Tomo (BPRI), and Mohammed Saleh Werdisastro (KNI and Lasjkar Rakjat, Jogjakarta). The officially stated purpose of the Advisory Council was to improve the liaison between the army and the badan perdjuangan. This can be understood as a response to moves being made by Amir Sjarifuddin to bring the badan perdjuangan under the influence of the Ministry of Defense by establishing a Resistance Bureau (Biro Perdjuangan) directed by Major General Djokosoejono.

shrewd enough to leave the choice of personnel up to the individual commander.[4]

Conflict also arose over the structures and jurisdictions of the Ministry of Defense and the Army General Headquarters, as well as over the appointment of divisional commanders. On February 23 a committee had been set up under Maj. Gen. Didi Kartasasmita to make basic recommendations for the reorganization of the Ministry of Defense, the structure of the army (its optimum strength, its organizational format, and the scope and limits of its authority), and the status of lasjkar not directly associated with the government.[5] While the necessity of rationalizing and centralizing the military command was agreed upon, the antagonism between Amir's and Sudirman's supporters made the committee's task delicate and difficult. Not until May 25 were its final recommendations officially announced.[6] On one level at least, the outcome was clearly a victory for the government. The Army General Headquarters, Sudirman's bailiwick, was to be confined strictly to planning and executing military operations. Its administrative structure would consist of a mere seven sections under the day-to-day supervision of General Urip Sumohardjo.[7]

[4] General Sudarsono, the divisional commander in Jogjakarta, included in his board of advisers two well-known oppositionists, Dr. Buntaran, the minister of health of the Sukarno cabinet, and his younger brother, Mr. R. S. Boeddhyarto Martoatmodjo, the recently deposed resident of Besuki. All three were to be deeply involved in the July Third Affair; see "SV," pp. 298–99 (Tirtawinata's speech for the prosecution).

[5] The members of this committee were Maj. Gen. Didi Kartasasmita; Maj. Gen. Kaprawi; the chief of the Airborne Section of the Armed Forces, Maj. Gen. Suriadarma; Lt. Col. Sukandar; Lt. Col. Sujoto; Lt. Col. R. Hollan Iskandar; Maj. T. B. Simatupang; Lt. Gen. Urip Sumohardjo; Col. R. Sutirto; Prof. Soepomo; Prof. Ir. Rooseno; Dr. Mustopo; and, as secretary, Mr. Sajid Mangunjudo. See *Antara*, Feb. 28, 1946.

[6] *Kedaulatan Rakjat,* May 27, 1946. Nasution, however, gives the date as May 21; *Tentara Nasional Indonesia*, p. 249.

[7] Under Urip were Col. Dr. Sutjipto (Peta), as chief of intelligence; Col. T. B. Simatupang (KNIL), for organization; Col. R. Hollan Iskandar (Peta), strategy; Col. R. Sutirto (Peta), command; Lt. Col. Sumardjono, transport; Lt. Col. Surjo, secretariat; and Major Mahmud, administration.

The Ministry of Defense, on the other hand, contained at least twice as many sections, indicating its much more complex bureaucratic structure and the broad range of its functions. Most important, the Military Police were made directly responsible to the minister of defense.[8]

On the question of the divisional commands, however, the ascendancy of the ministry was by no means so apparent. Didi Kartasasmita's committee had recommended that these commands be reduced in number from ten to seven. While this recommendation was accepted by all parties, there was no agreement on who should take up the new command positions. Since it seemed impracticable to break the tradition of filling senior army positions by election, the conflict took the form of lobbying for the votes of regimental officers. The first round of these elections was held in Jogjakarta on May 23. Some idea of the character of these proceedings can be gleaned from Nasution: "From [the new] Division I [which was to cover the old divisions I and III and part of II] 15 officers attended, to make a choice between the former divisional commanders, i.e., Maj. Gen. Didi Kartasas-

---

[8] The ministry was organized as follows: Director-General, Maj. Gen. Sudibjo (KNIL); chief of staff to the minister of defense, Maj. Gen. Muhammad (Peta); chief of personnel, Col. Sundjojo (Peta); advocate-general, Maj. Gen. Kasman Singodimedjo (Peta); chief of military education, Maj. Gen. R. Suwardi (KNIL); chief of military service, Maj. Gen. Suratman (KNIL); chief of artillery, Lt. Col. R. M. P. R. Soerjosoemarno (KNIL); chief of infantry, Maj. Gen. R. Didi Kartasasmita (KNIL); chief of topography, Lt. Col. Ir. Sutomo Wongsotjitro; chief of engineers, Maj. Gen. Ir. Hudioro; chief of supply, Maj. Gen. R. M. Sutomo (Peta); chief of administration, Lt. Col. Sudibjo; chief of procurement, Lt. Col. Partodidjojo; chief of ordnance, Col. Soerjosoelarso (KNIL); chief of health, Maj. Gen. Dr. Wirasmo; chief of military police, Maj. Gen. Santosa (Peta); deputy chief of military police, Col. Sunarjo (Peta).

Nasution accounts for the discrepancies in the ranks given these officers by stating that intense rivalries and pressures for promotions led the government to make large-scale upward revisions in ranks during the course of the Jogjakarta meetings. Cf. *Kedaulatan Rakjat,* May 27, 1946; and *Tentara Nasional Indonesia,* pp. 250, 255.

mita, Col. Kjai Sjam'oen, Col. Abdul Kadir, and myself. I was elected with 12 votes, and Col. Abdul Kadir was elected also as commander of [the new] Division II." [9] The results as a whole were as follows:

Division I (West Java minus Tasikmalaja and Tjirebon), Maj. Gen. A. H. Nasution (KNIL); chief of staff, Lieutenant Colonel Askari (KNIL)

Division II (Tjirebon-Tasikmalaja-Tegal-Banjumas), Major General Abdul Kadir (Peta); chief of staff, Lt. Col. Bambang Sugeng (Peta)

Division III (Pekalongan-Kedu-Jogjakarta), Maj. Gen. Sudarsono (Police); chief of staff, Lt. Col. M. Sarbini (Peta)

Division IV (Surakarta-Semarang-Madiun), Major General Soediro (Peta); chief of staff, Lt. Col. Fadjar (Peta)

Division V (Pati-Bodjonegoro), Maj. Gen. G. P. H. Djatikusumo (KNIL and Peta); chief of staff, Lieutenant Colonel Wadijono (Peta)

Division VI (Kediri-Surabaja-Madiun), Major General Sungkono (Peta); chief of staff, Lieutenant Colonel Marhadi (Peta)

Division VII (Malang-Besuki), Maj. Gen. Imam Sudja'i (Peta); chief of staff, Lt. Col. Iskandar Sulaiman (Peta). [10]

Three brigade commanders were also elected: Col. Kjai Sjam'oen, Col. Gatot Subroto, and Colonel Sutarto. [11]

From the beginning, however, at least in the politically sensitive divisions III (Jogjakarta) and IV (Surakarta), the appointments of May 23 would not stick, probably because the electors assembled were not regarded as sufficiently representative or be-

[9] Nasution, *Tentara Nasional Indonesia,* p. 252; see also Sedjarah Militer Kodam VI, *Siliwangi dari masa kemasa,* p. 79.

[10] Of these figures, Nasution had been commander of the old Division III; Abdul Kadir had been Sudirman's successor as commander of the old Division V; Sudarsono had been commander of the old Division IX; Soediro had been commander of the old Division VI; Djatikusumo had been commander of the old Division IV; Sungkono had been commander of the old Division VII; and Imam Sudja'i had been commander of the old Division VIII.

[11] Nasution, *Tentara Nasional Indonesia,* pp. 252, 256.

cause it was thought that government pressures had distorted the results. In the case of Division III, the nomination of Sarbini, the regimental commander in Magelang, as chief of staff was strongly resisted by the commander, General Sudarsono, and his closest associates. Accordingly, when the inauguration ceremonies took place on May 25, it was an old Jogjakarta hand, Lt. Col. Umar Djoy, and not Sarbini who was sworn in as chief of staff.[12] In Surakarta the rebuff was even sharper. The appointment of Soediro as commander of Division IV was taken as an attempt to oust Colonel Sutarto, the strong man of the anti-Swapradja movement, and the Colonel's backers refused to accept Soediro as their new chief. The Ministry of Defense was unable to shake his position and was ultimately forced to accept his appointment and promotion to major general.[13]

In both Jogjakarta and Surakarta, then, powerful local military commanders had won their way. But perhaps more important was the long-range aftermath of the battle, for all sides were increasingly conscious of the political implications of the encounter. Sudarsono and Sutarto, in particular, became aware of the need to defend their positions, and tended to move into closer alliance with the opponents of the government. It would be wrong, however, to infer from these conflicts that nothing more than position and power was at stake. From the start, as we have seen, Sudirman and Amir represented two contrasting views of the army and its role, and the disagreements over the Pepolit, the organization of the defense establishment, and the appointment of divisional commanders were in part expressions of an intense competition for the loyalty of the military as a group. If anything this competition grew sharper after March, because by then the battlefronts had stabilized and the tempo of fighting had slackened off, while at the same time the government was pressing ahead with its diplomatic initiatives.

It may seem difficult, in retrospect, to understand how it was

[12] For a nice description of Sudarsono's triumph, see *ibid.*, p. 192. See also *Al Djihad,* May 25 and 27, 1946.

[13] "Sedjarah TNI, Diponegoro," pp. 75–76.

that the young panglima besar was able to hold his own against the more sophisticated political leaders in the government and the ambitions of his fellow officers, particularly after the fall of the Persatuan Perdjuangan and the arrests of its chief promoters. Part of the answer can perhaps be sensed from a radio address delivered by Sudirman on April 9, 1946, reminding the army of its duty to defend the nation's integrity and liberty to the last:

All of you, my children! . . . Never let any soldier of ours break his promise and betray his country, his people and his religion. Fulfill the oath of service you have sworn. We have all sworn together, let us now fulfill that promise.

I know that all of you have suffered much in the army—so different from what most outside the army imagine. The army is a place for suffering, and a place for self-sacrifice. All of you, those who were once soldiers in the Dutch army, in the Peta, in the Heihō, all of you have suffered—in the Dutch period, the Japanese period, and now in the period of Indonesia Merdeka. But even though you are now suffering all kinds of hardships, these represent your devotion to your country, your people and your religion.

I know that there are amongst you all some who have entered the army and now wish to leave it, to carry on the struggle outside the army where everything is far freer. All of you, my children, who were once civilians and officials—among you there are many who are dismayed and disappointed. You believed that once inside the army you would live in comfort, and as freely as outside. All your wants would be satisfied—and yet it turned out not to be so. . . . You believed that all the needs of your families would be fulfilled, as in the days of the Dutch colonial army. But in the Japanese period, and now in the period of Indonesia Merdeka, the families of our soldiers are always like any other families, and like our people as a whole. . . .

It is indeed a hard and bitter thing to be a soldier. Particularly since you are all bound by the discipline of the army: Always carry out orders without dissent—No order may be bargained with. But you must all understand and believe that the high command of your army will not permit any orders to be issued that conflict with the ideology of the people and of the whole Indonesian nation. I myself deeply believe that all of you, as soldiers, will never despair and never run aground in your voyage. For all your sufferings and all your sacrifices have been sincerely made for a holy purpose, the defense of truth and justice. Self-sacrifice must become the armor of our struggle. Strengthen your conviction! Purify your hearts and your deeds! Make firm your unity! With God's Grace the victory will be with us, for God is All-knowing and Most Just.

All of you must remember: there will be no victory if there is no strength. There will be no strength if there is no unity. There will be no unity if there is no excellence [keutamaan]. There will be no excellence if there is no spiritual teaching that can consecrate all our endeavors.

Therefore our struggle from now on must be a struggle which is truly pure and holy. . . .

In conclusion then, my message to you is this:

Have faith in your own strength.

Continue your struggle.

Defend the homes and courtyards of us all.

Never let our army know any attitudes or acts of surrender to anyone whatever who tries to rule or oppress us once again.

Hold firmly to the discipline of the army, outwardly to the world and inwardly in your hearts.[14]

It would be hard to imagine words more different from those of a Sjahrir, an Amir, a Hatta, or even a Sukarno. The Dutch are barely mentioned. There is no appeal to the symbols of military glory. Indeed, nothing is more striking than the pervasive sadness. But Sudirman knew his audience, and spoke out of the culture he shared with his listeners. In his stress on spiritual purity and sincerity, on the moral qualities of the soldier, and on the need for austerity and self-sacrifice, one can see a harmonious blend of ancient Javanese conceptions of the satria-warrior and the values of the Japanese military ethos at its best. It was quite in keeping with his words that only a few days later he issued orders that the entire Indonesian army should fast for three days "to deepen our consciousness of the purity of our struggle to

14 *Antara,* April 10, 1946.

demand 100 per cent Merdeka, to strengthen the sincerity of our determination to attain our ideals, and to heighten our courage for battle." [15] In him a deeply rooted tradition found an authentic voice, and this was surely part of the secret of his charisma.[16]

While the malaise in the army grew, the government suffered a severe setback on the diplomatic front that eventually encouraged a partial revival of those political forces that seemed to have been decisively defeated in March. The delegation that had left for Holland early in April came away at the end of the month without having reached any agreement with the government in The Hague.[17] Both the Dutch and the Indonesians made what each felt to be far-reaching concessions, but the shadow of the imminent elections in the Netherlands lay heavily on the negotiations. And when the polling of May 17 was over, it was at once clear that Dutch public opinion had moved sharply to the right. The Catholic People's Party, led by the arch-conservative Professor Romme, emerged as the largest fraction in the Second Chamber, while Schermerhorn's socialists, in whom the Sjahrir cabinet had the greatest confidence, dropped into second place.[18]

In Indonesia the main consequence of these developments was to lessen optimism about a rapid diplomatic settlement and to strengthen the position of those who argued that the Dutch would soon undertake a military offensive against the republic. Renewed pressures began to be exerted for a further cabinet reshuffle "in order to strengthen the republic against the Dutch." Early in May, at the initiative of Sarmidi Mangunsarkoro, a conference attended by virtually all the major parties and badan

[15] *Ibid.,* April 13, 1946.

[16] Another aspect of this charisma may have been his austere, melancholy appearance. One can get a sharp sense of this from the photographs of him included in Indonesia, Kementerian Penerangan, *Lukisan Revolusi,* pp. 367, 395, and, in nice contrast with other senior officers, p. 207.

[17] For a full analysis of these talks, see Djajadiningrat, *Beginnings of Indonesian-Dutch Negotiations,* esp. appendix F, which shows clearly the precise differences between the final positions of the negotiators.

[18] *Ibid.,* p. 123.

perdjuangan was convened to create a loosely federated National Concentration to strengthen national unity in the face of the bad news from Holland.[19] When the National Concentration met in plenary session on May 25, the focus of its lengthy discussions was the failure of the negotiations and the steps to be taken as a result. While the group announced its general support for the government's position, it expressed the hope that this support would help to "strengthen the hitherto weak and hesitant attitude of the government." The leadership council voted narrowly in favor of the formation of a genuine coalition cabinet that would, however, continue to work within the framework of the Five-Point Program.[20] On the two following days joint meetings were held between the cabinet and the National Concentration's spokesmen, with the President and Vice-President also in attendance. The details of these talks were not made public, but it was clear from the tone of the statements subsequently put out by the various parties that the deteriorating diplomatic climate and the crisis in Surakarta had seriously weakened the cabinet's position.[21]

But still the cabinet leaders stubbornly held their ground. Their resistance was by no means simply the product of hunger for office and distrust of the opposition. It had been strongly conveyed to Sjahrir in Djakarta and to the Indonesian delegates in Holland that the most fundamental obstacle to a settlement

---

[19] Those attending included, *inter alia*, the PS, PNI, Masjumi, PBI, Catholic Party, Parkindo, PKI, Pesindo, Barisan Banteng, KRIS, BPRI, GPII, BBI, BTI, and Muhammadijah. It was agreed that the organization would have a leadership council in which the chairman would be drawn from the now pro-government PKI; the two vice-chairmen from Masjumi and the PS; the two secretaries from the PNI and the women's organization Perwari; the treasurer from the BBI; and other members from the PBI, Pesindo, and BTI. Obviously the position of the government in this structure was reasonably strong. See *Merdeka*, May 8, 1946, for full details.

[20] *Kedaulatan Rakjat*, May 27, 1946; *Merdeka*, May 28, 1946.

[21] See, e.g., the Joint Proclamation of the PNI, PBI, and Masjumi, contained in *Merdeka*, May 29, 1946.

was the Dutch public's uneasiness about the "radical" and "revolutionary" situation prevailing in Java. Both van Mook and the Schermerhorn cabinet had indicated that whereas they had full personal confidence in Sjahrir, negotiations would be considerably more difficult should he be replaced by another man who might be more acceptable to opinion in Central Java.[22] Sjahrir was thus in the paradoxical situation that a major element in his political strength, his acceptability to Dutch public opinion, prevented him from building a solid base of support in Indonesia. A broad coalition cabinet might have given him this kind of domestic backing (though this was by no means a certainty, given the intense competition for power in Jogjakarta), but it would have decisively weakened his bargaining power with The Hague. For any yielding to opposition demands would have been taken by the Dutch as a sign that the radicals were in the ascendant, and this in turn would have encouraged the "hawks" in Holland to redouble their pressure for a military strike against the republic. Sjahrir thus realized very well that his capacity to deal with van Mook depended in large degree on his success in silencing or winning over the opposition without making any serious concessions to it. While in pure logic this demanded a tough domestic policy, the crisis in Surakarta and the malaise in the army suggested that such a policy might be very dangerous.

The government's response to these growing pressures took two forms. The proclamation of a State of Emergency first in Surakarta and then in all of Java and Madura was designed not only to deal with the deteriorating situation in the "city of the opposition," but to create an atmosphere of national crisis that would rally public support to the government. The cabinet may

[22] See Djajadiningrat, *Beginnings of Indonesian-Dutch Negotiations*, pp. 92–94. Djajadiningrat notes that during the negotiations at Hoge Veluwe, "Minister Logemann underscored the revolutionary character of the Republic as the greatest obstacle to arriving at peaceful conditions in Indonesia. In this respect, the problem for the Dutch government was how to liquidate the revolutionary situation so as to make the Republic acceptable to the Dutch people."

also have calculated that by giving the military an increased legal role in government, the proclamation would mitigate some of the suspicion and discontent in that quarter. At the same time Sjahrir decided to reopen the stalled negotiations. On June 17 he forwarded to van Mook secret counterproposals to the standing Dutch position since the failure of the talks at Hoge Veluwe. The content of these counterproposals actually represented a hardening of the Indonesian stance by comparison with the proposals of March 27. There was now no talk of a Union with the Netherlands, but rather simply of normal international relationships between two independent states. Sjahrir also stood by his earlier insistence that The Hague recognize the republic's de facto authority over Java and Sumatra, and that the landing of further Dutch troops be halted.[23]

Though these counterproposals were supposed to be kept secret, word of their content quickly began to leak out in the Dutch press in Djakarta. Rumors spread rapidly to Central Java and were often highly distorted in the process. By June 25 the most influential newspaper in Jogjakarta, *Kedaulatan Rakjat,* was already publishing harsh editorials denouncing the government's silence and evasiveness on the nature of the rumored counterproposals, and noting that at the very least it might deny unofficial Dutch reports that Sjahrir had offered to accept de facto recognition of Java and Sumatra alone.[24] Since this offer was, in fact, a key element in the government's proposals, it is understandable that Sjahrir was reluctant to take up the challenge. But the atmosphere was so thick with suspicion that the silence had to be broken. Accordingly, on June 27, in a speech celebrating the Prophet's Ascension to Heaven, Vice-President Hatta explained the content of the counterproposals before a huge crowd in the main square of Jogjakarta, in the presence of Sukarno and most of the top political leaders. Immediately after the meeting he held a press conference in which he stated that

[23] Smit, *De liquidatie,* p. 37.
[24] *Kedaulatan Rakjat,* June 25 and 26, 1946.

he had been compelled to make the speech because of the poisonous cloud of rumors spread by the opposition press. He concluded by warning that the government was ready to take firm action if it should prove necessary.[25]

The government's anxieties were clearly revealed by two important decisions made at this time. It was announced that as of June 26, Sudirman was being promoted to the position of supreme commander of the entire armed forces, responsible directly to Sukarno; [26] and that within the week the national police would be removed from the Ministry of the Interior and placed directly under Sjahrir.[27] But if the government was worried, the opposition was no less so. Everyone remembered that the March arrests had virtually coincided with a diplomatic initiative, and there was wide concern that with the counterproposals now in Dutch hands, the emergency powers being assumed by the government presaged renewed repression against its critics.

In this atmosphere of anxiety and fear, events began to move with great rapidity. Among those who had listened to Hatta's speech with varying degrees of indignation were such well-known opposition figures as Buntaran, Boeddhyarto, Subardjo, Iwa Kusumasumantri, and Chaerul Saleh. After the meeting these men gathered at the house of Boeddhyarto, where they were joined by others of the same persuasion, including Sajuti

[25] "SV," p. 243 (testimony of Sumantoro, editor of *Kedaulatan Rakjat*).

[26] *Merdeka*, June 29, 1946. This promotion conferred prestige rather than power on Sudirman, and was intended to draw him to the government's side. The size of the republic's navy and air force was very small, and their organization was rudimentary. Moreover, their commanders sat on the State Defense Council along with Sudirman, and Sukarno stated that responsibility for the services' performance would continue to lie with their respective commanders.

[27] See Oudang, *Perkembangan kepolisian*, pp. 68–69; and Koesnodiprodjo, ed., *Himpunan, 1946*, p. 296. It should be noted that this move stemmed in part from long-standing rivalries between the police and the regular civil servants of the pangrèh pradja. In the Dutch period the police had been subordinated to the pangrèh pradja, but during the Japanese occupation they had won a large degree of autonomy.

Melik, General Sudarsono, the commander of the Third Division, and a young subordinate of his, Abdulkadir Jusuf, who happened also to be a relative of Iwa.[28] While there was a general feeling that something should be done, the long discussions produced no agreement on what concrete steps to take. When the group broke up Sudarsono returned home accompanied by Jusuf. The 23-year-old Jusuf, who had been a pupil at Maeda's Asrama Indonesia Merdeka and had won Sjahrir's approval as one of his best students, had made a reputation for himself in the Djakarta-Bogor area during the Siap period. Subsequently he had moved to Jogjakarta with the government, and by early March headed a so-called Red Pesindo battalion there, consisting mainly of migrant Sundanese. In the army reorganization of May he was given the rank of major, and his battalion was incorporated into Sudarsono's Third Division.[29]

At Sudarsono's house Jusuf spoke bitterly about the Sjahrir government's betrayal of Indonesia Merdeka and urged his commander to allow him to "remove" Sjahrir, on the assumption

[28] As we have seen, Buntaran and Boeddhyarto had recently been appointed by Sudarsono as his political advisers. For biographical details on Boeddhyarto, see the Appendix. Somewhat conflicting versions of what occurred during these discussions can be found in "SV," pp. 202 (testimony of Subardjo), 24 (Sudarsono), 216 (Boeddhyarto), and 236 (Sajuti Melik). According to Sudarsono, Subardjo remarked in Dutch that the "government has had its turn, and they've bungled it"—which would not be entirely out of character. The government was later to claim that the discussions focused on plans for kidnapping Sjahrir, but there is no real evidence to support this claim, and against it is the explicit denial of Sajuti Melik, who enjoyed a high reputation for honesty (and who was acquitted at the trials held in 1948 on the July Third Affair). It should be noted that none of these men had been arrested at the time of the March razzias with the exception of Chaerul Saleh, who was released without explanation on June 4. See *Kedaulatan Rakjat*, June 4, 1946.

[29] See Sjahrir, *Out of Exile*, p. 252. Jusuf is not named, but the reference is quite clear. "Sedjarah TNI, Diponegoro," p. 79. According to the latter source Jusuf's battalion had its headquarters in Kotabaru, the residential section of Jogjakarta, close by the Lempujangan railway station.

384 JAVA IN A TIME OF REVOLUTION

that with the Prime Minister out of the way Sukarno and Sudirman would take full power and reverse government policy toward the Dutch. Sudarsono evidently yielded to the young man's pleas, and signed written orders for the apprehension of Sjahrir, Dr. Sudarsono, and Abdulmadjid.[30] It may seem curious, even improbable, that the choleric, 45-year-old general would permit himself to be talked into sanctioning this classic daulat operation by a junior officer half his age. But the psychological ascendancy of the pemuda in the early revolution should not be underestimated. It was common enough for older leaders (perhaps especially in the military, given the peculiar history of its growth) to feel under great pressure to prove their audacity and selfless courage to their pemuda followers and thereby maintain their prestige as authentic revolutionaries.

In any event Jusuf left to find Iwa, and the pair proceeded to Surakarta late that afternoon.[31] It was known that Sjahrir would

[30] See "SV," p. 261 (speech of prosecutor Tirtawinata).

[31] It seems obvious that Jusuf would have shown Sudarsono's orders to Iwa, given the close family relationship between the two men. This was later averred by the government; see *ibid.*, p. 277 (speech of prosecutor Tirtawinata, on the basis of pretrial interrogations of Iwa). In Surakarta, Iwa spent the night with Dr. Kartono, an old friend and in one view at least the civilian *éminence grise* behind Sutarto, the military commander in Surakarta (see "Surakarta Hadiningrat"). At Kartono's house Iwa was joined by none other than Muhammad Yamin, who was presumably informed of what was afoot. Yamin had been held under detention since April in the mountain resort of Tawangmangu, about 40 kilometers east of Surakarta on the slopes of the Gunung Lawu. With him were other leading victims of the March razzias, including Tan Malaka, Abikusno, and Sukarni. The prisoners were allowed to move quite freely around the largely deserted resort, under the tolerant eye of the local battalion commander, Major Sastrolawu. They received occasional visits from such persons as Sukarno, Hatta, and Sudirman (the purposes of which are not at all clear). In April or May, Subardjo, and later Iwa, took up residence in Tawangmangu to be near them and to keep them in touch with developments in Djakarta and Jogjakarta. Yamin had evidently heard Hatta's June 27 speech on the radio and using the pretext of urgent family matters had persuaded his guards to let him visit Surakarta briefly that evening. See "SV," pp. 200–201 (testimony of Subardjo), 261, 285 (speech of prosecutor Tirtawinata), and

be spending the night there on his way back from a tour in East Java in the company of Dr. Sudarsono, Major General Sudibjo, Sumitro Djojohadikusumo, and others.[32] The Sjahrir group would be staying at the former residence of the head of the Javaasche Bank, and the responsibility for guard duty there had been assigned to the Military Police. Accordingly Jusuf went to the Military Police to gain their cooperation in the projected daulat action, but found them hesitant and confused. It was clear that nothing could be achieved without the approval of General Sutarto, the local "strong man," and so Jusuf set off to find him. Sutarto proved cooperative and gave orders to cut off all telephone communications out of Surakarta, halt all unauthorized motor traffic in and out of the city, and alert the Military Police posts in Gembongan, Kartasura, and Bojolali to permit free passage to Jusuf once the arrests had taken place. The guards at the Javaasche Bank were also silently withdrawn. At 11:15 P.M. Jusuf entered the building with four men, and in spite of Sjahrir's protests, forced the Prime Minister's entourage at gunpoint to get into the cars waiting below. The whole group then drove swiftly off to the hill village of Paras, about 35 kilometers west of Surakarta on the slopes of the Gunung Merbabu. There the prisoners were lodged in the unoccupied summer bungalow of the Susuhunan under the guard of Major Soekarto, the local battalion commander.[33] The daulat operation had thus been successfully completed. It remained to be seen whether the government would draw the moral lesson the operation, very much in the pemuda tradition, had been intended to convey.

156–57 (testimony of Yamin). Sastrolawu was responsible to General Sutarto in Surakarta.

[32] According to *Al Djihad* (June 26, 1946) Sjahrir arrived by plane in Surakarta on June 25 on his way to East Java. His group was scheduled to return via Surakarta to Jogjakarta to attend a plenary cabinet session along with Sukarno and Hatta.

[33] "Sedjarah TNI, Diponegoro," p. 27; and, for a detailed description of the preparations for the daulat operation highlighting Sutarto's role, "Surakarta Hadiningrat."

Any such hopes were rapidly dispelled. When the rump cabinet met on the morning of June 28, it was decided at the insistence of Hatta and Amir that martial law should immediately be declared for the whole of Indonesia, and that the State Defense Council should be installed at once with full powers to take any steps deemed necessary.[34] By special decree Sukarno took over Sjahrir's position as the council's chairman.[35] The news of the kidnappings was withheld from the public while urgent efforts were made to discover the missing Prime Minister's whereabouts and negotiate his return. At the same time the government wired Djakarta requesting a general cease-fire on all fronts, fearing that the Dutch might otherwise take advantage of the crisis in Central Java to launch an offensive.[36]

While the government extended its search for Sjahrir and tried to discover who had been responsible for his disappearance, the day passed quietly enough, the public being largely ignorant of what had transpired. In the morning Jusuf, Iwa, and Yamin drove up to Tawangmangu to inform the March 17 detainees of what had occurred. Reactions were evidently mixed, some feeling pleased, others alarmed at what they regarded as a rash action on Jusuf's part.[37] Their mission accomplished, the three men

[34] According to Koesnodiprodjo, ed., *Himpunan, 1946* (p. 251), the decree was signed at 1:00 A.M. on June 29; see also Jungschlaeger, "Double Coup," p. 1.

[35] Koesnodiprodjo, ed., *Himpunan, 1946,* p. 94. This decree was Peraturan Pemerintah Pengganti Undang-Undang 1946, nomor 4, signed by Sukarno alone on June 29, 1946. But compare Sukarno's speech of June 30, where he says that he took full power into his hands on the twenty-eighth. *Kedaulatan Rakjat,* July 1, 1946. The composition of the State Defense Council as given in *Merdeka,* June 29, 1946, was as follows: chairman, Sukarno; first vice-chairman, Hatta; second vice-chairman, Amir Sjarifuddin; members, Sudirman, Suriadarma (the air force chief of staff), Urip, M. Nazir (the navy chief of staff), and Sudibjo, acting secretary. However, the council's composition was considerably altered by the time the inauguration actually took place.

[36] Smit, *De liquidatie,* p. 41.

[37] "SV," p. 277 (speech of prosecutor Tirtawinata, on the basis of pretrial interrogations of Iwa).

headed back to Jogjakarta to give the news to Buntaran, Boeddhyarto, and Subardjo. Here the reaction was unanimous: all felt "excited and satisfied." [38] Unaware of what the government was doing, they clearly expected the rapid formation of a new cabinet, probably, like the Buchō Cabinet, under the personal leadership of Sukarno.

By evening General Sudarsono had become impatient. Accompanied by Colonel Sutjipto, the chief of army intelligence, he hurried off to find Dr. Sukiman, the most prominent of the civilian opposition leaders. They discovered him addressing a meeting at Masjumi headquarters, told him what had occurred, and invited him to inform the party members assembled that the Prime Minister had been kidnapped. Without much hesitation Sukiman did so, and raised the question that was on everyone's mind: what was to be done now that the cabinet had lost its leader? [39]

After Sudarsono's latest move the news of Sjahrir's kidnapping could no longer be kept from the public. With word spreading from mouth to mouth in the republican capital, the government now had no choice but to move slowly into the open. Accordingly, on the morning of June 29 Sukarno announced:

In connection with internal developments which endanger the security of the state and our struggle for independence, I, the President of the Republic of Indonesia, with the agreement of the cabinet in its session of June 28, 1946, have assumed all government powers for the time being until the restoration of a normal situation, which would permit the cabinet and other official bodies to resume work properly.[40]

[38] "SV," pp. 278 (speech of prosecutor Tirtawinata) and 157 (testimony of Yamin).

[39] "SV," p. 27 (testimony of General Sudarsono). Sudarsono claimed (quite plausibly) that Jusuf had still not reported to him precisely where Sjahrir and his entourage had been taken.

[40] Merdeka, June 29, 1946. It is interesting to note that political cognoscenti in Djakarta were still completely in the dark as to what really happening in Jogjakarta. Merdeka's editorial makes it clear that Sukarno's announcement was interpreted as a response not to domestic turmoil but to aggressive Dutch maneuvers.

With this public declaration by the President, the parliamentary cabinet system, which had operated since the previous November, gave way to a new form of the presidential government it had originally displaced.

That evening the government finally admitted publicly that Sjahrir and various other important political and military leaders had been kidnapped. The actions were strongly condemned as aiding the Dutch by weakening the internal unity of the state. Severe government action was threatened, and Sukarno called on all citizens "with a sane outlook" to stand behind the government and help secure Sjahrir's release.[41]

In the interim Sudarsono had not been idle. That morning he had gathered Buntaran, Boeddhyarto, Yamin, Iwa, Subardjo, and Chaerul Saleh together at division headquarters and informed them that Sudirman had ordered him to ask his political advisers and other politicians to draw up a new cabinet list that would be forwarded to the President. The Panglima Besar was leaving shortly for Surakarta and needed the list as soon as possible.[42] The little group proceeded to comply with Sudarsono's request, adding for good measure a "concept" drafted by the indefatigable Yamin, which envisaged the creation of a Political Leadership Council as a sort of inner cabinet analogous to the current State Defense Council.[43] With these documents in hand Sudarsono hurried off, and caught Sudirman as he was on the

[41] Raliby, *Documenta Historica*, p. 324. Meanwhile, on Amir's orders, pro-government troops, including heavily armed Pesindo units from East Java, converged cautiously on Surakarta, where Sjahrir had last been seen.

[42] "SV," pp. 157 (testimony of Yamin), 202–3 (Subardjo), 217 (Boeddhyarto), and 278 (prosecutor Tirtawinata). This was the first time Sudarsono met Yamin, at least according to Yamin.

[43] "SV," pp. 40 (testimony of Sudarsono), 208 (Subardjo), 217, 223–24 (Boeddhyarto), and 278 (prosecutor Tirtawinata). At the 1948 trials, the prosecution tried to show that the July Third Affair was the consequence of a long-laid plot hatched by the political prisoners in Tawangmangu. As evidence the state produced a large number of documents drawn up by Yamin while he was under detention. See "SV," pp. 270–76 (speech of prosecutor Tirtawinata). A perusal of these documents suggests, however, that they were the products of the energetic Yamin's

point of leaving Jogjakarta.[44] What precisely Sudirman intended to do with the documents is not at all clear.

In any event he was back the next morning in Jogjakarta in time to attend a meeting with top government leaders. It was evidently an angry confrontation. Sukarno, Hatta, and Amir suspected that Sudirman knew of Sjahrir's whereabouts and insisted that he use his influence to secure the Prime Minister's release. Sudirman seems to have refused to take any action; or perhaps he hinted that the price for his intervention on Sjahrir's behalf would be drastic changes in the cabinet and a guarantee that there would be no reprisals against the kidnappers. The meeting seems to have ended in deadlock. Sudirman left for Surakarta once again, sending private orders to Sudarsono to report to him there the next morning.[45]

---

frustration at the isolation and inactivity imposed on him in the remote hill resort. Most of them were examples of the grandiose, wordy, and fantastic schemata for which Yamin was famous. They included long, elaborately argued legal briefs for the defunct Persatuan Perdjuangan, as well as "concepts" for the drastic reorganization of the government. One such concept envisaged the creation of a government of the army and the people, in which the cabinet would be appointed by joint consultations between the president and the panglima besar on the basis of a broad national coalition; power would be exercised by an inner cabinet consisting of the ministers holding the most important portfolios. There is no evidence that the other prisoners paid much attention to Yamin's drafts. It is quite plausible, however, that when General Sudarsono presented Yamin and his friends with Sudirman's urgent request on the morning of June 29, the Yamin drafts served as the basis for a rapid and articulate response—particularly if, as seems likely, Yamin's forceful personality dominated the group.

[44] "SV," p. 45 (testimony of Sudarsono). It is not altogether clear why Sudirman was leaving for Surakarta, though probably the reason was to discuss the situation with Sutarto. Sudirman maintained an official residence at the Lodji Gandrung in Surakarta, so it would have appeared quite natural for him to stay there. According to Sudarsono, it was only after Sudirman departed that he finally received Jusuf's report on Sjahrir's whereabouts. "SV," p. 53 (testimony of Sudarsono).

[45] The only source for what occurred in these talks is the testimony of Sudarsono, who presumably got Sudirman's version ("SV," p. 28). Sudarsono was not a wholly reliable witness, however, for by the time of the trials he felt that he had been betrayed by Sudirman.

The government now realized that dramatic action was required and decided to play its trump card, Sukarno. That evening, June 30, the President made a masterly nationwide radio broadcast. Speaking "more in sorrow than in anger," Sukarno described an opposition group that did not understand the difference between opposition and destruction. While the state needed an opposition if it was to be based on democracy, the opposition must know its limits. Stability must be maintained. The kidnapping of the Prime Minister and other high officials would permit the Dutch to say to the world that Indonesia could not rule herself, and that chaos and disorder prevailed everywhere. The kidnapping of General Sudibjo, chief of the POPDA, would allow the republic's enemies to allege that Indonesia's promises to evacuate the internees herself were being broken. The people who had carried out the kidnappings imagined themselves to be "more left than the left," and more radical than the radicals, little realizing in their innocence that their actions played into the hands of the NICA and the Dutch fifth column. While subjectively their intentions might be good, objectively their actions were harmful and dangerous. Lenin himself had warned against radicalism as an infantile disorder of Communism. Slogans of popular sovereignty had been recklessly abused to turn "our children" against the government: some of the idealistic pemuda had fallen into the trap.

Since June 28 he had taken all powers into his own hands, not to become a dictator but to ensure short-term stability. When normal conditions again prevailed, he would return power to a regular cabinet. Everyone should stand behind the government against the folly of this "attempted coup d'état." However bitter the disagreement with and criticism of the government, this was not the proper way to express opposition. Anarchy and chaos would get no one anywhere. Sjahrir must be released immediately by his captors.[46]

[46] Paraphrased from the full text contained in Raliby, *Documenta Historica*, pp. 324–32.

Sukarno's strong denunciation of the kidnapping, combined with his rather kindly words for the pemuda who had carried it out, appears to have had its effect. Sometime during the night Sjahrir was released and escorted back to Surakarta.[47] From there he flew directly back to Djakarta.[48]

Thus when General Sudarsono presented himself before the Panglima Besar on the morning of July 1, the impasse of the last three days had finally been broken. Sudirman revealed that the President had requested Sudarsono's arrest, but he assured the anxious general that he was unwilling to comply.[49] While willing to accept Sjahrir's release, Sudirman was evidently determined that no reprisals be taken. It is in this light that one should probably interpret his order, following discussions with Col. Gatot Subroto, Col. Dr. Sutjipto, General Sutarto, and Sutarto's deputy, Major Mursito, to have an army-sponsored pamphlet written and issued describing the group that had carried out the daulat operation as a group "struggling for 100 per cent Merdeka."[50] After this meeting it was agreed that Sudirman would return immediately to Jogjakarta to prevent government retaliation against Sudarsono and the Surakarta commanders, while Sudarsono and Sutjipto would follow a little later.

But in the meantime the government had gone over to the

[47] The officers who released Sjahrir were all trusted subordinates of Sutarto: Lt. Col. Suadi Suromihardjo, commander of Regiment Twenty-six in Surakarta; Lieutenant Colonel Iskandar, who seems to have been a staff officer at divisional headquarters; and Major Soeharto, Suadi's subordinate as commander of Battalion Sixteen. See Indonesia, Kementerian Penerangan, *Republik Indonesia Propinsi Djawa Tengah,* p. 201; "Sedjarah TNI, Diponegoro," p. 82; and, with some variations, "Surakarta Hadiningrat," which indicates that one of the officers involved in the original kidnapping accompanied the rescue party. Since Sudirman was in Surakarta at the time, it seems likely that he knew of and approved the release, indicating that he had changed his mind since the morning confrontation with the government.

[48] "SV," p. 31 (testimony of Sudarsono); Jungschlaeger, "Double Coup," p. 1.

[49] "SV," p. 28 (testimony of Sudarsono).

[50] "SV," pp. 29–30 (testimony of Sudarsono).

offensive. It had already tried to undermine Sudarsono's hold over the Third Division by having his chief of staff, Col. Umar Djoy, appointed military deputy to the Sultan in the Jogjakarta Special Region Defense Council.[51] This was a choice made largely *faute de mieux,* since, it will be recalled, Umar Djoy had been made divisional chief of staff at Sudarsono's insistence over the original designee, Colonel Sarbini. But the government hoped that his ambitions might bring him to side now with it rather than with his commanding officer. The next step was a frontal attack on the opposition leaders suspected of being in league with the kidnappers. With Sjahrir now safely in Djakarta, there was no longer any reason to hesitate. On the night of July 1 the State Police were authorized to conduct a sweep through Jogjakarta. Buntaran, Boeddhyarto, Chaerul Saleh, Mohammed Saleh, Sajuti Melik, Subardjo, Ibnu Parna, Adam Malik, Pandu Kartawiguna, Sumantoro, and a number of lesser figures were quickly apprehended. Only Iwa and Yamin escaped the net. Early on the morning of July 2, the prisoners were taken to the Wirogunan Prison in the heart of the city.[52]

While the arrests were being carried out, Sudarsono and Sutjipto arrived in Jogjakarta and were at once alarmed by the unusual degree of police activity. Their alarm was not lessened when Sudarsono telephoned Umar Djoy and was told that it was unsafe to talk on public lines. When the two officers went to Umar Djoy's house, he showed them written orders from Sukarno which they interpreted as presaging at least Sudarsono's arrest, and possibly that of Umar Djoy as well.[53] To prevent this unwelcome eventuality, it was agreed to try to mobilize units of the Third Division. Sudarsono and Umar Djoy thereupon con-

[51] The order establishing this council was signed by Sukarno. Its composition is given in Koesnodiprodjo, ed., *Himpunan, 1946,* p. 300.

[52] For different descriptions of this razzia, see "SV," pp. 262 (speech of prosecutor Tirtawinata), 158, 161 (testimony of Yamin), 200, 203 (Subardjo), 218 (Boeddhyarto), 238 (Sajuti Melik), 249–50 (Pandu Kartawiguna), 241, 246 (Sumantoro).

[53] "SV," p. 32 (testimony of Sudarsono).

tacted Lieutenant Colonel Sukandar, the commander of Regiment Four (City of Jogjakarta), whom they believed sympathetic to their aims. He was to arrange for two battalions to take up defensive positions in the heart of the city to forestall any "unauthorized" raid against divisional headquarters, and also to patrol the main streets to discover what pro-government units, particularly from the police and Pesindo, might be up to.[54] Although Sukandar agreed, it is not clear that these orders were fully executed.

A few hours later Umar Djoy learned from the warden of the Wirogunan Prison that he had been instructed to make room for fourteen prominent political prisoners, including Mohammed Saleh and Boeddhyarto.[55] He immediately informed Sudarsono, and the two men agreed that the situation had become very serious, and their own arrests increasingly probable. Umar Djoy now decided to move his base out of the city to the headquarters of Regiment Three, situated in Wijoro, a small village about five kilometers southeast of Jogjakarta. There he could be sure of the protection of the regimental commander, Lieutenant Colonel Suharto (who two decades later would become president of Indonesia). Sudarsono stayed on in Jogjakarta until mid-morning,

[54] "SV," p. 32 (testimony of Sudarsono). There were four regiments in the Jogjakarta area: Regiment One (North Jogjakarta) under Lieutenant Colonel Sunarwibowo, with three battalions; Regiment Two (South Jogjakarta) under Lieutenant Colonel Palal, with three battalions; Regiment Three (Southeast Jogjakarta?) under Lieutenant Colonel Suharto, with three battalions; and Regiment Four (City of Jogjakarta) under Lieutenant Colonel Sukandar, with five battalions, including that of Abdulkadir Jusuf. Seven of these fourteen battalions seem to have been located within city limits or just outside. "Sedjarah TNI, Diponegoro," p. 79. The two battalions called up to guard the divisional headquarters were Battalion Fifteen in Djetis and Battalion Ten in Kotabaru. "SV," p. 32 (testimony of Sudarsono). Oddly enough, neither of these battalions was from Sukandar's regiment, the first being from Regiment One and the second from Regiment Three.

[55] There was a standing arrangement that the Wirogunan warden would regularly keep divisional headquarters informed of the identities of his charges.

when he received a telephone call from his chief of staff urging him to leave at once, since Suharto was afraid that any delay might mean his arrest or apprehension en route. Sudarsono let himself be persuaded and reached Wijoro unmolested at about noon.[56]

In the meantime Iwa and Yamin had taken cover in Jusuf's house. Iwa evidently decided Jogjakarta was too dangerous and left almost at once for Surakarta. In the afternoon Jusuf contacted Sudarsono and told him that Yamin was still at large under his protection. At the General's urging they too foregathered in Wijoro.[57] A little later Umar Djoy returned from reconnoitering in the city and brought Sudarsono a letter from Sudirman, summoning him and Jusuf to his residence in Surakarta. They had no recourse but to obey, and after darkness they set off, accompanied by Yamin. Evading various roadblocks, they reached Surakarta two hours before midnight and presented themselves before the Panglima Besar.[58]

The content of the four-hour talks that followed between Sudirman and Sudarsono is certainly the most obscure and controversial aspect of the July Third Affair. At his trial two years later Sudarsono claimed that Sudirman was very angry about the arrest of the fourteen political leaders the previous night and asked why nothing had yet been done to secure their release. He then ordered Sudarsono to go to Jogjakarta, release the prisoners, and confront the President with them, demanding the reasons for their detention and for the March 17 razzias. Sudarsono was to

[56] "SV," pp. 32–33 (testimony of Sudarsono). For some biographical details on Suharto, see the Appendix.

[57] "SV," pp. 158 (testimony of Yamin) and 282 (speech of prosecutor Tirtawinata). It should be noted, however, that Yamin's testimony is inconsistent. Later (p. 159) he averred that he had been "arrested" by the troops that took him to Wijoro.

[58] "SV," pp. 23 (testimony of Sudarsono), and 159 (Yamin). According to the prosecution, which in 1948 had a strong interest in minimizing Sudirman's role in the affair, Sudarsono was summoned to Surakarta because Sudirman had undertaken to arrest and interrogate him himself. As we shall see, this is clearly not true.

mobilize the Hizbullah and the Lasjkar Rakjat in order to emphasize the seriousness of these demands, and he was also to press for a cabinet change. It was understood that Dr. Sukiman should be asked to accompany the group, and possibly other still unarrested opposition leaders. Sudarsono was assured that the troops from East Java in Jogjakarta would not move against him, since they were under the command of Sudirman's trusted aide, Colonel Sutirto, who would be warned to confine them to barracks. Sudarsono further claimed that Sudirman told him to use Battalion Ten to guard the radio and telephone systems in the city.[59] Yamin's testimony for the most part confirmed Sudarsono's, though he evidently was not permitted to overhear most of the tête-à-tête. He recalled, however, that on leaving Sudirman embraced Jusuf in recognition of his bravery and daring. He also supported Sudarsono's story that Sudirman promised he would refuse to answer any telephoned requests for help from the presidential residence in Jogjakarta.[60]

While there is no reason to accept the self-interested testimony of Sudarsono and Yamin in its entirety, it certainly contains a considerable element of truth.[61] One can readily believe that Sudirman was highly incensed by the arrest of the fourteen opposition leaders and the blow to his prestige and authority this ac-

[59] "SV," pp. 34 (testimony of Sudarsono) and 282–83 (speech of prosecutor Tirtawinata, citing Sudarsono's statements in pretrial interrogations).

[60] "SV," p. 159 (testimony of Yamin).

[61] This judgment is strongly confirmed, in a negative sense, by the extremely implausible interpretation put on the Sudirman-Sudarsono talks by the state prosecution in the 1948 trials. Faced with the undeniable fact that Sudirman at the very least made no move to apprehend Sudarsono in Surakarta, though Sukarno had ordered his arrest, the prosecution explained Sudirman's behavior by saying that since he knew those orders had specifically been given to Umar Djoy, he did not wish to interfere! "SV," p. 286 (speech of prosecutor Tirtawinata). For its own reasons, of which more below, the government was anxious to draw public attention away from the military protagonists of the July Third Affair and focus it on the civilians—a precedent for political trials of a much later date.

tion implied. He was very probably not averse to Sudarsono's releasing the prisoners and confronting the President with them. That he ordered Sudarsono to mobilize troops to intimidate the government and to press demands for a change of cabinet seems less likely. Had such a move been his aim he would never have permitted Sjahrir's release, and he would have acted decisively shortly after June 27, when the government was at a clear disadvantage. In any case he certainly gave Sudarsono no written orders of any kind.[62] It must be recognized, however, that in Javanese social communication much is commonly left unsaid, great trust being put in intuitive understanding; this pattern, while sharpening subtle sensibilities, frequently leads to confusion and misunderstanding. Possibly, then, Sudarsono sincerely interpreted Sudirman's verbal instructions in ways that, while useful to himself, by no means accorded with the real intentions of the Panglima Besar.

At any rate Sudarsono was either permitted or ordered to return to Jogjakarta, and he promptly set out, accompanied by Jusuf and Yamin. The party went straight to the Wirogunan, and, claiming to speak for Sudirman, obtained the release of the fourteen prisoners. Though many of the prisoners wanted to go home to bed, Sudarsono insisted in packing them all into a truck and sending them off to Suharto's headquarters in Wijoro.[63] The one exception was Mohammed Saleh, who as chairman of the Jogjakarta KNI and chief of its Lasjkar Rakjat, had considerable pemuda backing in the city. Sudarsono dropped Saleh off with orders to mobilize the Lasjkar Rakjat in preparation for further instructions, and then hurried off to Wijoro himself.

[62] Interview with General Sudarsono, April 9, 1962. Sudarsono was very bitter about Sudirman's role, which he described as vacillating, deceptive, and unworthy of a satria. Since Sudarsono was sentenced to a long prison term in 1948 and was dismissed from the army, while Sudirman remained panglima besar until his untimely death in January 1950, this reaction is understandable, though by no means wholly fair.

[63] "SV," pp. 162 (testimony of Yamin), 218–19 (Boeddhyarto), and 246 (Sumantoro).

There he talked with Yamin and Subardjo, and asked them to prepare yet another "concept" to be presented to the President when they saw him. Without any sign of fatigue Sudarsono then rushed back in to Jogjakarta, located Mohammed Saleh, and went with him to arouse Frans Darmowardojo, the commander of the Lasjkar Rakjat division in the city. Darmowardojo was told to assemble his pemuda in the great square in front of the kraton and await further orders.[64] Similar contact was made with Djauzie, the leader of the local BPRI.[65] Finally, Sudarsono and Saleh called on Dr. Sukiman and the PNI leader Mr. Sunarjo to explain their alleged orders from Sudirman, the whereabouts of the released prisoners, and the plans for confronting the President. Both were urged to present themselves at the palace.[66]

Meantime, at Suharto's headquarters, while most of the exhausted prisoners slept, Yamin, Subardjo, and Chaerul Saleh had been busy typing up four proclamations for Sukarno to sign. They ran as follows:

Proclamation no. 2

At the urging of the people and the army in the second stage of the Indonesian revolution, who are struggling to defend the whole people and the whole archipelago under the sovereignty of the Republic of Indonesia on the basis of 100 per cent independence, I, the President of the Republic of Indonesia, this day dismiss the entire state cabinet of Sutan Sjahrir and Amir Sjarifuddin.

Proclamation no. 3

At the urging of the people and the army in the second stage of the Indonesian revolution, who are struggling to defend the people and the whole Indonesian archipelago within the sovereignty of the Republic of Indonesia based on 100 per cent independence, and with regard to the fact that the whole people and the whole archipelago are in a state of war, I, the President of the Republic of Indonesia,

[64] "SV," pp. 37–39 (testimony of Sudarsono).

[65] "SV," p. 259 (speech of prosecutor Tirtawinata).

[66] "SV," p. 39 (testimony of Sudarsono). Sunarjo, however, decided to accompany Sudarsono and Saleh to Wijoro, which they reached at about sunup.

deliver the powers of the people which are in my hands, in matters concerned with the defense and the security of the State, to the Commander-in-Chief of the land, sea, and air forces, together with his headquarters; and in matters concerned with political, social, and economic leadership, to a Political Leadership Council.

The members of this Political Leadership Council and of a new cabinet will be announced immediately.

Proclamation no. 4

In fulfillment of Proclamation no. 3, dated July 3, 1946, I, the President of the Republic of Indonesia, hereby appoint ten members of the Political Leadership Council: (1) Buntaran Martoatmodjo, (2) Boeddhyarto Martoatmodjo, (3) Chaerul Saleh, (4) Gatot, (5) Iwa Kusumasumantri, (6) Muhammad Yamin, (7) Subardjo, (8) Sunarjo, (9) Tan Malaka, (10) Wachid Hasjim.

Proclamation no. 5

In fulfillment of proclamations no. 2 and 3, dated July 3, 1946, I, the President of the Republic of Indonesia, hereby appoint as members of the state cabinet: minister of the interior, Boeddhyarto; minister of foreign affairs, Subardjo; minister of defense, to be announced; minister of justice, Soepomo; minister of prosperity, Tan Malaka; minister of religion, Wachid Hasjim; minister of social affairs, Iwa Kusumasumantri; minister of general development, Abikusno Tjokrosujoso; minister of finance, A. A. Maramis; minister of health, Buntaran Martoatmodjo; minister of information and mass communications, Muhammad Yamin; minister of education, Ki Hadjar Dewantoro; minister of communications, Rooseno; ministers of state, Chaerul Saleh, Fatoerrachman, Gatot, Kartono, Patty, Sukiman, Sunarjo, Sartono, Sjamsu Harja Udaja, Mohammed Saleh.[67]

It will be readily apparent that Yamin and Subardjo displayed little imagination in these draft proclamations. The proposed cabinet, for example, was virtually a replica of the discredited Buchō Cabinet that had fallen from power the previous Novem-

[67] "SV," pp. 60–61. The proclamations were numbered 2 through 5 to run in sequence from President Sukarno's Proclamation of June 28 taking full powers into his own hands. That proclamation presumably had laid the legal ground for the changes envisaged by the trio at Wijoro.

ber, for no less than seven of the proposed ministers had held the same position in that administration: Subardjo, Soepomo, Iwa, Abikusno, Maramis, Buntaran, and Dewantoro. The proposed cabinet was in no sense a genuine coalition government either: there was no representation from the Socialist or the Christian parties, nor, perhaps more significantly, was there any from the leading badan perdjuangan. Chaerul Saleh, Yamin's anak mas, was the solitary spokesman for the pemuda in the entire list. The only figure of real stature, Tan Malaka, was assigned the second-level position of minister of prosperity. The Political Leadership Council was little better. Such elementary steps as making Tan Malaka its chairman and including the names of Sudirman and other high military officers were unaccountably omitted. In general, the personalities named and the style and language of the proclamations evince clear signs of improvisation and haste. None of them indicate any serious thought about the real problems facing the Indonesian revolution—in sharp contrast to Tan Malaka's ideas and programs for the Persatuan Perdjuangan.

The documents were completed by the time Sudarsono reappeared at Wijoro, though the General showed little interest in them.[68] He was more preoccupied with his own problems. He accepted Jusuf's afterthought that Tan Malaka, Sukarni, and Iwa should be brought down from Tawangmangu to confront Sukarno, but telephone calls to the battalion commander there produced no results: Tan Malaka and Sukarni remained in captivity throughout the crisis.[69] He also allowed Jusuf to persuade him that Sukarno would be much more amenable if Amir and Hatta were neutralized. Accordingly Jusuf set off with a small group of men to kidnap these two leaders at their homes. But the mission

[68] Sudarsono did not even see the documents until some hours later, when the whole group arrived at the President's residence. "SV," pp. 176 (testimony of Yamin) and 227–28 (Boeddhyarto).

[69] "SV," p. 264 (speech of prosecutor Tirtawinata, citing testimony, possibly pretrial, given by Suharto). See also pp. 40 and 51 (testimony of Sudarsono).

was a fiasco. Amir's bodyguards drove off the would-be kidnappers, though two of them lost their lives in the skirmish. Jusuf did not even try to reach Hatta.[70] At the same time the sound of the shooting at Amir's house alarmed Darmowardojo, the commander of the city Lasjkar Rakjat, and he ordered his men to withdraw immediately from the square in front of the kraton.[71]

Unaware of this turn of events, the Wijoro group finally set off at about 6:30 A.M. on July 3 to confront the President in Jogjakarta.[72] The political leaders were bundled into a truck, while Sudarsono and his men filled four escorting cars. To their dismay they found the whole city quiet and still. A search for Sukiman proved fruitless. The Lasjkar Rakjat were nowhere to be seen. There was not a sign of the Hizbullah, and it was too late to call for reinforcements from Suharto's headquarters in Wijoro. The possibility of a show of force had completely vanished.[73]

But there was no turning back. The confrontation with the President had to take place, though there was now nothing more to face him with than fourteen exhausted former prisoners, a handful of troops, Yamin, and the choleric General.[74] When the

[70] "SV," pp. 263–64 (speech of prosecutor Tirtawinata, including excerpts from testimony, possibly pretrial, by Suharto), 40 and 63 (testimony of Sudarsono).

[71] "SV," p. 290 (speech of prosecutor Tirtawinata).

[72] Sudarsono had telephoned ahead to Kanapi Tjitrodiningrat, the head of the Military Police in Jogjakarta, who was also in charge of the presidential guard, instructing him to neutralize all the men on duty outside the palace. "SV," pp. 59 (testimony of Sudarsono) and 264 (speech of prosecutor Tirtawinata). It is not clear whether Kanapi pretended to agree and then informed Sukarno of what was happening, or genuinely agreed and later had a change of heart, for whatever reason. In any case, when Sudarsono reached the palace, he found the Military Police arrayed against him.

[73] Presumably word had begun to spread from Darmowardojo and others that things were not going as planned. For details of the hunt for support in Jogjakarta, see "SV," pp. 41 (testimony of Sudarsono) and 204 (Subardjo). Jusuf had been told to return to Wijoro and stay there.

[74] It was at this point that Yamin thrust the texts of the four proclamations into Sudarsono's hands. Perhaps he hoped they would look more impressive if delivered by an army general claiming Sudirman's backing.

disheveled band reached the palace gates, it was clear that all was over. The inner courtyard was full of heavily armed Pesindo and Military Police. Sudarsono's men were disarmed without resistance.[75] The whole group was compelled to wait outside under guard, while a stream of political leaders (including Sukiman and Sarmidi) who had been summoned by Sukarno filed past them into the audience-hall. It was only after Amir and Hatta arrived and had an opportunity to exchange information with the President that Sudarsono was finally permitted to present himself. The General tried to explain his activities as best he could, and played the only card he had left—that he was acting on Sudirman's orders. Although Amir, Hatta, and the others were very angry, Sukarno kept his composure, asked Sudarsono for his documents, and then ordered him to step outside. He was arrested there and kept in a side-room alone for the rest of the day.[76]

The one outstanding question was the attitude of the absent Panglima Besar. Negotiations were opened by telephone, and when Sudirman realized what had happened, he began to give ground.[77] In the evening he reappeared in Jogjakarta and at-

[75] It should not be supposed from this account that the government was not extremely alarmed by the release of the prisoners, the attack on Amir's house, Sudarsono's ability to move about Jogjakarta without being apprehended, and the continuing ambiguity of Sudirman's position. If Dutch intelligence sources are to be believed, sometime after June 27 Sukarno had wired General Nasution, commander of the First Division, urging him to remain loyal and to obey only his orders if Sudirman should launch a coup d'état. Only after the fiasco of July 3 was Sudarsono's name substituted for Sudirman's in the message. See Jungschlaeger, "Double Coup," p. 7.

[76] "SV," pp. 41 (testimony of Sudarsono) and 163 (Yamin).

[77] It seems probable, on the basis of indirect evidence adduced at the 1948 trials, that Sukarno tried to reach Sudirman by telephone very early on the morning of July 3, both to explore his intentions and to win his support. Prosecutor Tirtawinata, for example, in attempting to disprove Sudarsono's claim that Sudirman had promised him not to answer any calls for help from Jogjakarta on July 3, insisted that Sudirman had informed the government that, with East Java troops moving into Surakarta in great numbers, his continued presence was urgently required to control the tense and dangerous situation in that city. "SV," p. 286. This in

tended a long secret meeting with Sukarno, the cabinet leaders, and representatives of the major political parties and organizations.[78] Though no details of these talks were ever made public, the shape of the bargain that was struck soon became clear. Sudirman agreed to sign an order suspending Sudarsono from all military functions and appointing Umar Djoy in his place. He further acquiesced in the arrests of a large number of civilian and a smaller number of military leaders.[79] For their part, his opponents agreed that the Sjahrir cabinet would not be revived and that for the time being Sukarno would continue to head the government, assisted by the State Defense Council, on which Sudirman would retain his seat.[80] No action would be taken against the army high command or against party leaders who had had only "tangential" roles in the July Third Affair.[81] The KNIP

---

itself is an admission that Sudirman's help had been requested and diplomatically refused.

[78] Sjahrir arrived in Jogjakarta about 11:00 A.M. under heavy escort. He had flown to Surakarta, and from there traveled in a special train arranged by Amir. See *Aneta* (Djakarta), July 10, 1946; "SV," p. 163 (testimony of Yamin).

[79] Reportedly, 96 political arrests were made, in addition to heavy purges. Of these 96, 75 were civilians and 21 military men. Overdijkink, *Indonesische probleem*, p. 28. The men arrested at the palace were held for a week in Jogjakarta and then shipped off to Modjokerto in East Java, where they were imprisoned until shortly before their trials began eighteen months later. "SV," pp. 43 (testimony of Sudarsono), 164 (Yamin), and 205 (Subardjo). Iwa and Jusuf were soon rounded up. As for Tan Malaka, he remained in Tawangmangu, as he had done all along, until he was moved down to Surakarta on July 6. The following day he was brought to Jogjakarta and incarcerated in the Wirogunan Prison. Tan Malaka, *Dari pendjara*, III, 123–24.

[80] For the government statement on this settlement see Raliby, *Documenta Historica*, pp. 345–46. According to Koesnodiprodjo, ed., *Himpunan, 1946* (p. 253), the State Defense Council was officially inaugurated on July 4. In contrast to the membership originally envisaged, it was comprised of Sukarno, Amir, Sudirman, Dr. Sudarsono, Soerachman, Darmawan, Abdul Karim (all ex officio), Sardjono (PKI), Sumarsono (Pesindo), and K. H. Masjkoer (Masjumi). Sjahrir's name was notably missing.

[81] "Tangential" was stretched, for political reasons, to include such men as Sukiman.

would be expanded further to accommodate a wider range of interests; [82] and Surakarta's status would remain as it had been before the affair.[83] Implicit, too, in the bargain, was a tacit agreement that the policy of diplomasi would continue without further obstruction.

[82] Kahin, *Nationalism and Revolution*, p. 193.

[83] On July 3 Pesindo and BPRI units from East Java had entered Surakarta in force and virtually ransacked parts of the town ("Surakarta Hadiningrat"); these units were now gradually withdrawn (Jungschlaeger, "Double Coup," p. 14). But conditions in the "city of the opposition" remained troubled. On July 18 Iskaq Tjokroadisoerjo, an old friend of Sukarno from the prewar PNI, was inaugurated as resident of Surakarta with Sudiro, Muwardi's subordinate in the Barisan Banteng, as his deputy. *Al Djihad,* July 20, 1946. With this ceremony the conflict between the royal houses and the anti-Swapradja movement was settled largely in favor of the latter. While Jogjakarta remained a Special Region administered by the Sultan and the Pakualam, Surakarta sank to the level of an ordinary residency. But the position of Iskaq and Sudiro was by no means comfortable, and on November 9, 1946, they were the victims of yet another daulat operation. Surakarta, Djawatan Penerangan Kota Besar Surakarta, *Kenang-Kenangan,* p. 6.

Epilogue

The official government statement on the July Third Affair characterized it as a treasonous coup d'état masterminded by Tan Malaka.[1] A concerted campaign was launched to stigmatize him as an unscrupulous and ruthless adventurer of unlimited ambition. The aging revolutionary was given no opportunity to defend himself against this organized calumny. He was never brought to trial, and the final portion of his autobiography, written in confinement and entitled with some fitness *From Prison to Prison,* was not published until many years after his murder in 1949.

The leaders of the republic were well aware of Tan Malaka's innocence—and for that reason never dared to arraign him before a court of law. But reasons of state made it imperative that a powerless scapegoat be found, and no one was better fitted for this role than he. Public exposure of the deep cleavages within the political elite and the army that had precipitated the crisis of June 27 to July 3 would have seriously demoralized the nation and weakened its international position. Moreover, any such revelations would have virtually destroyed the delicate compromise reached in the wake of the crisis, which was designed to make possible a minimum of continued cooperation between the government and the army high command. For the purpose of safeguarding this tenuous understanding, Tan Malaka, always the outsider, was expendable.

But there was another reason why the wandering revolutionary

[1] The text can be found in Raliby, *Documenta Historica,* pp. 341–45.

404

had to be silenced and defamed. He was the one leader of stature who was fully committed to the policy of perdjuangan and who had the prestige to make it a plausible alternative. Now that the republican leaders, civilian and military alike, had decisively turned their backs on this alternative, they found it desirable, for domestic and external reasons, to write a clear *finis* to it. This could most simply be achieved by destroying the reputation and credibility of Tan Malaka, the living symbol of what they had renounced.

It remains to ask what, in retrospect, were the lasting consequences of the debacle of July 3, 1946?

In the first place, the affair resulted in a significant shift in the distribution of power and authority within the republican leadership. On the one hand, the position of Sudirman and the army high command was notably weakened.[2] There was considerable demoralization among the military, and the Third Division virtually fell apart. Not until three months later was a new commander successfully installed, and even then Sudirman was forced to accept the candidate of the division's junior officers after his own nominee had been humiliatingly rejected.[3] On the other hand, the

[2] His chief of intelligence, Col. Dr. Sutjipto, was among those arrested, and Sudirman could do nothing for him.

[3] This crisis is recorded in "Sedjarah TNI, Diponegoro," pp. 101–3. The first person to try to take Sudarsono's place was Lieutenant Colonel Sunarwibowo, commander of the First Regiment, who entered the divisional headquarters and declared himself Sudarsono's successor. This move failed because Sukarno had already made Suharto temporarily responsible for the Third Division. Then Lieutenant Colonel Palal appeared in a colonel's outfit, announcing that he would take over together with Umar Djoy. Major Bardosono and Captain Darjono were able to hold him off by telephoning for help to the commanders of regiments Seventeen, Eighteen, Nineteen, and Twenty. Many officers were then arrested. Finally, Major Moch, divisional chief of intelligence, called a conference to settle matters "within the Division." Since Suharto evidently refused to accept permanent command, for reasons that are not clear, the junior officers selected Colonel Susalit, then commander of Brigade V in Tjirebon. But Sudirman and Urip evidently disliked this choice, and nominated instead Major General Soediro from Kediri (who had

leaders of the political parties had scarcely come out of the affair
with much credit. Parliamentary-style government was eventually restored on October 2, when the third Sjahrir cabinet, a
larger, more unwieldy version of the second, was installed.[4] But
it was clearly lower in prestige and authority than its predecessor.

The one figure to emerge from the crisis with added stature was
Sukarno. While most of the members of the Buchō Cabinet disappeared behind bars after July 3, the leader of that first republican government assumed a more central role than ever before.
The crisis had shown that he was the one man whom all groups
would agree to support. The period of presidential government,
though short—from July through September—completed his re-
habilitation and created a powerful precedent for the future: in
times of national emergency and threats, internal or external, to
the state, it would be natural to turn to Sukarno, who had come
to represent Indonesian nationalism as no other man could.

In the second place, the silencing of Tan Malaka put an end
to whatever prospects there might have been of Indonesia's choos-
ing the path of perdjuangan rather than diplomasi. The chances
that the first path would be taken had perhaps always been very
small, given the nature of the Indonesian political leadership, its
social origins and political orientations, and its historical experience. But after July even this faint possibility vanished. In the
months that followed Dutch troops steadily continued to assemble in the archipelago. Combined with van Mook's shrewd policy
of mobilizing Outer Island groups against the republican center,
this military build-up gave the Dutch the leverage to force the

---

earlier been rejected by the officers of the Fourth Division in favor of
Sutarto). When the time for Soediro's inauguration came, none of the
officers showed up. It was not until September 25 that Sudirman and
Urip accepted Susalit as commander, and then only when he was brought
to Jogjakarta for this purpose by the junior officers. (Susalit was a half-
brother of the PS leader Abdulmadjid, which may have been one reason
for Sudirman's resistance.)

[4] The composition of this cabinet may be found in Finch and Lev,
Republic of Indonesia Cabinets, pp. 8–9.

republican leaders into ever greater concessions, culminating in the humiliating Renville Agreement of January 1948.

As we have noted before, the logic of diplomasi inescapably demanded the shoring up of traditional power groups and an adherence to conservative domestic policies, for the overriding necessity was to satisfy the expectations of first the Dutch and British, and later the Americans.[5] The ultimate result was to be that Indonesia attained her recognition as a sovereign state by the outside world, but not her 100 per cent merdeka. When the necessity of negotiating with the Dutch and the Americans passed, the groups whose power had rested largely on their ability to conduct these negotiations successfully found their authority gradually slipping away.[6] The recognition of Indonesia's sovereignty was not enough, in the long run, to fulfill the hopes and aspirations of Indonesian society. The subordination of everything else to its attainment, however, meant that the development of structures and organizations capable of giving that recognition lasting social form had been almost wholly neglected. From this came the deepening malaise of the post-independence years, and later tragedies.

Finally, the pemuda movement, which we have watched growing out of the late Japanese occupation, came by the end of the second Sjahrir cabinet to a historical impasse. The logic of diplomasi drove the government to curb and confine the movement, which for itself found no permanent, transcendent meaning in the government's policy.

The emergence of the pemuda as a political force was certainly the most striking aspect of the early revolution. It was on the

[5] Sutter's *Indonesianisasi* (pp. 407–8) contains an instructive description of the use made of the July Third debacle to pursue conservative domestic policies, particularly the removal of estates and factories from the control of their employees, and where possible, their restoration to their original owners.

[6] This process is superbly documented by Herbert Feith in *The Decline of Constitutional Democracy in Indonesia* (Ithaca, N.Y., 1962); see esp. pp. 19–26, 113–22, and 597–608, for a general analysis.

backs of the pemuda that the first Sjahrir ministry rode to power, with its promise of a freedom always denied during the Dutch and Japanese eras. Yet the promise soon proved illusory, the alliance a product of mutual misunderstanding. The longer the Sjahrir cabinets ruled, the greater the disillusionment in pemuda ranks, except among the educated few who found in Sjahrir a model for themselves, and in his private vision of a liberal-democratic Western-style society an acceptable spiritual anchor.

It was also largely with pemuda backing that the Persatuan Perdjuangan found its first powerful impetus. Tan Malaka appeared to offer, for a short time, the promise of a merdeka close to pemuda hearts. But after years of solitary wandering and without a devoted cadre of capable lieutenants, Tan Malaka was unable to protect himself from becoming the victim of elite rivalries and the mutual antagonism of government and army leaders.[7] In spite of his instinctive rapport with the pemuda and the pemuda-like character of his vision, he found the task of building a coherent and radical national front fueled by the pemuda movement beyond him. By July 1946 the promise of *Muslihat* was no less illusory than that of *Perdjuangan Kita*.

It was not that the pemuda rejected organization and direction as such, but that the organization and direction imposed would have had to have been rooted in the pemuda tradition. The pesantrèn and the asrama had, in different ways, offered a self-denying, disciplined way of life in the service of transcendent goals. From them the pemuda movement derived much of its special style and symbolism. But style and symbolism in themselves were not enough to channel the pemuda tide into a coherent,

---

[7] It must be recognized that Tan Malaka faced a formidable obstacle in Sukarno. But it was less Sukarno's prestige and power as such than his commitment to diplomasi that was decisive. Had Sukarno thrown his weight behind perdjuangan, the course of Indonesian history might have been very different. It is difficult to refrain from making the comparison with Ho Chi Minh, who built the radical organization that Tan Malaka lacked, and found in Bao Dai no serious rival as the custodian of his country's hopes.

politically revolutionary force. One can think of the pemuda movement as an engine running at breakneck speed without a driver to put it in gear.

The pemuda never found their driver. For a short time, in different places, the badan perdjuangan and the military partially fulfilled this function. (The parties, appendages of the political elite, never did.) But the army and the badan perdjuangan were themselves insufficient, and with the failure to weld them into a unified national structure, the pemuda movement was condemned to be frustrated.

Thus the revolution never became more than a "national revolution"; it ended in 1949, when the Dutch transferred legal sovereignty over the archipelago to Indonesian hands, and Sukarno moved into the palace where governors-general had ruled for generations. What it might have been can only be glimpsed in the short-lived, isolated social revolutions in the provinces, and in the memories of some of its survivors. Long after Indonesian sovereignty was recognized by the world, the search for 100 per cent merdeka was to continue, and was to remain sentenced to disappointment. But the hopes are still with us.

Biographical Appendix

Dr. ABDUL HALIM, son of Tuan Achmad gelar Mangkuto, was born on December 27, 1911, in Bukittinggi, West Sumatra. He was educated in a HIS, a MULO, and an AMS, all in Djakarta, and graduated from the Djakarta Medical Faculty in 1940. Though a member of the PPPI in 1932, he was not active politically before the war, except in the INPO (Indonesisch Nationale Padvinders Organisatie, or Indonesian National Scouting Association). During the Japanese occupation he practiced at the Djakarta General Hospital and was briefly arrested for listening to foreign broadcasts. He was regarded as close to Sjahrir. *Orang Indonesia,* p. 299; Deppen Files; Rasjied, *Riwajat orang-orang politik,* pp. 18–19. There is an excellent pen-portrait of his calm, correct, and cautious personality in Tjiptoning, *Apa dan siapa,* pp. 95–103.

Ir. Mas Endoen ABDUL KARIM was born on July 16, 1908, in Tjirebon, West Java. He was educated in a HIS, a MULO, and an AMS in Jogjakarta, before obtaining his engineering degree in Bandung in 1933. Thereafter he made a living as a teacher and businessman. In the Japanese period he headed the Djakarta Municipality's Public Works Division. *Orang Indonesia,* p. 220; *Antara,* March 16, 1946.

Mr. Radèn Mas ABDULMADJID Djojoadiningrat was born in Rembang, Central Java, on January 5, 1904, the scion of one of the best-known aristocratic families of Java. He was a close relative of R. A. Kartini, the founder of the movement for women's education and emancipation, and was connected to the Pringgodigdo family of Tuban

411

and to Kusumo Utojo, bupati of Djepara, one of the earliest strong advocates of Westernization among the upper prijaji class. Abdulmadjid was educated in an ELS, the elite HBS in Semarang, and at Leiden, where he received a law degree. While in Holland he joined the PI, and after Hatta's departure took control of it. Under his influence it moved steadily in a communist direction. *Sin Po,* Nov. 11, 1957; Kahin, *Nationalism and Revolution,* p. 89; information provided kindly by Daniel S. Lev. He himself eventually became a communist, indeed a member of the Dutch Communist Party's central executive. De Groot, *De dertiger jaren 1930–1939,* I, 198. He was in Holland during the war and took part in the resistance.

Radèn ABIKUSNO Tjokrosujoso, younger brother of H. O. S. Tjokroaminoto, was born in Ponorogo, East Java, on June 15, 1897. He graduated from an ELS and the Queen Emma School, and eventually got an architect's diploma at the Polytechnical Institute in Arnhem. Thereafter he worked as a free-lance architect. From 1917 to 1919 he headed the Surabaja branch of the Sarekat Islam, later becoming a member of the central executive board. In 1932, following his brother's death, he became general chairman of the PSII, and in 1939 headed the secretariat of the Gapi federation of nationalist organizations. During the war he was a member of the Consultative Council of Putera, and a member of the CAC. In December 1944 he was appointed adviser to the Bureau of Public Works, and on August 27, 1945, became chief of this bureau. *Orang Indonesia,* p. 470; Deppen Files; *Djawa Baroe,* Sept. 15, 1944; *Soeara Asia,* Aug. 30, 1945.

Dr. ABOE HANIFAH gelar Datoek Maharadja Emas was born in Padang Pandjang, West Sumatra, on January 6, 1906. He was educated in an ELS and in the STOVIA, and received his medical degree in Djakarta in 1941. Before the war he worked in various places as a doctor in government service. From 1923 to 1926 he edited *Jong Soematra,* the publication of the Jong Sumatranen Bond (League of Young Sumatrans). From 1929 to 1930 he edited *Pemoeda Indonesia* and *Indonesia Raja* (for the PPPI), and, in 1931, *Indonesia Moeda.* Thereafter he did not assume much prominence until the arrival of the Japanese, whereupon he became a leading member of the Barisan Pemuda Asia Raya (Great Asia Youth Corps). *Orang Indonesia,* p. 301; Amstutz, "The Indonesian Youth Movement," pp. 18, 29, 39.

Dr. Radèn Mas ADJIDARMO Tjokronagoro was born in Pradja, Lombok, on August 28, 1904. He was educated in an ELS, a five-year HBS, and the STOVIA, and received a medical degree from the University of Amsterdam in 1932. (He was thus, like Moelia, a contemporary of Sjahrir's in Holland.) On his return he practiced as a doctor in Surakarta and Banjuwangi. He had no prewar political record of note. *Orang Indonesia,* p. 375. During the Japanese occupation he was a top leader (*daitaichō*) of the Barisan Pelopor in Banjuwangi. *Kedaulatan Rakjat,* Dec. 18, 1957. According to *Harian Rakjat* (Dec. 18, 1957) he had been a member of both Jong Java and of the PI while in Holland. He was a Protestant.

D. N. AIDIT was born on July 30, 1923, in Sumatra. His formal education went no higher than an intermediate-level commercial school. After 1940 he joined the Gerindo. He was also deputy chief of an organization called the Persatuan Buruh Kendaraan (Motor Transport Workers' Union). See Parlaungan, *Hasil rakjat,* p. 268.

Dr. Mohammed AMIR was born in Talawi, West Sumatra, on January 27, 1900. He graduated from the STOVIA in 1924, and studied medicine in Holland, obtaining his degree in 1928 and marrying an upper-class Dutch girl. In 1937 he became personal physician to the sultan of Langkat. During the Japanese period he sat on the East Sumatra sangikai and later on the All-Sumatra CAC. He was also deputy chairman of the Badan Oentoek Membantoe Pertahanan Asia (Body for Assisting the Defense of Asia) or BOMPA, the Sumatran equivalent of the Hōkōkai. *Ensiklopedia Indonesia,* I, 68; Deppen Files.

Mr. AMIR SJARIFUDDIN gelar Soetan Goenoeng Soaloon was born in Medan, North Sumatra, on May 27, 1907. He received an unusually good education, graduating from an ELS, and later attending elite gymnasium schools in Haarlem and Leiden. In 1933 he obtained a law degree at the Law Faculty in Djakarta. Thereafter he worked as an independent lawyer until 1940, when he entered the Economic Affairs Department of the colonial government. In 1933 he had been second deputy chairman of the Partindo, the more popular of the two parties into which Sukarno's PNI split after its leader's arrest. From 1939 to 1940 he was chairman of the Gerindo. From 1938 to 1940 he headed the secretariat of the federation of Indonesian political organizations known as Gapi. See *Orang Indonesia,* p. 258.

Mas ARUDJI Kartawinata was born in Garut, West Java, on May 5, 1905, and was educated in a HIS and a MULO. He worked as a journalist in Garut in the twenties, and from 1927 to 1929 served the PSII executive as commissioner for West Java. From 1929 to 1931 he was imprisoned for seditious statements against the government. On his release he led the section of the PSII executive in charge of youth. From 1936 to 1940 he was the party's general secretary. During the occupation he was in the procurement section of the Bandung municipal government. *Orang Indonesia,* pp. 453–54. Later he was daidanchō in Tjimahi. In October 1945 he was the first commander of the Third Division, but he was soon replaced by Nasution.

ASKARI was born on October 4, 1919, and married Kawilarang's sister. *Pikiran Rakjat* (Bandung), June 6, 1960. No other biographical information on him has come to my attention.

Mr. Radèn Soendoro BOEDDHYARTO Martoatmodjo was born in Surakarta, Central Java, on November 16, 1898, the younger brother of Dr. Buntaran. He was educated in an ELS (Purworedjo), a MULO (Djakarta), and at the Law Faculty in Djakarta before obtaining a law degree at the University of Leiden in 1925. Thereafter he worked as a private lawyer. From 1920 to 1921 he was vice-chairman of Jong Java, and in 1926 he became chairman of the PI. In 1927 he helped found the PNI and headed its Djakarta branch. In 1928 he established and headed the PNI branch in Palembang; subsequently he led in turn the PNI and Partindo branches in Djember. In the Japanese period he became chairman of the Besuki Residency sangikai and a member of the CAC. *Orang Indonesia,* p. 273. He was also vice-resident of Besuki. Shortly after the proclamation of independence he became resident, but he was soon removed as a result of popular pressure, and retired to Jogjakarta. *Antara*, Oct. 8, 1945. For a time he had also been head of the Besuki Barisan Pelopor. *Djawa Baroe*, Oct. 15, 1944.

Dr. Radèn BUNTARAN Martoatmodjo was born on January 11, 1896, near Purworedjo, Central Java. He graduated from an ELS and the STOVIA, and got his medical degree in Leiden in 1930. He was not active politically before the war, working as a doctor in government service in various parts of Indonesia. In 1942 he was briefly general manager of *Sinar Baroe* in Semarang. In 1943 he became second vice-chairman of the CAC, deputy commander of the Barisan Pelopor, and in December 1944, adviser to the Health Bureau. *Orang Indonesia*, p. 328; Kanahele, "Japanese Occupation," p. 268; *Kan Pō*, no. 56 (Dec. 10, 1944).

CHAERUL SALEH was born on September 13, 1916, in Sawahlunto, West Sumatra, the eldest son of Dr. Achmad Saleh. He attended ELS in Medan and Bukittinggi, and subsequently HBS in Medan. In 1934 he attended the Normal School III in Djakarta before entering the Law Faculty. In 1937 he helped found the PPPI, the most radical of the student associations. He was the last man to hold the chairmanship of this organization before the war. In the occupation period he not only held a job at the Sendenbu, but was also a leader of the Baperpi, which was set up to look after stranded and destitute students. In 1940 he married the daughter of L. Datuk Tumenggung, a high Minangkabau aristocrat. *Madjalah Merdeka* (Djakarta), IX, 10 (March 10, 1956).

K. H. Muhammad DAHLAN was born on June 2, 1909, in Mandaran, near Pasuruan, East Java. He was educated in a Standaardschool and in Mecca. He was a member of the famous pesantrèn Tebu Ireng (Djombang) and Siwalan Pandji (Sidoardjo). Prior to the war he was an Islamic teacher and a member of the Nahdatul Ulama, rising from being chairman of the Bangil branch in 1930 and of the Pasuruan branch in 1935 to being consul for East Java in 1936. In 1939 he became a board member of the MIAI, in 1941 a central board member of the Nahdatul Ulama, and in 1943 general chairman of the latter organization. During the war years he also headed a traders' organization in Pasuruan. *Orang Indonesia*, p. 433; Parlaungan, *Hasil rakjat*, p. 227.

Dr. DARMASETIAWAN was born in Djakarta in 1911 of mixed Javanese and Bengkulu descent. After graduating from an ELS, a MULO, and an AMS, he obtained a degree at the Medical Faculty in Djakarta in 1938. Thereafter he practiced as a doctor and health officer to the KNIL. During the occupation he worked in hospitals in Djakarta and Semarang. There appears to be no record of his having any prewar political experience. *Antara*, March 16, 1946; Deppen Files (which give the year of his graduation as 1939). He was the son-in-law of Hilman Djajadiningrat, the bupati of Serang and brother of Lukman Djajadiningrat, who had fled with the Dutch to Australia in 1942 and, had he not died in 1944, would probably have become head of the Education Department in the postwar Netherlands Indies government.

Ir. DARMAWAN Mangoenkoesoemo, younger brother of the well-known prewar nationalist leader, Dr. Tjipto Mangoenkoesoemo, was born on May 25, 1901, in Purwodadi, Central Java. He was educated in an ELS and a five-year HBS before winning an engineering degree at the Technical College in Delft in 1924. On his return he worked for the Department of Economic Affairs, continuing this work under the Japanese. *Orang Indonesia*, p. 204. In June 1945 he succeeded Sudirman as the Surabaja representative on the CAC. *Asia Raya*, June 15, 1945. He was briefly active in the PI from 1922 to 1923 (Koch, *Om de vrijheid*, p. 100); and according to *Ensiklopedia Indonesia* (p. 372), he helped Sukarno found the Algemeene Studie-club in Bandung in 1927. Thereafter he played no political role.

Ki Hadjar DEWANTORO was born on May 8, 1889, in the Pakualam-an, Jogjakarta. His schooling included an ELS, the STOVIA, and a teachers' training school in The Hague. With Douwes Dekker and Tjipto Mangoenkoesoemo he led the Indische Partij; in 1917 he was exiled to Holland, where he worked as a journalist and teacher. In 1922 he started the Taman Siswa nationalist school system that made him famous. In the Japanese period he was one of the four top leaders of the Putera and became adviser to the Education Bureau in

December 1944. *Orang Indonesia,* pp. 386–87; *Kan Pō,* no. 56 (Dec. 10, 1944).

Boerhanoedin Mochamad DIAH was born on April 7, 1914 (or 1916), in Kutaradja, Atjeh. He was educated in a HIS, a MULO, and an AMS, and later studied journalism in Bandung. From 1937 to 1938 he worked as assistant editor to the Medan newspaper *Sinar Deli;* thereafter he was in Djakarta as editor of *Warta Harian.* After the arrival of the Japanese he became English-language commentator for the army radio and later assistant editor of the main Djakarta daily, *Asia Raya.* His wife, Herawati, was the niece of the prominent nationalist Mr. Subardjo. *Orang Indonesia,* p. 282; *Kedaulatan Rakjat,* July 16, 1957.

DJAWOTO, by his own account, was secretary of the Makasar branch of Tjokroaminoto's PSII in 1927, but later that year shifted to the local branch of the PNI, of which he became a leading member. When the PNI closed down, he became a member of the central board of the Pendidikan Nasional Indonesia under Sjahrir. Statement by Djawoto in *Sin Po,* July 7, 1955. During the war he worked with Malik at the Dōmei. During the fifties and sixties he was increasingly identified with the PKI.

Mr. DJODY Gondokusumo was born on June 7 or 12, 1912, in Jogjakarta. He obtained a degree from the Law Faculty in Djakarta. Thereafter, during both the Dutch and the Japanese period, he was an official in the employ of the Sultanate. In the thirties he was a member of the top leaderships of the PPPI, the Suryawirawan, and the Parindra, eventually becoming first vice-chairman of the last-named organization. He was active in the Triple-A Movement, and was regarded as friendly toward the Japanese. Parlaungan, *Hasil rakjat,* p. 136; Indonesia, Kementerian Penerangan, *Kami perkenalkan,* p. 22; Deppen Files; *Dokumentasi pemuda,* p. 29.

DJOHAN SJAHROEZAH was born in Muara Enim, South Sumatra, on November 26, 1912. He attended the Law Faculty in Djakarta but never got his degree. He was a founding member of the Pendidikan Nasional Indonesia, and was apparently a contact man for Tan Malaka's illegal communist party Pari. With Malik he was one of the founders of the Indonesian news agency Antara in 1937. During the occupation he worked for a period as Hatta's secretary, and then moved to Surabaja, where he was able to set up an underground group in the local oil refineries. He was also a son-in-law of Hadji Agus Salim. For a vivid sketch of his wartime role, see Kahin, *Nationalism and Revolution,* p. 113. Other information derives from Indonesia, Kementerian Penerangan, *Kami perkenalkan,* p. 84; and obituaries appearing in *Harian Kami* (Djakarta), Aug. 3, 1968, *Api Pantjasila* (Djakarta), Aug. 3, 1968, and *Nusantara* (Djakarta), Aug. 5, 1968. (In these obituaries his age at the time of his death is variously given as 55, 57, and 58.)

Ir. Radèn DJUANDA was born in Tasikmalaja, West Java, on July 10, 1911. He was educated in an ELS and a five-year HBS before graduating from the Technical Faculty in Bandung in 1933. Thereafter, until 1937, he directed a Muhammadijah secondary school. For the rest of the Dutch period and during the war, he pursued his profession as an engineer. From 1933 to 1942 he was a member of the executive of Oto Iskandardinata's Sundanese political party, Pagujuban Pasundan. *Orang Indonesia,* p. 223; *Antara,* Nov. 7, 1963 (his obituary).

Hadji Achmad DJUNAEDI was born on March 8, 1896, in Bodjong, near Tjiamis, West Java. He entered the Sarekat Islam in 1914 and chaired the Tjiamis regency branch. He was arrested early in 1918 in connection with the Afdeling B Affair in Garut and was exiled to West Sumatra. In 1922 he was released and became chairman of the East Priangan PKI. He was involved in the 1926 uprising and was exiled to Boven Digul. Freed in 1938, he returned to Tjiamis and was involved in underground activities there, and also during the Japanese period. *Harian Rakjat,* Nov. 10, 1964.

K. H. FAKIH OESMAN was born on March 2, 1904, in Gresik, East Java. He had an exclusively Islamic education, and later entered the textile and construction business in his home town. In 1922 he joined the Muhammadijah and became head of the Gresik branch. He rose steadily in the Muhammadijah hierarchy thereafter, becoming in 1938 the central board's consul for the Surabaja area. From 1938 to 1942 he was successively treasurer and secretary of the MIAI. He was active also in the Muhammadijah's publishing ventures, helping to edit the magazine *Bintang Islam* from 1925 to 1930, and acting as chief editor of *Siaran* (Surabaja) from 1938 to 1941. During the occupation he was a member of the Surabaja Residency sangikai. *Orang Indonesia,* p. 434; Parlaungan, *Hasil rakjat,* p. 152; *Madjalah Penuntun* (Djakarta), X, 4–5 (May 1956).

H. M. FARIED MA'RUF was born in the kauman of Jogjakarta on March 25, 1908. He was educated in a HIS, an Ibtidaijah school, and the Dar El Ulum high school in Egypt, and graduated from the Al Azhar University in Cairo in 1932. On his return in 1934 he became a teacher for the Muhammadijah in Jogjakarta and a member of the central board of the Muhammadijah. From 1938 to 1942 he was a member of the top leadership of the revived PII. He was one of the MIAI representatives attending the Tokyo Islamic Exhibition along with Kasmat. In 1942 he became a member of the central MIAI leadership, and later sat as a Muhammadijah representative on the wartime Masjumi's executive. *Orang Indonesia,* p. 439; Benda, *The Crescent and the Rising Sun,* p. 263; Kanahele, "Japanese Occupation," pp. 10, 248.

K. H. FATOERRACHMAN was born in 1904, in Tuban, East Java. He was educated in Mecca and at the Al Azhar University in Cairo. On his return he founded and headed the pesantrèn Hidajat in Tuban. He became a member both of the Muhammadijah and of Sukiman's PII. During the occupation he sat on the CAC. *Orang Indonesia,* p. 390; Benda, *The Crescent and the Rising Sun,* p. 252.

A. GAFFAR ISMAIL gelar Soetan Indra Maharadja was born in Bukittinggi, West Sumatra, in August 1911. He was educated in the modernist Islamic Sumatra Thawalib school system. Subsequently he was first a top leader of the local West Sumatran religious-nationalist party Persatuan Muslimin Indonesia (Indonesian Islamic Union), or "Permi," and then of the revived PII in Jogjakarta. During the occupation he was a member of the Semarang Residency sangikai, Sajuti

Melik's successor as an editor of the Semarang newspaper *Sinar Baroe,* and a spokesman at the Villa Isola Congress. *Orang Indonesia,* p. 283; *Djawa Baroe,* June 1, 1945.

Radèn GATOT MANGKUPRADJA was born on December 15, 1898, the son of Dr. Saleh Mangkupradja. He graduated from an ELS and later attended the STOVIA in Djakarta. He was a close associate of Sukarno in the prewar PNI and held a high position in its noncooperative nationalist successor, the Partindo. During the 1930's he developed relations with the Japanese. In December 1933 he attended the Tokyo Pan-Asiatic Conference sponsored by the prominent radical nationalists Tōyama and Uchida, and was much impressed with the pro-Indonesian views expressed there by the war minister, General Araki, the best-known representative of the radical Kōdōha faction in the Japanese military. During the occupation he became a member of the CAC. *Djawa Baroe,* Sept. 15, 1944; Kanahele, "Japanese Occupation," pp. 4–5; *Angkatan Bersendjata* (Djakarta), Oct. 5, 1968; Deppen Files.

Mr. GATOT TARUNAMIHARDJA was born on November 24, 1901, in Sukabumi, West Java. He graduated from the Law School in Djakarta at the age of nineteen and pursued his legal studies further in Holland. After five years there, studying under difficult financial conditions, he returned to Indonesia in 1927. Thereafter he worked as a private attorney. During the Japanese occupation he was chief judge of the local court in Purwokerto. He had a reputation of great integrity, and was a friend of Subardjo and Iwa from their student days together in Holland in the twenties. *Bintang Timur* (Djakarta), April 13, 1959; *Kan Pō,* no. 72 (Aug. 10, 1945).

Mr. Radèn HADI was born near Blora, East Java, on June 7, 1894. He was educated in an ELS and an OSVIA, and at the Law School in Djakarta, where he got his diploma in 1924. He then entered government service and rose steadily in the hierarchy of the Department of Education and Religious Affairs. From 1930 to 1938 he was a member of the Djakarta Municipal Council, and in 1938 became an alderman. He was in the Parindra for a short period, but otherwise confined his political activity to giving financial assistance to needy students. During the occupation he sat successively on the Djakarta and Surabaja courts of appeal. *Orang Indonesia,* p. 141.

HAMENGKUBUWONO IX was born in Jogjakarta on April 12, 1912. At the age of five he was lodged, together with his brother (Pangéran Prabuningrat), in the home of a Dutch family. It was a setting that laid strong emphasis on the bourgeois virtues of self-discipline and hard work. Subsequently he attended the HBS in Semarang, the Lyceum in Haarlem, and Leiden University, where he studied economics in the Indological Department. In 1939 he was called home by his father because of the imminence of war, and he never won his diploma. Deppen Files; *Sinar Harapan,* July 9, 1968 (interview with Pangéran Prabuningrat).

Anak Marhaen HANAFI was born on October 17, 1917, in Bengkulu, Southwest Sumatra. He became a protégé of Sukarno during the latter's exile there. On Sukarno's advice he went to Djakarta in 1938 and joined the Gerindo. He was made general secretary of the Barisan Pemuda Gerindo when it was formed that year under the leadership of Wikana. Biro Pemuda, *Sedjarah perdjuangan pemuda Indonesia,* p. 84; *Bintang Timur,* Dec. 19, 1963; Sidik Kertapati, *Sekitar proklamasi,* p. 47.

Drs. Mohammed HATTA was born in Bukittinggi, West Sumatra, on August 12, 1902. After graduating from an ELS, a MULO in Padang, and a commercial high school in Djakarta, he went to Holland, and in 1932 obtained a master's degree at the Rotterdam Business School. Prior to his departure for Holland he had been secretary and treasurer of the Padang branch of the JSB, and later treasurer at its headquarters in Djakarta. In Holland he was for almost a decade the dominant influence in the PI, which rivaled the PNI in its impact on prewar nationalist thinking. On his return to Indonesia in 1932, he took over the leadership of the Pendidikan Nasional Indonesia, one of the two groups into which Sukarno's PNI had split after its founder's arrest. In 1934 he was imprisoned and exiled, first to Boven Digul and later to the remote island of Banda. In February 1942 he was brought back to Sukabumi, and was eventually released by the Japanese. During the occupation he was the second man in the

Putera leadership, and was Sukarno's deputy in the Head Office of the Hōkōkai. *Orang Indonesia,* p. 44.

Radèn HIDAJAT was born in Tjiandjur, West Java, on May 26, 1916. After serving as a lieutenant in the KNIL, he worked during the occupation in the Bus Section of the Land Transport Division of the military administration. Indonesia, Kementerian Penerangan, *Kami perkenalkan,* p. 37.

Mr. Radèn HINDROMARTONO was born on December 31, 1908, in Rembang, Central Java. He was educated at a HIS, a MULO, and an AMS, before taking his degree at the Law Faculty in Djakarta in 1936. From 1929 to 1933 he helped edit *Indonesia Raja,* and from 1933 to 1934 headed the PPI. After leaving school he worked as a teacher, and from 1937 to 1938 sat as a member of the Djakarta Municipal Council. From 1937 onward he was active in labor organizations, becoming head of the PPST (Federated Union of Railway and Tram Employees), chairman of the PPPPK (Union of Harbor and Dockyard Employees), deputy chairman of the PPPM (Union of Oil Company Employees), member of the central leadership of the PVPN (Federation of Civil Servants' Unions), and deputy chairman of the Gaspi. During the Japanese occupation he worked in the Labor Bureau of the military administration. *Orang Indonesia,* p. 10.

ISMAIL WIDJAJA was Wikana's successor as chairman of the Barisan Pemuda Gerindo, after being a member of the Persatuan Pemuda Rakjat Mataram (Union of Mataram Youth), a mildly left-leaning youth organization in Jogjakarta in the early thirties. Biro Pemuda, *Sedjarah perdjuangan pemuda Indonesia,* pp. 76, 86; Sidik Kertapati, *Sekitar proklamasi,* p. 47.

Mr. Radèn IWA KUSUMASUMANTRI was born on May 31, 1899, in Tjiamis, West Java. After graduating from a HIS and an OSVIA, he received a law degree from the University of Leiden in 1925. In Holland he was for a while chairman of the PI. On his return to Indonesia he briefly joined the PNI before moving to Medan, where he opened a private law office. He was active in various labor organizations and was chief editor of the newspaper *Matahari,* for which

Subardjo was Tokyo correspondent. In 1929 he was arrested for his political activities, and in 1930 he was exiled to Banda. In 1941 he was transferred to Makasar, and only on the eve of the occupation was he released. He then returned to Djakarta and joined Maramis' law firm. He held no important position under the Japanese, and was appointed chief of the Labor Bureau only on August 27, 1945. *Orang Indonesia,* pp. 294–95; Deppen Files; *Soeara Asia,* Aug. 30, 1945.

Mr. Muhammad JUSUF was born on May 17, 1910, in Indramaju, West Java. He was educated in an ELS and a five-year HBS before obtaining a law degree at the University of Utrecht in 1937. On his return to Indonesia he went into private practice in Tjirebon. In 1942 he was a leader of the Gerindo organization in Bandung. During part of the occupation he was employed in the Health Bureau of the Department of Internal Affairs. *Orang Indonesia,* p. 10.

Muhammad Rachmat KARTAKUSUMAH was born in Tjiamis, West Java, on June 21, 1920. He was educated in a Christian HIS and a HBS, from which he graduated in 1938. In 1940 he entered the Bandung Military Academy, and on graduation became a section commander in Djatinegara. After the Japanese invasion he was briefly imprisoned in Tjimahi, but was released in May 1942. He was then posted to the central railways office in Bandung. He was also active in the Seinendan along with Nasution. *Madjalah Merdeka,* IX, 49 (Dec. 8, 1956); *Orang Indonesia,* p. 130; Deppen Files.

Didi KARTASAMITA (see Chap. 11).

Sekarmadji Maridjan KARTOSOEWIRJO was born in Tjepu, East Java, on February 5, 1905, the son of an official in the Opium Inspectorate; he was educated successively in a HIS, an ELS, and for four years in the NIAS (Netherlands Indies Medical School) before he was ousted for concealing books about communism and socialism. He was active in Jong Java in Surabaja from 1923, eventually becoming the local chairman. In 1925 he left Jong Java to join Wiwoho's JIB. From 1927 to 1929 he was private secretary to Tjokroaminoto. He then fell seriously ill and retired to the home of his father-in-law in Malangbong, near Garut. Evidently in this period he studied under various mystically oriented kjai such as K. H. Mustofa Kamil. It was probably at this stage of his life that he developed the intensely militant and mystical Islamic convictions he maintained until his death. In 1931 he became general secretary of the PSII, while still only 26 years old. Following the death of Tjokroaminoto he was made vice-chairman of the party. He was always uncompromisingly opposed to any cooperation with the Dutch, and supported the main body of the party in the expulsion of Hadji Agus Salim and Mohammed Roem for such activities in 1936. In 1939, however, he quarreled with the party leadership over what he believed to be their declining commitment to noncooperation, their willingness to work with the secular nationalist parties in the Gapi, and their support for the secular nationalists' campaign for a genuine Indies parliament. It is not clear whether he resigned from the PSII or was dismissed, but in any event he retired again to Malangbong, where he set up a Komité Pertahanan Kebenaran PSII (Committee to Defend the True Doctrine of the PSII). During the Japanese period he was made secretary of the Masjumi, but does not seem to have been very active. He spent most of his time in Malangbong, organizing an extremely militant asrama of his own, which he named the Institut Suffah. Noer, "Rise and Development," pp. 239–41; Pinardi, *Sekarmadji Maridjan Kartosuwirjo,* pp. 20–81.

Mr. Radèn KASMAN Singodimedjo was born near Purworedjo, Central Java, on February 25, 1908. He was educated in a HIS, a MULO, at the STOVIA, and at the Law Faculty in Djakarta, where he received a degree in 1939. Before the war he worked as a teacher in various modernist Islamic schools and subsequently joined the Agricultural Service of the colonial government. In 1923 he was a top leader of Jong Java. From 1925 to 1929 he headed the scouting organization of the JIB, and from 1929 to 1935 acted as general chairman of the JIB itself. From 1939 to 1941 he headed the Muhammadijah organization in the Djakarta area. During the war he became a daidanchō in the Peta in the Djakarta area. Indonesia, Kementerian Penerangan, *Kami perkenalkan,* p. 95; Parlaungan, *Hasil rakjat,* pp. 163–64; information supplied by Daniel S. Lev.

Mr. Radèn Achmad KASMAT was born in Kota Gede, Jogjakarta, on May 15, 1908. He graduated from an ELS and studied at the

Law Faculty in Djakarta before obtaining a law degree at the University of Leiden in 1934. On his return he opened a private law practice. In 1937 he was chairman of the Studenten Islam Studieclub, and in 1938 he became first secretary of the revived PII. In 1939 he was one of four young MIAI representatives sent to attend the Islamic Exhibition in Tokyo. During the occupation he worked in the administration of the Jogjakarta Principality. *Orang Indonesia,* p. 11 (which says he was vice-chairman of the PII); Noer, "Rise and Development," p. 255; Kanahele, "Japanese Occupation," pp. 10, 248.

Alex Evert KAWILARANG, a Menadonese, was born in Djatinegara, on the outskirts of Djakarta, on February 23, 1920. He was educated at a HBS in Bandung before entering the Military Academy. From 1943 to 1945 he was in Sumatra, his last job being that of chief of a rubber factory in Tandjung Karang. In 1945 he returned to Djakarta. Indonesia, Kementerian Penerangan, *Kami perkenalkan,* p. 48; *Almanak Angkatan Perang,* p. 154.

KEMAL IDRIS was born in 1923, the son of Prof. Muhamad Idris, a veterinarian and activist in the conservative and cooperative nationalist party Parindra. Kemal himself was educated entirely in Dutch-language schools: in an ELS in Purwokerto; then in an ELS in Utrecht, Holland, where his father was studying; and subsequently in elite HBS in Makasar, Jogjakarta, and Sukabumi. He was just nineteen years old when the war came to Java. *Kompas* (Djakarta), Aug. 16, 1968.

Biographical data on KRISSUBANU are contradictory. According to Indonesia, Kementerian Penerangan, *Kami perkenalkan* (p. 95), he was born on December 17, 1916, in Modjokerto, East Java. According to *Kedaulatan Rakjat* (Oct. 4, 1958), he was born in 1913 at Gresik, East Java, a descendant of Tumenggung Pusponegoro, who built the first mosque in the area and was a legendary figure to the local populace. Krissubanu's family for this reason had the title Kjai Ngabèhi. He finished MULO in Malang in 1932. While still at school he became the leader of the Malang branch of the SPI, the youth arm of the Pendidikan Nasional Indonesia. He was also the elder brother of Ibnu Parna.

Ir. Herling LAOH was born on August 23, 1904, in Tompaso, North Sulawesi. He was educated in an ELS and a five-year HBS, and received an engineering degree in Bandung in 1928. His prewar career was nonpolitical; he worked for both the Dutch and the Japanese administration on irrigation projects. *Orang Indonesia,* pp. 230–31.

Dr. Johannes LEIMENA was born on March 6, 1905, in Ambon. He was educated in an ELS and a MULO, at the STOVIA, and at the Medical Faculty in Djakarta, receiving his degree in 1939. Aside from his medical practice he was a founding member of the Perkumpulan Pemuda Maluku (Moluccan Youth Association) and of the Protestant political party Parkindo. Parlaungan, *Hasil rakjat,* p. 343.

M. H. LUKMAN was born on February 26, 1920, in Tegal, Central Java. His father was sentenced to serve a term in the Boven Digul concentration camp for involvement in the Communist uprisings of 1926–27, and he took the boy with him. Lukman was in fact educated in the camp. During the occupation he worked in the head offices of the Putera and the Hōkōkai under the eye of Sukarno and Hatta. He was active not only in the Menteng 31 asrama, but also in the Barisan Pelopor Istimewa. According to Communist sources, he and Aidit set up a small radical underground of their own called the Gerakan Indonesia Merdeka (Free Indonesia Movement), or "Gerindom." Parlaungan, *Hasil rakjat,* pp. 276–77; Sidik Kertapati, *Sekitar proklamasi,* pp. 43–45.

Mr. Radèn LUKMAN HAKIM was born on October 14, 1914, in Tuban, East Java, the son of a Solonese father, R. Abdoellah Koestoer, and a Tuban mother. He was educated in a HIS, a MULO, and an AMS in Jogjakarta, and obtained a degree at the Law Faculty in Djakarta in 1941. While still in secondary school he joined Indonesia Muda and later the PPPI. In 1938 he headed the Djakarta branch of Indonesia Muda. While studying at the Law Faculty he taught at the Perguruan Rakjat, a school system started and run by young nationalist intellectuals in the capital. During the Japanese period he worked in the government tax office in Djakarta. *Orang Indonesia,* p. 117; *Kedaulatan Rakjat,* Aug. 30, 1966.

Rear Adm. Tadashi MAEDA was born on March 3, 1898, the son of a school principal in Kajikimachi, a small town in Kagoshima province. At eighteen he joined the Marine College for three years and became a navigation specialist. In 1930, with the rank of first lieutenant, he joined the Naval Staff, and worked for one and one-half years in the European Affairs Section of the Naval Department in Tokyo. From 1932 to 1934 he worked at the Naval Station at Ōminato, where his wife died (he remained a widower). In early 1937 he was sent to England as adjutant to Rear Adm. Sōnosuke Kobayashi to represent Japan at the coronation. On his return he served in the Combined Fleet in Chinese waters, as aide-de-camp to the commander, Adm. Zengō Yoshida. In December 1938 he became aide-de-camp to Adm. Kiyoshi Hasegawa, commander of the Yokosuka Naval Base, with the rank of commander. In February 1940 he was sent to Holland as naval attaché. In October 1940 he went to Djakarta as a member of the Kobayashi mission, which tried to compel the Indies government to guarantee the supply of designated quantities of war materiel, especially oil, to give Japan unprecedented access to the Indies harbors and internal markets, and to allow a large increase in Japanese immigration. Maeda's specific task is said to have been to collect Dutch military secrets and, together with the civilians Nishijima, Ishii, and Machida, to set up a fifth column among the indigenous population. He returned to Japan in June or July of 1941 and in September was made deputy chief of the European Section of the Naval General Staff, which was then headed by his elder brother, Adm. Minoru Maeda. In August 1942 he was sent to Djakarta to become liaison officer between the Sixteenth Army and the naval administration in Makasar. See Tadashi Maeda, statements of April 4, 1946 (IC-RVO doc. no. 006812–3), April 20, 1946, and June 20, 1946 (IC-RVO doc. no. 006894–902); and Kanahele, "Japanese Occupation," pp. 17, 21, 253.

Adam MALIK was born in Pematang Siantar, North Sumatra, on July 22, 1917. His formal schooling did not go beyond HIS. In 1937 he was one of the founders of the first Indonesian press agency, Antara, in Djakarta, and when, in the Japanese period, this was merged with the Japanese news agency Dōmei, he joined Dōmei's staff. During 1932–33 he had been a member of the Siantar branch of the Partindo, and in 1933 a member of the East Sumatra Partindo leadership. From 1939 to 1941 he was a member of the Gerindo leadership of Djakarta. Just prior to the Japanese landings he, together with Sukarni, Asmara Hadi, and Wikana, was interned by the Dutch on suspicion of subversive activities. *Orang Indonesia,* p. 279; Parlaungan, *Hasil rakjat,* p. 314; Kanahele, "Japanese Occupation," p. 266. There is an excellent character portrait of him in Tjiptoning, *Apa dan siapa,* pp. 137–45.

Mr. A. A. MARAMIS was born in Menado, North Sulawesi, on June 20, 1897, and was educated in an ELS and a five-year HBS before gaining a law degree at the University of Leiden in 1924. Thereafter he worked as an independent lawyer in various towns in Indonesia. He was for a while secretary of the PI in The Hague, and later secretary of the Persatuan Minahasa (Minahasa Union). In the Japanese period he sat on the Consultative Council of the Putera. *Orang Indonesia,* p. 295. He eventually became an adviser to the Bukanfu. On September 25, 1945, he succeeded Dr. Samsi as minister of finance because of the latter's poor health. Finch and Lev, *Republic of Indonesia Cabinets,* p. 3.

K. H. MASJKOER was born in Singosari, East Java, in 1899 or 1902, and had a pesantrèn education. On completing his studies he set up his own pesantrèn, which in 1936 became a regular Nahdatul Ulama school. In 1932 he headed the Malang branch of the Nahdatul Ulama, and in 1938 he became a member of the staff of the Central Board in Surabaja. He was a member of the Investigating Committee in the late occupation period. Parlaungan, *Hasil rakjat,* pp. 241–42; *Madjalah Penuntun,* X, 4–5 (May 1956).

Mr. Dr. Todoeng gelar Soetan Goenoeng MOELIA was born on January 21, 1896, in Padangsidempuan, South Tapanuli. He graduated from an ELS and later from the Leiden Teachers' College before taking a law degree at the University of Leiden in 1932, and a degree in letters and philosophy at the same university in 1933. Aside from being a teacher, he was from 1927 to 1929 and from 1935 to 1942 a member of the Volksraad, from 1940 to 1942 as its vice-chairman. From 1936 to 1942 he was successively an official of

uprising of 1926 and was jailed for four years, then exiled to Boven Digul. In the Japanese period he headed the propaganda section of the Djakarta Hōkōkai, but was also jailed by the Kenpeitai for four months. He became a member of the Barisan Pelopor Istimewa. Parlaungan, *Hasil rakjat*, p. 76; *Berita Yudha* (Djakarta), April 29, 1966.

Radèn OTO Iskandardinata was born in Bodjongsoang in the Regency of Bandung on March 31, 1897. He graduated from a HIS, a Teachers' Training School, and a Higher Teachers' Training School. Before the war he was a teacher at various government and private schools, but made his name as editor of the Sundanese language newspaper *Sipatahoenan* (1935–42) and as the representative of the Sundanese political organization Pagujuban Pasundan in the Volksraad (1931–42). In 1942 he became editor-in-chief of the Bandung newspaper *Tjahaja*, and later sports chief of the Putera and a member of the CAC. In December 1944 he became adviser to the Security Department. *Orang Indonesia*, pp. 452–53; *Kan Pō*, no. 56 (Dec. 10, 1944).

PANDU KARTAWIGUNA was born in Tjirebon, West Java, on February 13, 1913. He was a close friend of Adam Malik and worked with him in founding the news agency Antara in 1937. Parlaungan, *Hasil rakjat*, pp. 320–21.

Mohammad PRAWOTO Mangkusasmito was born at Tirto-Grabag near Magelang, Central Java, on January 4, 1910. He graduated from an AMS in Jogjakarta in 1931 and at the end of the thirties studied for four years at the Law Faculty in Djakarta. In between times he worked as a teacher, and during the occupation, as a land surveyor. After periods of activity in Jong Java, Indonesian Muda, and the JIB, he became chairman of the Studenten Islam Studieclub and editor of the *Moslimse Reveille*. He joined the Sukiman-Wiwoho PII in 1940 and became one of its top leaders. He also joined the Muhammadijah. In early 1945 he was named to the official leadership of the Hizbullah. On a personal level he was a schoolmate of both Roem and Jusuf Wibisono. Parlaungan, *Hasil rakjat*, pp. 179f.; Indonesia, Kementerian Penerangan, *Kami perkenalkan*, p. 110; *Abadi* (Minggu), May 3, 1959; and *Soeara Moeslimin Indonesia*, III, 2 (Jan. 15, 1945), 12.

the Department of Economic Affairs and the Department of Education and Religious Affairs. *Orang Indonesia,* p. 398; Deppen Files. In the late Japanese period he held high office as the *kyōkakachō,* or chief of the Social Education Section within the Education Bureau. *Kan Pō,* no. 71 (July 25, 1945). He was also a second cousin of Amir Sjarifuddin.

Radèn Mas MOERDJODO was born about 1903 into the royal family of Jogjakarta. He had been a member of Sukarno's PNI. In 1945 he was active in setting up the local KNI in Jogjakarta. (Information provided by José Eliseo Rocamora from an interview with Hadiprabowo, July 1969.)

Dr. Radèn MUSTOPO was born on June 13, 1913, in Ngadiluwih, Kediri, East Java. After graduating from a HIS, he attended a MULO and the STOVIA for short periods. In 1939 he received a degree in dentistry. An eccentric, flamboyant man given to mysticism, he was briefly arrested by the Kenpeitai, apparently because his large build and strong features led them to assume he was a Eurasian, and therefore suspect. On his release he was employed as a dentist by the Japanese army. He was a member of the second group of men trained to be Peta officers and graduated at the top of his class of candidate chūdanchō. He returned to Sidoardjo to take up a position as chūdanchō, but apparently his prowess was such that he was moved up to daidanchō, a promotion achieved by only five other officers of his rank. *Orang Indonesia,* pp. 334–35; Deppen Files.

Mr. M. S. MOEWALADI was born in Sragen, Central Java, in 1907. He was educated in an ELS and a HBS before gaining a law degree at the University of Leiden. He was a member of the PI in the late thirties and was involved in the anti-Nazi underground in Holland during the war. Information kindly supplied by Daniel S. Lev; see also Sidik Kertapati, *Sekitar proklamasi,* p. 112.

Dr. Mas MUWARDI was born in Pati, Central Java, on January 31, 1907. He was educated in an ELS and graduated from the STOVIA in 1933. Thereafter he went into private practice in Djakarta. During the war he worked in the main general hospital in that city. In 1922 he was editor-in-chief of the Jong Java's magazine, and in 1925 headed the Jong Java's Djakarta branch. Beginning in 1926 he was a top leader of the nationalist scouting organization KBI. In the late thirties he was associated with the Parindra, as well as with a variety of sporting associations. During the occupation he was active in relief work before becoming top leader of the Barisan Pelopor. *Orang Indonesia,* p. 335.

Abdul Haris NASUTION was born in Kotanopan, Tapanuli, on December 3, 1918. He was educated in a HIS, a HIK (Dutch-Native Teachers' Training School), and an AMS. After spending a year as a teacher in Palembang, he entered the Military Academy in Bandung in 1940. When the war broke out in Java, he was a section commander in the KNIL, serving in East Java. During the war he worked first as a civil servant in the municipal administration in Bandung. While a student at the academy, he had lodged with the family of Sukanda Bratamenggala, and in 1944, when Sukanda left his position as head of the Seinendan in Bandung to join the Peta, Nasution took his place. He was also deputy commander of the local Barisan Pelopor. *Yudhagama* (Djakarta), no. 13 (Oct. 1951); *Orang Indonesia,* p. 131 (which gives his birthplace as Huta Pungkut, Tapanuli); Simatupang, *Laporan dari Banaran,* pp. 102–4; *Sinar Harapan,* June 18, 1968; and interview with Sukanda Bratamenggala, June 9, 1967.

Mohammad NATSIR gelar Datoek Sinaro Pandjang was born in Alahan Pandjang, West Sumatra, on July 17, 1908, the son of a lower-level government official. He was educated in a HIS and a MULO in West Sumatra, and then in an AMS in Bandung, where he took Latin and Greek as his specialty. From 1932 to 1942 he was director of the MULO and the Dutch-Native Teachers' Training School in the Islamic Education school system of the rigidly reformist Moslem organization Persatuan Islam (Islamic Union), or "Persis," centered in Bandung. On May 5, 1942, he was put in charge of education for the municipality of Bandung by the Japanese. Later in the occupation he became secretary to the board of the Islamic College established in Djakarta by the military authorities. He started his political career in the JIB in 1929 while still at school. In 1932 he became chairman of the so-called *kernlichaam* (core-

Ir. Martinus PUTUHENA was born in Ihamahu, Saparua, Ambon, on May 27, 1901. After graduating from a HIS, a MULO and an AMS, he obtained an engineering degree from the Technical Faculty in Bandung in 1927. Prior to the occupation he worked for the colonial government. In February 1945 he was appointed head of the Particuliere Landerijen Office in Djakarta. Like Darmawan, he was associated with Sukarno in founding the Algemeene Studieclub in Bandung, but seems not to have been politically active thereafter. *Antara,* Nov. 19, 1945, and March 16, 1946; Indonesia, Kementerian Penerangan, *Kami perkenalkan,* p. 40; *Ensiklopedia Indonesia,* p. 1150.

Ir. Baginda Zainuddin RASAD was born to a prominent Minangkabau family in Pariaman, West Sumatra, on November 21, 1890. He was educated in the Sekolah Radja at Bukittinggi, and later at a five-year HBS in Holland. In 1920 he received a degree in agricultural engineering from the Agricultural College at Wageningen. On his return to Indonesia he worked for the Dutch colonial government in various capacities. During the occupation he was attached to the municipal government of Djakarta. He does not seem to have been active politically at any time. Deppen Files.

H. RASJIDI was born in Kota Gede, Jogjakarta, in 1914. He was educated at an Al-Irsjad school in Djakarta before completing his studies at the King Fuad I University in Cairo. On his return in 1931 he taught at the Mualimin Muhammadijah and the Pesantrèn Luhur in Surakarta. He was a commissioner of the prewar PII, led by Sukiman and Wiwoho, and was subsequently active in the MIAI and the Masjumi. In 1945 he was a teacher at the Japanese-sponsored Sekolah Tinggi Islam (Islamic College) in Djakarta, together with Natsir. *Madjalah Penuntun,* X, 4–5 (May 1956); Noer, "Rise and Development," pp. 255–56; *Antara,* March 16, 1946. In the late occupation period he became deputy head of the Department of Religious Affairs under K. H. Abdul Kahar Muzakkir. Shortly after independence was proclaimed, Muzakkir left for Jogjakarta and was temporarily succeeded by K. H. Adnan. When the latter was unable to obtain his staff's backing for a move to Jogjakarta, he was replaced by Rasjidi. On these developments see the invaluable "Report on Religious Affairs during the Japanese Period," IC-RVO doc. no. 006599–611, prepared by an anonymous official within the department.

Mr. Mohammed ROEM was born in Parakan, Central Java, on May 16, 1908, the non-prijaji son of an urban *lurah* (headman) in Parakan. He was educated in HIS in Temanggung and Pekalongan, and in the STOVIA and AMS before shifting to the Law Faculty in Djakarta, where he won his degree in 1939. Thereafter he opened a private law practice. Though his earliest political activity was in Jong Java, during his STOVIA days he became, along with Kasman Singodimedjo, an intimate protégé of Hadji Agus Salim and was deeply influenced by the older man's thinking. He joined the PSII, but when his mentor was expelled from the party, Roem suffered the same fate. Thereafter he became head of the Working Committee of the Pergerakan Penjadar (Awakening Movement) established to spread Salim's liberal and cooperating political ideas. In 1937 he led the Studenten Islam Studieclub and for a year edited its magazine, *Moslimse Reveille*. In the Japanese period he played no important role. In early 1945 he was appointed vice-chairman of the Hizbullah, but he never took up the position. *Orang Indonesia,* p. 345; Tjiptoning, *Apa dan siapa,* pp. 76, 149–58; interviews with Roem in February 1968.

Mohammed Ibnu Sajuti, known as SAJUTI MELIK, was born in 1908 and by his own account entered politics in 1923, when he was just fifteen years old. He spent much of the prewar period in prison or in exile because of his radical left-wing leanings, including a stretch in the early thirties in Boven Digul and in the early forties in the Sukamiskin jail near Bandung. He was imprisoned by the Japanese at Ambarawa, probably because of critical editorials he had written for the Semarang daily, *Sinar Baroe*. In mid-1945 Sukarno discovered his whereabouts and interceded with the authorities to obtain his release. He reached Djakarta while Sukarno and Hatta were still in Saigon. On their return he was taken on as Sukarno's private secretary. Sajuti Melik, "Kenangan dimasa lampau" and "Proklamasi Kemerdekaan."

On Ir. Radèn SAKSONO Prawirohardjo little information is available except that in 1942 he served as agricultural education officer in

Central Java. He does not seem to have had any political interests.
Deppen Files.

Mohammed SALEH Werdisastro was born in Sumenep, Madura, on
April 6, 1908. He graduated from a HIS, the Teachers' Training
School, and the Higher Teachers' Training School in Magelang
(1930). He also studied in various pesantrèn between 1935 and
1940. Prior to 1941 he was principal of a private school in Sumenep.
From 1941 to 1943 he taught at the Muhammadijah MULO in Jogjakarta; then he joined the Peta and became a daidanchō. Before the
war he had been very active politically as a member successively of
Jong Java, the JIB, Indonesia Muda, the BU, and after 1932, the Muhammadijah. From 1933 until his move to Jogjakarta he was head of
the Pemuda Muhammadijah and the Moslem scouting organization
Hizbul Wathan for all Madura. After the independence proclamation he was elected the first head of the Jogjakarta KNI. Deppen
Files.

Hadji Agus SALIM, one of the best-known "characters" of the
prewar pergerakan, was born in Kota Gedang, West Sumatra, on
October 8, 1884. Coming from an aristocratic Minangkabau family,
he was educated in an ELS and a five-year HBS. For some years
before the First World War (variously 1906–11 and 1906–09), he
worked in the Dutch consulate at Jiddah. From 1915 to 1922 he
was active in the Sarekat Islam, becoming one of its top leaders.
When the Sarekat Islam broke up he led its right-wing rump, the
Partai Sarekat Islam (PSI), together with Tjokroaminoto. From
1922 to 1925 he served as a member of the Volksraad and was the
political mentor of the JIB. After the PSI became the PSII he served
on its executive board until 1936. It was as a result of his quarrel
with Sukiman that the latter left the PSII. But subsequent disagreements with other members of the PSII executive, partly personal,
partly over Salim's advocacy of a cooperative policy toward the
Dutch, led to his expulsion along with a number of his closest followers in February 1937. During the occupation he held a high
honorary position in the Putera and was a member of the Investigating Committee. He was closely related to Sjahrir, father-in-law of
Djohan Sjahroezah, and uncle of Tamzil, all top Socialist leaders, and
was politically allied with them, though he never became a member

of the PS. Though an influential Islamic politician, scholar, and controversialist, he was so fond of cigars and good drink that he was affectionately known as "Hadji Botol" ("Bottle Hadji"). *Orang Indonesia,* p. 461; Noer, "Rise and Development," pp. 174, 235, 255; Pluvier, *Overzicht,* pp. 71–72, 113–15; and Tjiptoning, *Apa dan siapa,* pp. 71–80.

Radèn SAMADIKUN was born on March 8, 1902, in Djombang, East Java. He was educated in a HIS, an OSVIA, and the Bestuursschool. Before the war he was nonpolitical, working his way up the pangrèh pradja hierarchy. In January 1944 he became bupati of Blitar, and in 1945, bupati of Kediri. *Orang Indonesia,* p. 73.

Dr. SAMSI Sastrawidagda was born in Surakarta on March 13, 1894. After being educated at a HIS and a teachers' training school, he obtained a doctoral degree in 1925 at the Rotterdam Business School. Subsequently he entered government service. From 1927 to 1929 he was a member of the top leadership of Sukarno's PNI in Bandung. According to Kanahele he was a member of the fifth column organized on the eve of the war by Maeda. During the war years he was appointed to the top leadership of the Putera and to the CAC. In December 1944 he became adviser to the Department of Finance. *Orang Indonesia,* p. 296; Kanahele, "Japanese Occupation," pp. 18, 251; *Kan Pō,* no. 56 (Dec. 10, 1944).

Mr. Radèn SAMSOEDIN was born to an Islamic family in Sukabumi, West Java, on January 1, 1908. He was educated in an ELS, a MULO, and an AMS in Bandung, and then went to Holland, where he gained a law degree at the University of Leiden in 1935. On his return to Indonesia he worked for a time in the Department of Economic Affairs and then as a private lawyer. He was a founding member of the cooperating nationalist party Parindra and sat on its central board. In 1940 he took the Volksraad seat of the eminent nationalist politician Thamrin on the latter's death. After the arrival of the Japanese he took a leading position in the Sendenbu and was the key Indonesian promoter of Shimizu's Triple-A Movement in 1942. In 1944 he was appointed head of the Public Welfare Bureau in the Putera head office. He also had a high position in the Hōkōkai headquarters. On November 2, 1944, he was appointed mayor of Sukabumi. Oddly enough, he later became a leader of the post-war Masjumi, even though his prewar and wartime activities show no connections with the Islamic movement at all. *Orang Indonesia*, p. 462; Rasjied, *Riwajat orang-orang politik*, pp. 20–21; Kanahele, "Japanese Occupation," pp. 47, 270; *Kan Pō*, no. 55 (Nov. 25, 1944).

Mr. Radèn Aju Maria Ulfah SANTOSO Wirodihardjo was born in Serang, Banten, on August 18, 1911. She was educated in an ELS and a five-year HBS before receiving a law degree at the University of Leiden in 1933. Before and during the war she worked in the legal departments of the provincial and central administrations. She was chairman of Istri Indonesia (Indonesian Wives) and was active in other women's organizations. Under the Japanese she was quite prominent in the Fujinkai, the women's affiliate of the Hōkōkai. *Orang Indonesia*, pp. 21–22; Rasjied, *Riwajat orang-orang politik*, p. 10. The daughter of a bupati, she was connected through her mother to the well-known Djajadiningrat family of Serang. Her younger sister married Professor Prijono. She was close to the Sjahrir circle.

S. SARDJONO was born in 1908 and eventually became a teacher and member of the Pendidikan Nasional Indonesia and the Gerindo. He was one of the founders of the BTI with Wijono and Soemartojo, and was elected second vice-chairman under Wijono at the Jogjakarta Conference in October 1945. *Kedaulatan Rakjat*, July 15, 1957; *Merdeka*, Nov. 28, 1945; *Antara*, Oct. 31, 1945.

SARMIDI MANGUNSARKORO was born in Surakarta, Central Java, on May 23, 1904. He was educated in a Standaardschool, a HIS, and a technical institute, and later attended classes at the Law Faculty in Djakarta. His prewar career was largely in the Taman Siswa school system pioneered by Ki Hadjar Dewantoro. By 1932 he had become principal of the Taman Siswa Teachers' College; subsequently he became head of the Taman Siswa in West Java, and from 1940 to 1942 he headed the education section of the Madjelis Luhur, the central leadership of the Taman Siswa organization. He was at various points chairman of the Jogjakarta branch of Jong Java; chairman of the Jogjakarta Jong Theosofen Organisatie (Organization of Young Theosophists); and a member of the central boards of the KBI, Partindo, and Gerindo. During the war he headed the Mass Education Bureau in the Hōkōkai central office and served as an official in the Education Bureau of the military administration. *Orang Indonesia,* p. 395; Indonesia, Kementerian Penerangan, *Kami perkenalkan,* p. 103; Deppen Files.

Mr. Radèn Mas SARTONO was born on August 5, 1900, in Wonogiri, Central Java. He was educated in a HIS and a MULO, and received a law degree at the University of Leiden in 1926. Thereafter he worked as a lawyer until the coming of the Japanese. He was secretary of the PI from 1922 to 1925, and deputy chief of Sukarno's PNI from 1927 to 1930. In 1931 he was a founder of the Partindo, and he led it until Sukarno's release from prison, whereupon he became deputy chief (1931–36). From 1937 to 1942 he was deputy chief of the Gerindo. In the Japanese period he was a member of the CAC and head of the organizational section of the Putera. He was adviser to the Department of Internal Affairs from December 1944 until he was relieved in June 1945. *Orang Indonesia,* p. 296; *Kan Pō,* no. 56 (Dec. 10, 1944). There is an excellent informal sketch of his personality and life in Tjiptoning, *Apa dan siapa,* pp. 19–30 ("Tacticus Mr. Sartono").

SETIATI was born in 1920 in Banjuwangi, East Java, and was active in Indonesia Muda and various women's organizations before the war. She was a pemuda figure in the Angkatan Baru and later in the BBI. *Harian Rakjat,* Sept. 26, 1955.

SIDIK DJOJOSOEKARTO was born on June 7, 1908, in Blitar, East Java, a distant relative of Sukarno, according to Herbert Feith. His education was confined to a MULO and the Middelbare Handelschool (Intermediary Commercial School) in Surabaja. He was very active politically, sitting on the executives of Jong Java, Indonesia Muda, the Partindo, and the Gerindo. During the occupation he headed both the Putera and the Hōkōkai for the Residency of Kediri. *Ensiklopedia Indonesia,* p. 1248; Indonesia, Kementerian Penerangan,

Kami perkenalkan, p. 119; *Suluh Indonesia* (Djakarta), Sept. 9, 1955; Deppen Files; Feith, *Decline of Constitutional Democracy,* p. 171.

Tahi Bonar SIMATUPANG was born in Sidikalang, Tapanuli, in 1920. After attending a MULO in Tarutung and a Christian AMS in Bandung, he entered the Military Academy there in 1940. When the war broke out he was an ensign and was captured by the Japanese near Tjiandjur, West Java. After a brief imprisonment he was released. He then went to work for the Department of Finance in the military administration. Indonesia, Kementerian Penerangan, *Kami perkenalkan,* p. 46; *Yudhagama,* no. 13 (Oct. 1951); *Almanak Angkatan Perang,* pp. 370–71.

Mohammad SJAFE'I was born in 1895 or 1896. He was active in the prewar PSII, but became famous for founding and leading a pioneering experimental nationalist school at Kajutanam, West Sumatra. During the war he headed the Sumatran CAC and the Sumatran version of the Investigating Committee. After the Japanese surrender he was briefly Resident of West Sumatra, but was removed as a result of popular pressures on December 5, 1945. *Ensiklopedia Indonesia,* p. 1259; *Berita Indonesia,* Dec. 8, 1945; *Sinar Harapan,* March 6, 1969 (his obituary).

Mr. Radèn SJAFRUDIN Prawiranegara was born of mixed Bantenese-Minangkabau descent on February 28, 1911, in Anjer Kidul, Banten, West Java. After graduating from an ELS, a MULO, and an AMS in Bandung, he took his degree at the Law Faculty in Djakarta in 1940. He was a founder of the Unitas Studiosorum Indonesiensis, a conservative student organization sponsored by the Dutch to counteract the somewhat radical PPPI. After graduation he went to work in the government tax administration, and during the Japanese occupation rose to be head of the tax office in Bandung. *Orang Indonesia,* p. 121; Indonesia, Kementerian Penerangan, *Kami perkenalkan,* p. 43; Amstutz, "The Indonesian Youth Movement," p. 46.

Sutan SJAHRIR was born on March 5, 1909, in Padangpandjang, West Sumatra, the eighth son of Muhammad Rasjad gelar Maharadja Sutan of Kota Gedang, a *hoofddjaksa* (chief prosecutor) and adviser to the sultan of Deli. He was educated in an ELS and a MULO in Medan, and an AMS in Bandung. At the age of twenty he was sent to Holland to study at the Law Faculty at Leiden. While in Holland he became briefly involved with the Socialistische Studentenclub in Amsterdam, developing a strong admiration for Dutch culture and for socialist ideas. He worked his way through school by taking jobs with the Metal Workers' Union and the International Federation of Transport Workers, and subsequently formed an attachment for a Dutch girl (a Miss Duchatau). He also joined the PI and was for a time its secretary. In 1931, his studies still incomplete, he returned to Indonesia and there helped set up the Pendidikan Nasional Indonesia. When Hatta came back to Indonesia in November 1932 and took charge of this organization, Sjahrir and he worked closely together. With Hatta he was imprisoned and in November 1934 sentenced to exile in Boven Digul. Early in 1936 the two were moved to Banda, and there Sjahrir was officially married for the first time, in a vain attempt to get permission in this way for Miss Duchatau to join him with her 14-year-old son. He was brought to Sukabumi in 1941, just before the fall of the Dutch. During the occupation he retired to a hillside bungalow in Tjipanas, claiming to be afflicted with tuberculosis. Salim, *Bung Sjahrir,* pp. 12–21; Sjahrir, *Out of Exile, passim;* Tas, "Souvenirs of Sjahrir," pp. 135–54; *Antara,* Feb. 25, 1946; Tijmstra, "Zoeklicht op Sjahrir," IC-RVO doc. no. 007946–8.

SJAMSUDDIN gelar SUTAN MAKMUR was born in Pangkalan Brandan, East Sumatra, on May 9, 1909. His schooling was confined to a HIS and a private MULO. Up to the occupation period he worked as journalist and editor for a wide variety of Indonesian newspapers in Djakarta, Medan, Surakarta, and Semarang, and from 1934 to 1942 was on the Semarang municipal council. From 1927 to 1928 he was vice-chairman of the JIB branch in Medan, and from 1936 to 1937 he was a propagandist for the Semarang branch of the Parindra. From 1938 to 1942 he was vice-chairman and member of the executive for press affairs of the same organization. From 1933 to 1940 he was a member of the executive and from 1940 to 1942 chairman of the Persatuan Djurnalis Indonesia (Indonesian Journalists' Union). Under the Japanese he was a reporter for the Military Propaganda Service in Djakarta. *Orang Indonesia,* p. 290; Indonesia, Kementerian Penerangan, *Kami perkenalkan,* p. 121.

SJAMSU HARJA UDAJA was born on March 23, 1913, in Binangun, Banjumas, Central Java. He was educated in a HIS, a MULO, and the Taman Siswa Teachers' College. In the thirties he worked as a journalist for various newspapers, and from 1941 to 1942 he was editor of the well-known Javanese-language magazine *Panjebar Semangat*. During the occupation he was on the staff of the Surabaja newspaper *Soeara Asia*. In 1933 he was elected vice-chairman of the SPI. In 1935 he was chairman of Indonesia Muda. He was also concurrently active in the leadership of the Taman Siswa student organization, the PPTS. From 1938 to 1941 he was in charge of youth activities for the central leadership of the cooperating nationalist party Parindra. In 1941 he became secretary of the Parindra. He also headed the Serikat Buruh Partikulir Indonesia (Union of Indonesian Workers in Private Enterprises) from 1941 to 1942. *Orang Indonesia*, p. 290; Biro Pemuda, *Sedjarah perdjuangan pemuda Indonesia*, pp. 74, 81.

Drs. Kandjeng Radèn Mas Adipati SOSRODININGRAT was born in Surakarta on December 1, 1902. After graduating from an ELS and a five-year HBS, he received a diploma from the Indological Department of the University of Leiden in 1935. On his return to Surakarta he rose rapidly in the kraton bureaucracy, becoming papatih dalem in November 1939, shortly after the death of Pakubuwono X. *Orang Indonesia*, p. 102.

SUBADIO Sastrosatomo was born on May 26, 1919, in Pangkalan Brandan, East Sumatra, and was educated in a HIS, a MULO, an AMS in Jogjakarta, and at the Law Faculty in Djakarta. He was mildly active in student politics before the war. Parlaungan, *Hasil rakjat*, p. 386.

SOEBAGIO Mangoenrahardjo was born in Tegal, Central Java, on September 5, 1905, the son of an irrigation official. He was educated in an ELS and a MULO, and then for a while in the machine-tools school attached to the Bandung Technical Faculty. After traveling widely in his youth, he joined the Jong Java in 1928, and in 1929 headed the Garut branch of Sukarno's PNI. In 1928 he founded the Tjahaja People's University in Bandung, at which Sjahrir taught for a while. He joined the Pendidikan Nasional Indonesia in 1932, and rose to become first the head of its Bandung branch, and ultimately its chairman after Hatta and Sjahrir were exiled to Boven Digul. During the war he worked in the Department of Internal Affairs. He was always close to Sjahrir, and was a founding member of the PSI in 1948. *Orang Indonesia,* p. 464; obituary notices in *Angkatan Bersendjata,* April 26, 1969, and *Harian Kami,* April 29, 1969.

Mr. Radèn Achmad SUBARDJO was born in Krawang, West Java, on March 23, 1897. He was educated in an ELS and a five-year HBS, and subsequently obtained a law degree at Leiden University in 1933. Prior to Hatta's rise he was chairman of the PI. Like many of the young Indonesian students of that period, he was associated with the left and even spent a short time in Russia. On his return to Indonesia he worked briefly as a lawyer before undertaking an assignment as Tokyo correspondent of the newspaper *Matahari,* edited by his old friend from Leiden days, Iwa Kusumasumantri. He evidently enjoyed himself in the culturally congenial atmosphere of Japan. Later on he took a position in the Economic Affairs Department of the colonial government. He held no office in any political party prior to the war. *Orang Indonesia,* p. 290.

Dr. SUDARSONO was born in Salatiga, Central Java, on May 9, 1911. He was educated in an ELS, a MULO, and an AMS before taking his degree at the Medical Faculty in Djakarta in 1938. Thereafter he worked as a doctor, first in Djakarta and after 1941 in Tjirebon. He was secretary and then chairman of the Pemuda Indonesia from 1928 to 1929; a top leader of Indonesia Muda after 1936; and eventually secretary of the Djakarta branch of the PPPI. During the Japanese occupation he headed the Tjirebon Residency branch of the Putera and was involved in Sjahrir's underground. *Orang Indonesia,* p. 358; Amstutz, "The Indonesian Youth Movement," p. 39; Kahin, *Nationalism and Revolution,* p. 112.

SUDIRMAN was born in Bodaskarangdjati, in the Regency of Rembang, Central Java, probably in 1915. Though of humble birth he was informally adopted by the local subdistrict officer, Radèn Tjokrosunarjo, who paid for his education. In 1932 he attended the Taman [Siswa] Dewasa school Wiworo Tomo, where he studied English, law, and religion, among other subjects. He later transferred to the Muhammadijah's Dutch-Native Teachers' Training School in Surakarta, but had to drop out when his adoptive father died. He then moved to Tjilatjap in southwestern Central Java and taught in a local HIS. There he became a member of the Muhammadijah and took charge of the local branch of its scouting organization, the Hizbul Wathan. When Tjilatjap was bombed at the start of the war, he enrolled in the Dutch-organized Air Raid Warning Service. During the occupation he sat on the Banjumas Residency sangikai and entered the Peta (second shift) as a daidanchō. After the independence proclamation he took the lead in forming the Banjumas Residency TKR. *Madjalah Angkatan Darat* (Djakarta) (Jan. 1956). There is some uncertainty about the date of his birth. The possibilities are 1912, 1915, and 1916, according to Kadarjono, *Swargi Djèndral Sudirman*, p. 11. The date 1912 was given by Sudirman's widow as the one he himself usually mentioned. But Sudirman's mother and the official biography in *Madjalah Angkatan Darat* both gave 1915, and therefore that date has been adopted here.

SUDIRO was born on April 24, 1912, in Jogjakarta. He was educated in a Dutch-language teachers' training school. Thereafter he became head of a MULO and Dutch-language teachers' training school created by the BU in Madiun, and later headed the Taman Siswa organization for the whole of the Madiun Residency. During the occupation he was deputy head of the Barisan Pelopor and chief of the Barisan Pelopor Istimewa. Indonesia, Kementerian Penerangan, *Kami perkenalkan,* p. 54; Deppen Files.

SUDISMAN was born in Surabaja on July 27, 1920, the son of a strongly nationalist lower-level municipal official. He graduated from a HIS and a MULO, and was in his second year of study at a local AMS when he was arrested by the Japanese in 1942 for being a member of the underground organized by Amir Sjarifuddin. In 1939 he represented the Persatuan Pemuda Indonesia Surabaja (Perpis) at the Third Youth Congress in Jogjakarta. In 1940 he was vice-chairman of the Surabaja branch of Indonesia Muda. He was also active in Javanese cultural organizations and joined the Gerindo. Together with Tjugito he edited the radical journal *Tamparan,* and was briefly arrested by the colonial authorities. He joined the Illegal PKI as a candidate member shortly after the Japanese landed, and thereby became involved in Amir Sjarifuddin's network. He was sentenced to eight years' imprisonment by the Japanese. On his release he became a top leader of the leading pemuda organization in Surabaja, the PRI, and also sat as a member of the East Java KNI. *Pendorong* (Medan), Sept. 10, 1955; notes taken by the author during Sudisman's defense before the Extraordinary Military Tribunal in Djakarta, July 1967.

SOEDJONO was born in Kebumen, Central Java, in 1915. He was educated in a Normaalschool, and later was active in the union and youth movements. In the Japanese period he worked as a teacher in Bandung. After the independence proclamation he moved to Surabaja and helped form the PRI. After 1950 he was associated with the PKI. *Harian Rakjat,* Sept. 26, 1955.

SOEGONDO DJOJOPOESPITO was born on February 22, 1905, the son of an official in the forestry service. After attending a HIS in Tuban, a MULO in Surabaja, and an AMS in Jogjakarta, he attended the Law Faculty in Djakarta for some years without obtaining a degree. Before the war he was active in the nationalist school movement, as director of the Perguruan Rakjat from 1930 to 1932, and of the Taman Siswa in Bandung from 1932 to 1934. He was then forbidden to teach for a year by the Dutch government. From 1935 to 1936 he set up his Lokasiswa school in Bogor and edited the weekly *Pasar Saptu* there with Dr. Tjipto Mangoenkoesoemo. The following year he moved to Semarang to work again with the Taman Siswa, and then from 1937 to 1940 established a new school of his own, while teaching at Douwes Dekker's Ksatrian Instituut. Afterward he returned to journalism and during the occupation worked in the Department of Justice. After being a member of Jong Java from 1920 to 1925, he was a cofounder of the PPPI in 1927 and became its first secretary. From 1927 to 1929 he was chairman of the PPI. At the celebrated Youth Congress in Djakarta in 1928, he was elected chairman (Amir was treasurer). He eventually became a key member of the Hatta-Sjahrir Pendidikan Nasional Indonesia, and after the war was a founding member of the Paras. Deppen Files.

SOEGRA was born on August 11, 1906, in Waled, near Tjirebon, West Java. He was educated in a HIS, a MULO, an AMS in Jogjakarta, and one in Djakarta. Before the war he headed the Tjirebon branch of the Pendidikan Nasional Indonesia. During the occupation he was a member of the Tjirebon Residency sangikai and headed the Koperasi Rakjat Indonesia in Tjirebon. According to Kahin this cooperative was a front organization for the Sjahrir underground group. Malik also identifies Soegra as a member of the Sjahrir underground. *Orang Indonesia,* p. 275; Kahin, *Nationalism and Revolution,* p. 112; Malik, *Riwajat,* p. 24.

SOEHADI was born in 1908. He was involved in the 1926 PKI uprising and spent six years in Tjipinang Prison as a result. Released in 1932, he entered the Pendidikan Nasional Indonesia, and later the Illegal PKI and the Gerindo. He continued his underground activities throughout the war. *Harian Rakjat,* July 2, 1962.

SUHARTO was born in Kemusu, near Jogjakarta, on either February 20 or June 8, 1921. In 1940, at the age of nineteen, he joined the colonial army and underwent military training at Gombong. When the Peta was formed, he joined it and was first stationed in Jogjakarta with the rank of shōdanchō. In 1944 he was promoted to chūdanchō and moved to Madiun. After the proclamation of independence, he returned to Jogjakarta and was active in the local BKR and later the TKR. *Berita Yudha,* Oct. 5, 1965; *Angkatan Bersendjata,* Oct. 18, 1965; *Merdeka,* June 8, 1967; Indonesia, Staf Pertahanan-Keamanan, Lembaga Sedjarah, *Siapa-apa* (*Who's Who*), pp. 53–54.

SOEKANDA was born on October 25, 1909, at Wahalartjageur in Kuningan, West Java. He was educated only as far as Standaardschool. In 1943 he became a member of Soegra's Koperasi Rakjat Indonesia in Tjirebon, and was presumably therefore a member of Sjahrir's underground group. *Orang Indonesia,* p. 275.

SUKANDA BRATAMENGGALA stemmed from an aristocratic Tjiamis family and was the son-in-law of Dr. Djundjunan Setiakusumah, one of the best-known physicians in the prewar Priangan. On the eve of the war he had led the youth organization affiliated to the conservative Sundanese regionalist party, Pagujuban Pasundan. *Berita Yudha,* Aug. 10, 1968; interview with (retired) Colonel Sukanda, June 9, 1967.

SUKARNI was born on July 14, 1916, in Blitar, East Java. He was educated in the Taman Siswa school system and in a MULO. He was active in a number of youth organizations in the thirties, including the Indonesia Muda (from 1930), the SPI (from 1931) and the Perpri (from 1934). His energy in helping to start a Partindo branch in Blitar was noticed by a senior party leader, Ir. Anwari, and he was sent to Bandung for cadre-training under Sukarno, along with other young leaders such as Wikana, Asmara Hadi, and Trimurti. After Sukarno's arrest and exile, Sukarni moved to Djakarta, where for a brief period in 1934 he was chairman of Indonesia Muda before falling foul of the Dutch security police. He was imprisoned in Jogjakarta and on his release dropped out of sight. He reappeared in 1940, after the fall of the Netherlands, when he was arrested by the Dutch police in Samarinda, Kalimantan, and brought to Djakarta. He was released from detention in Tjilatjap, along with Wikana, Adam Malik and others, after the Dutch capitulation in March 1942. During the occupation he worked for the Dōmei news agency, the Sendenbu, and the central office of the Seinendan. Along with Chaerul Saleh he was put in charge of the Asrama Angkatan Baru Indonesia at Menteng 31 in 1943. *Sinar Harapan,* May 8, 10 (obituary by H. Soebagijo I.N.) and 26, 1971 (biographical article by Soendoro); Sidik Kertapati, *Sekitar proklamasi,* p. 47; *Kan Pō,* no. 21 (July 25, 1943), pp. 9–10; Biro Pemuda, *Sedjarah perdjuangan pemuda Indonesia,* p. 71.

The official birth date of SUKARNO is given as June 6, 1901. The son of a Javanese school principal and a Balinese mother, he was among the best educated Indonesians of his generation. He graduated from an ELS, the HBS in Surabaja, and the Technical Faculty in Bandung. He rose to national prominence after the founding of the PNI in 1927. His extraordinary oratorical talent and political skill made him a natural leader. Though imprisoned by the colonial authorities from December 1929 to December 1931, and subsequently exiled to Flores and Bengkulu from February 1934 to the end of the

Dutch period, Sukarno's magnetism was such that he was accepted as the chief spokesman for Indonesian nationalism by virtually all groups during the Japanese occupation. He was the first of the four leaders of the Putera, and was the top Indonesian in the Hōkōkai. *Orang Indonesia*, p. 45. See also Dahm, *Sukarno, passim.*

M. Imam SOEKEMI was born on April 19 or 21, 1901, in Trenggalek, East Java. He was educated in a HIS, a teachers' training school, the Taman Siswa Teachers' Training School in Jogjakarta, and the Higher Teachers' Training School in Purworedjo. He joined the Taman Siswa organization in Jogjakarta in 1926 and rose to be a member of its supreme council, the Madjelis Luhur, in 1930. From 1927 to 1930 he was a top leader of Sukarno's PNI, and in 1932 he became the first chairman of the Pendidikan Nasional Indonesia before yielding this position to Sjahrir later that year. During the war he worked as Hatta's secretary in the central office of the Putera. In the fifties he was a member of the PSI. *Orang Indonesia*, p. 408; Indonesia, Kementerian Penerangan, *Kepartaian di Indonesia*, p. 173; Salim, *Bung Sjahrir*, p. 15; *Harian Kami*, April 29, 1969; Deppen Files.

Dr. H. SUKIMAN Wirjosandjojo was born in Sewu, Surakarta, Central Java, on June 19, probably in 1898. He was educated in either an ELS or a HIS, and in the STOVIA, before obtaining a medical degree at the University of Amsterdam in 1925. Either in 1924 or 1925 (probably the former) he was chairman of the PI. On his return to Indonesia in 1925 he opened a practice in Jogjakarta, where he resided from that time on. In 1927 he joined Tjokroaminoto's PSII, becoming first its treasurer and later its vice-chairman. In 1933 he quarreled with some of his colleagues in the leadership, most notably Hadji Agus Salim, and left the party to form his own party, the PII, together with Surjopranoto. This party, however, languished badly. Not until 1938 was it effectively revived and given a coherent organization under the triumvirate of Wiwoho, Sukiman, and Wali al-Fatah. It maintained its headquarters in Jogjakarta, where all three leaders resided. From 1933 to 1942 Sukiman was also chairman of the Perserikatan Pegawai Pegadaian Bumiputera (Union of Native Pawnshop Officials—pawnshops were a government monopoly). He was also a member of the Gapi, and MIAI. He was a deputy chairman of the Putera, representing Jogjakarta, but otherwise held no prominent position during the occupation. *Orang Indonesia,* p. 380 (which gives the years of his birth and chairmanship of the PI as 1896 and 1924); Parlaungan, *Hasil rakjat,* p. 192 (1898 and 1924); Rasjied, *Riwajat orang-orang politik,* pp. 12–13 (1887 and 1925); Indonesia, Kementerian Penerangan, *Kami perkenalkan,* p. 126 (1898 and 1924); and Deppen Files (1887 and 1925).

SOEKINDAR was a member of the Illegal PKI. He had been an original member of the PKI in 1920, and had subsequently been exiled to Boven Digul. During the war he was arrested by the Japanese and imprisoned near Semarang. *Harian Rakjat,* July 17, 1962.

Mr. SUMANANG was born in Jogjakarta on May 1, 1908. He obtained a degree from the Law Faculty in Djakarta. Before the war he was for a while attached to the Landraad (court of first instance) in Semarang, before moving to Djakarta to become editor of *Pemandangan* and head of the Perguruan Rakjat school in Djatinegara. He seems also to have been employed for a time by the Japanese consulate. During the occupation he was an editor of *Pembangoenan,* a member of the CAC, and a high official in the General Affairs Bureau of the Hōkōkai. He had been active in Jong Java, Indonesia Muda, the PPPI, and the Partindo. Indonesia, Kementerian Penerangan, *Kami perkenalkan,* p. 126; Deppen Files; Kanahele, "Japanese Occupation," p. 268; *Djawa Baroe,* Sept. 15, 1944; and "Who's Who in Java," IC-RVO doc. no. 007779–862.

Mr. SOEMITRO REKSODIPOETRO was born on September 3, 1907, near Tuban, East Java. He was educated in a HIS, a MULO, and an AMS in Jogjakarta before graduating from the Law Faculty in Djakarta in 1936. From 1940 to 1941 he worked for the Department of Education and Religious Affairs. In 1931 he had been chairman of the PPPI. During the war he was an official of the Education Bureau. *Orang Indonesia,* p. 15.

Mr. Radèn Mas SUNARIO KOLOPAKING was born in Bandjarnegara, Central Java, on October 15, 1906. His father was the local bupati,

R. A. A. Djojonagoro II, and his mother a daughter of the patih of the Mangkunegaran Principality. He was educated in a HIS, a MULO, an AMS, and the law faculties first in Djakarta and then in Leiden, where he took his degree in 1931. He returned to Indonesia in 1933, and from 1934 to 1940 worked as an official of the Algemeen Volkscredietbank in Djakarta, and as part-time teacher at the Law Faculty. From 1942 to 1945 he was top manager of the Mangkunegaran enterprises. In April 1945 he was transferred to Djakarta to become head of the Office of People's Economy. He was not active politically before the war. *Merdeka,* Nov. 17, 1945; Deppen Files.

Mr. SUNARJO was born on August 28, 1902, in Madiun, East Java. He was educated in an ELS and a MULO before getting a law degree at the University of Leiden in 1925. He had a legal career thereafter, right through the Japanese occupation, mainly working as an advocate. From 1924 to 1926 he was second secretary of the PI. In 1927 he helped Sukarno found the PNI in Bandung. From 1933 to 1935 he was a propagandist for the Partindo in Makasar, and in 1936 propagandist and commissioner (for the eastern islands) of the Parindra; in 1941 he held the same post for Central Java. He was also active in nationalist scouting organizations. *Orang Indonesia,* pp. 18–19; a somewhat different version of his biography is contained in Indonesia, Kementerian Penerangan, *Kami perkenalkan,* p. 19.

SUPENO was born in Tegal, Central Java, on June 12, 1916, the only surviving son of a railway official. He was educated in a HIS, a MULO, and the AMS in Semarang. Subsequently he studied for two years at the Technical Faculty in Bandung and then for four years at the Law Faculty in Djakarta. He was active in Indonesia Muda in Tegal, Semarang, and Bandung, and was involved in promoting the PPPI against the rival Unitas Studiosorum Indonesiensis, which was regarded as a tame, Dutch-minded student organization. In 1941 he became the head of the Baperpi. During the war years he was employed in the Department of Justice. *Orang Indonesia,* p. 491; Dwidjosugondo, *Peranan ramalan Djojobojo,* p. 233.

Prof. Mr. Dr. Radèn SOEPOMO was born on January 22, 1903, in Sukohardjo, Surakarta. He graduated from an ELS, a MULO, and the Law Faculty in Djakarta, and in 1927 from the University of Leiden. He worked in the Dutch period as judge, official in the Justice Department, and professor at the Law Faculty, but without any political affiliations. *Orang Indonesia,* p. 159. He became adviser to the Justice Department in October 1943. *Kan Pō,* no. 28 (Oct. 10, 1943). On August 27, 1945, he became chief of this department. *Soeara Asia,* Aug. 30, 1945.

Mr. SOEPRAPTO was born in the village of Senori near Tuban, East Java, in 1905. He obtained a degree at the Law Faculty in Djakarta in 1940. He was active in Jong Java, Indonesia Muda, and, like Sjamsu Harja Udaja, in the SPI. He was also secretary and later chairman of the PPPI. He engaged in union activity after his graduation, and took the leading role in setting up the Persatuan Supir Indonesia. He was apparently involved in some minor sabotage activities after the Japanese invasion, and was imprisoned by the military administration. *Harian Rakjat,* Sept. 23, 1955.

Ir. Radèn Mas Pandji SOERACHMAN Tjokroadisoerjo was born in Wonosobo, Central Java, on August 30, 1894. He graduated from an ELS and a five-year HBS and obtained an engineering degree at the Technical College at Delft. Before the war he was active in various economic sections of the colonial government. He had no political role of importance until he became a member of the Consultative Council of the Putera in 1943. In July 1945 he became chief of the Economic Affairs Department. *Orang Indonesia,* p. 208; *Kan Pō,* no. 71 (July 25, 1945).

Radèn Surjadi SURIADARMA was born in Banjuwangi, East Java, on December 6, 1912. He was educated in an ELS in Djakarta and in HBS in both Djakarta and Bandung. He graduated from the Royal Military Academy at Breda in 1934, and was posted as an infantry lieutenant in Magelang. In 1936 he took the opportunity to join the KNIL's infant air arm. After 1940 he was an instructor at the flying school at Kalidjati. When the war broke out he took part in the fighting, flying on missions against Japanese ships near West Kalimantan and in the Makasar Sea. During the occupation he worked as an administrator in the Bandung police. In August 1945 he helped form the BKR in the Priangan. *Orang Indonesia,* p. 133; *Indonesia,*

Kementerian Penerangan, *Kami perkenalkan,* p. 47; *Yudhagama,* no. 13 (Oct. 1951); *Madjalah Brawidjaja* (Malang), VII, 19 (Oct. 5, 1957).

Radèn Pandji SOEROSO was born on November 3, 1893, in Porong, East Java, and graduated from a HIS and a teachers' training school. From 1924 to 1942 he was a member of the Volksraad, and eventually he became a member of its executive committee, the College van Gedelegeerden. He headed various smaller unions of civil servants, as well as being active in the Sarekat Islam (from 1918 to 1922 he was assistant to its central leadership) and the Parindra (in 1942 he was a member of its central leadership). (See *Orang Indonesia,* p. 468, for further details.) In the Japanese period he became a member of the CAC and vice-chairman of the Investigating Committee, as well as resident of Kedu.

Mas SOETARDJO Kartohadikoesoemo was born near Blora on October 22, 1892. He graduated from an ELS, an OSVIA, and later the Bestuursschool. He made a brilliant career in the bureaucracy, and in 1931 became a member of the Volksraad, rising to be a member of its executive committee, the College van Gedelegeerden, in 1939. In 1943 he was made Resident of Djakarta, one of only three Indonesians to reach this position in the Japanese period. He had originally been active in the BU, but was better known for his tenure as general chairman of the PPBB from 1929 to 1942, and for his sponsorship of the famous Soetardjo Petition, a resolution passed in the Volksraad urging equal legal status between Holland and the Indies. *Orang Indonesia,* p. 48; Deppen Files.

SOETOMO (Bung Tomo) was born on October 3, 1920, in Surabaja, East Java. Largely self-educated, he was active in the local Indonesia Muda and was a secretary of the Surabaja branch of the Parindra. He helped edit the weekly *Pembela Rakjat* and was prominent in the nationalist scouting organization KBI. *Java Bode* (Djakarta), Aug. 13, 1955; Deppen Files.

Mr. Radèn SOEWANDI was born in Ngawi, East Java, on October 31, 1898, and was educated in a HIS, an OSVIA, and the Bestuursschool; he took his degree at the Law Faculty in Djakarta in 1938.

He worked his way up in the Department of Education and Religious Affairs, serving as its secretary in 1941 and 1942. On October 4, 1943, he became adviser to the Bureau of Education. Before the war he was at various points a leader of the Djakarta branches of the BU and the Parindra. *Orang Indonesia,* p. 20; Deppen Files.

Radèn SUWIRJO was born on February 17, 1904, in Wonogiri, Central Java. He was educated in a HIS, a MULO, an AMS in Jogjakarta, and at the Law Faculty of Djakarta. He held various unimportant jobs as teacher and businessman until the Japanese occupation, when he became head of the Activities Section of the Putera, and subsequently mayor of Djakarta. From 1920 to 1921 he was a member of the leadership of the Jong Java branch in Madiun, and from 1924 to 1925 he was secretary to its central leadership. He later helped found and lead the PPPI in Djakarta. From 1927 to 1928 he was secretary of the Djakarta branch of the PNI, and subsequently became the Partindo national organization's treasurer and the head of its Djakarta branch. He also, like Lukman Hakim, taught at the Perguruan Rakjat in Djatinegara. *Orang Indonesia,* p. 277 (which gives the month of his birth as July); Indonesia, Kementerian Penerangan, *Kami perkenalkan,* p. 44; *Suluh Indonesia,* July 31, 1956.

Mr. Muhammad TAMZIL was born in Kota Gedang, West Sumatra, on May 21, 1908. He obtained a law degree from the University of Utrecht. While still in Indonesia he was a founding member of Indonesia Muda in 1931. In Holland he became a leading figure in the PI and was active in the anti-Nazi underground during the war. Indonesia, Kementerian Penerangan, *Kami perkenalkan,* p. 57; Amstutz, "The Indonesian Youth Movement," p. 35. He was a nephew of the Sarekat Islam leader Hadji Agus Salim and a distant relative of Sjahrir.

TAN LING DJIE was born in Surabaja, East Java, in 1904. His education concluded with periods of study at both the Djakarta and Leiden law faculties. In the 1930's he was a member of the Sarekat Peranakan Tionghoa Indonesia (Association of Indonesians of Chinese Descent), and acted both as editor and correspondent from Holland of Liem Koen Hian's radical Surabaja newspaper, *Sin Tit Po.* In

1941 he joined Liem's pro-Indonesian PTI, which contained a number of noted left-wing intellectuals of Chinese descent, such as Oei Gie Hwat, Tjoa Sik Ien, and Sjauw Giok Tjhan, and represented it in the East Java provincial assembly. *Harian Rakjat,* Sept. 24, 1955; Somers, "Peranakan Chinese Politics," p. 95 and p. 100, n. 75; Soe Hok-gie, "Simpang kiri," pp. 20–21.

TAN MALAKA (see Chap. 12).

Mohammed TAUCHID was born in February or March 1915 in Krakal near Kebumen, Central Java. After attending Standaardschool he continued his education in the Taman Siswa system. From 1933 to 1936 he worked as a Taman Siswa teacher in Banjumas. In 1938 he became secretary to the Taman Siswa leadership council, the Madjelis Luhur. From 1933 onward he was also active in the scout organization KBI and in the Pendidikan Nasional Indonesia for the Banjumas area. In the Japanese period he continued his work as secretary to the Taman Siswa leadership. He was elected head of the information section of the BTI in October 1945. *Antara,* Oct. 31, 1945; Indonesia, Kementerian Penerangan, *Kami perkenalkan,* p. 134.

Radèn Mas Oetarjo Anwar TJOKROAMINOTO was born on May 3, 1909, in Surabaja, the son of the celebrated nationalist leader H. O. S. Tjokroaminoto. He graduated from an ELS, a MULO, and the Douwes Dekker Teachers' Training School (specializing in journalism), and also spent some time in pesantrèn in Rembang and Wanaradja. After working for his father's party, the PSII, in Sumatra, he returned to Djakarta to edit the newspaper *Pembangoen.* In 1944 he became deputy chief of *Asia Raya. Orang Indonesia,* p. 292. According to Tan Malaka (*Dari pendjara,* III, 69), Anwar wrote a number of very popular, subtly satirical articles about the evils of the occupation under the pseudonym Bang Bedjat.

Radèn Mas Harsono TJOKROAMINOTO, younger brother of Anwar, was born in Magetan, East Java, on April 24, 1912, and graduated from an ELS and a MULO. Until the outbreak of the war he was active in the PSII, particularly in its school system. In 1942 he joined the staff of Dōmei. He was also general secretary of the Djakarta branch of the MIAI and editor of the MIAI's organ, *Soeara MIAI*. *Orang Indonesia*, p. 444; *Hsin Pao* (Djakarta), Aug. 13, 1955.

TJUGITO was born in Blora, East Java, on January 21, 1921. He graduated from a MULO and in 1939 from the Surabaja Intermediary Commercial School. From 1939 to 1940 he worked for the Borsumij (Borneo-Sumatera Handelmaatschappij) corporation; subsequently he edited *Tamparan* with Sudisman and taught in a commercial school. From 1938 to 1940 he was a member of the Surabaja branch of the Parindra youth organization, Suryawirawan. From 1941 to 1942 he was a member of the Gerindo, and helped set up the Surabaja branch of the Persatuan Supir Indonesia, led by Mr. Jusuf and Mr. Soeprapto. He joined the Illegal PKI and Amir Sjarifuddin's group, and was arrested along with Sudisman in 1942. On his release he joined the PRI leadership. Parlaungan, *Hasil rakjat*, pp. 307–8.

S. K. TRIMURTI was born on May 11, 1914, in Bojolali, Central Java. She graduated from a HIS and a women teachers' training school. During the thirties she made her living independently as a journalist, mainly in the cities of Semarang and Surakarta. She was an aide to the top leadership of the Gerindo and of the union federation, Gaspi. She was the wife of Sajuti Melik, and like him was for a period detained by the Kenpeitai for suspected communist connections. Her release was arranged by Sukarno, and subsequently she worked under him in the central office of the Putera. *Orang Indonesia*, p. 293; Tjiptoning, *Apa dan siapa*, pp. 83–92.

URIP Sumohardjo (see Chap. 11).

Mr. Radèn USMAN SASTROAMIDJOJO, brother of Mr. Ali Sastroamidjojo, was born in Grabag, near Magelang, Central Java, on May 11, 1905. After graduating from an ELS and Queen Wilhelmina School, he obtained a law degree at the University of Leiden in 1934. On his return he worked as a lawyer in Bandung. He appears to have been politically inactive, except that in the late twenties he taught at Taman Siswa schools in Jogjakarta and Bandung, and in the thirties at Douwes Dekker's Ksatrian Instituut. *Orang Indonesia,* p. 296; Indonesia, Kementerian Penerangan, *Kami perkenalkan,* p. 59 (which gives his birth year as 1910).

K. H. WACHID HASJIM was the son of the great orthodox Moslem scholar K. H. Hasjim Asjari of the pesantrèn Tebu Ireng. He was born on February 12, 1913, in Djombang, and had a pesantrèn education. During the late thirties he rose fast in the Nahdatul Ulama. In 1940 and 1941 he was head of the MIAI. He later became a member of the CAC. During the later Japanese period he also effectively took over his aged father's job as chief of the Religious Affairs Department, which was temporarily discontinued after the republic was founded. *Orang Indonesia,* p. 435; Benda, *The Crescent and the Rising Sun,* p. 273.

Radèn WALI AL-FATAH was born on October 18, 1908, in Ngawi, East Java, and had no formal Western schooling. In the thirties he earned his living mainly as a journalist in Surakarta, Semarang, and Surabaja. In 1938 he was second secretary of the revived PII, and in January 1941 he set up and headed the Warmusi (Wartawan Muslimin Indonesia, or Moslem Journalists of Indonesia) in Jogjakarta. *Orang Indonesia,* pp. 470–71; Noer, "Rise and Development," p. 255.

Iding WANGSAWIDJAJA was born in November 1911 in Tjitepok, near Sumedang, West Java. Before the war he worked as a journalist for various Sundanese newspapers in Bandung, especially the *Sinar Pasoendan.* In 1932 he joined the Pendidikan Nasional Indonesia, and in 1934 he became the secretary of the Bandung branch under Soebagio. He was also secretary of the Central Priangan branch of the PPPB, and in 1937 became secretary of the Muhammadijah in the same city. *Orang Indonesia,* p. 293.

WIKANA was born on October 16, 1914, in Sumedang, West Java. He was the son of Radèn Hadji Soelaiman, a Javanese migrant to West Java from Demak. He graduated from an ELS and a MULO. For a time he was a protégé of Sukarno while the latter was in Bandung. He had close links with the Taman Siswa school system in

West Java, and he joined the Gerindo. When the Barisan Pemuda
Gerindo was set up after July 1938, he was chosen as its first chairman. Interview with Mrs. Wikana, Aug. 1968; Biro Pemuda, *Sedjarah
perdjuangan pemuda Indonesia,* p. 87.

Mr. WILOPO was born on October 21, 1909, in Purworedjo, Central Java. He was educated in a HIS, a MULO, and an AMS in Jogjakarta; after a spell at the Technical Faculty in Bandung, he obtained
a degree at the Law Faculty in Djakarta in 1942. Meanwhile he was
active in the Taman Siswa organization in both Sukabumi and Djakarta; he was also a founder, with Sartono and others, of the Perguruan Rakjat in Djatinegara. In 1933 he was vice-chairman of the
Sukabumi branch of the Partindo. In 1936 he became a top leader of
the PPPI, and subsequently he joined the Gerindo. He was high up
in the Putera during the occupation, and became a senior official in
the General Affairs Department of the military administration. He
was also Muwardi's immediate subordinate in the Djakarta Barisan
Pelopor. In August 1945 he was made head of the Djakarta branch
of the abortive PNI-Staatspartij. *Orang Indonesia,* p. 293; *Soeara
Asia,* Aug. 29, 1945.

Radèn Adipati Aria WIRANATAKUSUMAH was born on August 8,
1888, in Bandung. He graduated from an ELS, a five-year HBS, and
an OSVIA. He then entered the pangrèh pradja and became successively bupati of Tjiandjur and of Bandung. From 1921 to 1935 he
was a member of the Volksraad, from 1931 to 1935 as a member of
its executive committee, the College van Gedelegeerden. From 1929
to 1935 he was chairman of the PPBB, and from 1936 to 1942 of the
association of bupati, Sedio Moelio. *Orang Indonesia,* p. 110. In June
1945 he replaced Sartono in the senior post of adviser to the Department of Internal Affairs. *Kan Pō,* no. 68 (June 10, 1945). On August
27 he became chief of the department. *Soeara Asia,* Aug. 30, 1945.

Mr. Kandjeng Radèn Mas Tumenggung WONGSONAGORO (formerly
R. T. Djaksodipuro) was born on April 20, 1897, in Surakarta. He
was educated in an ELS and a MULO before receiving a law degree
in Djakarta in 1929. Afterward he worked for the Sunanate in Surakarta, primarily in a legal capacity. In 1939 he was made bupati of
Sragen. He was also active politically: in 1923 he was head of the

Surakarta branch of the BU; in 1925 he headed Jong Java and helped set up Indonesia Muda; from 1930 to 1939 he led the Surakarta aristocratic group Habiprojo; and in 1936 he became commissioner to the central leadership of the Parindra. In 1942 he headed the local Triple-A Movement in Surakarta. Late in the occupation he became vice-resident of Semarang, and after the independence proclamation, resident. He was related by marriage to the royal house of Surakarta. *Orang Indonesia,* p. 113; Amstutz, "The Indonesian Youth Movement," p. 23.

Mr. Muhammad YAMIN was born on August 23, 1903, in Sawahlunto, West Sumatra. He was educated in a HIS, an AMS in Jogjakarta, and the Law Faculty in Djakarta, where he obtained his degree in 1932. Thereafter he had a private law practice, and from 1938 to 1942 was a member of the Volksraad. He headed the JSB from 1926 to 1928, and Indonesia Muda in 1928. Subsequently he was prominent in the PPPI and the Partindo. Along with Gani and Amir Sjarifuddin, he was a founder of the Gerindo in 1937, but in 1939 he quarreled with his colleagues and formed his own Minangkabau-oriented party, the Parpindo (Partai Persatuan Indonesia, or Party of Indonesian Unity), and sat in the Volksraad as its representative. His quarrelsomeness was so legendary that the older nationalist leader M. H. Thamrin once called him "the eternal splitter." During the Japanese period he held high office, being appointed adviser to the Department of Propaganda in September 1943. In February 1945 he was relieved by Sukardjo Wirjopranoto and took a seat on the CAC. But the Japanese in the end found him a difficult handful, and after the GRB fiasco he was arrested as one of the instigators of obstructive pemuda activities. He was intimate with a number of the pemuda leaders, especially Chaerul Saleh, whom he had befriended when the latter was at odds with his family. He was a bitter opponent of Amir Sjarifuddin from the days of their quarrel in the Gerindo. *Orang Indonesia,* p. 472; Amstutz, "The Indonesian Youth Movement," pp. 18, 28, 30, 47; Pluvier, *Overzicht,* pp. 109–13; *Kan Pō,* no. 28 (Oct. 10, 1943), p. 29; *Asia Raya,* Feb. 12, 1945; Tjiptoning, *Apa dan siapa,* pp. 57–67 (which contains an excellent character portrait).

Tomegorō YOSHIZUMI had been a journalist and part-time businessman in Indonesia before the war. He ended up as an agent of

Toyoshima, the head of the Chinese Affairs section of the Japanese consulate in Djakarta, working among the local Chinese with the aim of persuading them to give financial and other backing to Wang Ching-wei rather than Chiang Kai-shek. He was first arrested in Bangka on December 8, 1941 and then expelled for subversive activities. He was taken to Australia by the retreating Dutch and later repatriated in an exchange of prisoners. On his return to Indonesia he went to Makasar and worked there to train Indonesians employed by the Hana naval intelligence organization. In 1944 he moved to Djakarta to work for Maeda as head of the Daisanka, the political intelligence section of Maeda's office. According to his friend Nishijima, he had been a right-wing Japanese nationalist before the war, but as a result of ill treatment at the hands of the Dutch and British, and of his interaction with young Indonesians, he eventually became a Marxist. After the Japanese collapse, wishing to continue his activities on behalf of Indonesian independence but fearing a second internment by the Allies, he moved to East Java. He died in Blitar in 1946, and was buried under the Indonesian name Arief. His gravestone can still be seen. Interview with Nishijima, May 27, 1967; and with Maeda, April 8, 1962. I have also relied on records of interviews with Nishijima by George Kahin in 1956, and by Nugroho Notosusanto at a later unspecified date. I would like to express my thanks to both for making these records available to me. See also Kanahele, "Japanese Occupation," p. 13; Tadashi Maeda, statements of June 20, 1946, and Aug. 26, 1946; Kishi et al., *Indoneshia ni okeru,* p. 432; and the "Addendum" appended to the statement of Hitoshi Shimizu already cited, prepared by Dutch intelligence, IC-RVO doc. no. 006585–92.

Foreign Terms
and Abbreviations

abangan — nominal(ly) Moslem, strongly influenced by Hindu-Buddhist and animist religious ideas

Algemeene Studieclub — General Study Club

aliran — lit., stream or current; a world-view and the social community that adheres to it

AMG&L — Angkatan Muda Gas dan Listrik (Gas and Electricity Youth)

AMKA — Angkatan Muda Kereta Api (Railway Youth)

AMPT&T — Angkatan Muda Pos, Telegrap dan Telepon (Posts, Telegraph, and Telephone Youth)

AMRI — Angkatan Muda Republik Indonesia (Younger Generation of the Republic of Indonesia)

AMS — Algemeene Middelbare School (General Middle School)

anak buah — younger associate, follower

anak mas — favorite pupil, follower

Angkatan Baru — New Generation

Angkatan Muda — Younger Generation

Angkatan Muda Gas dan Listrik — See AMG&L

Angkatan Muda Kereta Api — See AMKA

Angkatan Muda Pos, Telegrap dan Telepon	See AMPT&T
Angkatan Muda Republik Indonesia	See AMRI
Angkatan Pemuda Indonesia	See API
API	Angkatan Pemuda Indonesia (Younger Generation of Indonesia)
asrama	pre-Islamic, Hindu-Buddhist school; student dormitory or training place
Asrama Angkatan Baru Indonesia	Asrama of the New Generation of Indonesia
Asrama Indonesia Merdeka	Free Indonesia Asrama
Badan Keamanan Rakjat	See BKR
Badan Kongres Pemuda Republik Indonesia	See BKPRI
Badan Penolong Keluarga Korban Perang	See BPKKP
badan perdjuangan	lit., struggle body; armed resistance organization, paramilitary group
Badan Permusjawaratan Peladjar Indonesia	See Baperpi
bapak	father; patron, leader
Baperpi	Badan Permusjawaratan Peladjar Indonesia (Indonesian Students' Consultative Body)
barisan	front, league, paramilitary corps
Barisan Banteng	Wild Buffalo Corps
Barisan Buruh Indonesia	See BBI
Barisan Pelopor	Vanguard Corps
Barisan Pelopor Istimewa	Special Vanguard Corps
Barisan Pemberontakan Republik Indonesia	See BPRI
Barisan Pemuda Gerindo	Gerindo Youth Corps
Barisan Tani Indonesia	See BTI
BBI	Barisan Buruh Indonesia (Indonesian Workers' League)
bekel	bailiff, tax collector

Bestuursschool	School of Public Administration
BKPRI	Badan Kongres Pemuda Republik Indonesia (Council of the Youth Congress of the Republic of Indonesia)
BKR	Badan Keamanan Rakjat (People's Security Organization)
BPKKP	Badan Penolong Keluarga Korban Perang (Organization for Aid to Families of War Victims)
BPRI	Barisan Pemberontakan Republik Indonesia (Insurgent Corps of the Republic of Indonesia)
BTI	Barisan Tani Indonesia (Indonesian Peasants' League)
BU	Budi Utomo (High Endeavor)
buchō	department chief
Budi Utomo	See BU
Bukanfu	(naval) Office for Liaison
bupati	regent, administrative head of kabupatèn
CAC	Central Advisory Council (Chūō Sangi-in)
Chianbu	Department of Security
chūdanchō	company commander
Chūō Sangi-in	Central Advisory Council
daidan, daidanchō	battalion, battalion commander
daulat, mendaulat	kidnap for political reasons; forcibly remove from office
Dewan Perdjuangan	lit., Struggle Council; Resistance Council
Dewan Pertahanan Daerah	See DPD
Dewan Perwakilan Rakjat	See DPR
diplomasi	diplomacy; strategy emphasizing diplomacy as means to achieve independence
djago	fighting cock, champion; practitioner of traditional arts of self-defense
djawara	Bantenese variant of djago

djiwa	spirit, soul
Dōmei	Japanese news agency
DPD	Dewan Pertahanan Daerah (Regional Defense Council)
DPR	Dewan Perwakilan Rakjat (People's Representative Council), parliament
Drs.	title denoting that its holder has completed all requirements for a doctorate except the dissertation
ELS	Europeesche Lagere School (European Primary School)
Fujinkai	Women's Association
Gabungan Badan Perdjuangan Tiga Daerah	See GBP-3D
Gabungan Politik Indonesia	See Gapi
Gabungan Sarekat Sekerdja Partikulir Indonesia	See Gaspi
Gapi	Gabungan Politik Indonesia (Political Federation of Indonesia)
Gaspi	Gabungan Sarekat Sekerdja Partikulir Indonesia (Federation of Private Unions of Indonesia)
GBP-3D	Gabungan Badan Perdjuangan Tiga Daerah (Federation of Resistance Organizations of the Three Regions)
gelisah, kegelisahan	trembling, anxious; "tremblingness," anxiety
Gerakan Pemuda Islam Indonesia	See GPII
Gerakan Pemuda Republik Indonesia	See Gerpri
Gerakan Rakjat Baru	See GRB
Gerakan Rakjat Indonesia	See Gerindo
Gerindo	Gerakan Rakjat Indonesia (Indonesian People's Movement)
Gerpri	Gerakan Pemuda Republik Indonesia (Youth Movement of the Republic of Indonesia)

GPII	Gerakan Pemuda Islam Indonesia (Indonesian Islamic Youth Movement)
GRB	Gerakan Rakjat Baru (New People's Movement)
gunseikan	head of military administration
guru	teacher, especially in spiritual, esoteric lore
hadji	Moslem who has made the pilgrimage to Mecca
HBS	Hoogere Burger School (Higher Civil School)
Heihō	Auxiliary Forces
Hinomaru	Japanese flag
HIS	Hollandsch-Inlandsche School (Dutch-Native School)
Hizbullah	Army of Allah
Hōkōkai, Jawa Hōkōkai	Java Service Association
Ikatan Peladjar Indonesia	See IPI
ilmu kebathinan	mysticism; science of the inner being
Indonesia Merdeka	Free Indonesia
Indonesia Muda	Young Indonesia
"Indonesia Raja"	"Great Indonesia," national anthem
IPI	Ikatan Peladjar Indonesia (League of Indonesian Students)
Ir.	title denoting that its holder has an engineering degree
JIB	Jong Islamieten Bond (Young Moslem League)
Jong Islamieten Bond	See JIB
Jong Java	Young Java
Jong Sumatranen Bond	See JSB
JSB	Jong Sumatranen Bond (League of Young Sumatrans)
kabupatèn	regency, administrative district
Kaigun	(Japanese) navy
kampung	neighborhood, ward
kauman	devout Moslems' quarter in traditional Javanese cities

KBI	Kepanduan Bangsa Indonesia (Indonesian People's Scouts)
Kebaktian Rakjat Indonesia Sulawesi	See KRIS
kedaulatan rakjat	sovereignty of the people
Keibōdan	Vigilance Corps
Kenpeitai	Military Police
Kepanduan Bangsa Indonesia	See KBI
kerakjatan	"people-ness," democracy
Kidōbutai	Armored Corps
Kikakuka	Planning Bureau, Section
kjai	title of respect for holy persons and sacred objects; widely used specifically for Moslem scholars of the traditional type
KNI	Komité Nasional Indonesia (Indonesian National Committee)
KNIL	Koninklijk Nederlands Indisch Leger (Royal Netherlands Indies Army)
KNIP	Komité Nasional Indonesia Pusat (Central Indonesian National Committee)
Komité Nasional Indonesia	See KNI
Komité Nasional Indonesia Pusat	See KNIP
Komité van Aksi	Action Committee
Koperasi Rakjat Indonesia	Indonesian People's Cooperative
kraton	royal palace
KRIS	Kebaktian Rakjat Indonesia Sulawesi (Service of the Indonesian People of Sulawesi)
lasjkar	militia
Lasjkar Hitam	Black Militia (Army)
Lasjkar Merah	Red Militia (Army)
lasjkar rakjat	people's militia
Madjelis Permusjawaratan Rakjat	See MPR
Madjelis Sjuro Muslimin Indonesia	See Masjumi

Madjlisul Islamil a'laa Indonesia	See MIAI
Masjumi	Madjelis Sjuro Muslimin Indonesia (Consultative Council of Indonesian Moslems)
merdeka, kemerdekaan	free, liberated; freedom, liberation
MIAI	Madjlisul Islamil a'laa Indonesia (Great Islamic Council of Indonesia)
MPR	Madjelis Permusjawaratan Rakjat (People's Consultative Assembly)
Mr.	title denoting that its holder has a law degree
Muhammadijah	modernist Islamic social and educational association
MULO	Meer Uitgebreid Lager Onderwijs (More Extended Lower Instruction [school])
Nahdatul Ulama	Council of Moslem Scholars
NEFIS	Netherlands Eastern Forces Intelligence Service
ngèlmu kedotan	science of invulnerability
NICA	Netherlands Indies Civil Administration
OSVIA	Opleidings-School voor Inlandsche Ambtenaren (Training School for Native Administrators)
Pagujuban Pasundan	Sundanese Association
panglima besar	great commander, commander-in-chief
pangrèh pradja	lit., rulers of the realm; indigenous administrative corps (after 1946 known as pamong pradja, servants of the realm)
Panitia Oentoek Pengembalian Bangsa Djepang dan Asing	See POPDA
Panitia Persiapan Kemerdekaan Indonesia	See PPKI
Paras	Partai Rakjat Sosialis (Socialist People's Party)
paréwa	Minangkabau variant of the djago

Pari	Partai Republik Indonesia (Republic of Indonesia Party)
Parindra	Partij Indonesia Raja (Greater Indonesia Party)
Parkindo	Partai Keristen Indonesia (Indonesian Christian Party [Protestant])
Parsi	Partai Sosialis Indonesia (Indonesian Socialist Party)
Partai Buruh Indonesia	See PBI
Partai Islam Indonesia	See PII
Partai Keristen Indonesia	See Parkindo
Partai Komunis Indonesia	See PKI
Partai Nasional Indonesia	See PNI
Partai Rakjat Sosialis	See Paras
Partai Republik Indonesia	See Pari
Partai Sarikat Islam Indonesia	See PSII
Partai Sosialis	See PS
Partai Sosialis Indonesia	See PSI
particuliere landerijen	private estates, private domains
Partij Indonesia	See Partindo
Partij Indonesia Raja	See Parindra
Partij Tionghwa Indonesia	See PTI
Partindo	Partij Indonesia (Indonesia Party)
patih, papatih dalem	grand vizier
PBI	Partai Buruh Indonesia (Indonesian Workers' Party)
PDR&T	Pemerintah Daerah Rakjat dan Tentara (People's and Army Territorial Government)
Pembela Tanah Air	See Peta
pemuda	youth, especially politicized youth
Pemuda Katolik	Catholic Youth
Pemuda Protestan	Protestant Youth
Pemuda Puteri Indonesia	Young Women of Indonesia
Pemuda Republik Indonesia	See PRI
Pemuda Sosialis Indonesia	See Pesindo

Pendidikan Nasional Indonesia	Indonesian National Education [Movement]
pentjak	traditional art of self-defense; silat
Pepolit	[Staf] Pendidikan Politik (Political Education [Staff])
perdjuangan	lit., struggle, resistance; strategy emphasizing armed resistance as means to achieve independence
pergerakan	lit., movement; the anticolonial movement prior to World War II
Perguruan Rakjat	People's Education
Perhimpunan Indonesia	See **PI**
Perhimpunan Peladjar Indonesia	See **PPI**
Perhimpunan Peladjar-Peladjar Indonesia	See **PPPI**
Perkumpulan Pegawai Bestuur Bumiputera	See **PPBB**
Perpri	Persatuan Pemuda Rakjat Indonesia (Union of the Youth of the Indonesian People)
Persatuan Pemuda Rakjat Indonesia	See **Perpri**
Persatuan Pemuda Taman Siswa	See **PPTS**
Persatuan Perdjuangan	See **PP**
Persatuan Supir Indonesia	Indonesian Drivers' Union
pesantrèn	traditional rural Islamic school
Pesindo	Pemuda Sosialis Indonesia (Socialist Youth of Indonesia)
Peta	Pembela Tanah Air (Fatherland Defense [Force])
PI	Perhimpunan Indonesia (Indonesian Association)
PII	Partai Islam Indonesia (Indonesian Islamic Party)
PKI	Partai Komunis Indonesia (Indonesian Communist Party)

PNI — Partai Nasional Indonesia (Indonesian National Party)

POPDA — Panitia Oentoek Pengembalian Bangsa Djepang dan Asing (Committee for the Return of Japanese and Other Foreigners)

PP — Persatuan Perdjuangan (lit., Struggle Union; Union of Resistance)

PPBB — Perkumpulan Pegawai Bestuur Bumiputera (Native Civil Servants' Association)

PPI — Perhimpunan Peladjar Indonesia (Indonesian Student Association)

PPKI — Panitia Persiapan Kemerdekaan Indonesia (Committee for the Preparation of Indonesian Independence)

PPPB — Perserikatan Pegawai Pegadaian Bumiputera (Union of Native Pawnshop Officials)

PPPI — Perhimpunan Peladjar-Peladjar Indonesia (Association of Indonesian Students)

PPTS — Persatuan Pemuda Taman Siswa (Union of Taman Siswa Youth)

PRI — Pemuda Republik Indonesia (Youth of the Republic of Indonesia)

prijaji — member of the Javanese official class

PS — Partai Sosialis (Socialist Party)

PSI — Partai Sosialis Indonesia (Indonesian Socialist Party)

PSII — Partai Sarikat Islam Indonesia (Indonesian Islamic Union Party)

PTI — Partij Tionghwa Indonesia (Indonesian Chinese Party)

Putera — Pusat Tenaga Rakjat (Center of People's Strength)

rakjat — people, common people, the masses

RAPWI	Recovery of Allied Prisoners of War and Internees
rōmusha	(forced) laborer
Sabilillah, Barisan Sabilillah	lit., Path of Allah; Path of Allah Corps
sama rata sama rasa	on the same level, feeling at one
sangikai	advisory council
santri	student, pupil; member of the devout Islamic community
sanyō	adviser
Sarekat Islam	Islamic Union
saté	barbecued shish kebab
satria	warrior-aristocrat of Javanese legend and tradition
SEAC	Southeast Asia Command
Seinendan	Youth Corps
Seinendōjō	Youth Training School for Military Arts
Sekolah Radja	Kings' School
semangat	spirit, élan, spiritual power
Sendenbu	Department of Propaganda
Serindo	Serikat Rakjat Indonesia (Union of the Indonesian People)
shōdanchō	platoon, section commander
siap	ready, get ready
silat	traditional art of self-defense; pentjak
sōmubuchō	chief of the General Affairs Department
Southeast Asia Command	See SEAC
SPI	Suluh Pemuda Indonesia (Torch of Indonesian Youth)
Staatspartij	State Party
Staf Pendidikan Politik	See Pepolit
STOVIA	School tot Opleiding van Inlandsche Artsen (Training School for Native Doctors)
Studenten Islam Studieclub	Moslem Students' Study Club
Suluh Pemuda Indonesia	See SPI

Suryawirawan	Sun Corps, youth organization of the Parindra
Taman Siswa	lit., Garden of Pupils; nationalist school system founded by Ki Hadjar Dewantoro
Tentara Keamanan Rakjat	See TKR
Tentara Keselamatan Rakjat	See TKR
TKR	Tentara Keamanan Rakjat (People's Security Army); Tentara Keselamatan Rakjat (People's Salvation Army)
Tokubetsu Keisatsutai	Special Police Force
tonarigumi	neighborhood associations
Unitas Studiosorum Indonesiensis	Indonesian Student Union
Volksraad	People's Council
wajang	traditional Javanese drama, primarily the shadow-play
wedana	district officer, directly subordinate to the bupati

Bibliography

Documents and materials from the Indies Collection of the Rijksinstituut voor Oorlogsdocumentatie (IC-RVO), Amsterdam

"Addendum," appended to the "Statement" of Hitoshi Shimizu of Dec. 5, 1945. Doc. no. 006585–006592.

"Addendum on the East Java Situation," appended to the official Sixteenth Army report to Singapore and Saigon after independence. Doc. no. 005877–005878.

Amir, Mohammed. "Notes." Doc. no. 005936–005938.

[Anonymous, untitled document found in Sixteenth Army Headquarters by the Allies.] Doc. no. 006501–006506.

"Beschouwingen over de algemeene en financiele voorbereiding van de Indonesische onafhankelijkheidsbeweging door de Japanners." Doc. no. 059397ff.

"HQ Sixteenth Army Document on the Peta." Doc. no. 005118.

Huyer [Huijer], P. J. G. "Report on the Surabaja Affair." Doc. no. 007177–007179.

Kenpeitai (Semarang). "Daily Reports." Doc. no. 006743–006761.

Maeda, Rear Adm. Tadashi. "Statement" of April 4, 1946. Doc. no. 006812–006813.

———. "Statement" of April 20, 1946. Doc. no. 006830–006844.

———. "Statement" of June 20, 1946. Doc. no. 006894–006902.

———. "Statement" of Aug. 26, 1946. Doc. no. 006825–006829.

Miyoshi, Shunkichirō. "Statement." Doc. no. 005846–005847.

Mori, Rear Adm. Takeo. "Statement" of Aug. 2, 1946. Doc. no. 006969–006972.

Nishida, Maj. Gen. Shōzō. "Statement" of June 21, 1946. Doc. no. 041204–041205.

Nishijima, Shigetada. "Verklaring betreffende de Indonesische onafhankelijkheidsbeweging en de bijeenkomsten ten huize van Maeda op 16/17 Augustus 1945." March 10–13, 1947. Doc. no. 006076–006089.

Nishimura, Maj. Gen. Otoshi. "Statement" of May 31–June 6, 1946. Doc. no. 005815–005821.

———. "Statement" of April 10, 1947. Doc. no. 059331.

———. "Statement" of April 15, 1947. Doc. no. 006808–006811.

———. "Statement" of April 25, 1947. Doc. no. 059334.

Nomura, Lt. Col. Tetsu. "Statement." Doc. no. 059328.

"Official Statement of the Surabaya Contactbureau on the Death of Brigadier Mallaby." Nov. 1, 1945. Doc. no. 056029.

"Pemberitaan BP-KNIP tentang pekerdjaan dalam masa 27 Nopember 1945–28 Februari 1946." Doc. no. 008985–008991.

"Puradiredja-Mabuchi Agreement." Doc. no. 006626–006630.

"Report on Religious Affairs during the Japanese Period." Doc. no. 006599–006611.

"Report on the Semarang Incident." Prepared by officer commanding the Fifth Guard Unit. Doc. no. 00672–00673.

"Report on the Sulawesi Representatives' Journey to Java." Doc. no. 006009–006021.

Saitō, Shizuo. "Statement" of June 4–5, 1946. Doc. no. 00538–00542.

Shibata, Vice-Adm. Yaichirō. "Report" to the Allies. Doc. no. 059331.

———. "Statement" of July 31, Aug. 1, 3, 19, 1946. Doc. no. 006948–006967.

Shimizu, Hitoshi. "Statement" of Nov. 27–Dec. 2, 1945. Doc. no. 059815.

———. "Statement" of Dec. 5, 1945. Doc. no. 006580–006584.

Shimura, Maj. Gen. Fumie. "Statement" of June 13, 1946. Doc. no. 009402–009406.

Sukarno. "Letter to Maeda." Dated Nov. 26, 1945. Doc. no. 011240.

Tijmstra, L. F. "Zoeklicht op Sjahrir." Doc. no. 007946–007948.

"Tjatatan pendek sidang Sanyō Kaigi." Dated April 18, 2605 [1945]. Doc. no. 038861–038877.

Tjatatan stenografis sidang Sanyō Kaigi ke-empat pada tanggal 8 bulan 1, 2605." Doc. no. 036626–036655.

Tsuchiya, Capt. Kisō. "Statement" of March 3–8, 1947, in Tjipinang Prison. Doc. no. 00625–00635.

"Tull Report." Doc. no. 007414–007453.

Watanabe, Hiroshi. "Statement" of May 23, 1946, Doc. no. 005809–005811.

Weerd, K. A. de. "Prepared Statement" on the Japanese Occupation of the Netherlands Indies, International Prosecution Section, Netherlands Division, Nov. 1946. Doc. no. 059679ff.

"Who's Who in Java." Compiled by Dutch Intelligence. Doc. no. 007779–007862.

Yanagawa, Capt. Munenari. "Statement" of Oct. 14, 1945. Doc. no. 006508–006516.

———. "Further Statement." Doc. no. 006517–006522.

Other Sources

Aidit, Dipa Nusantara. *Pilihan tulisan.* 3 vols. Djakarta: Pembaruan, 1959–65.

Alers, Henri. *Om een rode of groene Merdeka: Tien jaren binnenlandse politiek, Indonesië, 1943–1953.* Eindhoven: Vulkaan, 1956.

Alfian. "Islamic Modernism in Indonesian Politics: The Muhammadijah Movement during the Dutch Colonial Period (1912–1942)." Ph.D. thesis, University of Wisconsin, 1969.

Almanak Angkatan Perang. Djakarta: P. T. Usaha Pegawai Nasional Indonesia, Bagian Pustaka Angkatan Perang, 1956.

Amrullah, Abdul Malik Karim, hadji [Hamka]. *Tenggelamnja kapal Van der Wijck.* 5th ed. Djakarta: Balai Pustaka, 1957.

Amstutz, James Bruce. "The Indonesian Youth Movement, 1908–1955." Ph.D. thesis, Fletcher School of Law and Diplomacy, 1958.

Anderson, Benedict O'Gorman. "The Idea of Power in Javanese Culture," in Claire Holt, ed., *Culture and Politics in Indonesia.* Ithaca, N.Y.: Cornell University Press, 1972.

———. "Japan: 'The Light of Asia,' " in Josef Silverstein, ed., *Southeast Asia in World War II: Four Essays,* pp. 13–50. Southeast Asia Studies, Monograph Series, no. 7. New Haven, Conn.: Yale University, 1966.

———. "The Languages of Indonesian Politics," *Indonesia,* no. 1 (April 1966), pp. 89–116.

———. "The Pemuda Revolution: Indonesian Politics, 1945–1946." Ph.D. thesis, Cornell University, 1967.

———. "The Problem of Rice," *Indonesia,* no. 2 (Oct. 1966), pp. 77–123.

——. *Some Aspects of Indonesian Politics under the Japanese Occupation, 1944–1945.* Cornell Modern Indonesia Project, Interim Report Series. Ithaca, N.Y.: Cornell University, 1961.

Angkasa Darma. "Sebelas tahun nan lalu," *Merdeka* (Djakarta), Aug. 16, 1956.

Bahsan, Oemar. *Tjatatan ringkas tentang: Peta ("Pembela Tanah-Air") dan Peristiwa Rengasdengklok.* Bandung: Melati, n.d. [1955?].

Benda, Harry J. *The Crescent and the Rising Sun: Indonesian Islam under the Japanese Occupation, 1942–1945.* The Hague: van Hoeve, 1958.

Benda, Harry J., and Ruth T. McVey. *The Communist Uprisings of 1926–1927 in Indonesia: Key Documents.* Cornell Modern Indonesia Project, Translation Series. Ithaca, N.Y.: Cornell University, 1960.

Benda, Harry J., James K. Irikura, and Kōichi Kishi, eds. *Japanese Military Administration in Indonesia: Selected Documents.* Southeast Asia Studies, Translation Series, no. 6. New Haven, Conn.: Yale University, 1965.

Brackman, Arnold. *Indonesian Communism: A History.* New York: Praeger, 1963.

Brand, W. "Some Statistical Data on Indonesia," *Bijdragen tot de taal-, land- en volkenkunde,* CXXV, 3 (1969), 305–27.

Brugmans, I. J., et al., eds. *Nederlandsch-Indië onder Japanse bezetting: Gegevens en documenten over de jaren 1942–1945.* Franeker: Wever, 1960.

Bruin, Theodoor de. "Gevolgen der internering van Nederlanders voor de economie van Nederlands-Indië tijdens de Japanse bezetting (Maart 1942–Augustus 1945)." M.A. thesis, Netherlands School of Economics, Rotterdam, 1962.

Budiman Djaja. "Mengenang seorang pahlawan: Tan Malaka, sepandjang hidup dan sepandjang perdjuangannja," *Tempo* (Semarang), March 28, 1963.

Chandra, A. M. "10 Nopember dan obor mental generasi muda," *Sinar Harapan* (Djakarta), Nov. 9, 1968.

Dahm, Bernhard. *Sukarno and the Struggle for Indonesian Independence.* Ithaca, N.Y.: Cornell University Press, 1969.

Darmosugondo. "Mengenang peristiwa sekitar 17 Agustus 1945," in Darius Marpaung, ed., *Bingkisan nasional: Kenangan sepuluh tahun revolusi Indonesia,* pp. 42–45, 48. Djakarta: Upeni, n.d. [1955?].

Dimyati, Muhammad. *Sedjarah perdjuangan Indonesia.* Djakarta: Widjaya, 1951.

Djajadiningrat, Idrus Nasir. *The Beginnings of the Indonesian-Dutch Negotiations and the Hoge Veluwe Talks.* Cornell Modern Indonesia Project, Monograph Series. Ithaca, N.Y.: Cornell University, 1958.

Djèn Amar. *Bandung lautan api.* Bandung: Dhiwantara, 1963.

Donnison, Frank Siegfried Vernon. *British Military Administration in the Far East, 1943–1946.* History of the Second World War, United Kingdom Military Series. London: HM Stationery Office, 1956.

Doulton, A. J. F. *The Fighting Cock: Being the History of the Twenty-third Indian Division, 1942–1947.* Aldershot: Gale and Polden, 1951.

Drewes, Gerardus Willebrordus Johannes. *Drie Javaansche goeroe's: Hun leven, onderricht en messiaasprediking.* Leiden: Vros, 1925.

Dwidjosugondo, R. W. [Tjantrik Mataram]. *Peranan ramalan Djojobojo dalam revolusi kita.* Bandung: Masa Baru, n.d. [1954?].

Encyclopaedie van Nederlandsch-Indië. 2d ed. The Hague: Nijhoff, and Leiden: Brill, 1917–39.

Ensiklopedia Indonesia. Bandung: van Hoeve, 1954–56.

Feith, Herbert. *The Decline of Constitutional Democracy in Indonesia.* Ithaca, N.Y.: Cornell University Press, 1962.

Finch, Susan, and Daniel S. Lev. *Republic of Indonesia Cabinets, 1945–1965.* Cornell Modern Indonesia Project, Interim Report Series. Ithaca, N.Y.: Cornell University, 1965.

Gandasubrata, S. M. *An Account of the Japanese Occupation of Banjumas Residency, Java, March 1942 to August 1945.* Translated by Leslie H. Palmier. Southeast Asia Program Data Paper no. 10. Ithaca, N.Y.: Cornell University, 1953.

Gatot Mangkupradja, Radèn. "The Peta and My Relations with the Japanese," *Indonesia,* no. 5 (April 1968), pp. 105–34.

Geertz, Clifford. *Agricultural Involution: The Processes of Ecological Change in Indonesia.* Berkeley: University of California Press, 1963.

——. *The Religion of Java.* New York: The Free Press, 1960.

Geertz, Hildred. *The Javanese Family: A Study of Kinship and So-cialization.* Glencoe, Ill.: The Free Press, 1961.

Goodman, Grant K. *Four Aspects of Philippine-Japanese Relations, 1930–1940.* Southeast Asia Studies, Monograph Series, no. 9. New Haven, Conn.: Yale University, 1967.

Groot, Paul de. *De dertiger jaren 1930–1939: Herinneringen en over-denkingen.* 2 vols. Amsterdam: Pegasus, 1965–67.

Hardjito, ed. *Risalah gerakan pemuda.* Djakarta: Pustaka Antara, 1952.

Hasjim Mahdan. "Prapatan sepuluh," *Indonesia Raya* (Djakarta), Aug. 16, 1955.

Hoeta Soehoet, Ali Moechtar. "Sedikit sekitar saat lahirnja R. I. Proklamasi," in Darius Marpaung, ed., *Bingkisan nasional: Kenang-an sepuluh tahun revolusi Indonesia,* pp. 27–34. Djakarta: Upeni, n.d. [1955?].

Idenburg, P. J. A. "Het Nederlandse antwoord op het Indonesisch nationalisme," in Henri Baudet and I. J. Brugmans, eds., *Balans van beleid: Terugblik op de laatste halve eeuw van Nederlandsch-Indië,* pp. 121–51. Assen: van Gorcum, 1961.

Idrus. "Och . . . Och . . . Och," translated by S. U. Nababan in *Indonesia,* no. 2 (Oct. 1966), pp. 129–34.

——. "Surabaja," translated by S. U. Nababan and Benedict O'Gor-man Anderson in *Indonesia,* no. 5 (April 1968), pp. 1–28.

Indonesia, Biro Pusat Statistik. *Statistical Pocketbook of Indonesia, 1961.* Djakarta: Biro Pusat Statistik, 1962.

Indonesia, Departemen Pendidikan Dasar dan Kebudajaan, Biro Pemuda. *Sedjarah perdjuangan pemuda Indonesia.* Djakarta: Balai Pustaka, 1965.

Indonesia, Departemen Penerangan. Unpublished biographical files [Deppen Files], located in the Department's archives in Djakarta.

Indonesia, Kementerian Luar Negeri. *Fakta dan dokumen2 untuk menjusun buku "Indonesia memasuki gelanggang internasional," Sub-periode: Kabinet Presiden Soekarno dari tanggal 17.8.45 sam-pai 14.11.45.* Kementerian Luar Negeri, Direktorat V, Seksi Pen-jelidikan dan Dokumentasi/Perpustakaan. Djakarta, June 1958.

Indonesia, Kementerian Penerangan. *Kami perkenalkan.* Djakarta: n.p., n.d.

——. *Kepartaian di Indonesia.* Tegal: de Boer, 1950.

——. *Lembaran sedjarah.* Djakarta: n.p., 1951.

——. *Lukisan Revolusi, 1945–1950.* Djakarta: n.p., n.d. [1954?].

——. *Republik Indonesia Daerah Istimewa Jogjakarta.* Djakarta: n.p., 1953–54.

——. *Republik Indonesia Propinsi Djawa Barat.* Djakarta: n.p., 1953–54.

——. *Republik Indonesia Propinsi Djawa Tengah.* Djakarta: n.p., 1953–54.

Indonesia, Staf Pertahanan-Keamanan, Lembaga Sedjarah. *Siapa-apa (Who's Who) Staf Pertahanan-Keamanan.* Djakarta: n.p., 1967.

Jay, Robert R. *Javanese Villagers: Social Relations in Rural Modjokuto.* Cambridge, Mass.: M.I.T. Press, 1969.

Jungschlaeger, Leon Nicolaas Hubert. "The Double Coup," *NEFIS Periodiek,* no. 13 (Aug. 14, 1946).

Jusuf Hasan. *Riwajat hidup ringkas.* Bogor: n.p., 1957.

Kadarjono, S. *Swargi Djèndral Sudirman.* Surabaja: Panjebar Semangat, 1961.

Kahin, George McTurnan. *Nationalism and Revolution in Indonesia.* Ithaca, N.Y.: Cornell University Press, 1952.

Kanahele, George Sanford. "The Japanese Occupation of Indonesia: Prelude to Independence." Ph.D. thesis, Cornell University, 1967.

Kishi, Kōichi, Shigetada Nishijima, et al., *Indoneshia ni okeru Nihon gunsei no kenkyu* [Study of the effect of the Japanese military occupation of Indonesia]. Okuma Foundation for Studies in the Social Sciences. Tokyo: Waseda University, 1959.

Koch, D. M. G. *Om de vrijheid: De nationalistische beweging in Indonesië.* Djakarta: Pembangunan, 1950.

Kota Jogjakarta dua ratus tahun, 7 Oktober 1756–7 Oktober 1956. Jogjakarta: Panitia Peringatan Kota Jogjakarta 200 Tahun, 1956.

Koentjaraningrat. *Some Social-Anthropological Observations on Gotong Rojong Practices in Two Villages of Central Java.* Translated by Claire Holt. Cornell Modern Indonesia Project, Monograph Series. Ithaca, N.Y.: Cornell University, 1961.

Koesnodiprodjo, ed. *Himpunan undang2, peraturan2, penetapan2 pemerintah Republik Indonesia, 1945.* Rev. ed. Djakarta: Seno, 1951.

——. *Himpunan undang2, peraturan2, penetapan2 pemerintah Republik Indonesia, 1946.* Rev. ed. Djakarta: Seno, 1951.

Mackie, J. A. C. *Problems of the Indonesian Inflation.* Cornell Modern Indonesia Project, Monograph Series. Ithaca, N.Y.: Cornell University, 1967.

Maeda, Tadashi. "On the Eve of Indonesian Independence." Typescript translation of an article in the *Sunday Mainichi* (Tokyo), March 12, 1950. In my possession.

Malik, Adam. *Riwajat dan perdjuangan sekitar proklamasi kemerdekaan Indonesia 17 Agustus 1945.* Djakarta: Widjaya, 1950.

Mangkunagara VII, K. G. P. A. A. *On the Wajang Kulit (Purwa) and Its Symbolic and Mystical Elements.* Translated by Claire Holt. Southeast Asia Program Data Paper no. 27. Ithaca, N.Y.: Cornell University, 1957.

McVey, Ruth T. *The Rise of Indonesian Communism.* Ithaca, N.Y.: Cornell University Press, 1965.

Mook, Hubertus Johannes van. *Indonesië, Nederland en de wereld.* Batavia [Djakarta]: De Brug/Opbouw, 1949.

——. *The Stakes of Democracy in Southeast Asia.* New York: Norton, 1950.

Mountbatten of Burma, Vice-Admiral the Earl. *Post-Surrender Tasks: Section E of the Report to the Combined Chiefs of Staff by the Supreme Commander, Southeast Asia, 1943–1945.* London: H.M. Stationery Office, 1969.

Nasution, Abdul Haris. *Tentara Nasional Indonesia,* Vol. I. Djakarta: Pembimbing, 1955.

——. *Tjatatan2 sekitar politik militer Indonesia.* Djakarta: Pembimbing, 1955.

Nawawi Dusky. "Hari proklamasi," *Abadi* (Djakarta), Aug. 22, 1955.

Netherlands, Staten-Generaal, Tweede Kamer. *Enquête-commissie regeringsbeleid 1940–1945, militair beleid, terugkeer naar Nederlandsch-Indië (8A en B).* The Hague: Staatsdrukkerij- en Uitgeverijbedrijf, 1956.

"Njala api 10 Nopember—Mengenal orang dibalik lajar," *Sinar Harapan,* Nov. 9, 1968.

Nugroho Notosusanto. "Instansi jang melaksanakan pembentukan tentara Peta," *Madjalah Ilmu2 Sastra Indonesia,* II (June 1964), 285–88.

Nuh, Muhammad. "Peristiwa Tiga Daerah," parts I and II, in *Penelitian Sedjarah,* III, 1 (March 1962), 29–32, and in III, 6 (June 1962), 31–36.

Noer, Deliar. "Masjumi: Its Organization, Ideology, and Political Role in Indonesia." M.A. thesis, Cornell University, 1960.

——. "The Rise and Development of the Modernist Muslim Movement in Indonesia during the Dutch Colonial Period, 1900–1942." Ph.D. thesis, Cornell University, 1963.

Olthof, W. L., trans. *Babad Tanah Djawi in proza: Javaansche geschiedenis loopende tot het jaar 1647 der Javaansche jaartelling.* The Hague: Nijhoff, 1941.

Orang Indonesia jang terkemoeka di Djawa. Djakarta: Gunseikanboe, 2604 [1944].

Oudang, M. *Perkembangan kepolisian di Indonesia.* Djakarta: Mahabharata, 1952.

Overdijkink, Gerrit Willem. *Het Indonesische probleem.* Amsterdam: Keizerskroon, 1948.

Pakpahan, G. *1261 hari dibawah sinar "Matahari Terbit."* n.p. [Djakarta?], n.d. [1947?].

Parlaungan. *Hasil rakjat memilih tokoh-tokoh parlemen di Republik Indonesia: Hasil pemilihan umum pertama.* Djakarta: Gita, 1956.

Pigeaud, Theodoor. *Javaanse volksvertoningen.* Batavia [Djakarta]: Volkslectuur, 1938.

——. *De Serat Tjabolang en de Serat Tjentini: Inhoudsopgaven.* Batavia [Djakarta]: Koninklijk Bataviaasch Genootschap van Kunsten en Wetenschappen, 1933.

Pinardi. *Sekarmadji Maridjan Kartosuwirjo.* Djakarta: Aryaguna, 1964.

Pluvier, Jan M. *Overzicht van de ontwikkeling der nationalistische beweging in Indonesië in de jaren 1930 tot 1942.* The Hague: van Hoeve, 1953.

Pramoedya Ananta Toer. *Tjerita dari Blora.* Djakarta: Balai Pustaka, 1952.

Pringgodigdo, Abdul Gaffar. *Perubahan kabinet presidensil mendjadi kabinet parlementer.* Jogjakarta: Jajasan Fonds Universitas Negeri Gadjah Mada, n.d. [1955?].

——. *Sedjarah singkat berdirinja negara Republik Indonesia.* Surabaja: Pustaka Nasional, 1958.

Pusat SBPI [Sarikat Buruh Pertjetakan Indonesia?]. *Dokumentasi pemuda: Sekitar proklamasi Indonesia Merdeka.* Jogjakarta: Badan Penerangan Pusat SBPI, 1948.

480   BIBLIOGRAPHY

Pusat Sedjarah Militer Angkatan Darat, *Kronologi sedjarah TNI 1945*. Bandung: Pussemad, n.d. [1963?].

——. *Peranan TNI-Angkatan Darat dalam perang kemerdekaan (Revolusi Pisik 1945–1949)*. Bandung: Pussemad, 1965.

Raliby, Osman. *Documenta Historica: Sedjarah dokumenter dari pertumbuhan dan perdjuangan negara Republik Indonesia*. Djakarta: Bulan-Bintang, 1953.

Rasjied, Zainal. *Riwajat orang-orang politik*. Medan: Bakti, 1951.

Reischauer, Edwin O. *Japan: The Story of a Nation*. New York: Knopf, 1970.

Roeslan, Toebagoes. *Sedjarah Tanah Banten*. N.p.: Arief, 1954.

Sajuti, Mohammed Ibnu [Sajuti Melik]. "Kenangan dimasa lampau bagaikan seorang purnawirawan," *Mahasiswa Indonesia* (Djawa Barat), Sept. 1968, Minggu ke-3.

——. "Proklamasi Kemerdekaan seperti jang saja saksikan," *Berita Yudha* (Djakarta), Aug. 16, 1968.

Salim, Leon. *Bung Sjahrir: Pahlawan nasional*. Medan: Masadepan, 1966.

Samudja Asjari. "Kedudukan kjai dalam pondok pesantrèn." M.A. thesis, Gadjah Mada University, 1967.

Santosa. "Serangan di Ambarawa, 1945." B.A. thesis, Gadjah Mada University, 1967.

Sartono Kartodirdjo. "Agrarian Radicalism in Java: Its Setting and Development," in Claire Holt, ed., *Culture and Politics in Indonesia*. Ithaca, N.Y.: Cornell University Press, 1972.

——. *The Peasants' Revolt of Banten in 1888: Its Conditions, Course and Sequel*. The Hague: De Nederlandsche Boek- en Steendrukkerij, 1966.

Sawer, Geoffrey. "Allied Policy in Indonesia," *Australian Asiatic Bulletin* (Melbourne), April 1946.

Sedjarah Militer Kodam VI Siliwangi. *Siliwangi dari masa kemasa*. Djakarta: Fakta Mahjuma, 1968.

"Sedjarah TNI Komando Daerah VII Diponegoro." Typescript in the archives of the Army Military History Center (Pussemad), Bandung. [1963?].

Selosoemardjan. *Social Changes in Jogjakarta*. Ithaca, N.Y.: Cornell University Press, 1962.

Serat Tjentini. Transcribed and edited by R. Ng. Soeradipoera with the assistance of R. Poerwasoewignja and R. Wirawangsa, and with an introduction by R. M. A. Soerjasoeparta. Batavia [Djakarta]: Bataviaasch Genootschap van Kunsten en Wetenschappen, 1912–15.

Sidik Kertapati. *Sekitar proklamasi 17 Agustus 1945.* 2d ed. Djakarta: Pembaruan, 1961.

Sihombing, O. D. P. *Pemuda Indonesia menantang fasisme Djepang.* Djakarta: Sinar Djaya, 1962.

Simatupang, Tahi Bonar. *Laporan dari Banaran: Kisah pengalaman seorang pradjurit selama perang kemerdekaan.* Djakarta: Pembangunan, 1960.

Singh, Rajendra. *Post-War Occupation Forces: Japan and Southeast Asia.* In the series Official History of the Indian Armed Forces in the Second World War, 1939–1945. New Delhi: Combined Inter-Services Historical Section, India and Pakistan, 1958.

Sjahrir, Sutan. *Our Struggle.* Translated with an introduction by Benedict O'Gorman Anderson. Cornell Modern Indonesia Project, Translation Series. Ithaca, N.Y.: Cornell University, 1968.

———. *Out of Exile.* Translated by Charles Wolf, Jr. New York: John Day, 1949.

Sjarief Hidajat. *Riwajat singkat perdjuangan K. H. Z. Mustofa.* Tasikmalaja: Soetraco, 1961.

Smail, John R. W. *Bandung in the Early Revolution, 1945–1946: A Study in the Social History of the Indonesian Revolution.* Cornell Modern Indonesia Project, Monograph Series. Ithaca, N.Y.: Cornell University, 1964.

Smit, C. *De liquidatie van een imperium: Nederland en Indonesië, 1945–1962.* Amsterdam: De Arbeiderspers, 1962.

Somers, Mary Frances Ann. "Peranakan Chinese Politics in Indonesia." Ph.D. thesis, Cornell University, 1965.

"Stenographisch verslag: Sidang Mahkamah Agung, dalam pemeriksaan proces Sudarsono cs., Maret 1948." Typescript in my possession.

Soe Hok-gie. "Simpang kiri dari sebuah djalan." M.A. thesis, University of Indonesia, 1969.

Sudijono Djojoprajitno. *PKI-Sibar contra Tan Malaka: Pemberontakan 1926 dan "kambing hitam" Tan Malaka.* Djakarta: Jajasan Massa, 1962.

Soehoed Prawiroatmodjo. *Perlawanan bersendjata terhadap fasisme Djepang.* Djakarta: Merdeka Press, 1953.

Sukarno. *Nationalism, Islam and Marxism.* Translated by Karel H. Warouw and Peter D. Weldon, with an introduction by Ruth T. McVey. Cornell Modern Indonesia Project, Translation Series. Ithaca, N.Y.: Cornell University, 1970.

Suputro. *Tegal dari masa ke masa.* Djakarta: Kementerian Pendidikan, Pengadjaran dan Kebudajaan, Djawatan Kebudajaan, Bagian Bahasa, 1959.

Surakarta, Djawatan Penerangan Kota Besar Surakarta. *Kenang-Kenangan Kota Besar Surakarta, 1945–1953.* Surakarta: n.p., 1953.

"Surakarta Hadiningrat dalam baranja api revolusi." Compiled by Toekiran Notowardojo, Sujatno Josodipuro, Sadjimin Surobusono, and Mardjio. Typescript, Nov. 10, 1963, in a private collection.

Sutter, John Orval. *Indonesianisasi: Politics in a Changing Economy, 1940–1955.* Southeast Asia Program Data Paper no. 36. Ithaca, N.Y.: Cornell University, 1959.

Tan Malaka. *Dari pendjara ke pendjara,* Vols. I, III. Djakarta: Widjaya, n.d.; Vol. II. Jogjakarta: Pustaka Murba, n.d.

——. *Moeslihat.* Jogjakarta: "Badan Oesaha Penerbitan Nasional Indonesia," 1945.

——. *Politik.* Jogjakarta: "Badan Oesaha Penerbitan Nasional Indonesia," 1945.

Taniguchi, Gorō. *Indoneshia to tomo ni ikite* [To Live Together with Indonesia], Vol. VI of *Hiroku Dai-Tōa Sen Shi* [Secret History of the Greater East Asia War]. Tokyo: Fuji Shoen, 1954. Mimeo. translation by Y. Sasaki in my possession.

Tas, Sol. "Souvenirs of Sjahrir," *Indonesia,* no. 8 (Oct. 1969), pp. 135–54.

Tjamboek Berdoeri [pseud.]. *Indonesia dalem api dan bara.* Malang: n.p., 1947.

Tjarly, S. T., ed. *Gelanggang repolusi: Sepuluh tahun proklamasi.* Djakarta: Badan Penerbit UPMI, 1955.

Tjiptoning [pseud.]. *Apa dan siapa.* Jogjakarta: "Kedaulatan Rakjat," 1951.

United States, Federal Broadcasting Intelligence Service. Daily Reports (1945).

United States, Office of Strategic Services, Research and Analysis Branch. Reports (1945).

Vlekke, Bernard Hubertus Maria. *Nusantara: A History of Indonesia*. Rev. ed. The Hague: van Hoeve, 1959.

Waardeburg, B. C. J. "KRIS," *NEFIS Publikatie*, no. 16 (July 23, 1946).

Wehl, David. *The Birth of Indonesia*. London: Allen and Unwin, 1948.

Wertheim, Willem Frederik. *Indonesian Society in Transition: A Study of Social Change*. 2d ed. Bandung: Sumur Bandung, 1956.

Widjojo Nitisastro. *Population Trends in Indonesia*. Ithaca, N.Y.: Cornell University Press, 1970.

Wulfften Palthe, P. M. van. *Over het bendewezen op Java*. Amsterdam: van Rossen, 1950.

Yamin, Muhammad. *Tan Malacca: Bapak Republik Indonesia*. Djakarta: Berita Indonesia, n.d. [1945].

———. ed. *Naskah persiapan Undang-Undang Dasar 1945*. 3 vols. Djakarta: Jajasan Prapantja, 1959–60.

Index

492   INDEX